JOHN SIMON ON FILM

JOHN SIMON
ON FILM
CRITICISM, 1982–2001

BY JOHN SIMON

INTRODUCTION BY BRUCE BERESFORD

APPLAUSE THEATRE & CINEMA BOOKS ▪ NEW YORK

John Simon on Film: Criticism, 1982–2001
by John Simon
Copyright © 2005 by John Simon
All rights reserved

These reviews previously appeared in *The National Review.*

Book design by Mark Lerner

Library of Congress Cataloging-in-Publication Data

Simon, John Ivan.
John Simon on film : criticism, 1982/2001 / by John Simon ; introduction by Bruce Beresford.
   p. cm. -- (John Simon on--)
Includes index.
ISBN-13: 978-1-55783-507-9
ISBN-10: 1-55783-507-1
1. Motion pictures--Reviews. 2. Motion pictures. I. Title. II. Series.
PN1995.S49397 2005
791.43'75--dc22

         2005009982

British Library Cataloging-in-Publication Data
A catalog record of this book is available from the British Library

Applause Theatre & Cinema Books
19 West 21st Street, Suite 201
New York, NY 10010
Phone: (212) 575-9265
Fax: (212) 575-9270
Email: info@applausepub.com
Internet: www.applausepub.com
Applause books are available through your local bookstore, or you may order at
www.applausepub.com or call Music Dispatch at 800-637-2852

SALES & DISTRIBUTION

North America:
Hal Leonard Corp.
7777 West Bluemound Road
P. O. Box 13819
Milwaukee, WI 53213
Phone: (414) 774-3630
Fax: (414) 774-3259
Email: halinfo@halleonard.com
Internet: www.halleonard.com

Europe:
Roundhouse Publishing Ltd.
Millstone, Limers Lane
Northam, North Devon EX 39 2RG
Phone: (0) 1237-474-474
Fax: (0) 1237-474-774
Email: roundhouse.group@ukgateway.net

To Pat, my wonderful wife, whose moviegoing was often soured by my cavils, in hope of forgiveness.

With special gratitude for his help in selection to Barry Monush.

And because film is such a popular topic of conversation among fellow enthusiasts, I thank the following with whom I had particularly stimulating and fruitful talks:

Jean-Jacques Annaud, Barry Boehm, Kevin Filipski, Michael Freidson, Michael Gallagher, Lenny Green, Clive Hirschhorn, Enrico Job, Dwight Macdonald, Patricia Mellencamp, Frank Noack, Frank Rich, Pierre Rissient, Charles Thomas Samuels, Wilfrid Sheed, Bertrand Tavernier, Jörg von Uthmann, Per Wästberg, and Lina Wertmüller.

Thanks also to the sundry editors of magazines where these pieces were published and to the helpful folks at Applause, notably Michael Messina and Kallie Shimek.

CONTENTS

Order of reviews and essays in each section is chronological according to the date it was originally published.

Introduction

Like most film directors I have a detestation of movie critics, based, of course, on their failure to recognise the amazing talent displayed in all of my works, while they all too often praise the feeble efforts of my contemporaries. Though I've never gone so far as a celebrated playwright friend of mine, in Australia, who has actually sought out his detractors and physically assaulted them, I have, with effort, followed the advice of Raymond Chandler and never responded to criticism.

The numerous readers of this collection of the film criticism of John Simon will no doubt attribute this introduction to the fact of his favourable reviews of my films *Tender Mercies*, *Driving Miss Daisy*, *Mister Johnson* and *Black Robe*—all found within these pages. He is even moderately kind about *A Good Man in Africa*, which I considered disastrous. Not included, though, are his dismissive if annoyingly acute reviews of *Paradise Road* and *Bride of the Wind*, both of which I still irrationally maintain were not all that bad.

I met John Simon for the first time in 1977 at the Berlin film festival. I was there with an Australian film, *Don's Party* which was written by my two-fisted playwright friend, David Williamson. After the screening, I went to one of those desultory drinks parties, where lots of people circle one another warily, not being too sure of who is associated with the film and who isn't. John, displaying no caution, was at the centre of what seemed to me to be an awe-struck crowd. I had no idea who he was. I had never been to America at this time and knew virtually nothing of the New York critics. I eavesdropped for a while, amused by John's precise and witty opinions. Being young and hardy, I introduced myself as the director of *Don's Party*. John nodded for a few moments then said it was "not without merit."

A couple of years later I was in New York, promoting *Breaker Morant*—though my major appearance on behalf of that film was an interview on an all-nude (except for me) late night talk show, which was being transmitted from a sleazy room in an even more sleazy building. John had given me his number and I tentatively called him, not expecting him to remember me. He did remember, though, and we met for lunch. We quickly discovered a mutual interest in theatre, as well as film, and a passion for the more obscure classical composers. For years now, we have jointly ransacked Tower records in search of the works of Granville Bantock, Xavier Montsalvatge, Lennox Berkeley, Albéric Magnard, Rebecca Clarke, Camargo Guarnieri, and others, near-forgotten but gifted.

By this time I'd read a lot of John's work, not just his film writing, but articles on theatre and music. He seemed to me to have more knowledge than it was possible to acquire in a lifetime, yet he was no pedant. He has a vast range of interests, speaks five or six languages fluently, and responds with vigour to everything that crosses his path.

The point I am lurching towards is that I find John's critical writing immensely entertaining even when I'm not in agreement—and who could possibly agree with a critic's views on every film? Mostly, I find, I do agree. More importantly, I find his reviews full of insights and perceptions that make reading a collection of this sort as exciting as reading a gripping novel. It is clear to me, too, that despite's John's extraordinary erudition his response to each film under discussion is fundamentally an emotional one. He is moved by the power of cinema—by its stories, its characters, its themes. He then has the gift, such a rare one (especially among film critics), of being able to analyse the work in question, to be able to say why it is that it's so powerful, so touching; or, on the other hand, so trite, so meretricious, or so banal. He is, perhaps, rather inclined to be more forgiving of the weaknesses of beautiful young actresses than he is of actors, writers or directors, but this is a factor I find perfectly understandable. I know it isn't politically correct to say it…but…watching beautiful girls can do a lot to relieve tedium.

John's wit is dazzling and is never displayed for its own sake, but to drive home an aspect of the review. Writing about Bergman's *Fanny and Alexander* he says "it is all dismally attitudinising and hollow, a sort of cross between Carl Dreyer at his worst and John Fowles at his best, which is not far removed from his worst." I feel he's being a bit tough on *Fanny and Alexander*, though it *is* somewhat sententious, but he couldn't be more on the money with the comment on Fowles. Reviewing Candice Bergen's performance in *Gandhi*, he writes, "though she is a bit of a real-life photographer, Miss Bergen does not even handle a camera convincingly, albeit this is nothing compared to what she does with acting."

It takes courage (sheer foolhardiness in my case) to speak out against widely held views relating to current films. One tends to end up being categorised with the man who said Beethoven was a lousy composer or that Tolstoy couldn't write. I recall being ostracized at dinner parties for my perhaps not too timidly expressed reservations about *The Piano* and *The English Patient*. It thrills me to read the abandon with which John Simon tears into a lot of the sacred cows of cinema—"how long has it been since an American movie has garnered a harvest of laurels like the ones being heaped on a piece of mindless junk called *Blue Velvet*." On Kurosawa's *Ran*: "I find it an almost total failure by a genius in his old age." His comment on Fellini must have outraged most of that director's vast following, but I feel that time will prove it to be correct: "When he made his early, wonderful movies, Fellini was a natural talent—perhaps the most natural of all. Despite a distinctly autobiographical flavour, the films managed to be sufficiently different." He considers the best of them to be *I Vitelloni* and thinks *8½* to be "his last film to show intermittent strength." What went wrong? "Success and egomania, and detachment from the world; withdrawal behind a living wall of amateur adulators and professional sycophants." Writing about *Europa Europa*, "the fact that it takes on an important subject seems to have guaranteed it good notices from the more Pavlovian reviewers." Simon examines, with characteristic logic, the many inconsistencies in the plot, finishing with the telling remark "what good is all the truth in the world if the work of art cannot make it feel true?"

It's been said to me, of John Simon's reviews in general, that he is merely iconoclastic, that virtually nothing has his approbation. The comment seems a bizarre one, as even the most cursory examination of this book will reveal enthusiasm for a huge number of films. It is much easier to write scathing reviews than adulatory ones, but Simon expresses praise as fluently and entertainingly as his dislikes. He begins a review of Bille August's wonderful *Pelle the Conqueror* with "it won the Golden Palm in Cannes and the Oscar for best foreign film of 1988. The remarkable thing is that, despite these awards, it is a very good film." Nor does he ignore or automatically dismiss mainstream cinema, even if he consistently shows a preference for the undoubtedly more personal products of the independents. He quickly dismisses both *Gladiator* and *Titanic* but finds Scorsese's *Goodfellas* "the most original and assured piece of American mainline cinema since—it's been so long, I've forgotten what." He considers Jim Sheridan's *In the Name of the Father* "a great film…it is something with which to bolster audiences: fill 'em up with pity and terror, with laughter, sadness, and rage. And perhaps even—the hardest reaction to elicit from moviegoers—thought."

It was exciting for me to read through this collection and see such warm praise for so many films that I feel have been unjustly ignored, or which have had only limited screenings—Zhang Yimou's *Not One Less*, Gillies MacKinnon's *Regeneration*, Cédric Klapisch's *When the Cat's Away*, Robert Benton's *Nobody's Fool*, Pavel Chukhrai's *The Thief*, James Ivory's *Mr. and Mrs. Bridge*, Francesco Rosi's *The Truce*. There are many others. Now, with the ubiquity of DVD, readers can rush out and rent or buy nearly all of the films John Simon is enthusiastic about. They are not going to be disappointed.

It is refreshing, too, to read a reviewer who is aware of the contributions made to a film by people other than the director and actors. These reviews often mention and discuss the work of cameramen, set designers, editors, costume designers and composers. The latter, whose contribution has assumed greater prominence in films because of developments in sound reproduction, come in for a broadside more often than not—"hack composers provide rampaging scores that tautologically hammer in obvious points—or, worse yet, blurt out that big moments are ahead…." Cameramen fare much better. Writing about *Faithless*, a superb film written by Ingmar Bergman and directed by Liv Ullmann, Simon says, "one of the film's remarkable features is the preponderance of scenes tightly confined within four walls, yet such is [Jörgen] Persson's artistry with light and shadow and shades of colour that his cinematography contributes as much emotion as some filmmakers' entire movies."

How do we know if it's a great film? I think John Simon's recommended test is infallible. In an aside from a review of Erick Zonca's brilliant *Dreamlife of Angels* he notes, "the surest way of testing a movie's greatness is seeing it a second time. If it is just as good, it is a good film. If it gets better in the fineness and fullness of its detail, it is great."

Bruce Beresford

Criticism from
the 1980s

To Russia, With Love

REDS

There were, I think, two ways of making a film about John Reed—author of *Ten Days That Shook the World*, the principal American buried in the Kremlin—and Louise Bryant, his fellow journalist, fellow Communist, and wife. Either you could stick to historical facts, with minor elisions, imaginative guesses, and clarifications added as necessary. Or you could create a fiction based on these real-life characters, preferably not using their actual names. *Reds*, which Warren Beatty co-scripted with Trevor Griffiths, directed, and starred in, falls squarely between the two stools.

We get such flimsy inventions as the now separated husband, Jack, seeking out Louise on a French World War I battlefront to persuade her, amid much marital infighting, to come to Russia with him to cover the brewing Revolution. Just when we assume that Reed is alone on the train to Petrograd, who should come flouncing in, plunking herself down opposite him, and announcing the ground rules that exclude sex, but Louise. And the Petrograd sequences duly switch between fighting, strikes, fevered politics, and Louise and Jack in separate beds (he on a nasty couch), throwing snowballs at each other, playfully tagging along in the march of history, and, as the Revolution succeeds, copulating to the loud strains of the "Internationale," to be, from now on, bedfellows as well as fellow-travelers. War and revolution are mostly an exotic background to spice up the screwball comedy of battling, wisecracking lovers:

while the Revolution is bringing up baby Jack, Jack is educating his
girl Friday—oops, Louise.

Fiction becomes even more arrant when, after the Revolution,
Louise travels from the U.S. under monstrous hardships to seek
out Jack in a Finnish prison whence he has just been sprung, then,
through further perils and privations, treks after him to Russia, in
episodes and shots that clearly derive from *Doctor Zhivago*. But,
at the same time, *Reds* tries to touch upon all the main points of
Reed's public and private life, from an almost subliminal sequence
of Jack as he covers Pancho Villa's uprising, through his quizzical
courtship of Louise, Greenwich Village bohemian days, literary ambitions and journalistic successes, co-founding of the Provincetown
Players and temporary loss of Louise to Eugene O'Neill, political
activism and brief stint in jail, gallant flouting of serious kidney
trouble, founding of the Communist Labor Party as an embattled
splinter group, trips (not quite all of them) to Russia, election to the
Soviet Executive Committee, all the way to his end as a quasi-mar-
tyred hero dying, after numerous marital ups and downs, nursed
by his darling wife. Cause of death: typhus; age: three days short
of thirty-three.

Though originally even longer, the film, as released, is not exactly
short at two hundred minutes; still, trying to cover all this and more,
it is forced to reduce its factual elements to something like a cross
between caricature and an illustrated primer. The cutting is often
so disastrous—surely through no fault of the gifted Dede Allen and
Craig McKay at the head of the team of editors—that we don't know
what happened. Thus when a Bolshevik train Reed is riding on is
ambushed by not clearly identified counter-revolutionary forces,
Jack, unarmed and on foot, chases after the mounted attackers. Cut
to something entirely different, and we are left wondering whether
our hero, steadily harassed by Zinoviev and other *apparatchiks*, was
trying (absurdly) to fight the assailants or merely join them.

Again, Reed's most significant achievement, his innovative journalism—Walter Lippmann said about *Insurgent Mexico* that "with
Jack Reed reporting begins"—is given short shrift; *Ten Days That
Shook the World* is barely mentioned in the movie. And the Jack-
Louise-O'Neill triangle, though dealt with at considerable length,
is greatly romanticized and made much less interesting than the
messier, almost sordid, truth. Yet the greatest problem is that political thought and action are grossly oversimplified if treated at
all. Figures like Kerensky, Lenin, Trotsky, or, even closer to home,

Emma Goldman, Max Eastman, Louis Fraina, etc., pop in and out of the film, but we get only the haziest notions of what they stood for and what Jack's attitude toward them was.

Indeed, the film's view of Communism and Bolshevism remains vague (characteristically, Emma Goldman even pronounces the word as "Boltchevism') as it keeps giving off contradictory signals about both American Communism and the Russian Revolution. There is not enough clarity even for artistic ambiguity; political issues mostly serve to make Jack and Louise appear more or less heroic, passionate, quixotic, or bumbling according to what strikes the filmmakers as most dramatic at any given moment.

There is also a curious device: 32 so-called witnesses appear from time to time, singly or in pairs, reminiscing in close-up about the Jack and Louise they knew. They include such figures as Roger Baldwin, Henry Miller, Adela Rogers St. Johns, Scott Nearing, Will Durant, Rebeca West, George Jessel, and Hamilton Fish, but they are never labeled, so that, if we do not recognize them and do not know their political histories, we cannot tell with how many grains of salt to take their testimonies. Yet these old, wise or childish, preternaturally unlined or movingly webbed and runneled faces—shot against blackness that has since then, in real life, swallowed several of them—are true and beautiful, and what they say, even when it is malicious or fey, irrelevant or riddled with touching memory lapses, has an aura of authenticity about it that is absent from most of the screenplay. Hence these talking portraits, exquisitely photographed by Vittorio Storaro (the rest of his camera work, though equally fine, cannot have the same haunting starkness), steal the show. For here, however faultily conceived or falteringly or mischievousy expressed, are ideas and some disturbing truths which most of the film proper carefully evades.

An additional deadweight is Diane Keaton's Louise. Always a mannered actress—if a few stock expressions mercilessly overused merit the term mannerisms—Miss Keaton is also totally out of place and period in her gestures, inflections, tics. This is not a World War I Oregonian who ran away from her dentist husband but a post-World War II escapee from a New York psychiatrist's couch. The real Louise Bryant was an even paltrier figure than her movie counterpart, but she was charming and vivacious; Miss Keaton suggests a perpetual, dreary analysand endlessly discussing her shrink with anyone who will listen. As Jack Reed, Warren Beatty is dashing and mercurial, but also too cute and less than convincing both in his political passion and in his private anguish over Louise or his failure as an artist.

Among the supporting players, though, only George Plimpton is an embarrassment; everyone else, however ludicrously skimpy the part may be, is at least good, and there is particularly impressive work from Maureen Stapleton as Emma Goldman, and the novelist Jerzy Kosinski as the sinister bureaucrat Zinoviev. Jack Nicholson, as O'Neill, is more restrained and to the point than he has been in a long while; but he is too laid-back, unintellectual, wise-guyish of voice, aspect, and manner for this tormented, complicated, much deeper figure.

Beatty and Griffiths's dialogue is adequate as long as it stays off the big issues and ideas, and not without its moments of cleverness. But the Greenwich Village and Provincetown sequences become tiresome with their mechanistic alternation of "seriousness" and bohemian frivolity, of partying and the Party. And much too much time is spent on "humanizing" Jack and Louise with their love of Christmas trees, bits of furniture, soulful children, and an ultrasoulful puppy that grows into the most golden of retrievers, whose scratching on the bedroom door becomes the obbligato for Jack and Louise's lovemaking. When the dog disappears—done in, it seems, by an ornery FBI agent—it comes as no surprise that the Reeds' lovemaking days are over.

Beatty's direction is commendable when it avoids dogs and tots. It is brisk, uses space and movement well, and can compete with Eisenstein when it comes to the taking of the Winter Palace. Not because of equal talent, to be sure, but because of superior technology and a budget of between $30 and $50 million.

Never exactly boring, sometimes entertaining, *Reds* is frequently irritating and finally disappointing. In a famous phrase, Hölderlin called the Germans "idea-rich and action-poor"; *Reds* is the exact, disconcerting opposite.

Wrong-Note Rag

RAGTIME; PENNIES FROM HEAVEN

For once I am in complete agreement with the majority of my colleagues: *Ragtime*, the movie, does not work, largely because one misses the kaleidoscopic construction of the Doctorow novel. Miloš

Forman, the director, and Michael Weller, the scenarist, chose what they felt to be the principal strands of th is multifarious web: Evelyn Nesbit and the celebrated murder case; Coalhouse Walker Jr., the black musician with his fanatical and fatal quest for justice; Tateh, the impoverished Jew immigrant who works himself up into a movie director; and the typical turn of the century American family that gets itself embroiled with all of them.

Some of the many subplots and characters beyond these make all but subliminal appearances (e.g., Houdini), some ended up on the cutting-room floor (e.g., Emma Goldman) and quite a few (e.g., Henry Ford, J. P. Morgan, Dreiser, Freud, Zapata) never even passed their screenplay test. So, instead of freewheeling ragtime, we get a fugue and a rather unbalanced one at that, with Coalhouse and his vendetta given top priority. A good deal of Doctorow's irreverent, ahistoric, but politically satiric jocularity bites the dust in the process. But could the filmmakers have stayed faithful to the novel? The printed page can work as a kaleidoscope because the reader takes the shuffling and reshuffling images at his own pace, making his quietus whenever he may choose; but a screen-sized kaleidoscope shimmying around relentlessly for several hours would leave audiences dizzy and confused—if it did not just make them leave, period.

So *Ragtime* was doomed from the beginning, and with what may well have been additional pressure from the crass producer, Dino De Laurentiis, Forman ended up making a predominantly earnest social document, a film whose piously liberal intentions, deprived of Doctorow's jazzy texture and mischievous mythmaking, emerge as conventional, indeed stolid, fare, with now and then a jaunty fillip. When history is monkeyed with as recklessly as it is in the novel, it turns out, paradoxically, more acceptable than when it undergoes fewer, lesser distortions, which now sound like false notes in a solemn music. And since the Coalhouse story becomes so important, it cannot help revealing how inferior it is in moral fervor, psychological complexity, and sublime irony to Heinrich von Kleist's masterly novella *Michael Kohlhaas*, from which Doctorow derived the tale as a respectful but reductive *hommage*.

We are left with some very handsome production values—John Graysmark's set designs, Anna Hill Johnstone's costumes, and Miroslav Ondríček's cinematography, individual scenes that work, but are surrounded by others that don't: and a mixed bag of performances. Howard E. Rollins is a superbly restrained, yet emotionally resonant Coalhouse, and there is excellent support from Kenneth McMillan, Elizabeth McGovern, Debbie Allen, Robert Joy, and a couple of others; acceptable performing from Brad Dourif, Mandy Patinkin, and quite a few more; but plodding contributions from James Olson and Mary Steenburgen as father and mother. Norman Mailer is rather stiff as Stanford White even before, mercifully soon, he becomes a stiff; and poor old Jimmy Cagney, as the police commissioner, even though one gets the feeling that he is moved about on casters, still manages to exude cocky authority. In this lean period of the cinema, I cannot reprove whoever admits to having caught the movie; but I doff my hat to him who can say: "No, but I've read the book."

Pennies from Heaven is also an adaptation, but this one from a British TV mini-series, written for the screen by its original author, Dennis Potter, with the help of Herbert Ross, the film's director, and owing a good deal to the choreography of Danny Daniels and the cinematography of Gordon Willis. Otherwise, this gloomy musical is distinguished mostly by its macabre eccentricity. If the trouble with the filmed *Ragtime* was that it lost its novelistic tricks in the translation, the problem with *Pennies* is that it preserves all the devices from the television installment plan and dumps them repetitiously into a full-length movie, where they are changed from flashy brainstorms into a long, soggy monsoon.

Steve Martin plays a sheet-music salesman at the height, or depth, of the Depression: an indefatigable optimist who believes the facile uplift in the pop songs he peddles, but whose life, like most of the circumambient lives, is sinking into poverty and sordidness. Martin himself, or his prudish and goody-goody wife, Jessica Harper, or Bernadette Peters, his girlfriend who goes from schoolmistress to mistress to prostitute, will at odd moments burst into big, period song-and-dance numbers, lip-synching the renditions of various Depression-era singers, sometimes even with a voice of the opposite sex seemingly issuing from their mouths.

The point is to show the disparity between people's fantasies and reality at a time when the gap was maximal, and to remind us of it further by the discrepancy between the seedy circumstances in which the songs begin and the lavish locales and trappings of movie musicals into which they are transported. We are to see minds mired in mirages even as bodies bog down in the morass of reality. Yet however potent a gimmick this may be, it is still only a gimmick, and once you have gasped, chuckled, and snorted at it, there is nothing left for you but to sink likewise into your own personal depression, aesthetic rather than economic. Daniels's dances continue to delight the eye, Ross's overall direction often stimulates the inner eye, and Willis's photography is so sensuous as to reach beyond the sense of sight to that of touch. But the device becomes more and more *device*, and instead of being supportive of the story, turns divisive. An idea, you see, goes somewhere: a device merely jumps around in a circumscribed space.

The tale is dreary without being hortatory, revelatory, or cathartic. If a repressed wife, after much urging, rouges her nipples to please her husband's libido, it doesn't help keep him from a more spontaneously erotic mistress; if said wife pours her little inherited nest egg into her husband's quixotic business enterprise, everything ends up lost. If the girlfriend loses her job, she also loses her unborn child by abortion, her respectability through prostitution, and, finally, her lover to the gallows for a rape-murder he did not commit. There is, to be sure, a tacked-on palinode of a happy ending, but I doubt if it washes even with the great unwashed. You begin to feel that the supposedly realistic miseries are piled on just as arbitrarily and factitiously as the slaphappy fantasies and self-delusions. Instead of tragic irony, we get excogitated trickery.

Nevertheless, there is much visual, musical, choreographic inventiveness afoot. But, again, there are even gimmicks within gimmicks. Thus the sympathetic wandering musician, affectingly played by Vernel Bagneris, turns out to be the supreme malefactor; the most electrifying character (smartly played and danced by Christopher Walken) has to be an odious pimp: and the most innocent person, a touching blind girl, must come to the most gruesome end. And a couple of showy shots skillfully but gratuitously recreate two of Edward Hopper's most famous paintings. Nothing kills affect like an excess of effect.

Steve Martin works hard, dances well, and is less Steve Martinish than one would expect: but he lacks the basic charm to make his character at least a winning loser. Jessica Harper; has, in a few short years, lost all her fresh winsomeness, though in this role that hardly matters. Bernadette Peters, however, is on the button and as cute as one, and there are also good supporting performances. *Pennies from Heaven* exercises a semi-morbid, semi-leg-pulling fascination; you might not want to walk a mile for it, but once there, a blend of incredulity and bedevilment will keep you from wanting to walk out.

Neither/Nor

VICTOR/VICTORIA

With *Victor/Victoria* Blake Edwards reconfirms his place as one of Hollywood's sleaziest directors, rivaled only by a select few such as Otto Preminger, Paul Schrader, Brian De Palma, and Richard Brooks. Edwards's particular forte is his often extolled "professionalism," but, as William S. Pechter reminds us, "the Hollywood film industry is one place . . . where professionalism and conformity all too easily merge." Two Edwards films, *Experiment in Terror* and *Days of Wine and Roses*, have their respectable champions; the numerous other productions of the master of *Operation Petticoat*, *Breakfast at Tiffany's*, *Darling Lili*, and the various *Pink Panther* movies (than which I would rather see pink elephants) appeal chiefly to crazed cultists and simpleminded pseudo-sophisticates.

Victor/Victoria is based on a 1933 Reinhold Schünzel film (and its clones), and looks for all intents and purposes like one of Billy Wilder's feebler efforts, which is to say very feeble indeed. This is the story of Victoria, a down-and-out English singer in the Paris of 1934, who falls in with Toddy, an aging homosexual entertainer of indeterminate nationality, who, likewise on the rocks, turns her into an alleged Polish count and purportedly the world's finest female impersonator. As Victor now, she proves wildly successful in one of Paris's leading nightclubs, and the two friends are rolling in money if not in bed. Along comes King Marchan (James Garner), a big Chicago nightclub owner with gangland connections, who may sign up the new sensation; instead, to his horror, he finds himself falling in love with what appears to be a man. So he hides out in Victor's bathroom, discovers the truth, then comically pretends to be succumbing to a homosexual passion. I'll spare you the various peripeties, among them the coming out of the closet of King's brawny but comical bodyguard (Alex Karras) but rest assured that all ends well for hetero- and homosexuals alike.

Edwards's screenplay, aside from the usual complement of sexual and other gags, has the principal aim of cashing in on the new trend of let's-be-sweet-to-homosexuals pictures, in which the idea is to make inversion as nearly indistinguishable as possible from so-called normality. (*Personal Best* and *Making Love* are two other recent and dishonest specimens.) Here the method is to talk grandly about the equality of all sexualities and of shame being "an unhappy

emotion invented by pietists in order to exploit the human race,"
while the seemingly homosexual relationship is, of course, a safely
heterosexual one: and also to show us the main homosexual, Toddy,
played by that fine, strapping fellow, Robert Preston, who, as we
all know, is synonymous with red-blooded manliness and, when
performing a musical drag act by way of the film's climax, wouldn't
fool an anchorite about his true sexuality.*

Yet Edwards's real feelings protrude from under the sanctimonious sugarcoating in the portrayal of a lesser homosexual figure
such as Toddy's castoff lover as an effete, nasty, mercenary, cowardly little bitch whom a woman, Victoria, can pulverize with a
single blow: or, again, in such jests as Toddy's line on waking up
sick, "There's nothing more inconvenient than an old queen with
a head cold," while the moviegoers roar with presumably unexploited, nonpietistic glee.

The writing in *Victor/Victoria* is, on top of its steady obviousness,
wholly anachronistic and insensitive to the alleged locale, what with
all these liberated and happily adjusted homosexuals in 1934 calling themselves "gay," and everyone in Paris quoting Shakespeare
or vocalizing to "Home on the Range" or even, in a workers' dive,
to "Sweet Adeline." This is made more ludicrous by bits of French
dialogue in the background and authentic posters near the edges
of a frame. And whenever we get one of Leslie Bricusse and Henry
Mancini's plodding song numbers, accompanied by routine dancing, we are once again solidly ensconced in the never and nowhere
of Hollywood through the ages.

More deplorable yet is Edwards's directing. Although his technique flows along smoothly, and he generally knows when an extreme close-up is called for or when to end a sequence with a blackout, we realize soon enough that we've seen it all before. Every shot
is dictated by conventional wisdom, no camera angle or movement
takes us by surprise, no piece of business (e.g., Victor's repeated
smoothing down of his shortcropped hair each time he removes his
feminine wig to display his masculinity) is anything but a cliché.
And Edwards has no sense of where to stop: scenes go on past their
comic point, a running gag must be practicing for the marathon,
undifferentiated brawls recur over and over again, window panes
obtrude at regular intervals so a scene can be shot in pantomime,

---

*That in real life Preston was a closeted homosexual, in no way detracts from the
intensely heterosexual persona he conveyed on screen and stage.

a private eye hiding in a closet not only gets his finger caught in its door but also, when he shows up later with a grotesquely bandaged index finger, is sure to have someone slam it with a mallet.

Mrs. Edwards, Julie Andrews, contributes woman- and manfully to this family enterprise. In her husband's *10*, she semi-revealed her bosom; in his next, *S.O.B.*, she unveiled it completely (though skeptics noticed certain underpinnings); now, even more daringly, she discloses her utter lack of sexuality. As Victoria, she comes across rather masculine; as Victor, as being in some sexless no-man's- and no-woman's-land. Her performance is mechanically precise, her singing soullessly correct, and her entire presence no more alive than a peg, on which the picture can hang itself. James Garner is considerably (and surprisingly) better: Robert Preston (unsurprisingly) better yet—though not, as some have claimed, extraordinary. Homophobia, Mr. Edwards informs us through his wife's mouth, has been created by "pious ministers and terrified heterosexuals." *Victor/Victoria* has been created by a non-risk-taking heterosexual and a pious fraud.

E. T. etc.

POLTERGEIST; E.T.: THE EXTRA-TERRESTRIAL

Every national magazine would seem to have had a cover story celebrating the simultaneous release of *Poltergeist* and *E.T.: The Extra-Terrestrial*, and the glory of their creator, Steven Spielberg—which is about as close to canonization as you can get in this secular society. Of the two films, *Poltergeist* is by far the lesser, so let's get it out of the way first. It takes place in a suburban housing tract, the residence of whose chief real-estate salesman, Steve Freeling, the poltergeists take over. At first they rather amuse him and his with-it wife, Diane (the couple smoke pot at bedtime), though they scare the bejesus out of their younger children, Robbie and Carol Anne. (Dana, the eldest, often sleeps out and seems to be a bit of a swinger.) So long as the poltergeists content themselves with raising fairly complete havoc with the house and its inhabitants, the Freelings, absurdly, try to cope with the situation. When the spirits spirit away little Carol Anne, the parents get frantic and call in a team of parapsychologists, who, however, prove even more incompetent than their hosts.

Eventually, a dwarfish spiritualist, Tangina, is summoned, and she challenges the poltergeists more seriously. I can't begin to summarize the absurdities—some of them stickily metaphysical—that Tangina rattles off, or explain the enigmatic machinations of the imps. Finally it is Diane who goes into what seems to be the maw of hell gaping inside a closet of the house (a concept borrowed from such equally dreadful movies as *The Sentinel* and *The Amityville Horror*) and, at the cost of enormous physical and psychic suffering, returns through the ceiling with her daughter, both of them covered with a writhing substance that appears to be part infestation of worms, part Jello. Do the Freelings now leave their house? No such brains; they stay on for another night of agony and special effects.

Only when the dead (whose burial ground has been violated by the housing complex—hence their photogenic revenge) emerge in various stages of grisly decomposition from the Freeling swimming pool and elsewhere to carry off the entire house does the family get the message and move into a motel. By this time I wouldn't have cared if it had been a roach motel.

Nothing that Spielberg writes, directs, or produces ever makes sense. Here he is billed as producer and co-scenarist, with the direction credited to Tobe Hooper, the director of the crude *The Texas Chainsaw Massacre*, but the fine Spielbergian hand is detectable everywhere. There is, to begin with, a fundamental self-contradiction. Spielberg the eternal adolescent wants his spirits jolly and likable; he has said there is "something wondrous and hopeful" about the hauntings. So these frolicsome cadavers are merely paying people back for the desecration of their resting place (shades of *The Shining!*), and are, initially, mostly droll and prankish. But Spielberg also wants horror, hence the abduction of the child, the terrible things befalling various people, and the rotting undead busting out all over.

Contradictions are even more plentiful than shocks. Thus there is a dread fight into which the spirits are dragging Carol Anne, and Diane receives contradictory instructions from Tangina and the rest about whether to go toward the light or away from it. This becomes utterly, though unintentionally, farcical, as do sundry other things meant to be frightening. Yet even the basic concepts of everyday living make no sense. Why should the flowered front lawn of the Freelings suddenly be dug up to make way for a swimming pool? What connection is there between a tremendous tornado and the poltergeists? How does a tree in the garden become allied with the poltergeists, who are, as everyone knows, household imps? No trace of consistency or credibility in any of this. Thus the spirits first emerge from the Freelings' television set; by way of a cute ending, after the family has moved into the motel, we see the door open and Steve Freeling toss the motel TV out on its ears, or antennas. Yet only an army of poltergeists or Superman himself could rip a chained motel TV from its moorings.

Even horror fantasy must play by certain rules to make us respect its premises, go along with it, and experience catharsis. *Poltergeist*, however, is the kind of movie where the reviewer needn't even worry about giving away the plot; the only thing not to be given away is the opticals—they alone matter. The writing—by Spielberg, Michael Grais, and Mark Victor—is execrable, and the character of the midget psychic, as enacted by Zelda Rubinstein, easily creepier than the corpses and special effects. The children are a perfectly boring trio, poorly acted to boot, and Carol Anne is so sickeningly sweet that we root for the poltergeists to keep her. Not even Jobeth Williams, an able and winning actress, can arouse much concern for Diane; as for Steve, if he is meant to be a consummate lug, Craig T. Nelson certainly meets the challenge.

E.T. is much more likable stuff, though scarcely more coherent. Here an extraterrestrial from a peaceably exploring spaceship is chased by mysterious earthlings (throughout the film we never see their faces) and the ship takes off without him. A series of amusing adventures brings the odd-looking but highly intelligent little extra-terrestrial—E.T. for short, which he is—into the sheltering care of ten-year-old Elliott (which, you might say, is E . . . t for long). Smart and adorable Elliott harbors and instructs E.T. in human ways; reluctantly lets his older brother, Michael, and younger sister, Gertie, in on his secret; and leaves loving Mom, still suffering from being forsaken by Dad, out of it. As an adult, she is out of it, anyway, not even noticing E.T. when he is underfoot.

Elliott develops a strange, telepathic kinship with E.T.; if the little creature, for instance, gets drunk on beer from the family fridge, the boy, at school, starts burping and crapulously ogling his prettiest classmate. As E.T. learns to talk human, he conveys an ever greater longing to return home. A Buck Rogers comic strip gives him an idea, and various household objects provide the means, for building a radar with which to signal his distant star.

Meanwhile he begins to sicken, even as the pursuing men zero in on his hiding place. They discover him, and NASA turns Elliott's dwelling into a superhospital in which the boy is medically parted from his spiritual Siamese twin just as the latter appears to die. He revives by a miracle left unexplained (like so many other things), and Elliott, Michael, Gertie, and their previously skeptical chums help him escape to his radar station in the woods. When the chasing men in their cars get too close, E.T. simply lets the bikes of his rescuers take to the air and fly into the forest. The spaceship returns, and there is a tearful farewell during which Elliott turns down an offer to accompany E.T. into space, but the sadness is mitigated by Mom's having found the one NASA man with a heart (played, characteristically, by an Indian actor, Peter Coyote), who'll doubtless replace her errant spouse, and by E.T.'s explaining to Elliott that they'll remain friends forever, even with a universe between them.

As others have pointed out, *E.T.* is derived from two sources: the child-and-animal story, where the growing child must finally give up or be given up by his pet, and *Peter Pan*, which, for purposes of self-protection, is actually read aloud by Mom to Gertie in one scene. But these are better archetypes than the wretched ones in *Poltergeist*, and Melissa Mathison's screenplay plays heartwarming variations on them. Nevertheless, there are glaring inconsistencies from the outset: How can the waddling, slow-moving E.T. escape from his human pursuers? And how can such superior intelligences not be equipped to deal with discovery by earthlings? Why can E.T. manage escape by flying at certain times, and not at others? Why does he need Buck Rogers to tell him about radar? Why does he sicken when, and in the way, he does; then recover in equally inscrutable fashion? And so, inconsistently, on. Most impenetrable is the physio-telecommunication between him and Elliott, as well as its fudged cessation.

But there are delightful compensations. First, there is more story, more characterization, more human interest than in *Poltergeist*, and the special effects subserve these rather than vice versa. Then too, the children here are more interesting, idiosyncratic, flavorous—even if still too good to be true—and they are enacted better by Henry Thomas, Robert Macnaughton, and Drew Barrymore. Again, humankind in general and NASA in particular are a more piquant set of antagonists (not to say heavies) than a bunch of preposterous and inconsistent poltergeists. Finally, the jokes here are more numerous and funnier. In fact, there are even places where you can suspend your disbelief; in *Poltergeist*, you cannot find one firm hook on which to hang it.

E.T. himself is a cunningly devised creature (by Carlo Rambaldi, whose progeny includes the ETs in *Close Encounters* and the second *King Kong*) in whom outlandishness and winsomeness are so intertwined that we can become neither repelled by nor oversentimental about him. Even his voice conforms to the schema: it is unearthly but affecting. There are many amusing references to the work of Spielberg's partner in other ventures, George Lucas, for those who like in-jokes. Allen Daviau's cinematography looks opulent without turning too gorgeous or cute, and most of the special effects work in an understated manner. Regrettably overstated, though, is John Williams's score: the more Wagnerian its aims, the more Jawsy the result. Its fishily Nibelungian ring and rant should be promptly put to rest.

An Intellectual Suspect

THE WORLD ACCORDING TO GARP

The Germans have a word for it: *Edelkitsch*, noble trash. Some recent fictional examples of it are *Fear of Flying*, *The White Hotel*, and *The World According to Garp*, John Irving's novel falling somewhere midway between D. M. Thomas's and Erica Jong's. As Calvin Bedient has remarked about another Thomas, R. S., his "poems have an almost visible brilliance," and so, too, has Irving's *magnum opus*: an intense, cute, rather labored brilliance that obscures all else—both the little that is there and the lot that pretends to be. The movie of *Garp*, written by Steve Tesich and directed by George Roy Hill, seems to me both more simpleminded and better than the novel. If this sounds like faint praise, it is meant so. Still, as movies go these days, it may not be all that faint after all.

Garp, as almost everyone knows—for almost everyone reads *Edelkitsch*, or reads enough about it to feel that he has read it—concerns well-born Jenny Fields, a nurse and fierce feminist, who wants a child but no husband, and so, during World War II, conceives by a dying ball-turret gunner, Technical Sergeant Garp, a child she names T. S. Garp. Already you can see the cutesiness of it. Even though young Garp explains to the girl he will marry that T. S. used to stand for Terribly Shy but now stands for Terribly Sexy, what reader will not associate it with T. S. Eliot? And since Garp is also Irving, the apotheosis is complete.

As you must further know, Jenny will write her autobiography as a "sexual suspect" and become a great guru for embattled feminists, including the Ellen Jamesians, who cut out their tongues to show their solidarity with Ellen James, a girl who was raped and had her tongue cut out to prevent her from betraying her violator. As you must also know, Garp, who, just like John Irving, turns into both a fine wrestler and a noted writer, is not so successful as his charismatically best-selling mother, but does well enough to marry nice Helen Holm, who becomes a professor of English. They have nice children whom they adore so much that a parental night out may consist of their getting into their car parked just outside, and watching through the windows their children playing with the baby-sitter. And yet they somehow start cheating on each other, and . . .

But why am I telling you all this? If you already know it, you surely want to forget it; if you don't and decide to see the movie, which greatly depends on oddball twists, you're better off if you're kept guessing. The novel's complicated plot and subplots have been considerably pared down. This makes the film less tricky and cloyingly sentimental than the book, and also less sadistic: the mutilations in which Irving revels have been omitted or toned down. On the other hand, certain absurdist elements that fit into the fabric of the book are doubly bothersome in the film. First, because film, unable to circumvent the real world, is intrinsically less hospitable to absurdism; and, second, because the screenplay winnows out so many absurdist elements that those left in stick out more jarringly.

Even so, one cannot but admire the talent for compression and suggestion that both Hill and Tesich exhibit. Take the very title sequence: to the accompaniment of the Beatles singing "Will you still love me when I'm 64?" an angelically smiling yet slightly befuddled baby keeps bouncing skyward. We do not see the cause of his soarings: is baby Garp being tossed up by his mother, or is he already on the great trampoline of life, treading air before even walking the earth? Then the film proper begins as Jenny announces her motherhood to her shocked parents (beautifully sketched in by Hume Cronyn and Jessica Tandy). Father blusters mutedly, mother exercises martyred self-control, Jenny glows with quiet arrogance; the whole family nexus is there in one quick epiphany. Tesich and Hill keep moving things along: if you don't like this scene, never mind, there'll be another one along in a jiffy.

Certain elements are handled more suavely than in the book, without, however, being shirked, e.g., the inadvertent emasculation by fellatio during the car crash. A potentially sticky character, such as Robert/Roberta, the transsexual football player, emerges charming, thanks largely to John Lithgow's thoroughly winning performance. The same goes for the brief appearance of Amanda Plummer as Ellen James. Even young Garp's fantasy about his aeronautical father's epic demise, done as a cartoon sequence partly drawn and partly dreamed by the child, comes off with flying colors. And though there are countless clever children pullulating throughout the movie, they do not, individually or collectively, sour us on their sweetness.

There are, however, less pleasant aspects. Garp, the delectable wrestler, writer, cook, and clown, is played by Robin Williams merely adequately; beware of television celebrities in even slightly more demanding movie roles. When the neighbors' dog bites off one of young Garp's ears, as the dialogue plainly states, Williams, no van Gogh, continues to display a matched set; a real actor would have done something about that. But it is not so much too many ears as too little variety that makes Williams mediocre. As his wife, Mary Beth Hurt is much better; as his mother, Glenn Close outclasses him totally. The film is a triumph for Miss Close; she makes the half-whimsical, half-insufferable Jenny, a sort of intellectualized comic-strip character, into a unified, flesh-and-blood being, believably strange and strangely likable. She looks right: asexually attractive; sounds right: calmly, crisply commanding; and acts right: adamantly wrestling Irving's flightiest fancies down to earth.

Most of the supporting roles are well handled, and Irving himself makes a congenial cameo appearance as a wrestling referee. Miroslav Ondríček's unassumingly authoritative cinematography makes the most of some extremely well-chosen locations. And, as I said, the film moves right along. But, as I also said, it is *Edelkitsch* or, *anglice*, garpage.

Time Stands Still

Nothing, however, is quite harmless in *Time Stands Still*, young Péter Gothár's second feature film. It begins with grainy black-and-white documentary footage of the 1956 Hungarian uprising, then switches seamlessly into the story: the freedom fighters have been defeated and a father is escaping to America, but his wife and two young sons refuse to follow him. An electric street sign—a circle of bulbs—flashes in the background; many bulbs are missing, like teeth from a defeated mouth. Mother and sons—Gábor, about ten, and Dénes, seven or eight—watch grimly as Father sneaks out of the country.

They are at the window again, but it is 1963, and the film, almost too brilliantly shot by Lajos Koltai, has taken on color. A quirky expressionist color, slightly unnatural and disorienting—as if a Käthe Kollwitz drawing had been casually tinted by Kirchner. It will become yet more eccentrically colored as the events become more lurid. The family of an escapee are semi-undesirables, and Gábor's chances of getting into medical school are slim. A sassy, sexy schoolgirl, Magda, has become smitten with Dénes and has infiltrated his cheerless ballroom-dancing class where kids learn obsolescent dances. Dénes responds to Magda's allure, but she used to go with the upper-form rebel leader whose *nom de guerre* is Pierre, and Dénes is jealous and a virgin. He suspects a trick and will not see her.

School life is a mess. A funny classmate of Dénes's has stolen some obscene photos from his father's drawer; the two boys try to sell them to the upper-formers, but are snubbed and denounced. The beastly assistant headmaster and his minions search the entire class, but the form master—a nice old Russian teacher who is deeply religious—covers up for Dénes, then lectures him in private about the sanctity of love and sex. Meanwhile, Bodor, Father's best friend, is released from jail and, in a scene full of bitter double entendres, gets Mother to take him in. He becomes her lover, but the boys drive a fairly hard bargain before they accept him.

Gábor fears that his chances at medical school are worse still with Bodor in the house, but Bodor's position (as a skilled technician) improves. Yet "they" may be setting him up as a fall guy. Magda, steadily rejected by Dénes, becomes Gábor's bedmate, which crushes Dénes. Bodor gives him some cynical advice. At school, a new form mistress—bright, perky, tough—replaces the old form master, who, in political disgrace, is transferred to a provincial school. But Dénes meets him in Budapest at a candlelight procession on Good Friday and, aching from Magda's betrayal, insults him and his ideas of love.

Dénes also has a strange love-hate relation with the new form mistress, and won't work for her. Mother visits the teacher in the latter's apartment; her husband, a former high-ranking Communist, is lavishly pensioned but in disfavor; he has become crazed, and his wife must lock him in his room. The two women begin to talk as mother and teacher but discover their past Political antagonism; the situation grows tense, even though the teacher warns about taking out their damaged lives on the kids. There is a national celebration, and the headmaster addresses the students in their various classrooms over a PA system; Pierre seizes the microphone and creates a funny "antisocial" disruption. Dénes and two other boys laugh at the address, and are grilled in class by the assistant head in a scene that, for wry comedy, would be hard to surpass. The new mistress earns the class's grudging admiration for her courage. Pierre, expelled, wrecks the school with his henchmen, jumps from a window, and lands in the hospital.

The plot goes on, extremely complex and always either funny and touching or sardonic and earthy. American popular music, Coca-Cola, and neon lights are allowed into Hungary. The kids are singing and dancing to Elvis Presley songs, getting high on Cokes that they believe to be drugged, and are seen in new, exotic illumination. Camera angles are slightly distorting; camera movements, explosive. The editing is elliptical, the color virulent. There are sexual initiations and plans to flee the country; an attempted suicide pops up in a comic context. Politics changes relationships; Bodor, who was gutsy and sarcastic when the going was roughest, is rising to the top and getting scared. A popular song of the period, "Time Stands Still," sheds its ambiguity on the proceedings: Does it mean *plus ça change*, or that timeless happiness is coming?

Toward the end, ironies, ambiguities, plot twists jostle one another. The circle of lights in the street is almost repaired: most of the bulbs are on. Events augur well, especially for Dénes and Magda. Then we skip to 1967 and an ironic epilogue. Things work out in a bittersweet, melancholy way. But all the lights in the circle are in full glow.

Both the older professionals and the young amateurs act splendidly for Gothár. No less splendid are the political ironies, the interaction of public and private happenings. Much is left ambiguous, but our concern can fill in the gaps. For an Iron Curtain film, *Time Stands Still* is remarkably courageous and provocative. For any kind of film, it is challenging and rewarding.

Harrowed Heroine, Harassed Audience

SOPHIE'S CHOICE

Suffering through the 157 minutes of pretentiousness and boredom that make up Alan J. Pakula's movie version of *Sophie's Choice*, I drew what consolation I could from having merely skimmed William Styron's underlying novel rather than wasting many more hours reading it. In his forthcoming book, *The American Novel and the Way We Live Now*, John W. Aldredge persuasively demolishes Styron's novel, and concludes that "with all it's pretensions to literary majorness, *Sophie's Choice* is clearly a phony book, as imaginatively inauthentic as it is intellectually without content." Aldredge points out that the terrible choice (an ss officer at Auschwitz threatened to have both of Sophie's children gassed unless she picked out one to be saved) was forced on the heroine, so that "the culpability belonged to the officer and not to her."

Aldredge may be a mite too rational, here, but he is right in saying that Sophie's sin, if sin there was—it was, after all, the only way of saving even one child—is too venal, and was expiated by many horrors undergone, not the least of which was the heroine's offering herself to Hoess, the commandant of Auschwitz, in exchange for her surviving child's life, being refused by him, and having that child perish too. A refugee in America, sick and starving, Sophie, a Polish Catholic, is rescued by Nathan Landau, ostensibly a biological researcher making important discoveries. By the time they are living together, however, Nathan has become viciously doubtul of her, and his beatings are as violent as their lovemaking, even though he knows nothing of her "guilty" past.

To quote Aldredge: "Nathan, after having been blown up by Styron into a kind of vengeful Old Testament Jehovah, is revealed to be . . . simply a paranoid schizophrenic and drug addict who has been lying about the important scientific work . . . and whose goal is to persuade Sophie to join him in a suicide pact. Her second 'choice' of death, therefore, seems not an act of atonement for a guilt which, after all, she lacks sufficient reason for having, but an indication that finally she is as insane as he is." Aldredge goes on to remark that Styron assumes that by going on for pages and pages he will "sooner or later blunder on his theme." Styron indulges "in sham

theatrics and specious intimations that there exist large meanings
just beneath the surface of his materials, that dark and inscrutable
fates, dooms and curses are hard at work shaping the grim destinies
of his characters," who, however, are too trivial, self-contradictory,
and boring to sustain "the great epic weight he tries to impose on
them."

All these flaws are inherited by the movie and augmented by
those Pakula, as writer and director, contributed to it. In the novel,
Stingo, the young Southerner who comes to New York to be a novelist, has guilt of his own involving the legacy of slavery, but these
have been excised from the film. Here Stingo, the author's alter ego,
is just a nice, innocent, lovable young fellow trying to write a great
novel and get himself laid. He is filled with admiration for Nathan
and secret love for Sophie, while having unsuccessful skirmishes
with other girls. When this perfect little Boy Scout finally loses
his virginity to Sophie, he proves a superb lover and is promptly
relieved from responsibility for this older, difficult woman by her
running back to the demented Nathan and the aforementioned
double suicide.

The film leaves far too much unexplored. Why do Nathan and
Sophie, who keep apart from the other tenants of the Brooklyn
boarding-house, befriend this funny little Stingo? And where are
all those other tenants and the landlady most of the time? The
boarding-house seems, day and night, a playpen for the exclusive
delectation of our three comrades. Where and how does Sophie
work? Where does Nathan, who has a menial librarian's job, get
all the money he throws around? Where do the elaborate Southern costumes with which the lovers tease Stingo come from? (Poor
costume design, as usual, from Albert Wolsky.) How does Stingo
support himself? Why does the non-Jewish Sophie, who goes to
Auschwitz for buying a contraband ham, take her children along
to the camp? The linguistically gifted daughter of a professor, who
taught her many languages, she speaks a German elaborate enough
for Martin Heidegger; why then does she butcher English in every
way, including such crudely audience-pleasing malapropisms as
when she congratulates Stingo on his nice "cocksucker suit"?

In the largely idyllic Brooklyn scenes, Pakula clearly wants to
rival the carefree threesome sequences from *Jules and Jim*. But here
the trio is not a ménage à trois, and the devoted Stingo is constantly
tortured by Nathan and Sophie's flagrant lovemaking, which turns
the relationship into something unequal, uncharming. And not

in the action, dialogue, direction, or acting is there the infectious spontaneity that implicates us in Truffaut's film. In fact, so graceless, repetitious, and doughy are these scenes that we come to yearn for a concentration-camp flashback to relieve the tedium—surely not the desired effect, aesthetically or morally.

The casting and acting do not help. Meryl Streep, despite a good Polish accent, is wrong for Sophie. Every five minutes, it seems, someone—man, woman, child, or beast gushes about Sophie's beauty. Even as a shorn-headed, emaciated camp inmate, she all but turns the commandant's head, not to mention softening the hard Nazified heart of his mean daughter, with her loveliness. Whoever looks at her, from Auschwitz to Brooklyn, is smitten: yet Miss Streep is only a decently ordinary-looking woman whose wide, angular face is imperfectly filled out by her features, even when they are as large and wavy as her nose. Though an impressive actress in comedy and character parts, she was not cut out for femmes fatales or ethereal leading ladies. It may well be her miscasting in *The French Lieutenant's Woman*, the worthless *Still of the Night*, and now this that propels her into compensation by overacting. She has become more mannered from role to role; as Sophie, she takes an unconscionable time to deliver her lines, what with *moues*, hesitancies, false starts, medial pauses, grace notes of every sort. A good quarter-hour of the film's unendurable length might have been lopped off had Pakula gotten her to play straight.

The two main men are likewise, and even more, wrong. As Nathan, Kevin Kline transports his flamboyant stage acting intact to the screen, where his ferocious exaggerations punch almost visible holes in the celluloid. As Stingo, the gifted comedian Peter MacNicol looks and acts like a dopey, wide-eyed and protruding-eared, gee-whiz-kid of 15, and reaches heights of the ridiculous in the love scenes with Miss Streep, who looks like his smothering mother. He is even harder to accept as a novelist than Styron himself, and his Deep Southern accent, never Virginian, vanishes as suddenly as it remembers to come. For further confusion, the wordy and supererogatory voiceover commentary by Stingo grown older, is delivered by Josef Sommer in an authentic Virginia accent. Among, the inconsequential supporting players only Karlheinz Hackl, as an uneasy Nazi doctor, scores by playing cleanly, without histrionic curlicues.

Nestor Almendros is a brilliant cinematographer, but here he cannot do much with the gooey pink walls of the boarding-house

(Army surplus paint, cheaply acquired by the landlady) among which so much of the maundering takes place. Pakula is running out of tricks: he shoots a library here with a similar crane shot to the one in *All the President's Men* and he makes the nocturnal railway station in Auschwitz so grandiosely sinister that it becomes less terrifying than in the seedily matter-of-fact treatment it gets in numerous Eastern or Central European films. The same goes for the other camp sequences, despite their having been shot in Yugoslavia under the usually gifted production designer George Jenkins. Even the music, culled from five or six classical composers, manages to be unfailingly pretentious.

In reviewing Styron's previous novel, *The Confessions of Nat Turner*, Wilfred Sheed raised the question: "Can a pastiche of this kind, however skillful, serve as a vehicle for genuine feeling? The answer, in terms of fiction, of the 'felt-life,' surely has to be no." It is no again in terms of this overblown, underrealized movie, which battens impertinently on the Holocaust even as it flattens out into depthless length whatsoever it touches.

Tootsie

Tootsie is fun. There have been years, perhaps decades, in film history when that would have been modest praise, but these days, this year, a film that is more or less adult fun (although children can enjoy it too) is worth, in E. M. Forster's phrase about democracy, two cheers, anyway. Many screenwriters worked on the project, which underwent radical changes; Sydney Pollack, the director, and Dustin Hoffman, the star, had grave disagreements—probably fights—in the making of it. Bill Murray's part, apparently, got slashed so heavily that he wanted no screen credit. The film took forever to finish. And yet the result is not a patchwork, but a nice, continuous piece of work. Not the comedy of the decade, not a laugh riot, and not a significant step ahead in man-woman relations. But fun.

Michael Dorsey (Hoffman) is one of those difficult New York "method" actors. Because of what he would call perfectionism and directors a pain in the ass, and because his looks, too, are against him, he hasn't had a part in two years. He works as a waiter, conducts informal acting classes (there is no hunger like that of struggling actors for a guru), and wants to raise money for an avant-garde play,

Return to the Love Canal, by his roommate, Jeff (Bill Murray). His hysterical part-time girlfriend, Sandy (Teri Garr), is turned down for the role of Emily Kimberley, the hospital administrator on the soap *Southwest General*, whereupon Michael disguises himself as one Dorothy Michaels and lands the part. His energetic, brusquely no-nonsense, tacitly feminist persona soon wins him adulation from the viewers, impresses the management (what with fan mail and ratings), and earns respect from his fellow actors. Though Ron, the arrogant director (Dabney Coleman), remains hostile, John Van Horn, the cast lecher who plays a doctor on the show (George Gaynes), is soon pursuing Dorothy, and Julie (Jessica Lange), who plays the promiscuous blonde nurse and is Ron's real-life girlfriend, develops a strong affection for her.

Only Jeff knows Dorothy's true identity. The imposture turns oppressive when Les, Julie's father and a goodnatured farmer (Charles Durning), becomes enamored of Dorothy and wants to marry her, and when Michael himself falls in love with Julie, and when, moreover, Michael's ruthless agent (very well played by the director, Sydney Pollack), who earlier refused to submit his client for more jobs, now won't let him get out of this one. There are double-entendres, misunderstandings, complications galore that I would not go into if I could; suffice it to say that every ounce of humor is gotten out of the situation without squeezing too hard and effortfully, and, better yet, without ignoring the pathos that is also inherent. For the imposture, like its unmasking, brings about disappointments for some, and the guardedly, intelligently happy ending is earned with wistfulness as well as wit.

Nevertheless, there are a good many improbabilities here, disbelief in some of which is suspendable, in some not. Chief among the latter are Hoffman's excessive homeliness as a woman (he's no beauty as a man, either) and his terribly strained, rasping female voice. And some of the goings-on on this TV soap are a bit too much even for satire. Still, this is less important than the maturity and taste with which certain dicey episodes are handled—for example, the scene in which Michael, revealed as a male, tries to make peace with the humiliated and incensed Les, or the one in which Julie, concluding that Dorothy must be a lesbian with designs on her, becomes hostile and turns away. Even some of the raucously comic scenes are imbued with a certain tact, as when the horny Van Horn bulldozes his way into Dorothy's pad and, finding Jeff there, retreats embarrassedly. Only in some sequences in the TV studio, and the lunch scene between Dorothy and her/his discomfited agent, is comedy pushed into farce; but these, as also the various audition scenes where Michael is comically rejected, being madly show-biz, lend themselves to hyperbole.

Larry Gelbart and Murray Schisgal, who are credited with the final screenplay; Sydney Pollack, himself a quondam actor; and, of course, the notoriously hard-to-work-with Dustin Hoffman—all know the milieu of desperate New York actors, so that the anguished acting-exercise scenes and the overcompensatory gaiety of the party scene have a comic-horrible authenticity. The frantic would-be actress Sandy is particularly well observed: it is merely unfortunate that Teri Garr is herself so charmless and untalented that, instead of acting, she lives the part, which makes the spectator uncomfortable. Nor is Jessica Lange quite capable of conveying the unease of being gorgeous outside and benighted within. But others are wonderful: George Gaynes, as the hack actor and hack Lothario, splendidly unaware of his ludicrousness and endearingly funny-sad because of it; Charles Durning, as Les, barely controlling his ultimate rage, yet precariously salvaging some comic dignity; Doris Belack, as the ultra-efficient producer of *Southwest General*, allowing the robot within her a smidgen of humanity. And there is a delightful *objet trouvé* (I assume) of a performance from a toddler, Julie's child, for whom Dorothy baby-sits with cataclysmic results in one of the film's least resistible scenes.

And Hoffman? He works hard, is almost too believable as Michael, and is, though not a flawless, a likable Dorothy. One wishes he wouldn't go around giving interviews about how playing Dorothy has changed his life (even if it's true), and one wonders whether his performance is worth the $3 to $5 million (the cited figure varies) he was paid for it. Still, what American actor could have done it better, or even as well? And with Pollack's direction, Owen Roizman's sensitive cinematography, and shrewd costuming by Ruth Morley, *Tootsie* falls happily into place.

Political Antitheses

GANDHI; COUP DE TORCHON (CLEAN SLATE)

Gandhi is oversimplification of the very best, most high-minded sort, but still oversimplification. It is a large-scale historical biography of the opulent, old-fashioned kind of which David Lean's *Lawrence of Arabia* is the finest specimen, and, indeed, Lean strove long and hard to get a crack at Gandhi himself. What Richard Attenborough has wrought is, finally, almost as much a tribute to Lean as to Gandhi, though the Mahatma was a more complex, quirkier figure than Attenborough's protagonist, and Lean's version might well have been, with or without a screenplay by Robert Bolt, a mite more idiosyncratic and unpredictable. John Briley, to whom the final screenplay is credited (though other hands may have left their marks on it), has done a neat, perhaps too neat, job of pulling things together, and for most of its three and a half hours, with intermission, it works.

Attenborough has done justice to both the South African and the Indian backgrounds, and the grandiose set pieces such as Gandhi's funeral work—well—spectacularly. Various scenes of brutality are carefully managed so as to convey the maximum of pain with the minimum of obvious gore, and, I suppose, that is to the good. The obvious problem with such a film is how to handle the politics without confusing or boring the average viewer, and without offending either India or Pakistan; formerly bloated but now shrunken Britain can be allowed to take its lumps all over again, and the Afrikaners are fair game for anyone. The slightly less obvious problem is how to avoid making Gandhi into a plaster saint.

Ben Kingsley's racy, sweetly ornery performance helps with the plaster, and when something of Gandhi's whimsical mulishness comes through, it helps with the sainthood. Though I know little about Gandhi, even I know that some of his strange sexual (or antisexual) *démarches* have been overlooked. As for the politics, a little too much attar of roses has been sprinkled over Gandhi, Nehru, and others, while the British tend to emerge as colonialist clichés. Only the figures of Mohammed Ali Jinnah and Gandhi's assassin (or assassins) are deeply shrouded in the mists of mollifying vagueness; but Jinnah is, at least, played by an actor so quietly ominous-looking that a little complexity does creep in. Still, *Gandhi* is meant to be a noble, idealized portrait dominating an immense series of heroic frescoes, and on that somewhat juvenile level it works splendidly.

Ben Kingsley, I repeat, does a marvelous job as Gandhi, not so much because he is half Indian and made to look wholly like the original, as because he is a solid, resourceful actor of unhomogenizable individuality and with sound English theatrical training. He clearly lived himself totally into the part, and was then able to *be* as much as to act. The supporting cast, which comprises many famous English actors in cameo roles and Indian actors in somewhat larger ones, performs extremely capably, even if not always inspiredly. Thus Roshan Seth, as Nehru, lacks the prototype's somewhat ambiguous charisma, and Martin Sheen, as an American journalist, has not enough to work with. Yet all goes more than adequately until near the end, when Candice Bergen enters as Margaret Bourke-White, and a pall of incredibility falls on every scene she is in. Though she is a bit of a real-life photographer, Miss Bergen does not even handle a camera convincingly, albeit this is nothing compared to what she does with acting.

Yet the real cinematographers, Billy Williams and Ronnie Taylor, have done most commendable work, using all available beauties and starknesses potently but not distractingly. Attenborough's direction, though sometimes routine, never lets the often unwieldy material slip out of its grasp. *Gandhi* may be as much a backward glance at the past of filmmaking as at that of India (where, incidentally, the past has a way of being scarcely distinguishable from the present); but the film has weight, intelligence, and an only slightly dishonest magnanimity going for it, as well as the occasional fortifying dollop of humor. As movies go these days, you could do colossally worse.

Bertrand Tavernier's *Coup de Torchon* (*Clean Slate*) is the exactly opposite kind of political—or even basic—filmmaking. Tavernier makes the most intensely personal movies: a large, hearty-eating man, he also devours all kinds of knowledge, especially from out-of-the-way books and from odd anecdotes, epigrams, quotations he gathers from everyone. Into his movies go these collected recollections, sometimes brilliantly bizarre and invigorating in the new context, sometimes merely an intellectual clutter in which story lines get lost. *Coup de Torchon* wallows in both the felicities and infelicities of this method.

Written in collaboration with Jean Aurenche, the 82-year-old *doyen* of French scenarists, the film is based on an American pop novel, Jim Thompson's *Pop. 1280*, about the Deep South of the thirties. The film transposes this to French colonial Senegal in 1938, to a little invented town where the protagonist, Lucien Cordier, is the solitary law officer. He survives by acting weak: allowing his slatternly wife to carry on under his nose with Nono, her alleged brother; letting two pimps run rampant in their vicious pursuits;

permitting Mercaillou, the nasty husband of his mistress, Rose, to beat her savagely in the streets; suffering a rich businessman to erect a stinking public privy right under his, Cordier's, own windows. Meanwhile a plague is decimating the black population, and when the film begins with a superbly photographed (and faked) eclipse of the sun already there is a bit too much symbolism for comfort.

Cordier's domestic and professional problems are funny and awful in an existentially gross yet elegantly written and filmed way, and the dialogue, especially above the subtitles, has the usual Tavernier dazzle. The characters exude a burlesque manginess, for which absurdity would be too grand a term. Cordier travels to the big city to consult Chavasson, his superior, about his problems; the fellow mocks and brutalizes him, but also tells him always to kick back twice as hard as he has been kicked. Like a holy fool, Cordier needs no more than this to go about suddenly, quietly, with just a little bit of droll speechifying, shooting the local varmints dead. As the executions are simple and summary, so the comic routines or lectures that accompany them have a galvanizing effect. There is an eerie, uncomfortable, *sui generis* humor afoot here.

Outwardly still playing the fool, Cordier develops a ruthless yet not quite untormented personality that even includes some vague Christ fantasies about himself. He has a wistful, platonic relationship with Anne, the pure, pretty new schoolteacher; with Rose, whose husband he dispatches, he now has even better, freer sex. Rose, perfectly played by Isabelle Huppert, is a joyously amoral creature, whose reveling in widowhood is as exhilarating as it is ethically equivocal, and there are also amusing incidents involving the military, the local priest, and that public privy.

But the canvas darkens not quite persuasively. Cordier sets up Rose as executioner to his wife and her lover (well played by Stéphane Audran and Eddy Mitchell), and the black humor curdles even more when an innocent native is killed for having witnessed the murder of Mercaillou; here Cordier's quasi-philosophical, proto-political rationalizing only makes the deed more depressing. But there is a wonderfully zany episode when the brother of the murdered brothel-keeper comes to avenge him (both men are superlatively played by Jean-Pierre Marielle); Cordier befuddles the avenger and sends him off to kill Chavasson, whom he has managed to incriminate. And there are other splendidly oddball episodes and incidents, such as a dialogue with a priest nailing an iron Christ to the third wooden cross, two previous ones having been eaten by termites.

Yet the gloom becomes overthick when Rose, too, is sent off into exile. Cordier is finally alone with his own soiled conscience and the untarnishable Anne; in the film's last, somewhat confusing, sequence, he teeters on the brink of quite senseless murder and suicide. France is hurtling into World War II, colonialism is doomed, but there is no satisfactory linking up of historical calamity with individual despair. Despite fine flashes, the film comes to nothing rather than to grand, nihilistic nothingness. Cordier is played by Tavernier's favorite actor and alter ego, Philippe Noiret, with grand hangdog self-irony and, later, merciless sarcasm. But the character, like the film, does not quite make sense, probably because the American pulp-novel base cannot carry the superstructure of all that sophisticated French existentialism and satire. Pierre William Glenn's cinematography and Alexandre Trauver's production design add further distinction, but the film finally sinks into an intellectual morass. Too bad.

Merciful Heavens, a Real Film!

TENDER MERCIES

Tender Mercies is winning, not only in the right moves it makes but also in the false steps it unerringly avoids. It is a small-scale but splendid triumph for Bruce Beresford, the Australian filmmaker (*Breaker Morant*, etc.), who, like his colleague Fred Schepisi, was drawn to the Southwest for his first American film. But Beresford's Texas is different from any other director's, Australian or American, by being ordinary and startling, idiosyncratic and utterly believable. Horton Foote (*To Kill a Mockingbird*, etc.), who wrote the pungent screenplay, is a Texan, to be sure, but that is no guarantee of authenticity.

Mac Sledge (Robert Duvall), a former country-music star, has become a drunken bum after his marriage to Dixie Scott, another country singer, ended in an ugly divorce and he lost all rights to his daughter, Sue Anne. As the film begins, he is stranded, broke and broken, at the Mariposa Motel cum filling station, three tiny buildings in the middle of a desolate, steam-rollered Texas landscape. The owner, a scrappy young widow named Rosa Lee (Tess Harper), whose husband was killed in Vietnam, lives alone with her small boy, Sonny (Allan Hubbard). Mac becomes her handyman, and, slowly and laconically, a nexus develops between the abandoned man and the lonely woman and child. Eventually, the no longer boozing Mac, in an emotionally strangulated manner, proposes marriage, and Rosa Lee, just as understatedly, accepts.

The film moves ahead somewhat elliptically through small, well-paced incidents. Dixie, who still sings Mac's songs, which have made her rich, though she hates their author, is appearing at the Austin Opry; Mac, who has picked up his guitar again, tries to interest her and her manager-lover, Harry, in a new song, but she furiously chases him away. Mac goes off on what may be a binge, and Rosa Lee worries stoically, but he returns sober. Meanwhile a group of young country musicians tracks down Mac despite his stringent retirement, first seeking his advice, then coaxing him into performing and recording his new songs with them. He may be on the verge of renewed success when tragedy strikes: Sue Anne, who has sought him out in spite of her mother, with faintly promising results (though he strictly avoided any incipient emotions), elopes with one of her mother's drunken musicians and, through his fault, is killed in a crash. Dixie seems to go to pieces, but Mac carries on, however grimly; while hoeing the vegetable garden, he asks the mutely empathetic Rosa Lee why things happen the way they do, and concludes: "You see, I don't trust happiness. I never did, I never will." But, later, as Mac and Sonny toss a new football at each other, and Rosa Lee watches from the house with inchoate hopefulness, a guarded optimism is in order.

You may ask how such a plot can hold much interest, and why I gave away what little of it there is. In fact, the plot is almost in-cidental, though neither hackneyed nor incredible; the telling of it—through direction, acting, and photography—is everything: an everything that no review can capture, let alone spoil, and that im-presses itself on you instantly and indelibly. There is so much even in the way the characters tend to be positioned, with more than the usual space in between; the way they look a little past and beyond one another; and the way they speak, unemphatically and haltingly and almost monosyllabically. This is life amid the curse and bless-ing of an excess of empty space; the film objectifies the vacuity and ennui seeping into the visual and aural patterns of these lives. Some visual relief comes from television, watched avidly but sometimes turned off in disgust; aural relief comes from country music, which, besides looming large in the plot, permeates the soundtrack. Sim-plistic as the songs may be, musically and verbally, they mediate between the people and the flat silence of the land, where the only other sound is that of cars whooshing by—an uncomforting sound that only emphasizes the elsewhereness of the world.

The isolation of the characters coagulates into emotional and conversational repression. The more citified Dixie can let her emotions, real or fake, hurtle out in song or griping garrulity; the others, though generally sincere, say less than they think and show less than they feel. There is a shyness even in much of their singing and dancing. No unequivocal explanations are suggested: is it the hard work of surviving, the temptation to run amuck in those gaping fields, or the resemblance between emotion and the devil drink that tires, tethers, or muzzles them? Or is it the strict Bible Belt religion? Still, Mac's nervous semi-laughs, Sonny's spontaneity, and Rosa Lee's evanescent smiles—sometimes expanding into the radiance of pride, love, hope—do usher in a gingerly, visiting joy.

Tender Mercies maintains an aura of honest, unforced mystery. People as constricted as these—and even Sonny, though more open, is not easily outgoing—can no more analyze than verbalize their feelings. Hence their actions are shrouded even from their own eyes in an ambiguity the viewer is challenged to grope through. When Mac and Sue Anne, after eight years of noncommunication, do not dare to touch or even call each other by their names, she finally asks whether Mac remembers a hymn-like song, "Wings of a Dove," he used to sing to her. Mac seems genuinely unable to recall it. As she leaves and he checks the hand that started to fumble for her, he stares after her car through the window and, in a small voice, sings the song. Was he punishing her for having forgotten that he used to call her Sister? Surely not. Has he only just recalled the song? Unlikely. Did he wish to protect Dixie, who has done everything to blacken him in Sue Anne's eyes, from her daughter's leaving her for him? Very possibly: he kept defending her to the girl. Is he afraid of unleashing excessive emotion in Sue Anne? More than likely. In himself? Almost certainly.

But nothing, you see, is spelled out. When Dixie, lying between pale blue satin sheets, is sedated yet frantic about her daughter's death, is she carrying on so out of love or guilt? Mac stands at the foot of her bed, yet Harry must point out his presence to Dixie. In a childish whimper, she asks twice: "Mac, why's God done this to me?" And she smiles a crooked, infantile smile. Coquetry? Whistling in the dark? Reversion to childhood? Perhaps all three. And the selfishness: Why has God done this to *me*? Violently she tries to rush out of bed and crawl into Sue Anne's coffin, which she has had brought to her mansion; is this disgusting or pathetic? Unlike lesser works, the film does not tell you what to feel. When a woman inquires, "Mister, were you really Mac Sledge?" and the chuckling answer is "Yes, ma'am, I guess I was," you have to deduce the modest pride in the past, the bemused acceptance of the present.

But it is not only the power of suggestion through taciturnity that works handsomely; there is also the amazing impact of lacunae, of what the film tactfully avoids. When Mac receives the news about Sue Anne over the phone, the camera is on Rosa Lee, waiting in the car, fiddling with the radio dial in search of Mac's new record; then Mac comes out to the car, turns off the radio, and says quietly, "My daughter was killed somewhere in Louisiana. I didn't catch the name of the town." It is only the second sentence that obliquely betrays grief; the camera averts its prying eye. When Mac stands by the coffin alone, we fear that he'll sing "Wings of a Dove." But he merely says "Little Sister." Earlier, when Mac tried to coax Rosa Lee into singing his new song with him, the stalwart choir singer refused—wouldn't even try. There is a quirky eloquence in the film's abstentions.

Religion, too, is treated with fine restraint. The dedicated faith of Rosa Lee climaxes in the astounding double immersion of Sonny and Mac: in church, but on a glassed-in stage with a painted riparian backdrop and a red, theatrical curtain. The baptism is potentially ludicrous, but Rosa Lee's transcendent smile and the quiet gravity of the others preclude, if not amusement, certainly all disrespect. Similar restraint informs relationships: Dixie's leg casually thrown over one of Harry's while she rants on about Mac tells all.

Robert Duvall proves that he can play an understatedly sympathetic character as trenchantly as he does fanatics; Tess Harper, an unknown local actress for whom Beresford had to fight, uses acting to conceal acting-magnificently; Allan Hubbard is the first totally convincing and likable American child actor in years. Betty Buckley is as brazen as she is pitiful as Dixie; Ellen Barkin heartbreakingly communicates Sue Anne's subtext; Wilford Brimley is a touchingly befuddled Harry; and the crackers in the band, so seemingly menacing when they first pull up alongside the Mariposa, are gems of bumpkinish joviality.

Beresford's camera placements and movements are as imaginative as they are inconspicuous. Consider Mac's angry departure for what may be a bender: without quitting Rosa Lee's anxious face, the camera catches hazily, at the bottom of the frame, Mac's car jerking this way and that before it careers off fearsomely. Or take Sue Anne's car nervously racing off in a long shot while, in the foreground, Sonny and Rosa Lee walk and talk constrainedly in the fields where they have come to leave father and daughter alone. So many shots contain layers of meaning. Russell Boyd's versatile cinematography is equally evocative with metallically luminescent skies and the purplish gloom of Dixie's boudoir. Beresford has served Foote's forthright script with fidelity and inventiveness; *Tender Mercies* is one of those rare films that grow with reseeing.

Grating Comedy

THE KING OF COMEDY

Martin Scorsese's *The King of Comedy* is on to something important, if only its aim were clearer and its movement more sure-footed. Rupert Pupkin (Robert De Niro) is a 34-year-old messenger boy who desperately wants to be a comedian. Downstairs in his mother's apartment, where he lives, he has created a mockup of the *Jerry Langford* (read: *Johnny Carson*) *Show*, where, between life-size cutouts of Liza Minnelli and his hero and model, Jerry Langford (Jerry Lewis), he practices his comic routines and talk-show blather. By helping Jerry out of the mauling clutches of rabid fans one night, then insinuating himself into the star's limousine, Rupert starts what he takes for a professional and personal relationship, and Langford for a mere *mauvais quart d'heure*. Not meaning it, Jerry asks for samples of Rupert's work: presently Pupkin is hanging around the Langford office's waiting room, sending in tapes, sticking around some more for results, and getting ever firmer, less polite, brush-offs from the staff.

Pupkin pursues his quarry—and his own goals—with the ineluctable doggedness that is an amalgam of uncritical self-esteem, total insensitivity to rebuffs, and a low-grade savvy that partakes less of intelligence than of marathon stupidity. With Rita, a girl he loved from afar in high school and who now works as a bartender, he goes for a weekend to Jerry's Long Island mansion, pretending to his date that he was invited. Thrown out conclusively, he plots, with someone even crazier than he is—Masha, a rich, weird-looking Langford worshipper and stage-door Johnny—the kidnapping of their common idol. It works, and Rupert demands as ransom a ten-minute monologue in the first segment of the *Langford Show*. And Masha? She tries bizarrely to seduce Jerry, whom they have taped as completely as a mummy into a chair in her absent parents' Park Avenue town house. By a series of comic-sinister, clumsy-shrewd maneuvers, Rupert gets on the show, is a smash hit with his fairly awful monologue, goes to jail (a six-year term, of which he serves less than half), and comes out to become the dreamed-of King of Comedy. Jerry escapes from Masha, who pursues him through the Upper East Side in bra and panties like some ghastly Maidenform Girl; Rupert isn't shown winning Rita, either; but, with his new celebrity, he ought to do all right.

The film, with a script by Paul D. Zimmerman, a former *Newsweek* film critic, is unsure of what it wants to do. Obviously, it attacks the power of the obscure and benighted, if not demented, over the stars they worship, emulate, and tyrannize in the attempt to become stars themselves. But Scorsese and Zimmerman seem uncertain in their attitude toward the Ruperts and Mashas of this world. Are they monstrously aberrant, or fairly typical, or even emblematic of universal stupidity and madness? Are we to shudder at them first in comic, then in real, horror, or are we to pity them for the perfunctorily thrown-in but undeniable implications of parental bullying or neglect they have suffered? Yet though there is a pathetic strain traversing Rupert's insuperable cockiness (he can sincerely deny his manifest ejection from a building to an eyewitness), and though there is a woefully lonely, infatuated girl in the homely and derangedly violent Masha, these characters lack the variety of detail to make us accept their contradictions as part of human complexity; rather, they remain grotesque caricatures (well-drawn, to be sure) on which we are jarringly asked to expend full-bodied compassion.

Still, these caricatures talk a good game. "Didn't anyone ever tell you you are a moron?" the exasperated Jerry blurts out in his country house as the butler is about to call the police and the apologetic Rita is summoning Rupert away, but the impermeable pest still refuses to leave. "I can take a hint," he finally concedes without budging, and adds, "So I made a mistake." "So did Hitler," snaps Jerry. Whereupon Rupert, with much-delayed hurt dignity: "So this is the way you guys are when you reach the top . . . I'll work fifty times harder, and I'll be fifty times more funny than you." To which Jerry: "Then you'll have idiots like you plaguing your life."

This dialogue has the proper ludicrousness and bite, but it is equally effective when Rupert is smarmy, dumb, or pitiful: "I see the awful, terrible things in my life and turn it into something funny." He is only mouthing a cliché, but, sad to say, there is the ache of truth in it: his comic monologue, which fractures the *Langford Show* audience, is partly based, we surmise, on genuine childhood traumas.

This is where things become particularly muddled. The monologue strikes me as only slightly less funny than most such monologues, which I don't find very funny, either. Are the filmmakers saying that Pupkin's comedy is junk, but that on the *Langford Show*, introduced by Tony Randall, it enchants an audience of Pavlovian fools? Or are they saying that Pupkin does have that minimal talent needed to make anybody's success in this abysmal business? Is the film about weirdos cannibalizing their betters, or are there no betters, and are large numbers of, if not, indeed, all-Americans a breed of imbeciles? Is the satire specific or all-inclusive?

If the latter, why doesn't the film prepare us for it? There are hints, but they are few and fuzzy. True, a middle-aged harridan talking on a street phone recognizes the passing Jerry Langford and, without letting go of the receiver, flatters him abjectly, extorts his autograph, but then, when he refuses to talk to her nephew over the phone, hideously wheels on the star: "You should only get cancer! I hope you get cancer!" Rita, mortally embarrassed at having been inveigled into invading Jerry's country house, nevertheless stuffs a bibelot from a side table into her pocketbook. Is this a pathetic attempt to recoup a little dignity, to have something to show for this unmerited humiliation: or is it, after all, simply a piece of thievery giving even the seemingly decent Rita her dram of vileness? And why does Jerry have only office staff, domestics, and a lapdog, but no trace of family or friends? Is that the proverbial loneliness at the top, or is he, too, merely a Pupkin on a pedestal? He does appear to be self-contained yet seething with something within, but what: frustration, repressed arrogance, or a nagging sense of unearned success?

Occasionally, there are lapses from credibility in an otherwise laudable attempt to emphasize reality in some of its more surreal aspects, but reality nevertheless. Though I have seen the film twice, I still miss a proper explanation of Masha's having the family townhouse to herself on abduction night. No parents, no servants; only this unhinged girl, scarcely to be entrusted with the safety of so palatial a domain. Again, if Langford is so wildly popular as to be mobbed nightly at the studio exit, would he quite so regularly walk alone through New York's threatening streets? And what about Rupert's job and financial status? He can take endless time off his messenger work and, although he complains of insolvency, is a flashy dresser (his outfits sometimes clumsily aping Jerry's), owns fancy sound equipment, and seems wanting for nothing. The gag whereby we only hear his always offscreen mother hectoring him does not clarify his presumable economic dependency.

Yet despite vacillations, there are respects in which *The King of Comedy* displays more assurance than any previous Scorsese film. The intermingling of Rupert's daydreams of glory with his shabby reality is strikingly managed; Rupert's psychology, language, and demeanor are presented with accuracy and the appropriate discomfiting humor, somewhere between laughter and wincing; and De Niro's performance perfectly captures the manic persistence of the idiot savant. When Langford tells him that he cannot begin at the top—the *Langford Show*—but must start at the bottom, catch De Niro's delivery of the reply, "That's where I am, at the bottom"; he is magisterially both ridiculous and chilling in proffering a confession of failure as a badge of honor and qualification. As Masha, Sandra Bernhard succeeds in being both frighteningly derailed and childishly pitiable; as Rita, Diahnne Abbott plays a once-popular high school cheerleader defeated by life with touching reserve. And Jerry Lewis's Langford—always wary, prickly, his face pulled in with uneasy self-control, like a waistline constricted by a Draconian belt—makes us squirmily aware of the constraints of fame. Minor roles are well taken, whether by celebrities playing themselves, little-known actors (notably the stunning Shelley Hack as Langford's cool secretary), or sundry members of the Scorsese family.

There is excellent production design by Boris Leven, the interiors of Jerry's two residences being particularly impressive in their expensively unlived-in looking frigidity. Scorsese's handling of the camera, ably seconded by Thelma Schoonmaker's editing, is equally compelling in the vividly orchestrated sequence of Pupkin being chased through the Langford offices by the security staff and in the patiently searching closeups in which De Niro deploys Rupert's bestial blatancy with disarming innocence. Rumor has it that there was studio interference obliging the filmmakers to make the humor less black; but even if *The King of Comedy* is often closer to Mel Brooks than to Evelyn Waugh, it still says more than most current American films.

Men in White

THE FLIGHT OF THE EAGLE

Jan Troell's *The Flight of the Eagle* is a deep and noble film of great
and subtle artistry about which it is impossible to write cogently
after only one viewing, and that a couple of months ago. So I have
the choice of writing a very inadequate review, or of filling you in
about the sad background of this film and about what prevented
me from reseeing it.

The Flight of the Eagle is based on the true story of Major S. A.
Andrée, a Swedish hero or fanatic or both, who believed he could
conquer the North Pole for his country by balloon. An engineer
with very little experience of actual ballooning, he had the charisma to get such diverse figures as King Oscar II and Alfred Nobel
to finance the construction of the *Eagle*, as the huge hydrogen balloon was named, despite expert testimony on the impracticability
of the quixotic scheme. In 1896, contrary winds made the takeoff
impossible; stung in his pride, Andrée set off from Spitsbergen the
following summer in spite of not much better winds, goaded on
by ambition, the cheers of a crowd of journalists and dignitaries,
the blaring of an army band. He had the blind faith of one crew
member, the sensitive young Nils Strindberg (a distant relative of
the playwright's), and the sardonic, needling camaraderie of the
other fellow, the husky, down-to-earth Knut Fraenkel. Two of the
three navigational guide lines were lost immediately, and they
could—should—have quit. But Andrée, driven and intransigent,
preferred death (his and the others') to dishonor, and his colleagues, inspired or bewitched, complied, soon frantically tossing
ballast, and even much-needed food, out of the snow-encrusted
balloon.

Within three days, they were grounded—or, rather, ice-floed;
Fraenkel and Strindberg favored walking south, the likeliest way to
unlikely salvation. But Andrée, hoping at least for scientific fame,
imposed an eastward trek for the exploring of uncharted regions.
For three months the men struggled on heroically against cold,
deprivation, and progress-foiling ice drift. Andrée was conduct-
ing maniacally scrupulous tests; Fraenkel distinguished himself
as a hunter and ironic, morale-building jokester; and Strindberg,
when not writing letters to his pianist fiancée, took photographs
of the expedition. As the men became more and more ravaged

and exhausted, eating polar-bear meat that seems to have given Strindberg fatal trichinosis, their infighting and underlying mutual loyalty increased *pari passu* with the dwindling of their hopes. Strindberg, the most delicate, was first to die; then (according to the film) Fraenkel, mauled in his sleep by a bear. Finally, there was only Andrée, keeping his diary to the end. In 1930, a ship discovered their remains at their last, island-based camp. The diary and letters were fairly well preserved, though chewed on by bears; 34 of the photographs could be developed perfectly. Troell's color film includes these even starker, black-and-white snapshots; they blend seamlessly into the magnificent work that earns the right to incorporate these lacerating, sublime documents.

After a state funeral, the trio became national heroes, even though some perceived Andrée as an unhinged megalomaniac. This unsympathetic view was espoused by Per Olof Sundman's fine documentary novel, *The Flight of the Eagle*, in 1967. Though the movie version is partly based on this book, Troell swings the balance more toward Andrée's heroism and good faith, while not overlooking the man's problematic aspects. Troell also takes some liberties: he has Fraenkel die before Andrée, for instance, and invents the bear-mauling in the absence of a stated cause for the last survivor's death. But he is very faithful in other respects: to Andrée's unfleshly love affair with a married woman and excessive devotion to his mother (both probable signs of latent homosexuality), and to all sorts of visual and narrative details for which he was as much of a stickler as Andrée for his scientific measurements. Troell is, I think, a filmmaker of genius whom we have too long described as "second only to Ingmar Bergman." On the strength of such films as *Here is Your Life*, *The Emigrants*, *The New Land*, and the marvelous short *Stopover in the Marshlands* (as well as some interesting lesser pictures), it seems more just to place him side by side with Bergman, who always admired and encouraged him. But the first three films I adduce were seen in the U.S. in savagely cut and mangled versions (a polar bear couldn't have done a better job on them), and the fourth hardly at all. It is in Troell's nature to make long films that, moreover, face up to unpleasant truths with signal honesty. So they incur chopping. A film brimful of questionable moral uplift, e.g., *Gandhi*, or exuding turbulently crowd-pleasing mendacity, e.g., *The Deer Hunter*, is allowed to be as long as it pleases; a morally impassioned work of truth-telling art had better be under two hours or else.

The Flight of the Eagle was cut down from four to three hours by Troell for German television, which so presented it. Jörn Donner, then head of the Swedish Film Institute and chief producer of the film, viewed it in this version with the representative of BBC television; the two men arrived at the screening late and talked through it frequently and loudly, to the discomfiture of others. Then Donner, himself a filmmaker, demanded cuts that Troell, under the circumstances, was more than usually loath to make. Still, the director (who is always both cameraman and cutter on his films) edited the work down to a two-hour-twenty-minute version that opened in Sweden to mixed response.

Bought for America by Summit Feature Distributors, a small West Coast outfit, the film was promptly handed back to Troell for twenty more minutes' cutting, the longer version to be shown only in New York, possibly in Los Angeles, and to the MPA board that nominated it for the foreign language Oscar. At a dinner with Troell and one of the heads of Summit, I pleaded for nationwide presentation of the 140-minute version—any further cutting would be vandalism if not sacrilege. For whatever reason, the man from Summit relented, and no two-hour version was made. As it is, in his very favorable but less than "money" review in the *New York Times*, Vincent Canby regretted that the film did not tell more of the earlier lives of the three balloonists; left to his own devices, Troell would have been only too glad to oblige.

Quite predictably, the senescent idiots who preponderate in the Academy of Motion Picture Arts and Sciences seconded, no doubt, by some of the younger academicians—chose a pedestrian Spanish film full of high sentiments and geriatric puppy love to crown (or bean) with the Oscar. This worthy turkey is now running, whereas the *Eagle*—without so much as a warning ("Last Four Days," etc.)—plummeted out of sight from the single New York theater where it was playing. How it has fared in L.A., I don't know—or whether it even opened in other cities. Ironically, the film closed here just as Pauline Kael's ecstatic and potentially life-prolonging review came out in the *New Yorker*—too late to do any good, Miss Kael's month-long vacation having delayed its appearance by several crucial weeks.

Let all this enlighten you about the vagaries of circumstance—or human stupidity—hounding a great film. But let me also urge you to read, in the May 16 *New Yorker*, Miss Kael's ample and perceptive review, to which, after one seeing and at this distance, I can add but little. Troell's mastery lies in the rhythm of his editing; in the incisive details of sight, sound, and spoken word; in the austere restraint with which the most heartrending scenes are presented, with camera placements and movements that, without calling attention to themselves, are nevertheless so apt as to make even a crusty old skeptic like me forget that he is watching a movie; and in the overwhelming, but again, unpretentious cinematography done on location—if not as far north as where the explorers perished, certainly farther north than most other filmmakers would venture. The film has a beauty that first enchants, then hurts—not only as sadness hurts, but also as so much truth does in the process of making us understand.

Jan Troell—a quiet, unassuming, yet also wonderfully dogged man—works with utmost ingenuity. Who else would have had young female ballet students long observe the polar bears at the zoo, learn their movements, and then, in bearskins, enact the most authentic on-screen polar bears ever—not excluding real ones (in documentaries), which, being amateurs, lack professional acting skills. The great wonder, however, is, as I said, in the rhythm, as, for instance, the doomed explorers recall scenes from the past or envision others in the future. Most strikingly, young Strindberg's visions of himself and his beloved burst forth suddenly in passionate summer colors from the polar whites, greys, and steel blues, only to be swallowed up by them just as suddenly.

Troell and his three co-scenarists were experts at conjuring up the slow, grinding stages of the three men's deterioration, their bickerings, and eventual desperate symbiosis; and also at chronicling the awesome phases of the emotionally frozen Andrée's spiritual thawing out even as their bodies succumb to the Arctic ice. But the earlier scenes of preparation, confrontation, and celebration are no less exciting. Brilliant, too, is the makeup that achingly chronicles the inroads of frostbite into the men's faces, and the sparing, suggestive hinting to which Hans Erik Philip's music limits itself. Max von Sydow is surely one of the greatest screen actors of our time, and his final scenes, as Andrée, with the Norweigen actor Sverre Anker Ousdal, as Fraenkel, are as moving as any I have ever seen. But Göran Stangertz, as Strindberg, and the rest are not a whit behind—yet another of the miracles Troell has carried off in this film. Wherever, however you can manage, buy, beg, bribe, or browbeat your way into it.

Farewell Symphony

FANNY AND ALEXANDER

Few things are sadder than the attempt of a great artist, hitherto fully appreciated only by a minority, to reach the masses—regardless of whether or not the attempt succeeds. This is what Ingmar Bergman has undertaken with *Fanny and Alexander*, supposedly his last theatrical film, though he proposes to continue working in theater, opera, and television, for which he has just made a film. Sure enough, *Fanny and Alexander* is Bergman's first box-office smash in Sweden, and bids fair to do well everywhere. It is also the most expensive Swedish film ever made, and it is certainly a work that Bergman views as a summing-up of his entire career—another fatal step for an artist. Recapitulation is for historians and philosophers: artists can only go forward, more or less successfully mark time, or indulge in sorry parodies of their past achievements.

Once before Bergman gave us an anthology of his previous work—in *Cries and Whispers*, a poor film but less so than this one. At least it was a pastiche of his harsh, uncompromising, personal films: here he is out for something more cheerful and crowd-pleasing, which he was never good at, except coincidentally, in such films as *Smiles of a Summer Night*. In fact, *Fanny and Alexander* is almost on a level with Bergman's biggest dud, *The Serpent's Egg*, where he was trying for a sociopolitical document, something entirely alien to his art. His great—indeed unequaled—strength lies in relatively short, intense, extremely personal films about relationships between men and women, or about individuals caught between the wish to live and the longing to die, between faith in divine or secular love and soul-crunching despair. Some of his pictures are referred to as chamber films, by analogy with chamber music: but even those with more players are concerti grossi in which a few instruments function as a chamber group against larger but almost undifferentiated background forces.

Fanny and Alexander conversely, is meant to be a huge canvas comprising a family chronicle, a Gothic romance, even a *roman fleuve*—with, actually, periodic shots of a river denoting, rather uninspiredly, the passage of time. It is also a foray into popular metaphysics and—another Bergman favorite—a disquisition on the relationship between art, here called "the little world," and reality, "the big world." The little world becomes, somewhat confusingly, identified also with the extended family in its room-temperature conviviality as against the wind-buffeted outside world of politics and society, for the ignoring of which Bergman here seems to ask for indulgence if not justification.

It is 1907 in Uppsala and we are in the great house of the Ekdahls, presided over by grandmother Helena, a benevolent matriarch just now overseeing the preparations for Christmas. Helena has three sons. Oscar, the eldest, manages the city theater, in which his wife, the lovely Emilie, is the star. They have two children: Alexander, ten, and Fanny, eight; the boy is clearly a stand-in for the young Ingmar, what with his puppet theater and magic lantern. The middle son is Carl (a professor according to the screenplay, which, as usual with Bergman, only this time more so, differs substantially from the finished film), who drinks and is unhappily married to a German woman considered beneath his station; she is devoted to him, but he treats her badly. The youngest son, Gustav Adolf, is a successful restaurateur and lecher, now carrying on with Maj, a sweet, buxom, lame chambermaid, whom his bouncy wife, Alma, jovially tolerates.

Nearby is the store and dwelling of Isak Jacobi, a Jewish money lender and dealer in antiques, with whom Helena (in the script, she is née Mandelbaum, but the film makes nothing of this) has had an affair followed by a steady friendship. He, too, is invited for Christmas, as are all family members with their children. The film is mostly a series of set pieces: Alexander alone in the still, pre-Christmas house; the nativity play at the theater, wherein Emilie plays the Angel; the uproarious Christmas feast at which Gustav Adolf plays Priapus with Maj, and Carl puts on a display for the kids of candle-snuffing by breaking wind; the death of Oscar, with Alexander's reluctance to come to his father's deathbed. Such scenes do not flow properly into one another because the point of view shifts too often, because we do not stay with any character long enough to care, because there is nothing here that Bergman hasn't done better before, and we get bored.

Whether Oscar is giving a self-effacing address to the actors about how the little world of the theater makes people understand the big world outside better—unless it merely allows them to forget it for a while (Bergman the escapist—my God!); whether Carl is berating his patient, hapless wife, only to hurtle sobbing into her lap the next moment; whether Gustav Adolf is having a minor extramarital fiasco in Maj's bed downstairs or, the next moment, a minor marital success in the conjugal bed upstairs—none of this has the reverberations of its antecedents in earlier, ground-breaking Bergman films. So the director resorts to trickery. Oscar, who played the ghost in *Hamlet*, returns as an ineffectual ghost in the white garb of memory we recollect from *Wild Strawberries*—where, however, the ghosts were remembrances; Helena reminisces with Isak about their former affair during a late-night session of nostalgia—the titillation of adultery with a lowly Jew; Alexander keeps his spirits up at his father's funeral by reciting sotto voce a litany of obscenities—again, the supposed shock effect. And so on, until Emilie marries the handsome but coldly self-righteous Bishop Edvard Vergérus, who officiated at Oscar's funeral. Significantly, neither of her marriages is made credible.

Edvard insists that Emilie and the children come to him with a minimum of possessions. They are now subject to insidious discipline and a variety of obnoxious female relatives such as Edvard's dour mother and smarmy spinster sister, as well as such treacherous servants as the masochistic maid, Justine (note the Sadian echo). The house is chill and austerely underfurnished; the kids are often kept under lock and key in their room with barred windows; there are dread rumors of how the first wife and *her* two children perished. Here one hopes for fertile cross-breeding of Gothic horror with Bergmanian sexual psychology, but gets instead chiefly supernatural hocus pocus, as when Isak springs the children from Vergérus's captivity by some not even very interesting magical tricks, or when, sheltered in Isak's domicile cum shop, Alexander is exposed to a number of supposedly scary experiences, such as the life-size puppets of Aron, Isak's nephew, or a session with Aron's brother, Ismael, kept under house arrest for alleged madness and indubitable supernatural powers. It is all dismally attitudinizing and hollow, a sort of cross between Carl Dreyer at his worst and John Fowles at his best, which is not far removed from his worst.

It all ends happily, with everyone in the right bed, more or less, and with the merrily widowed Emilie taking over the management of the theater with a production of *A Dream Play*, to star her and feature Helena in a comeback. It is a measure of Bergman's disingenuousness that the one quotation we get from the Strindberg work is optimistic, whereas the play as a whole couldn't be more pessimistic. And it is a measure of his eclecticism that the background music includes both an ingratiating Schumann piano quartet and Britten's forbidding Suite for Cello—something for everyone. And by way of trendiness, Ismael is played by a woman, and the bishop's aunt, Elsa, who sets the house on fire, by a fat man in drag—Bergman's bow to the loosening of sexual boundaries.

What is memorable here? Only two brief sequences. First, when Fanny and Alexander are awakened in the middle of the night by a shriek and timidly trek to their parents' bedroom. Mesmerized, they watch through a crack in the double door their wailing mother as she paces, arms flailing, up and down in front of the bed with her husband's corpse. The children in the dark, Emilie crossing and recrossing the narrow stripe of light, their silence and her ululation—this image haunts. Second, when, in Emilie's absence, Alexander is made to bend over with his pants down to receive Edvard's ferocious caning, and the bishop's mother holds the boy's head down against the table. She has been sewing, and one finger seen in close-up wears a thimble, thus equating sewing and sadism as routine household tasks. If only the rest of the film had such impact! Instead, there is even flabby dialogue, and the climactic christening speech by Gustav Adolf is an embarrassment of existential clichés.

It is nice, in this recapitulatory film, to re-encounter the old, unforgotten faces, even if the great Gunnar Björnstrand, his voice corroded by illness, gets only his now customary cameo role, and the once endlessly seductive Harriet Andersson is only too persuasive as the grizzled and desiccated Justine. The new actors are less resonant than the veterans, and Ewa Fröling, as Emilie, though pretty enough, lacks emotional range. As Alexander, Bertil Guve, of the cutely doll-like appearance, acts no better than a doll. Pernilla Allwin, as Fanny, is better, but has little to do. Children are not Bergman's specialty. Erland Josephson's Isak and Gunn Wållgren's Helena come off best, but even Sven Nykvist's fine cinematography is not up to top form. *Fanny and Alexander* is an overstuffed film, and, in this case at least, more is decidedly less.

$3 Bill, E2 Note

THE BIG CHILL; THE DRAUGHTSMAN'S CONTRACT

Certain decades are particularly nostalgia provoking; they even acquire colorful names in retrospect: the Yellow Nineties, the Mauve Decade. For today's Americans, the most longing-laden decade is the 1960s, which may in due time earn its psychedelically colorful epithet. Such special decades must contain some revolution, real or imagined, in politics, social conditions, or culture; John Updike called the sixties "the most dissentious American decade since the Civil War," and it had enough genuine protest and idealism in it—along with even more camp-following counterfeit—to inspire today's young-middle-aged to luxuriate in it with an exquisite sense of loss.

Unfortunately, this most up-to-date model of *illusions perdues* has turned into an instant cliché in the performing arts; it has produced a number of plays of which so far only one (Lanford Wilson's *5th of July*) has proved meritorious and is now beginning to yield movies that, if *The Big Chill* is any indication, are born old. Lawrence Kasdan, who wrote and directed the derivative and odious *Body Heat*, and scripted such stultifying blockbusters as *Raiders of the Lost Ark* and *The Empire Strikes Back*, has now directed and (with Barbara Benedek) written his "most personal film." Reminiscent of John Sayles's feeble but at least modest *Return of the Secaucus Seven*, and displaying startling analogies with Kathleen Tolan's play, *A Weekend near Madison*, *The Big Chill* reunites seven close friends from University of Michigan days in the sixties at the funeral, in some Southern town, of an eighth friend, Alex, who may have been the most gifted of all, but who, without leaving behind any explanation, committed suicide right in the summer house of two of his old buddies, Harold and Sarah, now married to each other.

Much of the film's maundering concerns why Alex did it. True, he kept changing professions, but he seemed to be good at everything—why, just the night before his suicide, he and his girlfriend, the very young and laid-back Chloe (Meg Tilly), had "fantastic" sex together. Of course, we never find out anything significant about Alex, though I am quite ready to believe that he was the most gifted of *this* lot. Harold (Kevin Kline) has become the head of a thriving shoe business, soon to do even better as part of a conglomerate; Sarah is a doctor (though none of her words or acts conveys it); and they have a couple of very nice houses and children. But there is implicit trouble: Sarah (Glenn Close) had a recent affair with Alex, and Harold is buying more and more redundant property.

Sam (Tom Berenger) has become the star of a popular TV series of which he is ashamed, and into which he desperately tries to inject morsels of artisic value. Meg (Mary Kay Place) is a lawyer who switched from defending the needy to remunerative corporation work. Her problem is finding a good relationship (which, apparently, is impossible), and she hatches the plan that, during this post-funeral weekend, one of her old dear friends will beget a child on her. She is conveniently ovulating, and will, whoever should be the father, happily bring up the child herself. Michael (Jeff Goldblum), who hoped to write the great American novel, now scribbles sleazy pieces for the great unwashed in *People* magazine. He plans a big business venture in Texas and tries, unsuccessfully, to seduce all the weekend's women.

Karen (JoBeth Williams), now a bored housewife and mother, is married to a square (Don Galloway), who, I must say, looks pretty good in this company. She tries to leave him for Sam, with whom she had a close nexus at college (Unfulfilled, I believe, but the old relationships are rushed past us in a multiplicity so bewildering as to defy my halting memory), yet who, when she throws herself at him with love and lust, rejects her out of a sense of his own failure. Later, however, on a night ramble, these cold lovers consummate on the cold ground out of hate and briefly, what they could not do more lastingly out of love.

Nick (William Hurt), who did well as a psychologist on a call-in radio show, came back from Vietnam impotent—we don't know whether physiologically or psychologically, and do not much care—and he now drifts through a life of drug-pushing and TV-addiction and cynical detachment. Chloe, for whom the 60's did not exist and who appears unaffected by her lover's death, floats through the weekend lives of these seven moral and intellectual dwarfs like a somewhat sullied but serene Snow White. She even ends up finding some mysterious form of happiness with Nick, which, like almost everything else in the film, must be taken on faith—thus, for instance the notion that Sarah's encouraging her husband to impregnate Meg somehow brings spiritual fulfillment to all three of them. And guess what? Even Sam, Karen, and Michael come away slightly sobered up from this weekend where nothing more occurs than a few flare-ups and a lot of boozy horseplay. Having achieved so much by his suicide, even Alex may now be rotting away more purposefully.

Some of the acting, notably that of Tom Berenger and JoBeth Williams, is solid; Kevin Kline and Meg Tilly are acceptable as, in a rather boring way, is Miss Place. But Glenn Close exudes more relentless warmth than a radiator whose knob is stuck, William Hurt's excessive mannerisms could use a little castration, and Jeff

Goldblum (who should only be cast in extremely repulsive roles) is too repulsive. Kasdan's direction is fluent enough, but his and Miss Benedek's screenplay is full of second-rate cleverness, third-rate melancholy and first-rate holes. Though there are some well observed details and sporadically funny lines, most of *The Big Chill* is badinage: nostalgic badinage, smart-alec badinage, mock-heroic badinage, and would-be-profound (nay, tragic) badinage. It is as if seven tone-deaf *pagliacci* were trying to render "Laugh, Clown!" as a barbershop septet, while a younger acolyte (and neophyte) tried to accompany them on the marimba. John Bailey's cinematography is stylish; the backgrounds, indoors and out, are appetizing; and the soundtrack resonates with the pop music of the sixties in what, by now, is the biggest and loudest cliché of all. The one talent Kasdan has is for slick, attitudinizing "significance." As talents go, it is one of the deadlier ones.

There is a kind of filmmaking that manifestly hates anything that smacks of coherence, warmth, humanity, even heterosexuality—of anything that, in less evolved times, we would have dared call morality. I am not saying that true works of art have not been achieved without some of those ingredients, only that for pretentious and unskilled hands to dispense with them spells disaster. So with the British film *The Draughtsman's Contract*, by Peter Greenaway, who wrote, directed, and drew the topographical drawings executed in the film by the eponymous draughtsman, Mr. Neville. This haughty and extremely unpleasant upstart contracts to supply, in the summer of 1694, 12 drawings of the Herbert manor, which Mrs. Herbert proposes to give to her philandering husband, off on a trip that turns out to be a cover-up for his murder. The contract also allows Neville the use of Mrs. Herbert's body, which he sets to with the same despotic brutality with which he attacks his work: whole areas have to be strictly evacuated while he draws them. Later Mrs. Herbert's daughter, who loathes her (equally) obnoxious German husband, enters on a similar contract with Mr. Neville, perhaps for a male heir, to prevent her husband from inheriting—but who can affirm anything here?

Mrs. Herbert angers the draughtsman by leaving irrelevant objects to clutter up his prospect, and he spitefully draws them in. These objects subsequently point to him as Herbert's killer. (Don't ask me why or how; in *Blow-Up*, from which the idea is stolen, things made a bit more sense.) Mrs. Herbert and her daughter may act out of hate for their husbands, Neville out of social spite against the upper classes—but, again, who knows? Residents and permanent or transient guests at the manor merely stuff themselves and insult one another in epigrams that Greenaway must take for Congrevian wit, but that are pure, witless malice in more or less eighteenth-century syntax. The plotting is inscrutable throughout, but the nastiness palpable and loathsome. For added humor, there is a naked man assuming the poses of various statues, including that of an overage *manneken pis*.

Mr. Neville finally meets his sticky end with an implausibility that harmonizes with the rest in positively Palladian symmetry. Neither on him nor on anyone or anything else can we expend a farthing's worth of sympathy. The acting, even by reputable actors, is routine, and the film is not so much directed as corseted. The very cinematography has a hard, pinched look, as if it were all painted on tin. If this soulless, unmerry chase has a beast in view, it is, quite simply, the author.

Under Fire

The most arresting political film recently made by what can still loosely be called Hollywood—even though the director is British and the location Mexican—is *Under Fire*. The immediately provocative aspect of this film about American journalists in Nicaragua is that it openly espouses the Sandinista cause: the more valuable contribution is that—despite a number of clichés, improbabilities, impossibilities, and views that you may not share—it is the most thought-provoking, intermittently perceptive, and generally well-made political film around.

The action begins in civil-war-torn Chad with a prologue that introduces the main characters. Russell Price is a renowned photo-journalist whose belly is as engirded with cameras as a hula dancer's bosom with leis, and whom we see fearlessly clicking away with his camera while elephant-enhanced ground troops are suddenly attacked by a large helicopter. Soon he finds himself on a military truck with one white man smirking among scowling black soldiers. This is Oates, an American soldier of fortune who thinks he is fighting for the government but, when informed by Price that these are the insurgents, proves just as happy to kill for that side. There is a farewell party for the press corps at which we meet Alex and Claire, whose love affair is ending. Alex, a famous *Time* correspondent, is about to take on a cushy TV anchorman's job back home and wants Claire to leave her work as a radio reporter and settle down as his wife. But Claire wants to go on as she is, though she also longs for her growing daughter, to whom she often talks by phone or tape recording. At the party, Russell, an old friend of Alex and Claire's, begins to fall for the woman and takes many pictures of her. Then all three are off to Nicaragua: the year is 1979, and there is "a dandy little war" going on there.

The prologue compactly establishes the strengths and weaknesses of *Under Fire*. The shots Price takes are recorded by freeze frames, in monochrome or color, that briefly stop the action to the accompaniment of the amplified noise of the shutter sounding like an elephant wheezing in orgasm. This annoyingly self-referential and self-regarding device recurs throughout (though less often later): I kept feeling displaced by its visual jazziness and aural stridency from a concert hall to a discotheque. However, John Alcott's cinematography is so lavishly alive, and Roger Spottiswoode's direction so Stendhalianly evocative of the chaos of battle and of human restlessness in general, that atmosphere promptly matures into communicated reality.

The three main Americans are efficaciously depicted (screenplay by Ron Shelton and Clayton Frohman), albeit as the conventional movie-made journalistic two guys and a gal hardnosedly triangling it up against a background of war; still, their conversation and behavior are a bit riper, more idiosyncratic, and at times even more vulnerable than those of the Hollywood prototypes. Similarly, the CIA presence is deftly, even wittily, sketched in, and Oates, the mercenary, is fleshed out with a couple of telling strokes as a clean-cut psychopath for whom carnage is a kind of college athletics minus the team spirit. He is the horrible hyperextension of Price, who says that he takes no sides, only pictures. And Alex and Claire are made more human by the conflicts of middle age, the temptations of easing up. But they can't say no to Nicaragua, where Somoza and his forces are on their last legs.

The atmosphere of genuine decadence and brittle bravado in Managua is well captured. Enter another major character: Jazy, a Frenchman working for the CIA and probably, as he says, for everyone else, too. Intelligent, luxury-loving, and sporting his jadedness like a perfect suntan, he carries on with Somoza's sexy and dumb mistress, plays cat-and-mouse with the American journalists, and spouts cynical, unsettling epigrams. Also well-drawn are Somoza's American publicist (played with just the right amount of oily sincerity by Richard Masur) and Somoza himself, with a megalomania that remains folksily puny, and a number of lesser figures. Against Mexican backgrounds, Spottiswoode re-creates a convincing Nicaragua in which tensions, menace, and outbursts of both meaningful and meaningless violence are framed by mingled lushness and poverty, natural opulence and human meanness or misery.

Stanley Kauffmann has stated the case against *Under Fire* well: Pauline Kael, the case for it rather too well. I am somewhere in between. The humanization-cum-radicalization of Price, and his consequent finding sexual favor with Claire, may be presented in too sentimental a way; the invention of a Guevara-like Nicaraguan leader, Rafael, and the role he plays in the revolution and in the lives of the principals have too much of the incredible about them: and the politically and amatorily happy ending seems rather too facilely upbeat.

I am not, however, particularly bothered by a journalist's losing his neutrality to the point of photographing a lie—Rafael's corpse as if it were alive—in order to help the cause he now espouses: I have never had much faith in the moral finickiness of the press, although I do wonder whether, even with rather persuasive motivation, Price would so endanger his future career. The casual murder of an American newsman (based on the case of ABC's Bill Stewart), though, and the conveying of various moods and attitudes in war, from fighting with sportively daredevil amateurishness to the hysterical or bored shooting of everything that moves (even a squealing pig), from the utter confusion of the populace to the sudden panic that seizes experienced pressmen—in short, chaos of every stripe—could scarcely be made more palpable. Thus it is the gruesome or ironic incidentals that carry the film more than do the major incidents.

Though there is no doubt of the filmmakers' pro-Sandinista feelings, there is some striving for critical balance. The three young Sandinistas who cannot decide whether to execute Jazy, whom they hold at gunpoint—and, along with him, Russell and Claire—are shown as bewildered and incompetent: Jazy's courage and shrewd anti-Marxist speech *in extremis*, wherein he questions easy sympathy for a revolution started by poets before twenty years of history make its true worth assessable, cannot be denied moral authority.

Even the disgusting Oates and the appalling Somoza are not entirely dehumanized, and there are oases of double-edged humor throughout.

Again, I don't believe that a wounded and bleeding man on the run could have the resourcefulness and stamina he exhibits here, or that a woman looking for him under circumstances that, by comparison, make a needle in a haystack more exposed than the Eiffel Tower would be able to find and succor him. Nor would the shooting of the American newsman be broadcast over the still Somoza-controlled television. But such things finally matter less than the authenticity of details laying bare the randomness, stupidity, and apocalyptic illogic of war—the surrealism of it, as if it were designed not so much by strategy and tactics as by a crazed Magritte or Max Ernst. And under the horrors and imbecilities, always the manipulativeness.

The dialogue is mostly simple, believable, and good. The American flack to a woman whose lover has been murdered by Guardsmen: "Jesus Christ! A human tragedy—what can I say?" A Nicaraguan woman to Claire: "Fifty thousand Nicaraguans have died, and now a *yanqui*. Maybe we should have killed an American journalist 15 years ago." And this, from a young female Sandinista ideologue: "The world is not divided into East and West any more. It's divided into North and South." Not true, of course, but wonderful rhetoric, music to ears seeking validation, and as emotion-charged as the love song Alex plays on the piano and sings in a Managuan nightclub as he tries to woo back Claire. But as the Nicaraguan poet Pablo Antonio Cuadra has warned in one of his poems, "*no recubras / de música tu oído*"—do not cover your hearing with music. Every "music" is delusive, as the film comes close to saying. Too bad it doesn't quite do so.

There are fine performances: Nick Nolte's Price, incredulously beginning to hear a voice other than his camera shutter's; Gene Hackman's Alex, with something battering from within his sly, comfortably rumpled, casually worn face; Joanna Cassidy's Claire, whose once girlish prettiness is molded before our very eyes into care-limned womanhood. Ed Harris is prodigious as Oates, with a smile like a jumpy hatchet that threatens to crack open both his face and your skull. As Jazy, Jean-Louis Trintignant is equally disquieting with a debonair suavity and with a disarming self-inculpation that are the distracting spiel of a sinister magician. Various Hispanic actors do splendidly in smaller parts.

Thanks to Agustin Ytuarte and Toby Rafelson's art direction and Alcott's camera work under Spottiswoode's guidance, everything looks devastatedly or devastatingly right—the spurious luxuries as well as the true exiguities. And Jerry Goldsmith has come up with a lean, sinewy score in which an Andean bamboo flute is discreetly reinforced by electronics, and not too much music, either. *Under Fire* is no masterpiece, but it gives you plenty to absorb and think about. How many films nowadays can make that claim?

The Right Stuff

Since my fellow film critic in these pages, Bill Buckley, has already reviewed *The Right Stuff,* and inasmuch as I substantially agree with his assessment, I shall keep this short. Philip Kaufman's script and direction try to be faithful both to Tom Wolfe's book (which I have read about enough to feel I have read it), with its arch-conservatism, and to Kaufman's own views, a mixture of San Francisco hip (i.e., liberal verging on radical) and Hollywood movie buff (i.e., retrograde). What emerges is a mighty peculiar hybrid, like a giant *nouvelle cuisine* hamburger. It isn't unpalatable, and it has both sociological and comic-strip interest, but it certainly isn't art.

"The right stuff" is, of course, unquestioning do-or-die courage, which Wolfe in his tongue-in-cheek way nevertheless celebrates, but Kaufman accepts only with modifications. Hence he makes Chuck Yeager—the test pilot who, with several broken ribs and a broken arm, broke the sound barrier—into the strong, silent hero of wagon-loads of Westerns, a fellow who breaks his silence only to drop a saltily laconic epigram or to pay his beautiful, strong-willed, toughly playful wife the odd, toughly playful compliment. This is the film's real hero, a combination Nimrod and Penrod, an airy Gary Cooper in times that test men's planes as well as souls, and as far removed from the wiles of Odysseus as from the sorrows of Aeneas. As Sam Shepard plays him, with a slightly snaggle-toothed countercultural charm, he is clearly meant as the hero who performs for neither money nor fame but only for the simple joy of excellence, to overshadow the seven dwarfed astronauts.

Yet the Mercury gang of seven are also viewed with warm sentiments, albeit with a collusive or even conspiratorial slap on the back rather than with the falling over backward reserved for Yeager. The

astronauts are jolly or grim, clean-cut or less than clean-living fellows from various branches of the service, and they go in for rivalries and razzing, pranks and put-ons, and the rest of the American
post-but-not-quite-past-school repertoire. There are even hard arguments between the philandering Grissom and the monogamous
Glenn, and, again, between foul-mouthed Alan Shepard and the
clean-spoken Glenn. But against exploitation by the media and oppression by NASA and the government, the astronauts form a kind
of comradely, indeed labor, union and—spunkily, cunningly, gain-
fully—outsmart the scientists and politicians (heavily caricatured)
as well as the media and medical authorities, including a stereotypical mannish tyrant of a nurse, who subject them to unspeakable
endurance tests.

What the film is saying—I don't know how consciously—is that
there is a supreme, solitary, epic heroism as well as, a step or two
below, in-group resilience, resourcefulness, and strength through
solidarity, and that there are moments when the seven commercially hagiographized, hosannaed, and well-remunerated heroes are
almost as valorous as the unsung and nearly unpaid Yeager. But by
far the most effective scenes are the ones involving Grissom's semi-
failed space flight (the capsule sinks, probably but not necessarily
through the astronaut's panicking) and its after-effects on Grissom's
marriage and mentality; and the one in which the congenitally badly stuttering Mrs. Glenn phones her husband awaiting takeoff into
space to ask, wretchedly and almost speechlessly, whether she must
go on TV with the publicity-seeking LBJ, and Glenn, despite the
threat of serious reprisals, indignantly and lovingly confirms her
in her wish for privacy. These sequences, and a few others, show
a rich blend of human strength and weakness, and if there were
more of them, the movie might have been major instead of merely
entertaining, uneven, and, at 192 minutes, overlong.

Still, there is enough right with *The Right Stuff* to earn recom-
mendation. There are a dozen or two superb performances, and
only two minor bad ones: Royal Dano's hammily symbolic Death
figure is a piece of cheap attitudinizing by the script and probably
could not be played well; but Pancho (a woman!), who runs a desert cantina with wall-to-wall pictures of dead airmen for Camp
Edwards pilots to noisily relax in—an *hommage* to *Only Angels
Have Wings*—is further damaged by Kim Stanley's mannered performance. The cinematography by Caleb Deschanel is first-rate,
whether in a genuine desert or in cleverly simulated outer space,

with fine special effects by Jordan Belson out of Moholy-Nagy. There are compelling sound effects (except for a mangy score by Bill Conte, a usable hack where a true composer was needed), good although old-fashioned direction (the hammered-in crosscutting between the astronauts at the Astrodome reveling in Sally Rand's fan dance and Yeager going it alone in a yet more ferociously intractable plane is clobbering rather than edifying), and ingenious fake location work with Northern California standing in for everything from New York to the Antipodes. This, along with often tart or canny dialogue, garners a sprinkling of esteem along with a good measure of enjoyment.

Star 80

Bob Fosse's *Star 80* deals, or pussyfoots, with a real-life horror story it will not, cannot, dare not fully explore. It concerns the hideous murder of a Playboy playmate and starlet, Dorothy Stratten, by her husband, Paul Snider—a con-man and pimp with aspirations of becoming another Hugh Hefner—who then killed himself. For three reasons, aside from the trashiness of the story, Fosse could not succeed. First, the truth was too grisly to avoid an x rating, meaning a loss in revenue no big-budget picture wishes to incur. And where a story registers, for better or worse, through its horror, soft-pedaling means a loss of nerve that infiltrates the entire operation.

Second, although Snider and Miss Stratten are both safely dead, and her mother and sister could be placated into permission, there is no way in which Hefner, who made Dorothy his Playmate of the Year, and Peter Bogdanovich, who directed her in his last picture show and wanted to make her his mate for life, would have permitted an excess of truth, against which the well-known and well-heeled can be legally immune. Hence any filmmaker undertaking to tell such a story knows ahead of time that he will have to skip, finagle, and falsify—another method from which little good can come. But the third and greatest drawback is that Fosse, a dancer and choreographer, is much less of a movie director and not at all a writer: There is not much communication between the dancing foot and the writing hand.

Now, it may not be of major interest how a nice but simple Canadian counter-girl falls for a flashy smalltime operator who prestidigitates with promises; but how she is persuaded to pose in the nude for a photographer friend of his, and becomes gradually sucked into the *Playboy* mentality and physicality, is a matter of some psychological interest if only Fosse—as director and his own screenwriter—knew how to handle it other than once over heavily. Although Eric Roberts manages to convey the obsession with luxury and fame of a sleazy fellow who gambles, not on cards or roulette, but on the crunchy freshness of a naïve young beauty (whom Mariel Hemingway, despite a silicone implant in her bosom, plays with a minimum of dimensionality, except a tallness that awkwardly towers over everyone else), there is much less detail and insight here than in Teresa Carpenter's reportage, on which the film is partly based.

One suspects that poor Dorothy perceived Hef as the Wizard of Oz, Kahlil Gibran, and Dear Abby rolled into one big, sexy Pygmalion, who (and this is one of the film's few authentic touches) always presided over the Playboy Mansion parties in pajamas, the appropriate uniform for dispensing what the Marquis de Sade, in a different context, called *la philosophie dans le boudoir*. But the script and Cliff Robertson turn Hef into a cross between a teacher of etiquette and a games master at a young ladies' finishing school, where all intercourse is supposed to be strictly social. And though the men she meets at the Mansion may have designs on her, Dorothy, despite her genuine upward mobility in contrast to Paul's ineffectual megalomania (while she poses for classy pictures in *Playboy*, he stages cheap sex shows in low dives), sticks to and supports her husband in almost the style he lusts after.

Following on a few awkward interviews watched over by *Playboy* mentors, Dorothy lands some trashy movie roles of which she makes a mess, until the classy director Aram Nicholas (i.e., Bogdanovich) makes her his star and mistress. Their cohabitation in New York is presented with a chastity that would do credit to a nunnery, until Paul, maddened with jealousy and the sense of losing his meal ticket to Fortuna's banquet, lures Dorothy to their Los Angeles house and there shoots her and himself. The particularly sado-pornographic details of the murder, as well as of some previous incidents, are merely lip-smackingly hinted at. Indeed, throughout the film we get flashforwards to Paul, bloody and looking into a mirror, railing against the world and his failure. Each sequence shows more gore on and around him, but the ultimate climax of obscene or, less likely, cathartic terror is thoroughly fudged, though doubtless not for reasons of taste. In fact, the movie lacks even the courage of its bad taste.

What, then, was the reason for making *Star 80*? Puzzled reviewers have postulated Fosse's disgust with the debasement of show business, or self-hate for former dabblings in commercial sleaziness, or an attempt to exorcise some of his ungallant attitudes toward women. Though there may be something to all of this, the finished film looks to me like an inadvertent tribute to false glamor as well as an attempt to titillate as much as an R rating can be stretched to. The only character who is even superficially examined is Paul Snider; the others, many of whom serve as narrators of segments of the story—a modish and tiresome device—get no real identities or, in some cases, even adequate identification.

Still more modish and annoying is the device of allowing, during Dorothy's endless photographic sessions, the soundtrack to resound with the clicking of shutters that won't shut up; it is hard to say whether this or Giorgio Moroder's score is more grating. Finally, Fosse's genuine cowardice is as great as his delusions of daring: Snider always wore a Star of David dangling from a chain round his neck; for fear of antagonizing Jewish viewers, Fosse substitutes a metallic S.

Little Big Screen

TERMS OF ENDEARMENT

Television, like a reverse Falstaff, is not only witless in itself, but also the cause of witlessness in other fields it has contaminated: theater and, especially, film. A flagrant example of this is *Terms of Endearment*, a movie that, besides being a crowd-pleaser, has already won numerous awards. Written and directed by James L. Brooks, it is loosely based on a novel by Larry McMurtry, and much more tightly on Brooks's experience as co-creator of such TV serials as *The Mary Tyler Moore Show*, *Lou Grant*, and *Taxi*. *Terms of Endearment* is the thirty-year story of love, and sometimes love-hate, between Aurora Greenway and her only child, Emma, who live out a tragicomic destiny while the film rattles through farce, comedy, drama, and tragedy as Brooks understands them, always with great concentration on the audience's anatomy: ribs to be tickled, sides to be split, eyes to be drenched, hearts to be broken—and carefully mended. A more calculating and manipulative movie would be hard to imagine, and yet there is a kind of innocence, too. Brooks seems to be the sort of con-man who cons himself into believing he is creating true art.

The film begins in Houston with a typical cabaret vignette in which young Aurora (Shirley MacLaine shot through a year's supply of Vaseline), coming home late with her husband (heard but not seen), finds baby Emma fast asleep. With farcical hysteria, Aurora overrules her sensible husband and insists that this is crib death. She tries to climb into the crib but is prevented, again farcically, by the tightness of her skirt. So she contents herself with banging the baby's back, which, of course, elicits howls from the baby. "Oh good!" exclaims Aurora. "That's better!" This slapstick preamble sets the tone for much of the movie: a rather sticky symbiosis played mostly for belly laughs. Aurora, insecure under her bravado, continually tries to climb, literally or figuratively, into Emma's bed while also soundly walloping her, ostensibly out of sheer maternal concern: Emma responds, consecutively or even concurrently, with affection, anger, vain outcries, and pity. It will be a lifelong hit-or-miss convergence.

But hack work cheats about human truths, and so Aurora is, for comic purposes, either overdependent on or excessively mean to Emma: later, for tragic purposes, she will be unbelievably devoted and self-sacrificing as her daughter is dying of cancer—a plot twist that must have leaked out by now, and, in any case, this film does not deserve critical discretion. The early-widowed Aurora is a fanatical pedant, puritan, and tightwad, and prefers surrogates to sex. Thus she has two men—a nice, grey Texas businessman and a short, cocky clown of uncertain provenance—in what looks like round-the-clock platonically adoring attendance, their passionate servitude rewarded with bullying and an occasional chaste kiss. Although meant to be charmingly zany, this strikes me as preposterous and mildly nauseating. The house next door belongs to the middle-aged ex-astronaut Garrett Breedlove (Jack Nicholson), who mostly swims, drinks, or orgies, using his space exploits as aphrodisiacs on very young girls, whom he prefers to bed in pairs. Lately, though, he is turned down more and more because of his age, potbelly, boozing, and crassness, but also so as to endear him to the audience, which might view a successful satyr with envy and resentment.

Aurora is secretly attracted to this jovially devilish lecher, which may make psychological sense. Yet I doubt if she would, after 11 years of ostensible contempt, accept his lunch invitation that is not kept: then, after four more years, suddenly coerce him into keeping it. And would she, after a wildly unsuccessful date, make a late-hour phone call to him inviting him over for the night? As for Garett, would the occasional fiasco with younger women be enough to turn this compulsive girl-chaser into the rapt lover of a woman of 52? Perhaps so, although his refusal to get involved in Aurora's family life—when Emma and her children show up in Houston because Emma has temporarily left her unfaithful husband, Flap—rings considerably truer. And whereas I can suspend my disbelief to the point of accepting Garrett's sudden turning up in Lincoln, Nebraska, where Aurora is tending her doomed daughter, I seriously doubt whether our man, about to board a plane back to Houston, would respond to Aurora's declaration of love with, "I was just inches from a clean getaway," and mean it. He is hooked, and will doubtless marry Aurora and be father to her motherless and, owing to Flap's incompetence, quasi-fatherless grandchildren.

And what about Flap (Jeff Daniels), who genuinely loves and is loved by Emma? Is he a wimpy English prof whose one strength is his enduring; though not undeviating love for his wife? Or is he a strong, silent man with strong sexual appetites whom one woman, however loving, and teaching jobs in the academic backwaters of Iowa and Nebraska cannot wholly satisfy? Does he have only one extramarital affair or many? How good a father is he really? And what of Emma herself? She is shown mostly as an ardent wife and dedicated mother, albeit rather untidy. Is there, besides her exaggerated involvement with Aurora (including enormous long-distance phone bills), something more—or less—to her? We are not shown this, even if Debra Winger, who plays her well, gives off a demotic aura that extends to a much lower-class accent than her mother's. As presented, she appears more than enough for Flap, whose two-timing could thus use a little exploration and elaboration.

To provide a little adulterous sauce for the goose, there is then a sweet Midwestern bank officer whom Emma meets cute at the supermarket. His wife has denied him sex for years which hasn't made him sour or greedy, only dripping or drippy with sweetness for Emma, and the gifted John Lithgow plays him not a bit against the grain, thus making him too adorably square even for a Des Moines bank officer. And there is, throughout, Emma's best friend, Patsy, who first has a marriage in Los Angeles to allow for some Hollywood jokes, then, unaccountably, lives in New York, where she can take the moribund Emma on a vacation for some New York jokes.

Brooks is so used to—and, alas, so ideally suited to—television serials that the entire film is made in their dishonest image. Characters are either oversimplifications such as the bank officer, or, like the plot, stitched-together bits of sitcom inconsistency. We go from episode to barely related episode, everything geared to the comic or tearjerking payoff of that particular segment. If the guffaws or sobs in this installment require a character to be thus and so, then thus and so he will be; if the climax of the next episode requires a radically different set of attitudes, the character promptly obliges with the needed inconsistency. So even the few genuinely funny or touching moments are corroded by contrivance. As soon laugh or cry at this as give alms to an arrogantly overinsistent beggar.

Indeed, by what sort of artistic integrity does a film go from freewheeling, or Catherine-wheeling, farce about seemingly invulnerable comic-strip characters to sudden troweled-on tragedy, from Mel Brooks to Erich Segal? A mother bidding final farewell to her two boys circa ten and six—especially with actors as good as Debra Winger, Troy Bishop, and Huckleberry Fox—is bound to elicit conspicuous Kleenex consumption among the gullible. But effects are not affects. Marionettes are not prone to mortal illness; cancer is no way of pumping blood into puppets. The calculation is salient: Emma is allowed to die—peacefully, nobly, with only one snappish moment for increased realism—because this enables Garrett to come through in the end, Flap to become integrated into the family, and Patsy to emerge as a surrogate daughter. It is all as spurious as that priceless Renoir (a fake, I presume, but ghastly in any case) with which Aurora brightens Emma's hospital room during the last days.

What real merit the film has—apart from the sporadic fun usually contributed by Nicholson and, in some cases, improvised by him—comes from the children. All the kids are splendid and well directed, no matter if some of the best things smack of improvisation. Yet even here there is cheating. The eldest child is aware of the rift in the parental marriage and resentful, which makes sense. But why should he resent his mother rather than his father, the manifest cause of the trouble. Because that makes for some added facile poignance in the parting scene between mother and sons and in the scene in which Aurora slaps the boy in passionate defense of her daughter. Shirley MacLaine plays a mostly ludicrous character mostly ludicrously, which may be right, but I find her a bit too obvious and coarse at times.

In one typical sequence mother and grown daughter are exchanging confidences while lying prone side by side in the same bed. In back of their heads, their legs can be seen intertwining in a sensual game of footsie. If this sort of thing chills you as it does me, you might as well hotfoot it out there and then.

Fustian

SILKWOOD; THE DRESSER

There are very serious problems with *Silkwood*. As I keep having to say, you shouldn't make biographic films about contemporary persons unless you know the facts and are in a position to tell them. This, however, is very rarely the case, and the films fall on their behinds between fact and fiction. Individuals from the distant past are fair game: The filmmaker can tell the known facts and then conjecture away to his heart's content. What about Karen Silkwood, though, the young woman from Texas who worked in a Kerr-Mc-Gee nuclear-fuel plant in Oklahoma, led a fairly loose life, became politicized and a labor-union spy, exposed laxnesses in the plant's safety procedures, and was allegedly about to make some tremendous revelations to a *New York Times* reporter whom she was driving to meet when her car went off the road and she died? It was 1974, and Karen was 28. Was it an accident or murder?

Though I haven't followed the case closely, this much is clear: We don't know what really happened, and probably never shall, but the available evidence suggests that Karen Silkwood had no sensational documents, and that it is unlikely that she met with foul play. Which is not to say that management wasn't remiss, that Karen (having become contaminated) would not eventually have died of lung cancer, and that it was mere coincidence that the Kerr-McGee facility in Crescent, Oklahoma, shut down a year later. But there just isn't enough hard evidence; so the writers, Nora Ephron and Alice Arlen, and the director, Mike Nichols, were forced to hint, waffle, and contradict themselves into a haze of innuendos, discrepancies, and, occasionally, total opacity.

Vital plot elements are missing because the filmmakers don't know much about the lives with which they are dealing, and because they desperately want management to appear guilty of murder, local labor repressed and slow to move, the heroine as nearly as possible a wayward saint and martyr—and all this without libel suits or charges of sentimental gloss. Thus the filmmakers had to walk on eggshells—if not, indeed, on water, for carrying off *Silkwood* would have required not so much delicacy as a miracle.

As things are, we never learn how, or by whom, Karen gets "cooked" on three ever more fateful occasions, why her house has to be stripped down to its skeleton, and why she hasn't more seriously contaminated her two housemates: Drew, her lover who also works at the plant, and Dolly, another co-worker and a lesbian hopelessly in love with her. The film equivocates fearfully on any number of subjects, e.g., what concrete proof Karen had of criminally covered-up imperfections in the product that might cause millions of deaths, and what really caused her own demise. Needless to say, the Kerr-McGee supervisors are presented as gross-looking lechers and exploiters if not actual killers, to which end they are given postures and expressions of advanced obtuseness, hypocrisy, or brutality, but without ever quite saying or doing the things that go with their stances. They emerge rather like filmed high-jumpers caught foolishly straining in mid-air by a freeze frame.

That, of course, leaves the "human" story of Karen; her three children whom she loves but left in Texas with the common-law husband she divorced; her fast living with various (mostly implied) men, booze, minor drugs; her relations with the sexually and convivially satisfying but morally and intellectually sluggish Drew, who wants to own a garage, marry her, and make her future even duller than her present; her tensions with Dolly, either because her own sex life disturbs the yearning lesbian, or because Dolly moves in with a mistress—the feisty but crass Angela, who verbally spars with Drew; her friendships and hostilities, her flirtatiousness and occasional slapdashness at work. Karen is a sort of Carmen at a plant more dangerous to her lungs than the cigarette factory was to the fiery gypsy's, until her nascent passion for union work, partly sparked by an affair with Paul, a union organizer, causes a rupture with Drew. And so on, through a reconciliation with her longtime lover up to the monumentally muzzy end.

Some aspects of this personal story are well enough developed, and scenes of the harrowing showers and scrub-downs given contaminated workers—not so unlike the flaying of Christian martyrs—are well directed and powerful. Yet in this area, too, there is trouble. Why does the otherwise sensible Angela make up her lover, Dolly—but not herself—the way she does her corpses? Why are we led to believe that Dolly ratted on Karen to the authorities—a curious plot development that is then feebly denied and left hanging? Above all, why is Meryl Streep allowed to play Karen as a sophisticated, middle-class New York neurotic with Woody-Allen-movie mannerisms rather, than as a believable Texas blue-collar worker?

This last is enough to cast doubt on any integrity the film might have. Miss Streep has developed—and overdeveloped—an acting style in which one clean gesture is never as good as three fussy ones. So a monosyllabic answer to a simple question is executed with 1) a turn of the head to profile enhanced with a Gioconda smile, 2) a return of the face camera-ward, with many tiny nervous nods, and 3) a sharp intake of breath, followed by the answer with a quaint catch in the voice. A cigarette is lit in the fruitiest Bette Davis manner, but Miss Davis was playing megalopolitan crazies, not basically sound hinterlanders. The entire performance seems to be carried out visually in a hall of mirrors and aurally in an Alpine valley famous for its multiple echo. To change tropes, there is a kernel of true feeling, but several layers of smug incrustation need to be scraped off it.

And then there is the question of the dialogue. The co-scenarists, two slick Eastern women writers, do not convince me they know how Oklahoma workers speak—or, for that matter, behave. There are moments, to be sure, when the conversation is tangy and unforced, but rather more when it sounds too clever and contrived; at other times, perfect banalities are delivered with a portentousness befitting Greek tragedy. There are such improbable bits as Drew's Hollywoodish parting from Karen and his ghostly return to their house after it has been gutted by the decontaminators, and a night scene on the porch wherein Karen and Dolly express their incommensurable loves for each other that ends with a sort of *pietà* from which the camera withdraws into a heart-wringing long shot. But the director's competence is not fully compromised until the final scene, in which Miss Streep drives to her death while her voice, endlessly and even posthumously, keeps singing "Amazing Grace" on the soundtrack—the cliché of clichés. Yet the supporting roles are all well taken, and Miroslav Ondríček's cinematography is fraught with hard-earned beauty even in humdrum or squalid surroundings. *Silkwood* is not a bad film, perhaps; merely an untrustworthy one, which may be worse.

The Dresser is one of those rare cases where a movie version, in this case Ronald Harwood's adaptation of his own undistinguished play, is better than the stage original. Dealing with the terminal day in the life of the last of the British touring actor-managers—a character modeled largely on Donald Wolfit, for whom Harwood once worked—it is an effective quadruple testimonial. It praises, first, the half-mad, half-inspired actor, an infuriating despot somehow awesome despite his senescent hamminess and loss of memory, here called simply Sir. It celebrates, second, his fluttery, florid, cluckingly overprotective homosexual dresser, Norman, without whose brooding-hen devotion neither Sir nor his company could go on—either on stage, or from one town to the next. Third, it is a tribute to the theater, which, even at its seediest and grimiest, manages to surpass itself and bring joy to the needy. Finally, it is a testimonial to Britain in World War II, when casts performed and audiences sat unruffled while bombs fell all around.

The film has two advantages over the play. It fleshes out some minor characters, notably the dour but efficient stage manager secretly in love with Sir (superbly played by Eileen Atkins): and it can provide glimpses, or even vignettes, of the audience, as when a man in uniform, his head bandaged, weeps during an intermission of *Lear*, while his civilian companion pats and consoles him with, "It's only a play!" Unfortunately, however, it does "open up" the stage play in two scenes neither of which quite works, and there is in Peter Yates's otherwise good direction a tendency to hystericize the manic relationship between Norman and Sir still further into convulsiveness by means of grotesque camera angles and distortions.

But Tom Courtenay, even goaded beyond the camera's tolerance for histrionics, remains a marvelous Norman; Albert Finney has some splendid moments, although he does not help us distinguish the abhorrent from the admirable in Sir. Also, Finney indulges himself in clever takeoffs on Olivier, Gielgud, and Richardson, instead of sticking to Wolfit's sui generis blend of the powerful and the repellent. Here too, however, the supporting cast is excellent, and *The Dresser*, coming on the heels of a batch of flops, very nearly redresses the balance.

Tightrope

It's a bit of a red-letter day when an American movie even flirts with maturity, and *Tightrope* certainly flirts with it. A trifle meretriciously, awkwardly, even immaturely, but it does try, within the format of the *policier* (strange that there is no English word for it) and the genre of the film *noir* (again!), for a significant statement and for a story that can accommodate such a statement. Written and directed by Clint Eastwood's protégé Richard Tuggle, and starring Eastwood, this is the tale of a capable New Orleans detective, Wes Block, whose wife has left him, and who lives with his two daughters, aged twelve and five, whom he adores. Though a good father, he sees with horror a kinky side emerging in himself.

Someone is murdering prostitutes in the French Quarter; he has more or less unorthodox sex with them, then strangles them. Although, under Block's supervision, some progress is made in the hunt for the killer, he leaves few, and rather confusing, clues. Most peculiarly, he seems to have it in for Block. For as Block ferrets around the good-time girls of the Vieux Carré, he gets little freebies from them: here a little oral sex, there a girl inviting him to manacle her to the bed, and so on toward a girl who proffers a bull whip. But no sooner has Block had sex with one of these ladies of the night than she is dispatched into eternal night, usually as the climax of the type of sex Block has had with her. We are shown the masked killer trailing Block, voyeuristically ogling his escapades, then striking. Since the police department is on to Block's kinkiness, there is some suspicion directed toward him; he himself seems to fear that, in a trance perhaps, he may be the killer.

Meanwhile he is accosted by a ballsy young woman he at first tries to shake: Beryl, who teaches self-defense at a rape crisis center and wants to know more about what the police are doing in this new emergency. An enlightened feminist, Beryl befriends Wes, and they eventually become lovers. She has a humanizing influence; asked by Wes what makes her so sure the women she coaches need help, she answers, "We all need it." Score one against Wes. When she asks how his experiences with homicide affected his relations with his ex-wife, Wes replies, "They made me treat my wife a little more tenderly."

"How did she respond?"

"She said she wasn't interested in tenderness." Score one for Wes; the film does not stack the deck.

For all of Beryl's wholesomeness, Wes is further demoralized the more he realizes that the killer and he are brothers under the foreskin. Even his love for his daughters begins to look ambiguous, especially where the elder, Amanda, is concerned. Shortly after he has learned that the killer went in for "sandwiches" (sexual threesomes), Wes passes out from exhaustion prone on his couch.

Amanda finds him there, tenderly climbs on top of him, and likewise falls asleep. Later, this incomplete sandwich will be figuratively completed. Whatever the killer does, Block has, in his own life, partially anticipated or echoed. Told that no one could have known what deadly thing the killer would do next, Wes says in bitter self-reproach, "No one but me." The thesis of the film is stated by a psychiatrist who is both black and a woman, which may be indulging in self-congratulatory liberalism: "There is a darkness inside all of us, Wes. Some have it under control, some don't. The rest of us walk a tightrope between the two." The image is somewhat imprecise and unoriginal; but then, the speaker is a psychiatrist, not a poet.

Clearly, *Tightrope* does a balancing act among three, not two, possibilities. It could have been a piece of soft-core pornography, and at times, alas, it is. It could have been a mere thriller, and, regrettably, it is that to a large extent. But it also could have been, and happily is in part, a searching examination of a psyche losing its balance, with distinct implications for the rest of us. I wish we could have seen something of Block's marriage. I wish we could see more sharply what self-realization does to him—beyond the fact that he does not handcuff Beryl to the bed. I wish the Beryl-Wes relationship were developed in greater, more rewarding detail.

I especially wish the film did not try to suggest more than it states without daring to pursue its suggestions. Thus when the killer tries to fix up Wes with a young male whore in a homosexual bar, another male hustler asks the non-consenting cop, "How do you know you won't like it if you haven't tried?"

"Maybe I have," replies Block, but there is no follow-through. Is this more than repartee, though? Later, when Block looks for the killer in a Mardi Gras-costume warehouse, the camera picks up among the grotesque disguises (some of which the killer is given to wearing) a Ronald Reagan and a Douglas MacArthur mask—but no Jimmy Carter or Harry Truman. Is a connection implied between leading Republicans and carnival madness? And murder? This is not just a cheap shot, it is also a red herring posing as something more.

Still, *Tightrope* makes some pertinent comments tersely and devastatingly. Thus Beryl, who is so good at kicking a male dummy in the groin during a demonstration, proves powerless to defend herself during a real assault. Thus Block is confronted in a terrifying way with his incestuous feelings about Amanda, though the film cannot quite show what this dreadful lesson does to him. Yet for all the weakness of his flesh, Wes is clearly superior to Dirty Harry, the cop who enjoys killing, whom Eastwood has portrayed in a progressively more odious series of films. Here, moreover, Eastwood, not exactly known for his histrionic range, manages to convey a troubled and troubling character without making him too antipathetic or too sympathetic.

But always the film rushes back to standard devices of suspense—for example, when the two frightened daughters huddle together while their father fights the killer, shots are heard, the door opens, and all we see at first the close-up of a smoking gun—but whose hand? Such tricks belong to a lesser genre; the suspense *Tightrope* could have generated, and does provide to an extent, is of a deeper, more existential kind. Similarly, I wish that after all that nagging doubt about Wes we were not treated to—and cheated by—a conventional happy ending.

In other ways, too, *Tightrope* is flawed. So Bruce Surtees, a cameraman who loves to underlight his films is here allowed to feast on darkness. Most of the film takes place at night, in dives, in heavily shuttered rooms; or in rainy weather; during the final chase there is even a thunderstorm. Like sunlight, the brighter sections of New Orleans are rarely visible. *Film noir*, very well, but is the epithet to be taken quite so literally? And there are other kinds of literalmindedness; Thus one prostitute is almost always provocatively licking a popsicle, which by way of underlining has to be red, And, worst of all, one of Wes's nightmares is shown, at first, as if Beryl were dreaming it.

Nevertheless, there is much stinging action and tingling dialogue, and generally compelling acting. Sadly, Geneviève Bujold (Beryl) is not aging well; but her performance, as always, is intelligent and persuasive. The various prostitutes, policemen, riffraff are shrewdly cast and make the most of their vignettes. And even though there is some hyperbole (a whore who handed out that kind of whip wouldn't last long), there is also understatement and ellipsis that allow seamy incidents to register without undue titillation. *Tightrope* is a film that points away from the American cinema's perennial adolescence toward an incipient adulthood.

Amadeus

Total eclipse overtakes what is now billed grandiosely as "Peter Shaffer's *Amadeus*," as if anyone else would be rash enough to claim it. Bad as the play was (though a huge success—what is the world coming to?), Shaffer's screenplay, written under the supervision of and directed by Miloš Forman, is immeasurably worse. This preposterous story contrives that Salieri—outraged that, despite a vow of chastity and service to God, he is gifted with only a middling talent, while the misnamed Amadeus, a licentious and scurrilous boy all his life, should be blessed with the most easefully copious genius of all—vows hatred for God and destruction to Mozart. Since, despite the baseless legend about the lesser man's poisoning his great rival, the facts cannot be easily squared with anything more than Salieri's animosity toward Mozart, it is Shaffer who is the real poisoner of the well of truth with a tale whose implausibility is matched only by its vulgarity. One, does, however, discern yet another chapter in Shaffer's continuous lament over his own mediocrity and inability to break with convention—themes that cropped up in *The Royal Hunt of the Sun* and *Equus* as well.

For the movie version of *Amadeus*, additional characters had to be dragged in—the allegedly despotic Leopold Mozart; the insufferable mother-in-law, Frau Weber; the spying maid, Lorl; and Schikaneder with his chicanery—while existing ones had to be beefed up. As a result, the new characters remain rushed and superficial, whereas Constanze becomes the stereotypical loving but nagging wife, a cliché from which the play's foreshortening dubiously saved her. The new scenes are often crass scatology, as when Mozart sticks out his behind at Archbishop Colloredo, or when he ends a pastiche of Salieri's music improvised at a revel by simulating a loud breaking of wind right into the elder composer's face. The play's crude Freudianizing, whereby the Commendatore is really Mozart's dead father, has been retained and grossly hammered in: "Wolfgang has actually summoned up his own father to accuse his son before the whole world" and "How that bitter old man was still possessing his son even from beyond the grave." And it has been expanded, by having Frau Weber's stridulous yammerings at her son-in-law turn into the coloratura aria of the Queen of the Night!

Forman has directed with his usual heavyhanded competence. That Leopold Mozart should wear by way of costume a domino with a grave mask before and a grinning one behind is effective when he makes a sudden turn, but he turns once too often; what is inexcusable is to have the man in grey who comes to commission a requiem from Mozart similarly accoutered. Or take the crosscutting between Mozart's dying and the homeward journey by stagecoach of Constanze and her children to the music of the *Requiem*: loud passages, the coach rattling through the night; soft passages, Wolfgang expiring or children looking forlorn. Particularly cheap is the conceit—new in the movie version—that the moribund Mozart dictated the *Requiem* to Salieri, who wrote it down in a prolonged ecstasy of love-hate. Here we are treated to an elementary music-appreciation lesson in dialogue form: "Identical?—Of course, the instruments doubling the voices. —I don't understand . . . Yes, yes, yes! I understand. Yes! Yes!" Salieri turns into an orgasmic Molly Bloom even as Mozart turns into an idiot requiring the Latin text to be translated for him by Salieri so that the great unwashed in the movie audience should be able to follow—which they won't anyway.

Most appalling is the ending, with Salieri dying illogically in a lunatic asylum. Here madmen more horrific than in *Marat/Sade* are hideously chained or caged along the walls of a corridor down which Salieri is being wheeled. "Mediocrities everywhere, I absolve you," he mutters. At least in the play this referred to the audience; in the movie, even that simplistic irony becomes an abject cop-out. Miroslav Ondríček's cinematography is splendid as usual, the Czech backgrounds are inspiritingly baroque (though the great innovator Josef Svoboda was the wrong choice for designing old-style operatic scenery), but the acting is routine or worse (Tom Hulce as Mozart), save for the sensitively muted Leopold of Roy Dotrice. Boo and *O, Weh!*

The Killing Fields

For all its flaws, *The Killing Fields* is an important, indeed necessary, film. Based on an article in the *New York Times Magazine* by Sydney Schanberg, it tells the story of the friendship between Schanberg, then the *Times* correspondent in Cambodia, and his Cambodian translator and guide, Dith Pran, before, during, and after the take-over of that luckless country by the Khmer Rouge. It also tells of Dith Pran's fearful ordeal in various labor camps after Schanberg's departure, of Schanberg's guilt feelings for not letting his protégé whose services he needed, escape with his evacuated wife and children before the fall of Phnom Penh (though he was eager enough to stay), of the American journalist's efforts to locate and rescue his companion, and of how the latter finally, with almost superhuman effort, did manage to escape to Thailand and fall into Sydney's arms. And also of Nixon-Kissinger's deleterious, disastrous involvement in Cambodian affairs.

The main problem with the film written by Bruce Robinson and directed by Roland Joffé (whose first feature film, after work in theater and TV documentaries, this was), is that it tries to do too much, which leads to oversimplification and superficiality in some areas, and the elision of relevant facts. For example, it does not show us how Dith Pran recruits the companions for his eventual escape, or that his wife, angry at him for staying with Schanberg rather than leaving with her and the kids, divorces him upon arriving in America. It glosses over Sydney's selfishness and doesn't adequately examine Dith Pran's motives for staying on.

There are other difficulties. Thus the foreground action, the friendship between the two men, is not written and directed well enough to make it worthy of a background so tragic and so graphically conveyed as the Cambodian genocide in which Pol Pot and his hordes exterminated some 40 percent of Cambodia's population, as stupidly as viciously, merely for having been able to function under the admittedly corrupt, American-backed Lon Nol regime, merely for speaking a foreign language. The background of senseless and exacerbating American bombings, of people dying and living coolly with the deaths of others (whether by foreign bombs or domestic ad hoc executions) as if nothing unusual were happening, of works of art perishing in the midst of cataclysm and silently rebuking the engulfing brutality—these things are brilliantly yet unostentatiously depicted, in the manner of Auden's Old Masters (in "Musée des Beaux Arts") who "never forgot / That even the dreadful martyrdom must run its course / Anyhow in a corner, some untidy spot / Where the dogs go on with their doggy life . . ." Accordingly, blood spurts in the most casual manner, heartrending amputees lie about inconspicuously bleeding, life-and-death operations are being performed with insufficient staff and medical supplies under enemy harassment—yet all this is portrayed from the point of view of war-hardened observers, from the corner of the eye and with a muzzled heart, and infinitely more shocking and shattering for it.

There are trenchantly observed episodes even in the more diffuse first half of the film. Take such a scene as the helicopter evacuation of the Americans and a select few natives while crowds of other Cambodians beat, like caged and frenzied birds, against the wire

gates that condemn them to probable death. Meanwhile the wind-
storms stirred up by the helicopters reduce figures like the athletic
American ambassador, who would normally tower over the Cambodians, to a humbled stoop if not a shamed crouch, which, makes
the exodus assume the air of a humiliating hugger-mugger. Even
more unforgettable are the incidents of the Khmer Rouge takeover
wherein teenaged Communists round up foreign journalists and
their retinue, arbitrarily killing some and sparing others, the way
capricious children squash one insect and ignore the next. Here
Dith Pran's self-abasing persistence as he grovels to these young
hoodlums in hero's clothing (often stripped off their victims), and
the untranslated palaver that circulates among them while journalists with their hands up don't know whether the jig is up and on
what this depends, incomparably convey the grotesqueries of high
tragedy.

In the second half, where the film chiefly records Dith Pran's
ghastly experiences and resourceful courage in captivity, *The Killing
Fields* rises to those heights where our tears flow even as our blood
is chilled. Seldom has man's inhumanity to man been shown with
such scrupulously understated harrowingness, and the scenes in
which green-behind-the-ears Reds murder innocent adults simply
because their hands are not callused enough are truly, earnedly horrifying—and also instructive. Consider especially the one in which
a zombie-like girl of perhaps 13 uproots the tomato plant Dith Pran
has clandestinely been growing in the labor camp: it is one of the
most frightening moments in recent cinema. For these young ones
have perfectly empty eyes, like the damned children or pod people
of sundry horror films, only this is fact. Dr. Haing S. Ngor, a refugee
Cambodian physician who experienced this terror and torture and
here enacts Dith Pran, raced away during the shooting of this scene.
"The Khmer! The Khmer!" he shouted.

The supreme lesson of the film is how much more ruthless
children can be than their toughest elders, how nothing takes to
murderous fanaticism like an unformed, brainwashed mind. But
there are many other scenes of overwhelming power in *The Killing Fields*, notably a sequence I do not wish to divulge that gives
the film its title. What does not convince, however, is the scenes in
New York, when we crosscut from Dith Pran's apocalyptic agonies
to Schanberg's more comfortable anguishings while, for example,
he listens to Franco Corelli singing "*Nessun dorma.*" (Is this meant
as mockery?) After a promising beginning, Mike Oldfield's back-

ground music becomes too loud, too cheap, too explanatory of the obvious, and, in the final scene, when it borrows John Lennon's trivial "Imagine" to celebrate the stirring reunion, it is totally off-key.

So, too, is most of the acting of Sam Waterston as Sydney. He is one of those unfortunate American performers who cannot grow up, who always look and sound like clockwork adult figurines wound up with a key and strutting on a table top. The peak of Waterston's passion is a sort of peevish pique. Conversely, Haing S. Ngor is extremely moving in his earnest, self-controlled way—an amateur actor who approaches his role from harsh experience with absolute histrionic abstemiousness. In supporting parts, John Malkovich and Julian Sands give idiomatic authenticity to an American photojournalist and British correspondent, respectively; Spalding Gray as a diplomatic, and Craig T. Nelson as a military ugly American are not far behind. The film, prodigiously photographed by Chris Menges on realistic Thai locations, tries hard to be evenhandedly objective. It does, however, have a few too many loose ends and thriller clichés; without them, it would be stronger yet.

And Lo! The Twain Shall Meet

A PASSAGE TO INDIA

How nice to have David Lean back with us after 13 years of absence, which was bad enough, and *Ryan's Daughter*, which was worse. For many years Lean wanted to make a film about Nehru, and when this was denied him, *A Passage to India* must have seemed the next best thing. Of course, my old caveat—or, better, my eternal lament—about *not* turning major novels into movies holds here, too. Something expressly and inspiredly created for the mind's eye and mind's ear cannot be adequately translated for bodily eyes and ears. The medium is not the message, but it is an essential component of the art: like Chinese ideograms, it has no true equivalents.

E. M. Forster's novel has a pervasive bitterness about it that Lean's narrower hatred of British bureaucracy in any case fails to match. Moreover, Forster's style hovers and darts; Lean's marches and pounces. In a fine essay in the *New York Review of Books*, Noel Annan describes how Lean came to Forster's literary executors, the scholars of King's College, Cambridge, to seek permission to make the movie, something Forster would have flatly refused for the duration of his life. Lean explained that "he was not prepared to make a movie whose climax would provoke ridicule and laughter from the audience—the climax of an old man smearing himself with butter . . . He was frank. No movie made for mass circulation . . . could ever be faithful to Forster's novel. What it could do would be to respect the novel. His final words . . . were that Forster's novel was eternal: movies were ephemeral."

I doubt whether a man who believes movies to be ephemeral can truly be an artist in that medium (though Lean succeeded several times with films not based on literary masterpieces, or on almost foolproof Dickens novels); in which case he should emphatically leave art alone. For, as Lean knows, movies are no longer ephemeral, and damage done by an adaptation lives impudently on. Most interesting, however, is the casuistry of respect without faithfulness. Among other things, Lean has, respectfully but unfaithfully, slapped a happy ending onto the story: Fielding and Aziz are and will remain friends, and there is no hint of anything wrong with Fielding's marriage to Stella. Yet what I consider the hidden homosexual despair is essential to the novel, transmuted as it is into the political and the metaphysical. Commenting on Forster's unhappiness at the time he was writing *A Passage to India*, Virginia Woolf wrote in a letter, "The middle age of buggers is not to be contemplated without horror." (Quoted by P. N. Furbank in *E. M. Forster: A Life*.) Aziz and Fielding, in the book, have an added reason—Forster's non-emergence from the closet—for remaining apart.

But, as Lionel Trilling pointed out in his *E. M. Forster*, "The separation of race from race, sex from sex, culture from culture, even of man from himself, is what underlies every relationship . . . The sense of separateness broods over the book, pervasive, symbolic— at the end the very earth requires, and the sky approves, the parting of Aziz and Fielding . . ." Yet the only separateness Lean (who wrote and edited as well as directed) stresses is that between the Indians and the British rulers, whom he hates. One is tempted to think this related to his being passed over until just now for a knighthood, while lesser directors made the Queen's List.

How, to be sure, could Forster's novel be honestly filmed? Take a passage quoted by Trilling in which Mrs. Moore—the elderly lady who has come to fictive Chandrapore to see Ronny, her magistrate son, and has brought along his intended, Adela Quested,

that "queer, cautious girl"—listens to Ronny, whose sahibifica-
tion both women deplore, as he defends the British attitude: "His
words without his voice might have impressed her, but when
she heard the self-satisfied lilt of them, when she saw the mouth
moving so complacently and competently beneath his little red
nose, she felt, quite illogically, that this was not the last word on
India. One touch of regret—not the canny substitute but the true
regret—would have made him a different man, and the British
Empire a different institution." No more than anyone else could
Lean, even had he wanted to, put these nuances, strictures, suggestive minutiae on film. In fact, so badly does he want to make a
popular movie that he even changes Fielding's somewhat precious
Christian name, Cyril, into the red-blooded Richard.

Altogether, Lean is prone to cinematic "bigness," and India lends
itself to that; even as intimist a filmmaker as Jean Renoir became
overblown in *The River*. Sure enough, Lean has the viceroy arriving on the same boat with Mrs. Moore and Miss Quested, thus
allowing for the hauling out of oodles of pomp and circumstance.
Presently, we get sumptuous views of the wonders of India from
the train carrying our two ladies to Chandrapore, and Lean's new
cinematographer, Ernest Day, perfectly emulates his former one,
Freddie Young, with colors almost too good to be true. Still, the life
of an Indian town is well captured, even if on a larger scale than
Forster's or reality's: the club grounds, for instance, could pass for
the Royal Enclosure at Ascot; the uniformed Indian orchestra playing for the members could double for Sir Henry Wood's Promenade
Concerts.

Yet there are beautifully realized scenes from moonlight on the
Ganges to the nocturnal meeting in a mosque between Aziz and
Mrs. Moore. Effective, too, is an incident Lean invented: Adela,
bicycling in the countryside, comes upon an overgrown temple
with carved erotic figures. Aroused and spellbound, she is soon
put to flight by a horde of angry monkeys that leap from the carv-
ings to chase away the intruder. For Adela's repressed sexuality,
nature is acceptable as statuary, but not as something animalisti-
cally alive.

However, with the centerpiece of the novel, the excursion to
the Marabar caves, Lean comes to, perhaps inevitable, grief. The
railway scenes are good, as is the ride on the ancient, painted and
bedizened elephant, what with the poor old beast heaving like
some superannuated and overrouged opera diva followed by the

native retinue as by scampering fans. But the panicking of the two women inside the caves falls flat. (Typically, Lean, dissatisfied with all natural caves, dynamited his own out of a rock wall: the result is too neat and symmetrical, with a kind of *nouveau* look.) The novelist can leave most of that mysterious, ineffable happening suitably nebulous; the filmmaker must show something, which turns out both too much and too little.

Forster's bizarre psychology also gets lost. Thus Mrs. Moore's departure without testifying for Aziz makes an odd sense in the book in the light of her loss of faith at Marabar. Lean, who does not want such potentially audience-alienating apostasy, leaves this crucial incident inscrutable. Such excisions help keep down the movie to a not inconsiderable 183 minutes, but they, along with the omission of almost anything subtle or demanding in the dialogue, render the film nearly as simple-minded as Richard Attenborough's *Gandhi*.

While the visual aspects are imposing, Maurice Jarre's music is mostly an imposition. Yet a good many performances are a joy to hear and behold. As Mrs. Moore, Peggy Ashcroft is superlative in her blend of sweet old lady and imperious crone, of initial humanitarian and ultimate solipsist. Her face perfectly captures the amiable reserve of trim British dowagers that may as easily cloak the reticence of wisdom as the blankness of inanity. With equal brilliance, the Adela of Judy Davis conveys the surface amenities and the buried, intermittently surfacing jaggednesses. She succeeds in being absolutely plain and yet indefinably appealing; her guarded animation is exquisitely poised between yearning and restraint.

As Aziz, Victor Bannerjee strikes me as overheated to the point of deliquescence, but perhaps that is the way to sublimate the hidden animosity of the resentful colonial. Nigel Havers may be a trifle too dapper for Ronny, but James Fox has an arrestingly cloudy intensity as Fielding. The minor roles, British and Indian, are exemplarily filled, but Alec Guinness's Godbole is a disaster. Though not quite a Peter Sellers pastiche Indian, the performance seems to come not from life but from a theatrical warehouse.

After the climactic trial scenes, the film flounders on for half an hour, faithful but not too faithful to the book. Still, as an example of commercial filmmaking that has both craft and intelligence, it easily outdistances most of the competition, whether mindlessly vulgar or mindlessly arty.

Witness

Peter Weir is far from being the most talented, but is surely the most successful, current Australian filmmaker. The combination is unsurprising: it tends to take history decades to evaluate talent or its lack accurately and the public is rather slower than that. With *Witness*, Weir (*Gallipoli*, *The Year of Living Dangerously*) has made his first American movie, and it is no better, no less phony, than his Australian films. It is visually arresting, it has spurts of melodramatic excitement, and it is about as artistic as "Waltzing Matilda" played by a two-hundred-piece symphonic orchestra.

Witness begins with an Amish funeral near Lancaster, Pennsylvania: black-clad Amish are walking through wheat as high as a donkey's eye. Why they should make things bad for the crop and hard for themselves instead of choosing the road is perfectly obvious: the shot is colorfully black-and-gold, quaint, and picturesque, with strange black hats barely bobbing above the wheat. For a director of Weir's stamp that is reason enough. Newly widowed young Rachel Lapp is off with Samuel, her eight-year-old, to visit relatives in Baltimore. Having missed a connection in Philadelphia, the two must bide their time in the railway waiting room. Here we get wordlessly cute touches, such as the quizzical glances exchanged between little Samuel and an old Hassid, first attracted, then estranged by their similar yet different garb. In the deserted men's room, Samuel witnesses a brutal murder (all murders are brutal, but Weir's more so) in which two cops who are part of a multimillion-dollar dope ring do in a third. That small, unworldly Samuel should be able to trick such experienced searchers into not discovering him firmly situates *Witness* in the flimsy realm of make-believe.

Rachel and Samuel are detained by the tough but honest police captain John Book (white), who, with his tough but honest sidekick (black), conducts the investigation. Pronto, we are doused with contrasts: violent Philly *v.* idyllic Lancaster, foul-spoken Book *v.* clean-mouthed Rachel, Book's fornicating divorcée sister (with whom John shelters the Lapps) *v.* the chaste widow Rachel—in short, urban sleaziness and dirt *v.* country purity and piety. That these Amish live in 1985 as if it were 1800 (no telephones, TV, radio, cars, music, dancing, close contacts with the outside world—or even buttons, those devil's baubles fostering human vanity) strikes the filmmakers as wonderful. No cameras or movie houses, either;

but such embarrassing virtues are overlooked. There is something distastefully disingenuous about the lip-smacking deference with which these Dream City slickers extol the exotic unworldliness of the Amish rustics, comparable to the eighteenth century's worship of the noble savage. But at least Rousseau, Diderot, and the rest had the excuse of never having known any savages, noble or otherwise: these filmmakers, however, spent a long time on location.

Samuel identifies one of the murderous cops, and Book in turn discovers that his own superior is running the dope ring. Severely wounded in a shootout with one of the malefactors, Book yet manages to drive Rachel and Samuel back to the Lapp farm, and there passes out. After some perfunctory compunctions, a good Amish leech (surely the *mot juste*) cures Book with natural remedies and Rachel's devoted care. Soon John becomes like one of the true Amish, even wearing the dead Lapp's clothes, which have to be way too short for him so that he may look "plain" (the Amish term for humble and devout) in the eyes of God, and a sight gag in the eyes of the moviegoers. Rachel and John start falling in love despite Grandpa Lapp's warning that she will end up being "shunned" (ostracized), after he catches them dancing in the nocturnal barn by the lights and radio of John's car.

Though Book's recovery is now complete, he does nothing about the dope ring beyond ringing up his partner from the area's general store. (The film's only good line is Rachel's telling John that the nearest phone is miles away on the farm of some—she utters the word with mild contempt—Mennonites.) Book and his partner contemplate calling in the FBI or the press but do nothing, whereupon the partner is duly bumped off. Book makes a threatening phone call to his murderous boss, but still does nothing else. The film proceeds to explore the joys of plain living, such as getting up before dawn to milk the cows, which Book does awkwardly; carpentering, which he does better; and exchanging loving glances with Rachel, at which he is best, especially during a barn raising at which he carpenters and she waits on the communal tables. The two swap so many *œillades* that it is a miracle the milk doesn't end up in a Lapp's lap, and Book's finger nailed to the roof beam.

Barn raising is the *locus classicus* for such works; we've had it in *Seven Brides for Seven Brothers* on stage and screen, and even in *Plain and Fancy* (1955), a Broadway musical about a pair of urban sophisticates redeemed by a stay among the Amish. But more than barns, hopes are being raised here as Rachel, one fine day—or, rather, one stormy night—is caught by Book during her evening ablutions, and with unaffected innocence reveals her proud, young breasts to him. (Some platitudes never droop.) But Book leaves her as untouched as the dope ring, explaining that, were he to yield, either she would have to leave or he would have to stay. This would not do—at least not that night. But a couple of nights later the affair is consummated, with neither of the aforementioned dire consequences. Instead, the bad guys come to get Book, and there is a showdown, marginally more thrilling than the barn raising. Now Book does have to leave, but coming in the opposite direction is the fine young Amish fellow (played by the Russian dancer Alexander Godunov) who all along was waiting to wed Rachel. A bittersweet ending, markedly and marketably more sweet than bitter.

Even the Amish speech is inconsistent here, let alone the thinking. When Rachel and John are dancing and romancing, emancipation seems to be the proper thing. But when herbal healing works wonders, when Book carves a new birdhouse for Samuel, and when at the end Godunov comes sauntering toward Rachel, the primitive proves sublime. Rachel and John have had their sweet fling and can share a rapturous memory (forget *nessun maggior dolore!*), then let each proceed along his nicely preordained path.

Harrison Ford does a decent, solid job of Book (though he needs to perfect his self-sacrifice before taking on the Book of Job), but Kelly McGillis is a real drama-school actress (as she was also in the dreadful *Reuben, Reuben*). Though she is very pretty from some angles, the moment her cast-iron jaw takes over the screen, she might as well be some country weather vane. Godunov knows how to look intensely casual, and little Lukas Haas is as good as golden wheat as Samuel. Even if the Amish have no telephones, the dialogue sounds phoned in; the camera work is steadily fetching. If film were, as is sometimes asserted, a purely visual medium, the visuals might be enough. But it isn't, and they aren't.

Lost in America

It is too bad that in *Lost in America* Albert Brooks is only kidding; all the film needs to be a devastating comedy is a little seriousness. The impossibility of breaking out of the system, the robotization of the career-oriented, upwardly mobile middle-class couple who, even with a shove of fate to nudge them along, cannot start afresh in some spontaneous, grass-roots, laterally mobile way, has powerful seriocomic potential; not for nothing has Preston Sturges's name been invoked in connection with this film. But despite a fine farcical frenzy, acute observation of everyday absurdities, and some wrenchingly comic episodes, the film cannot lift itself into high comedy, even if it towers over whatever else is around.

David Howard (Albert Brooks) is a Los Angeles advertising executive who expects to become vice president on the morrow. He and his wife, Linda (Julie Hagerty), have already made a $15,000 deposit on a $450,000 house; a yacht and a Mercedes are in the offing; and all that keeps him awake tonight is compulsive worrying. All that keeps Linda, a seemingly contented department-store personnel manager, awake is David with his nagging doubts. Small ones, mind you; the next day, he is totally unprepared for the blow of mere transferral to New York and a fancier account—no vice presidency, no immediate raise above the present $100,000, but a supposedly great opportunity to become even more "creative." First flabbergasted, then infuriated, David insults the boss and gets himself fired. He is hysterically exultant, gets Linda to quit, too (in his eagerness for freedom, he can barely be restrained from making love to her on the desk of her glass-walled office), and they both look forward to such neo-Rousseau-ish dreams as "touching Indians." For starters, they're off in their new mobile home, a thirty-foot Winnebago, to Las Vegas to remarry each other at the Silver Bell Chapel; then, supported by their $145,000 nest egg obtained from liquidating their possessions, they will realize David's fantasy of living out—with the minor improvements money can buy—his favorite movie, *Easy Rider*.

But, of course, the Howards are no Easy Riders: A real biker to whom David tenders a thumbs-up salute responds by giving him the finger. And when, at nightfall, they reach the seedy Silver Bell, Linda first wants a honeymoon night at the Desert Inn, complete with a gargantuan double bed in which to eat, watch porno movies on TV, and have sex, then let the new and simpler life begin. David, who depends on Linda as much as she on him for what she has once called a too "controlled," too "responsible" life, reluctantly agrees. At the Desert Inn, disaster first trickles, then hurtles, in. A heavily bribed desk clerk delivers only a "junior bridal suite" with no huge expanse of double bed, merely a pair of heart-shaped twins and a not quite heart-shaped gap between. Soon David is in the hole, for

Linda, unbeknown to him, has sneaked out to gamble away their nest egg in a trancelike fury such as only a long-repressed model working wife could muster up. The nest egg is down to $805—not enough shelter to keep the rain off an inchworm.

Although this infantile, atavistic, destructive self-assertion of Linda's is comic enough and makes primitive sense, it is also the first, and perhaps biggest, blow against the film's artistic integrity. To make valid satirical fun of the Howards and the society they suffocate in, *Lost in America* should have made their downfall—or the unviableness of their scheme—hinge on something less capricious, less facilely instantaneous. The nest egg should dwindle away in spite of their best intentions; its evaporation should tell much more about them (us) and their (our) world than that Linda had a rather unprepossessing flaw. Comic comeuppance is like coffee: the percolating kind tastes truer than the instant variety.

Still, the film bounces toward its predictable conclusion merrily enough. But just think what could have been done—assuming that money for such a conclusion could have been raised with an unforegone one. Yet even the present ending could have been arrived at more deviously, more compellingly, less prefabricatedly. There is also something wrong with the very structure and timing of the film: it is too short, and leaps from a rising (or falling) action to a denouement, skipping the needed climax. Even so, it scores in three distinct ways.

First, there are rich clusters of funny lines in this script by Brooks and Monica Johnson, as when David, no longer able to repress his slow burn at Linda's breaking the nest egg if not the bank, erupts into a conjugal lecture-philippic that forbids her the very use of the term "nest egg" and even its components: were they to drive through woods, a bird, for her, should be "living in a round stick," and they should be having "*things* over easy for lunch."

Second, there is perfect acting. Brooks has a way of turning manic without becoming over-ridiculous: he stresses the pre- or post-preposterous rather than the merely laugh-getting, as his namesake Mel usually does. Even his looks are neatly balanced between the wholesomely straightforward and the faintly ludicrous—a mite too pudgy, frizzy-haired, beady-eyed. And Julie Hagerty, attractive, sublime in her injured dignity, able to coalesce her wispiness in a twinkling into something sheerly demonic, is also (aptly) too sleek, breathy, and insubstantial, with a touch of Lehmbruckian elongation. The supporting cast is inspiredly chosen from little-known actors; thus the Desert Inn Casino pit boss is played by Garry Marshall, the TV and movie director, with a textured subtlety that does credit both to him and to Brooks, who directed him here. All the players in an almost uninterruptedly hilarious string of vignettes act with something like a rich, untapped vein of comic idiosyncrasy.

Lastly, the film has a visual imagination rare for comedies in this age of television-influenced moviemaking. The gags are always firmly situated within a setting, and often enough the inappropriate or disproportionate setting is the gag. At other times, with the help of his cinematographer, Eric Saarinen, Brooks achieves pungent visual effects, as when David's beige Winnebago chases after the red coupe in which the angry Linda has hitched a ride. The road winds around a hillside and we see, in extreme long shot, two miniaturized vehicles zigzagging athwart the screen in seemingly opposite directions. Even this shot, at first only beautiful, has comic reverberations.

Prizzi's Honor

Eureka! According to the *New York Times*'s Vincent Canby, we now have in *Prizzi's Honor* "the only other great movie of 1985," along with Woody Allen's *Purple Rose of Cairo*. That may be more greatness than this still relatively young year can bear. And let's remember that "eureka" is how a movie actor with a fake Italian accent would pronounce "you reek."

Actually, *Prizzi's Honor* doesn't reek; it is, just like *Purple Rose*, a mediocre film with delusions of grandeur, which make it slightly less than mediocre. It seems to be intended as a mordant satire on the Mafia, and, beyond that, American capitalism, and, beyond that, human nature, but it is too simplistic, too guarded, too farcical to be more than a modest entertainment with suppurating ambitions; I would love to know what Bertolt Brecht would have made of it, if someone could have coerced him to sit through its 130 minutes. *Prizzi's Honor* is based on a novel by Richard Condon, with a script by Condon and Janet Roach. Several novels by Condon have been made into movies—he is that kind of hack—most notably *The Manchurian Candidate*. But this one is no *Candidate*, not even a contender.

The director is John Huston, a man of genuine but uneven talent, whose besetting sin is a nonchalance that easily turns into indifference; when the project is *Beat the Devil*, Huston's slapdashness works perfectly. But he has done well with other kinds of films too, even as recently as *The Man Who Would Be King* (1975). Now 78, though, Huston has been showing increased nonchalance and diminished talent. For his latest films he has tended scarcely to rouse himself from his director's chair, a sedentariness particularly evident in *Annie* and *Under the Volcano*. If *Prizzi's Honor* shows rather more spirit than its immediate predecessors, it is wasted on material that never achieves the wildness and ruthlessness it requires.

Charley Partanna is the hit man for Brooklyn's Prizzi family, for which his shrewd, cynical father is the *consigliere*. Don Corrado Prizzi has joined Charley's blood to his own in a solemn ceremony, and blood is thicker (but only just) than Charley's head, which follows the Prizzi orders to the bloody letter. The Don's sons are the irascible Dominic, in charge of the family business, and the smooth Eduardo, who heads the family law firm. Under the circumstances, it is unclear why a *consigliere* without consanguinity is needed, but as with the charge at Balaclava, so with much of this film, ours not to reason why. Charley was once engaged to Maerose, Dominic's daughter, who ran off with another man and was, as the family scandal, banished to Manhattan and interior decorating, for which, given her Brooklyn accent and non-U ways, she is ideally unsuited, but again, remember Balaclava! At a Prizzi family wedding, Charley espies a beautiful blonde, and is instantaneously smitten.

Having tracked her down in California, he promptly flies out for lunch with her. Irene Walker turns out to be none of the fancy things her name, attire, and demeanor would suggest. She is, as she says, a "Polack" who changed her name; also, as she doesn't say, actively married, a participant in a major theft from a Vegas casino run by the Prizzis, and a hit man, or hit woman, whom the Prizzis hire when they need outside talent. Love blossoms between the two hit persons, and they marry, with Charley willing to overlook Irene's share in the theft, even as she sweetly overlooks his killing her husband. Were the film content with chronicling the fun and games of this respectably murderous pair, it could have been a fairly amusing blackish screwball comedy. But it isn't black enough—or, indeed, red enough, as shot people don't even bleed—and it tries to be a seriocomic comment on our society as well as a sendup of *The Godfather*, which is too much for its meager resources.

Most of the movie is taken up with purportedly comic double- and triple-crosses; according to Canby, also quadruple-crosses, but by that time I had lost track, comprehension, and interest. What is certain, and telegraphs itself, is that the Prizzis' honor will require Charley to dispose of Irene, who, however, is more disposed to have the gander in the sauce. The way the final conjugal showdown is written is particularly unconvincing, but it is clear that this marriage of true shots must end in a modified love-death—call it a love-hate death. In fact, the way it is staged and photographed, it looks as if both spouses kicked the bucket—which I rather suspect of being the original ending, disallowed by elementary market research. As it is, Charley gets off scot-free, and even gets the murdered Dominic's job, as well as his daughter (though why Maerose, who spurned him in his prime, should pant after his protruding paunch and receding hairline remains unclear), while Irene gets it, literally, in the neck.

This ending strikes me, even in its ludicrous context, as dramatically unsatisfying, inordinately improbable, and sexist. It is a harsh, pseudo-moral judgment on the female of the species, who, in this film, is not deadlier than the male, only equally so and disproportionately punished. True, she is also a bit of a liar and cheat; but, as Maerose says to Charley, "Just because she's a thief and a hitter don't mean she ain't good in all other departments." And, once married to Charley, she is a perfect helpmate or help hitter (even though Charley protests, "I didn't get married so my wife would go on working!") and doesn't commit any extramarital crimes—is, in fact, a square shooter. The difference in her destiny provides a rather rancid comedy with an indigestible close.

Whether one likes *Prizzi's Honor* depends largely on whether one likes lines like the ones I have quoted, or this apologia of Irene's: "I've been doing three or four hits a year. That may not be that many if you consider the population." I don't find any of that as funny as when, in the middle of a kidnapping-cum-murder, the spouses exchange this bit of stichomythia: "See you at dinner."— "Okay, dear." But where the Mafia should be treated with the blackest of gallows (Gallo?) humor, it gets sentimental-comedy treatment. This is particularly evident in William Hickey's Don Corrado, raved about by the reviewers who have not, like me, seen his appalling and never-changing stage performances, and have forgotten, or not realized, how bad he was in such screen outings as *Wise Blood*. Typically, Canby perceives Hickey as a "ferociously practical, wise, infinitely patient old Don"; whereas David Denby speaks of his "essential rattiness" and "enjoyment of evil [and] double-dealing [as] an end in itself." This seems to be contradictory, and a performance that is all things to all critics is not so much acting as a Rorschach blob. I am likewise unimpressed by the Irene of Kathleen Turner. Hailed by many reviewers as perhaps the funniest and surely the most gorgeously, steamily sexy Hollywood actress, she is, to me, competent by our screen standards and pretty from an angle or two—in repose and with ethereal lighting—but otherwise just another petty [*sic*] face.

Jack Nicholson, however, gives another of his highly accomplished, controlledly funny performances as Charley, and, as Maerose, Anjelica Huston, who previously always looked like the star's girlfriend or director's daughter, comes across, at last, as an actress. The supporting cast is solid, and Andrzej Bartkowiak, though he tends to mistake his camera too often for a Dutch genre painter's palette, delivers some piquant sombernesses. Alex North's score recycles Italian opera appropriately but predictably, and Huston's direction is sparing but at least not lethargic. How happy the spirit of Will H. Hays must be! Whatever American films have gained in sexual freedom, they have more than lost through social and political restrictions: The word Mafia is not mentioned once.

Tangled Web

KISS OF THE SPIDER WOMAN

The summer has acquired its second allegedly adult hit with *Kiss of the Spider Woman*, hailed as a masterpiece by Janet Maslin of the *New York Times* and acclaimed with resounding enthusiasm by reams of other reviewers. True, it is one of the two or three films these dog days that do not address themselves directly to adolescents of all ages, but from this to the nonstop greatness Miss Maslin and her ilk perceive in it is a longer way than to Tipperary. Hector Babenco's film adaptation, with a screenplay by Leonard Schrader, of Manuel Puig's novel is the reduction of a fairly clever piece of high camp to a cross between substandard Hollywood and rather low camp. But the supposed seriousness of the theme, the exotic locale, and the homoerotic orientation (William Hurt's performance as an outrageous but eventually heroic queen won a best-actor award in Cannes, where cinematic awards seem to be determined by a spin of the roulette wheel) give the film all the cachet needed for reviewers to start gibbering about genius.

Babenco, an Argentine-born Brazilian filmmaker, scored an honest success with *Pixote*, an unassuming, gritty, mostly unsentimental film about the garish world of a sweet little juvenile delinquent who coasts, almost blithely, from horror to greater horror. The home-movieish aspects of *Pixote* (and they were many) actually made for authenticity, much as early Italian neorealism profited from its filmmakers' ingenuousness and impecuniousness. *Kiss of the Spider Woman* was made on a low budget, too—though perhaps not so low for São Paulo, where it was shot—but it aspires to a professional slickness it fails to achieve.

The novel first. Puig's work is almost all dialogue, more precisely duologue between cellmates in a Buenos Aires prison. Valentín Arregui, a young left-wing activist from an upper-bourgeois family, shares a cell with Luis Molina, a 37-year-old homosexual window dresser, given eight years for corrupting a minor. There are no descriptions; whatever we know emerges, or can be inferred, from their conversation. This includes detailed recountings by Molina of movies he loved, which he relates with occasional embroideries to his cellmate, who (lucky fellow!) was too busy making revolution to attend movies. But these narrated indulgences, in which Valentín participates by adding his own interpretations and embroiderings, help while away the time for both men, and also conjure up other worlds and hopes of freedom. Valentín forgets the tortures he has undergone and may again undergo. Molina stops worrying about his beloved, ailing mother. On the wings of movie kitsch, the prisoners escape their cell and, eventually, fly into each other's arms.

The novel has technical ingenuity. Five films are retold: *Cat People*; a Nazi propaganda film, *Her Real Glory*; *The Enchanted Cottage*—though this one, too sentimental for Valentin, becomes an interior monologue of Molina's; a lurid Hollywood horror film about voodoo and zombies, with a happy ending; and a Mexican love story with songs, a sentimental melodrama with an unhappy ending. There are variations: one narrative is interrupted by bits of interior monologue of uncertain relevance and provenance (Luis's? Valentín's?); all narratives, like the dialogue itself, are interlarded with lengthy footnotes, mostly summaries of conflicting theories about homosexuality, from Freud to the present day.

There are other interruptions. Also in dialogue form, but more theatrical, are talks between Molina and the warden; near the end, there is a lengthy police report on the surveillance of Molina, now freed, with the spies baffled by homosexual smalltalk (Puig's little joke); finally another, quite different, monologue: a dream of Valentín's after renewed torture and a surreptitious shot of morphine administered by a kindly doctor. Out of these disparate strands, Puig weaves a thing of droll and touching rags and pretentious patches (e.g., the footnotes, not so much distancing devices as special pleading, a Marcusean defense of polymorphous perversity) and the ultimate banality of the well-known homosexual wish-fulfillment fantasy: getting a "real man," i.e., a very masculine heterosexual, to become your bona-fide lover.

To do him justice, Puig handles this unrealistic material with a certain resourcefulness. He uses any number of devices to suggest the merging, first, of the fantasies of the heterosexual and the homosexual, and then, gradually of their psyches and bodies. At last sexual union is meant to yield a humanizing fusion, whereby the masculine heterosexual is temporarily converted to sensitive homosexuality while the feminine homosexual achieves a spiritual virility, indeed heroism, and so each man grows in stature. Valentín's concluding dream, though perfectly heterosexual, nevertheless subsumes Luis's romantic, feminine, B-movie sensibility, viewed as an enriching element.

In the movie, thanks partly to a poor script, but partly also to the inapposite assertiveness of the visual medium, crudities and preposterousnesses proliferate. The action has been shifted from Buenos Aires to São Paulo, but dictatorships are interchangeable, and if the prison staple switches from rice to beans, no matter. Yet even in the book there were absurdities. For example, when the prison authorities want to make Valentín sick, they put much more rice (or beans) on one plate, and assume that the stronger man will take the larger portion. But Valentín gives it to Molina, who, although aware that it is poisoned, has to eat it, lest Valentín become suspicious. But what is there about rice (or beans) that makes portions indivisible? Why couldn't Valentín, upon Molina's urging, simply even out the size of the helpings? And when Molina eats the poisoned rice, he gets cramps, but not diarrhea; whereas, later on, when Valentín is similarly poisoned, he gets the worst possible case of the runs. Puig needs this, to give Molina a chance to play good Samaritan, but the diverse symptoms do not make clinical sense.

The film, however, is chock full of such illogic, starting with the principals' cell, a spacious, semi-private affair, bigger than most New York studio apartments. Molina, not a drag queen in the book, becomes one in the movie; he has turned his half of the cell into something like a bordello, and wears outré feminine gladrags much of the time without, it seems, incurring brutalization from the macho guards. The São Paulo police force is apparently three or four men strong—we see the same ones repeatedly; and even a high-ranking officer is reduced to chasing after Molina in the streets. When Molina is released, he and his homosexual friends go to a gay bar, where one of them works as a female impersonator; in the novel, nothing so blatant. The final pursuit of Molina and his death are written and directed so you don't know what's going on or how to interpret anything. If Luis doesn't know he is being followed, why does he keep looking at his pursuers: if he does, why does he lead them to the revolutionaries? His death is staged with surpassing hamminess, with allusions to Christ abounding.

But, then, whatever has been added to the book to open it up and make it more cinematic is either nonsense or sheer platitude. Thus the scene with Marta, Valentín's upper-class girlfriend (played, along with the two other main female roles, by Sonia Braga, who is too old and ravaged-looking), is pure persiflage. Valentín and two comrades are arrested in a subway station after he has given his passport to a leading revolutionary to escape with; but Valentín and the escaping revolutionary are so unalike in age and looks that the gesture is useless. Later, the man who is presumed to have escaped is put in the same prison as Valentín, who is supposed to see him from his cell and communicate this to his friends on the outside and so betray them. But the jailers always lead their new victim about with a black hood over his head, so he won't know his torturers; as a result, Valentín doesn't recognize him. But 1) torturers are too arrogant to worry about their victims' recognizing them, 2) other prisoners could easily tell the man who his tormentors are, and 3) how much brains does it take to figure out that Valentin doesn't have x-ray eyes?

And so on. But Schrader and Babenco's biggest mistake is to show only one of the five movies Molina relates to Valentín: the Nazi propaganda film. As Babenco crosscuts to bits of this film, we should see something glamorous that initially caught Luis's fancy and that he enhances with his own embellishments to triumph over dreary reality. Instead, we see a seedy, camped-up piece of shoestring filmmaking, mostly grotesque, in which we watch the

love story of a supposedly gorgeous French *chanteuse*, played by
the campy and cadaverous Miss Braga, and a dashing ss officer,
played by what looks like a bleached-blond, effete male hustler with
a collar two sizes too big for him. Furthermore, there is no sense
of Valentín's gradually increasing collaboration on these evolving
fantasies, which leads to the blending of identities. And the Spider
Woman, in the novel, is first a casual reference of Valentín's to Luis,
and then part of a psychologically intricate dream sequence. In
the movie, she stars in a scene from another film Molina narrates,
though this brief, solitary scene cannot carry the burden allotted
to it; and the final dream, without the Spider Woman, is flat and
trivial.

To top it all, Raul Julia (not bad as Valentín) and William Hurt
(who starts out overplaying Molina monstrously, and then settles
down to being merely boringly obvious) speak in their own voices—Julia's moderately Hispanic, Hurt's totally unaccented—while
the rest of the cast, dubbed in the United States by hack actors with
thick Latino accents, is bizarrely inconsistent. Much, if not all, of
Kiss of the Spider Woman is the kiss of death.

Compassionate Satire

WHEN FATHER WAS AWAY ON BUSINESS

Emir Kusturica, the 31-year-old Yugoslav film director, caused quite
a stir by winning the grand prize at Cannes with what is only his
second feature, *When Father Was Away on Business*. For once, the
Cannes jury was right: this film deserves the accolade. And apropos
of accolades, Kusturica told me that he doesn't like tepid films; he
wants a movie to hug you or slap you in the face. *Father* does both. It
is a film of undaunted honesty and unswerving intelligence, borne
aloft by humor, heartache, satire, and compassion—an unbeatable
combination.

The movie is based on a number of true stories, combining the
family experiences of both its director and its scenarist, the poet Ab-
dulah Sidran. I found it indebted also to Milan Kundera's novel (and
film) *The Joke*, as Kusturica willingly admits: he spent five years at
Prague's famous film academy, where, shortly before, Kundera had
taught, and admires the great novelist. In that novel, an innocent
political joke has dreadful repercussions under a repressive regime

that, axiomatically, has to be humorless. In *Father*, Meša, a minor government functionary who travels and womanizes a lot, refuses to divorce his wife, Sena, as the gym teacher Ankica, his current mistress, would have him do. Meša sees a political cartoon in the relatively liberal paper *Politika*, showing Marx writing at his desk and looking up for inspiration at a portrait of Stalin on his wall. We are in the late 1940s, when Yugoslavia is still paying official homage to Stalin while Tito is secretly jailing hard-core Stalinists.

"They're overdoing it a bit," is Meša's comment on the cartoon. Ankica, thwarted, remembers, and, having left Meša in a huff, passes on the comment to her new lover, who is none other than Zijo, Sena's brother and Meša's brother-in-law, a rather higher party official. Out of jealousy after what seems like a relatively amiable family dinner, Zijo has Meša carted off to an unknown destination. Seven-year-old Malik, the film's real hero, and his movie-buff brother, Mirza, *circa* 12, are told by Sena that their father is on a business trip. The locale is Sarajevo, where the Bosnians, whose ancestors were forcibly converted to Islam by the Turks, are especially patriarchal, rule over their wives and other women, and, by their absence, cripple a family doubly.

Malik is a sweet, chubby, dopey looking troublemaker. He is also a sleepwalker, but his somnambulism often seems to have a system to it: it can, to the confounding of his parents, divert attention to him; it can even lead him into the bed of a little neighbor girl, Mašenka, whom he is enamored of. He is passionate also about soccer (as are almost all true-blue Yugoslavs) and, with his fat friend Joža, is saving up to buy a real soccer ball, made of leather and with an inflatable inner tube. But, as Serbo-Croatian would have it, koža (leather) also means "skin," and duša (inner tube) also means "soul." The people around Malik have plenty of the former, with all its leathery toughness and erotic itches, but, for all their inflated egos, are short on inner tubes.

Sena is a decent, earnest, hardworking seamstress, now toiling twice as hard to keep her headless family going while Father, as it turns out, is doing two years of forced labor at the Lipnica coal mine. As the kids continue with their respective passions, soccer and movies, the country proceeds with the phasing out of Stalin and the monotheistic enshrinement of Tito, even opening itself up wide to Western tourism. Swiftly and unerringly, Kusturica sets the public and private tone *circa* 1950 with a couple of introductory sequences. While sundry agricultural tasks are being performed with a mixture of jollity, inefficiency, and just plain indolence, the town drunkard (who claims that his reflexes are quicker when he is soused) leads the assembled workers and children in enthusiastic renditions of various Mexican songs. Why Mexican? Because in these parlous times, they are the safest politically.

What makes the film so unusual, beyond its outspokenness, is the resonance of its generally unemphatic details, selected with precision and economy to convey a maximum of psychological and cinematic truth. A certain rough lyricism coats the most humdrum and harsh realities with wit and empathy, even where indignation would be so much easier. Kusturica, for all his youth, sees the humor in the horror as clearly as the horror in the humor. Take the scene where the parents fight bitterly with blows and rending words (the subtitles do not begin to do justice to the racy, often raunchy though simultaneously poetic, dialogue—least of all to the colorfully off-color expressions in which Yugoslav talk abounds), as the two sons, side by side in the same bed, watch. Little Malik, frightened, sheds silent tears; Mirza, precociously canny, observes with half-smiling fascination. Cut to the next sequence, with the entire family sitting on one bed, Mirza playing "The Anniversary Waltz" (the film's theme song) on the concertina, and all of them singing or stuffing sweets into one another's mouths. Which is sadder: the fisticuffs over Meša's infidelities or the facile, resigned reconciliation? Or, perhaps, which is more comical?

Conversely, there are moments of unadulterated beauty, as when Mirza brings Malik home after foiling his attempt to buy a soccer ball and makes him return his savings to their overworked mother, who, moved, stops the sewing machine to hug her sons. Sentimentality is avoided by bits of humor, and also by the loveliness and rhythm of the reverse angle shots, by the way the window frame through which the boys first see their mother (and vice versa) crisscrosses the image and, as it were, puts the characters behind bars. Or take the arrival of Sena and Malik at Lipnica, where Meša has a day off to spend with his family. Steam on a railway platform has often been used for dramatic effect, but never more suspensefully, never more Dantesquely than here. And the accelerating tempo with which the long-separated spouses converge is irresistibly involving: first a guarded, overwhelmed slowness, then an onslaught, then a fast cut to frenzied melting together. Meanwhile Malik, left out, tugs at his father's shirt tails. Hoisted, presently, on Meša's shoulders, he lets out a yowl of delight that the departing train whistle—which is it?—swallows up or makes epic. And as the happily riding Malik's jacket rides up on his midriff, we have just time, before the blackout, to glimpse a parental hand caringly pull it down.

Or consider the comedy of the scenes at the Koviljača Spa, where Meša, whose sentence has been commuted to managing a cafe-restaurant in the nearby godforsaken town of Zvornik goes to buy supplies. The angry Sena knows the lure of the loose women at the spa, and that some of the supplies Meša, the Zvornik doctor (a Russian émigré), and the local commissar are getting *will* serve appetites other than for comestibles. So Meša takes along Malik, as a supposed guarantee against concupiscence. Soon the men are in a car singing a ditty about three whoremongers—*kurvari* in Serbian—off on a jaunt; when we sight the gate to the spa, it still bears its pre-war (and faulty) German inscription, *Kur-Salon*, which now becomes an ominous pun. Forthwith, under a banner with the slogan CULTURE ART DIVERSION, the most grotesque singer and musicians dispense diversion or art, while our three middle-aged bucks are beginning to cultivate, with fatuous smiles and gestures, some girls sitting two tables away, over the heads of the doggier ones at the intervening table. Before long, all—well, three-quarters of—hell will break loose.

The film ends with a wedding that, for sustained tragicomic invention, has few if any equals. In the course of it, Meša drags Ankica, now Zijo's wife, into the cellar for a bout of revenge-intercourse that, along with its climax and anticlimax, encapsulates every contradictory emotion cohabiting in mankind. In the middle of it all, Malik kicks his new soccer ball toward the cellar window and glimpses his father in furibund adultery. Consumed though he is with curiosity, the boy nevertheless first carefully retrieves his precious new toy, only then to resume his voyeuristic activity. It is in such tiny but transfixing details, as telling as a poet's metaphors, that the movie triumphs.

Countless political allusions will, alas, elude American audiences, but the choral counterpoint of propagandistic orations, newsreels, and radio broadcasts should at least partly register as a sardonic, symbolic commentary. Thus the entire action is sandwiched between two broadcast soccer games: a pleasing victory over Denmark and a riotously intoxicating rout of Russia. But does this make up for a comment at the wedding that the country's coffers are empty and that there's no democracy without dough? The acting is flawless throughout, and only the final parting between

Malik and Mašenka (a children's love affair otherwise treated with matchless insight and tact) rings a bit too good to be true. But you need only compare *When Father Was Away on Business* with the highly touted Krzysztof Zanussi's current *A Year of the Quiet Sun*, which tries to do for postwar Poland what *Father* does for Yugoslavia: Zanussi's film is perfumed with artifice; Kusturica's gloriously stinks of life.

The Official Story

The historical and human elements are cannily blended in *The Official Story*, an Argentine film in which national calamity and individual tragedy answer each other like strophe and antistrophe. It is rare for a film to do equal justice to public and private problems, with subject and theme in such harrowingly close harmony. Furthermore, technique—a preponderance of short nervously edited scenes with many tight closeups (the director got his training in TV commercials)—is in flawless balance with content. For the slow dawning of realization must be shown in minutely scrutinized countenances; the frantic pursuit of an elusive truth, with jagged scenes hurtling from place to place.

It is 1983, after the Falkland disaster; an edgy dictatorship wages a secret, dirty war against so-called subversives. Argentina is suddenly full—or emptied—of *desaparecidos*, missing people who were tortured and killed in camps where the butchers often sold or adopted children abducted with their parents or born there. Unless, of course, the children, too, were killed. The story concerns Alicia, a middle-aged history teacher in an upper-bourgeois prep school, married to Roberto, a high-level executive in a U.S.-dominated multinational corporation. Childless, the couple has adopted Gabi, now five, from what Roberto vaguely described as a mother at some hospital who did not want her. Both adoptive parents lavish affection on the dazzling little girl, though they're not particularly emotional otherwise: Roberto is a slippery-smooth, cool businessman; Alicia a strict teacher preconizing hard grading and stringent discipline.

But when the beautiful Ana, back from long exile, meets her old friend Alicia again, she has a horrific tale of torture and rape to impart, along with the revelation that many recently adopted children belonged to murdered mothers. Here begins Alicia's awakening. She is a decent, intelligent person—one of those who are even more important to a dictatorship than active collaborators: the ones who see only what suits them. Most effectively, the scenarists—the writer Aïda Bortnick and the director Luis Puenzo—have chosen for their protagonist a history teacher and "mother"—showing how one who should know best and feel most can be rendered ignorant and apathetic by convenience. In class, when a student presents a seamy view of Argentine history that clashes with the official version, the incredulous Alicia asks for documents, for books supporting the pupil's report. Comes the cocky but credible answer: "History is written by the assassins."

Questioning her husband anew about Gabi, Alicia gets replies that are even shorter, shadowier, more snappish than before. At the same time, through glimpses of various students, teachers, business and political figures, and publicly protesting grandmothers, our boding unease is made to grow in unison with hers. There is, for example, a dinner party where all the men are in formal black, and only a young American, son of a partner in Roberto's firm, is wearing white. Nothing is made of this explicitly, yet the alien and alienating presence prefigures Roberto's involvement in foreign speculation. Also at the party is a particularly crusty ramrod of a general, which hints at Roberto's connection with the paramilitary forces. This scene is parallelled by a women's lunch at which Ana, who was jailed and abused for a long-since-concluded affair with a suspected and wanted revolutionary, rounds on a woman friend who, after not coming to her aid, presented the escaping, expropriated Ana with a set of silver salt and pepper shakers.

With many such fine, small, piercing touches, the film traces Alicia's awakening. When Alicia asks Ana why she didn't denounce her torturers and Ana replies with the question, "To whom could I have denounced them?" the chill is intensified by the setting: Alicia's comfortable living room, full of the gratuities of affluence punctiliously recorded by the camera. And as we observe the adorable but already spoiled little Gabi, we wonder how much of this parental overindulgence is expiation of repressed guilt. Alicia decides to investigate, and it is one of the film's multiple achievements to chronicle faithfully the tiny, worsening incidents that jolt the woman out of mendacious acquiescence into brave, eventually self-destructive but also redeeming, action. For although *The Official Story* wisely leaves some searing questions open, there is no doubt about the penultimate shot, in which Alicia, not unlike

Ibsen's Nora, leaves the keys on the inside as she departs. Her husband has just brutalized her for the first time; worse, he has been revealed as a liar and a fascist. A public tragedy has been brought home to a private, badly burnt heart.

Yet a film subtle enough to tell much through keys left in a lock on the inside is in no danger of portraying Roberto as a simplistic villain. (The nearest thing to that is Alicia's confessor, a priest emblematic of the complicity of the Argentine church, who keeps pushing Alicia back in blindness.) Roberto is the son of impoverished radical family whom he perceives as losers, a family that showers him with contumely while accepting his financial support. An otherwise devoted son and brother, Roberto simply wants to be on the winning team—a human enough flaw. The family conflict erupts in yet another brilliantly orchestrated eating scene—creature comforts in ironic contrast to the soul's discomfiture—as an uncomprehending Gabi and anguished Alicia look on. In such ways is our heroine's education frighteningly furthered.

Hectic scenes are cunningly interrupted by seemingly calm, tight shots, extended dwellings on a bedeviled face—at one point on no more than a single eye of Roberto's bulging out from behind a hand pressed to his forehead as to a wound—or on some leisurely object scrutinized in esurient closeup, and a delusive sense of peace is set up for puncturing. No less magisterial than the directing is the acting. Norma Aleandro, as the heroine evolving out of complacency into heroism, profits even from being unequivocally average-looking. Thus it is her performance (and a little cheating with hairdos) that makes her grow in beauty as well as perception. She has an intensity whose increase she can calibrate with uncanny control; even her reaction to her husband's final violence is more of an implosion, and more unbearably painful for that. As Roberto, Héctor Alterio is hardly less fine, with aggrievedness, crankiness, violence always aswirl under the rippling flow of his self-presentation. The actor, moreover, has the good sense to make Roberto more pathetic than vile.

The supporting cast is solid, and Félix Monti's camera reliable. Though the music has moments of overinsistence, it can also, at times, insinuate. Above all, the Puenzo-Bortnick screenplay, while maintaining an aura of sophistication and even humor, knows how to let horror creep in as a blur, then a glimmer, at last a conflagration. Even the pseudo-quiet of the ending merely bespeaks loss. At 39, Luis Puenzo has directed his first feature like a master.

Black and White in Purple

THE COLOR PURPLE; OUT OF AFRICA

What is an insuperable problem for a filmmaker who specializes in gadgets, sentimentalized children, and cute creatures from outer space? Adults—anything at all to do with grownups living their quotidian lives. To be sure, this is a problem for Hollywood as a whole; it is more intensely so for Steven Spielberg, for whom becoming a movie director seems to have been the surest way of trading in his toys for bigger and bigger toys while (in a juvenile version of *The Picture of Dorian Gray*) remaining himself forever small. In *The Color Purple*, based on Alice Walker's novel, the toys have become suffering human beings—blacks in rural Georgia between 1906 and 1940—and the film has become an infantile abomination.

Miss Walker's novel—far from the literary masterpiece it has been hyped into and unable to transcend the two humanly legitimate but artistically burdensome chips on its shoulder, feminism and black militancy—is still much better than the film, for which it wasn't suited. An epistolary novel, it thrives on the intimacy of one-to-one verbal confrontation, something that even maturer hands than Spielberg's could not have transposed onto film. But who would have expected *The Color Purple*, with its bitter hostility toward male blacks, and whites of either sex, to have the psychology of a *Dumbo* or *Pinocchio*, its feminist and lesbian coloration lost in a *mise en scène* doing its damnedest to look like a cartoon film, and pretty nearly succeeding.

Little Celie's cruel stepfather, after begetting two children on her and selling them to a childless couple on their way to Africa, marries Celie off to a young widower who really wanted her pretty sister, Nettie. The widower, whom Celie dares call only Mister, makes her clean and repair his shambles of a house and look after the wild, hostile children from his previous marriage. For her pains, he beats her and cheats on her, notably with the swinging singer Shug Avery, which does not prevent him from trying to rape Nettie, who comes to visit her sister. This unmitigated villain (who, needless to say, ends up getting mitigated in the movie) is frequently shown in a low-angle shot, exactly like the evil giant towering over his small-fry victim in a cartoon. And the perfectly competent cameraman, Allen Daviau (*The Falcon and the Snowman*), has been made to shoot the film as a series of picture postcards, whether the sisters are gambolling in a meadow whose pullulating flowers appear to have been planted in calculatedly swirling patterns, one by one; or whether Celie is seen reading a letter from Nettie in Africa, with Celie shot in silhouette a rocking chair against an improbably large window full of purple sky and a huge orange sun haloing not just her head, but her entire body.

Inadvertently, the film even turns racist, for the fulsomely sympathetic Spielberg cannot help patronizing his characters as he oversimplifies and sugarcoats everything, including the violence. Thus Harpo, Mister's eldest, is almost always seen falling off a roof or being flattened by his oversized wife, Sophia; thus all the other men are ravening beasts, whereas a lesbian relationship between Shug and Celie is made to look like a sequence from *Bambi*. But don't assume that the whites emerge any better; it's just that, not being a minority, they can more easily take the insults.

Credibility is at an all-time low here. Why would Mister hide Nettie's letters to Celie from Africa, rather than simply destroy them? Why would Celie not dare pick up her letters even when Mister is not around to forbid access to the mailbox? Why couldn't she at least enlist the mailman on her side? Why doesn't she answer Nettie's letters after she knows the address and has emancipated herself from Mister? And who is working those huge fields—Mister, by himself? And just who are those small children who hang around the house unchanged, decade after decade? The script is by the Dutch-born Menno Meyjes, and might as well have been written in double Dutch.

There are only three surviving performances. Margaret Avery exudes joyous vitality as her namesake, Shug Avery; Oprah Winfrey, a Chicago talk show hostess, is a good Sophia until she gets overdirected; and Desreta Jackson, as the young Celie is genuinely touching, because she is unsentimental. When, however, Whoopi Goldberg takes over as the grown Celie, mannerism takes over with her. The actress keeps covering her mouth in heart-melting shame while letting her saucer eyes practically fly out of her face. Her speech, moreover, is New York, 1985—not Georgia, whatever. The combination of souped-up yet sentimental violence and saccharine goody-goodiness makes *The Color Purple*, like a purple cow, something I would have hoped never to see.

If there is one art that cannot be rendered on screen, it is that of writing. There is some little drama in watching someone paint or sculpt; composing music at least livens up the soundtrack. But the writer at work is neither photogenic nor cinematically involving. So you might think that *Out of Africa*, which deals with Karen Blixen—who was to become the writer Isak Dinesen—*before* she started to write, has licked the problem: It tells of her life in Africa, as she was to write it later on in her memoir of the same title, on which the film is largely based. But its sources are as hard to find as those of the Nile, including as they do other works by Dinesen, her biography by Judith Thurman, and that of her lover (but was he really her lover?), Denys Finch Hatton, by Errol Trzebinski. That makes for heterogeneity; the screenplay itself, as written by Kurt Luedtke and directed by Sydney Pollack, makes for genteel, homogenized blandness, in which an occasional encounter with a lion or two is no remedy against creeping torpor.

The worth of the book *Out of Africa* is in Isak Dinesen's odd style: a somewhat Danish-accented, sometimes even faulty, English that nevertheless captivates with its archaizing newfangledness. It sounds like bardic Victorianism—a skald adapted by Charles Reade. There are Biblical overtones as well, and sensitive description mingles with despotic *hauteur*: Can one really write, well into the twentieth century, "Farah was my servant by the grace of God"? The blend of lyricism and arrogance, of heightened evocativeness and crass matter-of-factness, is what gives this writing its enticing/exasperating charm. Film cannot reproduce it.

The story itself—of hopelessly trying to grow coffee on a Kenya farm from 1914 to 1931, of being caught between a shiftless big-game-hunter husband and an eccentric hunter-*cum*-businessman lover, of having to be the Great White Mother to numberless natives, despite a World war, syphilis, and a passel of adventures—refuses to matter. Since neither the loveless (but not sexless or affectionless) marriage to Baron Bror Blixen-Finecke nor the relationship (whatever it exactly was) with Denys Finch Hatton, the younger son of an earl, has any pulsing aliveness in the film, which treads gingerly between meager facts and timid conjecture, why should we care about any of them? The film might have been better off as a documentary: When it isn't half-heartedly trying to churn up murky emotions, it drifts into impersonal chronicling. But, for a documentary, we would need much more about the lives of blacks and whites in Kenya, such as we do get in the book.

Bits of plot drift in as a new character crops up, remains undeveloped, and promptly disappears (e.g., the troubled young Felicity); and authenticity is seriously compromised when, for example, an

Englishman's native mistress is played by the New York high-fashion model Iman, unconvincing in both looks and demeanor. What action there is remains unpersuasive because its motives are unexplored; Denys in particular comes across as a huge blank. And one played by a cipher: Robert Redford gives the worst performance by a star in recent history. He won't try for a British accent, cannot do a drunk scene, renders aristocracy as brashness and romantic fervor as an ingrown toenail.

Meryl Streep, for the first time in a movie lead, gives a winning, unmannered performance, possibly because struggling with a Danish accent (imperfect, according to my Danish expert) preempted the energies she usually expends on overacting. No less fine is Klaus Maria Brandauer as Bror, a part that, unfortunately, allows for little scope. In a generally good supporting cast, Malick Bowens is outstanding as Farah, economically conveying dignity and depth. But the best thing about this mediocre film is the photography by the great British cameraman David Watkin: It all but captures the complexity and mystery of Dinesen's prose, and certainly equals its beauty.

The rest is vagueness and cliché.

Borscht-Belt Bergman

HANNAH AND HER SISTERS

In *Hannah and Her Sisters*, Woody Allen accomplishes the impossible: He makes that great actor, Max von Sydow, look bad for the first time. He who survived everything from *The Kremlin Letter* to *Three Days of the Condor*, from *The Exorcist* to playing Christ in *The Greatest Story Ever Told*, looks dull and insignificant as Frederick, the gruff and anti-social painter with whom sexy, flighty Lee, the youngest of our eponymous sisters, is living. But that is because Allen gives him only an attitude and no character to play. Frederick does not attend the family Thanksgiving dinners given by Hannah, the eldest sister, and he insults his crude would-be customers. He seems to have taught the dilettantish, ex-dipsomaniac Lee everything she knows, but we are not shown any of this; we don't see what brought and holds the two together. We do, however, hear him say to Lee, as she comes home late from lovemaking with her new man, that she missed a very dull TV show about Auschwitz, and that everyone is always asking the wrong question: How could it have happened? "Given that people are what they are, the question is why doesn't it happen more often?"

How are we to interpret this? The rock star who wants to buy paintings according to size and color is indeed a *nouveau riche* boor, so we sympathize with Frederick for refusing to sell to him. But what about the Auschwitz remark? Is it funny? (Many in the audience laughed.) Wise? Monstrously misanthropic? There isn't a clue in the film to help the actor—or viewer—decide. We get that typical Allen ambiguity that is really a way of shirking responsibility. You can read his characters as sage or silly; his films as tributes or satires. Creative ambiguity multiplies meanings so as to extend or deepen significance: Woody's antithetical meanings cancel each other out. But they are a way of hedging his bets.

That is how it goes throughout. Take this exchange: "Do you like Caravaggio?" "Oh, yes. W10 doesn't?" Is that answer informed, snide, or foolish? Or a bluff to cover up ignorance? Nothing about the speaker or the situation provides a clue. A highbrow moviegoer can laugh at the character; a middlebrow, empathize; a lowbrow, gape, awestruck. But the statement has no artistic value. One more example: Holly, the middle sister, a would-be actress and dabbler in cocaine—actually, an all-round dabbler—has met an interesting architect, but April, an actress friend with whom she just started a catering business, steals him from her. Holly fumes: "Where did April come up with that stuff about Adolf Loos and organic space? Well, naturally: She went to Brandeis." People laugh at this, but why? Is mentioning Loos to an architect automatically clever and funny? Or does it label one an intellectual phony? Or is Brandeis a school that breeds phonies, and so the butt of the joke? Or is the word "Brandeis" an immediate laugh-getter among anti-Semitic snobs? Or is the joke on Holly, for blaming April's education instead of her own ignorance? All are possible, but none is really funny: I think people laugh nervously and defensively, lest anyone suspect them of not getting some learned reference—which, for the most part, they don't.

All through the film, there are discussions of art, architecture, literature, and music (classical and popular) so trivial as to be meaningless. A poem by E. E. Cummings is "adorable," a Bach concerto is someone's "favorite"—and what are we supposed to do? Laugh or admire, feel superior or inferior? And even as the dialogue is an intellectual muddle, the characters are a psychological hodgepodge.

Thus Hannah, married to Elliot and mother of a numerous brood, is supposed to be the unwobbling pivot of this extended family, which, at the three Thanksgivings we witness, includes also her sentimentally show-tune-warbling or pettily squabbling ex-actor parents.

Hannah herself was a minor actress, but gave it up to be a terrific mother as well as superb wife to Elliot, an investment counselor, though from his speech and actions he could be an encyclopedia salesman. Her sisters describe her as "disgustingly perfect." Yet Elliot takes her sister from Frederick, and has a lengthy, affair with her without Hannah's catching on. Elliot's behavior and hints from Holly are dead giveaways, but disgustingly perfect Hannah remains a perfect dupe. Nor is there any evidence of wisdom from her as she lends Holly large sums for various harebrained projects.

As for Elliot, we see him only as a fool for love, torn between wife and mistress. As written, and as played by a now gross-looking Michael Caine—his Cockney accent as incongruous on Wall Street as in a Woody Allen menagerie—he remains nebulous and uninvolving. Allen cannot create rounded characters outside the artsy or bohemian milieu, and he specializes in intellectual drifters, usually show-biz and often female. Into the latter class fall Lee and Holly, women of the sort who go through life aimless and discontented. Yet Allen contrives happy endings for all concerned in the crassest Hollywood tradition—crasser, perhaps, because the old Hollywood puppets had no pretensions to being real.

Most preposterous is the fate of Holly, who, after aggressively failing at everything, suddenly becomes a gifted and successful writer, an amiable human being and happy wife to—of all people—Mickey (Woody Allen), the insanely hypochondriacal TV producer who could not make a go of his previous marriage to the wonderful Hannah, but is now headed for bliss with the radically reformed Holly. Yet when, earlier, he had a single date with her, it was a total fiasco: "I had a great time tonight. It was like the Nuremberg trials." Scarcely more believable is Lee, perennial student and member of AA, who goes from a long relationship with Frederick into a passionate affair with Elliot, and, when brother-in-law can't quite leave his wife, starts taking courses at Columbia and promptly marries the lit. teacher she got involved with. At the final Thanksgiving, four happy couples, including the girls' parents, sit down to eat turkey. Woody should eat crow.

Hannah and Her Sisters is a kind of remake of *Interiors* with bits of *Manhattan* humor grafted onto it. It may be that our Borscht-Belt Bergman, having found out that *The Passion of Anna* was a remake of *Shame*, felt the need to emulate the master in this too. So he naturally got von Sydow to play Frederick, a rethinking of the character of the same name in *Interiors*. And what about the *Manhattan* humor? It appears that writing Mickey—i.e., himself—into the movie was an afterthought: indeed, that the entire film was extensively reshaped during its editing. I've heard of performances being assembled in the cutting room, but to create a whole film there seems a very questionable procedure, not the way of an artist. Mickey, in any case, is the standard Allen persona yet again going through agonies with sundry tests and doctors over an imaginary brain tumor, then hoping to evade mortality by converting to Catholicism or, if that fails, the Hare Krishna cult. The jokes are schematic, the chief formula being the intrusion of an awesome term into a mundane context, as with the above-mentioned Nuremberg trials, or a mundane term into an awesome context, as when reincarnation elicits the comment, "It means that I'll have to sit through the Ice Capades again."

As for the "serious" dialogue, it's on the order of Elliot's, "For all my education and so-called wisdom, I can't follow my own heart." But is it perhaps Allen's directorial style that makes the difference? Yes and no. He has his tricks. He gets a good cinematographer, in this case Carlo di Palma, to shoot New York City so ravishingly that it looks like a cross between Paris and Paradise, he loads his sound track with good old show tunes, and sprinkles in some Puccini and Bach to cover all bases and trebles; then hauls out some putatively prestigious camera movements. Thus he shoots one scene in a bookstore, with the camera tracking back and forth, peering between stacks and intermittently catching the actors; a later scene, in a record store, has the camera tracking forth (but not back) as it follows the characters' heads and shoulders gliding above bins full of records. There are also the typical long shots of little Woody making his way through big New York's colorful streets—interchangeable with similar shots from *Broadway Danny Rose* and earlier Allen films.

Two scenes do come off. One has a friendly married couple slowly thrown into a tizzy as it dawns on them that their hosts, Mickey and Hannah, want the husband to impregnate Hannah because Mickey is infertile. (By way of a superhappy ending, the film concludes with Holly pregnant by Mickey: biology is no match for

Woody's imagination!) Another shows the three sisters at a charged luncheon get-together, with emotions running high as the camera waltzes around the women, catching them from curious angles in provocative juxtapositions. But, for the most part, Allen the director and Woody the scenarist are in unholy collusion: Whenever a scene reaches the point where a difficult insight is called for, they simply cut away to another set of characters and skim along those surfaces. But sets (Stuart Wurtzel) and costumes (Jeffrey Kurland) are contrived with extreme cunning to tell, by themselves, at least half the story. This is, undeniably, artful; but is it art?

The acting is generally satisfactory, though, as the sisters' father, the late Lloyd Nolan seems awkward and out of place. But such is the enthusiasm for this film (several major magazine raves well ahead of the opening date!) that Andrew Sarris could gush in the *Village Voice* about how Nolan's casting "contributes a ghostly poignancy." For Woody Allen, even the Grim Reaper puts out.

Lowering the Brow

SMOOTH TALK; A ROOM WITH A VIEW

As if the imbecile high-school movies that inundate our screens weren't enough, we now must cope with the stupidity and dishonesty of a supposedly serious film about teenagers, Joyce Chopra's *Smooth Talk*. Worse yet, Vincent Canby of the *New York Times* and other reviewers have hailed this as a remarkable movie. And worst of all, Joyce Carol Oates, on whose story "Where Are You Going. Where Have You Been?" the film is based, has published in the *Times* an apology for this travesty of her story, offering only the mildest, most wistful strictures concerning the disgraceful ending that turns allegory, Gothic horror, and tragedy into soap opera, and particularly mendacious and immoral soap opera at that.

The film, like the story, deals with 15-year-old Connie Wyatt during a school vacation. Her amiably superficial father is too happy to own the dilapidated Marin County farmhouse where the family now lives to worry about his daughters: June, 24, a dutiful drudge still living at home; and Connie, whose well-developed body is well ahead of her mind, and whose only interests are blasting the air with rock music and haunting beaches, movies, shopping malls, and hamburger joints with a couple of school chums in search of boys to neck with but not go all the way. Katherine, her mother, fitfully tries to paint the house, grouses at Connie for not helping in the least, and has one good line for her not-all-that-wayward daughter: "I look into your eyes, and all I see is trashy dreams."

The moment Connie, Laura, and Jill hit the shopping mall, Connie transforms herself: She sophisticates her hair, bedecks herself with lipstick and baubles, lowers her neckline to just this side of tartiness, and emerges as a precocious siren. The girls' dalliances at the mall with a variety of boys—those old and mean enough to be fled from on sight, those too young for anything but teasing, and those just right to go petting with only to escape when dress straps are tugged at—are well enough conveyed. Things go less well in the home scenes, where the mother-daughter bickering and sibling rivalry are much too perfunctory. This is not to be blamed on Miss Oates, but on the script by Tom Cole (who once wrote an honest, uncompromising play, *Medal of Honor Rag*), and on Miss Chopra's rote direction.

Less good yet are the hamburger joint scenes, inept imitations of *American Graffiti*, where youthful couples, self-consciously posed, flirt in unison. Here Connie attracts the attention of Arnold Friend, a man over thirty, who apparently haunts these juvenile fleshpots in search of game. Miss Oates tells that she derived this character from the Pied Piper of Tucson, who, in the Arizona of the early sixties, seduced and sometimes killed teenage girls with the tacit collusion of a circle of kids who never squealed on him.

On a hot summer day when Connie's exasperated mother slaps her, the girl refuses to accompany her family on a barbecue with relatives, preferring to laze about in and outside the house. Out of nowhere, up drives Arnold in his weirdly bedizened, gold-painted convertible, accompanied by an even weirder, silent pal. Introducing him as "Arnold Friend—A. Friend," he jumps out of the car and, with his reflecting sunglasses and James Dean manner, proceeds to hypnotize and smooth-talk Connie into going on a ride with him, declaring himself to be her lover. Vaguely fascinated as well as scared and repelled, the girl retreats into the house, whose screen door she latches. Arnold remarks that he could easily tear through the door, but won't; it behooves Connie to come out to him. He cajoles, bullies, soothes, and veiledly threatens, and seems to know preternaturally much about Connie and her folks.

Here the hitherto mediocre film goes to pieces entirely. Clearly, the insidious power of the story lies in Arnold's not entering the house. Cinematically, though, it would have required genius to shoot the scene from both sides of a screen door. Yet Connie cannot unlatch it without falling out of character and killing the suspense. So, from one shot to the next, the door becomes unlatched (by itself, presumably), and Arnold enters the house to lean against the nearest inside wall. This sabotages the symbolism of the Maiden seeking out Death and his chariot—the original title of the story was "Death and the Maiden," and it ended with Connie getting into the car beside Arnold and driving off into a land wider and vaster than she had ever noticed before.

Not so the film. While Arnold's loathsome friend brutally riffles through Connie's records, we see, through crosscutting, the car parked in a field; the camera pans to tall grass where something, anything may be happening. Presently, Arnold is driving Connie home. She gets out of the car in front of her house, and with a new-found authority, tells Arnold never to show his face again. The family has just arrived too. How come they don't see Connie getting out of a strange car? How does Arnold's pal dodge them and get back in with Arnold? Why isn't the disorder he left noticed? Why is Connie, who went off barefoot, wearing running shoes now? But she's even more different on top: Graciously accepting her mother's apology, she responds with easy affection to all. The film ends with the sisters dancing to a record that Connie finds less absorbing now.

This, I'm afraid, cannot be explained away, as Miss Oates has tried to do, as the difference between the mid-sixties, when the story was written, and the mid-eighties, when the film was made: "a girl's coming of age that involves the succumbing to, but then rejecting, the 'trashy dreams' of her pop teen culture." True, there is a chasm of time and sensibility between Oates '66 and Chopra-Cole '85. Today, Connie may well have had casual sex with the boys from the mall, and Miss Chopra, feminist that she doubtless is, would perceive her film as a 15-year-old *woman's* coming of age and self-assertion. But does her ending make sense? Is a tumble in the hay (or grass) with a cunning, ominous man twice her age and possibly a murderer the right rite of passage for a naïve young girl? Is that the way for her to gain the upper hand, a new self-assurance, and charity toward her kinfolk—not to mention the ability to outgrow a favorite rock record? And what about all the other garish rock songs on the soundtrack, the combined work of James Taylor and four other musicians—has she outgrown them as well? With feminists like Joyce Chopra, who needs male supremacists?

A less obvious, but no less deleterious, misadaptation is the film Ismail Merchant (producer), James Ivory (director), and Ruth Prawer Jhabvala (writer) made from E. M. Forster's *A Room with a View*. This team that, through a number of adaptations and original screenplays, has clung to a militant amateurishness that makes the crassest professionalism look good by comparison, is supposed to have scored a breakthrough here. In fact, the trio are back to their old tricks: disjointed scenes that do not flow into one another, a gently stinging irony in the narration sacrificed for sledgehammer effects, performances either un- or misguided by the director to the point where mostly competent or better actors overact brazenly, omission of most of the artistic and literary references in which the book abounds so as to make things easier for *hoi polloi* (who probably won't come anyway), cinematography by Tony Pierce-Roberts that makes not only Florence but everything else as well look like hand-tinted postcards, and, as a final insult, a score by Richard Robbins that leans on irrelevant and inappropriately lush Puccini arias, despite the fact that Forster approvingly quoted Beachcomber's epigram "Wagner was the Puccini of music."

So inept is the Merchant-Ivory-Jhabvala team that a refinedly lovely, fancily dressed and coifed blonde will be cast as a Florentine cabbie's girlfriend, or that the chance meeting between Cecil and the Emersons at the National Gallery, described in the book by Cecil as "They were admiring Luca Signorelli—of course, quite stupidly," will be shot smack in front of Uccello's *Battle of San Romano* panel. Neither the actors nor the camera moves in this static and stifling shot, which reveals nothing about the characters (as Cecil's remark in the novel does about all three of them), but exemplifies the filmmakers' catchpenny aestheticizing.

The ironic tone of the novel—"Of course [Santa Croce] contained frescoes by Giotto, in the presence of whose tactile values she was capable of feeling what was proper. But who was to tell her which they were?"—is replaced by blunt sarcasm. Even so important a theme as Forster's "feeling against religion . . . naïve and direct" (Lionel Trilling) is cravenly neutralized. Casting the cute but inexpressive Helena Bonham Carter as Lucy finishes off this jejune film. In a 1908 letter, Forster wrote about his forthcoming third novel: "[It] will probably gratify the home circle, but not those whose opinion I value most."

The movie forfeits the home circle's approval in a vain attempt to garner the kudos of those whom Forster valued least.

Clean Shaven

GINGER & FRED

There is a splendid story by the Italian humorist Massimo Bontempelli, *La barba di Federigo*, about a man with a gorgeous beard no woman (or anyone else) could resist. But the devil in disguise asked him with seeming innocence whether he slept with his beard inside or outside the covers.

Trying to figure out the answer drove poor Federigo nuts, to the point where he couldn't sleep either way and, in despair, shaved off his precious beard. "He no longer had a reason for living," Bontempelli concludes, "but he didn't die for all that, as one can live exceedingly well without having the slightest reason." This might almost be the story of Federico Fellini.

When he made his early, wonderful movies, Fellini was a natural talent—perhaps the most natural of all. Despite a distinctly autobiographical flavor, the films managed to be sufficiently different; indeed, in the greatest of them, *I Vitelloni*, Morando, Fellini's alter ego, is neither the most important nor the most interesting character. The last Fellini film to show intermittent strength was *8 ½*— even as it also admitted creative bankruptcy; after that came the vertiginous decline. Psychotherapy, which could have made him self-conscious, may be part of the explanation, but there is also success and egomania, and detachment from the world: withdrawal behind a living wall of amateur adulators and professional sycophants; indifference to what other artists, cinematic or otherwise, were doing; self-indulgent, obsessive involvement with a menagerie of international freaks and loonies; and supreme laxity as well as megalomania in the shooting of almost totally improvised, almost idiotically idiosyncratic movies.

I don't know whether it was in psychiatric or other disguise that the devil asked Fellini, "How do you do it, *maestro*? Do you spread your genius all over your films or do you keep it neatly tucked in?" But self-conscious as well as supremely self-regarding he became, watching himself for the provenance and quiddity of the Fellini magic. One of the old collaborators, Tullio Pinelli, was still there, but Ennio Flaiano died, and I'm not sure what became of Brunello Rondi. A new collaborator on scripts, Bernardino Zapponi, proved a disaster and was, I assume, dropped; by 1973, Fellini had latched on to Antonioni's chief scenarist, Tonino Guerra, for all the good that was to do him. The films became ever more horrible, and now, in this endless parade of artistic and moral collapse, along comes *Ginger & Fred*.

It is a case of arrested artistic development in tandem with ever growing delusions of grandeur. Take only the music. Even if the marvelous Nino Rota scores were getting a bit thin toward the end, the drop after Rota died was catastrophic: Fellini chose not to replace but to embalm him "Write me a Rota score," he presumably commands one of the rotating pseudo-Rotas—in this case Nicola Piovani—and the wretch coughs up some ghastly, watered-down imitation. In the same way, many of the scenes in the new film look like snippets of other Fellini movies (I noticed especially *Variety Lights*, *The Clowns*, and *Roma*), overproduced and underfelt. And as always when Fellini piles up huge sets and casts, more is less.

The story of a once-popular bush-league dance team, Ginger & Fred (in real life, Amelia and Pippo), who through thirty years of fascism and war entertained the provinces with their imitation of Rogers and Astaire, and who after years of separation are reunited for an appearance on a mammoth TV program, has undeniable potential. For it to work, though, the emphasis has to be on the personal element, as it would have been in early Fellini. Here, however, the story, which doesn't make sense in itself, gets submerged in all that late Fellini gigantism, exaggeration, and self-importance, in which crass exhibitionism and unrestrained manias crush the life out of human values. The film is ostensibly an attack on the commercialism and soulless vulgarity of television, but is really a flagrant example of the cauldron of pitch calling the kettle black.

That Fellini hates the dehumanizing materialism of television is all very well, but for a large-scale frontal attack on this subject it is a bit late in the game—especially if the attack is not accurate, not rich in fresh details and not properly integrated with what purports to be the story line. A major TV variety show, *Ed ecco per voi* (ineptly Englished as *We Proudly Present*), is offering a holiday special for which enough participants have been booked to make it an all-day affair. We get several kidnap victims and their lawyers, an old admiral who once performed a heroic rescue, a much-decorated civilian, a transvestite who caters to prison inmates, a defrocked priest and the woman for whom he lost his frock, a troupe of dancing dwarfs, a dapper and arrogant murderer with a retinue of guards, and numerous others. There are several look-alikes, including doubles of Proust and Kafka, as if there were a program in the world dealing in such esoterica. But Fellini must have his little joke at intellectuals, though its exact nature or relevance defies analysis.

In the immense shuffle, everything gets lost. What is the point of the old admiral, who has a fair portion of screen time but serves no discernible purpose? Though the transvestite seems to establish some genuine contact with Amelia and Pippo, nothing comes of this. None of the "acts" on the show is sufficiently developed to earn our interest: The clairvoyant and her son with their psychic tape recordings are as good for a giggle as the inventor of edible underwear, and nothing more. And Fred and Ginger, poor things, are themselves good only for a nervous titter, whether her moth-eaten old Ginger Rogers wig no longer looks right, or whether he cannot cadge another drink to screw up his courage.

Even amid hyperboles, some accuracy cannot be dispensed with. It is inconceivable that Pippo and Amelia, after thirty years of dancing and lovemaking, would completely lose track of each other, and that neither of them would make a serious effort to see a bit more of the other after the TV reunion. In any case, her *embourgeoisement* and his continued bohemian lifestyle deserve closer attention—and contrasting—than we get. But always now effect supersedes feeling. Thus when Amelia is alone in her impersonal hotel room, the revolving searchlight from the broadcast tower keeps invading her room at short intervals. This creates a prettily harrowing effect, but why doesn't she just pull down the blinds? So that Fellini can have his alienating effect, regardless of verisimilitude.

In the film's only location sequence, Amelia watches some of her fellow TV guests on the eve of the broadcast cavort across a misty, lamp-lit, desolate square to an all-night café, even as a gang of motorcyclists zooms viciously hither and yon. The forlorn, self-isolated woman, the dancing revelers, the mechanized brutes—it sounds so atmospheric and suggestive. But in the good, old Fellini movies, from which the components of this scene are lifted, something would have happened in such an episode, there would have been meaning as well as mood. Or take the scene where the head of the TV network visits the makeup room to survey the participants and ends up dancing with Ginger, whom he claims to remember with affection. The man speaks with a travesty of an upper-class Roman accent, and is presented as a total phony. An ounce of healthy vulgarity in the man, or a touch of self-irony, might have lent some acrid, aching truth to this moment. As Fellini now is, it exudes only perfunctory contempt. Indeed, all the TV personnel as well as sundry journalists are represented as either idiots or swine.

And even the climax is muffed. As Pippo and Amelia begin to perform, and we wonder whether they can make or even fake it, there is a power failure. The fulsome, tinsely MC (Franco Fabrizi, and good) asks for complete stillness until electricity is restored: on the pitch-black studio stage, amid Stygian silence, Amelia and Pippo have their moment of truth. But it isn't. No huge, modern studio would be without its own generators, and no audience, least of all in Italy, would observe pristine silence under such conditions. Against such flagrant untruth, even in a nonrealistic film, you cannot play out a compelling epiphany.

The very post-synching is wretched. Fellini makes the actors mouth anything, and their subsequently dubbed in dialogue distractingly bears no relation to lip movement. Dante Ferretti's production design is neither menacing nor mirthful enough. Even the subtitles are dreadful: *Paso doble* is translated as *pas de deux*, and the instruction to the participants backstage to be silent *come in chiesa* (as in church), one of the film's better ironies, is not translated at all. Marcello Mastroianni and Giulietta Masina give simple, faithful performances, but they cannot prevail against the surrounding farrago. Poor Federigo, without his gorgeous beard! Poor Federico, without what was once Fellini!

My Beautiful Laundrette

Last time round, I complained about the inability of Americans to make good small films of the kind an intelligent adult need not feel ashamed of in the unlikely case that their titles, advance publicity, and advertising were not enough to keep him or her away. Which is not to say that you cannot feel ashamed of most of them even without seeing them.

The problem, however, is not confined to the United States, for the garish, preposterous, or infantile effects that can be partly (but only partly) blamed on Americanization have extended way beyond the source, and if they only had the money and political freedom, there is no telling how many film industries would be indistinguishable from America's. It is, therefore, gratifying that an interesting movie has come in from England, even if it was written by a half-Pakistani and made for television.

I am referring to *My Beautiful Laundrette*, a film of undeniable quality, albeit not so great as the reviewers—eager to find their weekly masterpiece, which they seem to need as much as their daily bread—have tended to read into it. A critic, these days, cannot live by bread alone. More often he must make do with crumbs.

My Beautiful Laundrette was written by Hanif Kureishi, a young playwright born in the slums of London to a Pakistani father and English mother. Though he studied philosophy and had a play produced at 18, he supported himself as a writer of pornography. Such a Manichean—not to say manic—background provided good schooling for a screenplay about Pakistanis in London, some honest but poor, more of them hustlers or criminals with moments of nostalgia for the homeland and even for honesty. There is Papa, an ex-journalist whose wife committed suicide, and who now leads an Oblomovian existence of bed, gin, and hopes for his 18-year-old Omar at university next fall. But it's summer, and he calls his rich entrepreneur brother, Nasser, to give the boy a job at his garage, one of Nasser's many businesses, and to fix him up with a nice girl.

Omar does well at the garage, and impresses both Nasser and his pretty but aging English mistress, Rachel, whose only gift from Nasser seems to be a fur stole she wears in every scene. Is this an insight into Nasser's character, or a costuming error? Soon Omar is taken home to meet Nasser's family and friends, who range from Pakistanis of various degrees of Europeanization to fancy English racketeers. Tania, Nasser's eldest daughter, dissatisfied with her existence, promptly propositions Omar by baring her bosom to him in a scene that smacks of the overstatement that often mars this modest film. The only one who mistrusts Omar is Salim, a dapper young relative of Nasser's, prospering in the drug and porn trades, who uses Omar alternately as errand and whipping boy.

In due time, Omar runs into Johnny, a former school chum, now the head of a Pakistani-hating gang of punkers who shack up in abandoned houses often owned by Pakis. But Johnny has such affection for Omar that he agrees to help him run a broken-down launderette Nasser entrusts him with for a consideration. Omar refurbishes it with the price of some heroin he and Johnny lift from Salim; rechristened Powders, it is a huge success and makes

Omar, to his father's disgust, forget all about university, although the course of true greed does not run entirely smooth.

What makes *Laundrette* interesting is not so much the writing or Stephen Frears's somewhat overreaching direction, as the novelty of the problem of Pakistanis in England, a country where everything, good and bad, is laid out before you, "only you have to know how to squeeze the tit of the system." The alternative is going back to the fatherland, "but that country has been sodomized by religion: It is a bit hard to make money." So one stays "in this country we both love and hate." The imagery, whoever the speaker is, is sexual, and sexuality of one sort or another underlies everything here. Just as the new launderette is being ceremoniously opened to the strains of *Thus Spake Zarathustra*, Omar and Johnny are having intercourse in the office. Quite casually, they start nuzzling, then undressing each other and going to it. So that is why the hoodlum so eagerly embraced the "wog's" offer of a job.

Homosexuals have praised the casual way in which homosexuality is introduced; they find this scene and the final one liberating. Personally, I consider it artistically just as suspect to introduce pederasty so offhandedly and then more or less dismiss it as to make a huge fuss over it. But, then, the director is full of little tricks, such as the pre-title sequence that is all but incomprehensible except on second viewing, as well as other scenes that would not win prizes for lucidity.

Adding to the opacity is the lingo grunted by the young punks, a melancholy and ironic contrast to the high British spoken only by the Pakistani elders. And both author and director have to be blamed for such spurious effects as the scene where Tania, having, been spurned by both Omar and Johnny, leaves on her own. Nasser has gone to see his metaphysical slugabed of a brother, and they are having a touching reunion in the wretched bedroom overlooking the railroad tracks onto which Papa's wife jumped to her death. Outside, trains are clattering by in all directions, and as Nasser assures his brother that he is working on Omar and Tania's marriage, whom should he spot but his daughter, valise in hand, defiantly staring up at him from below. We weren't even aware of a railway stop and platform there, and, even if she had known that her father was visiting upstairs, each would have needed a telescope to see the other. As Nasser's face contracts in pain, a couple of trains whoosh by in opposite directions without stopping and, pronto, the spot where Tania stood is empty. This might go in Buñuel, but not here.

Still, *My Beautiful Laundrette* is different, genuinely small (it was even shot in 16 mm), and the youthful cruelty and ruthlessness with which it looks at the world is its very own. But it also has too many loose ends, e.g., where is Tania going, what does she want from life, and how will she subsist? Omar and Johnny will found an empire of launderettes—not beautiful, but, then, few empires are—but what becomes of rebellious, independent-minded women here? For that matter, what happens to old-fashioned Rachel, after Nasser's wife's voodoo gives her a terrible rash, and she regretfully walks out on Nasser? Even a modest little film could cover a bit more ground.

Not So Jocund

MONA LISA

Beware of the film that features a symbolic white horse! Even if it is the work of as fine a director as Andrzej Wajda (*Lotna*) or Ivan Passer (*A Boring Afternoon*), that snowy steed inevitably spells trouble: Something pretentious is afoot, or ahoof. There is a white horse—tethered, no less—in *Mona Lisa*, too; and, sure enough, this third picture by Neil Jordan, the Irish novelist and *cineaste*, is no exception to the rule.

This is the story of George, a petty criminal who took a seven-year prison rap for his chief, Mortwell, now a big boss in the prostitution and pornography rackets, with a little blackmail, it seems, on the side. George is rewarded with the soft job of acting as chauffeur and cover for Simone, a high-toned and high-priced black call-girl who, like George, works for Mortwell. It is also the story of Simone, who is desperately searching for a close friend from her streetwalker days, Cathy, a 15-year-old hooker hooked on heroin, from whom she has become separated, and whom she asks George to track down for her.

George's wife no longer allows her ex-convict husband to see his beloved daughter, Jeannie, also 15, to whom George now gives rides home from school on the sly in his spiffy Jaguar. His only other friend is Thomas, a fat, jovial, would-be writer of thrillers, who lives in a trailer inside a warehouse, and seems to be an auto mechanic and peddler of stolen goods (this is all very hazy) such as plastic mounds of spaghetti for restaurant display and light-up statuettes of Jesus and Mary. George, at first wary of, even hostile toward, Simone, gradually falls deeply in love with her, her chaste kiss on the top of his head acting as catalyst. The tall Simone, who at first despises this uncouth little man—squat, balding, plebeian, irascible, baby-bulldoggish—learns to respect him for his kindness, courage, and loyalty, and proceeds to buy him nice clothes, teach him manners, and turn him into the gentleman he always was at heart. But she doesn't reciprocate his love.

Neil Jordan—whose previous *Company of Wolves*, a revisionist fantasy on the Little Red Riding Hood theme, I missed—makes explicit reference here to the story of the Frog Prince redeemed by the maiden's kiss, but gives us another unorthodox recension of a fairy tale. Thus the obverse of Simone's kiss is the kiss George gives Jeannie, who asks him for one of those tricks "dads are meant to do," and then comments, "That's a good trick." The film marks the progress of George from seeming brute to "Mr. George," as Simone dubs him when, convinced of his decency, she asks him to find Cathy, and thence to "Father George," as Cathy, whom he finally locates in a church, jeeringly addresses him. And he has indeed become a shepherd, or would-be shepherd, to several prostitutes, whence he rises further, upon rescuing Cathy from the dragon's lair (in a scene that for sheer improbability would be hard to match) and reuniting her with Simone into Saint George, as he confronts that unlikely white horse tethered behind a roadside eatery.

And friend Thomas? He is nothing less than Thomas Aquinas, the Angelic Doctor. Early on, George informs him that "angels are men," not women; and, indeed, George and Thomas are the only active doers of good here. Thomas always asks for "the whole story," the *summa*, as it were, and it is he who produces those electrically lit holy statuettes, or brings the light of Aristotelian reason into Christian faith. He is, like Saint Thomas, a man of various skills and knowledge, his Italianness suggested by the plastic spaghetti, as well as by real ones he feeds to George. And there is also a reproduction of the *Mona Lisa* on his refrigerator, which connects the greatest medieval mind, Thomas's, with the supreme Renaissance one, Leonardo's. The eponymous Mona Lisa, of course, is the aloof Simone, whom George describes as a tart but a lady and, beyond that, feminine nature itself, underscored by Nat King Cole on the soundtrack at the start and finish of the film, as he sings, "Are you warm, are you real, Mona Lisa? Or just a cold and lonely lovely work of art?"

The mostly but not exclusively fairytale symbolism lurks in almost every aspect of the film. Thus the villain's name is Mortwell, dispenser of death; his chief henchman, a sadistic black pimp, is called Ander-

son, with indubitable (though obscure) overtones of Hans Christian.
Dwarfs appear both in the dialogue and in one actual sequence of
this screenplay by Neil Jordan and David Leland; in a scene of drastic revelation, Simone and George wear, respectively, heart-shaped
and star-shaped sunglasses that comment ironically on the situation;
during a deadly chase along Brighton Pier, the pursued George and
Simone knock over some large advertising-display hearts; after her
last, deadly act, Simone lifts her face to heaven and is illuminated by
the kind of oblique beam that descends on saints in baroque paintings; and so on, with various sorts of symbolism on the rampage.

There is, it seems to me, a very serious dissociation of sensibility
at work here. "The *Mona Lisa*, a disturbing work of art, has a kind
of sorcery about it that provokes disturbances," Mary McCarthy
writes; a work of high art, we might add, which is what Neil Jordan's
film aspires to, with its religious and fairy-tale symbolism. But the
sordidness of the story, its improbability the only high thing about
it, is in direct, jarring clash with its high-flown aspirations, each
getting in the other's way. A callgirl as Mona Lisa, a petty crook
who may or may not have killed someone (the film fudges a number of crucial matters) as Saint George, a dealer in stolen goods as
Aquinas—these and their likes do not elevate the meanness into
anything but pretension, while merely trivializing or demeaning
what is exalted.

Nevertheless, *Mona Lisa* does have its assets. In the exploration of
the worlds of sexual degradation—by having his production designer
(Jamie Leonard) and cinematographer (Roger Pratt) create a livid-
lurid environment of exotic aquarium colors for lower-class vice,
while reserving an elegantly cool palette for the Ritz Hotels and ritzy
fashions and furnishings (costumes by the aptly named Louise Frog-
ley) of upper-class perversion—Jordan comes up with some memorable images without much explicit detail, the horror made ineffable
by being merely suggested. By his evocations of three 15-year-olds,
the sweet but not saccharine Jeannie (Zoe Nathenson), and the two
pathetic but quite different child prostitutes—May (Sammi Davies),
wearing her crucifix earring and yearning for ice cream while she
walks her beat, and Cathy (Kate Hardie), heroin-ravaged and with a
system that can no longer digest anything but ice cream—Jordan tells
us, through partial contrasts and lopsided parallels, something about
the paradoxes and ironies of life, not least the curious emotional dependence of whores on the pimps they hate. And the dialogue is
generally tart, and not infrequently imaginative.

The central relationship between George and Simone, astutely observed with almost clinical astringency, is nonetheless also poignant and even poetic in its tender and violent hopelessness. But even here, there are flaws: How did an ex-streetwalker and present callgirl of about twenty acquire so much taste and such an upper-class accent? How can George, with his background, be so naïve about certain aspects of sex and drug addiction? And if Jordan avoids the Scylla of the whore with the heart of gold, is the Charybdis of the ex-con with the soul of a saint that much better? On the other hand, in Mortwell, in whom suavity and sleaziness have been raised to the ultimate degree of charming monstrosity, Jordan, with the help of a fiendishly persuasive performance by Michael Caine, has created an utterly fantastic and totally believable demon. Too bad that, on top of that white horse, there has to be a white rabbit in the film, preposterously present at the unlikeliest moment.

And besides some deft direction and dialogue and consistently fine camera work, there is the acting. George is played by Bob Hoskins, one of the most fascinating actors in today's cinema. The scarcely contained excess of excitability for good or ill, the aura of bewilderment under the surface security, and the sweet, sweaty, acrid sense of life being lived intensely every instant that Hoskins brings to everything he does here is, to use an overworked word judiciously, mesmerizing. Very good, too, is Cathy Tyson as Simone, devious and angry but also wise and touching, with an aura that combines the provocation of kinky sexuality with something still questing, still unspoiled. Everyone else is right too, notably Robbie Coltrane as Thomas, as well as all those girls and their exploiters and customers.

The mode of *Mona Lisa* is gutter Dostoyevsky, with the former, alas, outpulling the latter. But if I have devoted so much space to the film, it is because it is one of the painfully few movies these days whose appeal is to an adult audience; and because, though only intermittently warm and very seldom real, it at least strives to be a work of art.

Vagabond

Once again the Europeans are ahead of us. Even if Agnès Varda's *Vagabond* does not measure up to the masterpieces of the cinema, compared to what is around these days, it is at least an attempt to deal with a serious subject in an adult manner. Called in France *Sans Toit ni Loi* (*Without Roof or Law*), it is the story of an 18-year old drifter, Mona, found frozen to death in a ditch near Nîmes during an unusually cold winter in the south of France. Well, not so much her story as a pseudo-documentary of the last months of her life, told partly from her point of view and partly from the vantage points of the people she came in contact with. The film begins and ends with her corpse; in between, it tells us a good deal, though not quite enough.

Mona, whose motto is "Alone is good," has left her office work and despised petit-bourgeois parents in order to wander around the roads of Provence, occasionally doing odd jobs, or sponging and chiseling as best she can. She is not unattractive, and sometimes offers sex in exchange for creature comforts; all she needs is food, cigarettes, a place to sleep, and, if possible, her bit of pot. Sometimes she abuses people, sometimes she is abused, even raped; but, unsentimental almost to the point of stolidity, she is pleased enough with her mangy existence, her few belongings and fewer baths. When people are good to her, she may be as nice to them as her basic indolence allows, but without really opening up; when they are not (and sometimes even when they are), she can be pretty beastly, too.

The point of the film, however, is not so much Mona herself as the widely differing reactions she elicits from others. If for Stendhal the novel was a mirror in the roadway, the protagonist performs that function for Miss Varda. With her emotional minimalism, Mona brings out sympathy, envy, disgust, yearning, greed, even love in others, some of whom are concisely revealed. But she herself remains a cipher—or a mirror, which is a fine thing to be for a novel, but not for a heroine. As a result, a woman ecologist who takes Mona in for a short while, and a Tunisian guest worker in the vineyards who takes her in longer and genuinely cares for her (but must give her up when his fellow workers object), and several other characters emerge as more interesting than Mona, which unbalances the movie. Especially so since there is not enough time for developing these many secondary characters, and too much time for *not* developing her.

Can a young girl be such a near-perfect blank? Are we supposed to sympathize with her anyway? Is society to blame, or are some people born to be misfits? These are challenging, even if hardly new, questions, but Miss Varda refuses to answer them. Very well, an artist need not answer questions but must at any rate pose them better, more probingly, than this. Miss Varda is not much of a scriptwriter, and certain key scenes were left to improvisation—unsuccessfully, as is almost always the case with that tricky device. What, then, is good about *Vagabond*?

First, the atmosphere, the sense of subdued hopelessness: Many people are good, only a few are bad, but there is so little help one person can extend to another. Then, the beauty of nature: Agnès Varda was a still photographer before she made films, and there is, even though she is not her own cinematographer here, an extraordinary sense of composition in frame after frame. Sometimes the settings themselves are lovely, but even when they are not, the camera can extract a cool elegance from the mundane, the impoverished, the desolate. And it is against that dignity of the visual that the tawdriness or shabbiness of so many lives registers as particularly harrowing.

For even those people who have good reasons to be satisfied, if not happy, are able to conjure up, regardless of social class, some form of strain and discontent. Only a mild and meditative master of philosophy, who chucked it all to go into sheepherding with his young wife, seems to be at peace with the world and himself, but when Mona says that with his academic credentials she wouldn't be where he or she is, we cannot help sympathizing with her. Yet if the philosophical shepherd is hard to comprehend, Mona is even more so: How can someone so indifferent and indolent have elected a life where survival requires so much exertion?

The film, for all the nebulousness at its center, is greatly helped by the presence of Sandrine Bonnaire. Though not much of an actress, as she proved in *A nos Amours*, she is just right for Mona. She is the same age as the character, not pretty but not homely either. She has one of those very French, large-browed, oblong faces, prematurely canny, with beady eyes too close to a potato nose, yet capable of coming childishly, fetchingly, alive as well as lapsing into childishly implacable defiance. A face, in short, that can merge with its humdrum surroundings or take on the seductiveness of inner joy—or of someone else's desire projected onto it.

Finally, this is a film about the evanescence of things. Even as the colors are mostly sober, comely but sucked dry by winter, so lives are etiolated by something from within. Dutch elm disease is destroying the trees, and an ailment no less fatal gnaws at the souls.

There is something heart-rending about the way Mona deteriorates—about how her clothes keep getting more and more dilapidated, about how her boots become progressively mere leather rags
cumbrously trailing behind her, and, especially, about the seeming
insentience with which she accepts coming apart at the seams. True,
by definition, apathy is not pathetic; but that does not stop it from
being tragic—at the very least tragically wasteful. It is her former
imperviousness to deprivation that makes Mona's whimpers, when
they finally ambush her (and us), seem like tragic outcries with only
the sound turned down.

Ran

Readers have written in asking why I didn't review Akira Kurosawa's
Ran. Because I find it an almost total failure by a genius in his old
age, and tearing it apart would be worse than taking candy from a
baby—knocking an old man's crutch out of his hand. Kurosawa has
made several masterpieces and a good many outstanding films in
his long, productive life despite sad ingratitude from the Japanese
film industry in his later years; that, like other major film artists
(e.g., Chaplin, Buñuel, Renoir, Bresson, Welles), he should have
gone into a decline with age is profoundly sad. Since I am neither
a daily reviewer nor a Kurosawa monographer, I can pass over *Ran*
in silence. Besides a gesture of regret for his last few films, let that
silence also be one of respect for the many that went before.

Neat Trick

BLUE VELVET

How long has it been since an American movie has garnered a harvest of laurels like the one being heaped on a piece of mindless junk
called *Blue Velvet*? David Lynch's previous films were *Eraserhead*, a
grossout for cultists, and the inept and contemptible *Elephant Man*
and *Dune*. True pornography, which does not pretend to be anything
else, has at least that shred of honesty to recommend it; *Blue Velvet*,
which pretends to be art, and is taken for it by most critics, has dishonesty and stupidity as well as grossness on its conscience.

That the film deals—without much explicitness but with maximal striving for sexual arousal—with sadomasochism, voyeurism,
latent homosexuality, fetishism, and whatnot would be fine if the
goal were insight rather than mere titillation or shock. And though
it makes no sense on either the psychological or the narrative
plane—is, indeed, the writer-director's wish-fulfillment fantasy—
Blue Velvet pretends to comment on small-town American mores.
Add to this Lynch's primitive dialogue, jokes that in most cases are
not intentional but are pathetic either way, poor staging of individual scenes, and garish cinematography (extravagantly praised in the
reviews), and you have the archetype of a film in which mindless-
ness, pretension, and ineptitude vie for supremacy. Lynch is a naïf
from Montana who wants to be deep, but whose depth consists of
drawing huge sexual organs on a Norman Rockwell painting, and
of allowing his protagonist and alter ego, Jeffrey Beaumont, from
Lumberton, Middle America, hidden sadistic urges. Big deal.

In the movie's much-admired beginning, we see blazing red
roses and blatantly yellow tulips against a picket fence whiter than
the driven snow and topped by a baby-blue sky. We see a friendly
fireman on his truck, a crossing guard watching over babes in the
street. Suddenly, Jeffrey's father, idyllically hosing his front lawn,
has an accident with the hose and keels over; a dog cavorts in the
water jet still spouting from the supine man's hands. This is chilling
in its grotesquerie, but when the camera, to symbolize the horrors
under the surface of Middle American life, burrows into the lawn to
close in on a multitude of monstrous insects fighting to the death,
the effect is phony. The shot is clearly of a terrarium, and the whole
thing is clumsily derivative of the beginning of Peckinpah's *The
Wild Bunch*.

Returning from a visit to his father in the hospital, Jeffrey walks
through a field. (The topography of Lumberton makes as little
sense as its sociology: Sometimes it is a tiny burg, sometimes a
bustling town, and sometimes a deserted studio set.) Anyhow, in
that field, Jeffrey finds a severed and moldy human ear with a hunk
of hair attached to it (was the victim scalped?) and crawling with
ants. The ear, it will turn out, belonged to Don, the husband of
Dorothy Vallens, a tawdry chanteuse. Don and little Donnie Vallens were kidnapped (and dad-napped) by Frank—the local crime
boss, murderer, drug dealer and addict, sadist, fetishist, and latent
homosexual—as a means of coercing Dorothy into becoming his
abjectly masochistic sexual slave. Needless to say, that is not how

masochists of Dorothy's stripe (or stripes) are made; but, in any cast, what in tarnation was an ear of man—not corn—doing in that field? If cut off in an act of al fresco sadism, it would not have been left there, lying conveniently next to a brown paper bag in which Jeffrey can deliver it to Detective Williams of the police. If it was meant to intimidate and subjugate Dorothy, she wouldn't just have tossed it away.

This sort of preposterousness rules the film. Out of sheer perverse curiosity, Jeffrey sneaks into Dorothy's apartment one night and gets caught up in a sadomasochistic maelstrom as, watching through the slats of the closet where he is hiding, he pantingly witnesses Frank's torturing of Dorothy. Later, Jeffrey, who has already been forced by Dorothy at knife point to make love to her, is gradually coaxed into beating her during intercourse. Nevertheless, when Dorothy performs at The Slow Club (humor!)—where, incidentally, her entire repertoire seems to consist of a mediocre rendition of "Blue Velvet"—her bared back and deep frontal décolletage show not a bruise on her milk-white skin. When, later on, Frank and his henchmen work Jeffrey over in a way that would put him right beside his dad in the hospital, he walks home, and soon sports only a token bruise or two. Isn't it in pornography that the victim's body recovers miraculously from ever renewed tortures?

And how many closets do you know with slatted doors affording the voyeur a full, salacious view? The whole thing is pure swinish hogwash, the fantasy made more self-indulgent by the casting of Kyle MacLachlan (similarly used in *Dune*) as the hero: Untalented and with a cartoonishly doll-like face, he has the one virtue of looking like a young David Lynch. When Jeffrey watches Dorothy from that convenient closet, she strips to her tiny black bra and scanties for comfort, but keeps her uncomfortably stiletto-heeled red shoes on, to satisfy Lynch's fantasy. After an obligatory nude shot, she puts on a semi-eponymous blue velveteen robe: it has a sash, one of whose ends will be stuffed into her mouth and the other chewed on by Frank while he has brutal sex with her. (Frank, incidentally, has a repertoire of self-contradictory perversions that would have stunned Krafft-Ebing.) But the most amazing bit is Dorothy's removing at one random moment, and promptly replacing, what proves to be a wig she wears throughout the picture. Is this yet another Lynch fantasy, or Isabella Rossellini's desire to display her own hair, vastly inferior though it is to the wig's?

Because Jeffrey must have a blond, apple-pie-American sweetheart as well as a dark, sick, European-accented one, there is Detective Williams's daughter, Sandy, played by the cigar-store-Indian-faced Laura Dern. Though supposedly in love with Mike, one of her school's football stars, Sandy quickly switches to Jeffrey, so our boy can simultaneously enjoy kinky sex and puppy love. He and Sandy go to a diner for a date, dance cheek-to-cheek and then mouth-to-mouth at a high-school party, and, all along, Sandy plays Nancy Drew to Jeffrey's Sherlock Jr.

In one of the film's many climaxes, Dorothy shows up naked on Jeffrey's doorstep circa midnight, although she is in a complete daze and has never been given Jeffrey's address. She has been mauled by Frank—her lingered-on body is an anthology of scars and bruises—but Mike, who with his pals has come to beat up Jeffrey for stealing his girl, sneers, "Is that your mother?" Then he apologizes, and considerately departs with the gang. The nude Dorothy throws her arms around Jeffrey's neck, calls him her secret lover, and explains: "He [Frank] has put his disease in me." The agonized Sandy kicks out Jeffrey, then phones to forgive him. So much for psychology.

I could go on listing the absurdities and fudgings of this film—it is never even made clear whether Detective Williams is, like his partner, in Frank's pay, or whether he is just the most incompetent cop this side of Mack Sennett—but let me skip to the ending. While Dorothy, a fresh widow completely cured of her masochism, is blissfully playing with her restored son, the newly married Jeffrey and Sandy, with their extended families, are about to sit down to Sandy's dinner. Before that, in an elaborate process shot, the camera had entered Jeffrey's ear, as it earlier did Don's. But lo, there is a worm in paradise. A patently mechanical robin prances on the window sill with a huge black beetle in his beak. "It's a weird world, isn't it?" says Sandy.

This takes us back to the scene in which, in a car parked before a church, Sandy tells Jeffrey one of her dreams: "The world was dark because there weren't any robins," but then, "thousands of robins were set free" and there was the "blinding light of love." Jeffrey, smitten with so much poetry, mutters, "You're a neat girl, Sandy." That, and the leitmotivic line, "It's a strange world, isn't it?" should give you an idea of the dialogue.

The cinematography by Frederick Elmes is all poster colors, and the acting, especially Isabella Rossellini's, amateurish. Dean Stockwell is persuasive as a creepy, homosexual sadist, and Dennis Hopper (as Frank), who obviously improvised his dialogue—mostly roared-out f-words in every conceivable permutation—is an all too credible homicidal maniac. Otherwise, the only believable thing about this film is that the elevator in Dorothy's apartment house, out of order at the beginning, remains so throughout.

But why do the critics, from sophisticated magazines to family newspapers, rave about this trash? Let me tell you a parable—and bear in mind Jeffrey's above-mentioned declaration of love to Sandy. A friend of mine saw a youth of Jeffrey's age flanked by two Sandys, all in expensively casual clothes, standing in the Metropolitan Museum before a Martyrdom of St. Peter, in which the Apostle's garb, so as not to interfere with his upside-down crucifixion, is gathered at the ankles and wrists. Exclaims the awed youth: "Oh, wow! That's neat!"

Aimez-Vous Pascal?

MÉNAGE

Hardly have I got through decrying *Blue Velvet* for you before there is Bertrand Blier's *Ménage* to bemoan. The French title is *Tenue de soirée*, evening dress, almost never worn by the characters, which tells you right away what sort of contrariness is afoot. *Ménage* is a French *Blue Velvet*. Instead of being made by a primitive from Montana, it is the work of a slick Parisian; instead of being illiterate and, ultimately, stupidly optimistic, it is literate and steadily, cynically downbeat. But it makes just as little sense on any level, is equally eager to throw any ingredient into the pot as long as it passes for spicy, and is no less hotly in pursuit of the bizarre without the slightest regard for truth.

But in Blier there is something worse: contempt for all, and especially for women. The mockery lacerates everyone and everything without any hint of a moral or aesthetic value in whose name human shortfall may be assessed. In almost all previous Blier films—and certainly in the best-known ones, *Going Places* and *Get Out Your Handkerchiefs*—there are two male friends in implicit (or even explicit, though casual and random) homosexual involvement, even if they are always nominally heterosexual. Significantly, they compete for and share the same woman, whom they abuse or are abused by. This *folie à trois* reduces everyone, but tends to degrade the woman most.

In *Ménage*, the misanthropy, the repressed or downplayed homosexuality, and the rampaging misogyny are in full swing. Still, one could make a movie out of this, either painful or sardonic, either socially critical or blackly farcical, if only one played by some set of rules, maintained elementary coherence, and knew where one was going. Blier cannot claim any of these niceties, and has even admitted his dissatisfaction with the ending (one of several he toyed with); he depends, instead, on ever greater outrageousness, and on making his movie lurch forward in any direction save that of credibility.

An unhappily married couple is fighting in a café: Monique accuses Antoine of dragging her into abject poverty; he feebly apologizes and doggedly proclaims his love, which only makes her insult him worse. Along comes Bob, a strapping fellow who sits down with them and takes over their lives. He humiliates and wallops Monique over puny Antoine's attempts to defend her, then throws wads of money at the pair. Bob is a master burglar who can (literally) smell gold a block off, then walk into a house that simply opens itself for him, and head for the loot like a pigeon for home. The three embark on a fairy-tale crime spree: Besides money, the houses provide first-rate food and living quarters; if the owners show up, they are so jaded as to welcome the burglars: on the one occasion the police appear, they conveniently save the thieves from an unwelcome sexual orgy initiated by their would-be victims.

Monique falls for Bob and assumes reciprocity. But no: He rejects her even more brutally than she does her husband, and starts courting the mousy, unattractive Antoine with the most passionate dedication. The scorned and shattered Monique nevertheless hangs around and urges her shocked spouse to yield. Speaking from long, promiscuous experience, she assures him that anal intercourse is no picnic for women either, yet *they* have put up with it, so why not he? Like Antoine, Bob insists that he is no homosexual, and there is indeed some hanky-panky between Bob and Monique, but Bob's passion for Antoine duly wins out, even as the latter keeps asserting his love for his wife.

By now psychological veracity is all but expunged, but it gets the *coup de grâce* when Bob tries to lure Antoine into the clutches of a wealthy homosexual art collector, who, as it appears, had hired him to procure the little fellow. If Bob is, as suggested both before and after, madly in love with Antoine, what's this about having done it all for the art collector's money? And if he knows the Open Sesame

to every Parisian mansion and its treasures, why should this valiant burglar have to moonlight as a pimp? And even if Bob, out of
some quirk, should fall for a drab little nonentity, surely that is not
what a wealthy homosexual with lavish tastes would pay a boodle
for. In fact, such a man would scarcely need the services of a pimp;
he could get full satisfaction directly from the Parisian *demi-* or,
indeed, *beau monde.*

Forthwith, however, Bob, Antoine, and Monique are ensconced
in a cheerful little nest in Montmartre, where the two men live as
husband and wife, with Monique as their servant, menial and sex-
starved. In a much earlier scene, she was having intercourse with
a man whom Bob and Antoine were robbing while the man's wife
slept on the other side of the bed; the wife woke up, and clamored
for her share in the fun. Now the shoe is on the other foot—or,
more exactly, Monique's cot is smack at the foot of the big, comfy
bed in which Bob and Antoine, to her humiliation and chagrin, are
thrashing about in sexual ecstasy.

It is all as ugly as it is nonsensical, but, never fear, weirder permutations and peripeties are presently dragged in. Skipping over
much, I shall merely relate that Monique is turned into a cheap
prostitute in the very dance hall where Antoine, desperate and now
always in drag, chases after Bob, who is dancing and about to make
off with another man, a typical male whore. (Remember, Bob is
no homosexual!) Soon a murder takes place, without the slightest
legal or moral consequences, and, in the end, we find Monique
and the two men in drag doing the sidewalks together on a chilly
day (as if regular whores and transvestite ones worked the same
streetcorner). Business being slow, they take a break at a nearby
lunch counter.

Suddenly, one of the guys (I forget which, though by this time
they are pretty interchangeable, anyway) asks Monique whether she
remembers Pascal. I shuddered; here comes, I thought, the obligatory bit of philosophical attitudinizing with which to top off such a
Gallic confection. But it turns out even worse: Pascal is a son whom
Monique has abandoned somewhere. Heaven knows where or who
his father is, and why he has never been mentioned before. As the
two men in drag go back to ply their trade, Monique lingers at the
counter; she is lost in a teary reverie. If this summary gives away
too much and spoils your fun, I am truly sorry, though I cannot
imagine how something as thoroughly rotten as *Ménage* can be
spoiled. Neither can I imagine how this movie could become the

hit of France, then go on to garner high critical praise in America, and be headed for what looks like assured audience success.

What bothers me most is not the moral or sexual perversion; rather, it is the perverting of all narrative and structural logic. Here a dab of realism, there several dollops of out-and-out fantasy; here a person practices one kind of sexuality, there another kind; here a feeling is real, there it is shown up as phony, yonder it is more genuine than ever; here it is all a big joke, there a woman is reduced to abjection and a dead man bleeds. Forget about a sense of time and place: We don't know how much time elapses between scenes, or where we are at a given moment, or how we got from one point to another. And just when one character seems a trifle better, or at least more pitiable, than the others and begins to elicit a bit of sympathy, bingo, he or she proves viler than the rest. Even a satire (assuming that this is one) against the entire human race must allow us a glimpse of something better, if no more than a notion of lost goodness in the author's head. In *Gulliver's Travels*, there are the giants and the horses: in *The Dunciad*, there is the orderly mind of Alexander Pope. In *Ménage*, no one is any good, and the mind of the creator seems to be the most jaundiced, gloating, and spitefully destructive of all.

True, Blier knows how to write dialogue. Though extremely mean-spirited, the writing has sophistication and spurts of cruel wit, occasionally even innocent dementia. Some scenes, moreover, are well staged and neatly photographed, and the acting is fine. I am getting rather tired of Gérard Depardieu, even if it is traditional for French movies to overexploit periodically one star or another, whether it is Gabin or Montand, Belmondo or Ventura, or, long ago, even Bertrand Blier's unappealing father, Bernard. But here Depardieu takes impressive risks for a heartthrob, and his goofy, flabby Bob is an authentic creation. Miou-Miou is as winning as ever: She plays Monique as low as Blier wants her to, and even if she cannot salvage the character, she preserves her appeal as an actress and a woman. As for Michel Blanc as Antoine, he is, though extremely homely, instinct with charm and, even in this preposterous part, intermittently touching. That Bob should fall so in love with him is not made credible, but that is the fault of the poor script rather than of Blanc's measly looks.

What *Ménage* proves above all else is a need for and relish of anomie among audiences and critics alike. There is a tremendous craving, not just for some old-fashioned, harmless nonsense, but for the deliberate trampling of every kind of rationality or consistency: Human minds are turning into lemmings hurtling toward the sea of unreason. Even if the critics cannot stop them, must they join them?

Found in the Mud

PLATOON

The amazing thing about *Platoon* is that Oliver Stone, the writer-director, who spent 15 months fighting in Vietnam, managed to make a film scarcely different from the soap operas written by hacks who never got closer to the vc than their vcrs. Can you trust a movie that is finally going to tell you The Truth about the Vietnam War if it contains a smiling, ruddy-faced soldier passing around the picture of his girl with whom he will live happily ever after, only to be killed in the next reel? Can you swallow a film whose soundtrack, at a crucial moment of terror, erupts into an amplified heartbeat? Would you buy a used car from a filmmaker whose autobiographical hero, Chris Taylor, begins as a raw volunteer ("Why should just the poor kids go to war and the rich kids get away with it?"), only to emerge not only as a wily, wise veteran, but also as the supreme justicer?

Yessir, Chris shoots the demon, Sergeant Barnes, whom no one, foe or friend, was able to waste. But Chris, through supernatural sensitivity, deduces that Barnes, in a personal vendetta, perforated his nemesis, the saintly Sergeant Elias. The implications of *Platoon* are that if we had had a few more Oliver Stones, we might not have lost the war; but because we had at least one, we did not wholly lose our honor: Barnes got fragged by gallant Chris, as he deserved to be, and you should just hear the movie audience applaud.

Platoon is the film of a wild man who wants to be also a philosopher and a poet. Alas, Stone thinks in clichés and writes in tie-dyed prose, but as a wild man he is authentic enough. Having lasted one year at Yale, he next taught Chinese and Vietnamese students in Saigon; when neither this nor a stint in the merchant marines made a writer of him, he figured the war might do it. After two wounds, a bronze star, and some trouble because of insubordination, Stone returned a bona-fide druggie, but still no writer. Upon failing for Country and for Yale, the choice was either God or something equally hospitable to universal dropouts: film school. At NYU, the young man became a student of Martin Scorsese, not one to leave a Stone unturned.

After a false start or two, Stone wrote the screenplay for *Midnight Express*, which won an Oscar and more, and established the Stone style: brutal facts—in this case, the hair-raising real-life story of an innocent American pot-smuggler in a Turkish jail—that, however true, make the truth seem suspect. Or, if not the truth, the author's motivation for and mode of spelling it out. This became Stone's hallmark, climaxing in *Scarface* for Brian De Palma, the most gratuitously and mindlessly bloodthirsty film in years. I missed *Salvador*, which Stone co-scripted and directed, but *Platoon*, where he is the sole *auteur*, is clearly his supreme bid for fame thus far.

The film is not without some real, albeit submerged, merits. Shot in the Philippines, with the actors rigorously trained in enduring discomforts and deprivations, it is unsparingly detailed in evoking the full spectrum of horrors, from infestation with red ants and marching on ballooningly blistered feet to undergoing or inflicting the most appalling deaths. About those ants, for example, Chris is informed, while performing the perfect St. Vitus dance, that he is lucky: The red ones are less bad than the black. Which brings me to Stendhal, the first to show how utterly befuddled the combatant is in the midst of battle. Stone improves on Stendhal by keeping the audience equally confused: The barked-out commands are swallowed up by the noise of warfare; the hallucinatory images fall prey to darkness or the blinding light of flares.

When you add to this a large cast of grunts, most of whom look interchangeable, it is uncertain whether more is gained or lost by the scrupulous rendering of chaos. The effect, on the one hand, is to make horror more horrible by its very inscrutability; on the other, to make it more impersonal and abstract. After seeing the film twice, I still couldn't tell you just what happens to whom (let alone how or why) among the dramatis personae we are only superficially introduced to before we are supposed to care for or condemn them—or, more hopeless yet, feel provocatively ambivalent about.

There are, however, gripping scenes showing the grunts getting high and anarchic on drugs, and some of the dialogue has the right mixture of anger, wit, obscenity, and desperation about it. Even so, there are few moments that grabbed me by anything other than sheer brutality or pandemonium. Here are some. As Chris and the other cherries get off the transport plane that brought them to Nam, they file past their predecessors being shipped home by the same plane in body bags. After a horrifying Mylai-ish incident, when the order is to torch a village, a grunt uses the lighter with which he just incendiated a gook hut to light his cigarette. A shot from a helicopter carrying Chris and other wounded men: While battle still rages around them, the tarpaulin-covered American corpses are laid bare, row on row, by the gust of air from the copter.

But over against such strong, wordless moments, there is all the loquacity, pretension, and obviousness of the "serious" writing. Chris and his buddies are caught between two sergeants: Elias, the holy hophead turned into a good angel, who believes we shall lose the war by way of a much-needed lesson, but meanwhile does whatever he can to save lives; and Barnes, the evil angel, who pops up equally unexpected but to bloody purpose. His face is Elm Street-ishly stitched together after seven close encounters with death, all of which he survived because, it seems, only he can will his death. He fights like a demon, threatens (and probably secretly executes) his men, has murderous bouts with Elias, and is both hated and venerated. Chris declares himself, with the film's typical overexplicitness posing as profundity, "the child of these two fathers."

This internecine duel between good and evil is much too schematic and melodramatically manipulative (though Stone doubtless thinks it Melvillian) to serve as structural framework. And the ideological skeleton—"I can't believe we are fighting each other when we ought to be fighting them"—is a belated apotheosis of the Pogo philosophy, which can probably no longer be freshly expressed. But Stone trusts the audience's ability to infer things no more than the old-time cheapies by Sam Fuller and his likes did. At least Fuller and the rest did not go in for Art, as Stone presumes to, especially in the letters Chris writes his grandmother (and recites in voice-over), which contain the preceding quotation and repeat it, for bad measure, at film's end, embedded in a long, nauseatingly didactic and self-righteous homily. These letters abound in stuff such as this about the platoon members, in a repellent blend of folksiness and bathos: "Two years high school's about it . . . most of 'em got nothing [would anyone write 'em to his grandmother?], they're poor, they're unwanted, yet they're fighting for our society, our freedom." And "they're the best I've ever seen, Grandma, the heart and soul—maybe I've finally found it down here in the mud. . ." and so on and on.

The "poetry" is not confined to the letters home. Elias spouts it in the nocturnal jungle: "I love this place at night. The stars—there's no right or wrong up there," to which the awestruck Chris responds, "That's a nice way of putting it"—self-praise in its purest form. Even bestial Barnes verges on it when, bottle in hand, he drunkenly confronts his pot-smoking men contemplating his murder: "Trying to escape from reality? I don't need this shit: I *am* reality!" And the crude preciosity of the dialogue is echoed by Georges Delerue's abominably posturing score, which takes for its centerpiece an even soupier orchestration of Barber's Adagio for Strings, used for just about everything from rushing into battle to achieving existential epiphanies in the mud. This already stale piece of Barber's now joins the so-called Albinoni Adagio and Pachelbel Canon as one of the cloacas of classical music.

Typical of *Platoon*'s excesses is Sergeant Elias's double death. After being mowed down at night by Barnes at close range, he is seen by Chris from his helicopter the next day as, bloody but unbowed, he charges the enemy, gets plugged, and slowly collapses, his face and arms raised heavenward. If Barnes could almost die seven times, it may be all right for Elias to really do so twice, but it could have been shot less hammily and not viewed by Chris from so unlikely, godlike a perspective. Still, Tom Berenger is fine as Barnes, even if makeup does a good part of his work; Willem Dafoe is too actorish as Elias, but Charlie Sheen (Martin's son) is a likable Chris.

Keith David is excellent as King, a savvy black soldier; so is Kevin Dillon (Matt's brother) as a baby-faced gookbutcher:—"Holy shit! Did you see that fucking head come apart?" And we more or less do. There are powerful contributions from other Americans and Filipinos as well. But though *Platoon* may enlighten those who still harbor delusions about Vietnam, and serve the very young as an effective anti-recruiting poster, it is poster art. Even its most belabored point, that our defeat was caused by dissension, is not made compellingly enough.

Raising Arizona

I know of no profounder epigraph for a work of art than the one Odön von Horváth affixed to his play *Tales from the Vienna Woods* (1930): "Nothing gives us such a sense of infinity as does stupidity." In German, this reads *Nichts gibt so sehr das Gefühl der Unendlichkeit als wie die Dummheit.*" *Als wie*, however, is a solecism; *wie* by itself is sufficient and correct. It is as if, like those Renaissance artists who painted themselves in a corner of their large group canvases, the Austrian playwright had wished to inscribe himself on the passenger list of his ship of fools. Those, bear in mind, were the days when speaking your own language badly was still considered a sign of folly.

This melancholy truth was brought home to me again upon viewing the praised movie *Raising Arizona*, a farce by two young brothers, Joel and Ethan Coen, whose previous acclaimed film, *Blood Simple*, I found inept and detestable, though probably better than this, their second one.

The Coen brothers—Joel directs, Ethan produces, both write—are typical film-school products, which means that it is even safer than usual to assume that they know little about anything other than movies. Certainly there is no evidence in their pictures of exposure to any kind of culture or of observation of humanity in any but the two-dimensional, celluloid form. *Raising Arizona* is the story of H.I., a good-natured but mildy imbecile petty criminal in the Southwest, who holds up convenience stores with an unloaded gun—which, I think, is meant to prove his niceness, not his stupidity. A repeater, he keeps being sent to the same prison to confront the same inmates, officers and parole board, to the point where much of the film looks like stock footage, with the same shots recurring until you wonder just who is the recidivist, H.I. or the Coens.

He is always booked by the same female police officer, Ed (short for Edwina—this kind of nomenclature is typical of the upper reaches of the film's humor), who eventually marries him. Was ever woman in this humor won: while taking mug shots and fingerprints of a hood whose mug (he is played by the unprepossessing Nicolas Cage) is as godforsaken as his conversation, whose fingers are as black as the inside of his head? H.I. gives up crime and Ed retires from the police; forthwith she resolves that they must have a baby even though she is barren. Given H.I.'s record, they cannot adopt; kidnapping is the best bet, especially since Nathan Arizona, a loudmouthed furniture dealer, who personally advertises on TV, has just become the father of quintuplets. Ed deems five kids too much for any family, so she gets H.I. to abscond with one of them, who may be Nathan Jr., unless he is Barry, Garry, Harry, or Larry, as (I seem to recall) the others are named.

As it happens, Nathan Jr. is nary a baby, merely a filmmaker's gadget: Buffeted about, abandoned several times on the highway or on the roof of a speeding car, dangled from the arm of a bank robber during a robbery, etc., he never cries and never makes any demands; he must be the offspring of a punching ball and a bean-bag. The plot revolves—or rather careers or careens—around two jailmates of our hero's who escape and ensconce themselves in H.I. and Ed's ramshackle farmhouse and try to enlist H.I. in a series of bank robberies, but end up falling in love with Nathan Jr. and kidnapping him in turn. There is also a terrifying biker—a quasi-supernatural, seemingly indestructible murderous sadist—who sets out to recover the baby for the reward money; and, for good measure, a neighboring couple who propose wife-swapping and, re-fused, threaten to report H.I. to the police as a kidnapper; as well as H.I.'s boss, who is seen recurrently mangling the same Polish joke. Why an already unfunny farce needs even more appalling comic relief, only the Coens and the reviewers who abet them could say.

Almost the entire film is a car and bike chase, interrupted by oth-er, even cruder, forms of violence, or by somewhat quieter moments during which two or more characters vent their heaven-storming stupidity. Two of the more striking jokes are a) H.I., a complete illiterate, writing a farewell letter in perfectly spelled and gramati-cal Victorian-romance English; and b) the running gag whereby anyone in trouble—as anyone almost always is—starts roaring like a dumb, wounded beast. To be sure, no beast, however wounded, would roar that loud and long, but, then, no beast is as dumb as these characters.

So here is the problem with *Raising Arizona* and its ilk: they peddle the mere imbecility of their characters as humor. But though stupidity can be a fine subject for farce or even comedy, it has to be the recognizable stupidity of human beings who have *some* other characteristics besides stupidity. The idiocy of ordinary persons is funny; the idiocy of an idiot is sad and painful. And unrelieved idiocy is merely boring. *Raising Arizona* is an endlessly coarse, un-endingly mindless film, providing a fair idea of infinity in the way Odön von Horváth pinpointed it.

No Ordinary Joe

PRICK UP YOUR EARS

The playwright Joe Orton, who was bludgeoned to death in 1967 by his lover, Kenneth Halliwell, after a 16 years' relationship, is the subject of the most explicitly and exultantly homosexual mainstream film in the English language, *Prick Up Your Ears*. The educated, middle-class Halliwell met the eight-years-younger Orton, a working-class youth of 17 from Leicester, when both were students at the Royal Academy of Dramatic Art. They moved into a small flat paid for by Halliwell, who undertook the education of young John, the disciple subsequently changing his name to Joe, so he wouldn't be confused with John Osborne.

Halliwell, who was good-looking but began losing his hair by age 23, was an unsuccessful novelist, playwright, and (later) collage-ist, who nevertheless was able to stimulate and help develop his lover's talent. Their attempts at joint writing failed; their campy and obscene defacings of library books landed them in jail for six months. There Orton wrote—alone—what was to be his first produced TV play, which he later reworked for the stage, and so began a spectacular playwriting career that left Halliwell far behind.

Sexually, too, Joe surpassed Kenneth, who wasn't cut out for the life of promiscuous pickups, which Orton wallowed in more and more. This may have been partly owing to Ken's bourgeois upbringing (though neither was Orton's family, with the exception of sister Leonie, sympathetic to Joe's activities), partly to his fading looks and waning sexual powers, partly to his involvement with and investment in Joe, whom he did not want to lose. Above all, however, Halliwell envied his lover's growing success, wealth, and fame, even as he was sexually jealous of him.

Although Ken acted as secretary and housekeeper to Joe, he was mostly the older wife losing her hold on a younger, more successful husband. Ken made scenes at parties Joe took him to, bored or alienated the show-business and society figures Orton moved among, took profuse sedatives, and sought (as well as avoided) medical and psychiatric help. He was a fiasco and knew it, for all his assistance with Joe's plays and life. In the fear that Joe would drop him—a fear nurtured, by the extremely outspoken diary Joe kept leaving around for him to read, Halliwell took a hammer, went up to his sleeping lover, and methodically bashed his head to a pulp. Then he calmly stripped naked, swallowed 22 Nembutals with grapefruit juice, and died easily and much faster than Orton, whose brains and blood bespattered the walls Halliwell had covered with his photo-collages. This homosexual *Liebestod* was not of the Tristan and Isolde variety.

You get a sense of how the movie—based on the biography by

John Lahr, with a screenplay by Alan Bennett (playwright, scenarist, and Beyond the Fringer), and directed by Stephen Frears (of, rather overratedly, *My Beautiful Laundrette* fame)—errs or cheats from the very way it handles the murder-suicide. In the movie, Halliwell hammers away at his lover's back—not, as in reality, his head: It was Orton's brain, not his body, that he especially envied and desired. And, of course, there is absolutely no evidence for his lovingly muttering, "Joe! . . . John!" after the murder. And, like Lahr's equally mediocre biography, the movie begins with that murder, then moves back in time, and works up to—in fuller detail—the murder again. The pretense of explaining the social and psychological causes allows for much sexual and sensational exploitation, and the murder, which we get coming and going, crowns it all.

Just what is the film trying to say? At first, it uses a quasi-documentary structure, ostensibly chronicling how John Lahr (played by Wallace Shawn, who can't act but looks like Lahr, only worse) researches Orton's life to write the biography. Very sporadically, we get glimpses of Lahr dopily questioning people, notably Peggy Ramsay, the scrappy theatrical agent who helped make Orton a success, and members of Orton's family. This spurious and disruptive technique is soon abandoned, but not before it has served two tendentious purposes.

A parallel is implied between the heterosexual marriage of the American John Lahr and Anthea, his wealthy, upper-class English wife, and the homosexual quasi-marriage of Orton and Halliwell. The suggestion is that the same envy and rivalry obtain in both; so we are shown the Lahrs collaborating on the Orton biography (which in fact is credited to John alone, though Anthea doubtless helped), and also how Anthea sulks and carries on because John is getting all the glory. (Lindsay Duncan, who plays her, is much too good for the role.) We are not shown the Lahrs' son, however, lest the balance swing toward heterosexual unions.

The second implication is that bourgeois respectability—whether as practiced by Anthea and her stuffy mother on the upper rungs, or, up to a point by Halliwell on the lower—doesn't have a patch on the unencumbered, freewheeling fun of Orton's life, complete with orgies in public lavatories and Moroccan vacations where one revels with any number of boy prostitutes. The lower classes, as embodied by various lesser Ortons as well as by the couple on the ground floor of the house in Islington where Joe and Ken shared a last, still very modest flat, seem equally frustrated and edgy, as well as nosy and meddlesome; the elder Ortons, in fact, are shown living in a homemade inferno.

Contrariwise, all the casual homosexual relationships, notwithstanding Ken's jealous inveighing against Joe's promiscuity, are depicted as adventuresome and satisfying despite the odd narrow escape from that tool of hypocrisy and oppression, the police. Even where the scenario more or less follows Orton's diaries—now published, then available in large chunks from Lahr's biography, whose mainstay they were—there are some significant changes. Thus the debauch in "a little *pissoir*" on the Holloway Road, which involved Orton and eight strangers, took place in darkness because "somebody had taken the bulb away." In the film, there are several bulbs that get unscrewed in an elaborate choreography ("put out the light and then put out the light") involving lifts and going up on *pointes*—though what goes up must go down—and the whole thing takes on a romantic balletic quality. Similarly, the film invents a scene in which Joe loses his virginity to Ken as they watch on TV the coronation of Queen Elizabeth II (very jolly and iconoclastic, that!).

The problem with all this is that it mistakenly turns actual life into a cruel farce in the manner of an Orton play. Certainly that is how Orton perceived life, as his diaries make abundantly clear. A typical episode reported in them has Orton absconding from his mother's funeral with the corpse's dentures, only to hand them later, backstage, to a horrified actor about to go on in *Loot* in a scene involving comic business with *his* dead mother's dentures: "Here, I thought you'd like the originals." (This incident is, needless to say, in the film.) Oscar Wilde, from whom Orton learned so much, claimed that nature imitates art; it took Orton, however, to put that precept into action. And Alan Bennett contributes his own tuppennyworth. Thus to the factual scene in which Leonie Orton mixes the dead lovers' ashes, he adds this bit: LEONIE: "I think I am putting in more of Joe than of Ken." PEGGY RAMSAY: "It's a gesture, dear, not a recipe." Which doesn't even make minimal sense: Obviously one transfers the entire content of one urn into the other.

Unfortunately, what works in absurdist stage comedy does not work in a screen biography. The snuffing out of a gifted playwright's life so near the beginning of his dazzling career is humanly and artistically too terrible a loss to be laughingly digested along with irreverent jokes and casual copulations. Moreover, the film makes the life seem too easy, as if Orton had gone from success to success;

in fact, he also had some flops and other setbacks. Most disturbing of all is the inescapable feeling in the viewer of watching a film that would not have been made but for that grisly ending and the excuse for depicting explicit homosexual acts.

Gary Oldman's performance as Orton, whom he physically resembles, is an unqualified triumph; Vanessa Redgrave is fine as Peggy, and there's solid work from the entire supporting cast, save Wallace Shawn. A graver error is the miscasting of the talented Alfred Molina as Halliwell—a handsome man portrayed by a hulking cross between Lee J. Cobb and Peter Lorre. Was Molina cast to add a comic element to the film? Or was his goofy appearance meant to justify Orton's infidelities? Or are there some special, private reasons? By making the Orton-Halliwell relationship jokier than it actually was, the film gives up a further chance to be something more than a giggly whine about the heterosexual world's incomprehension of homosexuals and its allegedly fatal consequences.

Will Kids Be Kids?

RIVER'S EDGE; MY LIFE AS A DOG

The trouble with American moviemaking is that it is virtually impossible to turn out an honest piece of work any more. Costs have escalated well beyond sky-high (call it Warren-Beatty-and-Dustin-Hoffman-high), and sufficient returns are possible only if you can capture either the total youth audience or a fair cross-section of all possible audiences: young and old, urban and rural, illiterate and educated, assuming that the last-named category still exists. In the first case, you have to start with something infantile and stick to it as close as a Siamese twin; in the second, you begin as a whirling dervish trying to confront viewers from all points on the horizon, and end up dizzily staggering, exhausted, lost.

Take the case of what at least tries to be an adult movie—although, of course, with much of it aimed at the youth audience—*River's Edge*. Directed by Tim Hunter, whose earlier film, *Tex*, was straight youth exploitation, and written by Neil Jimenez when still in his early twenties, *River's Edge* tries to be an honest look at Middle American kids unmoored and drifting into disaster. It begins by focusing on a 12-year-old, Tim (why does he bear the director's name?); with his long hair, earring, and baby fat, we cannot at first glance tell what sex he is, though there is little doubt of his being up to no good. In fact, this grey dawn, he is pitching his sister's favorite doll into the river. The locale, although the story is based on events in a Northern California high school, is left deliberately indeterminate. As Tim looks across to the other bank, he sees Samson, alias John, a huge, fat 16-year-old, sitting in front of something white and letting out strangulated howls.

The something white is the nude body of 14-year-old Jamie, whom John has raped and strangled. The film will return to that body in progressive stages of discoloration as to a visual and moral refrain. But is it truly moral? Or is that body too sensuously perfect for an adolescent, too lovingly and, later, compulsively dwelt on? In any case, we are in the midst of moral quicksand. The implication is that Tim's drowning of his sister's doll is somehow tantamount to John's raping and killing his girlfriend. Is this meant to humanize John's guilt? The explanation we get later from John is that the act gave him a sense of total control; from Layne, the leader of this high-school gang, that Jamie had said something insulting about John's mother. Or is the meaning, conversely, that Tim is a budding murderer, a thesis later events tend to confirm? In any case, Tim won't squeal—or "nark"—if John will help him get some dope. So they're off to see Feck, their dealer.

Feck, as crazy as only Dennis Hopper can make him, is another problem with the movie. A one-legged former biker still hiding out since his killing of his girlfriend twenty years ago, Feck now lives like a hermit with Ellie, a life-size rubber doll, for sole sexual companionship, his dope and gun ever at the ready. When he and John compare notes on girlfriend-killing, it emerges that Feck shot his girl (a manlier way of doing it?), and that *he* did it out of love. "I strangled mine," John declares. "Did you love her?" Feck persists. "She was okay," John allows, and also concedes that he must be a psycho. Are the filmmakers saying that Feck is a better man than John? That his crime is nobler than that feckless riparian strangling? Or is it just a matter of fashions in murder: yesterday's crime of passion superseded by today's anomic *acte gratuit*?

Anomie is the principal theme here. John's high-school chums don't believe that he offed Jamie. (The film, by the way, cheats by never showing us her family.) So when, led by John and Layne, they go to view that voluptuous and unmarred corpse only just beginning to turn blue in the lips, Layne has to poke it with a stick to believe it is dead. "This is unreal, completely unreal. It's

like some fucking movie." The joke, if it is one, is that it is *real*,
more or less as it happened in Milpitas, California, where 12 kids
in the know did not nark on the killer for two days. But what is
like some movie is Layne, the leader, as played by Crispin Glover
who also struck me as the weakest link as the father in *Back to
the Future*. Sporting a black ski cap, black leather, and long, flut-
tering black locks, he speaks in a preposterous, whiny singsong
accompanied by effete, often frantic arm and body movements.
This is a stoned, juvenile version of the Jack Palance character in
Shane. Unreal, man!

Meanwhile, no one is too badly shocked by the murder. The
girls, pretty Clarissa and earthy Maggie, vaguely fascinated by the
thought of being raped and strangled, toy with calling the police,
and quickly desist. Layne declares that both Jamie and John were
friends, but you can help only the one still living. The argument
for hiding and helping John is bought, except, eventually, by Matt,
Tim's elder brother, the conscience of the group. Yet with his un-
kempt hair, sullen face, and mumbling speech, Matt is not markedly
apart from the rest. He argues bitterly with his mother (a belated
hippie), fights with her live-in lover, and, when mom goes to pieces,
has to act the paterfamilias. When he gives Tim a long-overdue
thrashing, the boy (almost too well played by Joshua Miller) vows
to kill him.

The kids drink, smoke pot, shoplift; by way of culture (or mythol-
ogy, or religion), they have rock and television. Looking at her dead
friend, Clarissa muses, "I cried when the guy in *Brian's Song* died.
Why can't I cry for Jamie?" What arouses Clarissa is an ex-activist
teacher who keeps telling his students about the glories of taking to
the streets in the sixties. They listen with apathy or shout him down
with obscenities (which he calmly tolerates) or, in Clarissa's case,
gaze at him adoringly. It is not clear how *he* responds to Clarissa,
an angel with a bestial mouth, not unlike that of Feck's doll.

Clarissa (well played by Ione Skye Leitch) seduces the lethargic
Matt into spending a night with her in the park. The sexual bout
in a sleeping bag, for which they hardly remove any clothing, is
singularly joyless; Clarissa is promptly tired, and when Matt craves
a little maternal affection from her, she counsels sleep. Meanwhile
Tim and his best buddy and coeval roam the nocturnal streets in a
stolen car and with a purloined gun in search of Matt, whom Tim
wants to kill. When asked, "Why are you two such delinquents?"
Tim's prefab answer is, "Because of our fucked-up childhoods."

What grown-ups we do see, rather sketchily, tend to justify Tim's glib sneer. *River's Edge*, to give it its due, spares no one. But it does dawdle or wander off, or underline too heavily from time to time, as well as remain a bit one-sided: Society is not shown in its full rivenness between the values of Norman Rockwell and Norman Mailer. Yet that may be too much to ask. There certainly is know-how in the dialogue of Neil Jimenez and in the cinematography of Frederick Elmes, who shows that, free of David Lynch, he can do much better than the poster art of *Blue Velvet*.

For all its earnestness, though, *River's Edge* is inferior to a Swedish film about adolescence, *My Life as a Dog*, by Lasse Hallström from an autobiographical novel by Reidar Jonsson (who collaborated on the script), exquisitely shot by Bo Widerberg's cameraman, Jörgen Persson. It tells of 12-year-old Ingemar, whose father is loading bananas in South America, mother is dying of TB, older brother bullies him, and dog is taken away from him. Ingemar hates being sent to rusticate in a southern-Swedish village with a sweet simpleton of an uncle, but consoles himself with gazing at the star-strewn sky while meditating on assorted horror stories he gleans from the papers.

In the village, he meets eccentric adults and nervy children, and has adventures involving soccer, boxing, sex and even the beginning of love for a tomboy whose nascent breasts he helps tape down so she can still be one of the boys. The adventures are jolly or wry, funny or wistful, and only rarely verge on cuteness. From Milpitas, California, in the eighties to rural Sweden in the late fifties it is, of course, a quantum backslip. Yet here, too, as well as back in town with the dying mother, there is suffering and anguish, and a kid may well resort to such a comic-symbolic remedy as pretending to be a dog.

Ingemar, compellingly played by Anton Glanzelius—an ageless, unsentimental child—is a racy mixture of decent and mischievous impulses; his faintly ghoulish nocturnal ruminations, like his daytime moments of wildness, are relieved by zesty humor. The film has that touching toughness I associate with Jules Renard's *Poil de carotte* (the novel more than the Duvivier movie): Even the handling of the mother's growing abstractedness, distance, and death refuses to beg for tears. There is a mature, mellow humanity about *My Life as a Dog* that neither the gee-whiz cutesiness nor the hell-bent rawness of its various American counterparts can begin to equal.

Ishtar

Everything is relative in this world, even criminal waste. When Michael Cimino spent $40 million on the god-awful *Heaven's Gate*, it caused the collapse of United Artists; when Francis Ford Coppola spent a similar sum on the somewhat better *Apocalypse Now*, he bankrupted his own American Zoetrope studio. Along comes Elaine May with Dustin Hoffman and Warren Beatty as stars (and the latter as producer, too) in a $51-million disaster called *Ishtar*, and though there is some finger-wagging and an acid review or two, where is the much-needed chorus of disgust?

Ishtar was meant as a takeoff on all those Crosby-Hope-Lamour *Road to . . .* movies, when the road had never a care or a Kerouac. But what could Miss May, the writer-director, have been thinking of? It was easy enough to spoof the Morocco of Valentino or Josef Von Sternberg. But if you invent the imaginary country of Ishtar, which by some geographical hocus-pocus becomes the buffer between the Western world and Qaddafi's Libya, and is ruled by a corrupt emir supported by our government, it is not quite enough to have two no-talent American musicians rattling around and getting into scrapes. There has to be genuine political satire, for which, Allah knows, we have more need than ever.

What is particularly depressing about the movie world is the magic power associated with a Big Name. Let someone have a sizable success once, and it doesn't matter how many failures follow apace, how many companies go bust because of him, how many crimes he commits (without going to jail, or barely); he can, henceforth, fail only upward—the Begelman Syndrome. Guy McElwaine, the chairman of Columbia Pictures (since dismissed, but surely about to resurface in comparable or greater splendor), bought the idea of *Ishtar* with, reputedly, nary a word on paper at a projected budget of $28 million—a rather hefty sum even today, but not quite the road to hell.

That, however, was reckoning without three gigantic egos, or what you might call threegomania. Aljean Harmetz's story in the *New York Times* about the making of the film was more hilarious than anything in *Ishtar*, which, by the way, was the name of the Babylonian goddess of love; after this movie, she might have to stand for self-love. Hoffman and Beatty each received between five and six million, with Beatty paid extra for producing; but that, gross as

it is, is not the worst of it. Miss May's misplaced perfectionism, seconded by the fanaticism of her cinematographer, Vittorio Storaro,
reveled in reshooting sequences (some of them forty or fifty times)
whose possible imperfection was as nothing to the staggering deficiencies of the grand plan. She ended up with a picture, part of
it shot in Morocco, that does not display anything looking like $51
million on the screen, but that would be just as wrong—overblown,
pretentious, top-heavy—if it did.

The film is really two films for the price of four: one about how
these two wretched songsmiths got together in New York, and one
about what befalls them on a booking in North Africa, the only
thing other than Nicaragua their disgusted agent (well played by
Jack Weston) could get them. The deliberately rotten pop songs are
not especially funny, first, because nowadays a parody can sound no
sillier than the real thing, and, second, because Hoffman and especially Beatty make badness seem more pitiful than amusing. And
no comic idea is really explored: Hoffman is a fake ladykiller, of
which nothing is made; Beatty a Texas nerd, hopeless with women,
of which nothing is made either. His feeble Texas accent comes and
goes, and how much comic mileage can you get out of such things
as Hoffman's prolonged attempt to teach Beatty that the word is
schmuck, not *smuck*, without ever succeeding?

There are a few funny lines and, when we reach North Africa,
even a couple of funny scenes—one involving a blind camel, the
other Hoffman's desperate attempt to pass as an Arab interpreter
with odd bits of Hebrew and doubletalk. There is visual fun when
our heroes, lost in the desert, are beak-smackingly contemplated by
some circumambulating vultures, and Charles Grodin is delightful
as a yuppified CIA operative who can make Realpolitik feel like a
game of squash. So much for *Ishtar*'s assets.

Elaine May is simply unable to follow through on a comic idea—
say, on the device of an ancient map and a prophecy that would
make our two bumblers the messengers of God and igniters of a
religious war. Even the political intrigue between Moscow and *their*
Arabs and Washington and *our* Arabs, with the two schmucks, or
smucks, caught in the middle, is either too muddled or not muddled
enough to pay off. Action scenes involving crowds are, moreover,
beyond Miss May's directorial ken. Hoffman manages to hold his
own pretty much, but Beatty seems to have become bleached out
both inwardly and outwardly. Isabelle Adjani, playing a beautiful
Arab Communist agent disguised as a boy (hence the numerous

jokes about her being mistaken for a boy whore), looks like nothing, which is most unusual for her, and acts like nothing, which is rather less so.

We have, then, a fiasco as good as any, and quite a bit costlier. But because reviewers are either dazzled by the blaze of a $51-million funeral pyre on which three big names are immolating themselves, or intoxicated by the headiest hype in some time, the wretched film is hanging in for the nonce. The only real laugh I got was from the report that, for a while, Beatty, Hoffman, and Miss May were working separately and at great expense, each with a personal editor, to come up with his or her version of a final cut. It would have been an interesting marketing device to play each version two days a week and, on the seventh, all three dogs in a row.

Nose Dive

ROXANNE

Is *Cyrano de Bergerac*, updated to America today, still possible? Steve Martin, who wrote the script of *Roxanne* and plays the hero—C. D. Bales, the fire chief of Nelson, an imaginary ski resort in Washington (shot in Nelson, a real ski resort in British Columbia)—obviously thinks so. I would say that in an age when chivalry is dead and plastic surgery prospering, the story no longer makes sense. Martin has solved the problem of chivalry by turning a piece of bittersweet heartbreak into a hearty comedy complete with happy ending; as for C. D.'s nose, though big enough to serve as the beginners' ski jump, it has apparently been bobbed already and is—for some mumbled, pseudo-scientific reason—by now inoperable. I don't buy either of these solutions: A C. D. who gets his Roxanne in the end, and whose only problem is how to kiss without his nose getting in the way, is no Cyrano—hardly even a Jimmy Durante.

So the nose stays the same, but everything else is pared down to puny, unheroic dimensions. The noble company of Gascon Cadets is now a bunch of Keystone firemen, volunteers who barely know a hose from a nose; Christian is Chris, a professional firefighter imported to bolster the volunteers, but also a stupid, illiterate lug who vomits from fright when the classy Roxanne addresses him; and Roxanne herself is a liberated astronomy student on summer vacation in sleepy Nelson, where she expects to track a comet she has discovered through a telescope hardly bigger than the smitten fire chief's proboscis. Some shreds of Rostand's tale surface now and then, but what has been substituted is a triple snub to that big-nosed, great-hearted, spotless-plumed hero and his story.

Chris actually gets to spend a night with Roxanne thanks to C. D.'s ministrations, but his performance is a decrescendo, and he promptly falls for a more congenial, undemanding barmaid, with whom he goes off to become a croupier at Lake Tahoe—so much for that visiting fireman. And C. D. himself, for all his verbal and physical prowess, is only a nostril-deep farceur whose suffering rings false, and whom a friend, Dixie, the local café proprietress, conveniently pushes into Roxanne's arms. I guess she represents the ragged remains of Ragueneau, and Shelley Duvall is wasted on the part.

There are a few clever snippets, notably a fight in which C. D. trounces two golf-club-wielding louts with a tennis racket for a sword, and the opening sequence, wherein C. D. walks from his house to the fire station and is photographed in long shot and head on, so that his nose appears, for the longest while, normal. Martin knows how to deliver a funny line when, on occasion, there is one, and we still get the nose tirade—now partly Rostand, partly Martin (more the latter) and still fun, though not followed by a *ballade*-cum-duel. *Some* of Martin's physical comedy is droll, too—e.g., his climbing up and down Roxanne's house less like a human fly than like a human flea. But hardly any of the firemen's shenanigans can elicit so much as a chortle, and that goes also for Michael J. Pollard's unimpressive comeback as one of the troop. Rick Rossovich must be the most unprepossessing Chris(tian) ever, but with quite a (real) schnozz of his own. Is this a deliberate joke, or Steve Martin's vanity at work in the casting? Daryl Hannah, as Roxanne, is better than usual, though she hasn't thus far set a very high mark for herself to surpass.

What is most disconcerting about the film is that it was directed by Fred Schepisi, who was a great director in Australia, but seems to have gotten the bends when he came up from down under. It is not that he does anything particularly wrong; it's just that he doesn't do anything especially right. Schepisi's Australian cinematographer, Ian Baker, fares much better: The views of Nelson nestled on the mountainside make a day in the Rockies more inviting than a night in Roxanne's bed. But Schepisi's Aussie composer, Bruce Smeaton, flails forlornly amid musical banalities.

In all fairness, I must report an amusing final fight between C. D.

and Roxanne, and, I repeat, scattered funny lines such as "What is a light year?"—"Same as a regular year, only it has less calories." Even this, however, could be improved with *"fewer* calories."

Twice-Bitten Bullet

FULL METAL JACKET

In his *Esquisse d'une psychologie du cinéma* (1976), André Malraux wrote: "The silent film knew sections [*les parties*]; the sound film no longer knows them, and editors encounter a permanent obstacle there. For the sound film does not want empty spaces and gives narrative continuity pride of place among its means of conveying action." I am always leery of theory, even if it calls itself psychology, and I don't know whether I would agree with Malraux in a blanket way; yet his statement surely applies to Stanley Kubrick's *Full Metal Jacket*, a film in two sections that falls apart largely because of that bipartite construction.

Though I haven't read Gustav Hasford's Vietnam novel, *The Short-Timers*, on which the film is based (screenplay by Kubrick, Michael Herr—the author of *Dispatches*—and Hasford), I gather that it has the same structure. This is a film based, in effect, on two novellas. One shows how a group of Marine recruits on Parris Island gets the basest kind of basic training from the relentlessly jeering, physically brutalizing, and probably sadistic gunnery sergeant, Hartman. The principals are Hartman; an unfortunate overweight recruit whom Hartman renames, as he does everyone in some cruel way, Pyle—after Gomer, but with a scatological pun; and Private (also renamed) Joker, whose wits and savvy make Hartman appoint him squad leader, and who is clearly Hasford's alter ego.

Of these three, only Joker shows up again in the longer second part, which concerns an incident during the Tet offensive; even of the lesser characters, only one or two reappear to continue being lesser. It has been argued that just as a book can consist of two related novellas, so can a movie. But a book is not consumed like a movie: in one continuous sitting and at its own imposed tempo—an unbroken impetus providing that kind of Aristotelian unity needed to keep our attention from flagging. There have been movies made up of separate tales—e.g., the ones based on three or four Maugham stories—but where are they now? Kubrick, however, wants to play for keeps. And three or four unrelated tales may even work slightly better than two that lay claim to an obscure, elusive connection.

And a connection can be forced onto the film: that the second part shows the former recruits as the efficient, ruthless combat machines they have been turned into. However (unlike, I hear, in the book), the connection does not arise from within, nor is it demonstrated that the most brutal soldiers fare better (or worse) than the others. And yet *Full Metal Jacket*—the very title, literally referring to the hard-metal coating over the soft lead core of a bullet, is mainly symbolic—comes across as a film that desperately wants to make a statement, if only it knew what.

The 45-minute opening section chronicles how Pyle is bullied from an inept meatball into a defective killing machine that devastates the wrong targets. This grimly ironic warning about the double-edgedness of violence was already well known to Hannibal when his fighting elephants turned around and trampled his own men. To make this come across freshly and plausibly, Pyle should not have been so grossly overweight and underbrained that he never would have made the Marine Corps: unable to make his bed, lace his boots, do a few pushups. And Sergeant Hartman (well played, and partly improvised, by a genuine Marine Corps veteran, Lee Ermey) is too unrelievedly beastly, which may be true to life but won't quite do as art. (Well, Iago, of course; but, except to himself perhaps, Kubrick isn't Shakespeare.) As for Joker, he comes perilously close to being a cipher. Hence the supposedly tragic climax of this section provides no more than some melodramatic horror, however artfully managed.

Yes, the cinematography by Douglas Milsome and Kubrick's way of shooting the grueling bestialization and sexual infantilization of the men in boot camp have suggestions—with the color-drained palette and extreme, head-on closeups, as well as obsessive Steadicam dogging shots (what else can I call them?)—of a perverted training film or a slightly unhinged documentary. But what do such touches, as well as some horrific bits of black humor, contribute when appended to characters who do not possess something that, however black or blackly humorous, can be called a soul? And it is quite a *tour de force* to have most of the first section's dialogue be a viciously comic series of insult monologues of Hartman's, sparing no one, not even Jesus Christ, as the sergeant leads his "maggots'" in a mock Christmas carol. But what good is this if he doesn't have even as much humanity as his counterparts in such B or C movies as *An Officer and a Gentleman* and *Heartbreak Ridge*?

The film lacks a human center. For in the second section, things are similarly lopsided. Joker is first seen as a *Stars and Stripes* reporter in what promises to be an interesting sendup of military journalism, but forthwith he is off to cover the Tet offensive, and we get the routine battlefield satire. Joker has BORN TO KILL emblazoned on his helmet, but his fatigues display a peace button. When an irate senior officer asks the meaning of such political Janus-headedness, he gets a wise-guy answer: "The duality of man. The Jungian thing, Sir." "Whaat??" There is a variety of sick jokes: "Inside every gook, there is an American trying to get out." Or: "How do you manage to shoot women and children?" "Easy. You don't lead them so far." Or, translated into action, a soldier from a helicopter grinningly shooting peasants at work while his buddy next to him vomits. And there is a whole contrived sequence in which documentary filmmakers interview front-line soldiers about what they are fighting for and get answers such as. "Freedom? If I'm going to get my balls shot off for a word, it will be 'poontang.'"

Finally Joker joins a mission (it used to be called "search and destroy," but has just been euphemized into "sweep and clear") with a squad containing one of his boot-camp buddies. Here things get exciting, and the encounter with a diabolically skillful sniper in the ruins of Hué, who kills any number of the men by installments, is staged and photographed with enormous skill, suspense, and terror; but the ending (which, alas, I must not reveal) presents a supposed dilemma that is no dilemma at all, merely a belated attempt to cram some specious humanity into a film that, shall we say, misfires.

For this is Kubrick's fatal flaw: He is a master technician, but at a loss when it comes to people. In his earlier movies, there was sporadic, rudimentary feeling for human beings; the later ones, however, showed no such concern, down to their very casting, e.g., in *Barry Lyndon*: Can one really empathize with the marital problems of the likes of Ryan O'Neal and Marisa Berenson? In *Full Metal Jacket*, Vincent D'Onofrio is good enough to make us commiserate with Pyle, compulsively smiling while being abused, then abused some more for smiling. But gifted as Matthew Modine is, Joker does not command an emotional response: The part has no depth, no reverberation, no meaning. When soldiers die, the piercing bullets and gushing blood are reproduced with chilling authenticity, but eliciting shudders is not the same as eliciting pity.

And what makes Kubrick shoot this in a war-ravaged English slum, furbished with two hundred palm trees imported from Spain, rather than on an authentic location? Is it laziness, arrogance, or insecurity? He cannot show us jungle warfare, and even the architecture and climate, the very texture of this war, is askew, compromised. The aim may be greater universality, so to speak, but the result is a certain depersonalization. Even the daintily built but war-hardened Vietnamese whores, and our boys' reaction to them, are viewed too superficially, they seem as adventitious as the scattered street and storefront signs, intended as earnests of topographical authenticity. Probably the most original contribution Kubrick makes is the shoddy pop-rock score with which he deliberately further debases the action. At crucial moments we get "Woolly Bully" performed by Sam the Sham and the Pharoahs [*sic*], "Surfin' Bird" by The Trashmen, and such.

Kubrick's main achievement in his films, early and late, has been a sense of alienation, most clearly felt in *Dr. Strangelove, 2001,* and *A Clockwork Orange.* I do not knock this: Alienation is certainly a major, perhaps even *the* major, element in our recent history. And portents suggest that it is here to stay, provided only that we do. But no matter how effectively Kubrick portrays the murderous robotization of Parris Island, no matter how swinishly alienated some of those "animal mothers" in Vietnam appear, whether they're killing or joking, I never feel—and neither, I bet, does the audience—the essential *de te fabula narrat.* From the reaction of moviegoers around me, I concluded that so far from recognizing themselves in these characters, they did not even recognize the bestiality as bestiality.

The Whistle Blower

There is something curiously slapdash about three British movies that have opened here recently, as there is also about a fourth, somewhat better one, *Withnail and I,* by Bruce Robinson, which I cannot review because, in a sold-out theater, I sat in front of someone who kept loudly talking to himself. Now, you can sometimes stop two-way conversations, but someone gleefully chatting with himself is clearly beyond reproof. The interesting thing, though, is that no one else seemed to mind this nut; who wants to hear everything said in a film, anyway? And, indeed, one of the things most recent British movies have in common is a great deal of incomprehensible lower-class and regional speech. It makes me wish I could catch them abroad, with subtitles.

The Whistle Blower is about the way GCHQ (a branch of British counter-espionage) kills off some of its lesser employees in the wake of one chap's defection to the Soviet Union. Some are suspected of collusion with the defector; others are dangerous because they might expose fascistic tactics within GCHQ or blow the whistle on a very high functionary who is indeed a traitor, but whose exposure might cause panic, to say nothing of queering GCHQ even further with the CIA, which is exerting pressure on British counter-espionage to tighten its security.

There is considerable potential in such a theme, and, for all I know, John Hale's novel, on which the film is loosely based, may have realized it. The film, however, was in immediate trouble when it engaged the screenwriting services of Julian Bond, who made such a mess of *The Shooting Party*, and whose principal work has been in TV mini-series. And again when Bond and his producer declared that "we wanted to go for a really positive ending." In the event, the ending is far from positive—though by no means honest, either—and the verdict on what precedes it must be largely negative, I fear.

One problem is that the film seems to have been edited down draconically, so that major plot elements are either truncated into inscrutability or simply missing. For example, the hero's son, Bob, who works as a Russian translator for GCHQ, with which he is getting progressively disenchanted, has a serious affair with Cynthia, the wife of his colleague Allen Goodburn. But we see Goodburn either not at all or barely (on one viewing, I cannot be sure) until Cynthia finds him slumped over dead in his car in their garage. So ineptly is the film made—or edited—that, because of their physical similarity, we at first think the dead man is Bob. Then it is not clear who he is, certainly not that he is Cynthia's husband; still less how Bob figures out that foul play was involved.

When Frank Jones, Bob's father, is about to learn from Pickett, an unsavory left-wing journalist, exactly whom the now dead Bob suspected of being behind it all, Pickett announces over the phone that he cannot name the person other than to Frank's face, and arranges a meeting. But if you suspect your phone of being tapped you don't say that much over it either, and, sure enough, driving to the tryst, Pickett is killed in a strange accident. This, and much like it, makes no sense. Where the film is not cut down to the point of nonsense, it is written or directed (by Simon Langton, a TV director) nonsensically.

Again, when Frank goes to see the traitorous muckamuck to extract from him a written confession, we see the panjandrum take out a sheet of stationery from a drawer that contains a gun. He proceeds to write and sign a confession while Frank turns his back on him to examine his rare books and costly bibelots. So why doesn't the traitor pull out that gun and perhaps even shoot? Instead, he hands over the paper and only then draws the gun. In the ensuing scuffle, the aristocratic swine (oh, how class-conscious British movies still are—in reverse) shoots himself dead. Tell me another.

Before the shooting, Frank accuses the bigwig of being a Communist while enjoying all the benefits of a British peerage. Why? The answer is a muddled speech of which only two words make some shade of sense: "aesthetic reasons." Something could be made of this if the moviemakers had any imagination and culture, or had been willing to credit the audience with some. But why bother when the average moviegoer is only too happy to assume the worst about aristocrats and eggheads portrayed by the likes of John Gielgud, and to hell with logical, psychological—or even aesthetic—explanations.

And so it goes in this movie, in which the best thing is the acting, especially that of Michael Caine as Frank. Always a good to excellent performer, Caine has tended to be kept by his material in the merely good category. Here he has his chance. No matter how preposterous a scene may be—as when Frank is kidnapped by GCHQ to a posh party, where they condescendingly spill the beans to him while telling him how powerless he is—Caine maintains dignity and credibility. His unerring way of finding the exact expressions and tones of voice with which to convey utmost fury and grief, while never losing heroic control of his speech and face—except, now and then, in a faint tremor or spasm: *that* is acting. The film has appreciable resonance in these days of the Iran-Contra hearings, but the real reason for seeing it is the mark of Caine imprinted on it.

Dark Eyes

The Russian director Nikita Mikhalkov and the Italian star Marcello Mastroianni have been gravitating toward each other for years.

Mikhalkov who adores Fellini's *8 ½* and resees it before he starts shooting any film, perceived the actor as the archetypal Italian lover and Fellini exponent. The actor, who saw Mikhalkov's *Slave of Love*, *Oblomov*, and *Unfinished Piece for Player Piano* (from Chekhov's *Platonov*), loved the atmosphere of not so much *dolce* as bittersweet *far niente* in those films, even as Mikhalkov is drawn to Western freedom of expression and lavishness. And so, as Hardy says in "The Convergence of the Twain," about the *Titanic* and the fatal iceberg, "consummation comes, and jars two hemispheres." In the movie *Dark Eyes*, watered-down Chekhov meets freeze-dried Fellini in an encounter that should jar both East and West.

It is a film of great opulence even in its locations—Italian spas, gardens, villas, Russian villages, churches, palaces, land- and townscapes—shot with eye-dilating, very nearly cloying beauty by Franco di Giacomo. No expense was spared by the production designers, Mario Garabuglia and Alexander Adabachian (one of the scenarists—beware of movies co-scripted by designers), the costumer Carlo Diappi, and, above all, the producer, Silvia d'Amico Bendico. She is the daughter of Suso Cecchi d'Amico—with Mikhalkov, the third co-scenarist—and one of Italy's most prolific screenwriters. But two hours of ravishing vistas and luxurious interiors cannot make up for that smidgen of intellectual and emotional authenticity nowhere to be found.

Even the film's title is a piece of vulgarity, deriving as it does from the best known and trashiest Russian song, which, moreover, is totally irrelevant here: Elena Sofonova, who plays the heroine, has grey eyes. To accommodate both Mikhalkov's and Mastroianni's fortes, something Russo-Italian had to be concocted. Four Chekhov stories, notably "The Lady with the Lapdog," were dimly drawn on, but mostly it is the three scenarists improvising in what they claim to be the Chekhovian manner. Actually, it is quite un-Chekhovian and utterly unmannerly.

The frame story has a rather slovenly, dilapidated Italian telling his life to a Russian passenger in the dining room of a ship sailing from Greece to Italy. Romano, the narrator, was a modest student of architecture when he married Elisa, an heiress who soon came into her fortune, which made Romano give up all work, to turn into a party clown, a Lothario, a hedonistic lazybones, who, when things get hairy at home, goes off to a spa. At a big party in his house, Romano eludes Elisa (Silvana Mangano), who has just learned that the family fortune may be lost, and a frolicsome mistress (Marthe Keller) to take a siesta. Pursued by the women, he packs himself off to a spa near Pisa, where, after one casual dalliance, he starts another with Anna, an unhappily married young Russian—the lady with the lapdog. Upset by their affair, the innocent Anna escapes to her distant province, leaving behind a passionate letter.

Back home, the letter haunts Romano, who journeys to Russia on the pretext of building a factory there, and manages to overcome bureaucratic opposition to a travel permit. (This is clumsy pseudo-Gogol.) He makes it to Anna's provincial town, where, after some ludicrous contretemps, the pair embrace again in a barn and resolve to marry, but Romano must first (improbably) trek back alone to secure a divorce in Italy—at that time! Confronted with Elisa, he loses his nerve and remains stuck. However, without our being told why and how, he finally left Elisa and has become, we learn, a waiter on this ship. His Russian interlocutor now summarizes *his* story: how, after years of persistent wooing, he managed to persuade an unhappy woman who doesn't love him to marry him. They're on their honeymoon, and she's about to join him and Romano. She is, of course, the woman with the grey—sorry, dark—eyes and we end on a closeup on her, looking not a day or a care older.

To turn Chekhov into O. Henry is bad enough. Chekhov's stories are not tied into neat little packages; rather, they end on ironies, uncertainties, aporias. Further, they are painted with quick little strokes of a dry brush: a wrenching detail here, a teasing wisp of conversation there. Mikhalkov & Co., however, go in for sprawl, lush exoticism, and lots of sight gags (Romano pretending that the mere Russian word *sabatchka*, lapdog, uttered by Anna cures his allegedly suffering legs). How would Chekhov, for whom Stanislavsky was too much, have taken to Mikhalkov?

The Italians are seen as decadent Westerners; the Russians are either slightly less decadent aristocrats or good creatures from the lower orders, including an ecologically concerned veterinarian who is a crushing, gate-crashing bore. Their convivial carousals are much nicer excesses than the Italians' sexual cavortings and balneary hysterics. The scenes at the spa, by the way, doubtless intended as an *hommage* to *8 1/2*, emerge as rather too rich for *Marat/Sade*, what with elderly patients racing about in wheelchairs as if in bumper cars or wallowing in mud baths like Disneyfied pigs, not to mention mealtime with a mountainous soprano yodeling a Rossini aria. Pauline Kael has rightly pointed out Mikhalkov's bungling of details: when Anna fingerpaints a line on the wall with her tears, the design does not evaporate; when a glycerine tear bejewels the corner of Anna's eye, it never rolls off. Not much better is a chorus of happily warbling gypsies riding past Romano's carriage, to be followed by his mother's voice singing a childhood lullaby on the soundtrack as saffron dawn breaks over the tundra. How life-affirming is a three-ring circus?

Even the music by the commonplace Francis Lai is a poor imitation of a Nino Rota score for Fellini. Mastroianni is still charmingly, fecklessly himself, but Mikhalkov does not push him to reveal the depth and daring he is capable of. Silvana Mangano is stylish and striking, Marthe Keller prettily bubbly, but neither has much to do. Only Elena Sofonova, as Anna, manages to contribute something fetching and moving, with little help from the script. There are implausible explanations for Russians hanging around Italy or speaking Italian, but the worst thing is to make Romano strong enough to reach Anna against overwhelming odds, then stupidly abandon her. In Chekhov's "Lady with a Lapdog," the quasi-happy but forlorn ending is much more depressingly true to life. And to think that there already exists a lovely 1959 Russian film by Iosif Heifitz from that story, which makes a mock of Mikhalkov's fatuous supererogation.

Fatal Attraction

Watching *Fatal Attraction* is like observing cinema blithely mutilating itself. Something that begins as an adult, psychological problem film splinters into glittering, schlocky shock effects, few of which make elementary sense, and many of which are stolen from earlier, better movies.

Adrian Lyne, the director, or footbinder, of the film, is one of those hotshots out of British TV commercials, like the Scott brothers, with a wealth of technical knowhow, some low-level intelligence or high-level cunning, and a cavalier contempt for integrity. There could hardly have been more dishonest movies than *Flashdance* and *9½ Weeks*, the latter about a sadomasochistic relationship with S and M excised from its alphabet, partly because feminists at exploratory advance screenings screamed bloody murder. Trashy though it is, *Fatal Attraction* had a rather more compelling ending until audience cards made Lyne and the producers change it to the present absurd and derivative one.

The screenplay by James Dearden, based on a previous short

film of his, now concerns Dan Gallagher, an unremarkable but upwardly mobile New York lawyer, long and happily married to pretty, mundane, uncomplicated Beth, and father to bright, six-year-old Ellen. His firm represents a publishing house, at one of whose parties he meets a provocative, faintly mysterious woman, Alex Forrest, a new editor at the publishers'. Soon after, at an editorial conference about a manuscript presenting legal problems, he meets her again. Beth and Ellen are in the country, it is raining heavily, and Dan and Alex duck into a nearby restaurant. Alex starts seducing Dan, and a no-strings-attached, hot one-night stand ensues, which, what with Beth staying away another day at her parents', and Alex proving devilishly persistent, evolves into a hot two-night stand.

When Dan wants to resume his normal life, and tries to call it affably quits with Alex—she a manifest woman of the world with no dearth of experience, he a monogamous fellow who yielded to an isolated yen—the unexpected happens. Alex, in ways we have noticed, is a bit odd: she now refuses to play by the rules and declines to let wholly go. Later, it also emerges that she is pregnant. In old-time movies, this required only one night's delirium. Now it takes two; otherwise nothing much has changed.

Well, yes, Alex refuses to have an abortion: she is 37, and carries a biological clock inside her along with the fetus; besides, Dan and she were great not only in the sack but also on her kitchen counter and on the floor of the elevator to her loft apartment—where their greed for each other and the film's eagerness to titillate had them fall to it. There is a real problem here: the neurotic, passionate woman who will go to any length to hold on to an ordinary, bedeviled man—slashing her wrists being only a modest beginning. This can happen to any married man, as profuse sympathetic male groans in the audience seemed to attest.

If *Fatal Attraction* had integrity, it would do two things: show equal sympathy for both its main characters, and remain in the realm of the plausible. Instead, it turns Alex into a ravening fury—the kind hell hath no like of—who could never obtain and hold an important editorial job with all the work and responsibility it entails. For Alex seems to have nothing else to do but to hound Dan in ever more bizarre, oppressive, and horrific ways, even as his responses go from the clumsily sympathetic to the exasperated and, finally, angrily retaliatory. What could have been interesting as a tragicomedy of manners, or even as a sourly disturbing view of liberated woman overshooting the mark, turns into a totally unbelievable shocker, with everyone behaving like a dangerous lunatic or a dangerous fool. Even Beth becomes more obtuse, more unforgiving than we can swallow.

But could an honest film about this situation—one in which Alex does not turn into a homicidal psychopath—be made in America today? After all, movies cost so much, and, thanks to our rapidly worsening education and sinking level of culture, audiences crave ever more drastic stimulants. Give them their quota of belly laughs and shrieks, then come up with a preposterous resolution that allows everyone to go home unchallenged and undisturbed to the comforts of oblivion. If movies started making sense, they might as well be life, right?

Though she is not a pretty woman, Glenn Close acts Alex with a sexy swagger and growing persuasiveness as the character gets madder; particularly good is that patronizing, demented, peace-offering smile lined with booby traps. As Dan, Michael Douglas is a credible amalgam of man and boy, sophistication and staidness, with penny-ante experience thrust into a high stakes game. Anne Archer is perfect as the anachronistic, transparent, congenially conjugal Beth, and little Ellen Hamilton Latzen plays Ellen with a minimum of cuteness and truly stunning veracity. But what can they do against a film that has school authorities allowing a perfect stranger, unknown even to Ellen, to pick her up without a note from her parents; that has endangered people not taking obvious precautions, and forgets all about Ellen during a night of terror involving her parents? For all its stylishness, *Fatal Attraction* is a piece of haute couture coming apart at almost every seam.

Even when the film has a genuine insight, such as making a near-murderous fight between Alex and Dan closely resemble their frenzied lovemaking, it does not know what to make of such an aperçu and rushes back to facile laughter and manipulative horror. It gets its shallow effects across, but how much better would be real anxiety than contrived fright.

The Dead

How many times must one let fall on deaf ears the elementary truth that no great work of literature can be turned into a comparable movie? We should all know by now that form is part of the content: a sonnet can't be turned into an epic, a mural can't be translated into a miniature, the most artistic photograph of a statue is nowhere near the statue. In a piece of great fiction, it is the descriptions, reflections, paragraphs, sentences, words, and cadences that make the art, not just plot and dialogue. And what writing leaves to the inner eye and ear is inevitably distorted or oversimplified by transposition for the outer senses. James Joyce's last and greatest story, or novella, "The Dead," is no exception.

Its film version, *The Dead*, is the last work of the multifariously talented John Huston, who once actually managed to make a very good film out of Flannery O'Connor's *Wise Blood*—significantly, however, not her finest or subtlest work. Moreover it is somewhat easier to cut down a short novel to movie format than to expand a story, even as long a one as "The Dead," to full film size. Tony Huston, the screenwriter and John's son, has had to add a passage or two from Joyce's other fiction to eke it out, but that is the least of the film's problems.

The film, like the story, concerns the annual party given (Joyce-lovers note!) on the Feast of the Epiphany by two old spinster sisters, Kate and Julia Morkan, and their middle-aged niece, Mary Jane. All three of them being singers or piano teachers, the large party is a dinner dance-*cum*-musicale. The story reports the feelings and conversations of those present, including Lily, the maid, but principally those of Gabriel Conroy (read: James Joyce), the favorite nephew, a teacher and book reviewer, who is to make the postprandial speech and generally keep order, notably where Freddy Malins, a garrulous, mother-pecked drunk, is concerned. There are oodles of revealing small-talk, tiny provocations and contretemps, and mostly the ruminations of Gabriel, the insecure intellectual unsure about his Irishness and his adored wife, Gretta.

At party's end, after much debating of the relative merits of various famous singers, Bartell D'Arcy, a local tenor, is finally prevailed upon to sing a bit of an Irish air, "The Lass of Aughrim," which puts Gretta, listening to it on the staircase, into a state of frozen melancholy. This arouses the sexual desire of her husband, and Gabriel can hardly wait to get to their Dublin hotel room, which he has rented in order to obviate a long nocturnal journey home. But Gretta now confesses her first love for a 17-year-old boy, Michael Furey, consumptive and in love with her back in

Galway, who, upon hearing she was off to convent school, came out into the icy night to see her once more and caught his death. *He* used to sing that song.

It had been fitfully snowing all day; now it snows through the night. Gabriel, unable to make love to the weepy Gretta and consumed by retroactive jealousy, stands at the window feeling sorry for himself, for her, for Michael Furey, for all the quick and the dead on whom the snow is falling. The end of the story is filled with *lacrimae rerum* and with some of the most exquisite prose written in English. Though Joyce was only 26 and not yet blind, his was already a largely aural sensibility, and the fineness of the story is in the way the language becomes spiritualized from its mundane beginnings, through anticipatory shudders of beauty, into that climactic litany of euphony and compassion.

Until the concluding pages of the story, the film jogs along merrily enough, though a bit cramped by that small house and the one recurrent, Ozu-like establishing shot of a lonely winter street. Huston was too ill to travel to Dublin, and shot instead in a California warehouse, himself confined to a wheelchair and connected to life by tubes, to his cameraman and actors by walkie-talkie. He finished the film in late spring, and a few months later started another, though he died soon thereupon of emphysema without having given up smoking. You must admire such indomitable mulishness, and there is something endearing, too about the film's connection to Galway, where Huston lived twenty of his best years. Yet the movie *The Dead* is small potatoes, if not a potato famine, to the story.

The film's end has Gabriel, in voice over, speaking the famous paragraphs, while the camera catches appropriate wintry scenes. It looks like a travelogue, the lowliest of cinematic genres, and no match for deathless prose. But all along there has been an inability to cope, as when Gretta stood on the stairs, rapt: "There was grace and mystery in her attitude as if she were a symbol of something. He asked himself what is a woman standing on the stairs in the shadow, listening to distant music, a symbol of." There are all sorts of ironies in this, but the film, which could bustle and chuckle along with the partying, is powerless here.

The Irish actors—mostly imported, some domestic—are good and racy, though Donal Donnelly overdoes Freddy Malins, and Helena Carroll exaggerates Aunt Kate even more. Anjelica Huston, who was born on that farm in Galway, manages the accent well enough, but not Gretta's depth. I especially liked Dan O'Herlihy's Mr. Browne, Rachel Dowling's Lily, and Donal McCann's Gabriel. It's an honorable try all around, with modest pleasures, but *The Dead* will stand as a testimonial to Huston's testy courage, not as the milestone or monument one had hoped for.

Broadcast News

The temptation to overpraise *Broadcast News* is great, but it mustn't lead us into the opposite temptation of underpraising it. I went expecting the worst, for James L. Brooks, who wrote and directed, was similarly responsible for the odious *Terms of Endearment*. Almost as if in reaction to the consummate speciousness of that movie, Brooks here devises a panegyric to honesty, as confused as it is fanatical, that does the film more harm than good. Luckily, there is enough else to save *Broadcast News* from drowning in its self-righteousness.

The central figure is Jane Craig, a producer of network news in Washington, a career woman and job-absorbed perfectionist, not so much sexually liberated as liberated from sex. Her work consumes her; yet sometimes she disconnects the phone to let her emotions—or frustrations—burst out as a quivering mixture of laughter and tears. The rest of the time, Jane is relentless in her pursuit of as much truth as a superficial and gimmicky medium allows; and though she thinks she despises the frills, she secretly enjoys even them. Like her laughter and tears, Jane is a mixed bag, and the more real for it.

To one side of her stands her longtime friend and co-worker, Aaron Altman, Pulitzer Prize–winning on-camera reporter, with great background knowledge, sangfroid, and ready wit, but quite unsuited for his dream of becoming an anchorman. For that, he hasn't the looks, suavity, and pseudo-solicitude. He and his epigrams are not casually charming, not photogenic. So, although Jane and he make a terrific work team and fine platonic friends, he dare not begin to admit his feeling for her.

To Jane's other side is Tom Grunick, Aaron's antithesis: a blond, goodlooking WASP, not very bright but eager to learn, aware of his limitations and not really a bad egg. He knows that his looks and laid-back way of hustling got him where he is—a young Washington anchorman going places—and he is neither arrogant nor falsely modest. He, too, wants Jane, and much as she, reluctantly, ends up reciprocating, something always gets in their way.

Tom, who has to learn everything from Jane and Aaron, ends up coaching his much smarter rival in anchormanship, but it doesn't work. Meanwhile the network, facing severe cutbacks, fires a good many people, even as some few are promoted. And that is what story there is, but it keeps things rolling. *Broadcast News* is not a trenchant satire on television news—and, beyond that, on television—but it is an amused, ironic, often deflating look at what goes on behind the scenes or screens. The writer-director, who used to direct the *Mary Tyler Moore Show*, knows whereof he speaks as long as he sticks to the world of TV; only when he tries to impose some improbable moral laws on his characters does he lose his footing, and the film falters.

But the movie has a lot more going for it than its insider's view. There is consistently clever, often very funny dialogue that makes its points without pushing, sometimes perhaps too subtly for the average moviegoer; there is remarkably smooth direction by Brooks; and there is, not merely in the principal roles, first-rate acting. The only real flaws are a supererogatory prologue (our leads as youngsters) that is forced and cute, and an even more expendable epilogue (our leads years later) that is forced and drab, even though, I am told, Brooks toiled over it for several months.

Dialogue. A woman subordinate, emotionally, to Jane: "I've got to tell you something. Except for socially, you're my role model." An executive, fired in the cutbacks after years of good work, to his boss: "I'm just old enough to be flattered by the term 'early retirement.'" "That's wonderful! Now, if there's anything I can do for you . . ." "I certainly hope you die soon." Her boss, sarcastically, to Jane: "It must be nice to always believe you're the smartest person in the room." To which Jane, vehemently: "No, it's awful." Tom: "I'm no good at what I'm being a success at." The jokes don't shout and gesticulate at you, they stay in character, even if the characters sometimes don't.

As for the acting, Holly Hunter manages admirably to teeter between work-mad sexlessness and nascent feminine longings, also between hoydenishness and winsome vulnerability. She is so tiny and William Hurt so tall that I often felt I was watching a split screen, yet her intensity easily projects into the farthest reaches of the frame. Hurt gives one of his best performances as a fellow in whom good and not so good are so thoroughly scrambled that his every move keeps us guessing, yet we always get something human and credible. Of course, most of this is in the writing, but it requires deft histrionic shading not to let the design down.

Most amazing among the leads is Albert Brooks, a comedian who himself has written, directed, and starred in some funny, underrated movies. His Aaron goes from seeming winner to nice loser, to not so nice loser, to quasi-winner—but always wisecracking—with exceptional poise and faultless timing, never missing or exaggerating a verbal or emotional beat. It is one of the great, seriously comic performances of recent times. No less remarkable, in an unbilled cameo role, is Jack Nicholson as a snooty, inflated New York anchorman. From his first appearance on a TV monitor, and thus at two removes from the movie audience, he has us in stitches, often with a mere look, for every one of his few onscreen seconds. In the strong supporting cast, Joan Cusack stands out as Jane's worshipful assistant.

Brooks has directed with unassertive fluidity, moving the camera around various interiors, notably in Aaron's apartment, with the sort of assurance the best television directors acquire from working in limited spaces in which camera movement is crucial. And no matter how propulsive the pace, he lets his actors breathe, expand, express themselves as if there were all the time of an unending sitcom at their disposal. But I wish he had allowed the ending to remain up in the air, rather than foist on us an unearned, not un- but non-happy ending, which, moreover, is rather self-consciously executed. Michael Ballhaus, the excellent German cinematographer, has given the film the spanking new, almost abrasively antiseptic look of certain TV studios and offices, a setting in which emotional sloppiness can look even funnier or more unsettling.

What keeps *Broadcast News* from making it into the first rank is chiefly an absence of self-irony. What is being held up as morally superior to the rest is never questioned, never analyzed, never considered possibly not so different from what it looks down on. But let us be grateful for a comedy that works, for the most part, handily, without insulting our intelligence or its own maniacalness.

Moonstruck

People are carrying on about how wonderful *Moonstruck* is, and Cher's equine visage nuzzles us from the covers of countless magazines. John Patrick Shanley, the screenwriter for this and *5 Corners* (a film of surpassing weirdness and very little sense)—hitherto an off-Broadway playwright of intermittent promise—grants interviews in which he sounds like D. W. Griffith and Orson Welles rolled together. Norman Jewison, America's most perfectly average director, is hailed for having made a truly charming, bubblingly human film. The whole world has become moonstruck.

Shanley, in his undisciplined way, can create bizarre but not uninvolving blue-collar characters who talk torrentially and behave violently, whether in love, hate, or madness. As a screenwriter—in *Moonstruck* more than in *5 Corners*—he has had to restrain himself somewhat, cutting down on the characters' garrulity, though not on their eccentricity. But, in *Moonstruck* especially, he has also been encouraged to overplay another streak of his—sentimentality—making everybody too lovable by half. This, I suppose, is to be explained by everyone's being working-class Italian, which, as moviegoers know, means some combination of mamma, Mafia, and scratchy Caruso records, though either the second or the third may be downplayed. Shanley repeatedly writes about lower-class Italians, whether because that is his maternal heritage or because the Italians can serve as convenient stand-ins for the Irish and make the nest-fouling less obvious, I don't know.

In *Moonstruck*, Cher plays a gutsy young-middle-aged widow who gets engaged to Danny Aiello, a timid fellow who must first return to the side of his dying mother in Sicily, but who wants Cher to invite his younger, estranged brother—Nicolas Cage, a baker—to their forthcoming wedding. Cher lives in the comfortable Brooklyn house of her father, Vincent Gardenia, as prosperous as only a plumber can be, and busily cheating on his wife, Olympia Dukakis, Cher's no less gutsy mother. I shan't go into the assorted picturesque members of this clan, most of whom are haunted by the full moon, but with a craziness, usually amorous, that couldn't be cozier. I'm not giving away anything, however, if I say that Cher is reluctantly drawn into a torrid affair with the baker, who blames his brother (hence the estrangement) for the loss of his left hand in the freakiest of accidents. As Nicolas Cage plays him, he is the comic wild man to end all comic wild men, as well as some not so comic ones.

That Cage's passion for Cher is equaled by his passion for opera is a bit harder to believe, but there again Italianness is supposed to justify anything. Cher's initiation at the Met is, however, one of the film's least amusing sequences, though the camera makes clearer than the naked eye can what a wretched piece of architecture the Met is. The film, in fact, is a series of set pieces, some of which work, some of which merely strain. An additional problem is the unprepossessingness of this pair of lovers. Cher has, on occasion, looked better; here, the more she puts on the dog, the rattier she looks. Her wan yet raspy, sleep-talking Italian voice is convincing but unappealing. As for her swain, with his mauled-looking ears, naturally punky hair, and watery, bulging eyes, Cage should be not his name, but his address.

Where the movie comes most to life is in the performances of Olympia Dukakis, more restrained than usual, and aptly blending a philosophical acceptance of her husband's infidelity with a nagging existential curiosity about why men must cheat, and John Mahoney, as an NYU professor of communications who has brief, unsatisfactory affairs with his students. Mahoney is an actor with perfect emotional pitch, and his wistful, platonic encounter with Miss Dukakis—an Italian mother may be a comic shrew, but she never commits adultery—is one of the film's more attractive episodes. Noteworthy, too, is David Watkin's cinematography, which can make even a paper moon appear to be made of the finest vellum.

The Burden of Lightness

THE UNBEARABLE LIGHTNESS OF BEING

It takes an unappetizing mixture of arrogance and folly to make a film out of Milan Kundera's *The Unbearable Lightness of Being*, a book about as suited for cinematic treatment as, say, Sartre's *Words*. What the director, Philip Kaufman, and his co-scenarist, the ubiquitous Jean-Claude Carrière, have contrived is, you might say, the movie version of the jacket copy. Kundera's later novels, this and the even more astounding *Book of Laughter and Forgetting*, have built-in booby traps for adapters. First, they emerge from an authorial monologue in which the plot and characters are treated as conveniences, mere pretexts for political speculations, existential philosophizing, epigrams, and games. Next, they are relentlessly elitist, literary, intellectual—presupposing a tidy packet of culture and sophistication from the reader. Lastly, their mode is ironic, making uncompromising fun of life and the people trying to master it with ideologies, beliefs, religions, and hopes. These books are calculated to ruffle every standard feather, to rub the conventional fur mercilessly wrong.

Any novel that abounds in poetic and witty descriptions should automatically be taboo to filmmakers, but *Lightness* goes way beyond that. Its main characters are not really Tomas, a middle-aged Czech brain surgeon and womanizer, Tereza, his guilelessly clinging and unsuccessfully undemanding wife, and Sabina, his off-and-on mistress—an experimental painter, experimental lover, and embodiment of assorted freedoms. The principals, in fact, are the absurdity of life, the ironies it pulls on us that can be met (and then only partially) with nothing but ironic detachment, and the kitsch that, however fastidiously avoided, lies in wait for us everywhere.

Essentially, then, we are charmingly inveigled into a dialogue with a writer who, frequently talking in the first person, keeps reminding us that his fiction is a kind of probe, and inviting us to join in his racy ontological investigation. To take a few handfuls of plot elements and dialogue from the book, add one's own narrative strokes, and turn the whole thing into a linearly forward-thrusting typical movie is as alien, indeed antithetical, to Kundera's purpose and spirit as would be transferring it all to the court of Heliogabalus or Caligula.

The author's main point is that life is "an unbearable lightness" in both the good and the bad sense, largely because those very terms are too relative to have much meaning. Out of our good intentions come disasters; out of our attempts at righteous retaliation comes, generally, nothing. This is the unbearable irony of life. Out of our attempts to rise above contingency, to float above vulgar causality, comes sticky, inextricable involvement. Our lightness turns into heaviness, our refined superiority into kitsch. And there is no assigning value to any of our actions, because life affords us only the one chance of doing them—*this* way, leaving no basis for comparison with any other way.

Such an ironic view of life comes naturally to Kundera, a Czech exile, who was first stripped of his passport, then of his past works and the right to publish future ones, and, finally, of his very identity, being declared a non-person. So life, for the contemplative mind, becomes unbearably ironic, unreal, "light"—a joke (*The Joke* is the title of one of Kundera's novels). But this airiness, insubstantiality, lightheadedness may be preferable to any attempt to make life heavy and regimented, the ballast totalitarian regimes foist on it. And out of a novel-essay-treatise that keeps going off on meditative tangents and revels in aphoristic asides, Kaufman and Carrière have made a three-hour film that is all political incident, sexual titillation, and sentimental gesturing—all beginning, middle, and end.

Well, they do make a few concessions to Kundera's concept and strategy, and that's where they come most to grief. Thus in the middle of their lovemaking, Sabina, the free spirit, tells Tomas, the Don Juan, "You are the complete opposite of kitsch," and it's left at that; whereas in the book the notion of kitsch is omnipresent and ceaselessly assayed. Again, Tereza, a photographer, takes risky snapshots of the Soviet invasion of Czechoslovakia, and later, in exile, submits these to a Swiss magazine editor, who turns them down as *passé*. At the same time, he praises shots by a staff photographer of a nudist beach, which, he concedes, are something totally different. "Not at all," says Tereza. "They're the same." "Even I find it difficult to explain what she had in mind," remarks the "I" of the novel, but proceeds to show how the nudist pictures reminded Tereza of her mother who used to run around naked with the shades up, causing her daughter intense embarrassment. That is part of a troubling parallel.

But there is also Tereza's recurring dream of Tomas in a basket suspended above a swimming pool round which he forces Tereza and other naked women to do kneebends while singing. At the merest slip, a woman is shot dead by Tomas's pistol, her body left floating in the pool. This ties in with Tereza's mother not allowing the girl privacy on the toilet by locking the door. In the film, the mother does not figure, and the dream is merely a fantasy in which Tomas gives some naked women suggestive diving lessons. Thus it does not connect with the nudist pictures and those of the enslavement of Czechoslovakia, but becomes pointless, and does not convey the chain of absurdism that encircles and binds the world.

Yet the film fails even in areas where it could easily equal or surpass the book, e.g., in the death from cancer of Tomas and Tereza's beloved dog, Karenin. Because Tereza was reading Tolstoi's novel when they met, Tomas, who claims to see a resemblance, names the pooch he gives Tereza Karenin, even though it is a female. Much later, when the pair live as agricultural laborers in a village, Tomas, no longer allowed to practice human medicine, administers a lethal injection to the suffering Karenin, who, ironically, seems to be smiling. Passages of exquisite melancholy in the novel, serving also to point up the dynamics of Tomas and Tereza's relationship, remain wholly unmoving in the film, partly because of inattention to certain telling details.

Typical of the movie is that it spends much time on the entry of the Russian tanks into Prague, which gives it a chance to display its technical prowess in seamlessly inserting Tereza and Tomas into documentary footage of the invasion. But Kundera scores precisely by downplaying the big historic events, and letting the horror sneak up on us in a sardonic remark here, a grotesque anecdote there. If Kaufman had to make a movie out of Kundera, why not *Farewell Party*, a much lesser work, but a straightforwardly narrative one with a rattling good story? In *The Unbearable Lightness of Being*, he does not even mention the eponymous trope, which suffuses the entire book, more than twice, the second time in an obvious, heavily underscored ending quite different from Kundera's oblique dying fall.

And, apropos dying, Kundera announces the accidental death of Tomas and Tereza midway through the book, whereas in the film we learn of it only in the penultimate scene—another irony gone. And the particularly emblematic death of Franz, one of Sabina's lovers, which is the subject of a long, characteristic digression that, nevertheless, subtly reinforces the motifs of irony and kitsch, is cut altogether. But, finally, the absence of the authorial "I"—the *compère*, cicerone, and conscience of the book, the Vergil of this tragicomic Inferno—is what most causes the sinking of the film into what, in an access of benevolence, I shall call mediocrity.

There is a problem with the casting, too. Lena Olin is a splendid Sabina, unself-conscious yet never brazen in her diverse erotic scenes, but her Swedish accent is no more Czech than Juliette Binoche's half-French, half- (by mistake) Polish one, or Daniel Day-Lewis's almost totally British one. Even so, Miss Binoche is exactly right as Tereza, not just endearingly vulnerable, but also conveying the toll vulnerability, innocence, childlike faith can exact from the most confirmed Casanova. Just as Miss Olin is beautiful and slinky, Miss Binoche is pretty and bouncy, and the scene in which the two photograph each other in the nude, along with one where the talented Polish actor Daniel Olbrychski does a government official attempting to brainwash Tomas, are the nearest in spirit to Kundera and, not coincidentally, the best.

As Tomas, Day-Lewis is more than competent but too Anglo-Saxon and young. It is the middle-agedness of Tomas that gives his philandering its philosophical underpinnings (brilliantly set forth in the book and cut from the film), its bittersweet authority, and, when ultimately sacrificed for Tereza, its pathos. The actor's youthfulness puts a different complexion on this promiscuity, deprives it of its comic poignancy. There are also charming performances by two pigs, as the young and grown-up pet porker Mephisto, almost good enough to turn me off pork. But the movie, despite lovingly insinuating cinematography by Sven Nykvist and some stunning Janáček chamber music on the soundtrack, comes rather closer to putting me off art movies by American directors.

Au Revoir les enfants

One of the hallmarks of a good film is that it stays in your mind: certain images, scenes, bits of dialogue—even a movement here, an expression there—become part of your experience just as if you had lived them, which, in a sense, you have. Not so in Louis Malle's Au Revoir les enfants, a film that goes by you with a minimum of lasting impressions, and which the memory seems almost eager to relinquish. Not because this would-be autobiographical story about Nazi persecution of the Jews in France hurts too much, but because a subject of immense import emerges rather disembodied, lightweight.

At the Petit Collège d'Avon, near Fontainebleau, the 12-year-old Louis Malle knew (though, apparently, not very well) a Jewish boy, whom, along with two others, the priests who ran the school smuggled in as a Christian. After only a few weeks, in January 1944, the three boys were (again apparently—Malle is vague in his interviews about what really happened) betrayed to the Germans, and shipped off to Auschwitz to die. Father Jean, as the school's admirable principal is called in the film, was sent off to a work camp, where he continued to be bravely self-sacrificing, but succumbed, shortly after his liberation, from the hardships he had endured. He strikes me as much the most interesting character in Au Revoir les enfants, and I wish the film were about him rather than about the two boys Malle fails to make vivid and remarkable.

The director claims that this film has haunted him for years, but that it was only now that he was capable of making it. The intent seems to be expiation vis-à-vis those less fortunate than rich little Louis, who survived the war, and a coming to terms with perhaps more than the possible betrayal of one Jewish boy—with leaving behind France and enjoying life in America. And, to be sure, France and Frenchness are easy to feel ambivalent about. For here are a country and a people that have, over the centuries, been leaders in intellectual and artistic accomplishments, but who have also displayed spectacular chauvinism, xenophobia, anti-Semitism, petit-bourgeois meanness, and bohemian anomie (just count the pejoratives in this sentence with which French has enriched our vocabulary). No country is riper for love-hate than France.

So we have Malle beating his breast while also beating his drum. There is something mighty curious about a man who tries to come to terms with his past by, first, making himself guiltier than he actually was by *inventing* the possible betrayal of a schoolmate, and, next, *inventing* the doomed friend's acquittal of him. This looks rather like attempting to accumulate brownie points both for over-self-incrimination and for over-self-exculpation, where, in truth, only demerits are called for.

We are given the largely fictitious story of how Julien Quentin, a spoiled *maman's* boy, yet also tough and, of course, sensitive and bright, becomes the only kid at the *collège* to befriend Jean Bonnet, whose Jewishness the fathers do not reveal to the students, but who nevertheless remains an outsider. Bonnet, whose real name and identity Julien eventually discovers, is, as exceptionally gifted as Julien, perhaps even more so; but how could even the second-best boy at the school have been such a fool as to stare at his pal in front of the Gestapo officer come to ferret out the Jews among the pupils? And would Jean have merely told Julien, calmly and politely, that it was all right, that he would have been found out anyway? Or is this hagiography, junior division?

The director has tried to make an understated film on a highly charged subject, in theory at least a canny choice. But it is well to remember Roy Campbell's lampoon, "On Some South African Novelists," which Stanley Kauffmann is fond of quoting: "You praise the firm restraint with which they write— / I'm with you, there, of course: / They use the snaffle and the curb all right, / But where's the bloody horse?" The clipped, fast-paced scenes in which the film soberly canters along manage to be almost completely devoid of any emotion. Take the opening scene, in which Julien, his older brother, and other boys are about to leave for school from a wartime Paris railway platform. Julien, who adores his superficial, flighty, elegant mother (the father is always absent on business), carries on and doesn't want to board the train, but finally must with her lipstick on his brow like the mark of Abel. This could be galvanizing in the emotional undercurrents connecting mother, crybaby older brother, jeering other boys. But nothing beyond the most obvious is conveyed.

At school, Julien is a bedwetter and standoffish, small but haughty, and fierce in defending his territory. Nevertheless, he eventually recognizes in Jean Bonnet an equal—or, indeed, a superior—and an uneasy, often frayed, but keen friendship develops. Malle does get across some of the rigors of schooldays under the Occupation, mostly in a few sequences involving inadequate food and heating, minor but scary harassment by Germans or collaborationists, and the rich boys' patronizing dependence on Joseph, the orphaned and gimpy kitchen boy and black-marketeer. But he does not succeed in enlivening the diverse relationships between boys and teachers and boys and boys—least of all the growing bond between Jean and Julien.

When one thinks of what successes the French cinema has scored with comic and troubled adolescents in and out of school—from *Poil de Carotte* to *The 400 Blows*, from *Zero for Conduct* to even such a small but racily authentic film as Jean-Loup Hubert's current *Le grand Chemin* (badly Englished as *The Grand Highway*)—*Au Revoir les enfants* is enervatingly lacking in resonant detail, wrenching perception, liberating laughter or tears. It is full of good taste and utterly lacking in savor. Typical is an episode in which, during an air raid, Jean and Julien play hooky from the air-raid shelter to play the school piano. Julien, a hopeless no-talent, is given a few pointers by the outstandingly musical Jean, and forthwith they are making four-handed music worthy of public performance. Such falsity of particulars hounds and mars the movie.

Malle is not especially lucky in his casting, either. Gaspard Manesse looks right for Julien (though not for Malle), but is neither a versatile nor an eloquent performer. And Raphaël Fejtö, as Jean Bonnet (whose real name, in a less than engrossing scene, is revealed to be Kippelstein), is stolid of appearance as well as of performance. Crashingly average, too, is Francine Racette, as Julien's supposedly spellbinding mother. The best work comes from Philippe Morier-

Genoud, who invests Father Jean (why are both the saintly ones called Jean?) with stunningly unsentimentalized moral strength—though would he, on a Parents' Day during the Occupation, deliver quite so impassioned a philippic against the rich, and alienate the wealthy parents in the pews?—and from François Négret, as the treacherous kitchen boy, whose character echoes that of the hero of Malle's earlier, and incomparably better, film, *Lacombe, Lucien*. But there Malle had the good sense to hire a co-scenarist, Patrick Modiano, to say nothing of his good fortune in having in the lead Pierre Blaise, soon after killed in a motorcycle accident.

There is fine, restrained but revelatory cinematography by Renato Berta, and the closing scenes, finally, do generate almost inevitable excitement (unlike, say, the parlous treasure hunt in Fontainebleau forest, which falls flat), but it is too little, too late. The film clearly lives off its topic rather than its achievement, which, given the enormousness and enormity of that topic, leaves us with a queasy feeling as we leave it.

Wings of Desire

Rarely has one seen so much slowness and so little going as in *Wings of Desire*, an obnoxious movie concocted by the trendy German director Wim Wenders from a screenplay by himself and the even trendier Peter Handke. Handke, the Austrian playwright and novelist, is curiously uneven and vastly overrated. At his best, as when he writes a substantially factual memoir of how his mother ended up a suicide. Handke can write arrestingly, the self-consciousness of his style and the self-servingness of his all-round condescension kept pretty much at bay. But at his worst—and film always brings it out in him—his humorless wit and smugly exhibitionist detail-mongering that ignores larger realities become insufferable. As for Wenders, after a couple of small, rather engagingly disheveled and obliquely affecting road movies, he has turned to ever bigger, figuratively or literally American films, which have landed him in Handkean pretentiousness.

Here the attempt is to create something part fable, part poetic and cinematic avant-gardism, part slaphappy improvisation—with a predictably untidy result. Two angels, Damiel and Cassiel, come to Berlin, hover about, observe without becoming visible (though sometimes dimly felt by people), until Damiel relinquishes his angelism to partake fully of humanity—more specifically, to become involved with Marion, a dull and unattractive trapeze artist of whom he is enamored. As the human scene is depicted here, it is only minimally preferable to the angelic one, which appears to be the ultimate in pointlessness and boredom.

Wenders, with the help of the veteran cameraman Henri Alekan, uses every conceivable cinematic trick—in particular irritating changes from black and white to greenish monochrome to full color—while the soundtrack alternates between mundane dialogues and existential-metaphysical monologues of several kinds, the worst of them obsessively refrain-riddled evocations of childhood by Damiel, who seems to be suffering from an advanced Rilke complex.

Peter Falk is on hand playing himself—an American actor making a stupid movie about the collapse of Nazi Germany—and most of his random conversations and voiceover soliloquizings have the awful feel of inept improvisation. We get everything from a travelogue through the seedier parts of Berlin to much milling around the Wall and the desert that once was the Potsdamer Platz. There is the good old German actor Curt Bois pretending to be Homer, the paradigmatic storyteller, uttering condign platitudes, and there are long, dull circus sequences for Marion to dangle from ropes, and garish punk-rock-concert sequences in which Damiel, deliquescently played by Bruno Ganz, can blissfully lap up the joys of being human, if that is what Nick Cave and the Bad Seeds and their fans are.

Much the worst, however, with the possible exception of the angels' rat-tail hairdos, are the endless voiceover poetasterings, with the perennial refrain, "When the child was a child . . ." leading into contrasts between the child as child and the child turned adult. On the evidence of this 130-minute mess, there are at least two adults who have succeeded in perfectly perpetuating their childishness on celluloid.

So Big

BIG

Hard as it is to believe, the American cinema has actually turned out an accomplished, endearing, and by no means mindless fantasy,

Big. It was written by Steven Spielberg's kid sister, Anne, in collaboration with Gary Ross, and was directed—when Steven, thank goodness, became unavailable—by Penny Marshall. It may be that the reason this story of a 12-year-old boy miraculously transmuted into a young man circa 35 works so well is that two-thirds of its creative team were women. Though the boys-will-be-boys—or, rather, men-will-be-boys—story has rightly not been subverted, the feminine sensibility must have tempered the rowdiness with delicacy. The film is understatedly funny and measuredly sentimental; what it lacks in sharpness and brilliance, it very nearly makes up for in sensitivity and restraint.

Just think how awful things could have been had Spielberg directed, as he had planned, with Harrison Ford in the lead; the result, at best, would have been an Edsel. Ford's boyish charm, or what there is left of it, and his macho persona would have been of no greater use to him here than his acting ability, or what there ever was of it. Tom Hanks, however, proves just about perfect for the role of man-child rousing himself into a boy-man: brazening it out, lucking out, and sometimes just failing upward into the part of the spurious American adult. This character is not in the least out of the reach of a clever 12-year-old, especially if, in the course of the impersonation, the boy turns 13. Clearly, the Jewish view is at work here, for, at 13, the boy has turned man enough to get the girl, even if that girl is a tough, downright predatory, attractive businesswoman in her late twenties.

Twelve-year-old Josh Baskin, living just across the Hudson in bridge-and-tunnel country, is getting a bit bored with the school and games he shares with his best friend, Billy (earnestly and deliciously enacted by Jared Rushton), and hates being spurned by the girl he pines for merely because another boy is a trifle older and a good deal taller. So, at a fairground, he puts a quarter into an antiquated slot machine (so decrepit it barely looks postmodern) and asks Zoltar, the turbaned robot whose eyes light up and mouth gapes fiercely, to make him "big." He gets a card confirming that "Your Wish Will Come True"; next morning, he wakes up in Tom Hanks's body, but with all his adolescent insides intact. His panic-stricken mother takes him for her boy's kidnapper, and all Josh can do is escape to New York City in the on-and-off company of faithful Billy, who alone believes in and wants to help him but cannot always get away from home. Josh registers in one of Times Square's seamier hotels, the St. James, which Billy deems suitable

because it is named after a saint. Actually, it's a den of pimps and
whores, and when, in one of the film's many delightful moments,
Josh turns off a particularly violent movie on television, what goes
on around him in the hotel and the street below sounds exactly the
same. Such touches in the movie are almost always handled swiftly
and uninsistently, and are all the more telling for it.

Josh gets a job as a computer operator in a toy company, an
unlikely circumstance made both amusing and just about believable, as is his promotion to head of product development, a job he
gets when he and his boss accidentally meet at FAO Schwarz's toy
emporium and have a riotous time tapping out duets on a giant
luminous piano keyboard laid out on the floor. Josh also makes
some rambling comments about what kids want or don't want from
toys. This speech may persuade only the boss, but for us there are
many other good things: Josh, with Billy's aid, furnishing his loft
as a child's dream playground; Josh arousing the jealous hatred of
Paul Davenport (John Heard), one of the company's most ruthless
operators, over whom he is promoted; Josh winning Paul's girl, the
equally aggressive and scheming Susan, away from his fuming rival.
Meanwhile he and Billy are still trying to track down Zoltar to get
Josh back from a Big Apple operator into a small apple-cheeked
boy: or will all that success as an adult businessman and Susan's
new—and first true—love lure Josh away forever from his grieving
parents, betrayed-feeling best buddy, and childhood itself?

The film, which wisely opts for infectiously droll scenes rather
than belly laughs, and which further mixes the humor with dollops
of wistfulness, depends crucially on Tom Hanks, who does not let
it down. He manages to look and behave like a flawless conflation
of child and adult without having to resort to any conventional
tricks or cuteness. There is an intrinsic innocence and joy in what
he does, and when he is puzzled by others or surprised by his own
emotions, it is always done with a spontaneity and purity to make
your very toes curl up in a smile. Take the office party where, in a
ludicrously Liberacean rented white tux, Josh encounters unknown
foods, including baby corn, which he proceeds to eat row by row,
as if it were full-grown and he still a voracious child. It is this that
draws Susan to him; and his subsequent delight at the gadgets in her
rented stretch limo, and her toughness falling away as he overcomes
her resistance to enjoying herself on the trampoline in his loft, are
scenes that keep on romping inside one's memory.

Especially nice about *Big* is the way it handles Josh's sexual awakening. When Susan expresses doubts about staying the night on their first impromptu date, Josh, who has bought a child's double-decker bed, says with perfect guilelessness, "You mean sleep over? Okay, but I get to be on top." This sort of thing is treated with stunning unsmuttiness, as is the much later scene of sexual initiation when Susan undoes her blouse and guides Josh's hand to her breast. To embrace her fully, Josh must remove his hand, but it remains cupped for a while, reluctant to relinquish the wonderful shape and sensation it has just discovered.

The theme, clearly, is the triumph of innocence, of what Nietzsche hailed as *das Kind im Manne*. When the vexed Paul asks Susan, "What's so special about Baskin?" she replies with infinite condescension, but also sincerity, "He's grown up." This paradox could have been of the essence, and, if the movie were not (almost regrettably) aimed at a family audience, it might have been more thoroughly explored. Are steady playfulness, unbridled *joie de vivre*, undiplomatic outspokenness, virginity at what seems to be age 35 really so grown-up? Of course, the statement can be taken as a mere amiable one-liner, but something—dare I say?—bigger seems to have been intended. Is the child father to the man in ways unsuspected even by Wordsworth and Freud? Is innocence not just enchanting, but also a form of superior wisdom? Or is American society, even in the realms of cutthroat business and sexual competition, so infantile that the most childlike shall lead them all?

In which case, is this a good or a terrible thing? Susan (very finely embodied by Elizabeth Perkins) thrives under Josh's influence, going from chilly promiscuity to faithful loving-kindness, from a severe look appropriate to relentless competitiveness to clothes and hairstyles of much greater femininity—without, however, sacrificing her business acumen. It is Josh who, though he seems to have everything, nevertheless wants to go back to his true childhood, and the choice, even if touchingly written and played, emerges a little less dramatically and humanly satisfying than one might wish. When Susan drives Josh back to the parental house in the suburbs, there are large letters embedded in the asphalt of the street: SCHOOL. SLOW. We must not rush our lives. But what is to become of Susan? Though she half-jokingly (and, therefore, half-seriously) allows as how Josh might catch up with her in ten years, is she not doomed, after such shared innocence, to a life of deprivation?

I don't wish to overpraise *Big*, but I want to give one more example of its freshness and suggestiveness. When Zoltar first grants

Josh's wish, confirmed by that card printed in solemn gothic letter-
ing, the boy discovers that the machine's cord was unplugged all
along. When he eventually comes back for his, as it were, return
ticket, Josh begins by carefully unplugging Zoltar. The miraculous
could not be more gracefully conveyed. This is only the second film
directed by the ex-TV actress Penny Marshall, and it is either a fluke
or a most auspicious augury. If I knew the right slot, I'd drop in a
quarter to make it be the latter.

But, please, whatever you do, do not confuse *Big* with *Big Business*, a dreadful film in which, playing two sets of twins, Bette
Midler and Lily Tomlin display how doubly unfunny they can be
in one long set of errors without much comedy.

Molly Uncoddled

A WORLD APART

White South Africa has morally and politically painted itself into
a corner. There is no way a minority, in this day and age, can keep
its country's majority as second- or third-class citizens and perma-
nently get away with it. On the other hand, I appreciate the problem
of giving up what you consider your rightful, hard-earned possession, and the near-impossibility of squeezing the Dutch South
Africans back into the tiny fatherland. There might, of course, be
some compromise solution, except that after all the sternness and
brutalities of the Afrikaners, there is probably no way of working out a peaceable settlement, so all that seems left is to keep the
screws tight or to tighten them further. Meanwhile apartheid is a
nightmare from which the only awakening I can imagine is into
another, reverse nightmare.

Until recently, the screen, unlike the theater, has hardly addressed
this problem at all. Now film treatments are beginning to spring up,
most conspicuously Richard Attenborough's grandiosely inept *Cry
Freedom*. Chris Menges's *A World Apart* is a markedly better film,
although, as praise goes, that is not the least faint. Still, by not attacking the problem head-on, but approaching it obliquely through
the miseries of 13-year-old Molly—whose parents' political activism
leaves her ever more lonely and deprived of affection—then gradually fanning out to encompass the full horror of apartheid, the film
manages to avoid the sense of agit-prop oversimplification.

Shawn Slovo's screenplay is the largely factual story of her family. Gus and Diana Roth (for which read Joe Slovo and Ruth First)
are white political activists: he a lawyer and a leader of the banned
African National Congress; she the editor of a small liberal newspaper; both Communists. They have three daughters, of whom Molly
(i.e., Shawn) is the eldest. Set in 1963, the film begins in the middle
of the night on which Gus must flee the country to avoid arrest.
The children are told he is off for a while on business; this vagueness, and spying on her parents' passionately sexual farewell, leaves
Molly feeling all the more left out. Diana carries on alone with
fanatical dedication to the cause both as newspaperwoman and as
participant in clandestine meetings; inevitably, she is a neglectful
mother. It is impressive how much the film can convey through a
single incident, the killing of a black cyclist by a white hit-and-run
driver. Impotent black anger, white indifference or cowardice, police unconcern, Diana's preoccupation with larger political issues,
making her barely heed Molly's excited eyewitness account—all
these are succinctly encapsulated here.

The movie affords us swift, nervously paced glimpses of Diana's
political and journalistic activities; of Molly's hopeless reaching
out to her; of how Diana's mother, Mrs. Abrahams, comes to help
out with the children; of the younger daughters' childish solipsism.
We follow Molly's growing dependence on Elsie, the black servant,
whom the law has cut off from her children; also the partial sol-
ace Molly finds in her one sympathetic school chum, the extroverted Yvonne, and in an understanding headmistress. In some
ways—with Spanish-dancing classes, garden parties, doing the
twist to American records—a semblance of normal middle-class
adolescence is maintained, even if most of her classmates taunt
Molly about the "cowardly" escape of her Communist father, and
her mother, though basically well-meaning, remains distant and
evasive. As much as a child can be, Molly is sympathetic to the
struggle around her, but the need for a mother is greater.

Diana not only shortchanges Molly emotionally, but also keeps
defying the authorities in ways that jeopardize the entire family.
Finally she is jailed under the monstrous Ninety Days Detention
Act—held in solitary for ninety days, without trial, books, writing
materials—and relentlessly grilled to induce her to name names.
She resists, is finally released, and is immediately jailed for another
ninety days (there is much of what Villiers de l'Isle-Adam called
"torture by hope").

Afraid she will crack and betray, Diana attempts suicide; she is hospitalized and released after 117 days, but only into strict house arrest and round-the-clock surveillance. Meanwhile Molly has been ostracized even by Yvonne and her family, and, Granny having taken ill, Elsie is all that is left to her. She visits with her the black township where Elsie's brother, Solomon, is one of the leaders of organized protest. By a number of harrowing and tragic incidents, Molly becomes politicized and Diana humanized; in the end, daughter, mother, and even grandmother form a united political front, but Diana's continued indomitable recklessness was to lead in 1982, as a final title card states, to her assassination. By letter bomb, as the card, perhaps tendentiously, fails to inform us.

There is much to recommend the film. Menges is a dazzling cinematographer (*The Killing Fields*, *The Mission*) and fine documentarist whose first feature film this is, and though the cameraman was Peter Biziou, the movie reflects its director's cinematographic and nonfiction expertise—as well as some of the attendant drawbacks. Meetings dispersed by the police with ferocious dogs and weaponry, Diana's disrupted interracial birthday party, a church service from which a number of worshippers are dragged off to jail and death, Diana's harsh treatment in prison, are presented with the swiftness and incisiveness of an inspired documentary. But the human story gets scanted: we do not find out how Diana got to be the way she is; we learn nothing about Gus and the grandmother (the family seems to be Jewish, but nothing is made of that); the plight of the blacks is communicated through effective vignettes, but mere vignettes nevertheless. Details are not overlooked, yet except for Molly, who preserves much naïveté amid her knowingness, no character has any complexity. This is especially true of the blacks, who are represented as plaster saints.

The cinematography is at times almost too artful, notably in the dark interiors in Solomon's house, where the camera plays at being Georges de la Tour, and gloom emerges as aestheticism. It is typically a documentarist and cameraman's approach to avoid analysis as much as self-analysis. Much of Elsie's scant dialogue isn't even in English; Diana's main interrogator shows some humanity, but remains a shadowy-figure. True, *A World Apart* is primarily about a mother-daughter relationship set against a terrible background, about how the larger damage done to impoverished blacks takes its toll also on bourgeois whites. Even so, there are too many missing depths and heights. Perhaps the most moving scene is one in which Harold, Diana's only white assistant on her newspaper, tries to explain her mother's imprisonment to Molly: the mixture of awkwardness and wisdom, the fumbling of a decent but ordinary mind trying to impart something huge to the even more limited understanding of a child, and the way this is shot—the pair tight against a wall, Harold hard put to meet Molly's appetitive gaze—holds helpfulness and helplessness in exquisite balance.

Equally fine is the brief glimpse of Elsie's collapse at Solomon's funeral, even though the rest of this closing scene cannot avoid looking like the poster art of *Cry Freedom*. Still, by moving fast, Menges minimizes his, perhaps inevitable, lapses. And if, for example, some of the prison scenes cannot avoid the déjà vu, there are others that truly score, e.g., Diana's effortful hoisting herself up by the bars of her high window to stare longingly at the humdrum city traffic outside, the banal suddenly becoming wrenchingly beautiful.

Expectably, Menges has an unerring eye for the right faces; unexpectedly, he proves expert at eliciting remarkable performances. Barbara Hershey, with a persuasive accent, does a compelling job as Diana, both in her basic stiffness and chilliness, and in her two very different kinds of warmth: the easy, almost exaggerated one for the cause and its fighters, and the repressed maternal one that intermittently breaks through, especially at the end. She may lack the ultimate histrionic greatness that fills in the gaps of a screenplay, but she restrainedly makes the most of what is there.

As Molly, Jodhi May, a 12-year-old British schoolgirl, does wonders. She starts out low-key: we are pleased to note an unpretty, slightly clownish face whose beauty comes from within, all tangled up with even an intelligent child's immaturity, but the performance almost imperceptibly deepens, and a sorrowing intensity pours out of the awkwardly forward-tilted head; the ungainliness is somehow transmuted into the tragic, yet the child never turns into a precocious quasi-adult. The little girls playing the younger sisters are first-rate, too, as are most of the supporting actors, black or white. Linda Mvusi exudes calm strength and cheer as Elsie, which makes her crumbling into grief all the more shattering.

Shot on location in Zimbabwe, the film has the right look about it. It has no flab, no sentimentality or self-pity. However, you want it to be great, the way *Shoeshine* and *Forbidden Games* are, and that, from a novice scenarist and first-time director, is not forthcoming. But, until the overexplicit ending, it works.

Pale Galilean

THE LAST TEMPTATION OF CHRIST

The Greek writer Nikos Kazantzakis typifies that mixture of driven, autodidactic erudition and primitive vitality that one often finds among Eastern European literati. Frenziedly seeking ultimate truths, he eclectically absorbed everything from Buddhism to Bergson (with whom he studied) and traveled restlessly across the world in search of reconciliation of our—or his—animal and angelic natures. This duality is portrayed in *Zorba the Greek* as two characters, and fused, in *The Last Temptation of Christ* (1951), in the protagonist.

I haven't read the latter novel, having had quite enough with *Zorba* and *The Greek Passion*, a piece of highminded drivel filmed by Jules Dassin in his fruitiest manner as *He Who Must Die*. So I can't say how many of the sillinesses in Martin Scorsese's misbegotten movie version of *The Last Temptation* (the Greek version of the title) are attributable to Scorsese and his scenarist, the obnoxious and untalented Paul Schrader, and how many are Kazantzakis's own. At least the novelist had (I gather) linguistic and evocative gifts that the movie lacks.

The film does not represent so much the fifties sensibility of the novel as the spirit of the generation of '68, which spawned Scorsese and Schrader. Rather than take more than a fleeting cue from Pasolini's *The Gospel According to Matthew* (which beats them hollow), our filmmakers have come up with a deconstruction of a Cecil B. DeMille Biblical epic, with the difference that DeMille did his homework and produced well-researched, genteelly stilted, British-style schlock, whereas Scorsese gives us sloppy, garbled, up-to-date schlock, with a hippie Christ and action and dialogue aimed at a contemporary know-nothing audience. I don't know which is worse, but DeMille was more fun.

Typical of Scorsese and Schrader's level of operation is the language of the movie. The Jesus of the Gospels speaks beautifully and commandingly, and I imagine that Kazantzakis, too, could make his Jesus articulate and even eloquent. In the movie, we sense immediate trouble as an initial quotation from the author crawls across the screen and we read, "My principle anguish . . ." People who don't know how to spell "principal" should leave Christ and Kazantzakis alone. But, of course, there is worse.

The woman caught in adultery is here Mary Magdalene, the most popular whore in Judea, whom the Jews are about to stone not, to be sure, for adultery, but for selling herself on the Sabbath, the day of rest. Jesus holds up two biggish stones and makes the following speech: "Who of you people has never sinned? Which of you has never sinned? Whichever it is, take this!" A bit later, Jesus says, with divine disregard for grammar, "Whoever is hungry for justice, they'll be blessed." He sits down with his followers and a group of Jews and says, "Come closer, we're all family." Later, an apostle remarks, "Move over, John, Peter wants to lay down."

Jesus asks the crowd, "What difference does it matter what you own?" This is so gross that I take it to be a slip of the actor, Willem Dafoe, which, in a lowbudget picture (such as this is) did not seem worth rectifying. At the Last Supper—where, to oblige the feminists, women are participating—Jesus says, "Take this bread; share it together." That I would not put past Schrader; as for Scorsese, language was never his bag.

But even the manner of speaking is a problem. Dafoe talks with a somewhat hippified Middle American accent, in which, for example, Jerusalem becomes "Jeruzlem." Harry Dean Stanton, who plays Saul not as a Sadducee but as a philistine, says, "He rose zup from the dead." Most wondrous is the speech of Judas, played with flaming red hair and a built-up hook nose (more Jewish? more heroic?) by Harvey Keitel, which is straight New York sidewalk. Particularly fine is the moment when Jesus, in the desert, having just been tempted by a cobra with the voice of Mary Magdalene (Barbara Hershey, in an impossible role), is accosted by a lion with the voice of Keitel asking preposterously, "Don't you reckonize me?" It used to be *exungue leonem* now it is strictly *ex voce*.

With updated (and diluted) language goes up-to-date sensibility. Thus Jesus reminds Judas, "You said if I moved one step from the revolution, you'd kill me." Judas is one of the Zealots, whom the film confuses with the Pharisees. It also presents the Essenes without naming them, thereby suggesting that contempt for the flesh was a universal Jewish tenet, which it wasn't, though it might have appealed to Kazantzakis—in theory, certainly not in practice—and to the kind of zipless Zen that Scorsese and Schrader may well be drawn to. So Christ will ask his auditors, "Who are you—I mean, really?" We're only a step from, not the revolution, but "like really, man."

When fancier diction is in order, we call on the British. Pilate is played by the English rock star David Bowie, because a Roman governor would have such a classy accent. So—in the final fantasy sequence, where Christ on the cross imagines at length the totally human life he might have led—the Lolita-ish guardian angel who uncrucifies him also speaks with a high British accent. In the *New York Times*, Janet Maslin claimed that Scorsese has, in another high-class touch, obviously studied Christian iconography. Not very well: though numerous Renaissance paintings show Christ standing before a majestically seated Pilate, Scorsese, contrary even to elementary common sense, has Dafoe sitting in his most laid-back way, while the mighty procurator, in his nervous (or is it rock-singerish?) fashion, jerkily dances around him. Most ridiculously, André Gregory, as a far-too-old John the Baptist, speaks in that fake upperclass accent of his—not so much Baptist as high Episcopalian.

The film is one of those cheesy attempts to have it both ways: be daring without offending anyone excessively. So high-ranking Jews such as Caiaphas and Herod are shown barely or not at all, and the populace is only very intermittently out for Christ's blood, lest present-day Jews take umbrage. The Romans, too, are fairly harmless—except when handed a whip or hammer and nails—lest, I presume, Italians take offense. These Romans, by the way, are a raggle-taggle crew of youths from Morocco (where the film was shot, on the optimistic assumption that it looks like Biblical Judea), equipped with the measliest hints of Roman armor—low budget, remember? In no way could *they* have conquered half the world; at the utmost, Hoboken. Finally, so as not to strain the patience of today's moviegoers with too much "heavy" stuff, we're given only an anthology of the best miracles (the raising of Lazarus, by the way, is played for horror, not tears) and one token parable.

There appear to be glaring historical inaccuracies, which makes the stray stab at authenticity seem forlorn, orphaned. The inscription on the cross of a Jew, whom Jesus, a carpenter for the Romans, helps crucify, is the only bit of Latin; there is no Hebrew whatever. When Christ reads from Isaiah, it is not from the Torah, but from some weird parchment he seems to be deciphering with his fingers, like Braille. Since, however, the film correctly shows the crucified as nude, it can crucify that first Jew correctly, because he disappears immediately; but how is it to dwell on Christ and the thieves without showing their genitals? Well, they are crucified in a bizarre crouching position, with one leg covering the pudenda; they look to be practicing some modern-dance routine.

Willem Dafoe, if you like your Jesus as a Zen hippie, is good enough, and very nice-looking, but wouldn't you think that the Son of God would have better teeth? It must be easier to change water into wine than Harvey Keitel into anything but Keitel; his tragic Judas, ordered by Jesus to betray him, emerges as a displaced person *avant la lettre*. At least he is no more ludicrous than those others who, unlike the apostles, don't have the good luck of being completely washed out by the film. This includes two unsightly actresses, who, as Mary and Martha, become Christ's wives in the final fantasy, giving fantasizing a very bad name indeed. They bring home the truth of Jesus' answer to Judas's question about whether he could betray his master, "No, that's why God gave me the easier job—to be crucified."

The Last Temptation of Christ is a perfectly excruciating 156-minute film (there seem to have been four minutes cut recently), but reprehensible for artistic, not religious, reasons. It is too bad that various religious groups have seen fit to persecute it and thereby provide invaluable free publicity to a movie that could have died promptly of its own boring ineptitude.

Midnight Run

There is the well-known genre of the buddy movie, but there exists also the less-chronicled genre of what might be called the anti-buddy movie, in which persons who hate each other's guts are thrown—often even chained or handcuffed—together and forced to make the best of it. *The Thirty-Nine Steps*, *The Defiant Ones*, *The African Queen* are typical, though unequal, examples. So is one of my favorite films of all time, the far too little known *Il federale* by Luciano Salce. *Midnight Run* is a pretty fair example of the genre—at least in the beginning.

Martin Brest, the director, is best known for what I consider a truly contemptible film, *Beverly Hills Cop*; here, however, in George Gallo's script, Brest has an initially appealing idea. Jack Walsh (Robert De Niro), an excop turned bounty hunter for a sleazy L.A. bail-bondsman, is bringing back from New York Jonathan Mardukas (Charles Grodin), a Mafia accountant by accident, whose boss was the very man who got Jack fired from the Chicago police force. Jonathan, called Jon, embezzled $15 million and gave most of it to charity; apprehended, he jumped bail and hid out in New York. When Jack tries to put him on the red-eye to L.A., Jon fakes a hysterical fit and the two are taken off the plane to continue their journey by train, bus, car, even as stowaways on a freight train. They are chased by the mob, the FBI, and another bounty hunter as double-crosses and other peripeties proliferate.

Jack is a taut, tough, impatient man who wants to make enough money to start a coffee shop: Jonathan is a basically respectable, happily married burgher on the surface, but reasonably crazy underneath. He assumes (rightly) that his former boss will have him killed once he gets to prison, and tries to befriend Jack, about whose tobacco and cholesterol ingestion he is genuinely concerned, and whom he professionally warns about the risks of the restaurant business. Jack does one slow burn as Jon gets more and more weirdly solicitous. This is fun until the movie turns into ever more relentless car chases and helicopter shootouts, whereupon most of the charm gets lost.

Nevertheless, the De Niro/Grodin relationship holds the interest even in the later, hokier sections of the movie. De Niro has a marvelous way of scrunching up his face into a smile of agony, as well as of exploding on the installment plan, and he somehow manages to play his part to the hilt even while faintly suggesting that he is kidding it. He oozes canniness and determination along with a lot of repressed decency, as his compact, streamlined frame races ahead on unleaded nervous energy.

Contrariwise, Grodin, though bigger, is also much softer (the actor seems to have put on considerable weight), and has a woebegone, slack-jawed look about him that can readily be heightened into noisy hysteria. Yet Grodin underplays the part, making one or two expressions and intonations leitmotifs, then subjecting them to highly suggestive variations. He is especially impressive when communicating with a bus-ticket seller by means of tiny head movements and eloquent facial play, meant to give De Niro surreptitiously the lie.

There they are, then, this not-so-wild boar and this not altogether cuddly teddy bear, always figuratively and often literally handcuffed together, making funny conversation or dropping even funnier throwaway lines. Suddenly the subtext dawns on us: De Niro is the goy and Grodin the Jew; they must make a go of it if the social fabric is not to rip. An interesting idea, but underdeveloped.

Seven Types of Exiguity

RUNNING ON EMPTY

It is almost impossible to make a serious movie in Hollywood these days. (Actually, it wasn't much easier before.) If the idea is a potentially good one, such as that of *Running on Empty*, the following requirements are sure to reduce it to pap by the time it comes off the production line.

1. The picture *must not offend anyone*. The story of Arthur and Annie Pope, who bombed a government-sponsored laboratory that made napalm for the Vietnam War, and who have been living on the run with their two sons, was triggered by the actual bombing of the mathematics building at the University of Wisconsin, where a graduate student, working late, was killed. In the movie, the victim was a janitor (less valuable than a grad student), and he was only blinded and crippled (no actual blood on the Popes' hands): the Popes need the blessing and forgiveness of the audience.

2. It must have *something for everyone*. Let's make Artie Jewish because so many radicals were, including, I dare say, the film's director (Sidney Lumet) and writer (Naomi Foner) and their families, as well as many moviegoers. Let's, however, be sure to make Annie not only Christian but also a runaway debutante—a WASP formerly in best standing—so we can make sure of the rest of the audience, especially those proper Republicans whose children rebel.

Weathermen and such, who went in for bombing and then went underground, were not burdened with offspring; but a whole family on the lam makes the movie a family picture, commercially very desirable. If the family survives by changing towns, names, low-paying jobs—well, that makes them appealing to the proletarians in the audience. If we see them moving from Florida to New Jersey, if a few scenes are shot in New York City streets, this makes the movie saleable abroad as a quasi-travelogue. But just how deadly dull those jobs—Annie's as a doctor's receptionist, Artie's as a short-order cook—are, must not be gone into.

3. Some element in the film must make it *attractive to youth*, the biggest group of moviegoers. So it is 17-year-old Dan Pope

who becomes the center of attention: he is a musical genius. With
initial lessons from his mother and constant practice on a portable soundless keyboard, he can elicit from a briefly encountered
Steinway the most gorgeous Beethoven or Chopin. So, at his latest
school, Mr. Phillips, his music teacher, wants to recommend him
for Juilliard, and the boy is itching to go. But he loves his boorish,
unreconstructedly and infantilely radical father too much to leave
him. What keeps volatile Artie going in his underground existence
is a loving wife and boy (Harry, the younger, is only ten and not
yet supportive).

But today's young, divided as they are, don't just want an obedi-
ent, respectful son; they also need a rebel. So the movie provides
one from column B. Mr. Phillips's daughter, Lorna, who falls for
Dan as he does for her, is a hellion who treats her doting, cowed
father with exemplary disrespect. Let him so much as enter her
room without knocking and he gets her lip, if not the back of her
hand. This elicits Dan's admiration, even as the sticky cohesion of
the Pope family stirs up Lorna's longings. The formulaic, manipulative script manages to have it both ways.

4. Indeed, the film must *have it both ways* about everything.
Though Dan is a studious, dedicated classical pianist, he is not
some sort of acned, highbrow nerd. No, as played by handsome
and virile River Phoenix, he plays baseball and knows pop music,
too; he will even tap his foot when Mr. Phillips plays some of it
in music appreciation class. (If high-school classes are indeed as
much fun as shown here, we are in serious trouble.) Notice especially how "the Revolution" is treated in the movie. The laboratory
bombing emerges as a one-time lark that accidentally went sour.
Since then the three (later four) Popes have been living in close
harmony, with only Arthur inveighing against capitalist evils such
as the chamber-music concert he wants to keep Dan from attending. Warm remembrance of flings past surfaces when, at Annie's
birthday party, the Popes and Lorna dance to James Taylor's "Fire
and Rain" in the most down-home American way, complete with
victrola, paper hats, candle blowing, and inexpensive presents as
prescribed by Artie, either found (sea shells) or homemade (whales
carved from bits of wood).

Dan, 17, and Harry, 10, driven from pillar to post in the family
van, remain pure as the driven snow despite all that name-chang-
ing, hair-dyeing, having to drop everything and run from the Feds.
No school problems, drug problems, sibling rivalry. How they man-

age to get into new schools each time without records from the former ones (*We lost our papers in a fire*), how new passports and identities are acquired by their parents—not to mention how wages are paid in cash—is adumbrated but not made believable. The kids don't even know what their parents' crime was or who their grandparents are until they find out from a newspaper article; but none of this makes them neurotic or intractable.

Yet tormented Arthur does needlessly heckle, yell at, boss around dutiful Dan—the one bad effect the underground life seems to have. But, never fear, he can also be wonderfully understanding: "You sleep with [Lorna]?" "Yeah." "Okay. Now hit the sack; you've got school tomorrow."

5. The film needs to *appear daring* while playing it safe. So Annie tells her staunchly conventional millionaire father, whom she meets for lunch at a fancy restaurant where he is well known (to make the scene more photogenic, though in reality such a meeting would have to be inconspicuous), that as soon as her younger son is old enough, she will give herself up, even if she cannot vouch for Artie's following suit. A good woman, truly repentant about that bombing—"Don't you think there were times when I'd have blinded and paralyzed myself to take that back?"—she doesn't permit herself the luxury of going to jail as long as maternal duty requires otherwise. As for Artie's being less reliably repentant—isn't that a proof of the film's adultness, its sense of reality?

Talk about reality! There is also an unrepentant sixties radical, the evil Gus Winant (played as a caricature by the untalented L. M. Kit Carson), who tries to put the make on Annie, with whom he once had an affair, even as he attempts to get the Popes to help him with a potentially murderous bank robbery by means of the arsenal he proudly displays in the trunk of his car. If Arthur is not noble enough, perhaps, ever to give himself up, at least he is superior to Gus.

6. *Tears must be jerked.* When Dan, in New York for his Juilliard audition, stumbles on his grandparents' address, he spends his scant money on a large pizza and, pretending to be the delivery boy, rings the grandparental doorbell. Grandmother answers, looks warmly at the strange, lovely boy, and offers to buy the pizza she didn't order. Dan gazes yearningly at the kindly, elegant old lady but neither accepts her money (attaboy!) nor reveals his identity (sob!). At the lunch with Daddy, Annie fights contradictory emotions but chokes back her tears. Daddy is full of reproaches, yet agrees to look after

Dan should he get into Juilliard. As Annie leaves (without having gorged herself on food unavailable to her loved ones), tough, righteous, self-righteous Daddy erupts into strangulated sobs.

There is a farewell scene, now that it's fleeing time again, for the young lovers that won't leave a heartstring unstrung or a hankie unwrung, even though we can guess that Dan won't have to leave. But his parents don't just tell him this. He must sadly jump into the pick-up truck for which Artie has exchanged the van ("Keep them guessing!") and still more sadly toss out, when ordered, his beloved bike. Only then is he, for a meretricious effect, told to jump out after it and head for his grandparents' and Juilliard. Earlier we were told that the Popes blew up the lab because they wanted "to make a difference." Now Arthur tells Dan, "Go out there and make a difference," implying with a self-abnegating smile that blowing minds at Carnegie Hall does as much for social justice as blowing up labs.

7. Very little about *Running on Empty* stands up to any sort of scrutiny, and *almost none of the dialogue transcends platitude*. That, I fear, is the seventh prerequisite for a current serious movie, lest it be too demanding for today's illiterate audiences, both lower and upper class.

Judd Hirsch makes Artie's interior as unappealing as his anteaterish exterior. One yearns for a shred of sensitivity, a touch of charm to explain what Annie saw in him. In vain. Conversely, the excellent Christine Lahti brings genuine down-to-earth humanity to her preposterous role in a phony script. River Phoenix, as an actor, just flows along (or goes with the flow) and doesn't look like Hirsch's boy by a long shot, never mind a close-up. As Lorna, Martha Plimpton is better, but what can the kids do in scenes that, despite a fake harsh touch or two, are glowing with the aura and smell of calculated innocence? At the end, the soundtrack reprises "Fire and Rain": this is not a movie that lets go of its gaffes easily.

Sweet Bird of Untruth

BIRD

Perhaps I am not the right person to review *Bird*, Clint Eastwood's biographical film about Charlie "Bird" Parker. With the exception of rock and other pop forms of today, nothing leaves me colder than bebop. I rather like jazz, but bop strikes me as an unfortunate

hybrid: a popular art form flirting with a highbrow one and falling between two schools. Classical composers could make use of
jazz because of its unspoiled folk quality; I cannot imagine another
Ravel, Stravinsky, or Martinů incorporating bop in his music.

I say this by way of laying my cards on the table. I would guess
that upward of half of Eastwood's two-hour-forty-minute film is
taken up with Bird blowing his alto sax: in a couple of early sequences, as he is growing up, by himself; later, in various groups.
The music has been carefully recreated for the film: Lennie Niehaus,
himself a noted alto saxophonist, "cleaned up the original recordings electronically and isolated Parker's solos," Eastwood explains.
Then some top jazz musicians were hired and offered the "unique
opportunity [of playing] with Charlie Parker thirty or so years after
his death." Since some of the tapes used were from the private collection of Charlie's last (common-law) wife, Chan Richardson, and
such previously unreleased material must thrill the aficionados, the
movie, for them, must be bathed in a sacred glow lost on me.

But Charlie Parker the man arouses my curiosity: not because he
changed the face of jazz forever, but because, to adapt Whitman, "he
was the man, he suffered, he was there." Yet, highly touted though
Bird was at Cannes, then at its release in France, and now here, it
doesn't tell me anything about how Parker got to be the musician
he was (was he completely self-taught?), about how he got hooked
on heroin and drink (yes, I know about jazz musicians in general,
but I'd like to know more about *this* one), about how his renowned
appeal for women functioned, chubby and undistinguished-look-
ing as he was. What about his three other marriages and countless
flings? The film, based mostly on Chan's memoir, *Life in E Flat*,
gets properly going only when Charlie meets Chan (no puns about
Chinese detectives, please!).

Eastwood says that when he bought Joel Oliansky's screenplay,
which had been lying around Columbia Pictures for years, he wanted to do a movie about "the mysteries of [Bird], his strengths and
weaknesses, gals and booze and drugs and stuff, but at the same
time his genius." Sure enough, it is a movie about the mysteries,
preserved intact with not a single veil lifted. Even the death of a
daughter that apparently causes Bird's suicide attempt with which
the film swings into action is not shown; we have to take everything
in the movie on faith. The story, what there is of it, proceeds by a
dotted line whose interstices we can fill ad libitum. Call it a do-it-
yourself biography.

To be sure, there were genuine obstacles. The filmmakers clearly did not want to spell out details of this interracial affair, especially since Bird is not one of your dashing Poitierish blacks but, especially as incarnated by Forest Whitaker, a heavy-set, almost obese man who (someone must have thought—perhaps rightly) would not go over well as an attractive white woman's lover. So we see one kiss between Chan and Charlie and one getting-dressed sequence—the late phase at that!—and no more. Oh, occasionally we see him being gazed at intensely by another white woman. But how is that going to tell us about Bird and his "gals," to say nothing of his "stuff"?

Nor are there any serious discussions of music between him and Dizzy Gillespie or other musicians who figure in the movie, from which we might learn about the genesis of bebop. The music is just there. Or not there, as in an early Kansas City sequence where young Charlie tries to qualify to play with a band, but elicits only ridicule and the drummer's pitching his cymbal at him. True, in a later scene, the crapulous Charlie offers "getting inside the music" as his method, but that is pitifully, or laughably, insufficient. It is also true that it is very hard to convey what bebop is by filmable events or words. Still, Bertrand Tavernier got much closer to it in 'Round Midnight by smartly engaging a real jazz ace to play his jazzman hero and then letting the camera linger on his playing. An actor's simulated fingering won't do the trick.

A serious drawback indeed is the Cannes-prize-winning central performance. A fine actor in supporting parts, Whitaker has proved himself in Platoon, Good Morning Vietnam, and especially in a stunning bit in The Color of Money. But he cannot as yet carry a whole long movie, or at least one in which he has to encompass such extremes as irresistible charm and tormenting tormentedness. Bird's dark, destructive side come through even less, as written and acted, than does his hinted-at charm.

Darkness of another kind, however, is all over the place. Almost the entire film takes place at night, in dimly lit space or, when outdoors, nearly always in both night and torrential rain. Often you cannot truly see the actors: quite often you cannot understand them either, what with opaque speech and naturalistic sound recording. I would say that roughly 30 percent of the film is invisible, and some 40 to 50 inaudible. I cannot remember when—in moviegoing or life—I so longed for an honest bit of daylight as I did while groping my way through Bird. Of course, we get the symbolic-didactic value of this murk with a vengeance, as we do that of the recurring shot of the Kansas City drummer tossing his cymbal at Parker, complete with visual and sonorous special effects—talk about the clash of symbols! But although the stygian dark may convey the mood of this life, it does not, so to speak, shed any light on it.

The sparse social details, though accurate, are not sufficiently helpful either. When Bird and his quintet tour the South, the white trumpeter, Red Rodney, is billed as an albino to enable them all to stay in black hotels. This is fine, as is showing the segregation of black and white audiences during the concerts. But it hardly begins to show how society affected Bird's psyche and his interracial marriage.

Similarly, we get a sequence where Parker, driven around nocturnal Los Angeles, asks that the car stop outside the Stravinsky residence, at whose outer gate he rings the bell. The far-off front door opens and two puzzled silhouettes, Igor's and Vera's, peer into the night, then shut the door again. Bird just stares, awe-struck. Now, it's interesting to learn that he revered Stravinsky. But just how did he discover him, how well did he know his works, and what did they do for him—such questions aren't even raised, let alone answered.

The best thing about *Bird* (other than the music, for those who fancy it) is Diane Venora's performance as Chan. Cocky in the flasback sequences, where she is a dancer and free spirit, she announces: "I've had my sweet sixteen at the Cotton Club. It's always been musicians." The way she speaks the line to Charlie, you don't know whether it's a boast, a promise, or a putdown. You are kept guessing, and it enriches the moment: perhaps it is all three. Venora gives us a Chan hot-blooded yet elusive, proud yet earthy. And when finally committed to Bird, devoted yet steely. The actress makes something full-bodied out of snatches, something fresh out of clichés. She lights up the film's darkness.

The atmosphere, the visual details may be authentic, but that does not guard against stereotypes in the telling. Bird's relations with a drug pusher, with a Javert-like policeman, with a fictitious jazzman representing the various ways of selling out are all staples of such bio-pics. And what, for example, is the function of that baroness to whom Chan introduces Bird and in whose Boston house he dies? And the famous line of the coroner who describes the dead Bird as aged about 65 (so in the film: elsewhere I have encountered figures between fifty and sixty), only to be told that he was 34, is not built up to. We do not see, for all the ulcers and addictions and hospital scenes, Charlie aging and deteriorating. But perhaps it merely gets lost in cinematographer Jack Green's chiaroless oscuro.

The film queers itself at the very beginning by sporting for its epigraph the well-known and well-worn Fitzgeraldian dictum, "There are no second acts in American lives." Yet we don't see Dizzy Gillespie or Red Rodney go down the tubes. But, then, the Diz tells Bird, "I'm a leader . . . a reformer. You're a martyr." Well, no. There are self-made men, but there are no self-made martyrs. It takes a higher cause to make a martyr; if there is one in *Bird*, it does not come across.

In Double Focus

A CRY IN THE DARK

With *The Chant of Jimmie Blacksmith*, Fred Schepisi had proved himself one of the most startlingly new directors since the New Wave. Leaving Australia for America, he floundered a bit (although *Barbarosa* was not without interest), but with *A Cry in the Dark*, he emerges as both a master of his medium and the kind of artist almost unknown these days: a true humanist, who would save mankind from itself. Hopeless as his hope may be, he has the artistry and endurance to give it a living and lasting form.

The film is the true story of an Australian Seventh-Day Adventist pastor and his wife, Michael and Lindy Chamberlain, who, with their two little boys and baby girl, were vacationing at Ayers Rock in 1980. At a moonlight barbecue with another couple at their campsite, the Chamberlains heard a cry from their tent, where the younger boy and baby Azaria were sleeping. Lindy hurried back; glimpsed a dingo (a wild Australian dog) rushing out and vanishing into the wilderness; found some blood but no baby in the tent. A search by campers, aborigines living nearby, and, eventually, police yielded no more than some dingo footprints near the tent. An inquest totally exculpated the Chamberlains.

Much later, Azaria's clothes were found in the wilds, torn, bloodied, and neatly folded (clearly because their stupid discoverer put them back that way), although a knitted jacket was missing. Testimony by questionable forensic experts and the belief that a dingo could not-carry so heavy a load that far (the aborigines knew better) caused the reopening of the case: Lindy was charged with murder,

Michael with being an accessory after the fact. All of Australia was agog as over no previous trial. Despite a patently sympathetic judge, the couple, who were tried as much by the media and the public as by the jury, were found guilty. Lindy was sentenced to life, Michael was given a suspended sentence, so as to be able to take care of the boys and a new girl baby, born in prison and snatched from her mother despite a petition to let her keep the child for a while.

Three and a half years later, further evidence came to light, and was released; but only last September did a high court clear the Chamberlains of all charges. They still have to convince many of their fellow countrymen of their innocence. The reason they persist in trying is encapsulated in the film's last line, which Schepisi shoots brilliantly, and which may be the most haunting utterance with which any movie ever left us; I leave you to discover it for yourselves.

The prosecution never tried to establish a motive for child murder in this manifestly close-knit, child-loving family. The unstated implication (it was voiced abundantly in cross-country gossip) was some bizarre rite of human sacrifice demanded by the Adventist Church. The principal reasons for the verdict were hatred for a little-known, fundamentalist religion; the seeming imperturbability of the couple and their willingness to discuss the case on TV and in the press; the popularity of the dingo as a national mascot; and various forms of legal incompetence, though not on the part of the judge, who clearly considered Lindy innocent. And, of course, encompassing everything, human stupidity and malevolence.

The Chamberlains, however hurt and grieving, believed in the will of God—even though, eventually, Michael lost his faith and gave up the ministry, as the film wrenchingly shows. Lindy and her Bible remained inseparable. Such faith strikes people nowadays as alien and suspect; Aussies were giving credence to a rumor that the very name Azaria meant "sacrifice to God." The media first conned the Chamberlains into cooperating under the pretext of helping the search for the baby; later, these victims of yellow journalism thought they could use the media for their vindication, a procedure for which the media have extraordinarily little stomach. Dingos, of course, are wild beasts, despite their lovable aspect; and that Lindy is not a warmly effusive woman, that she showed remarkable toughness under questioning, that she did not cry much at her trial, should hardly constitute evidence of guilt.

What is masterly about the film is that, in a mere two hours, the screenplay by Schepisi and Robert Caswell manages to touch upon any number of private and public aspects of this tragedy, which is both that of unjustly suffering individuals and that of mass hysteria and general benightedness. Schepisi ingeniously keeps the story in double focus: both on how it felt to those enmeshed in it, and on how it looked to the media, the police, the outsiders. He keeps inserting tiny vignettes showing how diverse people in a great variety of situations reacted to the case—mostly obtusely, and often obscenely. At the same time, having instructed every actor to enact his character as if motivated by the best of faiths, Schepisi was able to portray honest but horrible human stupidity with unsurpassable sharpness.

Aside from a hair-raising story, rivetingly told, there is—inconspicuous, and all the more affecting for it—Schepisi's superb technique. You have to be two persons watching this film: one for the plot and dialogue, the other for the sovereign cinematic know-how. I solved the problem by seeing the film twice. The camera placements and movements could serve as exemplars for any film course. Thus helicopter shots from a nose-mounted camera immerse us in the principal locations on the run, as it were; wideangle lenses keep straining to catch more, more searchingly, more bewilderingly. For bewilderment is of the essence here. Even the cogent alternation of close-ups and long or extreme long shots serves to evoke bewilderment on both intimate and public levels: we keep shuttling between the puzzled and anguished protagonist couple and the, with rare exceptions, unfeeling or hostile cast of millions.

How imaginatively, for example, Schepisi and his gifted longtime collaborator, the cinematographer Ian Baker, use Ayers Rock, that awesome monolith, as a visual refrain and emotional leitmotif. Often between what might be called acts of the drama, in harsh light or falling dusk, the camera flies furiously toward that natural wonder: holy to the aborigines, unholy to the Chamberlains' detractors, a Mecca for tourists, and a memento of horror for the parents. It is as if the latters' consciousness, their inner eyes, were irresistibly drawn to that cynosure; ironically, cynosure is Greek for dog's tail, or the rear view of a dingo heading for the dark. Or consider how magisterially shots of Azaria and of the dingo bursting from the nocturnal tent (was there or was there not a baby in its maw?) are intercut with the sequence of Lindy under cross-examination: the counterpoint of speed and stasis, of night and courtroom glare, objectifies the assault on her by the D.A. from without and by her memory from within.

Particularly subtle, often almost subliminal, is the recording of the tribulations and final triumph of conjugal love under trials greater than a mere tribunal—even one disposing over life and death—can inflict. The incisiveness of these scenes owes a lot to the performances. Sam Neill's is a vivid embodiment of Michael's mixed emotions toward God, wife, and mankind: of befuddlement, bitterness, and severely shaken but unshattered endurance. Even more astonishing is Meryl Streep's Lindy, not least for mastery of a difficult accent, but most for making this well-nigh granitic woman sympathetic without resorting to any sympathy-stealing device, despite plentiful opportunity to do so. As she proved in *Ironweed*, Miss Streep is of all our leading ladies the least vain about her appearance; here, even more touchingly, she conveys the depredations of inner anguish on outer comeliness. But by never visibly trying to move us, she moves us all the more.

To cover vast ground, the film must rocket forward; this, with all the often complex details and (to our ears) outlandish accents, makes it hard, though not impossible, to follow. But with such a director, such principals, and such a supporting cast—no one among these scores of people displays an iota of actorishness—the rewards for concentration are lavish. Consider the masterly way in which Schepisi conveys chaos in the crowd scenes, how the submersion of the principals in the multitude, the heterogeneous concurrent actions, the Draconianly cut short takes fitted together with a soupçon of disjointedness allow confusion to make its masterpiece. And notice how the camera will move in the opposite direction from the actors to crystallize the *dépaysement*.

No less fine is the technique in the private scenes: Lindy and Michael talking to each other stiffly, fumblingly across a room, or casually from one room to another. Or there will be one-liners delivered on the wing by someone flitting by, or shots so briefly held that their impact registers on top of that of the next sequence, or kinetic balances where a camera movement from left to right is complemented by one from right to left. How much, for instance, is told by a tight shot of two hands failing to clutch each other as Michael rejects Lindy, contrasted with a later one where they are defiantly clasped.

What to me, as an unbeliever, is particularly eye-opening is the variety of roles religion plays in this movie. For *A Cry in the Dark* is, among many other things, one of the most transcendent religious films since *Monsieur Vincent* and *God Needs Men*, which is saying a lot.

The Ophuls Truth

HÔTEL TERMINUS

What I love about the documentaries of Marcel Ophuls is that they are so far-ranging and dogged in their pursuit of the truth, so fastidious in their attempt to be fair to everyone. Even if the ultimate truth—as truth will—remains elusive and relative, Ophuls casts his net so skillfully and so wide that he catches the next best thing. And that is the complexity of the human condition, the contradictoriness of human nature, with its predictability shot through with surprises.

Ophuls is the bane of producers. He always shoots longer and more, and has a harder, longer time editing than they can bear. But how else can a man proceed if his passion is to get at what is morality, what is right, what is justice, the triune question that haunts him? This universal question must be approached in terms of specific murky incidents, which raise the anterior question of what really happened, of what is truth? And that, as Ophuls keeps discovering, is often impossible to ascertain.

His first documentary, *The Sorrow and the Pity* (1970), remains his best. It examines what happened during World War II in the French town of Clermont-Ferrand. It is about maquisards and collaborators, heroes and cowards, leftists and rightists, Christians and Jews, Frenchmen and Germans and the Allies. What did individuals do? How did that affect world events? How is history made? The problem was how to tackle these enormous questions. Happily, Ophuls hit on Clermont-Ferrand, at the *dead* center of France. It is the French Podunk: when benighted relatives in a Feydeau farce descend on Parisians, they're most likely from Clermont-Ferrand.

Some two centuries ago, the great German philosopher-poet Novalis wrote that the poet "needs nothing more than the decision to renounce infinite variety and its sheer enjoyment and to *begin* somewhere—but this decision costs him the free indulgence in an infinite world, and demands restraining himself to one single manifestation thereof." Though he roamed all over the world in pursuit of the problems of French resistance—the *Résistance*—or the lack or rivenness of it, Ophuls sensibly kept coming back to Clermont-Ferrand, for the necessary restraint.

His next documentary, about the "troubles" in Ireland, *A Sense of Loss* (1972), was a fascinating failure that lacked a self-limiting

focus; small as Ireland is, it and the British presence in it still proved
too big. *The Memory of Justice* (1976) was good but even messier
as it tried to figure out the truth behind the Nuremberg trials: the
nature and degree of the guilt of the accused, and the nature and
degree of the justice meted out to them. Though this documentary
shed infinitely more light than such a popular movie as *Judgment
at Nuremberg*, it fell almost as short of its aim as that Hollywood
movie fell of Ophuls's.

Now, with *Hôtel Terminus*, subtitled *The Life and Times of Klaus
Barbie*, Ophuls is again onto a manageable story. This is a good
place to begin yet another (alas, needed) investigation of monstrous
guilt and precarious justice. Exactly what did Major Klaus Barbie
of the ss do in Lyons, whose German commander he was during
World War II? And what sort of justice was achieved by his trial
in that city forty years later? The answers, even incomplete ones,
were hard to come by. For one thing, Barbie had escaped to South
America with the help of U.S. counterintelligence, which had enlisted him as a useful pawn in cold-war spying, and Ophuls had to
do much ferreting out in Bolivia and Peru, where Barbie and his
family functioned influentially and happily for decades. For another, French justice dragged its heels and did not bring the Butcher
of Lyons to trial until four years after his extradition in 1983.

So Ophuls's investigation had to be conducted in France, Germany, and both Americas, and ended up costing $1.6 million; a
trifle compared to a Hollywood blockbuster, but a lot for a much
less salable documentary. Yet what ought to win audiences for *Hôtel Terminus* is that Ophuls is a documentarian almost in spite of
himself; if he had his druthers, he would be making exquisite feature films like those of his late father, Max—something at which
Ophuls's films proved unsuccessful. Nevertheless, the fact that his
heart is really in show business, that he wants to entertain, enables
him to make documentaries that are not dry, private, or fanatical.
He looks for contradictions and ironies, for the absurd on both
sides of the fence, for what is covered by the Socratic term *aporia*:
the perplexity at the end of a Platonic dialogue. However, in *Hôtel
Terminus* he goes too far: sometimes he puts himself into the film,
being sardonic and clever—something he used to avoid.

Very few photographs of Klaus Barbie in his dread heyday survive; even his name is not pronounced alike by those who knew
him. Near the start of *Hôtel Terminus*, Peter Minn, a retired Wehr-
macht major and schoolmate of Klaus's (he was *Bub* [Sonny] in

those days), pronounces the name like the French *barbier* (barber);
much later, another informed speaker does the same. All others
pronounce the name like the well-known cute American doll's. In
that two-way name, what irony! For the same man was indeed a
Nazi torturer and butcher (the Demon Barber of Lyons?) and also
the respectable-seeming naturalized South American businessman,
whom his Indian gardener describes as "a noble man," and whom
his neighbors evoke as a jolly, round-faced gentleman—a Kewpie,
if not a Barbie, doll.

Such ironies abound. A former Gestapo man (or perhaps an
ex-ss officer—Ophuls interviews so many, it's hard to keep them
straight) recalls Barbie as a chap you could trust because "my dogs
took to him," and dogs always know. What breed? Ophuls asks with
mock gravity; "Dachshunds," comes the answer. Equally mistaken
as these badger hounds were the U.S. secret services. One retired
member, Eugene Kolb, says he is certain that Barbie couldn't have
been a torturer: he was too high up and too clever to stoop to such a
thing. (Any number of witnesses in the film testify that he stooped.)
Did Barbie have it in for the Jews? You could say he wasn't their
friend, Kolb replies, without a trace of irony. Barbie, he is confronted with having said, was "a Nazi idealist." Asked what he had
meant, he replies that he no longer knows. I could tell him. He was
clearly confusing "ideologue" with the similar-sounding and more
familiar word "idealist." Of such, and their bosses, are the makers
of history made.

But if you fear that we are alone in our malodorousness, relax:
the French and German professionals and such whom Ophuls
interviewed smell no more sweet. In fact, it is quite as revealing
to find out who behaved admirably as it is to learn who didn't.
For example, a simple French farm worker, Julien Favet, whom
the district attorney says he considered too benighted to testify
against Barbie, spoke out repeatedly—as he does here—about the
guilt of the people of neighboring Izieux, who betrayed 44 Jewish
children to Barbie, on whose orders they were deported to the death
camps. Favet bravely tells the truth, for which his fellow villagers
have repeatedly attacked him, physically and otherwise. The world
must not learn how shabbily Frenchmen could behave, so the D.A.
wouldn't let Favet testify.

Guido Vildoso, a former president of Bolivia, opens the gate to
his house and garden himself (can't he afford servants?), but courte-
ously refuses to answer any questions, claiming he needs permis-

sion from the present government. Conversely, Gustavo Sinchez Salazar, the Bolivian Minister of the Interior, who arranged for Barbie's extradition, speaks courageously about everything. Georges Neagoy, a retired CIA agent now working in television, refuses to be photographed or interviewed, but we hear his harshly curt refusal. Another former U.S. agent, Erhard Dabringhaus, speaks honestly and wittily from his poolside. One thing becomes evident throughout the film: people with a sense of humor behaved, by and large, much better than those without one.

The heroism of some of these people is almost as unbelievable as is their goodness. The cowardice of some of these people is all too believable, as is their rottenness. But some of the rotters are brave, whereas none of the good persons seems cowardly. Think about that; think about much else in this necessary film. Do not be afraid of its almost four-and-a-half-hours' duration: I have seen it twice and could easily see it again. Only the summit of Mount Everest might feel as exhilarating as the company of such unassuming heroes, such simple good people as you meet here. You will not be bored by any of them; nor will the evil ones bore you.

Perhaps the two most unforgettable figures are Barbie himself and the lawyer who defended him, Jacques Verges, the mysterious, Mephistophelean Eurasian (half Vietnamese) who has also defended a North African terrorist, claiming that what the French did in Algeria was the same as what Barbie and the Nazis did. (Yes, in a small way: no, in a big one.) I have seldom if ever seen such placid evil as these two serenely exude; much is to be learned from them. And the title of the film, *Hôtel Terminus*—the name of the hostelry that served as Barbie's headquarters in Lyons—is perfection itself. How's that "last stop" for an *objet trouvé*?

Rain Man

Rain Man is about a Los Angeles sports-car importer and feckless younger brother, Charlie (Tom Cruise), whose father leaves his $3 million to Charlie's older brother, Raymond (Dustin Hoffman), an autistic savant of whose very existence, in a Cincinnati institution, Charlie was unaware. Enraged, Charlie abducts Ray in the hope of somehow acquiring his inheritance, and drives him to L.A. in the white 1949 Buick convertible that is just about all his father left him.

There ensues a typical comic road movie cum mismatched-buddy movie (are those still two genres or have they become irrevocably fused?) as the brothers drive across Western America and each other nuts. Well, Ray already is, more or less, but he is also a mathematical and mnemonic genius who helps Charlie make a killing at blackjack in Vegas. In return, Charlie's Italian girlfriend teaches Ray to dance and kiss. Since that is as far as it goes, it may not be a fair exchange for the $80,000 Ray wins for Charlie.

By the time the brothers arrive in L.A., Charlie has become seriously fond of Ray—an affection not untinged by considerations of Ray's financial usefulness. By now, Charlie has become accustomed to Ray's weird ways, and Ray—to some extent—to Charlie's normally heedless ones. But the two can't go on together. As Ray is taken back to Cincy, he is close to feeling affection for Charlie, who, genuinely moved, promises to come visit soon. In the old days, when such efforts could be assessed as one-, two-, or three-handkerchief movies, this would have been a one-hankie one; in the era of Kleenex, it is harder to classify.

The problem with the picture is that the writing, by Ronald Bass and Barry Morrow, is sometimes illogical, often over-explanatory, and never more than serviceable. Though Barry Levinson's direction is competent, it allows Hoffman's performance as Ray to wag the movie. Now, Hoffman is an over-fussy (you could say egomaniacal) actor who worries every detail of his performance to the point where the actor's bravura matters more than the character's reality. And this Ray, instead of being offset by an equally vital Charlie, has no match in Tom Cruise. With one performance flapping at us from the chandelier, and the other mostly supine on the floor, it's hard to keep both in our field of vision.

The Frenzied and the Frozen

MISSISSIPPI BURNING; THE ACCIDENTAL TOURIST

Some movies, however defective, have success built into them. A picture such as *Mississippi Burning*, provided only that it does not shy away from violence—which, Lord knows, it doesn't—cannot but make a killing. To see sheeted or unsheeted rednecks beating, burning, and lynching away is irresistible to viewers outside the South (and perhaps also inside), and pyromaniacs should get their money's worth from the plethora of burning homes, schools, and churches crumbling rafter by lingered-on rafter. And then there is the cops-and-robbers story of how Ward, a prim FBI agent, and Anderson, a hearty former Mississippi sheriff, crack the murder case of three (here unnamed) civil-rights workers: the black James Chaney and the white Michael Schwerner and Andrew Goodman.

The film can be judged on three levels: as a thriller, as history, and as a human-interest story, what with the stiff Northerner Ward going strictly by the book and the easy-going down-home Anderson proceeding by folksy, unorthodox methods, as—once again!—two mismatched buddies come to respect and care about each other. For added human interest, there is even a platonic flirtation between Anderson and Mrs. Pell, a beautician and wife of Deputy Sheriff Pell, one of the men who murdered the civil-rights workers. It is Mrs. Pell who—at grave risk to herself, but because Anderson treats her so much better than her scurvy husband does—reveals the whereabouts of the three corpses, and so makes possible the victory of justice.

On the historic level, *Mississippi Burning* is mostly fabrication; for example, the way the FBI found the corpses was by paying an informant $30,000. Time was when such vital information cost only thirty pieces of silver, but 1,000 percent inflation over two thousand years is understandable. If this remark sounds flip, let me say that thinking about this movie—as opposed to viewing it, when it is perfectly possible to get sucked in—invites flipness. Thus the film shows Southern blacks in 1964 as patient victims, a sea of angelically anonymous faces, not in the least involved in their own liberation. Equally unhistoric is the presence of blacks in the FBI at that time, and more besides.

As a human-interest story, the film is not appreciably better. Anderson's warmth is conveyed mostly by his treating Mrs. Pell as a lady and not pawing her, and by handling the so-called law enforcers like scum and grabbing one of them by his testicles. But are we to believe that this is enough to get the woman to betray her husband and upbringing, and to stop the sheriff's boys (or the KKK) from gunning Anderson down, especially since he keeps laying himself open to such an exercise in marksmanship? And how are we to care about Ward at all, given that we never find out more about him than that he used to be in the Justice Department and was shot in the shoulder when "with Meredith at Ole Miss"? And how can our fine Anderson say good-bye to the severely husband-battered Mrs. Pell in her ravaged home (retaliation for her squealing) and not even offer to help clean up?

But as a thriller, the film has elementally effective moments, thanks to Chris Gerolmo's explosive script and Alan Parker's detonating direction. Parker knows the shortest way to the viewer's gut, having been a leading British TV commercial director. He jabs again and again from the very outset: adjoining drinking fountains, one labeled "White," one "Colored"; a white man drinks from the first, followed by a little black child drinking from the second. Next, a backwoods church is seen burning in such detail as Nero would have enjoyed accompanying, though here we get Mahalia Jackson singing a spiritual on the soundtrack. Then, in silhouette, lowly-looking graves. Now we are ready for the murder of the CORE workers.

Since no one living knows or will tell how it happened, the event had to be imagined. And what could be more alarming than to see in extreme longshot a car being pursued along a nocturnal country road by another vehicle whose headlights are turned off. The whole scene is imbued with precise nightmarishness, but the detail of the lightless pursuers gaining on the lighted victims is etched in unshakable horror. All of the early scenes work at least on the gut level, but the film starts losing points as it stops making sense, as when Ward, in a crowded noontime coffee shop, sits down at the back with a young black man and starts pumping him. The man silently moves away, but is nevertheless beaten to a pulp a bit later. Ward simply couldn't be that stupid and careless.

Still, Parker delivers some thorough Grand Guignol even when he ascribes preposterous methods to the FBI. What he should never do is sermonize. So when the town's mayor, who is not a Klansman, commits suicide, Ward enlightens a puzzled assistant: "He was guilty, just as guilty as the lunatics who pulled the triggers. Maybe we all are." Pathetic as this little preachment is, it was originally more extensively and grandiosely homiletic: Parker prints it all in the press kit, along with his intense regret at having had to cut it.

As Ward, Willem Dafoe plays a colorless part impassively; Gene Hackman, as Anderson, is in top form, convincingly Southern in his bluffness and pawkiness even when the material or his accent abandons him. Frances McDormand is first-rate as Mrs. Pell, able to wrest grandeur from weariness without resorting to trickery. Brad Dourif, as her husband, conveys chillingly the wretched insecurity behind evil, illustrating the story Anderson tells Ward about his own father, who once, without compunction, killed the mule of his hard-working black neighbor. The animal gave the man an economic advantage, and "If you ain't better than a nigger, who you better than?" If there were more of this stinging insight and less grandstanding, *Mississippi Burning* would not be in such desperate need of a mule.

The film does, however, have starkly imposing work from the British cameraman Peter Biziou, who served in the same capacity on *A World Apart*. Can this age of specialization have produced a specialist in racial-violence cinematography?

Over the vociferous bafflement of some of the fancier members of the New York Film Critics' Circle, *The Accidental Tourist*, then still unreleased, limped off with the Best Film award and, unusually, no award in any other category. Nevertheless, Lawrence Kasdan's movie, from his and Frank Galati's screenplay based on Anne Tyler's book, is not without its minor, almost marginal, virtues, not to mention the serious merit of being aimed at adults, not overgrown or undergrown juveniles. In its tight, perhaps excessive, restraint, it is the polar opposite of *Mississippi Burning*, and would deserve praise for that alone.

Miss Tyler's novel, which the adaptation follows closely, is high-minded schlock, but at least does not yield a film catering to any of the prevailing forms of tasteless craving, whether for the dialectics of yuppiedom or the metaphysics of the car chase. The main plot concerns Macon Leary, whose solid upper-crust Baltimore marriage to Sarah crumbles after the murder of their young son during an out-of-control holdup. Macon is a writer of travel books for accidental tourists, Americans who on business trips abroad—like himself on the journey through life—want to feel that they never left home. Accidental, too, is Macon's broken leg, caused by a panicky leap of his frightened corgi, Edward.

While his leg is in a cast, Macon moves into the Learys' ancestral home, shared by his spinster sister Rose, who alphabetizes the groceries in the pantry, and by two bachelor brothers even stodgier than Macon. But Edward must be taught some manners and is taken for lessons in canine comportment to Muriel, an extremely unconventional divorcée who lets her feelings hang out like laundry in Naples, and who, while teaching Edward how to behave himself, undertakes to teach his owner how not to. There is also a subplot in which Julian, Macon's spirited publisher, falls for and marries Rose, with seriocomic results.

Much about *The Accidental Tourist* is either too cramped and ossified—as is the nature of the tale—or, if dealing with Muriel, somewhat preciously eccentric. It is a film dealing in extremes, with very little in between, yet often seeming so low-keyed as if it were all in between. All the same, it deals with adult problems far more compellingly than its only recent American competitor, Woody Allen's stupefyingly contrived *Another Woman*. Above all, Kasdan's work manages not to look and feel like that of a Bergman epigone, no small achievement in American moviemaking, where an authentically grown-up voice seems hard to come by.

It is unfortunate that the best performances come in supporting roles, from Bill Pullman as a genuinely three dimensional Julian, and Amy Wright, whose quirkiness is unforced throughout. And, as Edward, there is Bud, the relatively rare canine actor who suggests that he might have studied with Stanislavsky. (Three other Cardigan corgis acted as stand-ins, but the triumph is Bud's.) William Hurt, Kathleen Turner, and especially Geena Davis (it's not easy to incarnate the life force) are all a shade overexplicit; but John Bailey's cinematography is a wonder of many-shaded restraint: a subdued palette that nevertheless encompasses a host of gradations. His camera is like fine furniture polish to the old mahogony of these surroundings and lives: it does more than just show, it reveals.

Torch Song Trilogy

As long as people lack original ideas for a movie, they will turn to adaptations. Short stories, novels, and especially plays are grist for the adapters' mills, which, unlike God's, grind fast and exceeding coarse. Theater, since the dawn of cinema, was considered the ideal source for photoplays, as moving pictures used to be called with *nouveau-riche* pretension. The prestigious thing for the movies was to capture some New York stage star in a hit vehicle for transfer to the screen; nowadays the traffic tends to be reversed, as Hollywood blockbusters are turned into Broadway musicals, and big- and small-screen stars are coaxed into offering themselves up live to their hungry fans.

Yet movie adaptations of plays have presented, from the beginning, pitfalls galore. Film is a restless medium, suffering from acute dromomania, and can stay put for any length of time only with great difficulty—or great directorial knowhow. Conversely, theater, though it too enjoys an outing or a change of scene, is perfectly content to tarry among the same three walls for an entire evening. Though in need of some action, theater dotes on talk; whereas nothing seems to make movies more nervous than public speaking. I could list further differences, but all this is well-known to everyone except the unfortunates who keep making movies out of plays; even if their tribe does not increase like Abou Ben Adhem's, it will never go begging for bridge partners.

The usual solution, of course, is to "open up" the play: to fill in the scenes merely reported or mentioned in the stage version, or invent new ones out of whole cloth for the celluloid version. This tends to be risky: the rhythms, strategies, cohesion of the play are tampered with; it is at the very least as if a drawing in charcoal on paper were translated into one in chalk on a blackboard. Say something in the enclosed space of a stage box, where the viewer sees the entire cast of reacting characters all the time, or say it on screen in a closeup or two-shot—or even in a long shot showing everyone present—and you always end up getting unbalancingly more or less than the play did.

As I write this, my eye catches an article in the *New York Times* about a debate in London's Merchant Taylors' Hall on adapting literature for the screen, won (if a show of hands counts) by those opposed. Most peculiar, however, was the novelist Salman Rushdie's contribution from the floor in favor of adaptations. It seems he failed in six attempts to get through *The Name of the Rose*, and was grateful to the movie for telling him how it all came out. I hope that Rushdie was being ironic; otherwise I must point out to him that the movie changes a key incident and that Eco's erudite potboiler isn't literature in the first place.

The classic case of trying to remain faithful to a play is Hitchcock's *Rope*, from Patrick Hamilton's stage thriller, where, after a scene on a park bench, the action stays within an apartment. But here, again, the play had scant literary merit, and the film adds little to it save technical bravura. The only instance of a film's improving on a play that comes readily to mind is Noel Coward's *Brief Encounter*; but the play was a one-acter that could use expansion, and Coward himself wrote the screenplay. Moreover, one seldom if ever sees the original play, *Still Life*, acted by the likes of the movie's Trevor Howard and Celia Johnson. Bruce Beresford's magnificent *Breaker Morant* is based on a play, to be sure, but I have neither seen nor read it; still, I expect it to be less good than the film. And though such exceptions may not prove the rule, they assuredly do not disprove it.

One current film version of a play is certainly not exceptional in any way; it is *Torch Song Trilogy*, directed by Paul Bogart. Harvey Fierstein's largely autobiographical trio of one-acters, *Torch Song Trilogy*, chronicled the happy or unhappy relationships of Arnold Beckoff, a female impersonator, until, in the end, he adopts a young boy, makes peace with his mother, who accepts his way of life, and gets a former lover who thought he could make it married to a woman to come back to him instead. These were funny and moving plays nine or ten years ago, and Fierstein, with his terminally gravelly voice, deliquescent eyes, and rawboned gawkiness that could turn surprisingly slinky in drag, was his own ideal interpreter. The play must have seemed still too outrageous for Broadway when it got there by a long and circuitous route; yet it won over even the blue-haired ladies from New Jersey, who could be seen laughing, crying, and rooting for Arnold, whom they recognized as droll, extremely likable, and, finally, even wise.

In the years since then, AIDS has changed the situation drastically, making one of the funniest scenes unreusable. Fierstein himself has grown older and harder-looking—especially for the camera's pitiless eye. And the author/actor has become more of a star, letting himself perform his transvestite nightclub routines in the movie, whereas the play featured a real chanteuse singing the blues, thus extending the work's range to the heterosexual world. The additional material Fierstein has written (mostly stuff at the homosexual nightclub) doesn't add anything substantial, and the casting is off: Bruce Kerwin can't act, Matthew Broderick is miscast as a homosexual male model, and Anne Bancroft is beneath contempt as the Jewish mother to end—not all Jewish mothers, but any shred of respect we might still have had for her even more exaggerated, brashly unnuanced (or, more simply put, gross) carryings on.

Above all other problems, though, there is the medium itself. The second play, *Fugue in a Nursery*, is literally a fugue with a homosexual and an uneasy heterosexual pair of lovers interacting in an enclosed space, with fugal background music by Ada Janik. The film does not and cannot duplicate this, and is much the poorer for it. Missing, too, is the hilarious yet also vaguely sinister monologue in the orgy room of the homosexual bar from *The International*

Stud, part one of the stage trilogy. Even if this scene had not been made obsolete by AIDS, it would not have worked on film. A stylized monologue with a blotted-out background, merely suggested by light or sound effects, is impossible on film; the almost unavoidable literalness of the camera would have made the needed distancing by stylization unachievable.

Plum Danish

PELLE THE CONQUEROR

Bille August's film *Pelle the Conqueror* won the Golden Palm in Cannes and the Oscar for best foreign film of 1988. The remarkable thing is that, despite these awards, it is a very good film. This adaptation of the first volume of a four-part work by the Danish novelist Martin Andersen Nexø is roughly comparable to Jan Troell's magisterial *The Emigrants* and *The New Land*. Though not quite so brilliant and wrenching as its Swedish counterparts, the Danish film (which August intends as the first installment of the full work) is a humane, beautifully constructed, and gracefully executed piece of moviemaking, an unmelodramatic but touching tribute to the defeats and victories of lowly people, and thus the sort of thing that is least likely to succeed in this country. That it has already been playing for a while and may, thanks to the Academy Award it received, maintain itself longer on our screens is a heartening sign.

Pelle, a boy of 11 or so, and his aging father, Lasse Karlsson, a widower, are emigrants from Sweden to Denmark, where, to believe Lasse's tales, a boy's life is all play, bread is buttered, and a man like Lasse might even get Sunday breakfast in bed. "We must not accept the first job offered us," Lasse declares when awakened from his drunken sleep by Pelle as the migrant-laden ship pulls into port. (Andersen Nexø wrote his semiautobiographical novel between 1906 and 1910, but the action must take place in the 1860s.) Already with its opening sequences, the movie scores.

There is, first, the superb cinematography of the Swedish cameraman Jörgen Persson, best remembered for the films of Bo Widerberg, notably *Elvira Madigan* and *Ådalen '31*. The way that shadowy clipper emerges from the morning mists in an evocative slow dissolve from long shot to medium shot against a grey-white background resonates with recollections of maritime myths. There follow shots of huddled emigrants on deck, then the hopefully rosy face of Pelle (Pelle Hvenegaard, whose mother named him after *this* Pelle) and the alcohol-incarnadined countenance of Lasse as he is shaken awake. A few brief shots, a bit of dialogue, and we are well into plot, characterization, and the populist ideology of the (then socialist) author. The director knows his job.

And forthwith the next glory of the film, its acting. Pelle Hvenegaard won out over four thousand other boys for this part, which he well deserved. He may be almost too good-looking, but he doesn't coast on that; he acts with an open, unaffected straightforwardness, as innocent as a freshly unwrapped pack of butter. And as Lasse, there is the hero of Troell's films (and of so many of Bergman's), the great Max von Sydow. One of the finest actors of this or any time, von Sydow has the kind of face that is (to quote Martin Walser's *Messmers Gedanken*) "a door through which you can come in but not go out." That most elegant and well-spoken of actors assumes here a weather-beaten, bloodshot aspect and a drink-sodden, gravelly voice to give us an unforgettable Lasse: a pawky poltroon, self-deflating blowhard, poetic liar—a weak, well-meaning, foolish fellow, as likable as he is fallible, whom Pelle must, and does, learn to outgrow.

Take the scene of the landing in Denmark, with numerous prospective employers driving up to this slave market to haul away their chosen serfs. Proudly Lasse touts himself and his son, only to be told repeatedly—by those who don't just ignore him—that he is too old and the boy too young. Ever more dejectedly—and touchingly—he keeps telling Pelle they must not accept the first offer that comes along as the chaos around them thins out and the square is finally empty except for the hunched figure of Pelle, in long shot and silhouette, seated on a suitcase, around him a sunny cityscape and harbor view. One last employer drives up in a carriage; Lasse crapulously staggers out of a pub to meet him. It is wonderful to watch von Sydow conquer his tipsy smile and titubation to assume an air of unsteady dignity. He and Pelle are driven to Stone Farm by the martinet-like Manager, there to work for the owner, Kongstrup, a notorious womanizer, and his wretched, loving wife whom he has driven to drink. Under the draconian supervision of the Manager and his mean-spirited deputy, the Trainee, the workers toil amid terrible conditions.

Covering just one volume of Andersen Nexø's huge novel, even

granted the 150 minutes' playing time, requires the film to hop
along expeditiously. August wrote the screenplay with the help of
that fine Swedish writer Per Olof Enquist, and it is an exemplar
of how to get maximum plot into minimum time. Even without
reading the book, one senses the determined and dexterous technique involved in not allowing all that foreshortening to foreclose
on lucidity, continuity, and poignance. A subplot such as the tragic
love affair between a rich young man and a pretty menial at Stone
Farm is edited down to within an inch of its marrow (never mind
bone), yet it works shatteringly. Again, the subplot about Kongstrup, his mistresses, and his suffering wife is handled with amazing succinctness and evocativeness: Kongstrup's last romance and
its tragicomic consequences are told in virtual jump cuts, yet the
pathos, horror, and black humor are all there; note how sparely
and suggestively Kongstrup's final fallen state is conveyed.

The strength of any film is its rhythm, and rhythm is what *Pelle*
excels in. Despite the breakneck (but not break-sense) storytelling, whenever slowing down is needed, the film knows how to exploit near-stasis. Thus the meeting of the tragic young lovers at the
well; thus, too, the scene in which Pelle rejects the job of trainee:
rubato could not be put to better use. Pelle was just being outfitted
with the trainee's white smock—the tailor was basting it on the
awed boy before his exulting father—when a crucial incident has
Pelle run out into the wintry courtyard and look on in helpless
heartbreak. The camera lingers on the stunned boy in white in
front of white Stone Farm, in front of the greater snowy whiteness beyond. There is the unfinished white smock flapping in the
wind—symbol of privilege and authority that Pelle refuses. Snow,
ice the mist-covered sea: much of *Pelle* is about whiteness—the
fierce, hostile pallor of a chillingly unyielding world.

Which returns us to Persson's cinematography. Note, for instance, the hues of a dawn sky: strips of the palest green, yellow,
rose—subtle, almost subliminal, and quite sublime. Or take that
entire final leavetaking, which movingly continues through the
closing titles: Stone Farm in the Nordic pre-dawn light, with the
buildings and a clump of trees etched in spidery tracery on a
bleached-out background: one of the rare moments on film when
reality turns into evocative abstraction. But as Pelle escapes, bits
of hopeful color on land and sea break realistically, vivifyingly
through.

And how marvelous are the supporting players. Consider, for

example, Björn Granath, who plays Erik, another Swedish laborer at the farm. Beefy and often stolid, Erik is also the embodiment of defiance with his raucous humor and hope of emancipation. He sustains Pelle even when he himself succumbs to a fate worse than tragic—grotesquely ironic, abjectly ludicrous. Granath, a bovine Scandinavian W. C. Fields, acts with childlike simplicity and wrenching transparence we are allowed to see repressed feelings mount in this slow but good man like a colored liquid carefully poured into a bottle. Or consider the *con sordino* acting of Astrid Villaume as Mrs. Kongstrup: both her agonies and her triumph are played with the mute pedal depressed—and how depressingly right it all is! And how fine, too, is funny-looking young Troels Rasmussen as the troll- or faun-like bastard son of Kongstrup who brings a much-needed panic element into the outdoor scenes. Yet even here the director wisely opts for understatement.

Not the least virtue of the film is the courage to leave some things unexplained. Which does not mean that the clues aren't there; only that, unlike in most Hollywood films, the audience is not absolved from thinking. The feeling in *Pelle* is so personal and intense—Andersen Nexø was himself, like his boy hero, a downtrodden cowherd—that the director does not need to editorialize; it suffices to use images imaginatively. Take, for example, the carriage imagery. When Lasse and Pelle come to Stone Farm, August shoots across the trotting horse's croup and head onto the landscape opening up in newness and (misplaced) hope. When Kongstrup rides forth in pursuit of pleasure, we usually see the carriage in profile, spreading possessively across the frame and scenery. Twice, when a sympathetic character is carted off to his doom, the last shot is from the rear, with the carriage a prison cell from which the victim stares back in a last, soundless call for help.

But the concluding words of praise must go to Max von Sydow. There is a scene near the end where his misery is shot almost entirely from the back, his face only briefly, partially visible. Yet there is more ineffable wretchedness in that rear view, as Lasse weeps in terminal defeat, than other actors could give us in full frontal closeup and twice the amount of time. Almost unprecedentedly, von Sydow, though in a foreign-language film, was nominated for an Oscar. Of course it went to the infinitely busier, showier, phonier emoting of Dustin Hoffman. But for the real thing—unaccommodated man, the poor, bare, forked animal—make mine Max.

Scanted Scandal

SCANDAL

A couple of reviewers having already quoted Philip Larkin's verses on the significance of the 1963 Profumo scandal for Britain's sexual mores, I shall have to forgo the pleasures of verse in dealing with the English film *Scandal.*

Too bad, because Larkin's "Annus Mirabilis" is ever so nice. In plain prose, however, the dalliance of John Profumo, the secretary of state for war, with Christine Keeler, an 18-year-old showgirl turned good-time girl, eventually toppled the Macmillan cabinet, and conservatism, in more ways than one, was out. At the storm's not so calm center was, besides Christine, Stephen Ward, the vicar's son and society osteopath, who also acted as unpaid pimp to the nobility. He groomed girls like Christine as "escorts" to the high and mighty, and enjoyed in exchange such privileges as the cottage on the estate of Cliveden, which Lord Astor rented him for a pound a year. It turned out, in the end, to be more like a pound of flesh.

After Christine, out of fear, spite, and greed, spilled the beans—and he himself made matters worse by blabbing—Ward was abandoned by his powerful clients and friends, and was brought to trial as the fall guy; he took his life before the guilty verdict was in. Profumo had to confess not only to adultery but also to lying; he had to resign, and he and his wife, the actress Valerie Hobson, devoted themselves to charitable works, eventually earning him a CBE. Miss Keeler spent nine months in jail for perjury, lost her good looks, and eked out an obscure existence, coming into slight prominence in 1983 with the publication of her autobiography, and now with this film. Her even younger fellow callgirl, Mandy Rice-Davies, was the only one tough and canny enough to emerge unscathed; she went on to a career as a songstress and owner of a chain of night-clubs in Israel.

Clearly there is a cinematic goldmine in all this, but Michael Caton-Jones, the director, and Michael Thomas, the scenarist, have not been able to make much of a movie. Some of the reasons are obvious. Caton-Jones wanted to direct a TV mini-series, allowing scope for details and full development; a feature film was deemed more salable. The result is ferocious foreshortening and severe stinting on character analysis. A bigger handicap was the draconian British libel law, not to mention the filmmakers' intent to make this an at-

tack on the class system and, as far as possible, to whitewash Ward
and Miss Keeler. So we do not get the man with the two-way mirror
in his living room, for him and others to watch the goings-on in
the bedroom; the man who, seldom if at all sleeping with his girls
(he lived, at different times, with both Christine and Mandy), nevertheless participated in orgies; the man who derived some latent
physical satisfaction from offering his Galateas to men he envied,
admired, longed to be. We do not even get the trendy osteopath
who treated the likes of Churchill, Averell Harriman, Danny Kaye,
and Elizabeth Taylor.

What we do get is the victim of class consciousness. Already at
public school, we learn, Ward was caned for an offense everyone
knew he had not committed, and though he became a successful
healer, drove a white Jaguar, enjoyed hobnobbing with the great for
whom he arranged sexual encounters, he never quite arrived. "It is
a closed society," we see him explaining to Christine, whom he has
just taken under his wing; "you have to be either beautiful or rich."
Ward was neither, but by supplying beauty (though never for actual
payment), he could barter his way into belonging.

Why was becoming a member of Society so crucial to him? This
is one question *Scandal* never really addresses; the other is exactly
what happened between him and Christine. All right, there was no
sex, we gather, though Christine, it seems, came to want it. Well,
why not? Was it Ward's voyeurism or sadomasochism, which bypasses normal fulfillment, or was it latent homosexuality, which
requires vicarious means for its satisfaction? The film takes Ward's
craving to become part of Society as a given and, except for tenu-
ous hints, does not concern itself with his sexuality. The platonic
quasi-romance between the principals is not even as believable as
that in John Schlesinger's *Darling*.

We do get some mild orgying with social-climbing and kinky
overtones, though here the film ran into censorship troubles in the
United States. A rather stylized bit of party sex on top of a piano
had to be cut, which is carrying soft-pedaling a mite too far. But an
aging, saggy-breasted, bragging hostess and former JFK playmate
is still there, unappetizingly embodied by Britt Ekland. So, too, is
the likewise naked elderly man (reputed to be a High Court judge)
serving drinks and wearing a placard round his neck instructing
those unsatisfied with his services to flog him.

Is this what Ward was trying so hard to break into? Either there
was much more to it, or else he was even shallower than all but

his worst detractors would have had it. No wonder the filmmakers tried to squeeze a specious love story out of these drab events.
But Christine, rather unromantically, got involved with a couple of
West Indians, lustier and nearer her own age. It is a savage knife
fight between those two that really precipitated retroactive revelations; that, and one of them shooting up the front door of Ward's
flat, where Christine and Mandy were cowering. In one of the best
scenes, a neighbor woman, witnessing the assault, phones Stephen
at his office: "Dr. Ward, I thought you should know there's a black
man shooting at your front door." Ward replies, "It's very kind of
you to call." This believably conveys Ward's gentleness. Not so the
unconvincing silent love scene at Ward's trial, where Christine and
Stephen exchange mutely adoring glances until he jumps up in a
self-damaging outburst, in an effort to spare Miss Keeler more excruciating grilling in the witness box.

But are Christine's other relationships shown any more compellingly? Those with the West Indians, although cursory, have a
certain aroma of truth. But the Profumo episodes barely scratch the
surface, and those with another simultaneous lover, Eugene Ivanov,
the Russian naval attaché (particularly damaging, when revealed,
to the Tory government in those spy-ridden times), merely tickle
the surface. Profumo, of course, is alive and, having gone from philandering to philanthropy, could easily have sued for libel. As for
the Russian, doubtless a KGB spy, why imperil détente for a mere
movie? Better concentrate on Profumo's white Rolls-Royce, even
more photogenic than Ward's Jaguar. But we miss Ward's pathetic
attempts to act as a James Bondish counterspy during the Cuban
missile crisis.

Stereotypes are everywhere, not least in the way Christine and
Mandy meet cute during a nightclub Indian-maiden number, sparring at first but quickly becoming fast friends. A scene with the
supine Christine bored while Profumo is heaving on top of her is
straight out of *Klute*. Another sequence, showing Christine and
Mandy getting dressed for a night on the town, though effective as
it delights in fetishistic closeup as each new garment is wiggled or
slithered into, is nevertheless too reminiscent of a similar scene in
Dangerous Liaisons. In another sequence, at Murray's Cabaret Club,
the scantily clad dancers and unclad showgirls are scrutinized by
a camera that pans in a tight shot across the chorus line forming
backstage; in extreme closeup, you can see strings of saliva in a
sensuously opened mouth, like stalactites in a cave. Good, but, for

the most part, the film seems to be spelunking without a strong enough flashlight. Its best ideas are minuscule ones, such as the cigarette lighter Ward keeps overeagerly thrusting at people, till it looks and sounds like a weapon for social climbing. So, too, that other lighter, from Asprey's, that Christine is given by a lover—so beautiful that it is never shown in closeup: a magic status symbol left to our imagination.

Undistinguished in its writing, the film is better in its casting, even if Joanne Whalley-Kilmer does not make it as Christine. A competent but hardly sexually arousing actress, her face has one good angle, from which the camera deviates at her (and our) peril: from many other angles, she looks almost grotesque. A tiny person, she has nowhere near Christine's body and legs; who would have thought the distance from Keeler to Kilmer so great? And John Hurt, though an outstanding actor, is also a rumpled one, his face like that of a sharpei pup. But Stephen Ward was smooth all over; even the man who stood bail for him (though this doesn't figure in the film) was smoothness itself: Claus Von Bülow. As the film portrays Ward, he is neither handsome nor witty nor polished enough to explain his success with either the ladies or the lords.

The others are fine. Thus Ian McKellen, as a boyishly avid Profumo with that Mohican-like hairline; given, for legal reasons, very few lines, the actor nevertheless creates a part out of looks and gestures. Thus Jeroen Krabbé, despite his Dutch accent, as a lustily vital Ivanov. And thus especially Bridget Fonda (Peter's daughter) as a demurely impudent Mandy exuding youthful irresistibility. Like the real-life Mandy from the scandal, Miss Fonda is the one person who truly profits from the movie *Scandal*.

My Thing, Right Or Wrong

DO THE RIGHT THING

Neither the cutesy, trivial sex carrousel of *She's Gotta Have It* (1986) nor the contrived, overstylized black-college musical *School Daze* (1988) prepared us for Spike Lee's third feature film, *Do the Right Thing*—which *he* spells with a capital T in "the," but we must not indulge him in everything. The earlier films showed skill, wit (though indifferent dialogue), and an eclectic, magpie-like ability to pick up bits from all over and make a personalized collage out of them;

they did not suggest that the young black writer-director would make his next film into something genuinely disturbing, strongly controversial, and nervily powerful. Not good, mind you, but slick, savvy, explosive.

Why not also good, then? Because though a work of art need not have the answers—indeed, it usually doesn't—it must ask its questions honestly. It must, even if it knows that there are no answers—and not just no easy answers—try to shed as much light as it sensitively and searchingly can. And it must be fair to all sides or be candid about which side it is taking. Above all, it must know itself. None of this is true of *Do the Right Thing*, a clever film that, every step of the way, outsmarts itself.

It concerns the "hottest day of the summer" on one block of Brooklyn's Bedford-Stuyvesant section, a poor neighborhood but not a slum. The brownstones lining the block are all tolerable, and there is also a storefront radio station, a church, a newly opened Korean market, and Sal's Famous Pizzeria, which Sal has run for many years. He and his two sons, Pino, 22 (a hothead and racist), and Vito, twenty (a nice but somewhat dim fellow), live in Bensonhurst, but drive over every day. Their delivery boy, Mookie (Lee himself), is a canny young hustler, always counting his money and nurturing nebulous dreams of advancement. He resides with his sister, Jade (played by his real-life sister, Joie, a pretty girl with a hairdo like a miniature car crash), but has a very young Puerto Rican wife, Tina, who, with their tiny son, lives at her mother's.

There are two choruses observing and commenting on the action. One is the three corner men, middle-aged guys lounging on a street corner and shooting the breeze while also taking potshots at one another and people around them. Though they seem to be penniless layabouts, they are well dressed and, apparently, comfortable. The second chorus comprises three young men and a girl who sit on stoops, dance around, turn on the fire hydrant for a street water-carnival, and frequent Sal's Famous. They, too, comment on the action, but from a youthful point of view. Finally, there are two old-timers who, without being a chorus exactly, give voice to the attitudes of the older generation.

Mother Sister (Ruby Dee) is a widow who lives in and off the brownstone her husband left her, and spends her time looking out the ground-floor window and condescendingly chatting with the passersby. Her opposite number is Da Mayor (Ossie Davis, Miss Dee's spouse), a beer-swilling street philosopher and self-appointed counselor to the neighborhood. He is in love with Mother Sister, who, however, berates, insults, or ignores him. He pays her elaborate compliments, buys her roses (with what money?), and humbly endures her contumely. Only when he throws himself into the street to snatch a kid from the jaws of an onrushing car does he earn a grudging compliment from his sassy Dulcinea.

The main action involves the conflict between Sal and two of the block's wilder inhabitants. One is Buggin' Out, a young man with distinctly neurotic symptoms, who objects to Sal's displaying pictures of famous Italian-Americans but none of famous blacks, even though most of the pizzeria's customers are black. Sal tells him that in his own establishment he can hang whatever pictures he wants; in the ensuing argument, he orders Buggin' Out out of his place, with the latter vowing to have the eatery boycotted. But he can enlist only two fellow boycotters: the block's other problem child, Radio Raheem, a huge, taciturn, unsmiling youth promenading about with his enormous boom box blasting away the same rap music (by Public Enemy) at top volume.; and Smiley, an unsmiling retardate who peddles hand-colored prints of the only picture ever taken of Martin Luther King and Malcolm X together.

The pivot around which much of this conflict whirls is Mookie. Working for Sal, and liked by him and Vito (though detested by Pino), Mookie has to an extent become part of that white family business, but, being black, tends to align himself with the black clientele, even the hostile ones. Still, being above all a me-firster and opportunist (he has ways of extorting sizable tips from the people he delivers pizzas to), Mookie is really on nobody's side but his own, always watching which way the wind is blowing—if we can talk of wind in this stifling heat—and acting in his own best interest. In a sense, then, *Do the Right Thing* is about Mookie's (Or Spike's) politicization, about his taking sides and starting the uprising.

There are minor confrontations with whites earlier: one with a loudmouth whose fancy convertible gets deliberately doused from the hydrant manipulated by a member of Chorus #2; the other with a yuppie who has bought a brownstone on the block and accidentally steps on Buggin' Out's new Air Jordans and soils them. In both cases, showdowns are avoided, perhaps a trifle unconvincingly. In fact, the episode with the yuppie (a cameo performance by John Savage) is one of the film's loose ends—probably intended as a "There goes the neighborhood" joke in reverse. Another is Mister Señor Love Daddy, the DJ of storefront station WLR (We Love Radio), who here fulfills roughly the same function Wolfman Jack did in *American Graffiti*—but if you must borrow someone else's idea you should do something more with it. Still another loose end, or red herring, is the homage to *Night of the Hunter*, where Robert Mitchum, a mad preacher, had his hands tattooed with LOVE and HATE, respectively. Here it is Radio Raheem who sports brass knuckle rings with these complementary legends, but for him they make very little sense, and his explanatory speeches, coming from a nonverbal person, still less. Yet remote, immaculate even in the heat and asserting his loud music, Raheem becomes for Spike an icon and, later, a martyred saint. But can sainthood be measured in decibels?

A more interesting near-confrontation occurs between Raheem and the hardworking Korean family running the market. Comments one of the corner men: "I betcha they haven't been a year off da motherfuckin boat before they opened up their own place." And later: "Either dem Koreans are geniuses or we blacks are dumb." Typically, Lee answers this question both ways. One corner man's "Nobody don't want the black man to be about shit," is rejected by another corner man as "Old excuse." But, a bit later, Da Mayor justifies his drunken indolence with, "Until you have stood in the doorway and heard the hunger of your five children, unable to do a damn thing about it, you don't know shit." This, apparently, is not the old excuse. Such duality, such ambivalence, runs through the entire film, from larger meanings to footling details, not, however, confronting the viewers with demanding quandaries but allowing everyone to come away with his own facile choice of answer.

Even before the violent climax and improbable denouement, there is troubling manipulativeness. By choosing a Saturday and Sunday morning for his time frame, Lee avoids the important matter of portraying many of his characters at work—or shirking it. By limiting his focus to one city block crisscrossed by the same principals and extras, a factitious intimacy is evoked, as in those old backlot movies with their cozily spurious sets. This absolves Lee (with one or two fleeting exceptions) from showing his characters involved with their families or friends living elsewhere. So relationships and interactions through which character is revealed can be finessed or left cavalierly vague. In fact, a whole larger social reality is ignored by omitting any reference to crack, even though the film crew had to dislodge crack dealers from two locations used in the movie. (They simply set up shop around the corner.) Mention this omission to Lee and he shouts "Racist!" at you.

Of course Lee's excuse—and it's a pretty neat one—would be that the artist must be selective, that he can't go into every detail of his numerous characters' lives. Furthermore, by using stylization, as in a sequence of monologues delivered straight into the camera by a number of characters reviling a member of another race, Lee can claim that his film is not strictly realistic (true enough) and can't be judged by naturalistic criteria. He might further argue that his characters are sufficiently defined by a symbol, a synecdoche, a fetish each one has: Raheem and his ghetto blaster, Buggin' Out and his unlaced sneakers, Mookie and the greenbacks he keeps smoothing out, rearranging, counting. Also Sal and his Mickey Mantle baseball bat, with which he metes out summary justice, Smiley and his photographs; and so on. Call it heightened, poetic realism.

But the questions raised clamor for more attention. What does it mean that these Koreans and Italo-Americans are working hard, while the blacks, all but Mookie, are taking it easy? Well, perhaps Saturdays are for relaxing. Then why does Mookie keep at it? Because he has a family to support? No—else why would both Jade and Tina keep upbraiding him? And considering his reasonable earnings from salary and tips, why does he mooch off Jade and let his wife and child live with the mother-in-law who hates him? And if Sal, who is shown as pretty decent, is mainly good to him, why is it Mookie who tosses a trashcan through the pizzeria's window to start the looting? Some argue that by attacking the pizzeria, he deflects the mob's rage from its owners. Yet nothing in the film as we see and hear it (which differs in some ways both from the intentions stated in the filmmaker's journals and from the screenplay published along with them) supports this. Indeed, the overwhelming use of the anti-Semitic rap group Public Enemy's song "Fight the Power," the cops' accidental killing of Raheem (never mind that he was deliberately trying to strangle Sal), the mob's yelling "Coward Beach" as they set fire to Sal's Famous, Lee's numerous references in the journals and screenplay to Michael Stewart and Eleanor Bumpurs (two black victims of alleged brutality), as well as the uprising finally bringing together the newly politicized Mother Sister and Da Mayor, all suggest that Lee advocates violence.

Or is there an honest uncertainty, a true *aporia*, expressed in the two quotations Lee appends to the film: one from Dr. King, decrying violence as a solution, followed by another from Malcolm X, saying that it is stupid not to resort to violence in "self-defense," i.e., in righting social inequity. But consider the running order:

Malcolm's solution comes last, as it were answering and supersed-
ing King's. I think it's also worth adverting to the closing words of
the epilogue Lee prints in the book version:

> Am I advocating violence? *No*, but goddamn, the
> days of 25 million Blacks being silent while our
> fellow brothers [*sic*] and sisters are exploited, op-
> pressed, and murdered, have to come to an end. Ra-
> cial persecution, not only in the United States, but
> all over the world *is* not gonna go away: it seems it's
> getting worse (four years of Bush won't help). And
> if Crazy Eddie Koch gets reelected for a fourth term
> as mayor of New York, what you see in *Do The Right
> Thing* will be light stuff. Yep, we have a choice, Mal-
> colm or King. I know who I'm down with.

I think there is little doubt about whom he is down with, despite his characteristic refusal to name him in a context where
other names are blithely bandied about. Koch, to be sure, has been
Lee's bugbear at the very least since Lee's graduation project from
NYU Film School, *Joe's Bed-Stuy Barbershop: We Cut Heads* (1982),
wherein a character—while playing the numbers!—declares that
four more years of Koch ain't gonna be no picnic. What this para-
graph seems to be saying is: I'm for peaceful solutions but, what
with Bush already in the White House, all that's needed is Koch's
re-election for all hell to break loose. And then there's no question
about whose side I'll be on.

There are three conclusions to be derived, I think, from this
generally well directed, acted, and photographed (by Ernest Dickerson) film. 1) The movie, consciously or unconsciously, intends to
be rabble-rousing. 2) It is highly unlikely to succeed, but if it does,
no one will be happier than Spike. 3) That happiness would have
less to do with the weal of "fellow brothers" than with the ego trip
of a middle-class armchair revolutionary.

Batman

You must have noticed that more and more American movies are
based on comic strips (the *Superman* series, *Batman*, the upcoming

Dick Tracy), or on what might as well be comic strips (the Indiana Jones series, the so far only two *Ghostbusters*, *Who Framed Roger Rabbit?*, and scads more.) You will also have noticed how many movies are sequels (the list is endless). What does this mean? It is the sinister confluence of two unwholesome manifestations: rabid nostalgia and a frenzy for playing it safe.

The comic-strip is the epitome of nostalgia, sequels, and playing it close to the vest. The nostalgia is for when one was young and devouring comic strips, sequentiality is built into the daily or weekly comic strip, and what could be financially safer than translation to the big screen—with stars—of a story that delighted fans for decades on end? In the case of *Batman*, there is also a TV version haunting the collective memory. So the public's attitude to this one is roughly what the ancient Greeks' would have been to a movie adaptation of the *Odyssey*. I have seen people in the *Batman* line picnicking on the sidewalk while awaiting their spiritual sustenance.

Well, *Batman* does provide spectacular production design. Gotham City, as dreamed up by Anton Furst, is an amazing amalgam of present-day New York, Fritz Lang's *Metropolis*, Victor Hugo's Notre Dame and environs, the Temple of Karnak, Art Deco as Edgar Allan Poe might have conceived it, and perhaps also postmodernism after acid rain has had its well-deserved way with it. It is a parody city, but with a certain sinister beauty about it as well as genuine horror. Furst is the relatively rare case of an art director who is not only a director of art but also a connoisseur. With sets like these, one could have made an adult movie, perhaps a satirical dystopia that might have commented sardonically, wittily, seriously on the way of our world. What a pity to waste such visual talent—not to mention such money—on a comic strip.

Of course, the film will recoup its investment many times over, and is very likely to become one of the top grossers in cinema annals. But isn't there something truly gross about such unmitigated waste, such downright concupiscent greed? If the history of trash is ever written—and, unbeknown to me, it probably has been already—wouldn't it have to distinguish between trash with some redeeming inventiveness and excitement, and trash of the callously exploitative and predictable sort, such as this *Batman*? (Not having ever caught Bob Kane's cartoon or the campy TV show it generated, I cannot speak about other *Batmen* or *Batmans*.) Will audiences never get tired of invincible Good disguising itself in mask and cape and, with or without a faithful companion (Tonto, Robin, Lois Lane), foiling vincible Evil in the nick of time? And what is so fascinating—except to nerds, who can identify themselves, realistically, with the Clark Kent persona while dreaming themselves into the Other—about the cut-and-dried dual personality of the superman-hero?

And speaking of Robin, he is conspicuous by his absence from the new *Batman*. The thinking was that, in this less innocent age, he would give rise to speculations about a possible homosexual relationship between himself and Batman, or Batman's other persona, the immensely wealthy playboy Bruce Wayne. That at least would have given the movie some crude interest of the do-they-or-don't-they kind. Instead, we get the glamorous photographer Vicki Vale, who is prompt to tumble into bed with Bruce but excruciatingly slow about deducing his other identity.

The entire story, after that dalliance, is a protracted coitus semi-interruptus until, at film's end, Vicki is reuinted with Bruce. Well, not quite with Bruce, but with his Jeevesian valet/chauffeur, Alfred, and Bruce's Rolls-Royce, comfier than the Batmobile, a product of miscegenation between a Maserati and a finned Cadillac. Alfred makes her get in and assures her that his master will join them presently. Yet the concluding shot offers Bruce still in full Batman regalia, surveying, from the pinnacle of the tallest building, his beloved Gotham City, temporarily purified by him. I am not sure what this mild ambiguity portends: most likely, heaven help us, a sequel.

There are only two scenes in the two-hour movie that have any resonance, and neither of them has anything to do with Michael Keaton, who spends much of his screen time in Batman costume, which exposes (other than those radar eyes) only the tip of his nose, the rosebud mouth (suggestive of Betty Boop or, just possibly, a fruit bat), and the chin, with which he is pretty much forced to lead. The scenes do, however, involve Jack Nicholson, as the petty thief Jack Napier, who, in his other persona, becomes the Joker, the hideously laughing supervillain with the disfigured mouth, supposedly caused by Batman's having tossed him into a vat of boiling, viridescent chemicals, but more plausibly derived from Victor Hugo's *L'Homme qui rit* (or its silent-movie version). Nicholson gives an inspiredly comic-epic performance as the cackling sadist whose rictus would spell the last laugh for the world, were it not for Batman.

In Nicholson's material there is even a smidgen of comic invention by the scenarists, Sam Hamm and Warren Skaaren. (Are these real names? Real people? I'd like to think that they are merely a team of screenwriting jingles. Surely "Warren" and "Skaaren" must be pronounced so as to rhyme, as "Sam" and "Hamm," and "love" and "dove," do.) There is a bit of cleverness in having the Joker poison various cosmetics so that, used in certain combinations, they will induce the same clownish grin as his, followed by swift death. Although such a conceit lacks the minimal illusion of credibility that lends piquancy to the incredible, it is still good for a disgruntled guffaw or two. But if Nicholson's performance steadily transcends the Joker's material, nothing much follows suit.

To return, however, to the two scenes that almost do. The first is the one where the Joker and his goons invade the local art museum and, while he sings and cavorts outrageously, deface the masterpieces from all periods hanging there—except for a Francis Bacon, whose work pleases the Joker. There is, thanks largely to Nicholson, a ghastly vandalistic humor to this, but the filmmakers missed a chance to do something positive by not showing Pollocks, Rauschenbergs, Warhols, and the like being defaced.

The other scene of some interest is the dark-garbed Joker's crazed skyscraper-top waltz with the white-clad, fainting Vicki (Kim Basinger), whom he intends to ravish and destroy as he already did a previous girlfriend, played, alas, by Jerry Hall (Mick Jagger's mistress), whose face before disfigurement is not much better than after it. As Nicholson whirls about laughing fiendishly with the limp and all but lifeless Vicki in his malefic arms, it conjures up images of Death and the Maiden, Dr. Miracle and Antonia. Svengali and Trilby, and other mythic or near-mythic archetypes.

The direction by Tim Burton is appropriately slick and mindless. Burton allows the scenarists to come up with several shaggy-dog plot elements (an imminent bicentennial celebration for which the city has no funds, a crusading D.A. who does absolutely nothing, a police commissioner who arbitrarily fades in and out of the action), and he cannot give shape to the material. But that is the occupational hazard in making movies out of comic strips, an art form that is all middle and no end. Kim Basinger has been lovelier and more effective in other movies: her main distinction here is that she sheds or loses her shoes in three separate scenes, either because she thinks she is playing Shoeless Joe or because she is taller than her leading man. Jack Palance, Pat Hingle, and especially the good Michael Gough are stuck with no-account roles: as Gotham City's mayor, Lee Wallace is a perfect Ed Koch lookalike, but nothing is made of that, either.

The Red, Red Robin
Comes Blabbin' Along

DEAD POETS SOCIETY

Let me come right out and say it: *Dead Poets Society* (naturally without an apostrophe) is the most dishonest movie I have seen in a long time. It is a particularly plummy specimen of the pseudo-sensitive, pseudo-serious, pseudo-real film. What is so distressing about the present state of affairs is that a picture as manifestly fake as this can get unlimited credit just for pretending to be serious. Here is what its producer says about the screenwriter: "Tom Schulman has done something remarkable. Instead of filling the screen with machinery, knights in armor, fast cars, or big guns—he has created an inspiring teacher whose warmth and ideas make him a larger-than-life character."

So it has come to that: merely because of what your film is *not* about, it has done something remarkable. That's like saying that because you do not pick fights with other bus-riders, do not run down pedestrians on the sidewalk with your bicycle, and do not relieve yourself on storefronts, you are a perfect gentleman. Sadly, though, when almost all movies are trashy and imbecile, seriousness of intent, however specious, is hailed as achievement.

And what about that "inspiring teacher whose warmth and ideas make him a larger-than-life character"—that Mr. Chips for our time; or at least for 1959, the time of the film? Robin Williams, who plays John Keating, makes his students rip the pedantic introduction (or, rather, absurd parody of an introduction) out of their poetry textbooks; has them walk around the courtyard each at his own pace only to fall into a common rhythm (to learn about lack of independence); gets them to attack a soccer ball after uttering some profound wish, and thus kick the ball with unprecedented force; invites them to follow him up to the top of his desk, "to look at things in a different way." When a boy is shy about speaking up in class, Keating writes on the blackboard: "I sound my barbaric yawp over the roofs of the world," and carries on like a raving (Whit)maniac to get the boy to utter loud yawps and free-associate while he whirls him about as the camera pans around with both of them.

Some of this may make a good English teacher, but much of it does not. Certainly saying, during that walking exercise, "Everyone started out with *their* own stride," is not worthy of a Groton—Exeter—Andoverish school, which this is supposed to be. But there are a great many more bizarre things here. For example, Keating conducts his first class out in the hall, with everyone standing and staring at framed photographs of students gone by: "*Carpe diem*, lads! Seize the day! Make your lives extraordinary. 'Cause we are food for worms, lads!" The class of 1902 is already "fertilizing daffodils." In 1959, these '02 graduates of Welton Academy would be in their mid seventies, and just as likely to be watering those daffodils as pushing them up. It's not a major lapse, but the movie is full of such disturbingly accumulating sloppinesses: "Gone, history," says Keating, in a way that smacks of the present-day "I'm history."

Such carelessness is everywhere. "I could care less about you," says Chris, the pretty blonde: her slip, though common now, was unknown in 1959. When Neil Perry, our sensitive hero, gets cast as Puck in the neighboring girls' school's production of *A Midsummer Night's Dream*, he tells Tom, his martinet of a father, "I have the main part." No one would describe Puck as the main part in *Dream*, and the further implication is that Tom Perry doesn't know the play, even though he is a Welton graduate, for shame! When the evil headmaster, Mr. Nolan (played, significantly, by one of Hitchcock's villains), takes over Keating's poetry class, he asks the boys what they have been reading; it was mostly the romantics. "What about the realists?" he asks. Answer: "I believe we skipped over most of that, sir."

Well now, just who are these realist poets one can leapfrog over? Carl Sandburg? Edwin Markham? Edgar Lee Masters? There are no realists in the poetry syllabus; but if they existed, Keating could not have just skipped over them at a school such as Welton Academy without getting into trouble. Nor could he have used all his other unorthodox methods without getting more than a mild, belated caveat from Mr. Nolan, who, though he appears to have more eyes than Argus himself, remains pretty much in the dark about Keating's pedagogy until there is a crisis. But the crucial absurdity is Tom Perry's going bonkers over his son's playing Puck.

Neil, a senior in this prestigious prep school, is getting an A in every course. Yet his father has forbidden his being on the yearbook, so, to have an outside activity, he takes on this play. His performance as Puck, we are to understand, rates an A, too. Not only Keating, not only Neil's fellow members of the Dead Poets Society (more about that anon), but also the entire cast of *Dream*, the teachers of both schools, the assembled students and parents—everybody goes berserk with enthusiasm: standing ovation, thunderous applause, kisses and compliments from all. But Tom Perry watches this with a mounting, white-lipped, icily psychotic rage. He drives Neil home and informs him that he is transferring him to military school, so that he'll get into Harvard College and Medical School—after he finishes those, he can do as he likes.

Let's face it, Neil, who has only a little way to go to graduation from Welton with top honors, has a much better chance of getting into Harvard that way than coming from some military academy—always assuming that such a transfer is possible at this late stage. Would not any normal father, however little use he had for extracurricular activities, consider his son's acting success a trump card, proving to the Harvard admissions people that Neil, with his straight-A record, isn't just some academic drudge? And would not Neil's mother, whom Tom makes witness to this angry scene, interpose some defense of her boy? No: she's just a repressed, frightened, chain-smoking housewife. Ditto the mother of Neil's roommate, Todd; in a later scene in the headmaster's office, this good woman exudes mere silent fright. And Todd's father proves an equally mindless bully.

Consider the clichés: all through the confrontation with his dad, Neil clutches a chaplet made of twigs and ornamented with holly and mistletoe berries that he wore on stage as Puck; before he shoots himself with his father's gun, the half-naked boy puts the wreath on once more. It dawns on us that Peter Weir, the Australian director (unless it is Tom Schulman, the scenarist), wants us to perceive Neil as a Christ symbol. This is all the more absurd because what we see of Neil's performance as Puck, for which he is being crucified, was perfectly awful. And what about the idiocy of casting a boy who seems well over six feet as the mischievous goblin? A Robin Goodfellow that towers above all the rest is no Robin—maybe an ostrich.

While on the subject of preposterousness, let's examine John Keating more closely. A graduate of Welton, where he founded the Dead Poets Society—a group of boys meeting in a nearby cave to recite poetry at one another, an activity Neil and six friends have revived—he has been teaching at a British public school and has (or had) an English girlfriend whose picture now graces his desk. Why would anyone leave a good school and sweetheart in England to come back to teach and chafe at a center of spiritual sclerosis such as Welton? Or was he fired by his English school, just as he is, unjustly, from Welton? For having encouraged Neil to get his father's consent to being in the play (something the boy seems to have extorted over the telephone—the film fudges this), Keating is blamed for the suicide and dismissed. Surely, if a school wanted to hush up a scandal, it would not do so by firing a fine and innocent teacher, thereby, as it were, admitting his and the school's guilt.

But Keating is preposterous in more ways, especially as Robin Williams acts him. Williams cannot refrain from indulging in his impersonations—of Brando, old-style Old Vic Shakespeareans, and a host of others—in mockery that is far more vulgarly crowd-pleasing than inspiringly educational. And for an alleged intellectual, Keating's literary tastes are stunningly clichéd. Every poem or piece of prose he tosses at his class seems to come from some *First Book of Quotations* for the use of young children. I even predicted the exact moment at which one boy, under Keating's aegis, would impress a girl with "She walks in beauty," right on the heels of "Shall I compare thee to a summer's day?"

Every adult in the film is either a tyrant or a hypocrite, a coward or a fool, or a combination of these. Except, of course, Keating. He can even perform miracles; how else would *Five Centuries of Verse*, a book that belonged to him as a student at Welton and bears his name, suddenly turn up in Neil's room, a mysterious materialization the film leaves unexplained? The ludicrous beastliness of the adults stretches to the point where boys to be questioned by the headmaster are summoned by a loud call from the bottom of the grand staircase by the slave-driving math teacher, only to be led up the stairs—in silhouette, no less—as if not to the headmaster's office but to the headsman's scaffold.

Still, why not? Tom Schulman was co-scenarist for *Honey, I Shrunk [sic] the Kids*; here, in the spirit of fair play, he shrank (or "shrunk") the adults. Why, Tom Perry, before going to sleep, lines up his slippers by his bedside as if they were soldiers on parade, to the millimeter. Earlier, Tom yelled at a teacher at his revered alma mater, "Keating, stay away from my son!" This desperately proper man would do no such thing. And he should not be played by Kurtwood Smith, who looks and acts like a model psychopath.

But, then, Peter Weir is one of the most overrated directors around; in *Dead Poets Society*, he revels in picture-postcard shots of the passing seasons and allows Maurice Jarre, his composer, to back up shots of soccer practice with Händel and Beethoven, even as his cinematographer, John Seale, backs them up with deliquescent sunsets. What Mary McCarthy said about Lillian Hellman applies to this film: I wouldn't even trust its *and*s and *the*s.

The Enemy Was Us

CASUALTIES OF WAR

Brian De Palma, who makes films in which women are brutally murdered, and David Rabe, a Vietnam veteran who writes plays about that war, have teamed up as director and screenwriter for *Casualties of War*, about an American platoon in Vietnam that kidnaps, gang rapes, and finally kills a pretty, teen-aged Vietnamese farm girl. The film is based on Daniel Lang's 1969 *New Yorker* article, later published as a book. This is the true story as told by Private "Sven Eriksson" (only the names have been changed), the one member of the five-man squad opposed to the rape, who tried to stop it but couldn't, tried to save the girl's life but failed, suffered terrible pangs of conscience but, against overwhelming pressure from above, managed at least to bring his comrades to trial. It is an ugly and important story, and although I admire De Palma for telling it—some of it very well—I deplore the way he ultimately flubs it.

The film is already stirring up controversy. Movie critics are vehemently divided, veterans' organizations have lodged angry protests in Washington, David Rabe has registered his unhappiness with what De Palma did to his script. There *should* be discussion of the movie and the events that prompted it, and it is good that the tale on film will get out among people who, alas, do not read. But it is disheartening that De Palma saw fit to fudge the ending—or was his arm twisted by Dawn Steel, the president of Columbia Pictures? Could that steely executive have insisted on giving the customers some release, some hope, some heavenly choirs?

I haven't read Lang's book, but gather that one-third of it deals with the court-martial of the four men. De Palma telescopes the trial scenes into a relatively brief montage and concentrates instead,

after some fictionalized combat scenes, on the true events involving the girl Oanh (the one name Lang did not change). For this he
has already caught some flak from Frances FitzGerald, Vietnam
correspondent and feminist, for having made "a sadoporn flick
coated with sentimentality and laced with every cliche of the Vietnam War." That is not a fair assessment. The sentimentality does
not come in till the end, the rape is treated forcefully but discreetly,
and though the dialogue has a few clunky moments, it is superior
to that of *Platoon*, *Full Metal Jacket*, etc.

Some military details are wrong, however, and there are other
lapses. Thus the scenes in which the squad engages the Cong across
a river, the endlessly drawn-out killing of Oanh, the absurd way the
hitherto canny Sergeant Meserve exposes his men and himself to
the enemy, the equally absurd way none of them gets hit even as an
American gunboat coming down the river is blown to bits by VC
copters—all this, though crudely effective, has unfortunate overtones of *The Wild Bunch* and even *Duel in the Sun*. Throughout the
film, De Palma will follow up something believable and powerful
with something contrived and crassly manipulative.

Take the opening scene, in which young Eriksson, new to Vietnam and with a wife and baby daughter back home, finds himself
in the thick of jungle warfare. The confusion is well conveyed. But
then he sinks up to his waist into a Vietcong tunnel that gives way.
He is stuck, legs dangling underground, shells bursting all around
him, palm trees turning into huge, closing-in torches. No one hears
his calls for help: nothing like a battle to leave you isolated, alone.
Next we see the Cong advancing through the tunnel, crouching as
they run; but one fierce fellow, knife in his teeth and headed for
those dangling legs, suddenly has to crawl—that way you can milk
the suspense interminably. But tough young Sergeant Meserve, in
the nick of time, pulls his man out and blasts the creepy-crawly to
kingdom come. A calculated effect, to say the least.

Next, we're in a peaceful-seeming village, where Eriksson helps
an old farmer plow with a team of buffaloes; Sven is so naive he
even accepts a gift of food from the villagers. Meserve and Brownie, a jolly black soldier (the two buddies are soon to be shipped
stateside), lecture him about gullibility. The peasants imperceptibly
make themselves scarce; VC, disguised as farmers, start hurling gre-
nades: Brownie, with his arm around Sven, is hit in the throat by a
sniper. Meserve performs wonders for his friend, stanching the jet
of blood, boosting his morale. A chopper appears and evacuates

Brownie, but we know he is dying. All this is shot, edited, acted dazzlingly. Best of all is the sequence back at base camp: Meserve shaves with a straight razor, says nothing while the camera seems glued to him; we sense that quietly, inwardly, he is going nuts. Sean Penn acts this superlatively.

Meserve and the chief brutes in his squad—Corporal Clark, a classic beast, and Hatcher, a grinning idiot—are unable to get release from their pent-up emotions with the local whores; an MP stops them from leaving camp: tonight it's the VC's turn with the girls. There is something monstrously preposterous about this punctilio at the heart of chaos. Enraged, Meserve announces to the squad, ordered on a five-day mission into the highlands, that they will "requisition" a village girl for "a little portable R&R." If anything goes wrong, she was just "a Vietcong whore" killed during questioning. The scene of the girl's night-time abduction—her and her family's terror, Eriksson's helpless consternation—is bone-chillingly effective. But then comes a false touch: the agonized mother runs after her captured, frightened daughter with a scarf for the "journey"—a scarf with which the bestial Clark promptly gags the girl who is crying out in her language.

This scarf does not belong in the steamy jungle. But De Palma needs it for a parallel effect in his epilogue, a bit of gimmickry that will prove profoundly offensive. On the march into the highlands, the wretched girl is obliged to carry the pack of one of her tormentors; it bloodies her back (Christ carrying the Cross?). Effective, too, is the capitulation of Diaz, the Hispanic squad member. He was going to help Sven defend the girl, but yields to vicious taunts impugning his masculinity and to his fear of being abandoned in combat. The gang rape itself is horrible though comparatively downplayed, the main horror is in the condition of Oanh, physical and psychological, after being ravaged for two days. Thuy Thu Le, a Vietnamese refugee who had never acted before, plays Oanh, who cannot even complain in English, heartrendingly, sublimely.

But now, again, two false notes: Eriksson, whose attempts to help have been beaten back by the others, stands on guard in a nocturnal downpour; though blameless, he is tormented with guilt. Now Meserve joins him, makes a ranting postcoital speech, misquotes the Bible, dispenses half-confessional, half-defiant madness. This is the movie's attempt to heighten mere horror into the hallucinatory, the surreal. It fails—as does Eriksson's riven silence in a long, tight close-up, the blue-green rain pouring off his face in a slow-motion

halo effect. Pauline Kael comments: "De Palma has such seductive, virtuoso control of film craft that he can express convulsions
in the unconscious." Maybe De Palma can; but Michael J. Fox, as
Eriksson, can't. He is an honest, small actor—and I don't mean his
5'2" frame but what is needed here is inspired acting of the sort
Penn sometimes achieves (at other times, he is forcing it). The real,
rending truth is in Thuy Thu Le's incomprehensible gibbering—in
a language the others don't understand, in a pain no one can comprehend. And, later, in her broken moans, and, still later, in her
lacerating cough, which Meserve claims will give away their position, and which he turns into an excuse for killing her.

I need not dwell on the horror that follows, but scarcely less horrifying are the vain attempts of Eriksson, driven by his Lutheran
conscience, to bring the others to justice. The ever-higher-ranking
officers, all bent on quashing his efforts, are pungently and ever-
more-appallingly conveyed. An attempt by Clark on Sven's life is
exciting, but out of key with the rest of the movie. And the retaliation—puny Michael J. Fox flattening the neo-Neanderthal Don
Harvey (a terrifyingly good performance) with one blow of a spade
as his buddies watch and daren't intervene—simply strains credibility. The foreshortened courtmartial, including some tricky dissolves, is all right, but we are cheated out of the final confrontation
between Sven and Meserve. Instead, the strongest encounter is an
earlier one, when Sven tries to help Oanh escape, but they hesitate
and are lost. That should be, and is, climactic: but not to match it
here with another climax is a miscalculation.

And now for the frame story. In a prologue, Sven sees a beautiful Vietnamese girl riding in his subway car in San Francisco; he
falls into a grief-stricken reverie. Is, then, the main story merely a
dream? Well might you ask. As the main story ends, and the culprits
are given stiffer sentences than they got in real life (a signal piece
of dishonesty), we are back on that S.F. train. The girl gets off at a
stop and heads for a lovely grassy knoll. But she left her scarf (!)
behind; Sven runs after her with it. She had noticed him staring at
her—does she remind him of someone? Yes. (She, too, is played
by Thuy Thu Le.) Out of left field, as the music swells, she offers
absolution: "You had a bad dream. It's over. I think." The music
swells some more.

Where are Eriksson's wife and child we have been hearing about?
Why does Eriksson/Fox look the same age as he did in Vietnam:
twelve? Why are we in this very lovely and very public setting? (The

real Eriksson, still afraid for his and his family's safety, hides somewhere in the Midwest.) Here all is well: the guilty are put away for
decades, Eriksson is absolved by an avatar of Oanh, our hero and
America are off the hook. If this unparalleled piece of cowardice—a
J'accuse turned into a *J'accepte*—was the price of getting the movie
made, better perhaps it had not been made at all.

Sex and Violence, Together Again

SEA OF LOVE; SEX, LIES, AND VIDEOTAPE

Is there such a thing as a totally persuasive thriller? One that doesn't
cheat by intentionally withholding information or deliberately mis-
leading you or playing fast and loose with character? Perhaps there
is, but all too often you end up with questions such as "How could
he have known this?" and "Why would she have done that?" Still,
most of us are ready to grab at any hook to suspend our disbelief
from; even so, doubts creep in. They creep all over *Sea of Love*, but
the film is fun to watch.

It seems that the connection among several New York City
murders is that each victim was a man who advertised for female
companionship in the personals of *New York Weekly*, and, what's
more, advertised in verse. God knows there are few enough lonely
hearts who espouse verse for their solicitations, and even fewer
souls who care enough about poetry to shoot those who abuse it in
the head at point-blank range. But it seems there is a young woman
who—apparently out of some less justifiable motive than love of poetry—does dispatch lyrically lustful swains in that manner, and it is
up to detectives Frank Keller from Manhattan and his new partner,
Sherman Touhey from Queens (site of one of the murders), to track
down a killer who must be quite a woman judging by the alacrity
with which the victims admitted her to their apartments.

The method our sleuths hit upon is placing just such a poetical
ad in said magazine and asking respondees to a tryst at a popular
restaurant, where one of them pretends to be the love-starved fellow, the other a waiter. Frank and Sherman take turns in each role.
Now, although service in most restaurants is shockingly amateurish,
a detective-waiter might still arouse suspicion. But let it go, especially

since the scenes of first meetings with women are among the movie's best. There is a problem in this kind of work for both detectives: for hollow-eyed Frank, a tense, overwrought twenty-year man whose wife has just left him for his former partner, and who needs a new woman almost badly enough to put a genuine ad into the personals, as well as for good-natured, roly-poly Sherman, a happily married man who can use a little relief from so much domestic bliss. Sherman, to be sure, connects with a harmless flake; but Frank may have hit on the perpetrator, or, in this film's parlance, the doer.

Or has he? Certainly, Helen is an alluring young woman in a broad-shouldered jacket crimson enough for an old-style executioner. Or is she that alluring? Ellen Barkin, a good actress who nevertheless has nothing like the looks of a femme fatale, a role in which she is repeatedly being cast, might still be tempting enough to a lonely versifier. Indeed, she is so sure of herself that, displeased, she can promptly walk out on Frank Keller. And given Al Pacino's appearance these days—midway between owlish and cadaverous—a woman might well think twice. But perhaps not if she is the kind that answers such ads, and with checkmating rather than mating on her mind.

In any case, we and Frank know that this fish should not get away; nevertheless she does, without so much as leaving a fingerprint on a glass for Sherman to match up with the killer's. But as luck or the screenwriter would have it, Frank and Helen meet again by chance and, this time, click. Before you know it, they hit the bedroom, but not yet the sack; this is one of those mature movies even heavier on foreplay than on copulation. After which the enamored Frank wipes off Helen's fingerprints before he could check them.

Sea of Love begins with the corralling of a number of minor criminals in an amusing but wildly unbelievable way. More credible is the edginess of a detective who has reached the point where he could retire at half pay, but would then have nothing to live for. Credible, too, are the crazy fights he picks with his partner who has taken over his ex-wife. But Keller's problems are almost too much for the film, too real for the titillating, contrived main plot.

Still, Richard Price, the novelist and occasional screenwriter (*The Color of Money*), has come up with an attention-holding situation: a woman who may be a man-killer but who may also have fallen genuinely in love with this particular man, who, however, may want to arrest her for murder; and a man who may be grossly neglecting his police duty, not to mention imperiling his life, by falling for that woman. From their tangled motives and conflicting behavior, the film derives suspense in the teeth of improbability, and Harold Becker (who has made at least one memorable movie, *The Onion Fields*) has directed with appropriate splashiness. Barkin, Pacino, and John Goodman (Sherman) do well, although the first two are no slouches when given the chance to overact. *Sea of Love* even begins with a striking piece of dishonesty, but by the time we realize that, we have been swept far enough out to make swimming back to shore impossible.

Sex, Lies, and Videotape may be the most overrated, and is surely the most irritating, movie in some time. Made by 26-year-old Steven Soderbergh in his home town of Baton Rouge, it won best-film honors at Cannes for its writer-director, and best-actor prize for James Spader, who plays Graham, a young man who returns to Baton Rouge after a nine-year absence. He comes both to see his old flame, Elizabeth, and not to see her, both with a wad of money and with no visible source for it, both to arouse the two women in the story and to declare himself impotent, both to seem a perfect scoundrel and to end up in what promises to be a good, fulfilling relationship with the wife of his ex-roommate and dear friend, John. John (Peter Gallagher) is an up-and-coming lawyer who has just been made a junior partner at thirty, but who is cheating on his pretty though troubled wife, Ann (Andie MacDowell), with her sexy and sexually voracious sister, Cynthia (Laura San Giacomo). Cynthia works as a bartender at a strange establishment that has a bar roughly a mile long but only a single, permanent customer, evidently glued to his stool, and played with notable lack of virility by Steven Brill. This barfly makes indiscriminate advances to Cynthia, with whom he has a nice arrangement: whenever one of them feels horny, a phone call brings the other one running. This seems to be no problem at the mile-long bar, but it does create difficulties for John. First, Ann is so furious at discovering one of Cynthia's earrings near the conjugal bed that she rushes off to be videotaped by Graham in one of those sex interviews he conducts with countless young women. Next, John loses some important clients as a result of his absenteeism and may forfeit his job.

Graham questions women on videotape about their sex lives and fantasies, then uses his collection of tapes to masturbate by, the only form of sex he can still muster. Cynthia promptly ferrets out Graham and not only talks but also masturbates for his camera. This doubly distresses her sister when Cynthia tells her about it because Ann, who has fallen for Graham, was shocked to learn about those tapes; now she is also jealous of Cynthia. Finding that earring is the last straw; Ann actually seduces Graham during her videotaped interview, then initiates divorce proceedings. Earlier, John had raced over to Graham's, punched out his ex-roommate, watched the tape of his wife, then bragged about his affair with Graham's chastely beloved Elizabeth. Whereupon Graham destroys his tapes and embarks on what augurs to be perfect bliss with Ann. Do you buy any of this?

It is the sort of plot worked out easily enough with a slide rule and a prurient, second-rate mind. The film sheds no genuine light, only a lot of spurious heat. The nearest it gets to enlightening us is during Ann's sessions with her therapist (played by Ron Vawter as someone who might have far greater need of psychiatry himself), and it isn't much: Ann assumes funny poses on the confessional couch and rattles on about her worries concerning what happens to all that garbage out there. (Quite a bit of it finds shelter in this film.) For the rest, we get Graham's soulful maunderings, and sex scenes between Cynthia and John that look more like parodies. We are to recognize Cynthia's nymphomania by her always running around barefoot, wearing an ankle bracelet, and taking some of her clothes off even when merely visiting her sister.

Yet it is the men in the film who are photographed nearly or wholly nude; the women show little or no flesh. Draw from this whatever conclusions you wish. What offends most, though, is the film's clearly improvised quality: much of the story and most of the dialogue must have been made up during the shooting (the press kit all but admits this). You can see the actors hesitate and fumble as they try to come up with the next line, and Soderbergh clearly encouraged vocal and physical tics as a proof of naturalness. This and confinement to four tight locations (to save money) make the movie look like a series of screen tests for actors trained in the pseudo-Stanislavsky Method.

Andie MacDowell, even if not really an actress, has some touching moments; Laura San Giacomo, though badly overdirected, has spunk and a genuinely erotic voice. Peter Gallagher, who can be good, is a cipher here; the cutesy James Spader comes across as an overweight girl trying hard to deliquesce, and is infuriating in his delusions of sensitivity. Soderbergh's *Sex, Lies, and Videotape* contributes handily to the moral untidiness it purports to anatomize.

And Justice for None

CRIMES AND MISDEMEANORS

One thing that distinguishes a work of art from mere entertainment is that you can give away its ending without doing damage. It hardly matters whether you know how *King Lear* comes out: plot is the least important thing about it, and the surprise is only in the magnificence with which the work strikes you anew, every time. So let me give Woody Allen's *Crimes and Misdemeanors* the benefit of the doubt and call it art, which absolves me from discretion concerning its plot (which, indeed, has holes in it). The chief strength of the movie is its courage in confronting grave and painful questions of the kind the American cinema has been doing its damnedest to avoid.

Allen tells, essentially, two interrelated stories. One is that of Judah Rosenthal (Martin Landau), a prominent ophthalmologist being feted at a testimonial dinner for raising the money for a new hospital wing, not to mention other achievements. But Judah—with a fine career, family, and reputation—has two secret blots on his scutcheon. He monkeyed around with the hospital funds, and had a two-year affair with Dolores, an airline hostess, who became threatening, wanted him to marry her, was about to break up his marriage, even reveal his financial machinations. Whereupon, despite considerable agonizing, he finally agreed to let his shady brother, Jack, have his underworld connections bump her off.

Judah has a patient and friend, Ben, a rabbi who is going blind. Ben is the link between the "Crimes" part of the film and the "Misdemeanors." In that story, Cliff Stern (Woody Allen) is a funny little fellow who makes high-minded cinematic documentaries that win footling awards and no audiences. He is married to Wendy, who will no longer sleep with him, partly because of his being such a flop compared to her two brothers: the saintly Ben, who takes blindness in his stride as the will of God: and the enormously successful and rich Lester, a TV-schlock producer who dictates his brilliant ideas into a tape recorder always at the ready in his pocket. Lester gives his brother-in-law, Cliff, the chance to direct a TV documentary extolling Lester's genius: it is produced by Halley, a young woman whom both men are after.

What the crimes are is obvious enough; what constitutes the misdemeanors is less clear. Lester's vanity, vulgarity, promiscuity, certainly; but Lester is not the one the film is about. The peccant fellow is Cliff, who cheats, or tries to cheat, on his wife (who, however, hasn't slept with him for a year-since April 20, he recalls exactly, because it is Hitler's birthday); Cliff, who tries to make an ass of Lester in the documentary (but, then, Lester is one); Cliff, who is consumed with envy of Lester. But what is all this compared to having a hysterical mistress rubbed out? Judah, as a boy, was taught by his father that "the eyes of God are on us always," which may be why, as he only half-jokingly says in his acceptance speech at the testimonial dinner, he became an ophthalmologist. But this is a non-sequitur: an ophthalmologist does not have a better, more godlike, eye than anyone else. And everything else in the film is similarly illogical.

Revisiting his childhood house, Judah sees a scene from his boyhood: a seder at which his father insisted that God was just and that all crimes were punished one way or another. A radical-feminist, chain-smoking aunt, leaning on the Holocaust, argues the opposite. The debate is unresolved, yet the vision somehow brings peace to the tormented Judah. Why? Cliff tries to impress Halley by showing her sequences from the documentary he is making about Professor Levy, an old Jewish philosopher and Holocaust survivor (a character based on Primo Levi), who argues that this is not a moral universe, but that we create the moral myths that act as a surrogate divinity. Levy sounds most compelling, and then, for no visible reason, he commits suicide.

Ben, the good, pious rabbi, can utter only comfortless platitudes when Judah spills out his guts to him; but that, surely, is no reason for him to be punished with blindness. Cliff's sister, a lonely divorcée, advertises for companionship in the personals, and gets a pervert who ties her to the bed and defecates on her face (true, as Cliff observes, he could have killed her, but still . . .). Only the worst people thrive: the ridiculous Lester (true, he has a certain fatuous charm, but still . . .); Judah, who gets away with the murder he instigated and even manages to clear his conscience; coolly ambitious Halley, who throws over the nerdy but loving Cliff for Lester the lecher.

I have read several reviews of the movie; they all disagree about its meaning, which, to me, seems perfectly clear: there is no justice, no rhyme or reason in the universe, no God. And whether you agree or not, you must admire a filmmaker who tackles *this* subject and has the guts to come up with *this* answer. Of course, good intentions in themselves are not enough, but the film, though flawed, delivers more than that. It is, I think, Allen's first successful blending of drama and comedy, plot and subplot. It is the Shakespearean technique of making the subplot comically echo and comment on the main plot. Judah, the big man, can get everything: the mistress he wants, when he wants her; her removal by assassination (at the cost of a little distress) when she becomes a burden. Cliff, the little man—less charming than Judah, but better and wittier—gets nothing. Crime pays; misdemeanor, like innocence (Ben, Levy, Cliff's sister), is severely punished.

Does this mean perhaps that the universe is ruled by a consistently evil spirit: a god or the devil? Not even that: the young people in the movie seem nice, get engaged or married, may escape unscathed. But we can't be sure. And there is the balm of humor. Yet it is no consolation to him who has it: Cliff, the wittiest and saddest of all. He warns a little girl about show business: "It's worse than dog eat dog; it's dog doesn't return another dog's phone calls." Or he observes: "Where I grew up in Brooklyn, nobody committed suicide. They were all too unhappy." Some jokes are cornball, but still funny, like Cliff's lament to his ungiving wife: "The last time I was inside a woman was when I visited the Statue of Liberty." But only we, the audience, are laughing.

What distinguishes the film most, though, is its technical savvy. Allen cuts between present and past, plot and subplot, the film and other films or videotapes within the film, grimness and levity with a sure eye and hand. With his great cinematographer, Sven Nykvist (whose work, by the way, never looks so good for another director as it did for Bergman, but even so is quite wonderful), he gives the film a consistently tasteful look, which reflects ironically on the tastelessness of the goings-on. Moreover, he frames his shots unusually—perhaps a bit too much so, and too self-consciously; but what a relief after the artlessly foursquare way so many directors use their cameras, or their cameramen. Study, for example, the scene in which Judah tries to reason with his rampaging mistress in her apartment: everything is off-center as it is out of kilter. Dolores is often partly or wholly hidden from view; there are many diagonal angles; Judah, alone in-the frame, is often very near the edge (on edge?) and facing out of the frame, not into it. It is disorienting, disturbing—as it should be.

Or notice Allen's handling of the music, more assured and less obtrusive than ever. It is nice to have Judah, in a flashback, sweet-talking Dolores—who has just said, "You can play me the Schumann"—with "The Schu*bert. Schumann* is too flowery; Schubert is . . . he reminds me of you," only to have, later, Dolores's murder performed to the strains of Schubert's Quartet No. 15. Both the use of Schubert in an otherwise pop score, and his use at this point, are daring strokes. Allen now uses art for purposes beyond mere namedropping.

But, yes, there are errors. Probably chief among them is the lack of sympathy for Dolores: there is nothing much to persuade us of her humanity, and a great deal—including Anjelica Huston's looks and performance—to make her unpalatable. And it is hard to believe that any wife in 1989—even an upper-middle-class, puritanical, Jewish one such as Judah's—could be as unforgiving as Judah imagines his to be, driving him to murder rather than confession. Some ambiguities are excessive: there would be no harm in delineating Ben's character a little more clearly; is he (as Richard T. Jameson has wondered) a saint, a fool, or a holy fool? There are also unnerving minor slips: Judah tells his wife to use the bathroom right away; presently, he himself will need it. In a luxury apartment such as the Rosenthals', there must be more than one bathroom.

The casting, however, is generally excellent. Alan Alda's Lester, Jerry Orbach's Jack, and Martin Landau's Judah could not be improved on. Even from amateurs, such as the psychotherapist Martin Bergmann, who plays Levy, Allen gets exactly what is needed. And Sam Waterston, whom Allen has often miscast in more dashing roles, is spot on this time as a well-meaning bumbler. Mia Farrow, though a bit blanker than usual, makes that blank work for Halley.

As for the injustice of the universe, consider this. Because of the bad reviews I've been giving Allen, Allen's people (I don't know whether he himself is in on this, though megalomania is not something he is lacking in) are denying me invitations to his screenings. And yet here I am giving *Crimes and Misdemeanors* one of its best reviews. Oh, the irony and injustice of it! Right again, Woody!

Criticism from
the 1990s

Wild Life

THE BEAR; MY LEFT FOOT

The Bear, by Jean-Jacques Annaud, based on *The Grizzly King* by James Oliver Curwood, takes place in the Canadian Rockies, but was shot in the Bavarian Alps. The big grizzly is played (mostly) by Bart, a Kodiak; the male bear cub—species unspecified—is played (mostly) by Youk, a female. Youk's mother, who dies and leaves our hero an orphan, is enacted (mostly) by a bear skin. But do not get the notion that the movie is unduly manipulative and specious. An adult film for intrepid children, a children's film for deserving adults, *The Bear* is one of those thrilling movies where you wonder how on earth the director could get such performances out of two bears, a puma, and even a frog.

From his frequent collaborator, Gérard Brach, Annaud elicited a first-rate script, except for one rather too cute scene in which the cub, having eaten hallucinogenic mushrooms, has a fantasy that is the only obviously anthropomorphic passage in the film. Otherwise, the story of how little bear finds and succors wounded big bear, loses his mighty friend when some hunters stalk the big fellow, and gets him and his protection back just as a murderous puma is about to do him in, feels completely fresh and believable, regardless of what human or ursine formulas may underlie it. And Annaud worked so closely with his four-footed actors that one mauled him fairly seriously. The human performers, though, emerge appropriately more brutish than the beasts, but in the end, both bears and men learn to forbear.

There is something exhilarating about the mountains as shot almost too refulgently by Philippe Rousselot (the cinematographer of the hour) and about all their creatures, directed here with enough wilderness to de-Disnify the proceedings. Philippe Sarde, who for years now has been the composer of choice in French cinema, is not really that good (think of Honegger, Auric, Thiriet, Jaubert), but at least he is not so gross as some of his colleagues. And there is something irresistible about a bear: the powerful build gliding with the grace of certain fat people: the billowing of the fur and the ripple of sunlight on it; the speed and dignity of the beast—something that only the elephant can match, but the hippo, rhino, or tapir never.

My Left Foot is a good, strong, unsentimental portrayal of Christy Brown, the Irish lad afflicted with cerebral palsy who grew up to be an acclaimed writer and painter—with his left foot, the only part over which his brain had control—and the husband of Mary Carr, a nurse supererogatorily assigned to watch over him. One of 13 surviving children in an impoverished Dublin family, Christy had a particularly staunch and supportive mother and an enlightened doctor, Eileen Cole, who helped him enormously, but set him back when she couldn't reciprocate his romantic feelings.

The story—as written by Jim Sheridan and Shane Connaughton, and directed by Sheridan—is one of those near-documentary treatments of stubborn courage triumphing over immense obstacles; it is told with grim honesty and raffish humor. Some reviewers have objected that it does not address the crippling role the Catholic Church plays (in their view) in Irish life, forcing a poor mother to keep giving birth to endless children, who then have to grow up in increasing poverty unless they die in infancy. That may be true, but it does not belong in this film: more troubling, I think, is the film's failure to note that Christy Brown choked to death on his Christmas dinner in 1981, at age 49. But the filmmakers are clearly more concerned with an inspirational happy ending than with the somewhat Pyrrhic victory that was the truth.

Still, the film is a considerable achievement, notably for Daniel Day Lewis. The actor immersed himself in the leading part both through previous study and by living in a wheelchair throughout the shooting; the result is a performance of awesome authenticity leavened by the roguish, iconoclastic wit Day Lewis conveys so well. He is backed up here by an extraordinary supporting cast, all of whom are fine, and some of whom—the late Ray McAnnally as the bitter father, Brenda Fricker as the indomitable mother, and Hugh O'Conor as the boy Christy—are outstanding. It is the kind of film that can help you not give up on the human race: its not being fiction adds the final fillip to a story with plenty of punch.

Born on the Fourth of July

Another remarkable movie also features a hero in a wheelchair: *Born on the Fourth of July*, by Oliver Stone. I have been anything but a fan of this director, but the new film, an adaptation by him and Ron Kovic of the latter's autobiography, is a gripping, unrelenting but extremely powerful work, whose shortcomings evaporate from the memory, but whose strengths are indelible. Kovic comes from a Long Island blue-collar family, and grew up to be a typical American boy with inordinate faith in his country, his Catholic upbringing, and his family. Especially Mom, whose sermons about Communist danger in Vietnam contributed to his enlisting in the Marines, leaving his girlfriend behind, and shipping off to Nam.

Scenes from Ron's childhood (the kids playing realistic war games, the little girlfriend full of love for Ron, the Fourth of July parade in Massapequa that coincidentally celebrates Ron's own birthday) artfully paint an American idyll that Norman Rockwell would have envied. But even here, there is a worm in the apple; in a somewhat later sequence. Ron loses a high-school wrestling match and cries like a baby. And Tom Berenger, as a recruiter for the Marines, is too steelily perfect for comfort: if the Rock of Gibraltar came to life, he could outwrestle it. Ron goes off to war directly from the prom where he and his girl (Kyra Sedgwick, insipidly sweet) chugalugged love's young dream.

The Vietnam sequences may be more frightening than anything in *Platoon*: the raid on a supposedly Cong-infested village that results in the butchering of civilians and a baby; the fighting in a cloud of confusion, during which Ron kills one of his buddies; Ron's attempt to ease his conscience by confessing to an officer who insultingly brushes him off with a blanket absolution; Ron getting shot in the spine more palpably than I can recall experiencing in any film; the field hospital in which mass amputations are hallucinatorily performed by a few, overworked medics with little or no anaesthesia; and more, still more.

But for intimate horror nothing can surpass the scenes in the Bronx Veterans' Hospital: understaffed and rat-infested, the mostly black personnel shooting up behind not even locked doors, the antiquated equipment falling and nearly costing Ron one of his nonfunctional but still precious legs. Particularly shattering, however, are Ron's fanatical yet hopeless efforts to regain the use of his legs through maniacal exercise, and the utter frustration when it all fails. Even so, Ron returns to his family a still dedicated American and ex-Marine, although his mother almost can't face her paraplegic son and his father now seems more ineffectual than ever. And for understated social criticism, little can equal the Fourth of July parade at which Ron, riding in full regalia in a car, keeps saluting but twitches painfully each time a firecracker goes off.

Tom Cruise, to my surprise, is intense and searching as Ron, impressive as he slowly, ineluctably turns from clean-cut hawk into rebellious, hirsute hippie war protestor. And every scene involving Raymond J. Barry as the well-meaning, befuddled father, and Caroline Kava as the angry, punitive, forever uncomprehending mother, is beautifully acted and almost unbearably painful yet absolutely necessary. I can't think of another American movie in which gaping family rifts are portrayed with such unblinking, gritty honesty.

Bizarrely disturbing but also highly revealing are the sequences in a paraplegic American expatriate colony somewhere in Mexico that involves the disgruntled, seedy Ron with an even more embittered fellow paraplegic, incisively played by Willem Dafoe, and a local prostitute who claims she can give him sexual satisfaction. The most searing scene has Cruise and Dafoe, having caught a cabbie trying to cheat them, dumped by him, wheelchairs and all, in a near-desert Mexican landscape, where they might easily have perished. How they fight, get overturned in their chairs, hurl impotent imprecations at each other—two tiny figures amid a starkly awe-inspiring nature—is fraught with nothing less than metaphysical significance.

Yet even this scene is dwarfed by Ron's trip down South to visit the exiguous family of the boy he shot and confess to them. This is one of those scenes in which a forgiveness that passes understanding breaks your heart: all that goodness in people going unrewarded, with no medals for the most self-lacerating candor, the almost superhuman gift of pardon. Love it or hate it, this is a film you cannot afford to pass by.

Driving Miss Daisy

Driving Miss Daisy accomplishes the impossible task of transferring a small, intimate three-character play that uses specifically theatrical, non-naturalistic devices to the realistic screen without losing its modest, bittersweet charm. Well, to be quite honest, it does lose some, but not enough to prevent the movie from being penetrant and affecting in its own right. For this we must thank Alfred Uhry, who adapted his own play, and Bruce Beresford, who directed with unostentatious finesse.

Miss Daisy, based on Uhry's grandmother, is a retired Jewish schoolteacher in Atlanta. Though she once knew hard times, now, thanks to the prosperity of the family cotton mill, currently run by her son Boolie, she lives in a grand house with a capable black housekeeper and a shiny new Packard. But she is 72 and wrecks her car; to drive her new Hudson, Boolie hires, very much against her wishes, a sixtyish black chauffeur, Hoke Colburn.

The film covers a quarter-century during which Hoke becomes ever more necessary to Miss Daisy, who warms to him with excruciating slowness, her wariness and niggardliness flaring up again and again. Yet, with Boolie occasionally intervening, Miss Daisy and Hoke find their way to a prickly but mutually helpful relationship.

Daisy's problem is that she can't accept her affluence and remains stingy with both her possessions and her emotions. Hoke, who says he likes working for Jewish people (there is some solidarity between these beleaguered minorities), nevertheless has rough going of it with the crotchety crone: his pride is often trampled on, his patience stretched almost beyond endurance. But they make progress through funny little misadventures, lopsided fights (he curses under his breath), and starchy reconciliations. Daisy helps the dignified yet illiterate Hoke toward literacy, while his ironic complaisance and tactful suasion end up by humanizing her.

Ultimately, the movie is about Daisy's growing dependency and Hoke's increasing ascendance. As Jessica Tandy and Morgan Freeman play these two characters, they become infinitely rich in shading. Under her unyielding hauteur, Miss Daisy nevertheless suggests the need for Hoke's reasonableness and strength; underneath his good-humored compliance, Hoke cannot quite hide some irony and resentment. It is all there in his variously intoned "Yes'm"—ranging from obligingness to tacit contempt, from sympathy to mild sarcasm—with which he responds to her genuine needs and absurd whims. Their mutual understanding evolves, yet for all her Jewishness and former penury, Miss Daisy cannot forget her image of herself as the white Southern lady, just as Hoke cannot forget that though he may be her superior in many ways, he cannot be her social equal.

It is not till long after Hoke has retired into rather easeful old age and Miss Daisy has been confined to an old folks' home and is on the threshold of death that the final epiphany occurs. Boolie takes Hoke along on a visit to his mother. Miss Daisy, frail and transparent as a paper flower, sends the by now greying and pot-bellied Bootie off "to charm the nurses," so she can be alone with Hoke, who helps her with her dinner, feeding her with spoonful by compassionate spoonful, his own hands less steady than when he used to drive her. Only then does the old woman admit that Hoke was her best friend. Even this scene, though, like all that preceded it, is directed as drily as possible; by not trying to break our hearts, it gently, sadly, humanely pervades our souls.

Driving Miss Daisy is a film made up mostly of very small incidents, many of them left unresolved except for the reverberations they set up in the characters and the audience. And although we see in the lives of Daisy and Bootie the growing acceptance of Jews by the Old South, and the loves of Hoke and his unseen daughter the integration of blacks into white society, the film does not cheat. Miss Daisy and Hoke may form a somewhat comic alliance against real and imaginary ills, but it never becomes a true friendship.

There are some oversimplifications. Bootie's parvenu wife (Patti LuPone) is a bit too obviously crude; Idella, the housekeeper (Esther Rolle), is as tall, dignified, wise as Hoke (are there no imperfect blacks?); a black, hymn-singing funeral is a trifle too resplendently life-affirming; the racist comment of a highway patrolman about Miss Daisy and Hoke is a mite too pat. But these are minor matters, and may even be necessary guideposts for an audience that cannot live with too much subtlety. And in the acting of Tandy, Freeman, and, yes, Dan Aykroyd (Boolie), the film gets plenty of honesty, humor, and understated forcefulness. That sentiment does not slide into sentimentality is Bruce Beresford's discreet directorial contribution.

Swords and Bullets

HENRY THE FIFTH; GLORY

There is such a thing as revisionist filmmaking: a movie that strains, kicking and screaming, to be different from what it is recycling. The process holds obvious pitfalls, but the *Henry the Fifth* that Kenneth Branagh has adapted and directed, with himself starred, avoids many of them. It takes great temerity to compete with Laurence Olivier's masterly *Henry V*, but with the brashness of youth, the arrogance of a rising actor-manager, and the luck of the Irish (Ulster division), Branagh has dived in, swallowed a few mouthfuls of salt water, and kept afloat.

If Olivier started his version with the re-creation of the Elizabethan playhouse in which *Henry V* is being performed, Branagh begins with a film studio in which it is being filmed. This is shaky, because starting with Shakespeare's "wooden O" is to begin appropriately at the beginning; a film studio, however, is more of a destination than a point of departure. Olivier's Chorus was Leslie Banks, a magnificent actor, in period costume, able to lead us seamlessly from the Globe to the realms of ostensible reality. Branagh's Chorus is Derek Jacobi, a very good actor, in modern dress, in which he remains throughout, walking through the film and creating a questionable alienation effect.

But this does clue us in to what Branagh is trying to do: a deconstruction of Olivier's movie, Shakespeare's play, and history itself. Olivier, you see, made his film in 1944, when Britain was in the throes of war and needed moral uplift: a sense that its sufferings had not been in vain. So the film was a glorification, a piece of propaganda (but, then, so is the play), and it was entirely right that a touch of the golden legend should mingle with that touch of Harry in the night. Agincourt was a battle fought in storybook sunlight, sparkling colors, and more panoply than agony.

Branagh, however, made his movie in a time of relative peace, loathing for war, and skepticism about patriotism, however artistically presented. Hence the battles are fought in rain and muck, in ghastly hugger-mugger, with scant heroics, and no glamor whatever. This, of course, is not a novelty; ever since Stendhal's *The Red and the Black* and Orson Welles's *Chimes at Midnight* (or *Falstaff*), specimens of demystification or deglamorization have abounded.

But Branagh knows how to deflate with style, how to make cutting down to size as exciting as epic idealization.

Yet, in so doing, he deconstructs not only Olivier and Shakespeare, but also, I repeat, history itself. When the longbows of the English release a singing tapestry into the heavens, they also explain history; when the arming of the French knights becomes the ultimate costume party, the gaudiest horse opera, it happens to tell truthfully why the French lost. When, in this revision, the English arrows wobble forth in hit-or-miss fashion, when confused hacking away creates a chaotic charnel house, we get no sense of strategy, no awareness of who won and why. And then to hear the reckoning of the huge French losses and minimal English ones is to lose faith in the furor that preceded it. If you are going to throw out the baby, at least don't splash us with the bathwater.

Nevertheless, Branagh's film accomplishes a good deal that is both original and believable in the scenes that Shakespeare meant to be depressing but couldn't, even as Olivier wouldn't, show in full detail. There is the death of Falstaff and the conspiracy of Cambridge, the hanging of Bardolph and Henry's carrying the dead Boy across the battlefield in a long sequence without any cutting. So, too, Henry in disguise, mingling with his men on the eve of battle, undergoes a genuine ordeal rather than merely playing a charming royal prank.

The main difference between the Branagh and Olivier versions, however, lies in the protagonists themselves and in the actors playing them. Olivier, even with his funny medieval haircut, was handsome, poetic-looking; like the historic Henry, though not in the same way, Branagh is not. Tow-headed and whey-faced, a bit chubby even, Branagh can show us leadership as a hard-won personal achievement, rather than, as with Olivier, the divine right of kings and movie stars. As Sally Beauman rightly remarked, Olivier "made many savage cuts, and removed from the hero's mind almost every doubt, and from his path almost every obstacle."

So Branagh's version, taken in conjunction with Olivier's—the two should be alternating on the same screen—acts not only as a gratuitous deconstruction but also as a useful corrective. Although William Walton's score for Olivier was better than Pat Doyle's for Branagh, Kenneth MacMillan's cinematography for the latter is, in its antithetical way, as good as Robert Krasker's for the former. And though there were spectacular performances in the Olivier, there are roughly comparable ones in the Branagh. Brian Blessed is a fleshly monument of an Exeter, Judi Dench a pungently gutsy Mistress Quickly, Robert Stephens a wrenching Pistol, Christian Bale a winning Boy, Paul Scofield a nobly careworn French king.

There is fine work, too, from Richard Bryers, Alec McCowen, and a number of others, and, astoundingly, the Mountjoy (French messenger) of Christopher Ravenscroft manages to be as brilliant as Ralph Truman was, maybe even more so. Ian Holm, a good Fluellen, is perhaps goaded into giving an overripe performance, and is made rather too much of—perhaps Branagh is doing his bit to stop Wales from seceding. And there is no way Michael Maloney's Dauphin and Richard Eaton's Constable can equal Max Adrian's and Leo Genn's, respectively.

But it's a bloody good—or good and bloody—showing all the same. Branagh has directed almost as skillfully as Olivier, and his education of a king says a good deal to all of us who have to assume responsibility by learning it the hard way, on the job, in the dirt.

When a new movie, not based on Shakespeare, addresses episodes from the American Civil War, and has most of the trappings of a historical document, adherence to history becomes more of a desideratum. *Glory* concerns the 54th Regiment of Massachusetts Volunteer Infantry and its role in the Civil War, which was to prove that black men could fight as well as white ones, and that black regiments were necessary for the North to win.

It is understandable that Kevin Jarre, the screenwriter, took some liberties in the interest of drama, but there are (as those knowing more about the subject have pointed out to me) excessive fabrications here. The direction by Edward Zwick, a TV director (*thirtysomething*, of all things!), is not bad, but depends on too many clichés or near-clichés. Still, some of the battle sequences, both at Antietam and in the 54th's climactic assault on Ft. Wagner outside Charleston (which, even at the cost of nearly half the regiment, did not fall), are effective, possibly because Zwick studied two other Civil War films—John Huston's *The Red Badge of Courage* and Robert Enrico's *Au Coeur de la vie*—both of them better than *Glory*.

But what makes *Glory* very much worth watching is the performances. Matthew Broderick plays the young Boston Brahmin, Colonel Robert Gould Shaw, who led the 54th and fell at the attack on Ft. Wagner. He is not ideally cast, since neither in sound nor in bearing does he suggest knowing beans about Boston Brahmins; but he does try hard to be as far removed as possible from his usual smart-alec, modern, New York self, and there is something appeal-

ing about the effort. The film's true distinction, though, comes from
a quartet of black actors obliged to play, not merely black but also,
weirder yet, white stereotypes.

Denzel Washington is Trip, the proud, cynical, white-hating
runaway slave; you just know that he will be "redeemed" before
gloriously dying. The part is the most anachronistic of the four: a
streetwise, scornful ghetto black, and Washington plays him for full
contemporary relevance. But the performance has such clenched
intensity, such primeval wariness about it that it becomes a kind
of histrionic emancipation proclamation, soaring well above the
scenarist's clichés. As an ex-grave-digger turned grave noncom,
and the moderating influence on Trip, Morgan Freeman gives yet
another one of his performances mingling quiet strength with wry
canniness (not unlike his Hoke in *Driving Miss Daisy*), and the
sheer economy of his acting is a streamlined joy.

Splendid, too, is Andre Braugher as a highly educated, intellectual Northern black, who grew up as a friend of Shaw's and now
finds himself in no-man's-land: no longer allowed to fraternize with
white officers, and mistrusted by his fellow black soldiers. Braugher
conveys the emotional quicksand, the nervous exhaustion of Sear-
les with such delicacy as to make us forget the basic ahistoricity of
the character. Finally, Jihmi Kennedy plays Sharts, a likable yokel
with intense country piety and a mild stutter, and turns what might
be pure platitude into the pepper of the earth.

Yet what's good is not only individual performances, but also and
especially the interaction of these four. There is a give-and-take, a
fierce complementariness as of a sports team, letting us see consummate ensemble acting as one of the prime expressions of co-operation
in a world lacerated by dissension. Add to this the work of the veteran
British cinematographer Freddie Francis, a triumph of *celare artem*—
things never look merely beautiful, they look believable, involving, inevitable, and therefore impressive and you have a movie that surpasses
its artistic shortcomings into something long on humanity.

Frissons from France

CAMILLE CLAUDEL

It is unusual for an actress in a foreign-language film to be nominated for an Academy Award (leaving aside the artistic value of

such an award, which I estimate at zero). But Isabelle Adjani has been so nominated for her portrayal of the eponymous heroine of *Camille Claudel*. It is equally unusual for me to urge you to see what I consider a basically unsatisfactory movie, but in this case I do.

Camille Claudel was the elder sister of the poet Paul Claudel, a sculptress of considerable talent, for many years the disciple, collaborator, model, and mistress of the great sculptor Auguste Rodin. With him, she compromised her reputation in the eyes of many in turn-of-the-century France, including those of her coldly proper mother and selfish younger sister. She never lost the support of her father and brother: but the former died, and the latter, a career diplomat as well as poet, was usually far away. The much older Rodin, though in love with Camille, could not give up Rose Beuret, his common-law wife and mother of his son. Eventually, he and Camille broke up, she to set up on her own, evolve a more independent style, and become a recognized artist in her own right.

But she also became more unhinged and antisocial. Living alone in colossal disorder and refusing to see most people, she changed from an extremely pretty young woman into an overweight frump while still in her early thirties, and developed an all-consuming persecution complex. She was certain that Rodin, who in fact was trying to help her (anonymously) in every conceivable way, was behind a sinister plot—involving everyone from art critics to officialdom, and even her family—to deprive her of her right to work, to succeed, to live. In time, this paranoia became so intense that, the moment her father died, the family had the 48-year-old Camille committed. For her remaining thirty years, she who had been on the verge of major success no longer worked, and became a more and more pitiful blank, until she died in 1943.

Perhaps the saddest thing about madness, for both the victim and those who care, is that it is almost never complete. The confined person may have many periods of lucidity, suffer monstrously from sequestration among the insane, write heartbreakingly sensible letters, and become madder yet. Such was the case of Camille, one that cried out for memorializing and got it in the concise, intelligent, fair-minded biography by Reine-Marie Paris, Paul Claudel's granddaughter and Camille's grandniece. The film—for whose realization Isabelle Adjani had to fight for several years—was made from this book, with Mme Paris as consultant. It was directed and co-scripted by Bruno Nuytten, Mlle Adjani's former lover and the father of her child—an outstanding cinematographer but neophyte director—and Marilyn Goldin, a Philadelphian in Paris, who has done quite a bit of, somewhat esoteric, film-writing. They made a three-hour film that has been cut in America by half an hour.

Such cutting is disastrous. Anyone who'll sit through two and a half hours of subtitled film will not demur at three. If the film was an enormous hit in France and elsewhere, winning numerous French and other awards, why butcher it for America? There is no hard evidence that cutting has ever saved a film: good tends to be even better when there's more of it; bad is bad at any length. The cut version does virtually nothing with Camille's horrible final decades, which surely deprives us of the sense of the unutterable sadness of this life.

Even so, we are left with a film that, until the last part, holds our interest with its story, though not with its filmness (if I may coin a word). For in the case of a film biography, it behooves us to distinguish between the informational excitement and the aesthetic mediocrity. As a rather faithfully reported true story, *Camille Claudel* rates a 9 ½; as a film, roughly a 5. The pacing, dialogue, and, above all, Gabriel Yared's vulgar and obtrusive music aren't good enough.

Isabelle Adjani would seem to be the ideal interpreter of Camille. Looking very much like that beautiful young artist—if anything, more attractive—she is also an actress of talent and temperament. Moreover, she has already excelled in a similar role, that of the protagonist in Truffaut's *The Story of Adèle H.* Finally, the story and role meant enough to her to fight long and hard to get them on screen. And indeed, much of the time Mlle Adjani is lively, volatile, impassioned, distraught, demented, as called for. But she also sports a slack, half-open, downward-slanting mouth virtually throughout. I've no idea whether she does this to suggest a disturbed creature, or because she thinks it is sexy, or because she has developed a tic douloureux. Whatever the reason, it makes Camille look slightly cretinous.

The other actors are mostly effective. Gérard Depardieu is a despotic, driven Rodin, lusty and saturnine in pungent conjunction. Alain Cuny, that problematic actor always a little too grand for whatever he is doing, is here a fittingly pompous yet loving father. The great Madeleine Robinson plays the mother with burning coldness; only Laurent Grevill seems somehow inchoate as brother Paul. In the small role of Mathias Morhardt, editor and art critic and Camille's first champion and biographer, the famed stage director

Roger Planchon contributes a dazzling cameo. I do wish, though, that Nuytten had not allowed the middle-aged and semi-demented Camille to look as young and pretty as ever; but perhaps a mere director and ex-lover is powerless in such situations.

There is one further aspect of the film that makes it, for me, a must: the photography. When the director is himself a superb cameraman (do you recall, for example, *Jean de Florette* and *Manon of the Spring*?), he will find, as Nuytten did, an extraordinary cameraman: Pierre Lhomme; this is the best cinematography I have seen all year. Good camerawork must look both as beautiful and as true-to-life as possible, and not call undue attention to itself. It must, in short, be notable and unnoticed. And that is the miracle that Lhomme and Nuytten accomplish here.

Bon Appétit!

THE HANDMAID'S TALE;
THE COOK, THE THIEF, HIS WIFE & HER LOVER

Dystopias are, by definition, unpleasant. But the two most celebrated English dystopias, *Brave New World* and *1984*, manage to be scary without stooping to gloating mean-spiritedness. That, along with a sadomasochistic brand of feminism, is what Margaret Atwood's novel *The Handmaid's Tale* is about, and that, too, comes across in Harold Pinter's screenplay as directed by Volker Schlöndorff. The film has been around too long for a detailed review now—especially since I have scant use for Atwood, Pinter, and Schlöndorff in general—but a few words about the acting seem indicated.

Faye Dunaway and Elizabeth McGovern give their by now customary mannerism-bespangled performances; Aidan Quinn refines his technique of tilting his face down and his gaze up; while Victoria Tennant, Blanche Baker, and Robert Duvall do nicely. In the title role of Kate, the young woman who becomes the joyless sperm receptacle for the Commander, and the character with whom Margaret Atwood identified herself, Natasha Richardson is miscast. Because she is the daughter of Tony Richardson and Vanessa Redgrave, she has it made on stage and screen, yet she is singularly unappealing: hard-featured, frozen, cocky, stolidly invulnerable. (With a little more smugness, she'd be the ideal Margaret Atwood in a film biography.) Yet the story depends on our concern for Kate.

About the cold, carapaced Miss Richardson, it's hard to worry: she'll make out all right even if she has to kill for it.

Still, *The Handmaid's Tale* is only inept and annoying; for true horror, I commend to you Peter Greenaway's latest, *The Cook, the Thief, His Wife & Her Lover*, a film whose detestableness is heralded by its ponderous title. Have you noticed, by the way, the depredations of the ampersand on film titling? It is a dependable harbinger of disaster, as recently in *Stanley & Iris*, and now in what I'll shorten to CTW&L. Why those ampersands? It wasn't *Romeo & Juliet* or *Crime & Punishment*. But, beloved of law firms and typographers, the ampersand has become chic & is here to stay.

But back to Peter Greenaway, a British painter, novelist, and filmmaker. His first full-length effort, *The Draftsman's Contract* (1982), was so pretentious, hollow, and odious that it set my teeth on edge; I had the urge to throw something equally rotten back at the screen. It was an attempt at a bawdy, witty, nasty Restoration comedy bolstered with the savagery of Jacobean revenge tragedy. But the comedy was not witty enough, the tragedy was gratuitously grafted on, and the whole thing made no sense. What could be more flavorous than an *olla podrida* of smuttiness, obscurantism, and self-congratulation?

As a result, I stayed away from Greenaway's next offerings: *A Zed and Two Naughts, The Belly of an Architect, Drowning by Numbers*, whose very titles inspired diffidence. But the glowing hullabaloo that greeted *CTW&L* demanded investigation. In the *New York Times*, where the two senior critics prudently abstained and let young #3, Caryn James, pluck this chestnut out of the fire, we could read that this "profound" film was, among other things, "a work so intelligent and powerful that it evokes our best emotions and least civil impulses." Where, I wondered, did this evocation take place: on the screen or in the auditorium? On film, it takes very little profundity to display noble feelings and bestial impulses. To evoke them in the audience—rather more interesting—would presumably mean causing you to make impassioned love to your neighbor on the left while urinating on the person sitting to your right.

It is with the latter that the film begins. In a garishly lit parking lot, the Thief (Michael Gambon), actually a major gangster, and his henchmen torture an unidentified man: they strip him, smear excrement on him, pee on him, and might go further if the Wife, impassively smoking in the car, did not advise the Thief to desist.

Albert Spica, the Thief, then vents his fury on Georgina, the Wife, as they enter his fancy restaurant. In the parking lot, savage curs roam about, getting in the pigs' heads and maggot-infested fish that fill garbage trucks seemingly uneager to cart them away.

One enters the restaurant, Le Hollandais, so named after a huge replica of Frans Hals's *Banquet of the Officers of the St. George Militia* that hangs on one of its walls, through the kitchen. This kitchen has a staff ranging from half-naked potbellied food handlers to a kitchen boy with punk yellow hair and an epicene persona, constantly singing hymns in a shrill voice. The saturnine Cook is played by Richard Bohringer, a posturing French actor with an impenetrable accent in English. Bohringer starred in *Diva*, Jean-Jacques Beineix's obnoxious and nonsensical film, a manifest influence on *CTW&L*, and the luridly green kitchen is his Plutonian domain.

From this we pass to the crimson dining room, where the Thief and his men, dolled up in quasi-Halsian regalia clashing with their oafish talk and foul behavior, seem to be regulars after all, the Thief owns the place. The Wife, in this swinishly illogical film, is especially illogical: for years she has tolerated the Thief's shoving, or making her shove, bottles, wooden spoons, etc., up her crotch by way of sex, and his beatings, buffetings, and cruel beratings by way of connubial bliss. Four times she has escaped, and allowed herself to be found and taken back. True, this is not realistic filmmaking, but some sort of stylized explanation, if I may put it so, wouldn't hurt.

The Thief, Albert Spica (is he so named that people addressing him should seem to be saying "Mr. Speaker," creating instant parliamentary satire?), roughs up everyone: henchmen, kitchen staff, waitresses, customers. He pulls off tablecloths with full dishes on them, pummels the diners, sometimes emptying a soup tureen on their heads before, literally, kicking them out. Just for fun, mind you, or to vent his anger at Georgina on them. The way the clientele on and off screen puts up with this suggests that Greenaway's view of people as sadomasochists may be justified.

Meanwhile, the Wife is making goo-goo eyes at a rather seedy youngish man in a rust-brown suit, who dines regularly at the restaurant in the company of two or three hefty tomes (some of them old and rare-looking), one of which he reads as he eats. The Thief likes to come up and toss some of these books on the floor, whereat the reader, who doesn't speak till midway into the film, smiles. Does the Thief do this because he realizes that Georgina's ever more frequent visits to the ladies' room allow her to make love in one of the stalls to Michael, as the bookish fellow is called? Not a bit; Albert is too thick to catch on to the obvious—maybe because the Cook's weird specialties are only too likely to induce diarrhea.

Finally, though, Albert does follow Georgina into the ladies' loo, but in lieu of catching on, merely makes himself gratuitously loathsome. The lovers must seek another hideaway, and the Cook first shelters them in the larder, where they have sex amid a legion of unplucked pheasants, literally making it in the feathers. When the Thief comes ferreting into the kitchen, the Cook hides the lovers in the cold-storage room, where love keeps them warm until he arranges their escape in a rotting-food truck, where their love is further fertilized by decomposing pigs' heads and fish innards. They find eventual refuge in the book depository, where Michael is cataloguing some half-million to a million volumes (I'm bad at guessing numbers), and where the hymn-squealing albino punker-castrato-hermaphrodite brings them meals from the Cook.

At this point, the film goes a bit queer. So uncouth, in fact, that I leave it to you to seek it out if your taste runs to tastelessness. I'll pass on to the music, costumes, sex, and *mise-èn-scene*. The music is by Michael Nyman, whose career is as bizarre as if it had been composed, or at least orchestrated, by Peter Greenaway. His score here is a queasy blend of baroque and rock, outlandish and insinuating, the aural equivalent of the Cook's cuisine, with perhaps the odd pig's head thrown in, to make sure it goes on your nerves, its ultimate intended destination.

The costumes are by one of the *enfants terribles* of *haute couture*, Jean Paul Gaultier. (The other two, Thierry Mugler and Claude Montana, are undoubtedly eating each other's heart out.) Their thrust is, besides jabots for the gangsters, fancy outfits and provocative undies for Georgina. These are an amalgam of cancan dancers' costumes out of Toulouse-Lautrec, whores' gear out of Genet's *The Balcony*, and saddles by Hermès—with, by the bye, coiffures to match. Though Helen Mirren (Georgina) is seldom wholly naked—at her age, it might not be seemly—her breasts and genitalia are dutifully exposed. As for Alan Howard (Michael), he's frequently in the buff to huff and puff with Miss Mirren in simulated sex that is less erotic than ornamental, presumably to better fit the décor.

That décor, surely, is what the film is about. Since I could hardly match such eloquence, let the press kit do the cataloguing: "1) the lavish restaurant dining room, where most of the verbal and physical abuse occurs, is blood-red, symbolizing danger; 2) the kitchen, where the lovers secretly meet, is jungle-green, suggesting safety; 3) the parking lot, where the lovers flee, is a cold ultramarine, connoting the netherworld; 4) the lovers' hideaway [book depository] is gold, to represent the golden age of learning and implying an Eden of reborn innocents; 5) a children's hospital ward, which is the yellow of eggyolk and spring [?]; and 6) the lavatories, where the lovers begin their affair, is [*sic*] the shadowless incandescent white of heaven."

Accordingly, when Georgina moves from one space to another, her dress changes from red (dining room) to white (lavatory) to green (kitchen). I have always considered the interior decorator one of the more sinister influences on modern life, particularly when, like Peter Greenaway, he sets himself up as a social-metaphysical moviemaker. *The Cook, the Thief, His Wife & Her Lover* is part post-modern vomitorium; part pseudo-Buñuelian existential parable, and altogether undesirable. Kathy Acker, the expatriate American punker-novelist, has characterized Greenaway: "If his films are—and are about—any one thing, it is the connection between perception, art, philosophy, mythologies, sexuality, and the political." That sure is some "any one thing."

Roger and Me

This is an age of eroding boundaries; the one between fact and fiction is no exception. For example, any performer on a major soap opera can tell you about stacks of warning letters he or she receives from viewers about some other character on the soap, about some secret vices that character has revealed only to a third one and some ten million TV watchers. Soap-opera fans can no longer tell that the show is not reality. And what about the much less sappy souls who nevertheless believe that what they see in a documentary is the truth *tout court*? It never occurs to them that there exists a thing called point of view, and that inclusion or exclusion of data is consciously or unconsciously affected by it, that the filmmaker's choices represent a slant on the facts, on the "truth."

This can get highly complicated. Take the recent *Roger and Me*, in which Michael Moore showed, or tried to show, how Roger Smith, the CEO of General Motors, brought misery to Flint, Michigan, by plant shutdowns and the laying off of thousands of workers. It was a grimly humorous and enormously persuasive film, and many people besides Roger Smith emerged as callous brutes or risible fools. Subsequently, it was revealed that Moore took many liberties with chronology and context to give the film dramatic shape and to make some people look worse and others (e.g., himself) better than they were. Anatole France, to be sure, spoke of *une histoire plus vraie que la vérité*, and Moore, too, defended himself as pursuing the spirit rather than the letter of the truth.

Then why, however, his anger when the film was not nominated for an Oscar in the documentary category? And why his anger now when video stores stock the film on the documentary rather than the feature-film (i.e., fiction) shelves, where, granted, rentals are considerably brisker? Can it be that what is fact on a reel becomes fiction in a cassette?

Pretty Woman

America today, when it wants to make a truly adult movie, comes up with *Pretty Woman*, rated R—nobody wants an X. And what is *Pretty Woman*? Worse than the old story of the whore with the heart of gold: the story of two golden-hearted whores who find each other, fall in love, and make honest, married lovers of each other. A first, I am sorry to say.

Edward Lewis (Richard Gere) is a New York corporate mogul known as the Wolf of Wall Street, who doesn't know his way around Los Angeles. Borrowing a sports car as he leaves a party, he zooms all over town in search of the Regent Beverly Wilshire, where, despite acrophobia, he rents the penthouse, because it is "the best." He asks directions from a hooker on Hollywood Boulevard, Vivian (Julia Roberts), who, for ten bucks, rides along to show him the way. Since Edward has just broken up with his latest mistress in New York and needs an escort, he hires Vivian—who, with better clothes and hairdo, would look just terrific—for the rest of his week's stay. A little sex thrown in will be fine.

So begins a double Pygmalion story: Edward turns Vivian into a lady in a matter of days; she turns the corporate raider into a decent, considerate, loving being, even curing him of his acrophobia. How this comes about has to be seen to be disbelieved. The very evolution of the sexual relationship is enchanting. Vivian produces condoms in all designer colors, and declares her readiness for everything except kissing on the mouth, which might engender cumbersome emotional involvement. Edward allows as how he doesn't go in for that himself, and they happily settle on fellatio. The affair progresses charmingly upward, including sex in a shared bathtub in which Vivian embraces Edward from behind (a position new to me), to end, after two hours plus of film, with a mouth-to-mouth kiss and an engagement ring.

Vivian is really a nice girl from Georgia, basically bookish and yearning to go back to school: she landed in her present profession by a series of unfortunate contretemps. She shares the flat of another hooker, Kit (the sexy Laura San Giacomo), who has a heart only of silver; but just as Vivian, thinking she has lost Edward, decides to go back to college in San Francisco, Kit, though still plying her trade, resolves to save up for beauty school. Let no one say education isn't the cure for everything.

The film, whose collaborative script is credited to J. F. Lawton, was directed by Garry Marshall, who himself worked his way up from the pavements of New York to the hills of Hollywood. It contains one bit of truth. When no one in the chic Rodeo Drive boutiques will wait on Vivian, even though she flashes a wad of Edward's greenbacks, Edward himself appears in the company of his credit card. The tune changes, and snooty *vendeuses* and sniffy homosexual salesmen vie to outgrovel one another. A nice bit, but no compensation for all the rest.

Richard Gere is, as always, dapper, dashing, and squinty-eyed; I believe him as a barracuda, but have trouble accepting his metamorphosis into a goldfish. Though not convincingly Georgian, Julia Roberts has charm and style. Asked how long I thought she had been a prostitute before the film begins, I said, "Somewhere between seven and 11 minutes, but I can't narrow it down any further."

The Freshman

I cordially detested Andrew Bergman's previous movies, such as *The In-Laws*, and his Broadway outing, *Social Security*, which defied even Mike Nichols's dexterity in the manufacture of silk purses. But when Marlon Brando makes one of his rare film appearances, even while bad-mouthing his very vehicle to the media, we critics snap to—even those of us who do not subscribe to the doctrine of his infallibility. In *The Freshman*, Bergman's latest, Brando's performance can again be debated. But not his judgment: the film is trash.

No need to bother you with the paltry excuse for a plot, but let's say that after the film sedulously constructs what looks like a chain of outrageous coincidences that is meant to seem, nevertheless, believable (not to me, friends!), it then completely reverses itself and pretends in the end that every specious link of that unendurably stretched chain was in fact cannily, cogently planned. Well, out of a sow's ear, perhaps; but out of a hog's wash?

Neither by chance nor by forethought could more than a fraction of these events have fallen into place; the film is like an attempt to solve an equation comprising nothing but unknowns. There are only two ways to make such a picture work: the absurdist (or surreal) approach or just plain devilish wit. Bergman's film has neither: it strives for a surface realism to set the tone and nudges itself forward by means of feeble, forced jokes. For a joke to be truly propulsive, however, it must have some significance or implication, some social, philosophical, or satirical content.

When Bergman is poking fun at the NYU film school (which, God knows, can do with some poking), he shows on the wall of a classroom life-size photo portraits of Truffaut, Spielberg, De Palma and Scorsese. But why not, and, therefore, so what? When, however, Mel Brooks, in *High Anxiety*, shows a psychoanalysts' convention with the wall behind the speaker displaying enormous photomurals of Freud, Jung, Adler, and Dr. Joyce Brothers, that gag makes a point.

Again, much is made of Brando's playing Carmine Sabatini, a very, very Godfather-like figure, and of how Matthew Broderick, playing the naive title character, keeps gulping and blithering about how Carmine is . . . looks like . . . doesn't he . . . isn't he? which Brando and the others acknowledge with a variety of literal or figurative shrugs. The audience is convulsed, but it does not take much to convulse an audience these days. What makes the joke less funny than it might be is that it is milked; one grand shrug from Brando—and it is grand—would have been funnier.

Further, Arthur Fleeber, the ghastly film-school prof who forces his students to buy his book as a text, would be funnier if he weren't played by that incurable ham Paul Benedict, and if his way of teaching film—playing movies with the sound off and mouthing each character's lines himself—were not shown some three or four times. And what's the use of casting Maximilian Schell wildly against type if you can't also give him some amusing lines and business? And though it is a nice idea to have the plot revolve around a Komodo dragon, an Indonesian lizard of giant size and (according to the screenplay) intimidating behavior, the role is played by a water monitor, a saurian of more modest scale and whose comportment is worthy of a pussycat.

There are two funny things in the film. One is Bert Parks's appearance to serenade the lizard at an unholy gathering for jaded millionaires, and his spoof of himself and implied jab at the Miss America Pageant. The other is the scene in which Brando comes to visit Broderick in his NYU digs and, taking in the dorm through dormant eyes, mutters, "So this is college? I didn't miss nuttin.'" Brando may well be a more endangered species than the Komodo dragon, and is certainly of more impressive size. He does play his part rather like a lizard sunning himself on a rock. But for his occasional blinking and emitting sounds that the trained ear will recognize as English, his craft seems to be less the actor's than the taxidermist's. Still, he has an undeniable mystique, and his waltz on ice skates is something not even one of those enchanting bears from the Moscow Circus would be likely to disavow.

Matthew Broderick preserves his perennial adolescence with grace and makes a delightful Candide from Vermont, nettled by New York but coping. Even though the amount of innocence with which he is saddled could make a Shetland pony buckle, he remains fresh and frisky. And he is ably supported by Bruno Kirby and Penelope Ann Miller. Yet, all in all, *The Freshman* falls—perhaps appropriately—a bit short of the sophomoric.

Movie Musings, 1990

The cinema is a user, and we, quite rightly, don't like users. But, quite wrongly perhaps, we often love them. Some of the most beautiful women I have known were users: so, I gather from women friends, are some of the most handsome men. Are these, then, not to be loved in a world where beauty, both the skin-deep and the deep-as-a-well kind, are all too rare? Plato, I think, did us all a great disservice when, in the Symposium, he postulated a hierarchy in the realms of beauty and made the physical kind the lowest, good only for a stepping-stone.

Beauty, as any number of *symbolistes* and *décadents* kept reminding us, is not a moral concept, which is what makes it interesting;
not enduring (at least when it's physical), which is what makes it
tragic; and not, in its full bloom, resistible, which makes it, after all,
a kind of absolute. And the movies, bless them, although equipped
to deal with all kinds of beauty, are of all the arts most suited for
the display of the physical sort.

But the movies, I repeat, are beautiful users. They use those
who make them, they use those who frequent them, they even use
themselves. In two hours or so they make you live a lifetime, laugh
yourself silly, scare yourself to death, fall in love with someone unbelievably yet (as it were) palpably beautiful, understand something about the world or yourself that you didn't even know needed
understanding, and think you are a better person for having seen
them. If they are good, that is—which they often aren't, but that is
another question.

Meanwhile, good or bad, they use you. Although pleasurably,
they take something out of you emotionally, sometimes even intellectually. And they are addictive: they make you want more, and
still more. They can cheat you out of the time you might have devoted to something better. And occasionally, when very beautiful,
they can leave you drained. As they can also, much more often,
when they are terrible. Either way, they use up a regular moviegoer's
innocence, though not necessarily his naïveté, but that, again, is
another story.

Similarly, only even more so, they use up their makers. A novelist
or dramatist, the closest thing to a filmmaker, can go on forever.
Well, almost. Just think of all those playwrights and fictionists who
wrote their masterpieces at the very end of their careers. Not so
a filmmaker: not Renoir or Kurosawa, not Pabst or De Sica, not
Hitchcock or Buñuel, not Chaplin or Bresson. Not even someone
like Truffaut, who died at the early age of 52. Bergman, wise man
that he is, stopped while still in possession of his full powers; even
so, I wouldn't give you one *Naked Night* or *Persona* for ten *Fanny
and Alexanders*. That is because film devours its creators as fiction
and drama do not.

It is all about showing, you see. A playwright doesn't have to
show all that much; words do most of his work. A novelist doesn't
have to show anything. But a filmmaker has to put in all kinds of
things he'd just as soon not. Suppose an important scene takes place
in a restaurant, where the hero meets the heroine or two people

conclude a crucial business deal. The filmmaker cannot limit himself to those specifics. He must show how the characters looked at that time, how they lifted their glasses to their lips, what and how they ate, etc. For this, the filmmaker may have to dredge up from his past anything from memories of waiters to recollections of flatware. And once recalled, they are used up: that kind of goblet, toyed with in that way, is finished for our filmmaker.

And film also uses itself up. In barely one century, what all hasn't been covered by the movies? Whole movements, such as surrealism, expressionism, absurdism, made it to the screen, also existentialism, nihilism, heaven knows what. Every type of story, plot, situation. All conceivable schools of acting and non-acting, by professionals and amateurs. And documentaries, and staged documentaries, and improvisation. There have been genres within genres—the Eastern Western, for instance, and the female buddy picture until it seems there is nothing new under the projector.

When film *was* new, Konrad Lange, a famous professor of aesthetics, denounced it as a thing made by "semieducated, aesthetically feelingless, ethically indifferent, in short, spiritually inferior people." After several strong decades, it now appears to fit that description all over again. At the just concluded 28th New York Film Festival, we saw such acts of desperation as the Bobbsey Twins of the Italian cinema, the Taviani brothers, reaching out to Tolstoy's *Brother Sergius* and converting it into *Night Sun*, a long, clattering exercise in sanctimonious mediocrity; also the sometimes stimulating French filmmaker Jacques Doillon reaching out to Dostoevsky's *The Eternal Husband* and making out of it something unrecognizable called *A Woman's Vengeance*. In it, two women claw and hack away at each other for 133 minutes, mostly in small apartments, with dialogue like rotten apples falling far from the Dostoevsky tree.

Yet even this fiasco had something to offer that only cinema can: closeups of Béatrice Dalle's fascinating face, angelic down to the upper lip, bestial thereafter. Not worth two-and-a-quarter hours, perhaps, but still . . . Otherwise, the film was so bad that even an audience of film-festival desperadoes was trickling out of it from beginning to end. Now, it's easy enough to walk out on something early on, but to do so after you have two hours of your life invested in it, you must have undergone extraordinary torture. The people who chose this and the 112 minute *Night Sun* for the Festival must have a very highly developed taste for excruciating boredom.

When you see such movies, you despair for the future of film, to say nothing of its present. And as you look at the audiences at the Festival's special screenings—ostensibly scholars, critics, distributors, and such, but actually also many rather more peripheral types—you see a lot of characters more suited to rock concerts, disreputable discotheques, late-night subway platforms, and cock-fights. Was the cinema intended for the likes of them? Or were they once wholesome human beings, gradually eroded, corroded, used up by moviegoing? Certainly the questions they ask during press conferences attest to an advanced state of cerebral atrophy.

Nevertheless, I refuse to believe that this is the final and irreversible phase of cinema: infantilism and dotage joining hands across an abyss of stupefaction. There were in this very same festival (and I didn't see everything) three good films and two interesting ones. So all is not lost. But it must become possible to attend movies without a sense of déjà vu, tired blood, the terminal exhaustion of an art form. Perhaps something truly new could come from the newly liberated countries behind the Iron Curtain—*ex oriente lux.*

And perhaps we are due for a new era in film criticism, beyond the raised or lowered thumbs of two television caricatures of film critics, beyond the perfunctory and insipid stuff we read in most newspapers and such magazines as deign to bother with movie reviews. If we could get film criticism on a par with the best in book reviewing in our reputable journals, we could perhaps experience something analogous to what happened in France after World War II, when a new wave in film criticism spawned a cinematic New Wave. To be sure, this was the rare case where the film critics themselves become the filmmakers.

There is one quality that more than any other could help revitalize the cinema: believableness. Characters in films must re-establish contact with social, economic, and political realities even where film style is non- or anti-realistic. We should not have to ask questions such as: How come she has that much free time? Where does he get his money from? Why would they have been so purblind as not to see *that* coming? And so on.

It may sound like rather simplistic advice, but, if heeded, it could make for major improvements. And truly persuasive critics could—maybe—teach their readers to demand that much. The problem with film critics, however, is that most of them aren't really critics, merely movie buffs who managed to preserve their childhood enthusiasms intact. They like movie movies, as they call them, much more than art films, as they call genres they don't care for. Can you imagine a literary critic preferring book books? Or detective stories to literature? On the other hand, can you imagine a book critic obliged to review most of what lands on his desk, the way movie reviewers are expected—indeed want to—see everything? Granted, a movie takes much less time and effort, but is that an excuse for critical omnivorousness, particularly if it results in your reading in the papers that such-and-such a film must be seen, only to have you feel, as you come out of it, the victim of highway robbery?

And now visualize, please, a bunch of grown men and women whose job it is to see movies as bad as that and worse, week in, week out. Or, more likely, day in, day out. If they weren't cretins when they started out, surely they must be feeble-minded by now.

Film criticism should be protected from our so-called critics. Movies should ideally be reviewed by persons well versed in all the arts, who, preferably, are also professional writers of something: plays, essays, poetry, fiction. True, some of the silliest film criticism I have read was signed Alberto Moravia. But then take someone, as early as 1928, writing sensibly about his enjoyment of "a touching screen love story, cast with actors who must be expressive, attractive, and agreeable, and are allowed to be vain, but never unnatural." That someone was Thomas Mann.

The trouble with an inexpensively available art form is that it is all but impervious to criticism. Asked to shell out fifty bucks or more for a play or opera, folks will consult a review or two first; but when something can be had cheap at a movie theater, or even more so at a video store, why bother? Now, if seeing films could only cost more money! But even if filmgoing never becomes expensive, that is still no justification for cheap reviews.

Reversal of Fortune

In *Reversal of Fortune*, as you may know, the millionairess Sunny von Bülow is lying in a coma that, unlike fortune, is unfortunately irreversible. Claus von Bülow, her playboy husband, has been found guilty by a Newport jury of twice trying to kill her with insulin shots. Alan Dershowitz, the high-powered Harvard Law School professor, is about to win an appeal for a new trial, in which von Bülow will be acquitted. Claus, a Danish quasi-aristocrat, as flippant as he is eccentric, is being flip again. Dershowitz exhorts: "This is life and death. Your wife is laying in a coma."

God knows, bad English is not the worst offense of this thoroughly offensive movie, written by Nicholas Kazan (son of Elia) from Alan Dershowitz's book, and co-produced by Elon Dershowitz (son of Alan), who is portrayed by Stephen Mailer (son of Norman). But in momentous moments of stress and tension, there is nothing like a piece of whopping illiteracy to reduce everything to a ridiculous shambles. I don't know who laid that "laying" on us: Alan D., Nick K., or Ron Silver, who enacts Alan—or, for that matter, Barbet Schroeder, the "highbrow" French director, whose English is usually good. Let them share the blame.

Respect for any rules or decencies, however, is not what this movie is about. For starters, the voiceover narration throughout is by Sunny (Glenn Close), the woman in a coma, as the camera promptly shows her (in flashbacks, she is vertical). To me, there is something ineffably tasteless, almost sacrilegious, about using someone brain-dead as a dramatic device, exploiting the disparity between her actual condition and the mischievously jocular things she says (totally out of character for the first shy, then withdrawn woman she was in her active life) to elicit a kind of metaphysical titillation. (Jack Kroll, in *Newsweek*, calls this one "of the film's many clever, unsettling, and even brilliant ideas.")

The film provides highlights from the first trial, and ignores the second. It concentrates, like the book, on showing how Dershowitz got Claus off the hook, even though he found him personally uncongenial: a hard-working, by no means uncelebrated or underpaid Jewish lawyer from a humble background, small of stature, casually dressed, and unsightly, confronting a tall, well-spoken (British accent with Danish highlights), elegantly attired and expensively groomed uppercruster, doubtless anti-Semitic. (His father, a drama critic, was one of Denmark's very few Nazi collaborators; his mother was indeed a Bülow, but the "von" is entirely of Claus's making.) Their verbal sparring is not uninteresting even in the movie (though doubtless juicier in life), especially when there are others present, e.g., Claus's new mistress, Andrea Reynolds, a Hungarian adventuress; or Dershowitz's Harvard students, a large team of whom went to work on every aspect of the case with the task of unearthing in a hundred days something that would justify a retrial. They did: a technicality.

And that's just it. The film makes much of several ironies. It is the crass Andrea who advised Claus, "Get the Jew!" And Dershowitz, who was at first sure that Claus was guilty, nevertheless managed to convince himself of Claus's innocence (though the film, finally, implies otherwise). He was paid an enormous sum by Claus, but, as the film keeps relentlessly and sanctimoniously reminding us, all the money went into the defense of two young blacks on death row down South, whom Dershowitz has thus far kept alive. What we see of Claus's home life—total frigidity with Sunny, both carnal and climatic, she insisting on open bedroom windows through the long winter nights at Clarendon Court, their Newport mansion—is contrasted with Alan's life as a mensch, a warm friend to his students, his son, and an ex-girlfriend especially invented for the movie, who comes to work on the Claus research team. Every chance they get, they play basketball; during these games Alan sprouts his best ideas.

But the main irony is ignored. It is that in working-class Providence, R.I., a city known for its political corruption, the case (unlike in upper-class Newport) was in the hands of a suspect legal apparatus and a benighted jury. Dershowitz, on the other hand, disposed of a battery of crack law students whom he did not even have to pay, and who worked their butts off for their famous and fatherly mentor. And indeed it is a student who makes the crucial discovery that his prof is able to parlay into a victory. And all the time Claus's case was financed by a son of his former employer, J. Paul Getty, who seems to have poured a cool million into it. We hear Dershowitz make some impassioned speeches about how even rich (well, richly married—Claus had no money of his own) immoralists deserve a fair trial, etc., etc., etc. But the final, unexplored irony lies precisely in that "even": I have very little doubt that the rich can buy themselves first-class consideration; it is the others I worry about—others who don't make such good political capital as the two blacks on death row in the South.

Some of those who knew Claus have pointed out mistakes in the film about the décor at Clarendon Court and some of the details of the von Bülows' daily life. What matters more is that all the major characters in the film are distortions of reality. Sunny was not the hard-edged, cigar-store-Indianish virago into which Glenn Close turns every character she plays; rather, she was a pretty, unbright, lost little rich girl who married consecutively two European aristocrats or pseudo-aristocrats with neither of whom she had much in common, and who, unsuccesful socially, withdrew more and more into neurasthenia. Miss Close's performance doesn't come close.

Claus was (is) a very tall, large-boned, sinisterly attractive man-about-town, a strange mixture of outward solidity and inner socio-pathic deviousness. The actor who could have properly portrayed him, starting with physical resemblance, is the late Curt Jürgens. Jeremy Irons, a charming lightweight and flibbertigibbet, too vain to espouse even Claus's near-baldness, gives the man an almost touching brittleness. He has clearly studied Claus's speech, and even though he can't get the soupçon of Danishness, the voice emerges so ponderously out of that weak face as to seem piped—or bas-sooned—in electronically.

Ron Silver comes nearer to being Dershowitz, but though he has the original's Jewishness and raffishness, he lacks his puniness and ferretiness. Still, he is at least in the ball park, or is it theme park? The only reality in the film is in the opening helicopter shot of New-port's Millionaires' Row; after that, tendentious fiction takes over. Particularly specious is the way the research team is cast: carefully balanced between men and women, blacks and whites, Occidentals and Orientals, WASPS and Jews and Hispanics. It's not so much the Harvard Law School as the Family of Man.

Especially hilarious is the early scene in which one bright fe-male student—self-righteously played by the smug Felicity Huff-man—starts to walk out on the team rather than defend the mani-festly guilty Claus. There follows a holier-than-thou Q&A session wherein Dershowitz, via Socratic dialectics, proves the nobility of the cause, as opposed to the man. But what the movie is finally sell-ing—aside from titillation (famous criminal case), catering to low curiosity (how do the very rich live?), and ego massage (the rich are weird and unhappy; yet are better and better off)—is an oddball fun couple, somewhat in the Schwarzenegger-DeVito mold: von Bülow and Dershowitz, the blueblooded Bluebeard and the ethnic legal beagle together in a glitzy caper.

GoodFellas

We were alerted early on that the battle of the films this year would be between two Mafia megamovies: Martin Scorsese's *GoodFellas*, which came out in September, and *The Godfather Part III*, which, with Francis Ford Coppola's customary last-minute fiddling, barely made it for Christmas. *GoodFellas* is based on *Wiseguy*, Nicholas Pileggi's nonfiction account of Henry Hill, a medium-sized Mafioso who ended up squealing on the mob; *Godfather Part III* is a continuation of the Corleone saga, a fiction devised by Mario Puzo. Both movies are superproductions even in length (*GF* is 146 minutes, *G III* is 161), but Coppola's is a tedious effort to flog an old hippopotamus into action, whereas Scorsese's is the most original and assured piece of American mainline cinema since—it's been so long, I've forgotten what.

GoodFellas, with a script by Pileggi and Scorsese, is a testimonial to the banality of evil as compelling as Eichmann's story and far closer to home. Henry Hill, a boy of half-Irish, half-Sicilian descent, is aware that the taxi stand across the street in his New York blue-collar neighborhood is a front for the mob, and he yearns to become a gangster, the way other kids want to be firemen or auto racers. He starts by, unbeknown to his parents, dropping out of school and performing menial tasks for the mob. When a mailman delivers a letter from school about his absences, and his father administers a thrashing, the mobsters give the postman a mighty scare, and no similar mail gets delivered again.

Already as a kid, Henry gets to meet the biggies, notably Paulie Cicero, who runs the show, and his various lieutenants, especially the still very young Jimmy Conway, a big-time thief and heavy tipper, who bestows a benediction of greenbacks all around like a rain from heaven. Also a coeval, Tommy, with a face like a beaked tomahawk, the future hitman extraordinary. Soon Jimmy, Tommy, and Henry are a trio of hijackers and high rollers, pulling off ever grander heists; goodfellas, as they like to call themselves, or wiseguys.

By this time, both script and direction have worked their wonders. When young Henry runs out of a Mafia pizza parlor to bandage a badly wounded Mafioso, he is rebuked, "You wasted eight fucking aprons on the guy!" Upon Henry's first arrest, he is greeted by Paulie, "You popped your cherry!" Later, Jimmy congratulates Henry on having learned "the two greatest things in life: never rat on your friends, and keep your mouth shut." Henry (he is heard most of the time in voiceover) exults: "If we wanted something, we just took it. If anyone complained, he got hit so bad, he never complained again."

The language is racy but simple, in the way of Satan's credo in *Paradise Lost*, "Evil, be thou my good." Camaraderie in the atmo-

spherically lit restaurants where the gang hangs out consists of telling about murderous exploits in ways that raise gales of laughter,
which, in turn, give rise to violent kidding that can lead to actual
violence. But it is all casual. If Tommy is dissatisfied with a young
waiter who is a bit slow, he shoots him in the foot; if, next time,
the boy gives him any lip, he shoots him dead. This elicits remon-
strances from Jimmy, but it doesn't stop the card game in which
everyone is immersed.

While the crisp narration alternates with sometimes broadly
comical, sometimes *sotto voce* conspiratorial dialogue, Scorsese
conjures with his camera. He introduces stop-motion at some not
obviously crucial moments while the voiceover commentary drives
a point home. Or he will repeat a short scene, either immediately or
much later on, with additional information. Or he'll tilt the camera
during a conjugal argument, then slowly straighten it while keeping the aroused spouses in the lower left-hand corner of the frame,
which shows a corner on the floor of the room where their sexual
reconciliation takes place, the placement within the frame replicating the position in the room.

Whenever possible, he shoots from a character's point of view.
When Henry drives up in front of the house of someone he'll beat to
a pulp, the person is first seen in Henry's rear-view mirror, as befits
the stealthiness of the occasion. When someone who hasn't paid his
dues to the mob is threatened by having his head bent back over
the railing of the lions' grotto at the zoo, the lions on their rocky
ledge are shot upside down, increasing the immediacy of the man's
terror. When Henry is being introduced to the goodfellas drinking
and eating at one of their joints, the camera weaves through this
long, sprawling, orange-dusky space in one uninterrupted shot as
various mobsters lift their heads long enough for a hello before the
camera meanders on. Again, when Henry takes Karen, his bride to
be, to the Copacabana, he beats the line outside by entering from
the rear, through the kitchen, tipping people as he goes along. It is
a single, very long take, often turning corners and brushing past
steam tables, with the camera traipsing behind Karen and Henry
like faithful Fido until, reaching the nightclub floor, it observes the
waiters, in a burst of groveling solicitude, setting up a choice table
for the newcomers.

The best thing Scorsese does is to use a freewheeling, uncon-
strained tempo. Most of the scenes are short and clipped, their beginnings and endings cropped, like fat sliced off the edges of a ham.

There is a sense of leanness and propulsiveness about the film, yet, when appropriate, the camera relaxes, even dawdles, in an inspired rubato, as in the aforementioned love scene on the floor. By casually using the extreme variety of procedures available to a director, Scorsese makes us accept them equally casually, until they seem as normal as the Cyrillic alphabet in a Russian text. And by cutting to the bone, Scorsese and Pileggi are able to crowd many more incidents into the film, and yet, by keeping the scenes short, never let our interest slacken. Here, too, Michael Ballhaus's cinematography helps enormously, with its almost clinical approach to every camera setup, as clean as Thelma Schoonmaker's editing.

Down to the last expendable mobster or mobster's girlfriend, the casting is impeccable. ("Saturday night was for the wives, but Friday night at the Copa was for the girlfriends.") The faces, the hairdos, the clothes, the intonations (Woman: "If I even looked at someone else, he'd kill me." Other woman: "Great!") all exude the most palpable, cozy vulgarity. And the major roles are filled to the brim, without a drop spilling over. As Harry, Ray Liotta is a black-haired, blue-eyed, sensual-mouthed fellow, his pale face, however, marbled with sinister rugosities. His performance is perforce less riveting here than it was as the heavy in *Something Wild*, but it neatly conveys the mixture of stupidity and cunning that jerks this man ahead. Robert De Niro's Jimmy, the corners of his eyes as soothingly rumpled as a comfortable jacket, tautens his face suddenly into chiseled ruthlessness. As Paulie, Paul Sorvino lowers and smiles, smiles and lowers like a two-faced walrus.

As Tommy, Joe Pesci is a bantam rooster crossed with a water moccasin, with a sleek, jeering voice; even his way of walking and speaking is a form of holstered trigger-happiness, his laugh the shortest distance between mockery and murder. When he jokes with his mother (played by Scorsese's mom), the joke is both funny and chilling: "Why don't you get yourself a nice girl?" "I get a nice girl almost every night." "I mean to settle down with." "I settle down. Then in the morning I'm free." But the most extraordinary acting comes from Lorraine Bracco (in private life, Mrs. Harvey Keitel) as Karen. She has the same devious sexiness as Debra Winger, exemplary timing, and, though Italian, can do New York Jewish as well as Shelley Winters. As Henry's put-upon but spunky, tenacious wife, her ferocity is always either droll or heartbreaking.

What makes *GoodFellas* unique is its exaggerated, comic-horrific mode that can with equal ease turn hilarious or deadly. When murder erupts, it does so quickly, almost subliminally, yet blood-ily—whether by gun, knife, or well-placed icepick into the back of the neck. These wiseguys live well even in jail—where nobody goes, we learn, unless he wants to: "Do you know why Jeanie's husband went to the can? Because he wanted to get away from her." There is much cooking, mostly by men, and the camera captures it as if gifted with a sense of smell and taste. Evil uses the spatula as natu-rally as the gun.

You remember those once-popular recordings of "Opera without words"? In it, blatancy and banality, *GoodFellas* is opera without mu-sic, and all the more funny-sinister for it. Even the word for killing used by these wiseguys—whacking—is characteristically prosaic and comic. But by the time one of the main characters gets whacked, we're laughing from the other side of our mouths, if at all.

Mr. and Mrs. Bridge

Mr. and Mrs. Bridge is based on the two celebrated novels that Evan S. Connell wrote ten years apart. In *Mrs. Bridge*, he told the story from the point of view of the docile upper-middle-class housewife in Kansas City, who lives only for her prosperous lawyer husband and her children, two girls and a boy. Though she has finer stirrings and sometimes even the tiniest rebelliousness in the name of self-expression, these are quickly squelched (usually by herself) as she goes on being a genteelly frustrated but exemplary wife and mother. In *Mr. Bridge*, a decade later, the same ground was covered from the husband's point of view, with generally different episodes neatly fitted in between those of the first novel. It was a genuine tour de force to get so much complementary mileage out of routine lives without letting the attention flag even if the two books were read in quick succession.

As it happens, I saw the film, which conflates the two novels into just 124 minutes of screen time, before I had read either book. So I was impressed by this, to me, most successful collaboration of the trio Ismail Merchant (producer), James Ivory (director), and Ruth Prawer Jhabvala (writer) since their first joint venture, *Shakespeare Wallah* (1965). As I keep saying, the producer-director team, with or without Mrs. Jhabvala, strikes me as invincible amateurs, their films betraying a certain shakiness, propensity for *faux pas*, home-movie-ishness despite good production values, and deliberate aestheticizing as of someone buffing his or her fingernails ostentatiously a few times too often.

In *Shakespeare Wallah*, the Indian locale that is the team's forte was still new to us. Satyajit Ray had tackled it from the native point of view; here, however, was a combined Indian and European sensibility at work: Mrs. Jhabvala is a German Jewess educated in England, married to an Indian and living in India. It was a sub-Forster sensibility (as the trio's version of *A Room with a View* made abundantly clear), but it had its midlevel charm. In *Mr. and Mrs. Bridge*, however, they seemed to me to have hit it just right.

Connell's novels are written in diminutive chapters a few pages each, each an epiphany of sorts and sufficient unto itself. But the gaps between are no more disturbing than the spaces between the tesserae of a mosaic. The stuffy Mr. B., good-natured in his pompous way; the faintly pathetic Mrs. B., saved by being only intermittently aware of her repression; the beautiful, flighty daughter; the level-headed, stubborn other daughter; the withdrawn, inscrutable son—all these are held together by a tone of understated satire. A satire more pitying than biting, but still laughing—sadly—at these lives on which the mute pedal is seldom released, and then only for willfulness or anger.

Or so it seems in the film. But upon reading the books, I find them considerably grittier, more penetrating, better. The lives of the Bridges, their friends, acquaintances, and servants are much more sharply dissected, to reveal deeper flaws, more acrid conflicts, more disturbing victories and defeats. There is a bracing toughness about Connell's writing that the movie frequently Jhabvalizes away. Thus both Mr. and Mrs. Bridge die in the fiction, and die deaths emblematic of their essences: the movie, however, keeps both of them alive and adds shamelessly ingratiating endings for the rest of the family as well. These are not even dramatized, but relegated to those irritating final title cards that, ever since Costa-Gavras's *Z*, have become the lazy or evasive way to end a movie. Good when they serve an ironic purpose, they are intolerable as sappy glossings over.

What greatly helps the movie despite the edulcoration is whatever of Connell does survive, plus the better than usual production values. Thus Tony Pierce-Roberts has evolved into a keen cinematographer, Richard Robbins has toned down the boisterous eclecticism of his scoring, David Gropman's production design is unassumingly astute. Above all, there is some noteworthy acting.

As Mrs. Bridge, Joanne Woodward is, in a word, perfection. There is in her performance the histrionic equivalent of a singer's perfect pitch: pathos, absurdity, staunchness, vestigial self-assertion, compliant self-effacement, intense (but not exaggerated) solicitude, benighted provincialism, tremulous openness to higher things, and boundless decency are all there in just proportions, sometimes warring with one another, sometimes in meek harmony. It is a performance that moves you so deeply precisely because it does not stink to please, as Hollywood star turns, however deft in other ways, so often do.

As Mr. Bridge, Paul Newman is thoroughly workmanlike, though no more than that; yet in the part of a straight but blinkered, attractive but emotionally hobbled man, this will suffice. In the supporting cast, only Kyra Sedgwick, as the rebel daughter, is unsatisfactory; everyone else does well or better. There are outstanding contributions from Blythe Danner, as a wife driven mad by suffocating *embourgeoisement*; from Diane Kagan, as a faithful secretary for twenty years whose secret passion for Mr. Bridge finally bursts out, only to leave him more emotionally constipated than ever; and from Austin Pendleton (finally not miscast), as an art teacher reduced to door-to-door salesman. And there are pungent contributions also from Simon Callow, Gale Garnett, and others.

The ultimate cravenness of the Merchant-Ivory-Jhabvala team does, however, exemplify what keeps our cinema from coming of age. As independent filmmakers, they could set an example to Hollywood instead of toeing the line. Though they can, left to their own devices, come up with such horrors as *Savages* and *Slaves of New York*, here—prodded by Miss Woodward, who initiated the project—they were on the verge of genuine, major achievement. And, thanks largely but not wholly to her performance, they come within striking distance. Alas, you can't get the full benefit of the film without rushing home and reading the books.

A Couple of Contenders

THE NASTY GIRL; OPEN DOORS

European film has traditionally been the thing we could turn to when American movies became, as they often did, too frivolous or empty for anybody's good. But now that most American movies are worse than ever, hang it if the films from Europe do not manage to be as trivial as our own. There are, however, some fortunate exceptions.

The Nasty Girl, a film from Germany (submitted for an Academy Award and, if anyone cares about that dubious honor, a strong contender), is based on—or, as they would pretentiously say in Hollywood, "upon"—a true story. The real-life tale is that of Anja Rosmus, a young Bavarian woman from Passau, whom conditions in her town spurred on to become a respected historian of what happened under the Nazis. Like Anja, the movie's Sonja begins as a carefree but intellectually curious girl who, having won one international high-school essay competition, tries again the following year. This time the assigned topic is "My Home Town During the Third Reich."

Sonja, who opens the film acting as cicerone to a television crew—and to us in the audience—is shown posed against or perched on the most picturesque locations in Pfilzing (as Passau has been fictionalized), and we are lulled into assuming that this will be a witty fashion-layout type of film about a quaintly photogenic town and its quaint, telegenic little people. And, true enough, there is comedy aplenty in the early sequences of the movie, written and directed by Michael Verhoeven, a German director not to be confused with the Dutchman Paul Verhoeven, who made Robocop and such. Indeed, so skillful is the workmanship that the comedy never stops even after the film has become scary.

For as Sonja starts rummaging in the town library and elsewhere in pursuit of the past, bureaucratic roadblocks and personal hostilities are thrown at her in funny, exasperating, and finally sinister ways. But her stubborn courage will not be deterred even after a vicious and life-threatening campaign is launched against her, her family, and even household pets. For by this time Sonja has married her (and everybody else's) favorite schoolteacher and become a mother herself. Yet with heroic mulishness or foolish temerity she pushes on.

I am a trifle regretful that Verhoeven feels obliged to Brechtianize and introduce alienation effects. That he sometimes uses outdoor photomurals for indoor backgrounds doesn't bother me; but to have Sonja's room during a family council turn into a sort of ferris-wheel gondola whirling about against a Pfilzing cityscape strikes me as excessive. Alienation effects work better on stage, a slightly artificial medium that adapts more readily to the studied, the deliberate; on film, which is by nature realistic, such devices work only if the style is antirealistic throughout—but in that case what need is there for alienation effects in the first place?

This, however, is almost nitpicking. The marvelous thing about *The Nasty Girl* (*Das schreckliche Mädchen*, by the way, should have been translated as *The Dreadful Girl*, which makes quite a difference) is that it so smoothly functions as both everyday story and cautionary parable. Aside from dialogue so pointed that it handily survives even subtitling, as well as fine direction, there is also splendid casting and acting, beginning with Lena Stolze as Sonja. Miss Stolze is equally believable as a spirited schoolgirl, a sexy woman, a noble but quixotic heroine, a canny strategist and tactician in knight errant's armor. Besides her great acting talent, she has a kind of looks that are ordinary yet enchanting, never movie-starrish yet nowise resistible.

The supporting cast is equally flawless, with Robert Giggenbach, as the devoted husband who nevertheless abandons Sonja, and Michael Gahr, as her father, especially noteworthy. But no less good, really, are all the townspeople by no means all black or all white—who glibly reverse themselves about Sonja—for, against, for, against again—as the winds of opportunism are blowing, until her equally intransigent granny remains her sole ally.

The film is beautifully shot in color (the present) and monochrome (the past) by Axel de Roche; but even more arresting is its tempo. When you look carefully at a fully accomplished film such as *GoodFellas* or *The Nasty Girl*, you notice its supreme virtue: a generally fast tempo that is not afraid of either speeding up even further or slowing down to the point of seemingly dawdling, whatever best serves the narrative or psychological needs—so that rhythm actually becomes content. And all this inconspicuously, without calling smug attention to itself.

What a thoroughly absorbing film Gianni Amelio has co-adapted and directed from a novel by the late great Leonardo Sciascia, *Open Doors!* This time, unlike in other Sciascia works, the Sicilian locale does not involve the Mafia but something worse: Mussolini's Fascists in 1917, adjudicating a triple murder that seems to have some vaguely political motivation. Sanna, the president of the court, is not a bad fellow, but he goes along with the Fascists, and since the killer, Scalia (Ennio Fantastichini, and fine), is only too proudly eager for the death sentence, what's holding up the show?

What's holding it up is one conscientious judge, Di Francesco, and one thoughtful juror, Consolo, a highly literate farmer. Both of them basically oppose the death penalty, and both of them perceive Scalia's killing of his superior, of his successor to the humble bureaucratic job he was fired from, and of his wife as something not quite ordinary but covering up bigger and fouler things. What is remarkable about this film is that it is almost entirely a character study of both the major and the minor personages. Old and young, adults and children, good people with flaws, bad people with patches of virtue, peripheral figures barely glimpsed—all contribute something to a story told so elliptically that it makes serious demands on the viewer, but also offers abundant rewards. Dostoyevsky figures in the film, too, and rightly so: *Open Doors* is Dostoyevskian—no small compliment.

Next to character, there is atmosphere, searchingly brought out in Tonino Nardi's unflamboyant cinematography of Palermo and environs, with many long and extreme long shots, where backgrounds are calibrated to enhance the soul of the story; Franco Piersanti's restrained musical underscoring likewise contributes incisively. But the ultimate glory of the film is Gian Maria Volontè's Judge Di Francesco. Playing a widower considerably older than he is, Volontè, famous for his violent or trenchant roles, proves equally superb as an introspective, hunched-up-on-himself character—note especially how he eats. This is not one of your simple, radiantly good men—Consolo, the juror played sensitively by Renato Carpentieri, is that—but one capable of outbursts, albeit more implosive than explosive. Volontè may be the greatest leading man cum character actor in movies now that Olivier is gone: he gives off shudders of concentration that are spine-tingling in the *positive* sense.

Amelio's film is really a philosophical combat between conflicting ideologies. Chief Judge Sanna declares, "I don't like zealous people. They are capable of breaking a priceless vase to kill a fly." Sanna, a half-hearted fellow-traveler and amateur conchologist, wants to play it easy; but what if the vase is an overinflated piece of Fascist art, and the fly the carrier of a major disease? A high Fascist observer from Rome goes further: he would like a magic ring that could make troublemakers disappear. Failing that, he'll settle for speedy executions: the good peace-loving citizens ought to sleep safe behind open doors. Di Francesco answers soberly, wearily: "I always keep my front door locked." He is not an idealistic zealot; he merely believes in reckoning with human frailty.

How this conflict works itself out is the subtext of Amelio's calmly unsettling film, another Oscar nominee. What the two decent men, Di Francesco and Consolo, achieve may go for naught; or it may be that the uprooted vine of a goodness can, fragmented, retain a foothold from which to sprout, surprisingly, anew, as the farmer says from experience.

On the Richter scale on which our movies are foolishly measured, *Open Doors* may be only a four; but on the scale of human content, this Sciascia-Amelio-Volontè teamwork rates something more like a ten.

The Silence of the Lambs

Besides sex and violence, there is a third perennial favorite among movie genres: horror. And the horror film is particularly effective when, rather than dealing in monsters or the undead, it grafts itself onto another genre, the film noir, turning it into the thriller-chiller.

Such is the current hit *The Silence of the Lambs*, faithfully adapted by the playwright Ted Talley from Thomas Harris's best-selling novel. It has an unusual and complicated (but not overcomplicated) plot, idiosyncratic characters who interact provocatively, suspense and surprises galore, and unless, like me, you are among the impervious few—it can scare the bejeezus out of you.

It is the story of a highly gifted and attractive FBI trainee, Clarice Starling, chosen to help catch "Buffalo Bill," a serial killer of young women, whose bodies are found horribly flayed. The person who, it seems, could greatly facilitate the FBI's efforts to nab Bill is Hannibal "the Cannibal" Lecter, a distinguished psychiatrist and psychopath, who likes to eat his victims and is now in his eighth year in a maximum-security prison. In exchange for certain alleviations of the mode of his lifelong imprisonment—and because he might lust for Clarice—Lecter, who hitherto has refused to answer questions, might talk and provide useful hints.

Or so special FBI agent Jack Crawford believes when he sends Clarice to Dr. Chilton, the repulsive head of the prison-cum-asylum where Lecter is kept. Over Chilton's misgivings and, later, protests, Clarice proceeds to have some sessions with Lecter as she sits outside his special glass-walled cell. In a quid pro quo, he will tell her things about Buffalo Bill (who, it emerges, was the lover of one of his male patients) if she tells him things about herself, her childhood and adolescence. Her mother died early on, it turns out; her adored policeman father was killed by thugs when she was ten. Farmed out to a farmer relative in Montana, little Clarice could not stand the bleating of the lambs about to be slaughtered. She tried to escape with one of them, failed, and was sent to a foster home. She has yet to exorcise—to silence—the cry of the lambs in her mind's ears.

Meanwhile, she has Lecter in her ears: this demonic superman cajoles, humiliates, insults with gross sexual innuendo, compliments, and bullies her almost irresistibly. The girl stands up to him admirably, and does get helpful suggestions from Lecter, even if couched in anagrams and other puzzles that she cleverly solves. Meanwhile Bill has struck for the sixth time, this time abducting a woman senator's daughter. Catherine, whom he holds at the bottom of a dried-up well inside his ramshackle house somewhere in the Midwest.

From further grisly evidence that surfaces, Clarice correctly deduces that Bill kidnaps big overweight girls whom he starves for a while until their skin becomes loose for easier flaying. It also emerges that, a homosexual whose transvestism is literally skin-deep, he is sewing a body suit for himself out of women's skins; why it should take so many is not made clear. In any case, Crawford, Clarice, and the FBI are racing to catch him before he murders Catherine; meanwhile, through a series of bizarre maneuvers, Dr. Chilton's and his own, Lecter escapes in a particularly gruesome way, and here one has to be as gullible as a five-year-old or one of my fellow critics if one is not to laugh the horror out of its efficacy.

For example, even though he warns Clarice not to take sharp objects such as pencils into Lecter's vicinity, Dr. Chilton nevertheless toys with his Cross ballpoint pen while questioning Lecter on a later occasion, and the last we see is his leaving it lying around and Lecter eyeing it. But since Lecter is strapped into a sarcophagus-like cage, and even his face is in a metallic muzzle, how could he have absconded with it, short of having telekinesis in his repertoire? Moreover, he has whittled it down later on into something like a long nail—how? He is now held in a cage put up in the middle of a huge room of the Memphis art museum (or so it looks), with a pair of cops providing round-the-clock surveillance, and he is certainly not accorded tools with which to pare down pens. The escape, moreover, hinges on a piece of surgery that Lecter—a psychiatrist, not a plastic surgeon—performs brilliantly with a mere penknife.

Altogether, this Lecter is endowed with supernatural powers, being able to smell through a glass partition what Clarice's perfume is—*L'Air du temps*—even though Clarice is not wearing it that day. But still more amazing is that Lecter—intellectual, man of culture, gastronome—would enjoy feasting on raw human tongue and entrails with mere Chianti, when caviar with Cristalle or Perrier-Jouët would be so much more appropriate. There are aristocratic types of psychopathology, but the film is capable only of the mass-audience variety, unsuitable to Lecter's elitist character.

Still, *Lambs* does have its strong points, too. Jonathan Demme is a very savvy director who knows how to establish the feel of a locale or the essence of a character with a few, telling brush-strokes. To such evocativeness and economy, he adds exact casting, fitting the right actors into even the smallest parts, down to Bill's toy poodle, perkily enacted by Starla. And Demme puts cross-cutting, a by now often tired-looking device, to a new, yet more stunning, use. And though Tak Fujimoto can photograph gorgeously, which he proves in the few instances where this is appropriate, Demme keeps his cinematographer mostly in low gear, giving the film the proper clinical look. Thus, too, he gets from Howard Shore, his composer, a score that is chillingly suggestive, without ever, like so much cheap horror-film scoring, warning you ahead of time with tautologically churned-out fright music.

Jodie Foster, surely the toughest of current Hollywood leading ladies (even her voice is an octave lower than the competition's), is a persuasive Clarice, balancing strength and vulnerability, and producing a superb West Virginia accent: let me hope she isn't a native West Virginian, which would minimize the achievement. Anthony Hopkins is galvanizing as Lecter; his accent may occasionally slip into British, but in every other way he is uncannily, hypnotically the bad doctor of every patient's nightmares. The goofier American version of this is well embodied by Anthony Heald's Dr. Chilton, and Scott Glenn, angular and anhedonic, is the perfect intransigent FBI agent, ascetic even in his infrequent forays into banter.

More disturbing to me than the violence and horror—which, for such a film, are handled with relative restraint—is the amorality of *Lambs*, the effect it has on the audience. I don't mind Lecter's getting away—such things happen in real life, alas. But that he should be presented as the wittiest and most ingenious character in the film, and that the further murder he plans should actually be cheered by the audience is morally wrong. In an age in which mayhem thrives, a mass medium should not be savoring one of the perpetrators quite so gleefully.

O Rare *Mister Johnson*

MISTER JOHNSON

Bruce Beresford's *Mister Johnson*, from Joyce Cary's novel, was favorably reviewed on the whole, but not in a way to send people racing to the box office. When I saw it a second time, I was one of four people in the theater. Too bad, because *Mister Johnson* is a work of genius.

I regret not having read the novel, but, knowing Cary's work, I have no doubt that it is a major achievement. And knowing Bruce Beresford, I have no doubt that he and his screenwriter, the novelist William Boyd, were faithful to Cary's spirit and, wherever possible, letter. Beresford is occasionally obliged to make a predominantly commercial movie, and acquits himself honorably. But he is incomparable when he gets hold of a story that really gets hold of him, and he works, as an artist should, primarily to please himself. Such films from his Australian days, were *The Gaining of Wisdom, Don's Party*, and the magisterial *Breaker Morant*: such, in America, were *Tender Mercies* and *Driving Miss Daisy*. There are also virtually unknown films of his, such as the haunting *The Fringe Dwellers*, about Australian aborigines in a white culture, which American audiences, white and black, completely ignored.

Such may yet be the utterly unwarranted fate of *Mister Johnson*, which also deals with the clash of two cultures, black and white, only this time in Nigeria. Cary's 1939 novel was based on his African experiences. It is the often comic tragedy of Mister Johnson, a mission-school-educated African who thinks of himself as English, and who, by not fitting in anywhere, perishes. But what is so beautiful and moving is that Johnson's failure is not seen as a mere part of the clash of black and white, but as the problem of any dreamer and schemer crushed by his own ambitions as much as by his environment.

Moreover, this is also the near-tragedy of Harry Rudbeck, the British district officer who, as Johnson's employer, in many ways benefited from his chief clerk, yet, in the end, had to become his executioner. Such, however, is the irony and complexity of the work that, although it is tragic, it is also full of astute and sovereign humor, and bristles with insights into colonialism, progress, civilization that provide everything save easy answers; in fact, they are those nagging uncertainties—or profound aporias—with which Platonic dialogues end, and which constitute the sobering glory of the Socratic method.

Mister Johnson—even his not having a first name but being called either, by his aspirations, Mister, or, by his job, Clerk, makes a strong point—is the quintessential misfit. Because he has had some education from the missionaries and speaks something closer to English than the prevailing pidgin, he sees himself as an Englishman, though he never set foot outside Africa. (And, speaking of foot, his relationship to his one pair of English shoes is one of the sublime leitmotifs of the film.) He is equally distant from the tribes working the land, to whom his beautiful wife, Bamu, belongs, as from the native rulers, such as the Muslim emir and his oily deputy, the waziri. Nor is he accepted as one of the British, either by the good-natured district officer, Harry Rudbeck, who is trying, with inadequate finances, to build a road that would bring trade to Fada, this deep-sleepy outpost, or by Sargy Gollup, retired British sergeant and owner of the Fada general store, who despises the "nigs" but is, like Rudbeck, impressed by Johnson's intelligence and enterprise.

On his clerk's salary, Johnson, who likes to give parties and indulge himself and his friends in beer, cannot afford his fine village-girl wife. He lives with Bamu on a sort of installment plan, and her father and brother keep reclaiming her whenever Johnson, always in debt to everyone, cannot meet the latest payment. Even Bamu does not understand his living beyond his means and treating her so indulgently because, as he says, "In England, we do not beat our wives." Finally, though he loves his employer, Johnson agrees to spy on the district officer's secret correspondence with the emir for a fee from the corrupt waziri.

What is so shattering about the film is that it sees equally clearly the predicament of all the characters: the ambiguity of the British, doing good with one hand and bad with the other, the precariousness of the Nigerians with their ancient traditions and barbarous rulers—let us recall their active participation in the slave trade until the British at last put an end to it. Also the confusion surrounding Rudbeck's road, its shady financing unmasked by a British subaltern, Tring, as meticulous as he is loathsome. And how touching is Rudbeck's sweet young wife, Celia, who begins by hating Africa but ends up loving it, only to suffer dumbly as the road brings trouble to Fada and to Mister Johnson, who has been so good to her.

Beresford never spells out anything: he always ends a scene a bit sooner than another director would. Take the one where Harry gives Johnson a taste of the plum pudding his mother sent him from Hertfordshire. "Hertfordshire," Johnson mumbles munching the novelty, "one of the most beautiful villages back home." Then, as the taste sinks in, his expression becomes puzzled, disappointed. Two seconds, and the camera moves on: we must be quick to keep up with the ambivalent moods and contradictory insights.

And when Beresford and his superb cinematographer, Peter James, show the gorgeousness of Africa—charcoal-grey nights with huge platinum moons suspended in them, sun-burnished days in which the world is orange shading into ecru—there is always something to cast doubt on the magnificence. Sometimes it is the ferocious hyenas straining against the leash by which they are led in a procession, sometimes it is the waziri's catamite sullenly defying his master's commands and blandishments, sometimes it is Sargy Gollup's comic-frightening condescension to the natives, sometimes it is a splendid jar left exposed to the inclemency of a rainy night.

Even the love and sex scenes between Harry and Celia restrainedly subserve the needs of characterization, and so does everyone's impeccable acting. As Johnson, Maynard Eziashi is a marvel of easeful authenticity, and his tragicomic last scenes should bite through the toughest of hearts. Hitherto only superior window dressing, Pierce Brosnan gives an ungainsayable performance as Harry Rudbeck; Beatie Edney is subdued yet splendid as Celia; Nick Reding icily scary as Tring; and Dennis Quilley on the button as a kindly but ineffectual superior officer. Several others, black and white, contribute memorably, but none more so than Fermi Fatoba as the waziri, and Edward Woodward as Gollup—both ignoble, yet achingly human. Like Georges Delerue's unusually understated music, the film is subtle but pervasive; it makes unaccustomed demands on us, but repays them munificently. Please see it.

La Femme Nikita;
Everybody's Fine

The French film *La Femme Nikita*, which has been breaking attendance records in Paris and London, and may yet do so here, is as peculiar as they come. It is a Frenchified, and therefore much more chic, version of that notorious American genre, the political-paranoia picture, of which *Three Days of the Condor* and *The Parallax View* were prime examples. If there are any shreds of Cartesian logic still left in France, this movie could put an end to them.

The underlying idea in such a film is that there exists some top-secret government agency that specializes in activities such as political assassination and the overthrowing of foreign governments. In this case, a beautiful young woman who is a streetwise punk, a zonked druggie, and a ruthless killer is apprehended during an armed robbery in which the store owner and the male members of her gang are killed and she shoots a policeman dead point blank. Condemned to death, she is given an alternative: to be proclaimed dead and trained for three years in a subterranean complex—under the surveillance of Bob, a man of iron—in everything from computers to karate, from sharpshooting to female allure (in which she gets some highly improbable lessons from Jeanne Moreau), until, because her deadliness is controlled, she becomes even more formidable than before.

We learn little about her beyond that her name is Nikita, an unlikely monicker, but Luc Besson, who wrote and directed, once on an airplane listened to Elton John's record of that name, and the lightheadedness of high altitude combining with Elton John can spawn just about anything. Anyway, Nikita, no longer a punker but a lethal weapon in enchanting female guise, leads a normal life under an assumed name except that, every now and then, she is ordered by phone to dispatch this or that person, which she does with great efficiency under titillatingly bizarre circumstances. This done, it is back to normality again, especially after she meets an adorable supermarket clerk, the sweet and dreamy Marco, and they become sweet and dreamy lovers. Thereupon complications ensue, not so much from the odd assassination, on which Marco traipses along uncomprehending, as from the reappearance of Bob, which pushes the film into a much older French genre, the love triangle, albeit of a very queer sort.

The film does, however, have two assets. The more dubious one is its ability to mix brutal actions with an offbeat, devil-may-care humor. The less dubious one is Anne Parillaud, a former dancer, in the lead. Her legs cavort through the world even as her body revels in its corporality. As talented as she is pretty, she makes the movie throb with aliveness.

Giuseppe Tornatore, who made the insufferably sentimental Oscar-winner *Cinema Paradiso*, is back with *Everybody's Fine* (*Stanno tutti bene*), starring Marcello Mastroianni as Matteo, a 74-year-old retired civil servant in Sicily, who talks to his dead wife, Angela, as though she were still alive. Films whose protagonists conduct dialogues with the dead constitute a subgenre to be shunned.

Matteo's five grown sons and daughters lead busy, ostensibly thriving, lives on the mainland, and have no time for papa. He puts up beachside bungalows for their summer holidays, but the *disgraziati* don't even bother to call—never mind write—to say they can't make it. Still self-deluded, Matteo resolves to travel north and surprise them in their five respective cities. The film thus becomes a meditation on a hustling, desperate, confused, and dissembling Italy.

In Naples, son Alvaro is nowhere to be found, barely even in the computer of the university where he teaches; only his phone answering machine dispenses ghostly messages. In Rome, son Canio pretends to be a serious political contender, but is actually a lowly Communist Party hack. A mugger robs Matteo, and smashes the camera containing the pictures the old man has promised Angela he'd bring back for her. Still, his obsession to reunite his family around a dinner table continues unabated. In Florence, the beautiful Tosca (Matteo, an opera lover, has given all his children operatic names) is not a successful actress, but mostly a model for pornoid cameras; her elegant apartment is really her ex-lover's, who wants it back; the baby of a friend, which Tosca looks after, is really, albeit illegitimately, her own.

Matteo doesn't cotton on to any of this. He journeys on to Milan, and meets on the train an exquisite older woman (Michele Morgan, as fine as ever), has a sweetly melancholy time with her, and ignores her advice to give up on his children as she has on hers. He travels on alone, congratulating himself on having remained, as he puts it, faithful to Angela. In Milan, Guglielmo is not a successful concert artist, but a humble percussionist in a marginal orchestra. His 15-year-old son, at least, is unevasive enough to admit getting his girlfriend pregnant. In Turin, Norma is not the big phone-company executive, but a mere telephone operator, her marriage a shambles. At the festive dinner Matteo throws for all in Rome, only Canio and Guglielmo show up, and finally admit their cover-up: Alvaro has actually committed suicide—something Matteo can't bring himself to believe.

The point here—conveyed in part through flashbacks, dreams, fantasies—is that Matteo (Italy) won't face the truth even when hit in the face by it. The story, if it weren't so mechanistic, might just barely work, but the attempt to revivify it with mildly surrealist touches and faintly absurdist humor merely reminds us how much not only such stories, but also the strategies for their updating, have aged and paled.

Aged, too, has poor Mastroianni, whose very real charm now seems a bit sweaty under the collar. The supporting cast is undistinguished, although Valeria Cavalli, as Tosca, is quietly enchanting. Tornatore's dialogue, on which everybody's perennial collaborator, Tonino Guerra, duly collaborated, is routine stuff, not helped by Blasco Giurato's boilerplate cinematography. Another very old hand, Ennio Morricone, managed some still respectable, but by now second-best, background music. Sad.

Movie of the Moment

THELMA & LOUISE

There is almost always a Movie of the Moment, which sometimes, though far from often, proves a lasting achievement. Currently, that title goes uncontestedly to *Thelma & Louise*, Ridley Scott's film from a first screenplay by Calli Khouri, a former pop-music video producer. It has been described as a combination road movie, (female) buddy picture, and crime-spree film, as if these were three separate genres, whereas, because of the customary overlapping, they are more like one and a half.

Louise (Susan Sarandon) is a waitress in an Arkansas eatery. She is mad at her traveling-musician boyfriend, Jimmy, who won't commit himself to her. Her good friend Thelma (Geena Davis) is married to Darryl, a domineering and patronizing narcissist who treats her as a backward child—a treatment, it must be said, not entirely unearned. Louise, needing a change, proposes a weekend trip to the mountains in her 1966 Thunderbird convertible, and Thelma, though afraid to ask Darryl for permission, accepts after some hesitation anyway.

We now encounter the visual leitmotif: the two women side by side, with Louise driving, shot from every conceivable angle and then some. With the winds of freedom playing in their liberated tresses, the car topless and the journey aimless, their joy is bottomless. In a roadside honkytonk, however, their lives change irrevocably. A darkly handsome, soft-spoken but swaggering stranger in his sexist prime joins them uninvited, pays compliments to both, and soon gets the somewhat drunk Thelma to dance with him in complete, newly emancipated abandon. You'd think that a woman, even a quasi-runaway, would not trust a man who dances with a beer bottle in one hand poking his partner's shoulderblades, but Thelma does, and even follows him out into the parking lot for a breath of sobering air. Provocative as she is, she gets not air, but attempted rape.

Louise appears just in time to find Thelma tossed over the hood of a car, and the man on top of her. As it happens, Thelma brought her husband's handgun along on the trip; as it further happens, she put it in Louise's pocketbook for safekeeping. With the gun, Louise pries the man off Thelma, then gives him a well-deserved dressing down. As the women start to leave, the fellow becomes defiant and insulting; Louise turns around and plugs him. With one shot from some distance, she gets him right through the heart.

Let's take stock here. We've never been told that Louise is such a marksman and how she got that way. Was she shooting to kill, which seems excessive, or was it just luck, which seems unlikely? Nor were we shown why this tough, savvy, not-so-young waitress pals around with this immature, silly housewife who married foolishly at 18, and still doesn't seem much older in years or experience. The man has slapped Thelma around: from mouth to thigh, she is covered with bruises. There are no other witnesses, and the man, as a friendly waitress warned the women, has a bad record. So why not go to the police?

No. Louise decides to escape to Mexico. But, to the dismay of Thelma, who is studying the road map, her friend, because of something terrible she won't talk about that happened to her there, refuses to drive through Texas. They must, time-consumingly, circumnavigate it along unpoliced back- and dirt-roads. Why can't Louise just tell Thelma? Oh, she explains, Texas policemen would be beastly to women on the run after killing a male. Would they be any worse than the ones in Arizona or New Mexico?

The journey now proceeds along a route that makes no sense, not only navigationally but also geographically. There is no way in which one shown location could connect with the previous or succeeding one, and sometimes the same locales pop up at very different stages of the trip. Ridley Scott clearly disregards continuity or logic for the sake of visual effects. Antonioni similarly skewed the landscape of Sicily in *L'avventura*, but that was not a naturalistic film and could absorb arbitrariness. Here such aestheticizing rings false. Scott started in commercials on English television, and he and his British cinematographer, Adrian Biddle, go in for a studied gorgeousness more suited to Pampers and Doeskin commercials than to a realistic movie. A veritable Babel of filters has been tapped, and the images speak in color tongues that are intoxicating but, in a realistic setting, unsettling to the human eye. The very composition of the frames is often artier than the subject and situation can bear. This is not the objective correlative for women's liberation; it is more like transfiguration.

Then again, there is that favorite road-movie strategy, whereby our heroines keep running into the same guys over and over. One such is a handsome young con man, JD, who rather unconvincingly pretends to be a student and finally hitches a ride with the women to Oklahoma City. There he talks his way into Thelma's bed for a night, and promptly steals the money that Louise's repentant lover, Jimmy, personally delivered to Louise earlier. Thelma, idiotically entranced by JD's sexuality and his accounts of liquorstore holdups, left the money lying around and even invited JD to join them in Mexico someday. Now, suddenly smart and effectual, Thelma herself robs a liquor store by the JD method, and replaces the money. Meanwhile, JD, on his own, falls into the hands of Hal, the friendly Dostoyevskian policeman, who gently but doggedly pursues the women.

At Louise's urging, Thelma calls home, but it is immediately clear that Hal, the FBI man Max, and their wiretappers have moved in with Darryl. Still, Louise conducts numerous brief phone conversations with Hal, evading the tappers but enjoying the badinage. Who knows what might have happened if the women had not met up again with a male-chauvinist gasoline trucker, who each time they passed him made rude gestures and overtures. This time they decide to humiliate him, which is fine; but they also shoot the hell out of and blow up his truck, which (the Big Bang theory of liberation?) may be a bit too much. In any case, they are total outlaws now.

What was mostly comedy turns into drama and ends in what Unamuno would have called tragic joy. I don't think I am giving anything away here, since Scott and Miss Khouri clearly think they have created a work of art, and no one was ever turned off *Hamlet* by being told it ends badly. But what exactly is this work of art trying to say? Miss Khouri (married to another producer and writer, and thus no innocent, wide-eyed outsider) seems a trifle confused. In an interview with the *New York Times*, she first says that Thelma and Louise are "outlaws . . . never intended as role models, for God's sake." Their actions are criminal, and they duly pay for them. "I don't want anybody doing anything they saw in this movie," she says with perfect genderless syntax.

A tad further on, though, Miss Khouri says, "I also wanted, as a woman, to walk out of the theater not feeling dirty and worthless… like I had compromised the character of women… So many times you go to the movies, and what woman up there would you want to be? None of them." Well, what woman up there in *Thelma & Louise* would you want to be? There is that nice waitress (Lucinda Jenny, and good), on screen for three minutes; could she be a role model to leave women viewers feeling clean and worthy?

Another objection addressed by Miss Khouri is that all the men in the film are pigs—that she is male-bashing. There she has an out: as Hal, the good cop, Harvey Keitel is almost too sympathetic; and Jimmy, the errant lover, reforms, albeit too late; moreover, as played by Michael Madsen, he is such an Elvis clone as to be repellent even when reformed. But the others are truly scum. Darryl, the husband, especially as performed by Christopher McDonald, could give narcissism, sexism, even marriage a bad name. As the proto-rapist, Timothy Carhart invites instant castration; shooting is really too good for him. Brad Pitt, as the fuck-'em-and-pluck-'em JD (for juvenile delinquent?), overacts mightily and keeps displaying his near-nude body almost gloatingly. (Or does this tell us something about Ridley Scott?)

Then there is Max, the Fed, played by Stephen Tobolowsky (the ex-husband of the playwright Beth Henley), who manages to be as mean as he looks dumb—with a head like a vegetable (eggplant? turnip?) on which someone has painted a face. Finally, the highway policeman (Jason Beghe) who tries to arrest Louise is portrayed as another narcissist and uniform-happy fascist, coward, indeed a sissy. The cover of the press kit inadvertently lists a further principal, Marco St. John, who was evidently cut out of the movie. Was he too monstrous even for Miss Khouri? There seem to have been other extensive cuts: Louise and Hal appear to be intimates after their second phone conversation, intimating at least a couple of other excised chats in between.

But there is something Ridley Scott does have: a strong visual sense. The way a helicopter suddenly, scarily pops out of a canyon to block our runaways' path: the way a whole brigade of squad cars springs up before and behind them like Cadmus's dragon seed, and similarly self-destructs. Or the way he will fade back and forth between the two women in the T-Bird's front seat, until it feels as if there were only one person there, her face changing in a lazy rhythm from Louise's to Thelma's and back again. Does this suggest an emotional merger? Are these women, consciously or unconsciously, in love with each other? Is this perhaps not just a feminist but also a lesbian feminist movie? There are clever effects here, but, like those slow cross-fades, there is something too chic about them—as is this entire film, which treats the great outdoors with an interior decorator's sensibility.

Undeniably, the performances of the leading ladies are powerful. Susan Sarandon, her face aged into a fine scrimshaw—a tracery of experience that deepens her womanliness—can switch from truculent waitress to blissful free-wheeler, from adolescent playing hooky to fugitive gambling her life at a happy or unhappy moment's notice. The tautness around her eyes and mouth is relieved by the fullness of her body; this is a woman used by life, bent on using what's left of it; she is both young and no longer young, both giving and hardened, and you feel with and for her.

And Geena Davis, with puppy fat still padding her jaw, an awakening greed for freedom dancing in her pupils, her rangy limbs loosening further with every new picaresque adventure, is all burgeoning sensuality triumphant over postcoital disappointments. She manages to smooth over the contradictions in the writing of her part, and almost brings off the too sudden, unlikely transition from the early, unfocused Thelma to the later, cooly efficient one.

Yet for all the talent of the actresses, this overlong, underrealized, and overmanicured movie reflects the deludedness of its makers. They think that, by exultantly sacrificing their lives, Thelma and Louise somehow justify their anti-social anabasis. They think that feminist liberation, even if hurtling into destructive excess, is somehow glorious, which is surely the way benighted moviegoers are encouraged to view it. But it leaves a bad taste in the thinking mind—as did *Butch Cassidy*, *Easy Rider*, *Sugarland Express*, and countless others.

All these films, whether all-male, male-and-female, or all-female, are a glorification of, apology for, violence; they pander to piggery, masculine or feminine. The sole notable exception is Terrence Malick's *Badlands*, a true work of art, which managed to view a crime spree as both enchanted and horrific, and to connect it to the rootlessness and sleazy values of our time.

The Case of the Missing Prepuce

EUROPA, EUROPA

Europa, Europa, we are told by a title card, is a true story. It is what happened to Solomon Perel, a Jewish teenager, before and during World War II. At the end of the film, we see the real Perel, now 66, in front of a beautiful landscape in Israel, as he intones a Hebrew chant. As at the beginning, authenticity is affirmed. But the hell of it is that almost nothing about this movie, as we are watching it, rings true. Any number of avowedly fictional films come across infinitely more believable, more moving, more real.

The Perels were a German Jewish family of Polish origin living in a small German town in 1938, when, during a pogrom by Hitler Youths on the eve of Solly's bar mitzvah, his sister Bertha was killed. The family relocated to Łodz, Poland, only to have Hitler invade a year later. The eldest son deserts from the Polish army and brings news of imminent catastrophe; the father sends the two younger brothers, Isaak and Solomon, off eastward to seek refuge among the Russians. At a crowded river crossing, they become separated and Solly ends up in a Soviet orphanage in Grodno; his parents, he later learns, have been confined to the Lodz ghetto. Forswearing his religious background, Solly becomes a good enough little Communist to be eventually admitted to the Komsomol.

But Hitler breaks his pact with Russia, and forthwith Solly finds himself in a Nazi roundup where Jews are being screened out and shot. With his flawless German, he convinces the Nazis that he is

Josef Peters, a transplanted German Aryan, and he is promptly annexed to this German military unit as a Russian interpreter. He becomes a dutiful German soldier until, in an attempt to surrender to some Russians across a bridge, he looks as if he had singlehandedly spearheaded a successful counterattack, and ends up as a hero.

Solly is sent to an elite Hitler Youth training school, where he does well, though he lives in constant fear that his circumcised member will give him away (the film began, effectively, with his circumcision ceremony), and his painful attempts to make himself a new foreskin are, of course, doomed. Eventually, Leni, the prettiest of the girl students, falls for him and takes him home to her widowed mother, where Solly, for the first time in years, experiences a sense of family. But when Leni tries to seduce him, he is afraid, though he returns her feelings, that she would recognize his Jewishness by his penis. So he refuses and, when she talks of cutting the throat of any Jew she'd meet, slaps her. The romance is nipped.

Earlier, Solly's commanding officer had talked about adopting the boy after the war was over, and the ex-CO's wife now invites her future son on a vacation from school. Instead, he goes to Lodz, where he catches a streetcar that runs through the ghetto. Though the tram's windows have been painted over to make them opaque, through a gap, Solly catches, both coming and going, horrifying glimpses (a little too conveniently panoramic) of ghetto life, including, he thinks, of his suffering mother. Back at school, much later—one of the film's most irritating weaknesses is its inability to convey a clear sense of time elapsed—he visits Leni's mother and learns from her that Leni, in an ecstasy of young-Nazidom, is about to bear a child as a gift to the Führer. In an outburst of misery, he confesses his Jewishness to the woman, who claims to have guessed it all along. How?

What a charmed life Solly has! The good woman mothers him, and warns him not to tell Leni, who wouldn't understand. Only once before did Solly's Jewishness come out, when, back with that army unit, a soldier—a homosexual and actor in civilian life—chases the naked Solly around a barn, and makes the genital discovery. He, too, is a good German and becomes the boy's brotherly protector. When he gets killed in his trench and all other Germans flee, Solly remains seated by him, mourning. Evidently, no Russian bullet is disrespectful of his grief. The writer and director, Agnieszka Holland, gives us a fancy crane shot and achingly pulsating music—and an altogether unbelievable scene.

I have skipped much so far and have reached nowhere near the end of the film, but let me retrace my steps and examine some of the holes that *Europa, Europa* sports as if they were so many medals. To start with that *Kristallnacht* pogrom, it catches Solly reading in the tub as rocks come flying in the bathroom window. He jumps out naked into the courtyard below, climbs across a dividing wall, and hides in an empty barrel in back of the neighboring beerhall. But why would a 13-year-old whose house is being besieged leap out naked unto his enemies and risk being beaten or killed? Is it not logical to hide inside with his family behind locked doors? And why, coming home much later, would he find his sister dead and bloody on a tabletop, and the rest of the family grieving? Why was only Bertha killed? Why wasn't her body properly attended to?

There may be explanations to such questions that keep cropping up throughout the film, but Miss Holland will not or cannot give them. Why, for example, when the Nazis doubt the veracity of Solly's Aryanness, do they not make him, like some others, drop his pants? And why doesn't anyone—in the army, at the school—get to see his circumcised organ? Once, when a medical exam is imminent, Solly fakes a sore tooth in need of extraction. He howls like a banshee; would a star student and leader of a victorious attack on the enemy carry on so in front of everyone over a mere toothache? And, after the tooth is pulled, wouldn't he still have to have his physical?

Earlier, when the kids from the Grodno orphanage were escaping under the leadership of a highly attractive woman teacher (quite improbably smitten with Solly), this young woman, in the midst of panic on the teeming road, forcefully requisitions a truck for her wards. A German plane strafes the escapees, then the truck gets going and only Solly, who was hiding under it (is he the smartest or the cravenest?), cannot hoist himself into the vehicle and is left behind. Why can't this powerful and loving woman get the truck to stop for a few seconds? Too much in this movie looks manipulative.

Again, a middle-aged woman in uniform, some kind of officer, is escorting Solly from the front to that elite school on a train. She, too, falls for the sexy kid and seduces him in a railway compartment. Granted, the lights are out, but if this experienced woman did not notice anything, why would Solly fear that the innocent Leni, who probably never heard about foreskins, would spot such a lack? Again, much later during a battle scene, despite the urgings

of an officer behind him, Solly refuses to shoot a young surrender-
ing Russian, and defies repeated commands to fire. Wouldn't that
officer have pistol-whipped him for insubordination? And, would
you believe it, everyone around Solly is killed, so no one can incriminate him later on.

Unlikely coincidences, unlikely hairbreadth escapes, contrived
little setbacks—the film abounds in them. True, war is a hotbed of
confusion, rampant with absurdities. Still, if you added up all the
elements in *Europa, Europa* that would strain the greatest talent for
credulity, the figure would be too large even for the most brazen
fiction: but this, we are told first and last, is the truth. Which raises
two questions: Just how much stranger than fiction can the truth
afford to be? What good is all the truth in the world if the work of
art cannot make it *feel* true?

Miss Holland commits every kind of error. I'll instance half a
dozen types. First, she doesn't know where to stop. It's fine for a
Russian teacher to say to a Polish boy to pray to his God for some
candy and have nothing happen, then have him pray to Stalin and
promptly have goodies shower down from an airduct above. But
to follow this up immediately with an air raid and debris failing
through the same duct is heavy-handed symbolism—too much.
Second, she doesn't know how to evoke atmosphere, except in some
easy cases. Thus when the Nazi soldiery adopts Solly as a mascot,
she cannot convey what about him was so captivating—the telling
remark, incident, touch. Granted that Marco Hofschneider, though
pleasant-looking, does not convey quick intelligence, the filmmaker
could still have found ways to stage such key scenes more flavorously, flexibly, incisively.

Third, Miss Holland needs a better aural sense. The dubbing of
this international cast is atrocious. You don't need to know German
and Russian, the film's main languages, to realize the delinquencies
of synchronization here: there's many a painful slip between the dub
and the lip. Fourth, she needs a better editorial sense. The inclusion
of dream sequences in which, say, Hitler and Stalin dance together
is pretentious and alien to the rest of the film. Only if there were
more fantasy in the realistic sequences could such outright fantasti-
cation be absorbed. Fifth, she needs more of a sense of history. Yes,
the Nazis had one branch of their propaganda representing Jews
as hideous, subhuman creatures. But would a teacher at an elite
school with older pupils not realize that some of them would have
known Jews very much like themselves? Would he not have taught

hatred in subtler terms than the *Stürmer* caricatures? It would have eliminated some cheap humor from the scene and made it more chillingly effective. But, of course, Miss Holland is telling her story often on a low-comedy level. I wonder how Perel does it in his book, not yet available here.

Finally, Miss Holland lacks plain sense. You do not in an epilogue show the present-day, real-life Solomon Perel a homely little man bearing no resemblance to the cute kid who portrays him up to then. There are not enough hooks on a movie theater's wall—or in the world—from which to suspend that much disbelief. The fact that *Europa, Europa* takes on an important subject seems to have guaranteed it good notices from the more Pavlovian reviewers, even if the story-telling is faulty, the humor often feeble, and the persuasiveness minimal.

Growing Pains, Growing Joys

BOYZ N THE HOOD; MY FATHER'S GLORY; MY MOTHER'S CASTLE

It does set my teeth on edge to write out *Boyz N the Hood*, but John Singleton's film is vastly preferable to the spelling of its title. Singleton is a 23-year-old graduate of the University of Southern California Filmic Writing Program (another grating piece of nomenclature) whose first feature this is. His writing and direction tend toward the schematic, and there are a few passages that strain credulity rather badly; all in all, though, I would rather have made this film than any one of Spike Lee's, or the lot of them rolled together.

The action is situated in south central Los Angeles, a black tract-house neighborhood—or hood—where young Tre Styles, the quasi-autobiographical hero, is growing up. His parents are divorced (Singleton's never married), and his mother, who wants to go back to school, turns the boy over to his father, Furious Styles, for the kind of upbringing whose lack makes so many kids in the hood go bad. A former army man now working in home mortgages, he is a calm, strong fellow whose hands keep skillfully revolving those Chinese metal balls, suggesting that Furious has gained his peace by learning to control the fury within.

The early sequences show us Tre aged ten with his buddies, in particular the Baker boys, Ricky and his half-brother Doughboy, whom their hardworking single mother does her best to keep in line. The hood is almost continuously overflown by jet planes that fray the nerves; shiftless young men, sometimes cruising in cars, terrorize the boys; a corpse in the streets is both an attraction to gape at and a thing to ignore a minute later as one plays ball close by; a young girl does her homework, ignoring as best she can the gunfire in the street outside.

In the main part of the movie, Tre and his pals are 17, but no better off. Gang members take potshots from their cars at whoever displeases them, bloodshed begets more bloodshed. There are raucous parties and sexual adventures for some others are sustained by wish-fulfillment fantasies. Doughboy and his friends sit on the porch, drink, and talk big. Ricky, married already, studies hard to get test scores that will earn him a college scholarship. Tre is still undecided, but thrives under the guidance of Furious, who in one disturbing scene lectures him on the need to avoid the gunfights among black "brothers" that the whites, he says, encourage in order to decimate the black population. This is the only overtly white-hating speech, but as it is delivered by Furious, the film's *raisonneur*, one suspects that it issues from the filmmaker's mouth as well.

Tre finds a nice girlfriend, although his sexual initiation is one of the movie's most awkwardly shot sequences; Ricky is mowed down by those gun-happy hoodlums on his way home one time with Tre. In this least believable scene of all, Tre and Ricky, rightly feeling threatened, escape by climbing over various backyard walls, then split up, whereupon Ricky proceeds to lope homeward fully exposing himself and ignoring Tre's shouted warnings. He is promptly killed; with ponderous irony, the next mail brings his test results: he passed with flying colors. Aside from a few such heavyhanded plot maneuvers, there are scenes that seem directed too stiffly, or simply underpopulated. But, then, retakes and extras are costly, and low-budget pictures can ill afford them. What is more remarkable is how much of this film rings true. It accomplishes most of its bitter aims with unsensationalistic honesty.

Singleton does have problems with his cast, though. A number of the performances, including Cuba Gooding Jr.'s as Tre, are either histrionically or charismatically deficient; the young actress who portrays Ricky's wife is particularly unconvincing when she first glimpses her husband's corpse. But there are also successes. The rap singer Ice Cube is an entirely credible Doughboy, Morris Chestnut makes Ricky's almost too-good-to-be-true goodness sweetly believable, and as their tense, beleaguered mother, Tyra Ferrell, so good in an entirely different role in *Jungle Fever*, scores again. Much of what is so moving about this taut, edgy character comes from her acting rather than from the writing. And that experienced stage actor Larry Fishburne makes Furious into an alert, complex, sympathetic character without sacrificing any of the man's basic hardness.

Almost eclipsing the merit of the film, though, has been its effect on black audiences, even on people outside the theaters where it has been playing. Both inside and out, in several cities, there have been shootings, injuries, some deaths. The terrifying paradox is that a work condemning shooting and killing among young blacks should elicit the opposite effect. What does this tell us? That tension has gotten so out of hand that anything, or nothing, can trigger violence? What is ultimately so discouraging is human—and I mean *universal* human—stupidity. Wherever one looks, there are people unable to understand what is plainly put before them. I am reminded of the Austrian playwright Ödön von Horváth's epigram, "Nothing conveys so well the sense of infinity as human dumbness."

Singleton's film ends with title cards summing up the characters' future, a tired and here also supererogatory device. Tre, we learn, went to Morehouse College, an apparent *hommage* to Spike Lee. But, I repeat, Singleton is already the more interesting filmmaker; let's just hope that he knows where and how to go on from here.

If, however, you are looking for something gentler and sweeter, but that still eschews the vulgar escapism thrown at you nowadays from every side, there remains an attractive tertium quid in the double-header the gifted Yves Robert has fashioned from the childhood reminiscences of that racy and jovial French writer, Marcel Pagnol. Remembered most for his plays *Topaze* and the Marius Trilogy, Pagnol was also a filmmaker of distinction. Recently, we had Claude Berri's twin films, *Jean de Florette* and *Manon of the Spring*, based on Pagnol's most ambitious novel; now Robert has made his sibling movies, *My Father's Glory* and *My Mother's Castle*, from the first two tomes (1957) of Pagnol's four-volume memoirs of his childhood and youth.

Yves Robert, a marvelous comic stage actor and director of lively film comedies, made these films as a septuagenarian, and though he is a northerner, his feeling for Provence, the wonderful herb-scented hills of southern France, and for Marseille, the two locales of the movies, is as acute as it is sympathetic. Most of all, though, Robert has a splendid sense of children, as he demonstrated with *The War of the Buttons* (1961), and of the childish foibles and entanglements of adults, as recorded in *Salut l'Artiste* (1973), two films that should be on everybody's hit parade.

The subject of *Glory* and *Castle* is the way Marcel's somewhat giddy schoolteacher father and his lovely and earthy seamstress mother gravitated from the city to the country, leaving Marseille ever longer behind for enchanted sojourns in Provence. It's a film not so much of a boy's growing up as of an entire family's falling in love with nature, and of how one painstakingly learns to meet the demands of that exacting mistress. It is also a film about being a family—father, mother, two boys, spinster aunt, with occasional incursions by a rich, rambunctious uncle and how these people make out with one another in one of the world's most beautiful countrysides, condignly photographed by Robert Alazraki. What gets lost in the translation and the foreshortened subtitles, alas, is the language, e.g., "a little winter sun, pale and tonsured like a monk."

Glory is good, but *Castle* is even better; still, one must see both, and in that order. The performances are all solid and idiosyncratic—the cast was chosen for being, among other things, able to sound genuinely southern—and, as usual, it is precisely the authentic sense of time and place that makes these films truly universal. I particularly enjoyed Nathalie Roussel, whom every man and boy in the audience will recognize as his dream spouse or mother, yet who exudes not a trace of treacle: and also the faunlike Victorien Delmare, as Paul, the mountain boy who befriends Marcel and teaches him the ropes of outdoor living. As Marcel, Julien Ciamaca is a trifle too beautiful and passive, but the world that swirls around him is full of recognizable, merrily invigorating, and cherishable life.

Rambling Rose

The American cinema today is a cheerless place for anyone seeking quality. When the products are not obvious children's movies, they are children's movies disguised by super-budgets, with Arnold Schwarzenegger saving the future or Kevin Costner redeeming the past. Or else they are sappy and sickening, like Mary Agnes

Donoghue's *Paradise*, or worse, the mindless attitudinizing of the Cannes Grand Prize winner, *Barton Fink*, by the Coen brothers, those scavengers and refurbishers of other people's offal, which they serve up as art.

On such a scene, it is inspiriting to welcome even an imperfect yet in many ways alive and pulsating little film such as *Rambling Rose*, which Martha Coolidge has made from Calder Willingham's script based on his own novella. The book, I suspect, may be tougher, but even the screenplay contains enough elements of Southern Gothic, that bone-deep quaintness that can amuse, unnerve, charm, and, finally, bemuse.

This is the story of Rose, an exotic-looking young woman who arrives as servant to a Deep Southern family from an even Deeper South, where she seems to have gotten knee-deep into trouble with men. For her employers, the kindly Hillyers, she resolves to be on her very best behavior, which proves just sufficient to throw the entire family, if not the whole town into first-class dithers. Well, the younger Hillyer children, Waskie and Doll Baby, can handle it, with only intermittent outbursts of voyeuristic glee. But Daddy, a once impoverished fellow who married a rich woman working on a nebulous master's degree for Columbia University, and who now runs the hotel her family left her, can barely cope with it, narrowly escaping the girl's prompt and thorough infatuation with him. The worst thing he can call Rose, however, is the touchingly off-center "nincompoop."

Mother, who is hard of hearing and soft of heart (she disconnects her hearing aid whenever she is working on her thesis and, as Daddy puts it, "lost in the fourth dimension"), is Rose's staunch supporter, and will hear nothing, which is easy enough for her, and see nothing, which is difficult for anyone, against the girl. She prevents Daddy from firing Rose even when the bushes around the house fill up with pining suitors or satiated ones whose postcoital fun has been cut short when their noises awakened the household and they had to leap out of her window naked as jaybirds, as the charmingly illogical Southern phrase has it.

Most keenly affected by Rose's presence, though, is Buddy, the 13-year-old eldest Hillyer kid, possessed of considerable, mostly lurid imagination, precocious smarts, and a cruel streak—clearly an authorial alter ego. His burgeoning sexual appetites partially indulged by Rose, who, however, saves her body for the town's eligible blades, and her heart for the elusive Mr. Right, whom she seeks by trial and not unpleasurable error. Daddy (Robert Duvall), Buddy (Lukas Haas), and especially Mother (Diane Ladd) are so well and controlledly acted that the comedy spins like a top with—in defiance of physical laws—increasing rather than diminishing energy. As a Yankee doctor, Kevin Conway contributes a wholly exaggerated performance, but even that does not dampen the centrifugal fun.

What does impair the film is a totally inept prologue and epilogue, in which the now grown-up Buddy, played with insufferable smarminess by John Heard (once a good actor), comes back to visit his widowed Daddy to find out also what has become of Rose. These sequences are highly unconvincing, with even Duvall's performance thrown off by the corny writing and direction. Too bad that Miss Coolidge allowed her otherwise winning film to lose its grip and go as limp as a dying limpet.

Johnny E. Jensen's cinematography tries too hard to look sunburnished and earth-saturated: all those ambers and ochers get to be a bit unrelenting. Although conventional, Elmer Bernstein's score is apposite enough. But what might have been the film's biggest problem proves no sweat. The rather beanpole and hatchet-faced Laura Dern—proclaimed a beauty by tasteless reviewers possibly further blinded by her genealogy—is not one to make a population's gonads go hogwild. But she manages a good accent, gets into the spirit of things, and, with her not overgenerous thespian endowment nevertheless falling into the required slot, carries off the central role more than acceptably.

Aimez-Vous Aymé?

URANUS

Marcel Aymé (1902–1967) may not have been one of the greatest French writers of this century, but he certainly was one of the most diverse, most prolific, and most charming. He wrote in every genre from fiction to poetry, essay to children's fantasy, drama to journalism. Some of his novels, stories, and plays are very near top-grade, and there was always, even in his harshest works, a lightness of touch, a floating irony that was Aymé's hallmark, and very probably one reason for his not being more widely appreciated. The other was that, though never an actual Nazi or Pétainist, Aymé did contribute to some Vichy journals during the Occupation, and was friends with such fascist writers as Céline and the very gifted Robert Brasillach, the only major talent executed after the war, despite efforts by Aymé and others to save him.

Aymé was never even tried after the Liberation, which suggests that the case against him could not have been strong. As for his strong talent, it can be approximately described as lying at the juncture of Jean Anouilh and Colette, if those two could be said to intersect. Aymé had the discrimination to reject membership in the French Academy, and the courage to publish as early as 1948 a novel, *Uranus*, whose subject is the question of guilt and innocence during the Occupation. It is an ironic assessment of the self-righteous meting out of "justice" by people who, under the best of circumstances, would not have been qualified to cast stones, but who under the worst ones, in 1945 France, used the cloak of justice to hide a cloaca of the basest motives.

Claude Berri's movie version of *Uranus*, written with his sister, Arlette Langmann, is, on the whole, a faithful adaptation, departing from the novel in only two major ways. It does not go into the most bestial horrors perpetrated on the collaborators, and it does not get inside the collaborator Maxime Loin, around whom the story revolves. Aymé neither justifies nor excuses him, but movingly explains him, thus making a case, not for clemency, but for retribution less extreme than the firing squad. There is also a third, less obvious but even more important, difference: the movie fudges the implication of universal guilt, the omnipresent suggestion that nobody is without taint.

In the small village of Blémont, partly destroyed by *American* bombs (another detail glossed over), people made homeless have been billeted with those whose homes have been spared: the result is not only overcrowding but also grating juxtaposition, where ideologies collide and hatreds flare up. Thus the local factory's chief engineer, Archambaud, who lives with his overripe bourgeoise wife, his pretty but somewhat flighty daughter, Marie-Anne, 18, and his younger son, Pierre, has been saddled with the Gaigneux family. Gaigneux is a lower-level employee of the same factory, the village's leading Communist, and has a pugnacious wife as well as a band of small, squalling brats. Gaigneux, like most men, hankers for Marie-Anne, and tries to keep peace between his defiant wife and sniffy Mme. Archambaud, who have turned the shared kitchen into a battleground. Also assigned to the apartment is the merry widower

Watrin, the high-school lit. teacher (in the book, it's math), an incurable optimist who insists on perceiving the world as beautiful, and man as the fairest thing in it, his evil deeds only "less good," even the concentration camps merely "pranks and turbulences."

If Watrin is a Pangloss, he is nevertheless no fool. He accuses other people, justly but ever so gently, of the useful flaw of hypocrisy, and loves rain almost as much as sunshine as he glories in a world that includes the wonder of dragonflies and elephants. His glorying, though, is hard-earned. At 11:15 on the night of the bombardment, he had been reading a book on astronomy, and had just reached a passage about "the dark, icy planet Uranus" when all hell broke loose. He managed to sleep through some of it, but woke up in the morning in a house reduced to rubble except for a bit of second-story floor on which his bed miraculously survived. Since then, every night at 11:15, he must, with "the infinitesimal light" of his being, fight Uranus, this "crushing mass of blackness and negativity, of desolation and despair." And every morning he wakes to renewed joy and confidence.

One dark night the collaborationist Maxime Loin, hunted everywhere, sprouts up before the rather ordinary Archambaud and begs for asylum—life. Archambaud takes him into the three rooms left to him, though he doesn't like him, and makes him share the bed of son Pierre, who detests him. The danger of discovery by the Gaigneux, and other Communists who keep calling on them, is great. Meanwhile an innocent party gets into trouble because of Loin: Léopold, the owner of a popular local café. He is a former strongman and current alcoholic, whom we see in a very Gallicly bittersweet scene reproaching his wife, Andrea, for getting old and ugly, while he, thanks to his modest daily ration of 12 litres of white wine and the discovery of poetry, has stayed young. For, the village school having been razed in the bombing, classes have been reassigned to cafés during their off hours. From behind the bar, Leopold has listened to Watrin teaching such masterpieces as *Andromaque*, and feels another Racine stirring inside himself. He stumbles on an accidental alexandrine in his utterance—a perfectly ludicrous one that he thinks magnificent—and forthwith, working out the scansion on his fingers, finds himself in dogged pursuit of a rhyming second. Eventually, he hopes to have ten, thirty, fifty, and then . . .

Because he throws a misbehaving little Communist, Rochard, out of his café, the fellow, a railroadman and prime witch-hunter, denounces Léopold, claiming to have seen Loin skulking about the premises. Léopold seeks out Rochard in his habitat, roughs him up, and, oddly, turns him into his slave. Later (in a scene not in the book), using information extracted from Rochard, he goes to the house of Monglat, the billionaire war profiteer, whose wealth guarantees impunity, to help keep him, Léopold, out of jail. Monglat, a marvelous creation, glides smoothly between slimy pathos and harrowing menace. At the last minute of the war, he pressed his dopey son, Michel, into the Resistance to help keep their asses covered; now Michel is the lover of Marie-Anne Archambaud, who is both drawn to his healthy vulgarity (and vulgar wealth) and slightly repelled. Monglat makes vague promises of help, but when Léopold threatens to denounce the enormousness of the wine merchant's ill-gotten gains (he knows because, in a very limited way, Monglat let him in on his deals), Monglat merely reminds Léopold that it was thanks to him that he, too, thrived under the Nazis.

When the well liked and falsely accused Léopold is led off to jail—denunciations by Communists carry particular weight—the local Party is embarrassed. That hothead Rochard will have made asses of more than himself. Gaigneux is for expelling him, but he is defended by Jourdan, the story's most complex and distressing character. A 27-year-old classics teacher and intellectual from a well-heeled petit-bourgeois family, Jourdan is a passionate renegade, a vest-pocket Robespierre, but a physical coward and mother's boy, who keeps writing *maman* detailed letters about his Communist activities. (The film doesn't quite do justice to this last, absurd aspect.) Gaigneux, the leftist of humble origins and practical concerns, must bow before the windy ideologue Jourdan.

The interactions of all these characters and a few lesser ones are the action of *Uranus*, which I won't go into. There is, granted, much talk in the movie, but it is not boring, even though it forfeits some of the richness and pungency of the book's dialogue. Claude Berri, who began as a mediocre, if not downright poor, director, has improved over the years; his *Jean de Florette* and *Manon of the Spring* were respectable efforts. With *Uranus*, he goes up another notch or two. But then, it would be hard not to with material this good, especially if you cast in it just about every major French movie actor going.

As Léopold, Gérard Depardieu is a bit of a problem. He is too young for this "Racinian gorilla," as Aymé describes him, and, unlike his colleagues, overacts even beyond what this seemingly ham-proof part can take. Moreover, he looks a bit too dashing for a man whose homeliness is part of his pathos. But Depardieu is to the French cinema what the Statue of Liberty is to New York: like it or dislike it, it is there. And Depardieu does know how to play a line such as the one to his lawyer, who visits him in jail: "Poetry is my thing. Give me some verse and my ration of white wine, and I'll stay in jail all my life . . . Wretched business to have to say it, Monsieur Mégrin, but I'm forced to admit: white wine comes even ahead of poetry."

The others, however, are sublime. Philippe Noiret makes Watrin adorable without making him cute; let him say the most outlandish things with that benignly droopy tapir's face of his, that insinuating voice full of mellow ritardandos, and you believe, nay, you *feel* every syllable. Jean-Pierre Marielle is a wonderful Archambaud, a plain, practical man with a plain, practical face, but in whom finer things bubble up from time to time, only to let him, soon enough, sink back into the quotidian. As Gaigneux, Michel Blanc offers another of his zesty little guys, unsightly but soulful; a redoubtable Communist, but not without his small vulnerabilities. As Monglat, Michel Galabru is magisterially chilling precisely because his evil is worm-like one moment, dragonish the next—a dread metamorphosis in the twinkling of an eye.

As Loin, Gérard Desarthe is not given much to work with by the script, but does manage to look hunted, humbled, hungry second to none. Florence Darel is the ideal Marie-Anne: like her name, she is an archetype of the French girl with her high forehead and somewhat angular face: coolly pretty, and as willful as she is lyrical. Most astounding, perhaps, is the Jourdan of Fabrice Lucchini: you feel the wetness behind his ears as well as the ooziness of his entire being; yet there is pure, angelic fanaticism darting out of those watery eyes.

There are indelible supporting performances by older actresses, notably the controlledly moving Andréa of Josiane Lévêque. Everyone and everything is captured faithfully by Renato Berta's camera, which, less bent on beauty than in previous outings, makes nature look rapturous enough, but concentrates on the ruins all around and the cluttered interiors with an aptly sober-to-somber palette. It must finally dawn on the most casual spectator that the earth is threatened every night at 11:15 by the monstrous mass of Uranus, by coldness and inhumanity. And that only the inconspicuous, irrationally hopeful Watrins, sweating in unequal dream combat, can stave that obliterating weight off our imperiled bones.

My Own Private Idaho

Gus Van Sant Jr. made a fine, small, dark, honest movie with *Drug-store Cowboy*, where, however, the film was based on someone else's writing. In *My Own Private Idaho*, he is both writer and director, and gives us an unbridled homosexual fantasy that has no logic, no credibility, and much unfortunate pretentiousness. And, on top of that, sentimentality.

This is the story of two young male hustlers in America's North-west: Mike Waters, a genuine drifter and derelict, who suffers from narcolepsy and is haunted by memories of his lost childhood; and Scott Favor, son of the mayor of Portland, a rich bisexual in the hustler's life for a lark—someday he will straighten out and prob-ably become mayor like his father. The two of them become friends for a while; there is also a fat, elderly, drunken homosexual, Bob Pigeon, with whom they get involved in a petty crime. It soon be-comes clear that they are, respectively, Hotspur, Prince Hal, and Falstaff from Shakespeare's *Henry IV*, Parts 1 & 2. Sometimes the dialogue actually switches into speeches taken over verbatim from Shakespeare.

Poor Gus Van Sant! During a press conference, he told us that male hustlers are really sweet, romantic creatures underneath. I believe in sweet, romantic male hustlers as I believe in the whore with the golden heart, who is the mother of them all. A great ho-mosexual artist can make us accept that myth—Jean Genet almost carries it off, and so, perhaps, might Jean Cocteau have done, had he been less devious. But self-taught, sentimental Van Sant is the dupe of his primitivism. He is, however, honest, and admits that he had never known the Henry plays until he encountered them in Orson Welles's *Chimes at Midnight*; he was so impressed that he started a screenplay that would be an updating of them. But he also wrote a screenplay about male hustlers cruising in Boise, Portland, and Seattle; eventually the two scripts fused into *My Own Private Idaho*.

Needless to say, neither Shakespeare's ideas nor his language can be made to apply to Van Sant's present-day hustlers, and the parallels pressed on the plot are much too vague and unresonant to come across as anything but the vagaries of a cultural parvenu. To give you an inkling of the arbitrariness of the script, let me say that Mike decides, out of nowhere, to visit his long-lost mother. So he and Scott ride off on a stolen bike to the obscure Idaho hotel where she last worked. They find an Italian forwarding address, and, presto magico, they're in Rome, mingling with their local colleagues. (Clearly Van Sant wanted a free trip to Italy.)

We next see them on an Italian farm; the owner is absent, and his 14 or 15-year-old niece seems to be running things by herself(!); Mike's mother used to be there (why?), but is gone or dead. Scott promptly turns heterosexual and has lusty sex with the girl, whom he takes back to America to marry. Poor Mike is left hustling for himself again. We last see him, during an episode of narcolepsy, being stripped of his very clothes by some steal-and-run drivers on that same two-lane blacktop in Idaho where he fell asleep at the start of the film. (Good thing there isn't much traffic on those Idaho roads.)

To make it more modish, the movie is divided into largely disconnected chapters, each with its heading on a title card. The photography is pretty in a self-conscious way, and the lead actors—Keanu Reeves (Scott) and especially River Phoenix (Mike)—are fine. But this kind of filmmaking, to quote *Henry IV, Part 1*, "Loses men's hearts, and leaves behind a stain."

The Fisher King

The Fisher King received generally warm notices, and is being touted as Oscar material. Let me say categorically that it is one of the most nonsensical, pretentious, mawkishly cloying movies I have ever had to retch through. An attempt by Richard LaGravanese to write a modern New York Holy Grail story in which the Grail turns out to be a school trophy won by an eccentric nabob, it brings on Jeff Bridges as a contemporary knight errant—not quite Lancelot and certainly no Galahad; also Robin Williams as a combination Percevalesque holy fool and wounded Amfortas-like fisher king. Under Terry Gilliam's frenetic, Roger Rabbity direction, full of obnoxious artinesses, the film indulges Williams's unholy foolishness.

As a mighty peculiar waif, Amanda Plummer indulges her shuddery talent for being simultaneously eight and eighty, and thus a fittingly spooky love interest for Williams. But the film wastes the considerable knowhow of Jeff Bridges and Mercedes Ruehl, as his lover. He plays a ruthless disk jockey (straight out of Eric Bogosian's

Talk Radio) who unintentionally but irresponsibly instigates a mass murder; she is the jolly proprietress of a seedy video store for whom he now works behind the counter and under the sheets. Any film that hinges on whether Bridges can cast off convention and spend a (platonic) night lying naked with Willams on a Central Park lawn as both gaze at the moon is, at best, wholly frail; at worst, a bitter chalice, dregs from the first sip.

Despair Not

BLACK ROBE; LET HIM HAVE IT

Bruce Beresford goes from extreme heat to extreme cold, and from strength to strength. Close on the heels of *Mr. Johnson*, based on Joyce Cary's novel and made in remotest Africa under unusual rigors, comes *Black Robe*, shot in the wilds of freezing Canada under no lesser hardships, and no less a masterwork. Indeed, this film, with a screenplay by Brian Moore from his own novel, may be an even greater artistic triumph. But the public does not want serious films: *Mr. Johnson* disappeared from the theaters almost immediately; *Black Robe*, so far just managing to hang in there, does so because its subject appears superficially less controversial.

The time is 1634, and the French under men like Champlain are conquering Nouvelle France, the future Canada. Meanwhile Jesuit priests are trying to convert the mutually warring Algonquins, Iroquois, and Hurons to peaceful Christianity. Young Father Laforgue, from an aristocratic family in Rouen, was inspired by seeing the mutilations wrought by the Indians on an older priest, a priest who can hardly wait to return to Quebec. Now Laforgue sets out from Quebec, together with another young Frenchman, Daniel, and an escort of Algonquins, in four canoes; the aim is relief for Father Jerome at his distant outpost among the Hurons, whence no word has come in a long time. If Jerome is dead, Laforgue is to take over; back in Rouen, his mother had rejoiced in the family's acquiring a martyr: "God has chosen You to die for Him."

The canoe expedition is led by the Algonquin chief, Chomina, whose wife and lovely daughter, Annuka, are also along: soon Daniel and the girl are exchanging significant looks and curt but loaded words. The Indians call the Jesuits Blackrobes, and the film begins brilliantly with a screenwide shot of blackness that begins to move and proves to be Laforgue's cloak seen from the back. What better visual metaphor for ambiguity? Paddling up the St. Lawrence and Ottawa rivers, amid an austerely sumptuous autumnal landscape of wooded hills, Chomina and Laforgue get to understand each other less and less. The priest's reading from a book (the Bible) confirms the illiterate Indians in the belief that he is a demon, as does his baptizing of a dead baby. The Algonquins believe in dreams, animals, animistically worshipped nature, dead warriors hunting in nocturnal forests, and a hideous dwarf shaman who counsels them to kill the black-robed demon in their midst.

Laforgue zealously reads his Scriptures, talks fervently but uncomprehendedly, and becomes prey to yearnings of the flesh as he watches Daniel and Annuka falling in love and coupling with the reluctant consent of Chomina. Tensions grow, and the Indians abandon Laforgue in the wilderness, though Chomina won't let them kill him. Even Daniel follows his love in his own little canoe at a just barely safe distance, for the Algonquins, other than Annuka, don't want him around either. The Jesuit continues alone, on foot, just as the bloodthirsty Iroquois start popping up all around.

I will not continue with the story, which gets fiercer, deeper, more emotionally and intellectually involving with every frame. Sex and violence, torture and heroism are there without embellishment or exploitation, depicted with intensity and economy as phenomena of nature—or human nature—that have their beauty, their horror, their occasional humor, and their seemingly permanent, impenetrable mystery. Indian language (with subtitles) is used sparsely, as is English, but most of the story is conveyed in actions and images of astonishing starkness, lyricism, trenchancy. Nothing is emphasized, yet nothing is less than compelling. Two antithetical cultures with their conflicting motivations keep confronting each other, subdividing into even trickier antagonisms and loyalties, with nature always all around, turning wintrier and snowier as clashes intensify, a love affair lurches ahead, and every major character undergoes extraordinary, shattering changes.

Perhaps the most moving aspect of the film is its refusal to take sides, its avoidance of easy—or indeed, any—solutions, coupled with its ability to speak volumes with a few monosyllables (Friendly Indians who save Laforgue lost in the forest, "How can anyone get lost here? The woods are for men"), to express history with images (Peter James's superb shots of a land of cold, harsh magnificence), and to encourage the viewer to think without any buttonholing and hectoring. Nothing is shortchanged on either side of the religious-cultural fence: generosity and intolerance and an understatedly ironic questioning of the seemingly noblest motives—all are given their full self-contradictory due. The film is so totally in command of itself that a birchbark canoe scraping aground on suddenly unnavigable ice is just as dramatic and fraught with meaning as a man's finger being cut off with promise of deadlier tortures to come. In a supreme final irony no one emerges a long-range winner in this or any world; only feelings have value, however transitory, however doomed.

Indians in movies, to this day, have been noble or ignoble savages, food for one or another kind of mendacity and sermonizing. Here they and their beliefs come to extraordinary, absorbing life, as do Catholicism and its representatives, though neither party gets the final nod. The actors, white or red, are mostly Canadians and mostly unknown to us, which works very well. We do know Lothaire Bluteau from *Jesus of Montreal*, where, like the film itself, he was dreadful; as Laforgue, he conveys movingly the uncertainties lurking under religious certainty, even as the remarkable August Schellenberg (half Indian, despite his name) subtly suggests the doubts that infiltrate the strong Chomina. The beautiful Sandrine Holt (Annuka), though a trifle too pretty, and Aden Young (Daniel) are good, too; she especially, with a wonderful toughness under her exquisite exterior.

Even the neatly interpolated flashbacks to France, fitted in with masterly matching shots, make their sardonic points laconically but powerfully. And Moore's dialogue accomplishes the best and hardest thing movie dialogue can do: full characterization through minimal palaver. The audience must participate with its own intuition, inferences, insight. With *Black Robe* and *Mr. Johnson*, Bruce Beresford proves himself conclusively not just an Australian director who can speak to the world, but a world director able to direct anywhere (an almost unique achievement) and speaking to everyone, Australians, naturally, included.

Peter Medak's *Let Him Have It* is the true story of an English court case that shook up the early postwar years. A 19-year-old Londoner, epileptic and not very bright, Derek Bentley, was drawn into minor crime by a precocious youth of 16, Chris Craig, leader of a gang of boys who had access to handguns and a fast life. Though Derek was far from a bad fellow, the guns, the girls, the aura of Chris's world were hard to resist.

In an attempted nighttime burglary, Chris and Derek were surprised by police. Soon the crazed, gun-wielding Chris confronted
a policeman, Fairfax, on a dark rooftop. Fairfax shouted to him
to hand over his gun. Derek, who had already given himself up,
yelled out, "Let him have it!"—meaning the weapon. Chris took
it as meaning a bullet: he shot and wounded Fairfax. Under-age
Chris got away with a prison sentence Derek, despite his own basic
decency, his father and family's no-stone-unturned support, and
the efforts of a few enlightened public servants, was—amazingly—hanged. There was no clemency from on high: conditions in
England were bleak and tense, and unconducive to mercy.

Neal Purvis and Robert Wade have written a first-rate, no-nonsense script, and Medak has directed with heroic straightforwardness and empathy. The not-to-be-denied grandeur of the film lies
in the humanity of the homely people depicted, the sublime dignity
with which they struggle against the blows they incur for offenses
hardly of their own making. Justice untempered by compassion,
which crushes them, proves more abhorrent than awesome.

Although the method used is that of the feature film, the even-
handedness with which the story is told, the meticulousness rather
than grandstanding with which scene after scene unfurls, the refusal to milk even the most legitimate of emotions invite comparison
with the greatest cinematic documentaries. I am not the first to notice that Paul Reynolds does not quite possess the charisma needed
for Chris; otherwise, a very large cast performs to—a word I do not
use lightly—perfection. Many of the actors are old hands, many
new to me: all are, down to those in the tiniest roles, flawless.

Chris Eccleston's Derek is an achingly real compounding of
childlikeness and fallibility, likableness and mediocrity, trusting-
ness and incomprehension. Chris's father, a man whose lowliness
in no ways lessens his magnanimity, is played by the marvelous
Tom Courtenay with acting that no longer seems to have surface of
any kind, but is all utterly from within. In the much smaller part of
Chris's mother, Eileen Atkins reveals herself yet again the supreme
character actress of the English-speaking world; somehow, while
sticking unconditionally to her role, she always presses forward to
embodying the joys and sorrows of humanity itself. The scene in
which the Bentley family huddles together in excruciated solidarity as the parlor clock strikes the hour of Derek's execution belongs
in the pantheon of cinema as well as in every moviegoer's stock of
memories.

But what actors the English have! Consider, for example, Michael Gough as Lord Goddard, the judge at Chris's trial. It is a very small and unsympathetic part, almost limited to reaction shots. Yet so good is Gough that, without the slightest underlining, he can make indelible the obtuseness, prejudices, obsoleteness of the establishment couched in the acrid decorum and seeming judiciousness of the judiciary. Or take a somewhat bigger part, that of Derek's sister, Iris. As played by Clare Holman with wry affection, and without a trace of glibness, glitter, or gush, Iris (whose real-life counterpart, the last of the Bentleys, still wages the fight for Derek's posthumous rehabilitation) emerges as a figure to tug at the very roots of our being.

Peter Medak, the Hungarian-born British director, first impressed us with the delightful satire *The Ruling Class*. Since then, he has made interesting movies that, for one reason or another, do not quite make it. But with *Let Him Have It* he is once again firmly in the saddle, directing with utmost simplicity and an unerring eye for detail. As long as there are films like this one and *Black Robe* to escape to from the highly touted but worthless hits of the day, nobody need despair.

Bugsy

Bugsy is the story of the notorious gangster Benjamin "Bugsy" Siegel, who was deputized by the East Coast racketeers to colonize the West Coast for them. His ruthless takeover executed with movie-star charm, his passion for Hollywood, where he had aspirations to acting, his close involvement with celebrities such as George Raft, his stormy relationship with the scarlet starlet Virginia Hill, and his "vision," to quote the press kit, "of a hotel in the desert, a palace, a city: Las Vegas," are the stuff of this long, resplendently produced, slickly accomplished, and dazzlingly hollow film.

The gangster movie, formerly one of Hollywood's staples, has latterly grown much more sporadic, but also opulent, elephantine, and portentous—witness *Godfather I*, *II*, and *III*. When it does not take itself too seriously and is executed with savvy and authenticity—as in *GoodFellas*—it remains as viable as before. *Bugsy* falls midway between the elegance of the latter and the bombast of the former. It has a screenplay by James Toback, who, in several movies he has written and directed, has shown a certain perverse flair along with unsavory excesses and clumsinesses, but who here, under the supervision of the proficient director Barry Levinson, spins out this tale of (to quote the same source) "a media celebrity . . . as appealing as he was dangerous" well enough while it is fictionalized biography, poorly when it turns into romanticized hagiography.

Contributing to the movie's glamor are the high budget and Allan Daviau's almost too ravishing cinematography. Incidents and dialogue tend to have punch and style, except, where Toback overshoots the mark into unhinged sex-and-power fantasies. Acting more incisively than usual, Warren Beatty makes a compelling Bugsy, with Harvey Keitel and Ben Kingsley outstanding in the supporting cast. However, Elliott Gould overdoes the underwritten part of a pathetic mobster, and the gifted Joe Mantegna does not find his way into George Raft's persona. As Virginia Hill, Annette Bening will do, but she is fast losing the edge that not so long ago made her one of the best and loveliest New York stage actresses.

Reshooting the President

JFK

There are three distinct angles from which Oliver Stone's *JFK* must be considered: artistic, historical, and political. For it is not only a feature film but also a polemic revision of history and an incentive to political action. Oliver Stone clearly implies that he has given us a riveting entertainment, the probable (or, more likely, definitive) reconstruction of the assassination of John F. Kennedy, and a clarion call for the release of documents ordered sealed until 2029—and thus started a political process that will lead to truth and justice and better government.

One can no more oppose these motives than be against sunlight, fresh air, and good health. But one may question the credibility of Stone's movie, based on the books *On the Trail of the Assassins*, by Jim Garrison, and *Crossfire: The Plot that Killed Kennedy*, by Jim Marrs. Many, including prominent journalistic and political figures, have done that, finally rejecting the film as hogwash. There is, to be sure, an aura of arrogance and sensationalism about the filmmaker that invites skepticism and dismissal.

Personally, I know very little about the Kennedy assassination and, worse yet, am open to charges of political analphabetism. I have always sympathized with the autobiographical hero of Anatole France's *Le Lys rouge* who declares, "I am not so devoid of all talents as to occupy myself with politics." Yet this credo, which makes some sense coming from a French artist and intellectual, would foul the breath of an American speaker. For if politics has been one of the two enervating preoccupations in France (need I name the other?), it has trailed just about everything, notably sports, in this country.

Now, I have nothing against sports, but for an entire nation to be besotted with them to the point where for every thousand Americans who can rattle off a litany of football scores and batting averages there may be one who can name his representatives in Congress is another matter. If a fraction of the time America spends on rehashing a basketball game could be reclaimed for informed political discussion, the quality of life would improve immeasurably. This is why I consider *JFK*, even if it makes a slice of Swiss cheese, by comparison, as solid as a glass brick, a salutary phenomenon.

By all means let us reconsider the assassination, remove the seal from all documents for qualified examiners (scholars, elected officials, journalists), and question the motives of all who might have been involved. Even the most far-fetched questioning seems to me healthier than indifference and complacency. And if it takes a movie such as *JFK* to get the ball rolling—well, did anyone ever claim that *Uncle Tom's Cabin* was a work of art? Stowe or Stone, bluestocking or loudmouth, nemesis or nudge, they also serve.

JFK, though sometimes long-winded, ponderous, or hard to follow, is not to be sloughed off easily. It makes its troubling points forcefully, and at the very least persuades that a single assassin could not have done it all. That it turns Jim Garrison into a much more appetizing figure than he seems to have been or be strikes me as a footling misdemeanor. Whatever its shortcomings, the film conveys the sense of confusion, panic, and impotence at such a dread event, the way witnesses cannot sort out what they have seen. A similar problem confronts me as I try to make sense of what this three-hour movie kept thrusting at me. The trouble with *JFK* is that whereas it solicits a second seeing to unscramble it, it does not offer enough aesthetic compensation to warrant the effort of reimmersion.

Yet what technical knowhow! The interweaving of documentary footage (the Zapruder film) and the stuff shot by Stone, the feel of authenticity and immediacy as these historic scenes are recreated (thanks in large part to Robert Richardson's canny cinematography), and the highly charged, redolent work of performers in small roles—all these dazzle. There are exceptions, though. Garrison himself turns Earl Warren into a denizen of the ghoul-haunted woodlands of Weir, and the gifted English actor Gary Oldman is too rich a presence for the puny Oswald. It may also have been a mistake to cast stars in cameo roles, e.g., Ed Asner (who at least tries to act), Walter Matthau, Donald Sutherland (who are just themselves), and John Candy and Jack Lemmon (who overact).

But what might have been the biggest miscalculation, the casting of Kevin Costner as Jim Garrison, proves a coup. Costner not only delivers a sound performance, but also, by being cast against type, manages to make us—and even himself—forget that he is Kevin Costner. As Mrs. Garrison, Sissy Spacek cannot, for all her good efforts, save the part of the workaholic's neglected wife from the clichés with which Stone and Zachary Sklar's script has bedizened it. Stunning work, however, from Laurie Metcalf, Jay O. Sanders, Kevin Bacon, and many others. Most impressive is Tommy Lee Jones as the smooth, homosexual businessman-playboy Clay Shaw, followed closely by Joe Pesci as David Ferrie, one of those seemingly over-the-top Pesci performances that, in the end, register conclusively right.

Fried Green Tomatoes

On the contrary, *Fried Green Tomatoes*, from which the very title might scare off faint hearts and city slickers (especially those who are not Southerners), proves to be an unassumingly graceful and, aside from a few heavy touches, fulfilling film. Based on a novel by Fannie Flagg, a former actress and stand-up comedienne, and co-scripted by her and the late Carol Sobieski, this is a "woman's picture" that nevertheless should go down pleasurably with male viewers, demonstrating that not even feminism, of which there is plenty in the movie, can drive an undislodgeable wedge between men and women.

It is the story of two female friendships. One in the present, between Evelyn Couch, an obese and unloved wife who, visiting a relative in the hospital, is befriended by a feisty octogenarian, Ninny Threadgoode, who regales her with tales of her home town, Whistle Stop, Alabama. They center on Idgie Threadgoode, an unconventional, spirited young woman who ran the Whistle Stop Café, a railside eatery where the specialty was fried green tomatoes. Idgie the tomboy had for best friend the town beauty, Ruth, and for advisor the family's black seamstress, Sipsy. Idgie and Ruth's friendship is the corresponding bit of female bonding in the past. When called upon, all four friends can show resourcefulness and guts.

Idgie and Ruth have two enemies: the railroad, which kills or maims some of their menfolk; and Frank Bennett, Ruth's vicious ex-husband, who mysteriously disappears in the process of trying to abduct his baby son from Ruth's loving care. Frank is a much greater threat than the railroad; though duly gotten rid of, he resurfaces posthumously and gets Idgie and her friend Big George, Sipsy's son, into a passel of difficulties with the law, intensified by Idgie's never having discriminated against blacks, in her café or elsewhere.

The film does have its melodramatic moments that do not play as smoothly as they might, and here and there a touch of improbability. But both pairs of friends, Evelyn and Ninny (Kathy Bates and Jessica Tandy) and Idgie and Ruth (Mary Stuart Masterson and Mary-Louise Parker), are idiomatically conceived and racily played. And the way the two stories come together in the end, though by no means unpredictable, is a model of skill and finesse under the directorial guidance of Jon Avnet. Miss Parker, a pretty young woman who, not unlike Belloc's Maria, is given to making faces that produce a horrible effect, is here kept free of mannerisms and gives a restrained performance as Ruth, which I attribute to Avnet's acumen.

Jessica Tandy is just as sublime as she was in *Driving Miss Daisy*, though this old woman is very different from that one: and Kathy Bates is good both as the initially downtrodden and miserable fattie and as the later self-respecting and self-assertive one. Mary Stuart Masterson is unbeatable in tomboy roles, and there are several relishable performances in smaller parts. The Whistle Stop Café, with its bustling and egalitarian atmosphere, does not come fully to life—I never got the taste of fried green tomatoes in my mouth—but the ending succeeds in being both extremely affecting and wholly life-affirming, as befits a picture that means to make few waves our spirits can't go surfing on. Some Flagg-waving is due this modest American film that can be enjoyed by adults and children, natives and foreigners, feminists and male chauvinists, Southerners and even Yankees who never so much as saw, let alone ate, a less than rubicund tomato.

Howards End

Merchant and Ivory should have been ivory merchants, a field in which fakery thrives. Not to worry, though: they have made a phenomenal career out of peddling plastic as cinematic art, as their latest, *Howards End*, triumphantly confirms. Let us recall that M & I, with their devoted screenwriter Ruth Prawer Jhabvala, have already laid waste Henry James's *The Europeans* and *The Bostonians*, and have similarly attacked two by E. M. Forster, *A Room with a View* and *Maurice* (not to mention a foray into Jane Austen). Though they successfully demolished *Room*, *Maurice*, Forster's sentimentalized fictionalization of his own homosexuality, had a tone congenial to the filmmakers, who, in this instance, were also helped by the master cameraman Pierre Lhomme.

When they are not razing masterworks but addressing Indian matters, M & I do better. Merchant, after all, is Indian, as is the husband of Mrs. Jhabvala, who has lived in India and written about it. But with *Howards End*, the Merchant-Ivory-Jhabvala team is firmly back in Masterpiece Theatre, which is where their talent for subversion leaps to the fore.

I approached this film with benevolence, because I happened to like the trio's last venture, *Mr. and Mrs. Bridge*, based on two novels by Evan S. Connell, although even there the ending was a bathetic failure of nerve. With *Howards End*, however, it is business as usual, start to finish. When Forster's novel appeared in 1910, the *Saturday Review* (to quote P. N. Furbank's *E. M. Forster: A Life*), wrote that "to express his genius in using everyday speech to betray 'cunning shadowings' of personality, the term 'Forsterian' was now a necessity." Forster's Bloomsbury colleague, Virginia Woolf, writes more critically: 'We are to notice this, take heed of that. Margaret or Helen, we are made to understand, is not speaking simply as herself, her words have another and a larger intention.' So, Mrs. Woolf argues, we are repeatedly forced into "the twilight world of theory."

In the movie, we are also shoved into another world, though not one of subtle shadowings or larger, symbolic intention. No, it is a smaller, indeed diminutive, world of farce, of rather mechanistic, caricatural exaggeration. If I do not go into the plot, consider this my attempt to get you to read the novel, marvelous even if flawed, and to find out for yourselves just how far short, for all its superficial faithfulness, the movie falls.

The reductive technique can be demonstrated with the treatment of the famous passage near the beginning, where two of the principal characters are deeply affected by the Beethoven Fifth they hear at a concert. Forster's description both of the music and of its effect on the listeners is a justly famous purple patch in modern literature, perhaps even in music criticism. Granted this is hard, even impossible, to translate to the screen, surely better could have been found than having Simon Callow, in an uncredited cameo performance as a music appreciation lecturer, whose mother plays illustrative passages on the piano, act smug and condescending to his audience. The scene does incorporate passages from Forster's text, but it reduces them to comic rubble.

There are fine British actors in the film, doing their level best to stem the leveling into farce; I feel especially for Anthony Hopkins and Emma Thompson. One thing, though, works: wonderful English landscapes and houses, flashily but still invitingly shot by Tony Pierce-Roberts, the M & I house photographer.

Basic Instinct

We were teased by the advance reports: parts of *Basic Instinct* were so sexually explicit, they had to be cut. Of course, in Europe the film would be shown uncut, as presumably in the cassette version to be eventually released in the U.S.: but here and now puritanism would be served. In such a climate of illogic, it may be too much to expect the movie to make sense.

Basic Instinct was directed by Paul Verhoeven, the Dutch director, whose American hits, *Robocop* and *Total Recall*, I somehow managed to miss. But the two Dutch films of his I did catch were advancedly loony stuff: bizarre, well made, and creepily magnetic. And now he comes on with his first doubly attention-grabbing film: first, because of the sequences cut from it; later, because of the protests it has generated. Two scenes, we gather, had to be trimmed: one in which, during some intensive police questioning, Sharon Stone, wearing the miniest of skirts with no panties, crosses and uncrosses her legs for a voyeuristic camera; and one in which she and Michael Douglas are having no-holds-barred sex. As for the protests, they are from various activists objecting to the film's villains being wholly or partly lesbian.

A third point of interest is that the outwardly and inwardly unprepossessing scenarist of *Basic Instinct*, Joe Eszterhas, was paid three cool millions (or can only one million be cool?) for his hot screenplay, whose two chief distinctions are sex, ranging from innuendo to obscenity, crammed into every possible line or situation; and total incoherence. Whereas the former is considered a plus, the latter is, in today's world, of no consequence. So the movie glides along with maniacal skill unconcerned with logic, consistent characters, or minimal verisimilitude.

Nick Curran (Michael Douglas) is a San Francisco police detective who has been jinxed lately. He has had problems with drink, drugs, a broken marriage, and a few accidental killings in the line of duty that have earned him the sobriquet Shooter. He has also had an intermittent affair with Dr. Beth Garner (Jeanne Tripplehorn), a police psychologist of uncommon seductiveness, who alternately recriminates with him and protects him against dismissal. Needless to say, Nick is basically a nice, vulnerable guy, even if his one sexual encounter with Dr. Beth recorded here is clearly of the S&M variety, but so carefully staged every inch of the way as to be a possible turn-on only for choreographers.

When a wealthy rock-club owner and playboy is found dead, nude, wrists bound to his bed with an Hermes scarf, his body (appropriately for that of an art collector) turned into a piece of bloody pointillism with an icepick, Nick has a hunch that it must have been the victim's girlfriend, the millionaire playgirl-novelist Catherine Tramell, who did it in an untrammeled moment. (We were shown the kinky sex cum murder scene, but the killer woman's face remained hidden.) Catherine writes mysteries that come to life—or death—exactly as she wrote them. Yet no one but Nick suspects her; surely nobody would be that self-incriminating? The killer must be some copycat reader, perhaps trying to do Catherine in. Since the police cannot produce another plausible suspect, but consider Nick's notion quixotic, we are already on shaky ground. That ground soon earns an even ten on the Richter scale, with Eszterhas's computer doubtless placed squarely athwart the Saint Andreas fault. Suffice it to say that Nick finds himself falling heavily into bed and love with Catherine, even as she flaunts her capacious files of clippings about him, and her work on a new novel in which the detective falls in love with the heroine, who not so much melts him as turns him into finely chopped ice.

Except for the clever direction by Verhoeven and the lush cinematography of another Dutchman, Jan De Bont (who also shot *Shining Through*), there is nothing here worth further rehashing. But I must stress that Catherine has, or has had, several lesbian lovers, including a current live-in one, Roxy, whom she lets spy on her bed bouts with men. When this leads to Roxy's violent death, a momentarily distraught Catherine exclaims, "I shouldn't have let her watch us!" Late learning is one of the several buried themes of the movie.

It would be otiose to discuss performances in such a piece of hokum, unless one had in mind another type of performance altogether, which, however, given the infinite manipulativeness of the camera, is equally unassessable. That leaves what is essential here: looks. Sharon Stone, an ex-model, is decidedly beautiful, although in a manner too cosmeticized for my taste. Jeanne Tripplehorn (a name that unduly panders to punsters) is enormously sexy on stage, especially when, in a recent play, her body was being languidly soaped in a protracted bathtub scene; she suffers, however, in cinematic closeup, where her lips hog more screen expanse than any other Caucasian's I can think of. Leilani Sarelle (Roxy) looks like one of those dolls on late-night commercials whose conversational skills are hawked at $2.95 a minute, and whose acting is worth two cents an hour. Michael Douglas, women tell me, has a sexy mouth. Here, unfortunately, you can see the rest of him, too.

To the sundry homosexual organizations up in arms, I have two things to say. First, the lesbian scenes in this movie would not persuade the most susceptible 12-year-old of any sex that there are real lesbians here; second, the treatment of heterosexuals is ultimately every bit as insulting. So if we are going to take offense, it should be as thinking, not as sexual, beings.

The Player

The raves are coming in for Robert Altman's *The Player* from reviewers of every stripe. It is as if Leonardo da Vinci, after not death but merely a few centuries' snooze, were back again with an even more mysterious *Mona Lisa*, a more mystical *Last Supper* than the last.

What, in point of fact, is or was Robert Altman? A converted television director who made *M*A*S*H*, an amusingly absurdist army satire, and *Nashville*, a sprawling, overambitious movie that, after being repeatedly cut in half like the Sibylline books, emerged both prophetic of cinematic things to come and arresting in its own right. Good accomplishments, to be sure, but Altman's other films, both before and after *Nashville*, were so doggedly experimental, such mulishly avant-garde H*A*S*H, that Altman's chief contribution to film history may yet be the muddied soundtrack. For, starting with *McCabe and Mrs. Miller*, Altman's main trick was the systematic overlapping of several conversations, making us strain to decipher the dialogue. If we failed, the failure and loss (we thought) were our own; if we succeeded, we were so elated with our unscrambling that we overlooked the paltriness of what was decoded. Besides, Pauline Kael pronounced *McCabe* sublime, and goaded her numerous fans into advanced Altmania.

But unlike most major directors, Altman appears to lack a literary sensibility of any kind, and displays along with a bloated ego a remarkably shriveled intelligence. Thus he turned out ever more muddled and pretentious atrocities until he ended up unbearable, unbankable, and unemployable. Now, after a ten-year hiatus, he returns with trivia worthy of Jackie Collins or Judith Krantz, hailed as a sublime comeback. Let us not forget that the screenplay, based on his own novel, is by Michael Tolkin, the man who last year gave us *The Rapture*, starring Mimi Rogers, a piece of apocalyptic trash megalomaniacal to the point of near imbecility. *The Player*, which purports to be a wicked satire about Hollywood's greed, corruption, and stupidity, is a prime symptom of them rather than a lancing or curettage.

Griffin Mills, a rising studio executive, though suitably crass and unscrupulous, is made jumpy by an impending shakeup that may replace him with the even more crass and unscrupulous Larry Levy. Mills is rendered even more jittery by anonymous missives, on postcards and faxes, that threaten his demise in retaliation for what he has done to writers. He manages to track down the rejected scenarist whom he suspects of hounding him and, in an ensuing fight, batters him to death. Suspected in his turn by the police in the person of the black female detective Avery—Mills finds partial respite when his victim's toothsome mistress the supposed Icelander and self-proclaimed painter June Gudmundsdottir, promptly transfers her affection and favors to him.

What does not help, however, is that the threats continue coming—not least in the shape of a rattlesnake smuggled into his car—

which convinces Griffin that he has offed the wrong hack. But, in the end, all comes right: the police are thwarted, Griffin and June are married and expecting, and Griffin and Larry Levy, in a marriage of true hucksters' minds, are producing monstrous movies that promise megabucks. The next one, in fact, will be the story of *this* film, to be called *The Player*, and scripted by the very anonymous epistolarian whom Griffin failed to kill.

I have, of course, greatly simplified the plot here, but nowise betrayed the film's pristine primitivism. *The Player* is essentially an anecdote stretched out to over two hours' duration not by digging into the characters and their relationships, but by routinely stringing together episodes. We never learn much more about Griffin and June than we knew shortly after meeting them, and their adventures are not breathtaking enough, the Hollywood ambience not devastatingly enough portrayed, to cloak a mounting sense of sameness. There is even a nagging suspicion that some of the funding might have come from the fancy restaurants and hostelries that periodically pop up in the proceedings. Such excitement as the film proposes—wit, sex, suspense—flags alarmingly fast; what is meant to compensate, perhaps, is a superabundance of atmosphere: old movie posters and stills on the walls, references to old movies in the conversations, and certain techniques evocative of the films of the past.

So, for example, even as one character is overheard praising the long tracking-shot opening of Welles's *Touch of Evil*, an even longer and more elaborate tracking shot, including that bit of dialogue, marks the beginning of *The Player*; in its course, we are exposed to the hurlyburly in and around the studio. Again, the cinematography, which in the outdoor sequences tends to go grainy even as in the indoor ones it is often murky, seems to be intended as a tribute to the old B movies—unless it is merely a testimonial to the falterings of Altman's favorite cameraman, the Canadian Jean Lepine. And again, as in the old genre movies, the colorfully bizarre minor characters look like the triumph of Central Casting. Yet such devices, while delighting movie buffs and nostalgia hounds, add relatively little to the quality of the work.

A more striking device here is Altman's recruitment of any number of Hollywood stars and near-stars to appear in cameo—sometimes almost subliminal—performances. At times, these celebrities are identified in the dialogue; at others, they are offered as challenges to the moviegoers' ability to spot and identify them. This game, though not without its amusement value, detracts from rather than adding to the sense of reality (this is Hollywood and, of course, stars are everywhere!): the viewer, hellbent on catching the luminaries, loses sight of the story. The strategy also suggests a—by no means unwarranted—directorial lack of faith in the merit of the material at hand.

As usual, Altman strains after Effect with a capital E. For example, he shoots the major sex scene in extreme closeup of two profiles, one above the other, with the dialogue dissolving into moans and panting. The result is stark and startling, but also self-defeating: seeing every blemish on those complexions, hearing all that heavy breathing and grunting, is not a turn-on—any more than is another scene showing these lovers stretched out in parallel mud baths at a desert resort. Tim Robbins, a good but funny-looking actor, has little to lose by such maneuvers; but the lovely Greta Scacchi is abused for no good reason. To cover these already morally compromised lovers with layers of mud and ridicule is to nudge us into withholding that bit of lust and sympathy even unsympathetic characters need to subsist on.

Satire? Not really. Nothing here really punctures, really deflates, except the initial sequence that has aspiring scenarists pitch their screenplay ideas at Mills in 25 words or less—though, of course, profusely groveling, they exceed the allotted amount. And casting the insufferable Whoopi Goldberg, whose smugness knows no bounds, as detective Avery is the next-to-last straw. The last is Lepine's way of shooting her, so that her black face emerges in medium shots as a mere dark blur. An aesthetic and moral blur is what the entire movie is, too.

A Woman's Tale

With his latest, *A Woman's Tale*, the Dutch-born Australian director Paul Cox has won me over completely. This is a rare, honest, moving but not maudlin, melancholy but not depressing film about old age, illness, and dying. Cancer here is not a tear-jerking or "artistic" element, but a simple fact of life with which you live as best you can.

Cox saw the distinguished Australian actress Sheila Florance in a play over a quarter-century ago and vowed to make a movie with her. After two lesser efforts, he wrote *A Woman's Tale* for her. Miss Florance was dying of cancer, so the script is about an old, cancerous, but infinitely brave woman, and the result is a film that could make you live your life better, something you cannot say about many movies, these or any days.

I'm not sure whether it was a good idea to make Martha, the protagonist, not an actress. The pictures and mementos around the apartment bespeak one (they are clearly Miss Florance's own), as does much about Martha's personality. But by turning her into a generic old woman, Cox has made her more ecumenical, even if slightly less credible. Her speech, for example, is much too fine for your ordinary middle-class Australian; that superb diction is the legacy of the London stage, where Miss Florance plied her craft between 1935 and 1950. Yet such elocution serves the character of Martha in good stead: it conveys a gentility that labels her not arrogant or snobbish, but simply a person who believes in crisp, clear speech as a token of civility, a way of partaking in and spreading the grace of culture.

The characters surrounding Martha are flavorous, too. There is, first, the visiting nurse, Anna, a young Polish woman whom Martha calls Malinka (Polish for Little One), and whom she has totally won over by such kindnesses as letting her use her apartment and bed for trysts with a married lover. This situation is handled with consummate tact. The lover is no Romeo, but an unremarkable, shy, middle-aged fellow; Anna herself is appealing and decent, but in no way idealized. Their affair is a basic necessity for two otherwise savorless lives.

Martha's immediate neighbor is Billy, an even older and much lonelier person. Martha has joy and energy and a son who, in his clumsy way, loves her, even if his wife does not; Billy's family takes no interest in him. Martha has a cat and a canary; Billy, only an old record-player. But Martha looks after Billy, and also has other friends: Miss Inchley, a cheerful ninety-year-old whom Martha slightly patronizes for being a virgin (she has to have someone to feel superior to); and the streetwalker who operates nearby. The landlord, to be sure, is a typical feelingless clod, as landlords are everywhere; but the downstairs neighbors, two excitable French homosexuals, are an interesting couple, laconically but cannily observed.

Above all else, though, it is Martha's friendship with Malinka that grows and flowers. The symbiosis of these so different women is sympathetically but unsentimentally set forth. Film has generally been able to depict romantic love, family love, even more specialized loves—a boy's for his dog, say, or a dog's for his boy. But affection—pure, simple affection, or what Goethe called "elective affinity"—has rarely been filmed with such pristine dignity. Cox never says anything so banal as "surrogate mother finds surrogate daughter"; indeed, he never *says* anything at all; we are left to figure out the nature of this profound, realistic, and moving bond.

The film features two kinds of effective slowness. The direct kind, as when Anna takes Martha out of the hospital so she can die in her beloved apartment, which the landlord has repossessed but Malinka reclaims for Martha. The first outdoor sight that catches Martha's eye is a tree in the hospital parking lot. As a botanical illiterate, I can only say that it is a fairly humdrum tree with long, willowy branches and tiny or no leaves. But the wind soughs in this tree, and the branches dance to his song. The camera holds on this. It is up to us to discover what nature means to a human being in extremis.

And then the delayed-effect slowness: Martha's beloved canary is called Jesus, which gives rise to all sorts of minor merriment. But the payoff comes when Anna sneaks into the now dead woman's apartment to rescue the bird that has been solemnly left to her care. The landlord materializes and points suspiciously to Anna's bosom, which must hide something precious. Asked what she's got there, she answers, "Jesus," and the landlord dismisses her with a condescending laugh. This double entendre achieves a funny and solemn sense of reverence that touches even a nonbeliever.

There are many kinds of relationships in *A Woman's Tale*; in fact, the movie is almost all relationships, with hardly any plot. Some of these are warm and sweet, some ugly and cold. But all are thoroughly human and minutely observed. Art is everywhere: in the writing (by Cox and Barry Dickins), in Cox's direction, in the unassuming camerawork of Nino Martinetti, in the unobtrusive music of Paul Grabowsky. And, of course, in the acting.

Sheila Florance received the Australian Best Actress award in her hospital room, nine days before she died at age 75. Never was an award more merited. Not because the actress was moribund, but because, like the movie, she was full of enjoyed, exuded, freely shared life; and because she was able to communicate goodness without sanctimoniousness or sugariness or (a protective device that often backfires) a trace of gruffness. Many of the film's episodes were taken from her life, and devolve to her further glory. As Anna/ Malinka, the Polish-born Gosia Dobrowolska is also outstanding, of a spontaneity utterly devoid of sappiness, of a self-renewing boun- teousness like the waterfall that is one of the film's loveliest images. The other performances are spot on as well. Perhaps the best way to describe them is to say that in them professional actors come across as natural as characters in a documentary. See this film.

The Waterdance

The Waterdance is a semiautobiographical film written and co-di- rected (with Michael Steinberg) by Neal Jimenez, scenarist of the splendid *River's Edge* and co-scenarist of the mindless *Something for the Boys*. Jimenez broke his neck in a hiking accident and is now a paraplegic; one of the film's principals, Joel Garcia, is a Hispanic novelist hospitalized under similar circumstances. He has a mar- ried girlfriend, Anna, whom he wants to detach from her husband, and two zestful ward mates, the racist biker Bloss and the black ladies' man and bon vivant Raymond.

There is a sassy candor about this movie, an attempt to tell the defiant truth about men trying to come to terms with being re- duced by roughly one half: they can no longer indulge in many of their former activities, and their chances of sexual fulfillment of a normal sort are extremely slim. The movie is most concerned with its three main characters' relations to women and sex, and also to one another: their attempts to overcome their social, racial, and intellectual differences.

A hospital film, alas, is not unlike a Grand Hotel film: too many principal and even ancillary characters battle for our attention, too many lives are displayed in excessive foreshortening, and the danger of being told too little or too much, or the wrong things, is ever present. What exactly happens during Joel and Anna's sexual bouts, lovingly scrutinized but never clarified? Why would his long-neglected wife want to leave Raymond now that she has him in her power and that he desperately wants to dedicate himself to wife and daughter? Why does the blowhard Bloss not have a woman other than his mother? Not quite enough attention is paid to anything besides the sensitive maunderings of Joel, and because he is so obviously the author's alter ego, the film cannot escape an odor of self-importance.

Good, though, that the film avoids the agonies of physiotherapy and the sadistic male or female nurses we know from too many other movies; but it is strange that none of the main characters has much of a family—not one relative visits Joel. Bloss, besides his mother, has some biker friends who drop in noisily; otherwise the three men live in a peculiar vacuum. Though we are not allowed to forget that Joel is a writer, we learn little or nothing about the others' occupations. Further paraplegics are used mostly as sight gags: Victor, a Latino, has a numerous family loudly but otherwise anonymously milling around him; Vernon, a presumed pathetic nonentity whom we only hear but do not see, is all too briefly revealed to us as a handsome fellow with a smashing wife. We see a bit more of a young Korean and his people, but he too remains a cipher.

When Raymond takes off for an old folks' home, the move and his existence there are shrouded in undue mystery; when Anna finally manages to break away from her husband and find a suitable place for herself and her lover to move into, Joel tells her to go back to her husband. Out of foresight, nobility, or cowardice? We're not told. When she returns in the end, is it merely as a pal? And, above all, who pays these men's hospital bills? And how will they manage, once out? This is not a veterans' hospital, and these are not your standard war victims. A little ambiguity or openendedness can be good for a movie, but leaving us in complete darkness about major issues is another matter.

Still, there is much keen, first-hand observation here—for example about how the kindnesses of well-meaning bunglers can humiliate these men. A visit to a strip joint (though how one of the guys manages to steal a hospital van, and how another drives what is clearly not a specially equipped vehicle, remains uncertain) is persuasively rendered, rather than being a mere exercise in rollicking screen rowdiness. Relationships are searchingly explored, and the character of an unsappily compassionate nurse is well written and restrainedly enacted by Elizabeth Peña. Eric Stoltz (Joel), Wesley Snipes (Raymond), and William Forsythe (Bloss) are all very fine, but Joel can't be made as juicy as the others. And some vignettes are powerful, e.g., a demented-looking figure in an electric wheelchair, which is viewed as less couth than a manually operated one.

Pretension does creep in, as in some facile literary references and the film's title, derived from an all too patly symbolic dream. Yet for addressing a genuine problem tactfully, for featuring authentic dialogue, and for allowing Helen Hunt (Anna) to give a fine performance even in sex scenes (for once, not exploitative), *The Waterdance* deserves attention and gratitude.

The Best Intentions

The Best Intentions is Ingmar Bergman's account of his parents' precarious courtship and toilsome first decade of marriage. As directed by Bille August, the Dane who gave us *Pelle the Conqueror*, it won the Grand Prize at Cannes, a prize gravely compromised by the likes of *sex, lies, and videotape*, *Wild at Heart*, and *Barton Fink*. This time the jury did not fink out, though the film does have its problems.

The work, initially a six-hour TV mini-series, is now edited down to a three-hour movie, pretty much as was the case with one of Bergman's masterpieces, *Scenes from a Marriage*, which, however, was no longer quite such a masterpiece in its final 158-minute trimming. *Fanny and Alexander*, the last solo cinematic venture by Bergman, similarly suffered from shrinkage. *The Best Intentions*, whose full-length version I haven't seen, does not exactly feel like *disjecta membra*, which is good; but neither does one feel the steady presence of the *poeta*, which is not so good.

After many troubles with social inequality, ill health, family disapproval, and a rival relationship, the upper-class and snobbish (but otherwise charming) Anna Åkerblom marries the impoverished, tormented, indecisive Henrik Bergman, first a starveling divinity student, then a minister who takes his bride to a godforsaken northern parish, where he becomes the assistant pastor. They have their contretemps and even major fights, but they stick it out through the birth and childhood of a son, and are expecting another child (the future Ingmar), when an offer comes from the Queen (a splendid cameo by Anita Björk) for Pastor Bergman to become chaplain of the Royal Hospital. Henrik refuses to leave his working-class parishioners, whereupon Anna leaves *him*. But there is a final reconciliation.

It is instructive to compare *The Best Intentions* with that other scrutiny of a conjugal minefield, *Scenes from a Marriage*, and so figure out the reasons for the current shortfall. The easy (and insufficient) answer would be that Bergman is a better director than

August; but *Pelle the Conqueror* was no mean achievement without any help from Bergman.

The main problem is that there is not much change in either Henrik and Anna or their circumstances as they lead to an ending predictable for anyone with the slightest knowledge of Bergman's life. The only real conflicts involve Nordenson, an atheistic manufacturer who does not want his daughters confirmed, and a strange young boy, Petrus, who seeks shelter from a harsh family with the Bergmans, but to whom Anna cannot really warm up, especially when her second child is on the way. In the three-hour version, at any rate, neither of these plot elements achieves sufficient dramatic stature. In the uncut version, the political struggle of the exploited factory workers, barely touched upon here, and the more fleshed-out presences of colorful townfolk may have enhanced the atmosphere and texture.

And whereas *Scenes* enjoyed the freedom of fiction, *Intentions* is saddled with the constraints of biography. In the cut version, moreover, the colorful lesser members of the Åkerblom clan get much less of a chance to add to the film's ambience and aroma. Even the kind but ailing paterfamilias, beautifully played by Max von Sydow (whose very face seems to have so filled up with lived and acted experience that it is an eloquent scenario in itself), is here shortchanged. Ghita Nørby, the Danish actress playing Anna's mother, comes off best, but in a rather monochromatic role. The delightful Lena Endré, who plays Henrik's supposedly older, working-class mistress, inappositely looks (and probably is) younger than the heroine.

Samuel Fröler, as Henrik, is not a bad actor, but must, without much personal magnetism, play a rebarbative personage. As for Pernilla August (Östergren before she married the director, when she dazzled us on the New York stage with her Ophelia and Nora), she is saddled with a role nearly too noble. And, though neither pretty nor young enough, she has such talent, presence, and inner beauty as to unintentionally overshadow her partner. One misses the complex, evenly matched characters and performers of *Scenes from a Marriage*. Still, there are the achingly authentic psychological details, the intricate social and gender balances and imbalances, and the striking land- and cityscapes poignantly photographed by Jôrgen Persson (who did such masterly work for Bo Widerberg's movies): enough to make this a rewarding, adult movie, a rare thing in our era of infantilism.

One False Move

American movies today are aimed at three kinds of audiences: kids, cokeheads, and those seeking any kind of loud and vulgar stimulation with which to fill up a gaping inner emptiness for a couple of hours. Under those circumstances, story is the first thing that goes out the window. Cheap laughs, cheap thrills, bloated production values will do quite nicely.

One False Move is a modest B picture, but, wonder of wonders, it tells a real story. A trio of drug addicts cum criminals—the black sociopath, Pluto, the psychopathic redneck, Ray, and his mulatto girlfriend, Fantasia—"cold-bloodedly rip off a large stash of cocaine and cash from two families, killing six people." I take David Denby's word for it because the film begins so confusingly that it is hard to tell how many houses, families, victims are involved. But if Carl Franklin, the black actor turned director, and his white screenwriters (Billy Bob Thornton, who plays Ray, and Tom Epperson) are not good at that kind of clarity, they are adept at creating suspense and at conveying brutality and horror in a way that reaches the precise last limit of the bearable.

The police in Los Angeles, where the murders took place, figure out that the trio is headed for tiny Star City, Arkansas, where both Ray and Fantasia (whose real name is Lila) have family; Pluto is from Chicago, and met Ray in San Quentin. Star City is a good place to hide out. First, however, the trio, unbeknown to the police, heads for Houston, to sell the dope to a dealer there, but things go bloodily wrong. As they also do elsewhere along the highway, where a state trooper grown suspicious stops them. Corpses mark the trio's path.

In Star City, another trio awaits them: a pair of detectives dispatched from L.A., one white and one black, and the local sheriff, the good ole boy Dale "Hurricane" Dixon. Married, the father of a small daughter, and bored with small-town police work, Dale dreams of joining the L.A. Police Department. His delusion fills the Angelenos with sarcastic merriment, which Dale, unfortunately, overhears. Now he must prove himself to these sneering cops whom he and his wife entertained so hospitably. And he does so—in the most disastrous fashion.

If the near-parallel configuration of the two multiracial trios is supposed to have some deeper meaning, it escapes me. But each

trio is skillfully drawn. Pluto is a buttoned-up, respectable-busi-
nessman type, a cool strategist; he just happens to enjoy carving
up people with his handy knife. Ray is a tattooed, pony-tailed, trigger-happy slob, yet he has something that appeals to the sexy, inscrutable Fantasia, whose attitude toward men, sex, and crime we
must gradually piece together. Similarly, we have to figure out why
someone as smart as Pluto teams up with someone like Ray. Is this
cat using this ape to remove hot chestnuts from the fire for him? Or
is it the fun of bossing a white man around? On the other hand, in
the motel rooms they share on their flight, Pluto must put up with
the greedy lovemaking of Ray and Fantasia.

Again, the trio of lawmen is an interesting study in contrasts,
although the white and the black detective are alike in their scorn
for Dale, who, poor soul, began as their devoted fan. But such admiration is hard to take. So the potential for some sort of eruption
is always suspensefully present.

Especially right is the atmosphere of the conversations and silences these juxtapositions generate. And finally, albeit briefly, racial undertones do come to the fore as Dale, a/k/a Hurricane, and
Lila, a/k/a Fantasia, meet up as something, it turns out, more than
strangers. It is one of the strengths of the film that matters of black
and white are *not* treated in a black-and-white way. One of the
funniest, and also wisest, scenes is the meal at the Dixons' during
which the sheriff, forgetting the blackness of one of the detectives,
casually refers to "niggers." Here as elsewhere there is awareness of
bonds between people that defy the divisiveness of language, mores,
and social structure.

Ultimately, though, it is acting and directing that make the difference here. As noted, Franklin's direction botches the topography
of the early scenes. Later, it goes in sporadically for arty camera
angles. In the death of the state trooper, what really happens remains hidden from view—a deliberate effect, perhaps, but ill-ad-
vised, I think. And in the climactic finale there is an impassive
black shanty-dweller somewhere at the periphery of the action; he
is playing his mouth organ, and the camera periodically cuts to
him as a quasi-symbolic refrain, and to increase the suspense by
delaying the main action. It is both a cliché and artsy-fartsy. But
all this is more than made up for by pacing that knows the value
of leisureliness in the right places and the worth of leaving certain
things to the imagination.

Moreover, humor is put to excellent use in unlikely situations, as when everything depends on a child's erratic responses. Humor, too, mitigates the foolishness of the sheriff, who, for a film noir, is an unusually complex character. Though childish and even obtuse, he is allowed to transcend his limitations and achieve something damn near tragic stature. Similar claims can be entertained for Fantasia. And then there is that admirable lightness of touch, as in the fleeting but highly idiosyncratic caress Dale bestows on his sleeping wife.

There is very fine ensemble acting from Bill Paxton, a fully rounded Dale; Michael Beach, a coiled cobra of a Pluto; Billy Bob Thornton, an all too humanly inhuman Ray; Jim Meltzer and Earl Billings, the megalopolitan detectives stymied by rusticity; and any number of others. It may be unfortunate that Dale's wife is somewhat patronized by the script and casting; though here, too, there are redeeming touches. And best of all, perhaps, is the Fantasia of Cynda Williams, a performance that brings thoroughgoing emotional confusion into sharp and touching focus. Only near the end, when she is given a rather too literary and philosophical speech, is there a touch of preciosity and propaganda that even Miss Williams cannot completely salvage. But she and Bill Paxton, in their crucial encounter, elevate a coolly efficient genre picture into something higher, more human.

Unforgiven? For What? By Whom?

UNFORGIVEN

Just what kind of a western is Clint Eastwood's highly touted *Unforgiven*? Revisionist? Postmodern? Deconstructionist? Or merely adult? Mostly, I would say, confused. It is one of those well-meaning liberal attempts to do right by all current politically correct notions, and the penalty it pays is self-contradiction, muddledness, moral fog. These are not mortal flaws or sins—a fuzzy enthusiast will remain gleefully unaware of them—but they make for a movie that wobbles, lurches, and variously trips itself up.

The so-called adult western has been around for some time. In Henry King's *The Gunfighter* (1950), the protagonist was a gunslinger trying to put his past behind him, but in vain. Essentialism wins out over existentialism in *Shane* (1953) as well, where neither the love of a woman nor a youngster's idolatry can keep the reformed gunfighter from riding off into his lonely sunset, after duly risking his life for the homesteaders. Still, he at least rides away; the hero of the earlier film is gunned down from behind by a glory-seeking young punk. In David Shipley's words, "a rotten tradition will have been passed on."

Alternatively, the adult western's protagonist may be someone like the marshal in *High Noon* (1952), virtually the only brave and honest person in town; he must take on the vengeful outlaws nearly alone, the solid citizens having cravenly forsaken him. In any case, as aging gunfighter or beleaguered upholder of the law, the hero is a pariah: a loner unsuited to a world too naïve or too corrupt. And there you have pretty much the entire repertoire of the adult western, those pictures from the early fifties encapsulating most of what followed. Pauline Kael may sneer at them—"the message is that the myths we never believed in anyway were false"—but that isn't the whole story. The pariah-hero is a hero yet; those surrounding him are piddlers, poltroons, or worse.

The ambivalence in the adult western is what makes it potentially absorbing. That is what Sergio Leone, the father of spaghetti westerns, tapped into when he engaged an American television cowboy, Clint Eastwood of *Rawhide*, to portray the Man with No Name in *A Fistful of Dollars* (1964), and the rest is movie history. And now, 36 starring roles and ten westerns later—some of them directed by himself—Eastwood is back as director and star, playing William Munny, a former outlaw who robbed trains, shot up towns, and killed women and children. Then he married a good woman from New England who made a new man of him. But she died (of illness, not Munny), and here he is trying to run a pig farm to eke out a grim living—the hogs become diseased—for himself and his two young children.

A cocky pipsqueak, who calls himself the Schofield Kid and claims to have killed five men, rides up and asks Munny to team up with him to collect a thousand-dollar reward for the killing of two men guilty of brutally slashing the face of a young prostitute, Delilah, in the saloon-cum-brothel of Big Whiskey, a small town run despotically by Sheriff Little Bill Daggett, a reformed but sadistic ex-gunman. Over the protests of Strawberry Alice, the madam (Frances Fisher, and good), Daggett lets the culprits go; they must, however, provide several horses for Skinny, the weasely saloon owner, by way of restitution for Delilah's permanent impairment. Skinny is content, but Alice contemptuously rejects a very fine colt, offered to Delilah by the younger and less guilty of the men (he was an unwilling accessory). The men are chased away by the prostitutes, who pelt them with mud.

Already the politically correct features are manifest. The women, although whores, are basically moral: they have pride, spunk, and solidarity, and offer up their collective savings in their passion for justice. The minimally guilty and repentant younger guy must perish too; if a woman has been injured, it's a die for an eye. What was Delilah's offense? Ingenuous and inexperienced, she couldn't suppress a giggle at the smallness of her client's member. The slasher acted out of hurt male-chauvinist pride: sexism and suprematism out of male inferiority feelings, Freud enlisted in the feminist cause.

More PC: the police are brutal (memories of *Dirty Harry*!), and all authority corrupts. Daggett is an autocratic brute who compels everyone staying in Big Whiskey to deposit his firearms with him. Noncompliers will be savagely beaten by him, even jailed; this is the fate that befalls the dapper British bounty hunter English Bob (Richard Harris at his arrogant best). But he has it coming to him: his job had been to shoot Chinese laborers who displeased the railroad barons. Killing workers of color is, of course, the most heinous crime. Yet isn't it the liberals, not Daggett, who are supposed to abrogate the right to bear arms? Haven't Eastwood and his scenarist, David Webb Peoples, slipped up here?

Munny, poor soul, has been farming for 11 years and he can hardly mount his horse any more, though once in the saddle, he's okay. His marksmanship with a six-shooter is all shot to hell, but with a rifle, he's still a crack shot. (Never fear: when called upon later on, his sidegun skills will be restored to him.) He spouts pious platitudes and keeps sanctimoniously extolling his dead wife's salutary influence until it begins to sound like a sendup. But his humility is clearly genuine, unless it represents some unconscious resentment on the filmmakers' part of the anachronistic feminism informing the rest of the film.

Political correctness is firmly in the saddle again when Bill Munny calls on his old friend and fellow ex-ruffian Ned Logan to enlist him in the enterprise, even if it means splitting the reward money three ways. Logan is played by the terrific black actor Morgan Freeman, whose race is, even more anachronistically, never commented on, not even by that loudmouthed Texan, the Schofield Kid, who objects only to his diminished profit. Ned, the black man, proves to be the noblest person in the movie. It is hard to persuade him to revert to his killing days, and he does it only because a woman has been abused. When the shooting starts, he can summon up no taste for it, and sorrowfully quits, offering his rifle to Bill, who returns it.

Needless to say, Ned falls into Daggett's hands, but even under merciless flogging refuses to reveal Bill and the Kid's whereabouts. Only when the torture becomes infernal does he spill a bean or two. His mate is an Indian woman (the only Indian in the movie), and she is just as humane as he. When he rides off with Bill and the Kid, she says nothing; she merely looks at the gun protruding from his saddle pack, and her expression is one of ineffable sadness. True, she is silent throughout her single, brief scene; but here her silence reaches the height of nonviolent protest.

There is also W. W. Beauchamp, the writer of cheap westerns, who travels with English Bob as his portable Boswell. This is the cowardly intellectual, ignorant about what really matters, misdirecting his adulation, and officiously getting in his betters' way. And there is Skinny, the saloon owner, a craven, crawling capitalist exploiting his women workers, and valuing a girl no more than a horse. This is even better than political correctness: this is populism. One wonders to what extent the filmmakers believe this stuff and to what extent they are only pandering to their actual or presumed audience.

Nevertheless, there is also much solid craftsmanship here. As director, Eastwood knows the virtue of not rushing things, of allowing talk, fumbling words, stumblings into silence to make their points. He and his cinematographer, Jack N. Green, avoid shooting for obvious beauty, picturesqueness, and the Canadian Tourist Office. (Most of the filming took place around Calgary.) Outdoors it is usually overcast or snowy or, most often, storming or raining polecats and dogeys. Indoors it is generally dark, and what light there is is often moody backlighting. There is relatively little shooting, and even that frequently erratic. But it hurts: people die painfully, sometimes, indeed, grotesquely.

Certain characterizations and relationships have originality. The Kid behaves less than entirely predictably, and Munny himself, the most cliché-ridden figure (he even rides a near-cliché—an off-white horse), has his atypical moments. There is a nice scene between him and Delilah, and even the obligatory give-and-take between him and the Kid manages to sprinkle some idiosyncratic spice on the standard fare. Still, the most interesting character is that doggone Daggett, and Gene Hackman plays him to the hilt, and not an inch beyond. By far the best scene is the nocturnal one in which he has English Bob and Beauchamp behind bars, and he sits at a table outside their cell. Jeeringly he reads Beauchamp's penny-dreadful novelization of Bob's derring-do out loud, sneering at writer and wrongdoer alike. Saul Rubinek (Beauchamp) is superlatively unctuous and spongy, and Richard Harris offers bravura seething as Daggett taunts and tempts him with a tossed-in gun into a duel Bob is bound to lose.

But such good moments are possible mostly when there are no righteous characters around (and they are fairly ubiquitous) to nudge their righteousness, however modestly and self-effacingly, into self-righteousness. Eastwood's own acting is adequate; the others, several of them Canadians, are admirable, including Jaimz Woolvett as the Kid. Yet almost everything Fenin and Everson say apropos of *The Gunfighter* in their seminal study *The Western* is pertinent here:

> In films whose theme has been that of the young hoodlum out to make his reputation by killing a wanted man, sympathy has always been with the older outlaw and almost never with the younger would-be fighter, who is invariably presented as sadistic or maladjusted. While this in a sense whitewashes the older outlaw, especially since he is also presented as a man weary of killing, aware that he is doomed, at the same time notions of violence for glory's sake and the temptation to take the law into one's own hands are heartily condemned. But in essence, one is asked to sympathize with the killer and to reject a man whose actions, if not motivations, will benefit law and order.

True, the Kid here doesn't try to shoot Munny, and Bill neither is nor feels doomed, but the situation is just as stereotypical—and morally ambiguous. Here Munny gets his money and, as a title card informs us, moves with his kids to San Francisco, there to become a successful businessman. Virtue is and isn't its own reward. *Unforgiven* isn't and is forgiven.

Worst Guys Finish First

BOB ROBERTS; GLENGARRY GLEN ROSS

All extremism—Left or Right, black or white is heinous. Conservatism can be perverted into sclerosis; radicalism easily turns into despotism. The satraps of the Right are as atavistic as the firebrands of the Left, and the permissiveness of the knee-jerk liberals does at least as much damage as the stodginess of the reactionaries. A movie such as *Bob Roberts*, pretending to be a courageous political fable, is only an elaboration of radical-populist skits and songs from the old Greenwich Village cabarets and jazz joints—as brave as, say, a satire on some snake-handling cult pretending to be an attack on Christianity.

Tim Robbins, the writer, director, co-songwriter, and star of the film, who grew up as the son of a Greenwich Village folk-club manager, says his parents weren't radicals or hippies, though his mother aroused him one night when he was 11 with the news that he should be very proud of his sister: "She was arrested for protesting the Vietnam War." The mentality that informs *Bob Roberts* is the spirit of 1968, which, for all its gallant attitudinizing, was not quite the equal of that of 1776. Bob Roberts is a young right-wing demagogue from Pennsylvania, a candidate for the Senate on a platform that ostensibly stands for solid yuppie values such as fighting drugs, and thereby deflects attention from graver issues. For behind genial, clean-cut Bob, campaigning by means of folk-like songs he writes and performs accompanying himself on the guitar, lurks the threat of right-wing totalitarianism.

The Roberts campaign team, with everyone looking like a cross between a debutante-partygoer and an IBM office manager, is targeting straight-arrow yuppies and their megabucks-toting parents, with the slyly treacherous Bob using the folk music of the sixties' youth movement with wickedly reactionary lyrics to infiltrate the psyches of disenchanted ex-flower children and back-to-basics backlashers. Oh, the sacrilege of it! The songs of freedom subverted by Richard Nixon masquerading as Phil Ochs, an act at least as iconoclastic as turning *Madama Butterfly* into *Miss Saigon*. If the noblest thing the liberals can find for the conservatives to besmirch are the songs of Joan Baez, and if the best values the liberals can uphold are the natterings of Brickley Paiste—the incumbent old-style-liberal senator played by Gore Vidal, who improvised much of his dialogue—the world is well lost, no matter who stays un-besmirched.

The film's artsy format has Terry Manchester, a British filmmaker (nicely played by Brian Murray), shooting a documentary on Roberts as he stomps around Pennsylvania. Interviewing Bob, his staff, his fans, and his detractors, Terry becomes more and more disgusted. Much of the film uses the possibly ingenious and certainly economical device of shooting itself through the eye of a documentarist's mostly hand-held camera. This saves a lot of money on elaborate camera set-ups, and allows all kinds of booboos to look like the realistic portrayal of chaos.

The result, however, is a movie very hard to watch. Following that frantic hand-held camera, you feel chained into a canoe shooting a nasty set of falls, and this with a stomach already nauseated by the crude oversimplifications, the stretchings of credibility, the self-congratulatory smugness of sequence after sequence. No major character emerges as sympathetic in the least. Obviously, not Roberts; but not Bugs Raplin, either, the muckraking reporter for an underground paper, who in the process of getting the goods on Roberts proves himself obnoxious to the point of insanity.

Nor can one have much warm feeling for Brickley Paiste, whose very name suggests a stuffiness that Gore Vidal supplies in spades. It's hard to tell what Robbins had in mind here; he may have wanted the senator to be touching in his inability to counter with reason the smear tactics of his opponent. But Robbins may have been so awed by Vidal as to be unable to control him (he felt that the film project had been "validated" by Vidal's acceptance of the role). In any case, Vidal's delivery, quite aside from the content, is so filled with effete snobbery and languid condescension that Paiste emerges pastily unsympathetic.

Nor is Robbins the right actor for Roberts. Though talented, he conveys more smart-ass brattishness than—what would be more believable and frightening—solid Middle American values corrupted by greed. There should be something more archetypally spic-and-span about him, grinningly slippery. Again, Giancarlo Esposito, a charismatic actor, goes, or is made to go, way over the top as Bugs. As Lukas Hart III, Bob's aptly named campaign manager, the able British actor Alan Rickman overplays cobra-eyed Machiavellianism exponentially, and June Stein manages to lose sympathy for a righteous staffer of *The Cutting Edge* show (read: *Saturday Night Live*) by overdoing hysteria.

The best performances come in tiny roles, many of them from famous actors impersonating a variety of news-casters and TV personalities, though even these are sometimes conceived and executed too broadly, notably by Susan Sarandon, Robbins's companion and the mother of his children. And the movie's latter parts escalate unbelievability into utter preposterousness. Most discomfiting, though, is the self-contradictory message the film gives off. It is supposed to remind people, Tim Robbins has said, of the importance of their vote. Yet in portraying a political scene so scurvy, a nation of stooges so easily manipulated by scoundrels, whom does it encourage us to vote for?

All-pervasive corruption is also the subject of *Glengarry Glen Ross,* which David Mamet has adapted from his own Broadway hit. It concerns a handful of seedy real-estate salesmen in a shabby workplace, run from "downtown" by their ruthless bosses, Mitch and Murray—never seen, but always dreaded. Right now the salesmen are supposed to be selling plots of Glengarry Highlands, actually worthless Florida wetlands, and the "leads" they get from downtown are mostly clients who have either been bled dry or who never had any serious intention of buying. There are also some live leads, kept carefully locked up by Williamson (Kevin Spacey), the office manager, who is a kind of miniature Mitch or Murray. These good leads will presumably go to Ricky Roma, the salesman on a fantastic lucky streak, a piece of favoritism bitterly resented by the rest.

Blake (Alec Baldwin), described as a "hot-shot consultant," comes in to conduct a sales meeting in which he sarcastically and threateningly informs the men—except Roma, who, riding high and setting up a sucker for the kill, doesn't ever bother to attend—that this month's prize to the best salesman will be a Cadillac Eldorado; the second prize, a set of steak knives. Third prize? You get fired. The men are seething, demanding better leads to no avail.

Who are these men? Shelley "the Machine" Levene (Jack Lemmon), sixtyish, with a daughter in the hospital needing an expensive operation has been off his form for some time. A former winner, he exudes spurious confidence and charm as he goes off on house calls ("sits") or tries to bribe Williamson into giving him better leads. An even more luckless and desperate version of the same man is George Aaronow (Alan Arkin), whose conversation is virtually reduced to blankly repeating bits of what his interlocutor has just said. Dave Moss (Ed Harris) is younger, meaner, more scared, and more dangerous; with George's help, he wants to break into the safe holding the leads. Ricky Roma (Al Pacino) is both phonily impassioned and supremely cool as he cons a pathetic victim, James Lingk (Jonathan Pryce); this Roma could coax money, if not blood, out of stones.

The plot leads up to an office burglary, an inside job, and the ensuing police investigation. But the film is mostly about the scams these salesmen come up with, the dog-eat-dog rivalry among them, and also, at the same time, the solidarity that unites them against their evil superiors, making them as tightly knit as a football team, a happy family, or the inmates of Death Row. And, as always with Mamet, the film is about language.

These salesmen share the lingo of the damned, which consists chiefly of the F-word in every known permutation and combination, sometimes rising to unparalleled heights of—not invention so much as repetition. It's a litany, a chant, a howl of anger and attempted release. It is an incantation to squelch your enemies, boost your morale, establish your potency (of every kind), call down on you the favor of the gods. It is by no means Mamet's discovery— though he must have personally encountered it in a Chicago real estate office where he worked for a while—but none of its practitioners in literature has carried it to such depths of perfection. I myself am neither fascinated nor disgusted by it; merely, as by all forms of fanatical reiteration, bored.

There is no character in *Glengarry Glen Ross* whom one can sympathize with. Everyone lives by rotten values and practices fraud and self-deception with equal zeal. Success is as contemptible here as abject failure; and, unlike in *Bob Roberts*, there are not even redeeming minor characters. The one outsider, Lingk, is almost too pathetic to elicit any pity. Predictably, the small-time crooks come to grief, while the big ones prosper. The offensive thing here, however, is the implication that this is the world: our entire, beastly capitalist society.

Now, I am willing to entertain any notion provided it is proffered by a genuine artist. There is about almost everything Mamet writes, though, such an aura of self-admiring smugness, of authorial oneupmanship, that I feel untempted, let alone compelled, to trust him. His view is not darkly tragic, or even darkly comic, his concern is to render everything as glossily black as the best-shined shoes. I remain unimpressed by an author who tries to dazzle me with the sheen of his footwear.

But James Foley has directed with great liveliness and variety in what is, for the most part, a tight, non-cinematic space. And the actors are a spectacular ensemble. Jack Lemmon gives a performance of terrifying realism—like watching a burning candle in the image of yourself guttering to slow, inexorable extinction. Al Pacino starts out too abstractedly, his far-roving gaze apparently out for some sort of long-distance record, but then settles into an image of heaven-storming fanaticism that makes his cajolings and outbursts better than dramatic, operatic. Alan Arkin is the epitome of devertebrated defeat, and Ed Harris oozes such dirty malice, you'd think he'd have to change shirts hourly. Alec Baldwin turns contempt into a deadly weapon, Jonathan Pryce displays an inimitable hangdog hopefulness, and Kevin Spacey, perhaps most remarkable of all, conveys complete sliminess convinced of its own integrity. But even the best acting and directing can only turn a sow's ear into a full, but not a silken, purse.

Van Gogh

There has been a proliferation of films about Vincent van Gogh, the painter who, along with Rembrandt, most exercises the popular imagination. And van Gogh has the edge over Rembrandt for having been mad; there is nothing the public relishes more than the image of the artist as madman and failure. A painter who in his 37 years sold only one painting—there's something to feel comfortingly superior to! "And yet what beauty the poor fellow created," the prosaic burgher sighs with patronizing melancholy, to show that he is no philistine, after all.

Whatever one may say against Maurice Pialat's *Van Gogh*, one must concede that it is the most detailed scrutiny yet of van Gogh's last phase, and the least conventional. It's the final 67 days of the painter's life, under the supervision of Dr. Gachet at Auvers-sur-Oise, that this 155-minute movie examines Pialat is in some ways a kindred spirit of van Gogh's: he, too, was a painter; he, too, tried various things before finding his real calling; he, too, is said to be hard to get along with. The film is an interesting combination of telling all (including some apparently new findings) realistically, and also respecting the ultimate mystery of genius without trying to explain it away.

I am insufficiently versed in the vast literature on van Gogh to say how much of the movie, which Pialat both wrote and directed, is documented fact, and how much surmise or pure invention. But as Pialat conceives Vincent, and as Jacques Dutronc plays him, this is more of a normal human being tormented by syphilis-induced headaches and outbursts of fury than some sort of divine madman lightly touching the earth on his transit to the stars. He has an affair with Marguerite, Gachet's spirited but undisciplined daughter: abandons her for his former favorite among prostitutes, then resumes with her; has a complicated relationship with his devoted brother and keeper, Theo, and Johanna, Theo's wife, whose financial concern for their growing family conflicts with her husband's fraternal charity; and finds Dr. Gachet rather less tolerant after he discovers the dalliance with his daughter.

Dr. G. Kraus, the Dutch alienist who published a 49-page analysis of van Gogh's "illness" in 1941, could not resolve what it was, though he did call it psychopathic: "In his art no less than in his 'illness,' [van Gogh] was an individualist," he concluded. But the painter Paul Signac, a friend of Vincent's, wrote, "Never did he give me the impression of being a madman. Though he ate hardly anything, what he drank was always too much . . . absinthes and brandies would follow one another . . . He was charm personified. He loved life passionately." There are as many van Goghs as there are people writing about him.

Pialat's Vincent does not drink all that much, but he is intense, unpredictable, sometimes violent. Mostly, though, he is silent and aloof. The talking is done chiefly by others, notably Marguerite, who chatters on and on. Although the cut-off ear is mentioned, when the camera zeroes in on it, we see it is unscathed. Is Pialat trying to tell us something, or was it simply easier and cheaper not to bother? Dutronc, though a good actor, evidently did not take the role seriously enough to sacrifice so much as a lobe to it. The actor did not even make much of an effort to achieve physical likeness to Vincent, just as the excellent Bernard Le Coq is not made up to look like Theo. A beard is as far as either will go toward visual verisimilitude—perhaps just as well.

Authoritativeness is achieved in other ways. What little we see of Vincent's hand as it attacks a canvas looks authentic, as do the sitters and landscapes of Vincent's paintings. But the paintings are not brought to life in showy, extended fashion; they are tossed off with canny casualness. So, too, fellow artists such as Toulouse-Lautrec and Suzanne Valadon (then still an artist's model) make appropriately throwaway appearances, even as life in the bistros and brothels is swiftly but flavorously captured.

There is good acting from everyone, notably from Gérard Séty as a well-meaning, supportive, but not especially competent—and eventually torn and exasperated—Gachet, and from Leslie Azzoulai as the quietly devoted innkeeper's daughter who intermittently looks after Vincent. The film is rich in atmosphere, and conveys moods incisively, but answers no previously unanswered questions. Two and a half hours plus is a long time, and there are moments when we do yearn for that gunshot to ring out across the wheatfields.

For my money, the finest evocation of van Gogh's spirit is still the shortest: Jacques Prévert's magnificent poem "*Complainte de Vincent*," with such verses in it as "*Il a le regard bleu et doux / Le vrai regard lucide et fou / De ceux qui donnent tout à la vie.* " I cannot translate this—nobody can—without losing the music, the poetry: the very things that Pialat's film cannot catch for all its dogged sincerity.

Not for Enlightened Buddhists

BRAM STOKER'S DRACULA;
TOUS LES MATINS DU MONDE

Why the perennial fascination of horror movies? If we are to believe Gore Vidal (in *Screening History*) it is that "any confirmation that life continues after death has an appeal to almost everyone except enlightened Buddhists. No one wants to be extinct." But extinction may be preferable to afterlife as a vampire in a Francis Ford Coppola movie. The latest, *Bram Stoker's Dracula*, tries to be for Dracula what *Apocalypse Now* was for Vietnam, and the *Godfather* trilogy for the Mafia: gigantism as an end in itself, *lusher* as a synonym for *better*.

Perhaps I am being hopelessly old-fashioned but I don't trust people who can't tell the difference between *lie* and *lay* as far as I can throw up. In this movie, we keep hearing "lay down" and "lay back," and in the screenplay by James V. Hart (scenarist also of the hopeless *Hook*) we read: "Panels pull apart to reveal Dracula laying in his 'day coma.'" Would you, *mutatis mutandis*, commission a score from a tone-deaf composer?

If you lust for luxury, to be sure, *Bram Stoker's Dracula*, i.e., Francis Ford Coppola's *Dracula*, may be your *Dracula*, too. But if you want a film that knows what it wants and goes about its business efficiently, don't touch this one with a ten-foot stake. Coppola has engaged the services of a talented jet-set crew. The Japanese designer Eiko Ishioka has dreamed up her most nightmarish costumes, the German cinematographer Michael Ballhaus has come up with his customary spellbinding images, and the Polish composer Wojciech Kilar (best known for his work for Wajda) has concocted music that is no joke. Countless craftsmen, technicians, and special-effects wizards—and no fewer than three editors—have contributed their skills. The eye and the ear are dazzled, but the nose must be held.

The movie may be faithful in its fashion-show fashion to Bram Stoker's fustian novel, but faithfulness is a virtue only if its object is deserving. The film does not know what it is doing. It tries to make Dracula as sympathetic as he is horrible, for which the genius of a Shakespeare would be required. It makes Mina, the lovable heroine, love Dracula more than she does Jonathan, her fiancé, which does not make our hearts go out to her. It tries to give us the historic background of Dracula, the Romanian despot Vlad the Impaler, but in a kind of foreshortening that turns history into a comic strip. The protagonist is allowed so many different shapes that we perceive him more as a quick-change artist than as a vampire. And Coppola and Hart do not know how to invest the preposterous with the slightest aura of plausibility.

The film steals from all over. Its debt to Murnau's *Nosferatu* and Tay Garnett's *Dracula* is understandable, but must there also be cribbing from Cocteau's *La Belle et la bête* and Fellini's *Casanova*? I refer to the human arms as flambeaus, and to the twin peaks sausage-roll hairdo for Dracula, which makes his head look impaled on the horns of a dilemma. But the worst theft may be replicating a dated novel about Victorian dread of sexuality instead of imaginatively rethinking it along modern lines—or, better yet, dropping it altogether.

Gary Oldman, a fine actor, strives to play a thinking man's Dracula, but between that effort and the straining to sound Transylvanian, he ends up giving a performance so carefully calibrated as to lose all semblance of trash-movie spontaneity. As Doctor Van Helsing, Anthony Hopkins has an even harder time with his Dutch accent, and ends up merely peppering his lines with random *jas*. But what to do with a part that calls on him to answer Mina's anguished "You want to dissect her?" with a casual "Not really; I just want to cut off her head and take out her heart"? Winona Ryder, as Mina, manages a better British accent than one might have expected, and is very pretty except for her slightly batlike ears, which may explain her susceptibility to vampires. As Jonathan, Keanu Reeves looks befuddled, and delivers his lines in an electronically amplified whisper. Tom Waits, as Renfield, swallows various insects with real gusto, which may account for his patented growl as mere flies on the voice box.

A young English actress, Sadie Frost, plays the campy role of Lucy rather too cloyingly, but with a persuasively bared left breast. Three international models play the brides of Dracula even more bared—from fangs to (nearly) crotch—and would do any burlesque house proud. Coppola indulges himself in any number of such fancy touches. Thus he makes Dracula wear contact lenses of various colors to match the degree of luridness of the situation; allows "Dracula" to be pronounced in three separate ways; and cuts whimsically from a stake being driven into someone to someone eating steak, which makes the more sophisticated punsters in the audience squeal like a bunch of moon-mad paronomasiacs.

Arguably the strangest film I've ever seen is *Tous les Matins du monde*, which won seven Césars (French Oscars) in 1991, as well as other prizes, and turned all France baroque-happy. It is the fictionalized story of two real-life baroque musicians: Monsieur de Sainte Colombe, so reclusive that his first name remains unknown, and Marin Marais (1656–1728), whose viola da gamba gambols are much better known. The film is based on a novel by Pascal Quignard, who co-wrote the script with Alain Corneau, the director.

Although *Matins* has a plot of sorts, it is mostly about playing the bass viol. The film flaunts almost continuous bass-viol playing, on the soundtrack by one, two, or three instruments; on the screen by Sainte Colombe, his daughters Madeleine and Toinette, and Marin Marais in various combinations. If in a moment of charity the bass viols stop their infernal scraping, the characters discuss bass-viol playing and musicianship in general ad nauseam.

Let not Bill Buckley read this review, for I am about to confess that I know of no sounds less bearable than those of baroque music, unless it be baroque music played on one, two, or three bass viols, than which I can think of nothing more base and vile. Since the two-hour film seems to go on for centuries, I kept hoping we would get to Berlioz, where French music gets bearable, but no such luck. Jordi Savall and his consort of musicians just kept fiddling away on the soundtrack; not since the unendurably 'umble Uriah Heep has there been such bowing and scraping.

The story, or what passes for it, concerns Sainte Colombe's rude refusal to play for the king at court, and eventual ceasing to play even for his fellow villagers. He now makes music only at home with his daughters. In the end, he has a cottage built on the grounds where he plays for no one but the ghost of his beloved dead wife, who sits there, untouchable but undeterred, raptly listening to him. Brash young Marais intrudes on the master's isolation and demands lessons; the contemptuous master listens to him and sneers, "You make music; you are not a musician." But with support from the sex-starved daughters, Marin gets reluctantly taken on as a pupil by Papa, and taken into her bed by Madeleine, the elder sister.

In due time, however, nothing can keep the virtuosic Marais from abandoning Madeleine and artistic purity ("Life, to be sweet, must be cruel!") and hotfingering it to Versailles to become Musician Ordinary to the King's Chamber and, later on, time beater (there were no conductors yet) to the Paris Opera. Still, for three years running, he keeps riding back clandestinely every night to glue his ear to the master's cabin in the hope of overhearing his secret. (Earlier, he and Madeleine used to hide in a ditch under the cabin, listening, but were discovered by Papa and chased away.) When he comes upon Sainte Colombe dying, Marais is let in for a final debate about music and a last session of battling bass viols.

But no summary can do justice to the absurdity of the film, with its alternating dawdlings and lurchings forward, static camera setups, hopelessly arty visual compositions, and sublimely artsy-fartsy dialogue. Yet it exercises a horrible fascination, like watching midgets playing basketball or listening to stutterers discussing Wittgenstein. Any moment, you feel, you might lapse into helpless giggles or a rampaging rage. But you end up just sitting there, as if suspended by your disbelief, anaesthetized by your incredulity at such toweringly arrogant kitsch. If hokum has a stratosphere, you are in it.

Jean-Pierre Marielle is a marvelously sourpussy Sainte Colombe of whom you can easily believe that he would punitively lock his daughters into the cellar and forget them there—the baroque precursor of *Home Alone*. No less superb is Anne Brochet as Madeleine, the *jolie laide*, love-starved virgin who falls hard for young Marin, and, ditched, dies lingeringly of accumulated bitterness. Mlle Brochet in a nightgown ugly enough to become her shroud, and tossing about and out of her sickbed as she lets the camera scan her ravaged-looking legs and pudenda, offers a vision of spurned femininity powerful enough to make watching her an almost guilty pleasure.

As young Marin, Guillaume Depardieu seems quite untalented, but wonderfully doltish and loutish. Papa Gérard, as the aging—bloated, beribboned, bedizened—Marais, looking in a peruke like a mastiff masquerading as a poodle, is at least more credible here than as Columbus elsewhere. Yves Angelo's cinematography and Alain Corneau's direction are appropriately stilted and emphatic, but the English subtitles try to jazz up things by translating the decorous *sexe* (penis) as prick. It doesn't work; baroque will not be jazzed up.

Malcolm X

Into his short life, *Malcolm X* (1925–1965) packed many careers, from criminal to ascetic; and many ideologies, from extremist white-hating black nationalism to some sort of incipient tolerance and ecumenism. I know no more about the Black Muslim orator and organizer than anyone would who lived in New York City during the first lustrum of the sixties, when Malcolm X's rise within the Nation of Islam, expulsion, and murder made headlines, and I am not especially qualified to assess the value of Spike Lee's three-hour-and-twenty-one-minute *Malcolm X* from the historical standpoint (for that see "Bad Rap for Malcolm X" by Carol Iannone, *National Review*, Dec. 14, 1992).

Even so, having read some of the printed matter that has recently been gushing forth on the subject, I can safely say that although Lee has not turned out a hagiography, neither has he gone into the particularly spiky aspects of Malcolm's history: his negotiations on behalf of Elijah Muhammad with the KKK, his excursions into homosexuality and male hustling, and the Nation of Islam's anti-Semitism, which he espoused. But even without those elements, and the alleged burning down of his own house for propaganda purposes, Malcolm

X leaves room enough for the filmmaker to cover all kinds of ground, from rough to smooth to tragic: from Malcolm Little, the preacher's son in Omaha, whose father is allegedly murdered by whites and whose mother goes mad, to El-Hajj Malik El-Shabazz, the independent black leader gunned down at the Audubon Ballroom less than a year after his eye-opening pilgrimage to Mecca.

In between, we get Detroit Red, the red-headed hustler in Roxbury, Massachusetts, and, later, Harlem—the fellow who dabbled in pimping and robbery while living with Sophia, a Cadillac-driving white good-time girl; Satan, the recalcitrant inmate who, during six and a half years in jail, went from hell-raiser to self-taught intellectual (with guidance from the fictitious Baines, a fellow prisoner and Elijah Muhammad henchman who turns Malcolm around); and Malcolm X, the beloved lieutenant of Elijah Muhammad, whom Malcolm worshipped for years until he discovered his polygyny, and, denouncing it, got himself drummed out of the Nation of Islam. And, of course, the loving husband of Betty Shabazz and father of three daughters, all of whom his political activities kept him away from far too often and, at last, irrecoverably.

Such a life guarantees a filmmaker the virtual impossibility of boring his audience, however long his movie. For my money, this is the first film with which Shelton Jackson Spike Lee, assistant professor of Contemporary American Cinema in Harvard's Afro-American department, has made a genuine contribution to Contemporary American Cinema. I do not think that *Malcolm X* is a totally honest movie—if it were, it would offend almost everybody—but it is a genuine piece of filmmaking, with a savvily paced story, bustling and bristling atmosphere, security of technical execution, and devilishly good acting.

Marvin Worth—who bought the rights to *The Autobiography of Malcolm X* from Betty Shabazz and Alex Haley, who, with Malcolm, wrote it (neither Malcolm, embellishing his past, nor Haley, the plagiarist and mythologizer of *Roots*, is to be entirely trusted with words)—has for a quarter-century struggled to get the film made. At first, James Baldwin, the black novelist, joined by Arnold Perl, a blacklisted screenwriter, tried to come up with a script. They died, and Calder Willingham, David Mamet, David Bradley, and Charles Fuller made unsuccessful stabs at a screenplay. Finally, Spike Lee revised the Baldwin-Perl script, from which, for reasons that remain murky, Baldwin's name was dropped, leaving Perl-Lee victorious. Someday a student of Contemporary American Cinema will have fun writing a dissertation on who wrote what in this screenplay, which, barring a few anachronisms, sounds authentic enough.

Even so, what was needed was a charismatic actor to portray the red headed firebrand; in Denzel Washington, Lee was lucky to find the ideal interpreter. If anything, too good, for though Denzel resembles Malcolm a lot, he is better-looking and does not have the slightly desiccated quality one associates with that haggard figure in the sixties. Washington manages to be playful and formidable, touching and terrifying, without once seeming excessive in a role that must have been an invitation to excess. Angela Bassett plays his wife with the straightforwardness bordering on cliché with which the part is written. Al Freeman Jr. conveys admirably the disquieting singsong and ominous jollity of Elijah Muhammad, and as Baines, the man who converts Malcolm in prison to the Nation of Islam, Albert Hall is stunning.

There is similarly magnetic work from Delroy Lindo as West Indian Archie, the drug dealer who recruits Malcolm into crime, and Kate Vernon as Sophia, Malcolm's white mistress, particularly convincing in the bedroom sequence in which Malcolm makes her kiss his foot. Theresa Randle is touching as his black sweetheart who ends badly; Lonette McKee is perhaps a touch too glamorous as his mother, but good, as are countless others. Some famous black or white actors, and no less famous non-actors, appear in cameo roles, and it is equal fun to spot them or to discover only afterward who they were.

Lee himself plays Shorty, an early companion of Malcolm's in mischief, and though he is all right, he is the only cast member who makes you aware that you are watching an actor—or, in this case, director. The zoot suits he and Malcolm wear in the early sequences are flamboyant enough to start a conflagration, and contrast expressively with Malcolm's later Ivy-League-cum-IBM-office-manager look. As ever, Ernest Dickerson is Lee's cinematographer, and he once again indulges his trademark juxtaposition of warmly lit and broodingly dark areas within the same frame, suggesting not so much chiaroscuro as a divided screen. There is a brief recurrence of Lee's crazy effect from *Jungle Fever* of keeping the actor static while ostensibly moving the background, and one or two other indulgences recalling *School Daze*.

None of this matters much; the film charges ahead with such a voracity to fulfill itself that you cannot but bobsled along. Terence Blanchard's original score is unobtrusive, and the exteriors look consistently right. It's nice that Lee was allowed to film—a world first—in Mecca, and make us all vicarious hajjis. The one thing that does not get fully conveyed is Malcolm's conversion on this pilgrimage upon encountering blond, blue-eyed, fair-skinned Muslims. How many of those could there have been? And can one be sure they didn't wear contacts and dye their hair?

On the other hand, Lee makes no bones about blaming the NoI for Malcolm's assassination, albeit with the tacit collusion of the FBI. That scene is staged with tremendous urgency and persuasiveness. Genuine flaws occur only at the beginning and end. In the pre-title sequence, we get the videotaped beating of Rodney King by the Los Angeles police; at the very end, we watch black schoolchildren jumping to their feet one after another in a classroom to shout: "I am Malcolm X!" At such times, an otherwise dignified work stoops to agit-prop.

Antiestablishmentarians

A FEW GOOD MEN; LORENZO'S OIL

On Broadway, *A Few Good Men* proved good, gripping boulevard fare, albeit a great wide way from art; I wish that at least that much could be claimed for the movie version. But thanks to the adaptation by Aaron Sorkin, the playwright himself (with an assist, we hear, from William Goldman), and the direction by Rob Reiner, just about everything that could go wrong did; even so, the movie, based on an actual incident, should not be dismissed by those who missed the play: it could have some educational value for people who depend on movies for their education. (Their numbers may well be legion.)

Two Marines from the U.S. Navy base at Guantanamo Bay are on trial in a Washington military court for the murder of another marine, Pfc. Santiago, to whom they administered a supposedly unordered Marine Corps hazing (Code Red), in the course of which they allegedly stuffed a poisoned rag into Santiago's mouth. With a weak heart, and unable to keep up with Marine rigors in a subtropical climate, Santiago—denied a transfer by the fanatical commanding officer, Colonel Nathan Jessep (even though his adjutant recommended it)—has been writing desperate letters to influential Washingtonians, offering to reveal details of an illegal "fence-line shooting" at a Cuban watchtower in exchange for his transfer. One of the accused killers is Corporal Dawson, a gung-ho black Marine, fiercely dedicated to the code of "unit, corps, God, and country." The other is his taciturnly reverential, possibly slow-witted sidekick, Pfc. Downey.

The Navy assigns to their defense Lieutenant (j.g.) Daniel Kaffee, a snide young man 15 months out of Harvard Law School, the son of a legendary Navy lawyer, and himself a brilliant plea bargainer, a talent he is expected to use here. And so he intends, preferring to shine on a softball field rather than grub away in a courtroom. He assumes the men to be guilty; not so Lieutenant Commander JoAnne Galloway, an attractive, idealistic Navy lawyer, likewise assigned to the case, though in a less important capacity, who believes in their innocence. The third member of the defense team, Lieutenant Sam Weinberg, Kaffee's friend and an expert at research, perceives the accused as unsavory American equivalents of Nazi soldiers blindly executing grisly orders, but believes in justice for them all the same.

Gradually, thanks to JoAnne's dedication, Jessep's manifest amorality and near-dementia, and the keenness of his own intelligence once aroused, Kaffee goes into action—spurred on also by Corporal Dawson's contempt for the seeming time-server assigned to defend him. Many aspects of military life get touched on lightly—too lightly—as the movie works up to the climax even the converted Kaffee long resisted: an apparently unequal confrontation between himself and the much-decorated model martinet, Jessep. There are veiled allusions to the uneasy interrelations among different ethnic groups, to the ambiguities of men and women together in uniform, to the conflict between robotic obedience and high-risk personal morality, to the differences between branches of service (the more relaxed Navy, the more fanatical Marines), to latent homosexuality (Downey's feelings for Dawson), and so on.

Yet all this impinges only very shadowily on the proceedings, which in the play at least were not further diluted with Rob Reiner's irrelevant inferiority feelings toward his famous father, superimposed on the movie version. Sorkin's real aim was simple: a good yarn and plenty of excitement, which he duly delivered on stage with the help of a better director, Don Scardino, and a generally more believable cast. Tom Hulce, though no favorite of mine, was a more credible Kaffee than pretty-boy Tom Cruise, whose high-pitched voice has to be electronically transposed downward to make it aurally palatable, and whose acting has an inescapably gee-whiz quality about it. Demi Moore, as JoAnne Galloway, gives an earnest, balanced performance, but she lacks the fetching spontaneity of the actress who, on Broadway, played the part so well that the playwright married her.

The movie's biggest loss is the absence of Steven Lang, who made Jessep into an absolutely persuasive, bone-chillingly scary, and ultimately pathetic monster. But Hollywood wanted a "name," and got it in Jack Nicholson. What made Lang so fine was that, even though unhinged, he had the unfussy, self-assured dementia that might do for a potential trouble spot such as Guantanamo, where a maniac who identifies himself with the safety of the nation might find favor even with judicious heads. Nicholson, however, who recycles his Joker from *Batman*, comes across frequently laughable, full of jeering malevolence, as one using his power for some insidious, perverse purpose of his own. Instead of the intended Creon figure, we get a sinister mountebank, whose patent anomaly lets the system off the hook. Thus Sorkin's Antigone—Kaffee—is reduced from a potential reformer to a mere jolly giant-killer.

One thing the movie makes abundantly clear is that Rob Reiner has an excellent reason for feeling inferior to his (not all *that* wonderful) father: Rob is a hack director. The concatenation of three shots in which we see Kaffee meditating in the shadow of the Jefferson Memorial while a hammy sunset haloes his head is a good example of the film's shopworn aesthetics. Perhaps the best thing in it is the solid performance by Kiefer Sutherland as Lieutenant Kendrick, the executive arm of Jessep's Machiavellianism, and the ominous reminder that the Jesseps of this world are self-perpetuating, even if the film's happy ending would have us believe otherwise. Even the final irony—that Dawson and Downey are saved in a way they don't want to be is all but lost in Reiner and Sorkin's sanitizing glibness.

If *A Few Good Men* halfheartedly questions the sacrosanctness of the military establishment, *Lorenzo's Oil* does much better with the medical establishment (including the FDA), sensibly allowing the antagonist some dignity and credibility in wrongheadedness. This is the story of a married couple, the Italian economist Augusto Odone and his Irish-American linguist wife, Michaela, whose sweet five-year-old son, Lorenzo, starts weirdly misbehaving at school for reasons neither his teachers nor his parents can fathom. After much parental anxiety and medical befuddlement, one doctor makes the correct diagnosis: adrenoleukodystrophy (ALD), an ailment that was as yet very little known in 1984, and for which no therapy existed. The Odones are directed to Washington and Dr. Nikolais, the leading expert on ALD; but all he can do is describe and explain how the patient—always a boy to whom the mother, herself unaffected, transmits the malady—will lose more and more of his faculties, and, in two years, die. Already Lorenzo is suffering from loss of speech and hearing.

I shan't go into the etiology of ALD here, or into the vain attempts at combatting it by Dr. Nikolais and others. The film, directed by the Australian George Miller, himself a physician by training, explains it all very well, without boring and losing the audience. There are visual aids for every theoretical discussion, and the way Miller and his co-scenarist Nick Enright dramatize the sessions with sundry doctors and the diverse ineffectual experiments inflicted on Lorenzo is always lucid, dispassionate, and profoundly affecting; Miller's background as director of the Mad Max action films may have come in handy.

The Odones refuse to take no for an answer. They won't take it from the doctors, and keep reading medical books and journals until they find some useful hints in related research. They don't take it from nurses, as they fire any who won't do the utmost even in seemingly useless care. They won't take it from the government, as they go abroad—to England—for a certain acid that the FDA will not authorize. They won't take it from their own human limitations: performing their other work and duties, they still find the time and strength to give Lorenzo round-the-clock love and care; they stretch their brain power, puzzling out answers to why certain enzymes are shirking *their* duty by the boy. With crayons and boards and diagrams, with paper clips representing molecules, with tired but persevering minds, they go over the same problems, the same lack of answers, again and again. And they certainly don't take no from the ALD support group, headed by a married couple advocating resignation and compliance with the doctors. Instead of going along with them, the Odones proclaim their defiance at the meetings and gain the adherence of another doughty mother.

They have one further, major ally: little Lorenzo himself; with almost superhuman strength, he helps them fight the illness. Even when reduced to an apparent vegetable, he refuses to comply with ALD's supposedly irreversible schedule, and becomes an inspiration to his parents in their struggle. But united as the Odones are against the world, they—understandably enough—sometimes take things out on each other. Yet when one of them temporarily weakens, there is always the other to carry on for both. And Michaela's sister, Deirdre, proves a substantial ally, even though at one point, when—rationally, persuasively—she advocates giving up, she, too, is temporarily banished by her implacable sister.

Step by exhausting step, these no's begin to add up to an enormous yes, as the Odones reverse the path of ALD, and various members of the worlds of business, medicine, and other sciences come to their aid. The story is full of human interest in the best—most unsentimental and, therefore, most moving—sense. It is a remarkable display of what a father's predominantly intellectual passion and a mother's overwhelmingly emotional one can, as complementary equals, do to keep a child alive, and, beyond that, help discover what promises to be a complete cure for a previously fatal illness.

Nick Nolte has obsessively studied Augusto Odone's accent and movements from tapes, and has worked for months with an Italian teacher and a dialect coach. Augusto himself has declared Nolte's accent "just right." I am sorry to have to dissent, but the actor does not convince me with his fine Italian ham—visually, vocally, or histrionically (by which I don't mean histrionics); but I do appreciate his effort. Conversely, Susan Sarandon is entirely persuasive as Michaela, in a performance that, well-nigh miraculously, manages to be both no-holds-barred and subtly controlled. It is uplifting to contemplate how the enchanting sexpot of *Joe* (1970) has evolved into one of our finest dramatic actresses and has, in her last half-dozen movies, proved no less remarkable for her incisiveness than for her range.

Peter Ustinov contributes a nice, understated performance as Dr. Nikolais, who embodies both the strengths and the limitations of the medical establishment, and there is good supporting work from Gerry Bamman, Margo Martindale, Maduka Steady, and James Rebhorn and Ann Hearn as the unctuously superior couple who, prudently and purblindly, make the ALD support group ineffectual. I have difficulties with Kathleen Wilhoite as Deirdre, but this may have to do with her looks rather than with her acting. A special word of commendation for young Zack O'Malley Greenburg, who endures the physically difficult role of Lorenzo with exemplary fortitude and finesse.

Under George Miller's efficacious direction, all technical elements fuse flawlessly, though the production design of Kristi Zea

must be praised as *primus inter pares*. I recommend this film especially to those who might deludedly avoid it as "depressing."

The Smell of the Arty

SCENT OF A WOMAN; THE CRYING GAME

In 1975, Dino Risi, who had directed the brilliant *Il sorpasso* (*The
Easy Life*), made a pleasantly mediocre movie, *Profumo di donna*
(*Scent of a Woman*), from a novel by Giovanni Arpino. It starred
Vittorio Gassman as an ex-army captain who lost his sight and
one hand in a freak accident, and who, too proud to let the world
know he is blind, lives a sequestered life except for occasional jaunts
around Italy, for which he hires some young soldier on leave to be
his seeing-eye boy, whom he always calls Ciccio. His adventures
with the current Ciccio are told with a mixture of comedy and
sentimentality, ending in a specious romance.

Hollywood has bought the title, *Scent of a Woman*, and the basic situation. But Bo Goldman's screenplay upgrades the captain
into Lieutenant Colonel Frank Slade, and downgrades everything
else into the crassest and crudest comedy-drama. Slade is even allowed to keep both hands: Al Pacino, who plays him, must not look
crippled in any way, and besides . . . but let's not anticipate.

In Goldman's version, the point of view is that of the boy,
Charlie Simms, a poor young man on scholarship at a posh New
England private school, who sees some of his rich, spoiled classmates pull a naughty prank on Mr. Trask, the nasty headmaster,
who is evidently also stupid enough to fall for it. Charlie (Chris
O'Donnell) won't squeal on the perpetrators, and Trask gives him
the upcoming Thanksgiving weekend to come across or lose his
chances at Harvard the next fall. In the midst of this quandary, the
poor (in both senses) boy takes on the job of looking after Colonel Slade while his niece, with whom he grudgingly lives, goes
off on a weekend vacation with her family. Why the enormously
self-sufficient Slade would need Charlie's reluctant services at all
remains unclear.

Slade, a drunkard and a bully, immediately bellows at and brutalizes Charlie; he proclaims preppies "a bunch of runny-nosed snots
in tweed jackets, all studying to be George Bush." He so intimidates
Charlie that the boy almost turns down the job. And then the sur-

prise: Slade has planned a weekend in New York City. They are to stay at the Waldorf, eat at the Plaza's Oak Room, get a woman for Frank, and (as Charlie learns later on), at the end, Frank will blow out his brains with his old service revolver.

In New York, things become more preposterous by the minute. Getting from the Waldorf to the Oak Room proves a bit of problem (couldn't they have stayed at the Plaza?) until a nice cabbie is finally found. At the Oak Room, Frank shouts in his usual drillmasterly way, but no one minds in the least. A visit to Frank's brother in suburbia ("Let's surprise him: give that fat heart of his an attack!") ends disastrously, but during cocktail hour at the Trump Tower, Frank gets to dance a mean tango with a young woman whose date is late. Though Gabrielle Anwar is charming, the scene is remarkably unpoignant. For one thing, although it was possible to believe of Vittorio Gassman that he could identify the scent (perfume) of a woman and base on it an accurate character analysis, the only thing we could believe from Al Pacino is a disquisition on body odor.

The first peak of absurdity is reached when Slade, having wangled a Ferrari from the dealer for a test drive, proceeds, in the wee hours, to race the sports car at top speed in downtown Manhattan. At this point, we are forced to draw three conclusions: first, this man is a swine, so to endanger the life of his passenger, Charlie; second, Charlie is an imbecile not to jump out of the car at whatever cost; and third, the director, Martin Brest, is a fool to allow Bo Goldman to write such nonsense.

Almost equally pitiful is the scene in which Charlie tries to talk Frank, by now his surrogate father, out of committing suicide. Pointing the gun at him now, Frank growls, "I don't know whether to shoot you or adopt you," which gives Charlie and the audience a pretty fair example of Hobson's choice. But the second peak of absurdity is not reached until Mr. Trask conducts a McCarthy-style hearing in his school's auditorium, complete with microphones and the presence of all students, teachers, and parents. Frank Slade, claiming to be a relative, acts as Charlie's counsel, and delivers an oration of epic length full of heroic platitudes.

I am surely betraying no secret if I tell you that the devil (Mr. Trask) is shamed, Charlie exonerated, the bloom back on the rose, and Hollywood knee-deep in the usual self-righteous saccharin. It takes the wretched movie two and a half hours, and Pacino enough decibels to stun an ox, to arrive at its foregone conclusion. Even those reviewers who had doubts about the picture tended to extol Pacino's performance as great. For a chaingang boss or a carnival barker, it would be.

In Neil Jordan's *The Crying Game*, Jody, a black British soldier, is held hostage in Northern Ireland by the IRA. He was enticed by a girl, Jude, from a fairground to a deserted spot and, just as he mounted her, nabbed by the IRA (one of whose regulars she is), crowned with a ghastly black hood, and spirited off to a distant hideaway. Unless the British release an IRA bigwig they are holding within three days, Jody dies. Fergus, the IRA volunteer who guards him most of the time, is a decent fellow who takes the stifling hood off Jody whenever he can. Step by step, the two men become friends. Interestingly, the two most intimate things they share are, first, the picture of Dil, Jody's attractive girlfriend, whom Fergus is to look up if Jody is shot: and, second, the fact that, the handcuffed Jody being unable to urinate otherwise. Fergus must take out his penis for him and, later, tuck it back in, midst embarrassment that turns into loudly shared laughter. (We are not shown the modus operandi for defecation.)

When he must be led into the surrounding woods to his doom, Jody runs ahead of Fergus shouting, "You would not shoot a brother in the back?" We don't learn how Fergus would have acted (cheap trick No. 1) because a British tank, a *machina ex machina*, conveniently runs Jody over. The IRA group is seemingly exterminated, but Fergus escapes to London, changes his looks and name (to Jimmy), and becomes a construction worker. He is haunted by the image of Jody, and finally looks up his sexy black girlfriend, Dil, at the shabby hair salon where Jody told him she works, and gets a haircut from her.

He now hangs out at the shady bar Dil frequents, and eventually befriends her, especially after he beats up an obnoxious former lover whom he catches beating *her* up. He is taken into her apartment, full of snapshots of Jody. It is under his, as it were, approving gaze that Jimmy and Dil become lovers. But Jimmy must surmount a big hurdle: to accept that Dil is not what she seems to be. At first he is, literally, nauseated and brutalizes Dil. Gradually love prevails.

Cheap trick No. 2 is that it should have taken Jimmy so long to figure things out; No. 3 is that kind of moral blackmail the filmmakers have practiced on reviewers and audiences not to reveal the Big Surprise. At this point, Jude and Maguire, the leader of the IRA group, who also managed to escape, reappear, and, having (unexplainedly) tracked down Jimmy-Fergus, threaten to kill Dil unless Fergus performs a political assassination for them. As has been remarked by others, *The Crying Game* (titled after a song Dil performs at the said shady bar) does not truly cohere. The IRA thriller and the love triangle cry out for separate movies; though they can, as here, be mashed together, it shortchanges both.

But there is an even graver problem, the Big Surprise that we have all been harangued into not divulging. At what time may a critic address such an issue? Is it all right by now to discuss how the witches' prophecies in *Macbeth* come true? After all, there is one person born every minute who has not yet seen or read the play. Can one evaluate a work of art—and I am quite sure Jordan views his film as such—without going into what most of it hinges on? And is *that* kind of surprise honest art or merely sensationalism? In which case, might not part of the critic's task be warning his readers?

Let me say, then, that *The Crying Game* is homosexual propaganda and not art: not because of the kind of propaganda it is, but because it is propaganda at all, and so the opposite of art. This said, the film, aside from its loopholes, is well written and directed by Jordan, and has some terrific acting. The American Forest Whitaker manages a tolerable accent for Jody, and gives a decent performance, although he ought to shed some weight if he is to play romantic roles. As Jude, Miranda Richardson, a usually fine actress, overacts ferociously, but has moments. As a quizzical bartender, Jim Broadbent is smashing.

Capital work comes from the two leads, Stephen Rea, as Fergus-Jimmy, and Jaye Robinson, as Dil. Rea is the kind of actor who strikes you as homely, but grows on you tremendously as you realize the humanity in and behind his face. Similarly, his apparent underacting slowly but surely builds to revelations of great inner depth and complexity, and becomes their truest expression. *That* kind of surprise is the very essence of art. (You can see Rea now on Broadway in *Someone Who'll Watch Over Me*, and I cannot urge you strongly enough to do so.) Jaye Davidson is, appropriately, much more flamboyant, yet never hammy, and becomes very touching in the enactment of a near-impossible role with great persuasiveness. I am not sure that Davidson's looks and voice are exactly right, but they, too, manage to come extremely close. Although I do not buy the thesis of *The Crying Game*, it holds the interest and is, at times, genuinely moving.

Mighty Oak

THE OAK

"If we have a child," says Nela to her lover, Mitica, "it will be either a genius or an idiot." "If it turns out normal," answers Mitica, "I'll strangle it with my bare hands." So ends *The Oak*, the movie with which the Romanian director Lucian Pintilie may rightfully claim to be the heir apparent of those great Italian masters, Fellini and De Sica. It concerns Romania during the last phase of the Ceausescu dictatorship, but it applies equally to any country in which a despot with a servile bureaucracy at his command holds sway. And there still are, and perhaps always will be, such countries in our hapless world.

What that exchange means is simply this: to survive intact in a totalitarian bureaucracy, you have to be either a person of exceptional skill and intelligence or a holy simpleton. In *The Oak*, Mitica is a bit of a genius, and Nela a magnificent fool. Both are completely honest and fearless, and complement each other perfectly; they could have managed even if Romania had not ridded itself of the Ceausescus. But, then, Romania is not quite like the former Soviet Union or Nazi Germany. It is, for all the Ugric and Slavic admixtures, a Romance country, in which (to adapt Lucchino Visconti's *mot* about the Fascists versus the Nazis) the horror was more operettaish than operatic. But we must not forget that such an operetta is as lethal as it is comic.

In Romania, as elsewhere, the one most in danger of becoming dehumanized by totalitarianism is indeed the "normal person," as Pintilie's film shows with a dazzling but unblinding clarity. It opens with a modern Bucharest housing development that the camera approaches during the title sequence through a wilderness of weeds and stray dogs. But inside the rundown apartment of Nela, the schoolteacher heroine, things are exponentially worse. Nela and an older man are in bed together watching home movies of a happy Christmas party for a little girl. In Nela's apartment ashtrays overflow with generations of cigarette stubs, the kitchen is a graveyard for appliances buried in alimentary debris, the bathroom looks like a promoter rather than a challenger of filth; here, as elsewhere in the movie, if water comes from the taps at all, it is the color and consistency of cocoa—or something worse.

As for the double bed that Nela and the man occupy—the latter in some sort of stupor as he lets a crumpled *Paris Match* and an overturned glass of milk add to the dismalness—it is the ultimate, ineffable disaster area. Nela, disheveled, smokes ferociously as she watches the movie—projected by the whirring mechanism beside her onto a wall impinged on by Soviet airplane models—with a mixture of contempt and loathing. Who are this young woman, striking even in disarray, and that seemingly passed-out, fine-looking man? Spouses, lovers, prostitute and client? In the home movie, the little girl plucks off Santa's beard, rejects all toys but a handgun, and, transported by Santa, gleefully shoots all the party guests who collapse in sham deaths as the camera dollies after that doll-like would-be murderess. We come to realize that the man in bed is Nela's father, to whom the young woman administers a belated injection: Dad is dead.

The next events, leading up to Nela's leaving home, are among the finest examples of sardonic grotesquerie I have ever seen: a series of incidents as absurd as comic, as funny as garish. I won't spoil it for you, and will mention only Nela's subsequent confrontation with the surgeon who operated on her colonel-father, and who now rejects the father's wish that parts of him be donated to science or needy human beings. The grounds for refusal encapsulate a cross-section of what is wrong with economically and morally bankrupt Romania. Eventually Nela, about to transfer to an elementary school in a provincial town, has Dad cremated. In a marvelous shot, we see the good hand of that one-armed man crumble into cinders. Collecting the ashes in a Nescafé jar, Nela proceeds to a farewell call on a lover, with the jar sometimes in a brown paper bag, sometimes exposed, giving new meaning to Jules Laforgue's verse, "*Les morts, ça voyage,*" where, of course, the genius is in the tiny *ça*.

In the film, too—with Pintilie's script based on a novel by Ion Baiescu—the genius is in the details, though the larger aspects of construction and characterization, verbal and visual narration are by no means neglected. When Nela, in a rage, demolishes her telephone and overturns her projector, the latter keeps turning, slapping its images at a drunken angle wherever they fall. So, too, the past, recent or distant, obtrudes indiscriminately, creating sardonic superimpositions, jangling paradoxes. Most appallingly, that mock holocaust wreaked by the little girl—Nela as a child—will return to haunt her (and us) in the film's most shocking scene near the end. Yet even there Pintilie works a bit of comedy into the horror—legitimately, and with exquisite perception.

Take the delineation of Nela. This woman is totally fearless, except that, when she must change trains in the night because a bridge may not hold, she refuses to wade across the swollen stream: she is—of all things—afraid of snakes. Even more peripatetic than her father's ashes is her Polaroid camera. Why does this unsentimental, untouristy traveler take pictures of everyone and everything? Because in a society where death and enforced decay devour life with heightened voracity, you need something to conjure up an illusion of survival. So Nela's pocketbook and wall space are always full of snapshots, happy or sad, of creatures without other memorial except the Polaroid, prodding memory into becoming a cenotaph. In a wonderful late scene, Nela buries these pictures.

The Oak is a picaresque story, for Nela, even when not on the go, is never static. She has the good fortune of meeting an ideal fellow *picaro*, the young doctor Mitica, who saves her from being raped by four thugs. Mitica is such a strong man—muscular of body, stout of heart, irreverent of mind—that he is only bruisable, never breakable. This is, to be sure, partly because he is the only true healer in these parts where shortages proliferate. That makes him close to impervious to party bosses, hospital superiors, the Securitate (the secret police), and other forms of chicanery. And his sense of humor, joined to a relish for people (well, those who haven't lost their savor), stands him in good stead.

Having been plundered, Nela has no shoes. In response to Mitica's invitation for a weekend in the country, she remarks, "If you buy me a pair of sneakers, I'll go with you anywhere," and, as so often, puts a bare foot on the table. "No need to buy any," he replies, "I'll give you a pair of mine: we have the same size feet." A large (but not heavy) woman, this Nela; we see her in the next shot enjoying the country with Mitica and taking a Polaroid picture of those sneakers on her feet. Thus she and he approach the world on equal footing. And the picaresque outing evolves into a journey through other dimensions: the impacted mentalities of army personnel, petty officials, lawyers, teachers, Securitate agents, priests and their wives.

Nela even recaptures some of the past: she finds out the true answer to why her supposedly noble father placed one of his arms before an oncoming train, and about what her mother had to put up with. And she gains a catastrophic insight into the smarmy, hated sister who tauntingly dogs her almost every step. That last encounter with the sister is so hallucinatory that one doesn't quite know what to make of it; but this whole twilight of the Ceausescus is the world at its bewilderingly topsy-turviest. Yet it is thanks to this world—more upsidedownness!—that Nela and Mitica find love, notably during two burials: that of Titi, a young religious cultist and favorite patient of Mitica's, whom the doctor cannot save, but whose precious diary he rescues from the Securitate; and that of the father in the Nescafé jar, interred, as he requested, under a superb oak. Here Nela and Mitica play out one of the most strangely beautiful, and beautifully shot (with a camera, but almost with a gun as well), love scenes in movie history.

Aside from a few cogent rubatos, *The Oak* moves at an insistently breakneck pace, as befits the madness it chronicles. You have to read the subtitles (good, but not good enough) quickly, so as to have time to take in the riches of throwaway details providing a wry obligato to the main action. Note, for instance, the recurrent images of forlorn faces staring out of windows across the street, the ludicrous code names of army radio operators during maneuvers, the one-line definition of the burg in which Nela may be stuck forever, certain expressions on the faces of embarrassed sergeants, the farcical way in which Mitica treats his oafishly adoring nurse, the exasperation of Nela when she swallows some suicide pills and there's no water from the faucet, so she has to dump a bunch of flowers and drink up the contents of their vase. And much, much more.

And also note the sensitively understated cinematography of Doru Mitran, in, for example, the gorgeous backward-tracking shot at the end of Nela's last visit to her ailing mother, where the camera seems to take discreet leave of the dying old woman as, supported by Nela, she moves down an alley of trees in the opposite direction. The scene is bathed in an unearthly wash of blue, as if Mother were fading into Heaven.

All performances are fine, but the two leads are spectacular. Maia Morgenstern is of the family of such rawboned, powerful actresses as Christine Lahti and Sigourney Weaver, with the added zaniness of a Mary Steenburgen, and the veiled sexiness of a Kathy Baker. Her beauty sneaks up on you, then ambushes you with frightening intensity. She acts from the bottom of her being—even her quiet moments seem to be eruptions shot in slow motion. There is passion in her wit, wit in her passion; can you ask for more? As for Razvan Vasilescu, he has one of those slightly crooked, sly, almost homely faces that light up with intelligence, humor, and a perverse joy of living just when every hurdle is higher than the last. There is a restless alertness about his gaze from behind narrowed lids, a quickness of comprehension one jump ahead of everybody else's. Without the least effort to please, these two compel you to root for them with all your being.

Lucian Pintilie, now 59, made this film in 1991. His persona contains elements of both Mitica and Nela. He has done distinguished work in Romanian film, theater, and television, and had the honor of being repeatedly censored by Ceausescu himself. With his first film, *Sunday at Six*, and especially the second, *The Reconstruction*, he demonstrated (in Mira and Antonin Liehm's phrase, in their book *The Most Important Art*) "that Romanian film finally had a director of international stature." His stage production of *The Inspector General* was banned after three performances: his 1979 film, *Carnival Scenes*, could not be shown till 1991; finally Ceausescu personally saw to it, with sarcastic politeness, that Pintilie be granted his exit passport. For 17 years he lived in France and America, directing controversial stage productions. Now he's back in charge of Romanian film production with the suitably operettaish title Director of the Cinema Creation Studio of the Ministry of Romanian Culture.

I could detect only one false step in *The Oak*: some time after death, Titi's corpse still shows no sign of rigor mortis. But even that may have been right in Romania: where every sort of rigor besets the living, how could death be anything but a loosening?

Frail Fantasy, Forceful Fiction

GROUNDHOG DAY; RICH IN LOVE

I am for method in madness, a touch of reason in rhyme, and a bit of logic even in fantasy. If the hero of *Metamorphosis* wakes up as a beetle, let him be a beetle for all concerned. And sure enough, the mailman does not perceive him as a kangaroo; the family does not farm him out as an ox at plowing time. The picture of Dorian Gray does not turn into a self-portrait by Rembrandt setting a record at Sotheby's. There are rules, limits, even to fantasy.

The new movie *Groundhog Day*, for all its incidental pleasures, is a cheat. Its hero, Phil Connors, a jaded, arrogant, insufferable cad of a Pittsburgh TV weatherman, is sent out, as on every February 2, to cover Groundhog Day at Punxsutawney, Pennsylvania, and report on the prognostication of his colleague and namesake, Phil the groundhog. Bored stiff and insulting everyone at the bed-and-break-fast where he is billeted (his woman producer and his cameraman, on a flimsy pretext, stay at a hotel), he gets up grouchy at 6 A.M. and sulkily narrates as the other Phil faces his shadow. And indeed, winter resumes as a huge blizzard forces him, the attractive Rita, and the nerdy Larry to spend another night in the snowed-in burg.

But when Phil (the grinch, not the groundhog) wakes up, it is Groundhog Day all over again. And the next day, and the next; he seems hog-tied into an eternity of Groundhog Days. But there is a catch: he can live the day any way he wants to. He can seduce any town belle by trial and error, or commit any kind of suicide out of sheer exasperation: he will awake under the same flowered quilt, to the same silly song and inane radio chitchat, punctually at 6 A.M., to report the same shadow play. But although he may behave bet-ter or worse, the townsfolk, though they react appropriately to his changes, go on living their own unchanged lives, convening in the town square for the groundhog ceremony, then proceeding with their admittedly uneventful existences.

This is where the rules are broken. It's fine for wretched Phil to be punished by a spell of repetition, but why would all others have to groundlessly groundhog it up, without even being, like Phil, aware of it? Why should their guiltless lives be implicated in his comeuppance? And if they do not change in any other way, why would they change in respect to Phil? The attrition grinds down his haughtiness, he becomes involved with others: he changes a flat tire for helpless old ladies, he runs to catch a young boy falling from a tree. Yet Punxsutawney, unlike Brigadoon, is not under an enchantment: it participates in Phil's fantasy without sharing in it.

Phil discovers that Rita, the producer, is really a charmer. Having used his privileged position—learning daily from his nightly mis-takes—to seduce the local sexpot, Nancy, he switches his attentions to the demurely desirable Rita, and tries to conquer her by fair or ever-so-slightly foul means. Yet why should poor Rita be forced to relive this miserable day just to give Phil a chance to evolve from crafty Casanova into selfless swain? Though snooty Phil may not be missed back in the real world, why should Rita and Larry, the cameraman, be trapped in the same nightmare? Why should Rita be educating Phil? Compared to this, *Back to the Future*, which also cheated, was as pure as this movie's artificial snow.

If you can accept the inconsistent (much harder than the improbable), the rest is mildly pleasant going. Bill Murray knows how to make the initial Phil deplorable without being disgusting, and both the increased self-indulgence in his furious early repeat performances, and the gradual redemption through love for Rita, are skillfully managed. The body of the film is the rehabilitation of Phil, as Rita's recurring slaps in his face slowly dissolve into reciprocated feelings. And here the character of Rita, too, falls prey to self-contradiction. Rita, now thoroughly answering Phil's passion, nevertheless refuses to spend Groundhog Night with him even on his umpteenth try. Very well: perhaps Rita, improbably for a sophisticated TV producer who majored in nineteenth-century French poetry (!) wants to remain a virgin till marriage. Yet at film's end, as a reward for his by now enormous goodness, Phil is astounded to find her in bed with him as another Groundhog Day dawns—or the first non-groundhog dawn breaks.

But the pusillanimous filmmakers—Danny Rubin, the writer, and Harold Ramis, the co-writer and director—have another twist up their tricky sleeves. Phil, it emerges, was too tired to possess Rita (monumental goodness can be exhausting), as she, rather regretfully, remarks to her now fully redeemed bed partner. This sexual shell game, these moral tergiversations, attest to the film's queasily exploitative values. In the end, all is contrivance, to maintain an anodyne PG rating. *Groundhog Day* makes a pig of itself, and it's no use saying, "But it's only a fantasy." Tell that to Franz Kafka.

Still, for folks who can enjoy ice hockey played with soccer goals, there is something here. Andie MacDowell is an endearing Rita, though rather overshadowed by the luscious Marita Geraghty as Nancy—and the minor roles are all well taken. The movie is nicely shot by John Bailey, agreeably scored by George Fenton, and atmospherically designed and directed. But where the fantasy goes overboard is when Murray (and he a Canadian, too!) utters some unspeakable gibberish and Andie rhapsodizes, "You speak French!" On the whole, Hollywood should stay away from culture (references to Baudelaire and that most prestigious composer of soundtrack music, Rachmaninov); but *Groundhog Day* is clearly unafraid of turning into groundhogwash.

Minor novelists remain a wonderful source for movies, provided they are not married to the director. I refer to the Mexican Laura Esquivel, the spouse of Alfonso Arau, who produced and directed the initially attention-grabbing, but soon fulsome, overrich, and indigestible *Like Water for Chocolate*, based on his wife's novel and screenplay. Miss Esquivel represents the feminist branch of magic realism, the Latin American fictional mode that swept the world ever since García Márquez won the Nobel Prize with his *One Hundred Years of Solitude*, which reads more like a thousand to me.

Conversely, the zesty movie Bruce Beresford fashioned from a novel by a minor South Carolina novelist, Josephine Humphreys, *Rich in Love*, is a winsome delight. It, too, has quite a bit about food in it, but eating it is neither deified nor demonized à la Miss Esquivel: it is merely a vehicle for characterization and comedy, as it should be. When Helen Odom, after a long marriage to her amiably eccentric but relentlessly self-absorbed husband, Warren, suddenly disappears, the good old boy (not quite a duffer yet) is more shocked than hurt, and consoles himself with weird but easily come-by sustenance: bananas dipped in peanut butter and potato-chip-and-mayonnaise sandwiches. And, eventually, with another woman: Vera Delmage, a slightly overripe unisex hairdresser, who, however, bakes a mean angel-food cake.

To be sure, Warren's younger daughter, 17-year-old Lucille, proposes to cook for him, but he kindly rejects her offer: he has always kept children and other concerned parties at a friendly arm's length. Earnest Lucille, the family's mainstay, was the one who found Helen's good-bye note, and quickly composed and substituted a warmer, less grating kiss-off. And it was she who drove Warren all over tarnation comically searching for Helen, whose defection to start "a second life" makes no sense to persons whose first life fits them like a frowzy but comfortable old slipper.

Helen, however, remains unfindable. But such is the economy of Southern exotica that for one family member lost, another promptly turns up. It's Rae, the somewhat wayward elder daughter, who got herself spliced up North to Billy McQueen, a likable Yankee who had to punch minuscule holes into his condoms to get Rae pregnant and willing to marry him. Exactly why the couple have to move in with Warren while awaiting the baby somehow slipped by me, but it matters little as one watches them enjoyably make love *and* war. Such fine points are immaterial here: the film is about how to live with one's idiosyncrasies and take pleasure in the vagaries of existence. Instead of endowing the irrational with magic status, it contemplates it like an ever-changing landscape in which everybody can find a pebble or weed to his liking.

Beresford and his screenwriter, Alfred Uhry (the same team as in *Driving Miss Daisy*, which this film in unobvious ways commodiously resembles), respect the work's gently provocative ironies. Over everything hangs a doom of human bumbling, but it's a doom that can be domesticated, made downright cozy. Thus Lucille experiences sexual initiation at first vicariously, then actively, but, in antithetical ways, less than fulfillingly. Yet she is not discouraged. We know that as some relationships are dissolved and others entered on—while still others loom just beyond the horizon—life with its seriocomic surprises will come up with something for everyone.

The director, who is capable of major wonders, here contents himself with minor ones. He guides people with his usual sure hand through puzzling yet ultimately life-asserting imbroglios, making individuals and their surroundings interact in a quizzical yet also comradely symbiosis. To this end, Beresford makes the ambience delicious, but casually, modestly so. He bypasses the obvious, renowned beauties of Charleston, and concentrates on the homelier, homier ones. He and his superb cinematographer, Peter James, capture loveliness where you'd least suspect it, say, in an Erector Set-like drawbridge, over a mundane waterway, where telephoto lenses and a few filters transmute highway and canal traffic—with a bit of help from sunsets and moonlight—into a companionable dreamscape. Always there is the eye for soul-satisfying shots, e.g., one in which the ramshackle, plantation-style Odom house, with its upper- and lower-story veranda, fills out precisely the widescreen frame. On the upper level, there are minor dramas taking place both left and right, while another spills over to the center of the lower level. This inverted triangle fitted into a rectangle, the rectangle itself perfectly covered by the camera's compass, is sublimely suggestive: there's a divinity that shapes our ends, roughhew them how we will.

The other Beresford triumph is the performing. All the actors—some cast against type, and none of them obvious choices—act winningly. You'd never believe England's Albert Finney isn't a major Southern actor—but, of course, he is major wherever you set him down. And Kathryn Erbe is an unwobbling pivot amid this whirligig, bearing the brunt of growing up and the weight of the movie with equal grace. But all are perfect in this small-scale but big-hearted picture.

Precocious Children, Childish Adults

IL LADRO DI BAMBINI; THIS BOY'S LIFE

There is no subject more popular in movies (or literature) than growing pains, but the possible divergence of approach is well illustrated by *Il ladro di bambini* (*Stolen Children*) from Italy, and *This Boy's Life* from Hollywood, U.S.A. The American film is optimistic, the Italian pessimistic, yet with glimmers of hope. Unbounded optimism is what made America strong; guarded pessimism is what makes Europe wise.

To be sure, *This Boy's Life* is made from Tobias Wolff's autobiographical novel, and has to end well because Wolff is now an established writer who teaches at Syracuse University. *Il ladro di bambini* (literally, though less euphoniously, *The Child Thief*) on the other hand, is fiction, albeit based on a news photograph and other documentary evidence. Toby (i.e., Tobias) in *This Boy's Life* is saved presumably by his special talent; the brother and sister in *Ladro* have no such prowess, and their future remains a question mark. But the real difference is that Toby, even when doubting it, always had the love of his mother; whereas 11-year-old Rosetta was turned by her mother (the father left long ago) into a prostitute at age nine, and nine-year-old Luciano, who cannot be commercially exploited, gets only jeers from his mother.

Il ladro di bambini begins in a so-called dormitory neighborhood on the outskirts of Milan, where immigrants from the south lead precarious existences. The economy, incisiveness, honesty yet restraint with which the initial situation is established are exemplary. The mother indulges Rosetta, whom she has debauched into a breadwinner, but nags and bullies Luciano, who is merely in the way. Still, the rich client who comes for Rosetta's services is not an obvious ogre; he goes about his monstrous pleasure with urbanity and even a surface benignity, which says much more about human corruption than making him a patent heavy would.

It is heartbreaking to see Rosetta pray to the Virgin before she plies her trade, but even this is shown in a soberly understated way, with not a trace of smuttiness. The emphasis is on the dissension the situation creates between the siblings. Luciano bitterly resents his sister's privileged status even as he angrily senses her degradation; she, scorning him as a useless brat, doubtless envies his freedom from sexual enslavement. The script by Gianni Amelio (the director), Sandro Petraglia, and Stefano Rulli conveys all this without resorting to exposition, excessive emotionalism, or an iota of sentimentality.

Two *carabinieri* are assigned to take the kids, after the adults are apprehended, to a religious home in Civitavecchia. The elder *carabiniere* goes AWOL in Bologna, leaving the sticky job to Antonio, a very young man studying on the side for a university diploma. He has a hard time marshaling these siblings who, disliking each other, have no affection or respect for anyone. The first great accomplishment of the movie is to show how genuine feeling from Antonio eventually enables the kids to care for each other as well as for him. The second is that this happens gradually, with an avoidance of big scenes, and believably. The third is that, in the end, love has conquered much, but not all. The individual is still in thrall to society and its Draconian laws.

One of the means by which this fine picture attains its aims is Hollywood's chief anathema: leisureliness. In Amelio's film things happen at a pace as close to that of life as a movie allows. The wanderings of the central threesome are fraught even more with frustrating noncommunication than with actual mishaps. Therein lies the misery that Antonio overcomes only with utmost difficulty. Although, like the kids, he, too, is prone to anger and sulky silences, his basic humanity lies in his patience. He does not give up on the children: he does not give in to indifference. In fact, he goes slightly AWOL with them, out of genuine affection.

Slowly, then, the asthmatic and proudly withdrawn Luciano, the prematurely independent but vulnerable Rosetta, and the exasperated yet concerned Antonio become a kind of family. The film has sympathy for almost all; even the purblind priest who refuses to take the children into the home (Rosetta might corrupt the others!) does not elicit outraged condemnation. Antonio now has to take his charges to their native Sicily, to a home for disturbed children. Foreseeing the joylessness in store, he decides on a stopover at his sister's in Reggio di Calabria, the last mainland stop. Here the kids are fed, cleaned, and clothed, but here, too, Antonio explodes at a woman who, recognizing Rosetta from a magazine cover, exposes her as a prostitute. The hurt girl runs away, Antonio takes off after her, and Rosetta ends up sobbing in his embrace. It is only now that Luciano, who has all along been suspiciously watching from the sidelines, realizes that his sister is not vamping the young man, and that his feelings for her—and him—are sincere and pure.

For the careful viewer, the film provides many collateral pleasures. Take Antonio's reaction to his sister's new establishment, a sprawling restaurant with adjoining living quarters she is trying to whip into shape. The restaurant looks like your average soup kitchen, the residence like the temporary dwelling of itinerant mountebanks. Yet to Antonio, it's the kind of place where he might want to settle down. By showing us the pathetic modesty of its characters' aspirations, the film eloquently conveys the depth of their deprivation.

The ending is as compelling as the beginning. Discover it for yourself, but be sure to note how realistically the resolution—if it is one—is presented. Enrico Lo Verso, the *carabiniere*, is a professional; the two children are amateurs, in the great tradition of those unforgettable finds in the heyday of Italian neorealism. Or is every child in Italy a born actor? None of the principals has cinematic good looks, but all three light up with inner beauty. And you root for them long after the movie is over because Gianni Amelio (who also gave us the wonderful *Open Doors*) has the gift of making you realize that a shattering movie is not just a movie.

The good thing about *This Boy's Life* is that it likewise tries to be honest and stick to (I imagine) the book on which it is based. When Caroline Wolff was divorced, she kept her younger son, Toby, to share her straitened circumstances; Geoff, the elder, remained with his father, to lead a posh East Coast and eventually Ivy League existence. Unlucky with her boyfriends, Caroline developed a special closeness to her young teenage son; together, they set out for Utah, where, the time being the fifties, they hope to strike it rich as uranium prospectors. But the unwelcome pursuit by an unwanted lover, the end of the uranium rush, and the vagaries of bus schedules propel them to Seattle, where a kind of last-frontier spirit still prevailed.

Life is Spartan and humdrum until a new beau appears in the person of Dwight Hansen, a blue-collar charmer from the small hill town of Concrete, a name that thuds louder than a thousand bricks. Dwight, a single father with three maturing children, appears to be a good risk, especially as his courtly wooing of Caroline, his easy (though unreciprocated) camaraderie with Toby, and his boundless cheerfulness enchant the young mother, whose melting point is not particularly high. She marries Dwight, and six people are forthwith

ensconced in his abjectly ramshackle house, not even made of concrete, where his three well-disciplined but clearly unhappy children
can hardly wait for the day they can escape.

Mother and son are promptly confronted with major disappointments. Dwight, whose lovemaking is fairly animalistic, will
not have face-to-face sex with Caroline. And Toby is condemned
to a crack-of-dawn paper route whose earnings he is not allowed
to keep; ostensibly Dwight is holding them for the boy's future use.
He has also enrolled Toby in the boy scouts, but buys him only a
faded and ill-fitting second-hand uniform. And life with Dwight
becomes worse and worse for both Wolffs as monotonous days drag
on. Dwight's affable smiles have become sarcastic sneers, dispensed
mostly while he pummels the boy on the pretext of teaching him
self-defense.

The ingredients for a solid movie are here, but the Scottish-born
Michael Caton-Jones (whose dubious claim to fame is *Scandal*),
and his screenwriter Robert Getchell (remembered for the not
dissimilar *Alice Doesn't Live Here Anymore*) cannot make things
jell. They concentrate on the more heavily dramatic incidents, and
rather neglect the daily drudgery. They do not establish a convincing rhythm, and the picture lurches or skips ahead. We see how bad
the family's bad moments are, but not enough of how bad the good
ones can be. Why would Caroline have married Dwight in the first
place? His jollity was put on with a trowel. But everything in the
film is either overstated or underdeveloped.

The three principals, unlike those in *Ladro*, are all a bit off. Robert De Niro has played small-time sociopaths (as well as big-time
psychopaths) too often for comfort—or even the proper kind of
discomfort. His dishonest smile now looks like painting by numbers, as if his face were engraved with dots that merely have to be
connected with crinkles to produce an instant grin of deception.
Ellen Barkin always struck me as having a quality I can describe
only as asking for trouble, which makes it hard to perceive her as
the innocent victim of circumstance. Leonardo DiCaprio as Toby
would be fine but for his rather girlish looks. No matter how macho
you act or are, you will be undercut by the face of a young Betty
Hutton.

The best thing about *This Boy's Life* is David Watkin's cinematography, which unobtrusively creates the right atmosphere. Since
both Tobias Wolff and his brother, Geoffrey, under vastly different
circumstances, ended up as writers and professors, I'd like to see

something of these strong literary seeds developing. Some final title cards contain more curious and tantalizing information than does the whole body of the film.

Shakespeare Without Tears

MUCH ADO ABOUT NOTHING;
LA GUERRE SANS NOM

Kenneth Branagh's film adaptation of Shakespeare's *Much Ado about Nothing* raises some interesting and important questions that go beyond the specifics of this enterprise. Thus it seems to me that no matter what they do, American actors will never equal British ones in Shakespeare, at the very least because they have not the right language. British English has a melody: American English has not. More precisely, British English is like classical music; American English is like a marching band.

I am, of course, aware that Shakespeare's own English sounded more or less like that still spoken in parts of West Virginia, and not at all like the "high" English my generation associates with Oxford, the Old Vic, and the BBC. No matter: once you have gone forward with linguistic evolution, there is no turning back—at least no turning back with impunity.

At the risk of incurring another reprimand from Bill Buckley, I permit myself a further musical analogy: Beethoven may have composed for the old fortepiano, because that is what was around. But in his innermost ear, where he wasn't deaf, he heard a more evolved sound, that of the great pianofortes to come: the Bechsteins, Bösendorfers, Steinways, and the rest. That is the piano music for today, and what the great composer, ahead of his time, must have heard in his mind's ear. I like to think that Shakespeare's ear was a similar time-traveler; in any case, after hearing Gielgud, Olivier, Redgrave, and Richardson, who would go looking for Shakespeare in Appalachia?

In this *Much Ado*, we have along with the British actors four from the United States and Canada, who labor under a further disadvantage. There is such a thing as Shakespearean training, such as very few American actors get at all, and even fewer with anything resembling adequacy. This is chiefly a problem on the stage, where diction cannot be electronically augmented, or sounds funny if it is. But even the best cinematic sound cannot get around the level-ing of American accents, a flatness harder to climb over than the Himalayas.

Robert Sean Leonard, as Claudio, comes off best, which is to say not very well rather than embarrassingly. The beanpole-ish, coltish actor (remembered especially for the wretched *Dead Poets Soci-ety*), has an undeniable boyish charm and a nice General American speech. He is a sincere and earnest actor but lacks the ultimate inspiration, the difference between a *routinier* and a pathfinder, a solid workhorse and a star. I always find myself sympathizing with his effort rather than thrilling to his achievement.

The Canadian actor Keanu Reeves plays Don John, usually des-ignated as the Prince of Aragon's bastard brother, but here called his "half brother," as a stock, bearded villain, undistinguished by verve, flamboyance, or mere individuality. His heavy-lidded eyes are usu-ally at the same aperture as the mouth of a child being force-fed spinach, and he snarls his way listlessly through his lines. At that, he is better than Michael Keaton, who manages to play Dogberry, one of the funnier parts in the Shakespeare canon, as a very tight cannon. There is no comic looseness here; instead, Keaton steps into his part as into someone's discarded wad of chewing gum. You cannot play Dogberry's pomposity condescendingly from the out-side; Dogberry does not perceive himself as a pompous fellow, he merely is one.

As Branagh has instructed his designers, the period could be anywhere between 1700 and 1900, but the locale is not a never-nev-erland. His *Much Ado* is a weekend-long country-house party in the most magnificent of Renaissance houses. It is the fifteenth-century Villa Vignamaggio, the Gherardini family's Tuscan pleasure dome at Greve. To transfer the play from the now industrialized Messina to this nook in mid-Chianti country was a neat idea—especially when you consider the production designer's addenda. Tim Harvey has added to the villa of Mona Lisa's parents a small private chapel, incremental formal gardens, and the quattrocento's answer to a Bel Air swimming pool, an Etruscan-style open-air bathhouse. Still, it all manages to look authentic, which is where the trouble comes in: What is Denzel Washington, a black Prince of Aragon, doing in such a persuasive period setting?

A black prince, whose name isn't even Edward, and who has a white bastard (or half) brother? Let me get this straight: The Moors were never driven out of Spain. In fact, the African-Aragonians ruled enlightenedly over the Iberian peninsula, and only when they, occasionally, wanted to make whoopee with members of the lowly white minority did this produce such amazingly pure-white bastards as Keanu Reeves—I mean, Don John. Washington is a fine actor in the right part—consider his searing Malcolm X. But he has no Shakespearean training, as he painfully demonstrated in the title part of the New York Shakespeare Festival's hapless *Richard III*. Moreover, his idea of sounding genteel makes him talk with a kind of fake finishing-school accent; he is also too young for the part and lacks royal bearing. Furthermore, a black actor presents a technical problem in a nocturnal torch-lit scene. If you light the scene so that it really looks like torchlight, a black face merges with the ambient dark. To watch a white actor talking to a uniform from which no head protrudes reminds one of Archibald MacLeish's *Fall of the City*, wherein an empty suit of armor on horseback conquers a cowardly town.

Though the American contingent was obviously brought in with an eye on the box office, the result, I repeat, is that the humblest Briton outshines the most stellar Yankee. Thus Hero, played by a mere Oxford student on temporary leave—the enormously personable and spirited Kate Beckinsale—totally overshadows her Claudio, even though he is the best of the Americans. It makes you wonder why she would be so upset to be ditched by such an insignificant popinjay, an obvious upstart trying to marry above his station.

The married couple Kenneth Branagh and Emma Thompson do very well by Benedick and Beatrice. Helped considerably by being able to play their scenes in the proper al fresco environment, where certain kinds of ambushes and eavesdroppings look more plausible and picturesque, these merrily sparring lovers have themselves—to use a suitably rustic trope—a field day. Miss Thompson may be a shade too mannered even for the madcap Beatrice, and Branagh a tad too earthbound for the fantastical Benedick, yet even this has its uses: it makes their coupling more promising than the mere gravitation of like to like.

The best acting, however, is to be found among the supporting players. Those often dullish greybeards, the brothers Leonato and Antonio, come to scrumptious life in the hands of Richard Briers and Brian Blessed. They are so good that you wish the play were about them, or that they set up forthwith as a satirical comedy team under the name Blessed Briars. Imelda Staunton is a disadvantaged Margaret: a good but homely actress, she could not, even on the darkest of nights, be mistaken at the window for the exquisite Hero. On the other hand, Phyllida Law, Emma Thompson's real-life mother, is almost too well-spoken and aristocratic for Ursula.

What the movie confirms is Branagh's directorial talent. The actor-director describes his way with Shakespeare as "that sort of blood-and guts, high-octane approach," which he convincingly exhibited in his *Henry V*. Here he applies the high octane to high comedy with similarly fueling results. But he is good with the more introspective passages, too, notably the grand Beatrice-and-Benedick scene (IV, i), which in the play takes place at the very church where Claudio repudiates Hero. Branagh transposes it to that chaste, little chapel he had especially built, where it takes on a bittersweet intimacy: this is the Chapel Perilous where the knight is tested to the utmost by his lady.

Consider also the clever beginning. In white letters on a black screen, we gradually get the text of the song we'll later hear sung to Patrick Doyle's fetching music, "Sigh no more, ladies, sigh no more." Here the unfurling text is accompanied by the offscreen voice of Beatrice reciting it as a motto for the entire play. The audience is invited to mentally recite along, and thus is promptly transplanted into a Renaissance whirligig, ready for a romantic rigadoon. Equally enchanting is the first view of the Aragonese cavalry arriving behind the film's titles. A telephoto shot in slow motion, it introduces the male principals slowly bobbing up and down on their mounts, and clearly spoiling for livelier mountings.

Branagh has cut and transposed much of the play, making for less ado and more nothing. But that's what you get when you compress the locale and time frame and cater to a youth culture impatient with too many fine points, too much poetry. On the other hand, the authentic locale, the extensive outdoor shooting, the long hot country weekend help make some things more credible. "People fall in love through this fury of summer madness," Branagh has said, and he has pretty much conveyed it. But how much he has forfeited. By making Don Pedro a young man, for instance, he loses the ruefulness of the older man's Cyranoesque wooing of Hero. By speeding things up, he minimizes Claudio's act of Christian contrition. But he does give us a rollickingly extroverted *Much Ado*, quickly converting its sounds of woe into hey nonny, nonny.

Shown only at the Human Rights Watch Festival in New York, Bertrand Tavernier's 1991 TV documentary, *La Guerre sans nom* (*The Un-*

declared War, but also, punningly, *The Unspeakable War*) may never be in public release here, so only brief mention of this sublime and shattering film seems warranted. Modeling himself on Marcel Ophuls's *The Sorrow and the Pity*, Tavernier picked a single city—Grenoble—and interviewed at great length several men (and, more succinctly, two women) whose lives were affected by the never officially recognized eight-year war that cost France, besides Algeria, some thirty thousand dead and tens of thousands of physically or mentally injured. The exact figures were never released by the French government, and though some of the maimed received financial help, full compensation was never granted. This was, after all, not a declared war.

Tavernier limits himself to showing the faces of those he and his associate interviewed, and sometimes a bit of their immediate surroundings. Also occasional shots of Grenoble and the relevant Algerian landscapes. Further, snapshots taken by these men, or of them by companions in arms. Save for a few explanatory words, Tavernier lets the men speak for themselves. There is no commentary from other sources, but their answers are often presented in such a way as to corroborate, elaborate on, or dispute what another of them has said. The result is four hours that are moving, funny, horrible, and absolutely riveting.

There is more here about war and peace, nobility and stupidity, men's strength and weaknesses than in almost anything else I have ever seen. Strong men who have not talked about their experiences even to their families now do to the camera. Someone asks whether he has to reveal all, and, urged to do so, gets all choked up and has to make a fresh start. Some men weep. Some don't, but you can see what thirty years of wrestling with unquellable memories has cost them. Some have learned awesome lessons; some nothing. In the end, you find out what each of these men does in civilian life, and how his social position colors his views. Without voicing a single opinion, Tavernier gives you a seminar in history. Also in living.

Technology Triumphant

JURASSIC PARK

Frankly, I don't give a damn about dinosaurs, perhaps because I'm one myself. But next to swapping baseball cards, nothing seems to me as bootless as becoming a dinosaur maven. For a layman, that is; savants are free to mix it up with the giant saurians. I thrill to a Mercedes or Volvo, but for a brace of Velociraptors or a prime Tyrannosaurus Rex I reck not. Which is not to say that one cannot marvel at Steven Spielberg's *Jurassic Park* for its conspicuous technical achievements; but I agree with Orson Welles's remark: "The directors I admire most are the least technical ones."

People who read such books inform me that Michael Crichton's novel *Jurassic Park* is much tougher and tauter than the screenplay, even though Crichton himself collaborated on it with David Koepp. The problem is not with the high-stepping lizards, but with the human lowlifes, whom Spielberg chronically edulcorates. The two most repellent characters in the story—Hammond, the venal owner of the theme park, and Nedry, the corrupt employee who sabotages it—are both turned into clowns of one sort or another. What I imagine to be one of the novel's points—that modern man is as feral as any prehistoric predator—is promptly lost.

Has there ever been a director as unable as Spielberg to tackle the relationships of grown human beings? His characters are by preference children, and true relationships are formed with sharks or extraterrestrials. I am, of course, speaking of his successes: in his fiascos, he has tried to deal with men and women—with paltry results. He reminds me of those artists who never quite managed to draw the human figure, and sought refuge in abstraction or dribbles. But whereas the abstract painter can avoid what he cannot handle, Spielberg is obliged to include human beings in his movies and the result is oversimplification, abstraction, cliché.

Hammond, the avuncular entrepreneur whose technocrats have recreated the dinosaurs from their blood preserved in mosquitoes, in turn preserved in amber, has erected his theme park on an island off Costa Rica. He flies in a trio of scientists to preview and endorse his enterprise: Grant, a paleontologist: Ellie, his girlfriend, a paleobotanist: and Ian Malcolm, a mathematician specializing in chaos theory, whose presence is less logical, but allows for sardonic commentary. And there is also a lawyer, who serves as the butt of anti-lawyer jokes that dependably elicit enthusiastic audience empathy.

The appointments for the park staff are downright sybaritic, whereas visitors are conveyed through the park in safari-style vehicles along programmed trajectories. The great beasts are kept safely sequestered behind electrically charged fences; computerized surveillance from the control center guarantees smooth traversal. Oddly enough, though, it is possible to step out of the vehicles and so invite trouble. Trouble reciprocates in spades when a double-dealing overseer causes an electrical outage, and the freed megamonsters expand their gastronomic horizon from steers and goats to human flesh.

The real problem with Spielberg is that, for all his technical cleverness, he keeps falling back on the same tricks. If in *Jaws* it was effective to start with someone being devoured by an invisible killer, that's the way to begin *Jurassic Park*: if in *Close Encounters of the Third Kind* it proved impressive to pan across a row of awestruck faces gazing at a phenomenon withheld from the camera for as long as possible, that shot goes straight into the new film. And once more John Williams has written redundantly overexplanatory background music that refuses to stay in the background.

Again, take the two adorable, blond, picture-perfect (i.e., picture-book, not just movie-perfect) children in the film. They get variously chased and roughed up by ravening dinosaurs, but neither of them—even after a rather severe electric shock—incurs serious damage. The only people who get eaten are two blacks, one lawyer, and one Englishman, none of whom the core audience feels overwhelmingly kin to. One of them—the lawyer—is roundly cheered when, ignominiously hiding in an outhouse, he becomes Tyrannosaurus fodder.

Needless to say, acting in such a movie consists mostly of reacting. Sam Neill, a good actor, dwindles as Grant to the stature of a B-movie hero: Richard Attenborough, the last word in sanitized heavies, bumbles all too benightedly as Hammond; Laura Dern, as the palest of paleobotanists, displays those elongated features of hers that should make any saurian cozy up to her amorously. Jeff Goldblum injects some genuine chaos as the mathematician, but does not look like an Ian Malcolm. The show is obviously stolen by the dinosaurs, who take to computerized acting far better than such fine human performers as Samuel L. Jackson and Bob Peck, reduced to similar robotics.

The screen brims over with *Jurassic Park* artifacts that should be available at your neighborhood stores and, unlike the book, ends with the prehistoric protagonist, T. Rex, merrily multiplying in preparation for the sequel. My own wish is that, like other Model Ts, he may soon find his proper habitat in a junkyard.

Sleepless in Seattle

Is the women's picture still a reputable genre? At a time when women have just about achieved equality with men, does the two-handkerchief movie still make sense? Back in 1939, Leo McCarey, with the help of such able scenarists as Delmar Daves and Donald Ogden Stewart, turned a story by Mildred Cram and himself into a directorial triumph. Charles Boyer and Irene Dunne enacted it to sheer tear-jerking perfection, spicing the weepy sentimentality with healthy dollops of wit, and out came one of the most romantic love stories in screen history, *Love Affair*. It was one of my 14-year-old self's favorite Hollywood movies, right up there with *Wuthering Heights* and *Dark Victory*.

Since Hollywood can never leave well enough alone, the picture had to be remade in 1957 in not quite glorious Eastmancolor, updated and expanded from 89 minutes to a soggier 114. The writers were again Daves and McCarey, with the latter again directing. The stars, this time, were Cary Grant and Deborah Kerr, a shade less romantic, but for those like Nora Ephron, too young to have known the original version, sublime. With *Sleepless in Seattle*, Miss Ephron has, fairly shamelessly, endeavored to direct a kind of variation on that film, producing a Nineties equivalent with the same mixture of laughter and tears, side-splitting and eye-wetting. A very, very little of it comes off, but a great deal merely looks retro, manipulative, contrived—an exploitation of the soft center that presumably lurks under the toughest feminist carapace, and that putatively thrives in the newly sensitized male bosom.

Sam Baldwin (Tom Hanks), a charming young Chicago architect, has just lost his beloved wife, Maggie. He is inconsolable, far more so than his sweet but practical eight-year-old son, Jonah (Ross Malinger). Sam moves to Seattle, to start afresh, away from haunting memories. He settles into a well-appointed house by the water, and obtains a comparably desirable job. But Maggie (Carey Lowell) haunts him even there, and he cannot so much as go out on a date. It promises to be a very bleak Christmas, so Jonah calls up a phone-in show run by a phony woman therapist—Dr. Marcia, as she likes to be called—and tells her about his dad's plight. Soon she gets Sam on the phone and coaxes out of him a confession of how much he misses his dead wife. Jeff Arch, who wrote the arch story on which he, David S. Ward, and Nora Ephron based their screenplay, probably thinks that Sam's platitudes are enchanting, and so manifestly do two thousand women who send Sam love letters and marriage proposals pronto.

Meanwhile back in Baltimore, there is Annie Reed, a feature writer for the *Baltimore Sun*, who hears that broadcast. She is engaged to and living with Walter (Bill Pullman), a nice enough fellow, though abounding in assorted allergies. But once she hears how wonderfully Sam is in touch with his emotions, she is a goner. Her eyes fill with tears, her heart with overgrown puppy love, and she practically drives off the road. Her yearning for him grows, and finally she too writes a letter that a friend forwards to Sam, whom Dr. Marcia has dubbed Sleepless in Seattle. It is, however, Jonah, not Sleepless, who screens the love mail that is still coming in, and Annie's cunning missive, mostly about baseball, grabs him. Pretty soon Jonah is telling Sleepless that this is the wife for him, and the mother that he, Jonah, must have.

I could go into a recital of the various cutesy devices Miss Ephron & Co. come up with to bring Annie and Sleepless together, as well as of the tricksy devices with which they come up to keep them apart. Annie, it seems, is the sort of person who'll travel three thousand miles to Seattle, only *not* to have the guts to accost Sleepless and son, by whom she is, from a safe distance, entranced. And Sleepless, seeing her, and promptly falling in love—even without knowing that she is the Annie who homered her way into Jonah's heart—is the sort of person who'll say a tongue-tied, smitten hello to her, and, upon getting back an equally love-sick hello, let the beloved run away. True, he has been halfheartedly involved with Victoria (Barbara Garrick), a young woman who guffaws so ghoulishly at every unfunny thing he says as to make the angels weep. Still, even this Rabelaisian rictus proves enough to drive a preposterous wedge between Sleepless and his Dream Come True!

So the movie spends most of its slumberous hundred minutes on keeping Sleepless and Annie sundered, and it is hapless little Jonah who must resort to a stratagem, as hazardous as it is unbelievable, to bring the predestined lovers together in the last reel—on top of the Empire State Building, where else? The entire picture is a collection of nauseating quotations from and references to *An Affair to Remember*, both visual and verbal. And as it wiggles on, it becomes a pre-coitus interruptus of gigantic dimensions.

If it had any bearing on reality—which the film proudly and repeatedly denies—Annie could very happily marry Walter, a decent fellow who takes rejection with touching magnanimity. But no, Sleepless and Feckless must finally take each other by the hand to the sound of Jimmy Durante croaking out "Make Someone Happy," and go off together with eight-year-old Reckless to stop being sleep-less—in Seattle, or Baltimore, or Timbuctoo, for all anyone not par-tial to cutesypoo, but also amazingly smartass, soap operas cares. Perhaps a sequel, *Smartass in Smyrna*, is indicated.

In the Line of Fire

Thrillers seem to proliferate in the summer, perhaps on the assump-tion that in the hot weather chills are especially welcome. And so they are when they are as well made as *In the Line of Fire*. Written by Jeff Maguire, a 41-year-old who was about to quit Los Angeles in disgust, his screenplay was accepted, then rejected, by a number of stars until Clint Eastwood took it on. Eastwood gives it one of his by now customary solid and intelligent performances. The cur-rent buzz is that he keeps getting better and better, and surpasses himself in this one. Actually, he has been good for a long time, and he is no better here; it is just that American audiences and reviewers wax sentimental about stars with prolonged staying power. If Lassie were still with us, she'd be right up there with George C. Scott.

This is the story of Secret Serviceman Frank Horrigan, who is close to retirement age but still a top agent, except that he is haunted by his one fiasco: he did not take a bullet for JFK when he was guarding him in Dallas. Now he finds himself looking for a man who is threatening the current, fictional President on his re-election campaign trail. Presidents are menaced by all sorts of cranks, but this threat, Horrigan feels, is serious. For this potential killer, by a trail of newspaper clippings he deliberately plants, reveals that he knows exactly what he is doing, including disturbing allusions to Horrigan's one costly failure. And forthwith Horrigan starts getting nocturnal phone calls from this man of many aliases and faces, whose deadly skills are no less numerous. He has even built a de-vice that makes it virtually impossible to trace his calls although Horrigan's phone is bugged.

The self-proclaimed assassin-to-be is both psychotic and infer-nally clever, as movie psychos invariably are. He was once with the FBI and has a great many tricks up his sinister sleeve, even though he also has a sick need to expose himself (he fully expects to pay with his life for his ultimate crime), and an equally sick one to play on Horrigan's nerves and pangs of conscience while purporting to be his friend. The nature of this game is fascinating, but remains underwritten, as is also Horrigan's romance with an agent, Lilly Raines, which begins as mutual teasing but evolves into a potentially absorbing love affair. This aspect of the plot is especially underdeveloped, but it is hard to sandwich in a mature love story amid all that elaborate thriller stuff, commendable as the human value of the effort may be.

No new heights are scaled in the film, but neither does the tension ever sloppily subside. The overconscientious and aging Horrigan is hampered by colleagues and superiors, there are costly rivalries between members of the Secret Service and the CIA, there is a series of well-staged ancillary killings and many a rousing foot chase, always more rewarding than car chases. True, all good thrillers are forced to cheat a bit, and this one is no exception. But it cheats as little as possible, and neatly avoids expeditions into the heartlands of the preposterous. John Malkovich, always dubious when cast as the hero, makes a most satisfying heavy. He is both suave and creepy, and although he looks naturally weird, it is a fascinating, eloquent weirdness. The script, moreover, allows him to say horrible things that do make some dreadful sense. He manages to convey real intelligence along with the dementia, and just as he is able to get under Horrigan's skin, he gets past our own defenses and makes us forget that in this sort of movie—unlike in life—crime never pays, thus heightening the suspense.

As a capable Secret Service agent and reluctant love interest, René Russo is almost too well cast. She has the unyieldingly clean-cut quality one associates with policewomen from meter maids up, and palpable sturdiness in her features. But there were moments when, watching her, I longed for a touch of delicacy about her face, for a brow not quite so beetling, a nose and chin less monolithic; why, even her name, René Russo, lacks that feminine and vulnerable mute second "e." Lesser roles are also savvily cast, with actors—other than the excellent John Mahoney—not overfamiliar. It is sad, though, to see John Heard, usually a fine leading man, reduced to a minuscule role.

Wolfgang Petersen, the German director, scored a well-deserved international success with *Das Boot*, and has other interesting European films to his credit. I am happy to report that I was instrumental in winning for him the Best Director award at the now defunct Paris Film Festival for *Black and White like Day and Night*, the best film ever about chess but a flop in America, perhaps because of the jarring jingle in its English title. His American movies hitherto were less than felicitous. Now, however, he finds the right tempos, and some excellent, lightly stressed visual effects, such as the sudden appearance of the Capitol dome behind the criminal's head. He has a true flair for camera placement, as in the low-angle shots of Malkovich fabricating his weaponry, and with such a strong, no-nonsense cinematographer as John Bailey at his side, he gives the film a sharply etched, vibrantly colored, but never arty look. And however brutal *In the Line of Fire* gets, Petersen does not let it get out of control: the horror is mostly psychological, the menace potent but subtle.

The Fugitive

I know a little about the Dr. Shepard murder case, but nothing about the TV series it inspired, so I came to *The Fugitive* relatively unencumbered. The first reel left me reeling. The director, Andrew Davis, and the screenwriters, Jeb Stuart and David Twohy, try to pump up excitement by means of some visual and aural tricks as obnoxious as they are obstreperous, and totally unnecessary. But once you get past this *mauvais quart d'heure* or so, you can settle down to the back or edge of your seat (depending on your susceptibility) and a very good couple of hours of thrills.

Despite that repellent opening—and even there—the movie does not waste time setting up the story. We learn swiftly that, coming back from late-night emergency surgery, Dr. Richard Kimble found a giant one-armed intruder in his house, grappled with him, and put him to flight, but could not save his wounded and dying wife. In fast, efficient strokes we see the police disbelieving the dismayed Kimble: then the trial, and his death sentence. On the way to the final prison, Kimble and some fellow inmates are in a phantasmagoric bus and train collision, and he and another prisoner escape. The other guy, less smart, is caught; Kimble proceeds to track down the murderer of his wife.

In his pursuit of the killer with the prosthetic arm, Kimble is, of course, himself pursued by the police, and even more fiercely by Deputy Marshal Gerard (do I detect an echo of Javert in his name?) and his team, and the cat-and-mouse game between these supersmart men is as exciting as a duel between master swordsmen. Unfortunately for the reviewer of such films, there is little he can say without giving away too much, and if the picture is this good, even a little can be *de trop*.

Let me commend the filmmakers on several things. First, they have come up with some unusual locations: the inside of a large drainage pipe, various parts of a vast city hospital, and Chicago's boisterous Saint Patrick's Day parade. Here and there, as usual with this genre, the film strains credibility, but less so than most. Next, although the plot is properly convoluted, even someone as unsleuthy as I was able, for once, to keep up with the proceedings. The pace, though taut, stops short of being relentless. Furthermore, the casting is expert: everyone looks right for his or her part, although the *New York Times*'s woman reviewer objected to the murdered wife's being too pretty. I don't think Sela Ward, who plays her, is: but if so, Harrison Ford, who plays her husband, can handle that.

Very sensible, too, is the way the murder is set up: it leaves no doubt that Dr. Kimble is guiltless. We need to worry whether an innocent man can save himself, not wonder about whether he might not, after all, be guilty. Finally, the relationship between the surgeon and the marshal is fascinating in its Dostoyevskian way. They hardly meet, but the manner in which each is trying to outguess the other constitutes an interaction of minds at least as gripping as any other, more physical, contact. And the way the sundry strands of the plot come together is highly satisfying.

The acting is proficient and efficient, all one can ask for in such a movie. Ford, who does most of his own stunt work, looks convincingly harassed through long stretches of action, and steady harassment is even harder to sustain than a slow burn. It is as if his parents had named him foreknowingly; he seems to defy the unjust forces of justice with a "Harass on!" as he plows on unstoppably toward his rehabilitation. As his nemesis, Tommy Lee Jones is equally solid. An actor I have never much liked (there is something fishy about his face), he is best precisely in such on-the-cusp roles: the good man who is nevertheless unlikable; the bad man who may not be so bad after all.

The minor rolés are all well taken, the various lawmen having an authentically dogged and often dumb quality, all too believable. The guilty are also shrewdly chosen. The only trouble is the cornball music by James Newton Howard, but I guess we must resign ourselves to trashy commercial scores in American films. Michael Chapman, who also photographed *Rising Sun*, does much cleaner work here. If you see large crowds outside theaters showing *The Fugitive*, don't run: the only way to lick them is to join them.

Betty

Claude Chabrol hasn't been heard from much lately. Now he is back with *Betty*, based on a Georges Simenon novel. Betty, an attractive, 28-year-old, obviously affluent woman, sporting a strange look—is it hostile, preoccupied, weirdly detached, downright crazy?—finds herself, drunk on a terribly rainy night, in a homey bar in Versailles, where a kindly-seeming doctor has brought her for dinner. Yes, it was a pick-up in a Paris bar, and there is something odd about driving all the way to Versailles in a downpour to a place that offers only one main course. But Betty seems to need protection, and who better to give it than a respectable-looking, fatherly physician?

Sitting there in the warm, familial Hole (*Le Trou*), as the hangout sheltering all kinds of misfits is called, the doctor suddenly starts talking weirdly, and is about to do something very, very queer. The way the mood imperceptibly changes from the mundane to the bizarre, the precise manner in which the nightmarish infiltrates the commonplace, immediately proclaims the master, or masters: Simenon the novelist, and Chabrol the screenwriter-director.

A middle-aged *habituée* of the Hole, Laure, comes to Betty's rescue. She and the proprietor (who, it turns out, is her lover) get the by now quite drunk young woman out of the doctor's clutches, and Laure takes her to her suite at the posh Trianon Palace in Versailles, where she has been living for the last three years since her husband's death. She has one special thing in common with Betty: they both like to hit the bottle. Next morning, the two women start to communicate, even though Betty is extraordinarily vague or taciturn about certain things. It does emerge, though, that she has "sold her children."

What does this mean? It means that she loved but never intended to marry Guy, her rich young husband from a suffocatingly bourgeois family, in which Guy's mother, Mine Etamble, rules the terribly proper, terribly constricting roost. Whether such a softspoken, despotic matriarch can still thrive in Paris (Simenon wrote this some thirty years ago) I doubt, but the director makes you believe it by his sheer command of detail. Chabrol knows what artists know: if the tiny things ring true, the hard-to-credit big ones will sound no alarms.

Take the scene where Betty, having been caught in adultery within earshot of her children, is made to sign a contract whereby, in exchange for never seeing her two little girls again, she will be provided with a decent living for the rest of her life. In full family gathering, a lawyer dictates and she write: "I, Elisabeth Etamble…" etc. etc. By force of habit, Betty writes "I, Betty." When the lawyer finally notices this, he takes the paper and slowly, deliberately, almost artfully, tears it into two strips (not four or eight pieces), and lets them float onto the tabletop. It is the quiet elegance with which he does it that breaks your heart.

After she has signed, and is about to leave this house, these lives forever, Betty approaches the door behind which her girls are sleeping to kiss them goodnight and goodbye. The very nice but mother-ruled Guy tells her no, this is out of the question. What gets to you is the sweetly reasonable way he says it (his heart isn't really in it): it's late, they are already asleep, what's the point? His considerate tone, as if he were merely correcting a slight lapse in grammar, gives you cold shivers. As does the docile expression with which, after a slight hesitation, Betty walks on—like a naughty, semi-contrite child being sent to bed without her dinner.

But the final wonder of the film is the personality of Betty, who is not just the victim she seems to be, but also a victimizer. There is something spectrally affectless about her as she goes around not connecting with people, repaying good with evil, being a pathological case. As Marie Trintignant superbly plays her, she is an unforgettably disturbing character, walking in a cloud of otherwhereness, yet somehow knowing, in that sleepwalkerish way of hers, where to stick in the knife. As Laure, Stéphane Audran is equally fine, and the rest are not far behind. Understated and aristocratically poised (and with minimal background music), *Betty* is one of the most well-behavedly bone-chilling horror stories of all time.

Boxing Helena

To anyone interested in sampling the rottenest apple from the bottom of the cinematic barrel, let me commend Jennifer Chambers

Lynch's *Boxing Helena*, a film acclaimed at the Sundance Festival, success at which is a guarantee of mediocrity or worse. Kim Basinger backed out of the lead, causing her to incur a ruinous seven million-dollar lawsuit. Believe me, though: every lost penny of it was well spent. Miss Lynch, whose sole claim to fame is her vastly overrated father, the director of *Blue Velvet* and *Twin Peaks*, manages to go Papa David one better in tastelessness, incompetence, and benightedness, unaware even that the accent in "Helena" does not go on the penult, for which offense alone I'd banish her to St. Helena.

Miss Lynch wrote the screenplay from a story by Philippe Caland, of whom I have never heard, and sincerely hope never to hear again. This is the tale of Dr. Nick Cavanaugh (an unlikely name for a surgeon), who is effete, namby-pamby, and supremely masochistic (an unlikely personality for a surgeon). He falls abjectly in love with the gorgeous, haughty Helena, who, after an unsuccessful initial date, keeps icily rejecting him, as well she, or anyone, might, given the mewling pest he is. When, trying to escape his crawling advances, Helena is hit by a car, Nick performs an operation on her in his private mansion that leaves her legless. Now in a wheelchair and his love prisoner, Helena can still verbally cut off Nick's attempts to wriggle into her affection: so the worthy sawbones operates away her remaining limbs, turning her into a nice little torso to feed, cosset, and blissfully toy with.

There are only two ways to make such a film. Either you have to be a tormented genius like Luis Buñuel, and turn out a dark, Sadean phantasmagoria, or you must be a clever outright pornographer. Not having the talent for the one, or the stomach for the other, Jennifer Lynch proffers unerotic titillation, sexless nastiness, mindless temerity. But also ultimate cravenness: the picture ends with a huge copout, denying all that went before. Reviewing it in the *Times*, Janet Maslin finds the movie not contemptuous of women, because "even without her arms, the cruel, beautiful Helena manages to hold all the cards." Miss Lynch displays "talent" and "control" as "no visible bloodshed is involved in transforming Helena from a cursing, prop-throwing hellion to the enshrined beauty Nick . . . wanted her to be." Just think what Shylock could have done with Nick's talent for bloodless surgery!

Divesting Helena of her limbs is, for Miss Maslin, a therapeutic act, cutting short her short-temperedness. The "engrossing" Miss Lynch, it seems, exhibits an "odd but coherent imagination," which may be true if wall-to-wall nonsense is construed as coherence. Miss Maslin's main reservation concerns Nick's neglectful mother, the cause of his subsequent troubles, being played by "an actress who looks like a *Playboy* bunny." If only Nick's father had deboned this bunny, she might have lost her *Playboy* look and become a nice domestic plaything.

Miss Lynch, I fear, is no cutting-edge director. She has cast two conspicuous no-talents in the leads. Julian Sands is a horse-faced British actor with a shoulder-length blond mane, whose voice drips with castor oil and whose manner is so mawkish and languid that the most pacific spectator would want to kick him. Sherilyn Fenn, the celebrated corpse from *Twin Peaks*, is so devoid of all ability that you wonder whether some previous surgeon might not have removed her cortex. In a meaningless supporting role, Art Garfunkle is his customary egregious self, but even such good actors as Bill Paxton and Kurtwood Smith are dragged down to Art's artistic level. And compared to Miss Lynch as screenwriter, Jackie Collins reads like Colette.

As I watched scene after flatfooted scene (is there no surgery for fallen arches?), I was reminded of one of Karl Kraus's apothegms: "Why do some people write? Because they don't have enough character not to write." The same applies to certain filmmakers, especially if they have powerful filmmaker fathers.

The Age of Innocence

How does an action director handle an inaction movie? How does a kid from the mean streets direct a picture about genteel upper-class New York in the 1870s? Will it be like unleashing Jesse James on Henry James? Or will Martin Scorsese find a way of making love not war to Edith Wharton's prose? I am happy to report that *The Age of Innocence*, though not quite a knockout, wins on points.

I must make the shameful confession of not having read Edith Wharton, though I have always suspected I would like her, if for no other reason than as an antidote to Henry James. So I came to this movie with the disadvantage of unpreparedness, of not knowing more than the average moviegoer, who may have heard of *Ethan Frome* (or *Ethan Fromme*, as the press kit squeakily puts it), but who certainly hasn't read *The Age of Innocence*. This may have proved, in the event, an advantage, for I kept hoping against hope that the principals would not end in quiet desperation: that the terribly well-bred and enormously eligible Newland Archer and the lovely, but semi-besmirched Countess Ellen Olenska would find the courage to do the unthinkable—defy the proprieties, kick over the already loosening conventions, and head for a life of unwedded bliss in Paris or the South Seas.

The best thing to announce about the film is that it looks, plays, and feels like nothing the Merchant-Ivory team of oxen could have plowed up with their plodding, methodical obtuseness. The some-what less good news is that Scorsese, striving hard to get away from the mendacious Gates of Ivory, ends up a bit out of breath. He certainly leaves viewers breathless as they try to keep pace with a movie that seems terrified of lapsing into the doldrums of respect-ability, into the pace of drawing-room conversation rather than the propulsion of a boxing match or a Mafia caper. Yet hard-pressed by the stasis of his material, he sometimes has the good grace to succumb to moments of stillness.

Nevertheless, watching the film is an exhausting experience. The director tries to make the material more cinematic in three ways: he keeps the characters on the go, or at least pacing about; he gives the camera a steady workout, sending it scurrying hither and yon, and frequently cutting on the move from one bit of kinesis to the next. Sometimes you feel as if you were on a people mover going one way, while the film was on a conveyor belt going in the opposite direc-tion. The cross fades between scenes in the sound editing reinforce the sense of speedboats that pass in the night, and although this tempo is not right for the inertia that is one part of Mrs. Wharton's subject, it is right for the other: the attempt to escape the forces of conformity driving this society. Thirdly, Scorsese directs his prin-cipals to convey pressures from within propelling their speech and movements.

This is not without interest for the viewer, and does help set off the moments of quietude. But the film can be dizzying even when Newland Archer is doing no more than looking at pictures at the Louvre. All the same, *The Age of Innocence* never falls into the sort of Merchant-Ivory amateurishness where you feel that a text is being illustrated instead of lived. Yet both Michelle Pfeiffer, as the separated but undivorced, dashing but ineligible Ellen Olen-ska, and Winona Ryder, as her cousin, the sweet but pedestrian May Welland—Archer's fiancée, with an unsuspected instinct for manipulativeness—have problems with their speech. Miss Pfeiffer seems to be urging her words along with a whip, as if they were circus horses being made to perform stunts; Miss Ryder strains for well-bred maidenliness and ingénue deliquescence, and becomes a mite gooey.

Still, these are not grave matters, and the supporting roles are filled with an Anglo-American cast that blends just about seamlessly. Especially notable are Alec McCowen as a smugly gossipy old bachelor, Mary Beth Hurt as an anguished wife, and Richard E. Grant as a social arbiter of exquisite odiousness. And it is nice to glimpse for the last time the late, beloved Alexis Smith. Everyone is good, even the unseen narrator, Joanne Woodward, whose reading steers a middle course between solicitude and reserve.

Narration of any kind, however, is a dubious blessing. It does allow Jay Cocks and Scorsese, who collaborated on the screenplay, to bring in a good deal of welcome Wharton prose; but it often sounds like someone reading out the stage directions while a play is in progress. There is an attempt at originality even here, as when the narration, as it were in mid sentence, glides into dialogue and action. This is only a mite self-conscious; more bothersome is when a letter on the sound track is begun in the voice of the reader, then continued in that of its writer, or versa, or when what starts as a letter suddenly turns into an acted-out scene. But better to err on the side of artfulness than on that of banality.

What holds the movie together is the performance of Daniel Day-Lewis as Newland Archer. As in a double exposure, the actor manages to convey both what the character is saying and the very different things he is thinking, and even the things he himself is not aware of thinking or feeling. Yet these warring emotions are conveyed not in sequence or even juxtaposition, but in perfect fusion. Compare his way of suffering with that of Miss Pfeiffer: she does everything she can, and she looks wonderful when she is distraught. But she comes across merely harried, buffeted; Day-Lewis, under a brave or dazed façade, is clearly collapsing inward.

Scorsese has paid fine attention to the look of things. Shooting New York City in Philadelphia and Troy, and Paris in Paris, he makes me believe that this is the 1870s, and as they were already somewhat nostalgically, but also bitterly, recollected by Mrs. Wharton a half-century later. An evening at the opera (*Faust* in Italian, as it well might have been) or a fancy dinner party is scrutinized with equal ritualistic fervor; the food, prepared under the supervision of Rick

Ellis, a culinary historian, and shot by Michael Ballhaus, the superb cinematographer, makes your taste buds stand up and cheer. But even as the sound of a roast duck being carved resonates crunchily from the screen, you are allowed to feel that all this overindulgence is compensation for the other freedoms denied this society.

Equal attention has been lavished on decor and costumes, for which Scorsese imported the talented Italian duo of Dante Ferretti and Gabriella Pescucci. The clothes are sumptuous without seeming ostentatious, and the sets, never much dwelled on, reek of authenticity—note especially the brilliantly chosen art works on people's walls. An experienced vocal coach (Tim Monich) and consultant on manners (Lily Lodge) also contributed to the feeling of not just looking at the 1870s but being inside them. Indeed, there is a certain fanaticism afoot here: cigar smoking is anatomized in choreographic detail; the wood burning in the fireplaces is not just a visual refrain, not just an occasional ominous rumble as a particularly fat log crumbles to ash, but also a faint obbligato humming behind the conversations even when the grate is not in the frame.

I cannot quite believe Archer's final act of abnegation, which may be my fault, the filmmakers', or Mrs. Wharton's. In fact there hovers over this entire sad tale a slight sense of the contrived, the *voulu*, as if some sort of Providence were watching over these characters to make sure that nothing comes out right for them. Where Scorsese is definitely to blame is in the music, which is by Elmer Bernstein, a typical Hollywood hack; its churning out of grandiose platitudes undermines everybody else's fine efforts. What a chance was missed here to press into service the works—particularly the chamber music—of American composers of the period, say, George Chadwick and Arthur Foote. Still and all, the film makes you feel acutely for its characters; of how many current American—or other—movies can that be affirmed?

Short Cuts

You can look at Robert Altman's *Short Cuts* in two ways. You can say that, as an adaptation, however loose, of nine stories and one poem by Raymond Carver, it turns something very close to gold into something very close to dross. Or you can say that, as a more or less original creation by Altman and his co-scenarist Frank Barhydt, it is vulgar, pretentious, voyeuristic, overlong, and, above all, contrived. After that, you can add that Altman has all kinds of technical prowess. But is that adequate compensation for a gross insufficiency of artistry, intellect, and taste?

Item: Three men on a weekend fishing trip discover the nude body of a girl floating in a river (Carver). How? By one of them taking a leak just where the body bobs among some rocks. In subsequent shots, bubbles of urine surround the body (Altman).

Item: A jealous surgeon asks insistent questions about a party three years ago, where his wife may have drunkenly kissed and even yielded to another man. She is expecting guests and trying to remove a spot from and iron her skirt as this interrogation proceeds (Carver). As she is not wearing panties, her blouse leaves open her front and rear, over both of which, especially the red pubic hair, the camera lingers lovingly. Thus her confession, eliciting lubricious laughter from the audience, is wrongly imbued with humbling hostility (Altman).

Item: The surgeon's wife is a painter, and her nudes, with the pubic hair often managing to loom large behind the actors' heads, are prominently displayed. When she is painting her sister in the nude, the surgeon comes home, and an awkward threeway conversation ensues (Altman—not in Carver).

Item: One of the anglers, on his return home, makes love to his wife, but then alienates her by relating how he and his friends fished through the weekend with the dead girl there in the water, and reported it only afterward (Carver). On first hearing this in the middle of the night, the wife gets out of bed to sit on the edge of the bathtub—to do what? Wash her feet, it seems. Why? So the camera can fondle her naked buttocks (Altman).

Item: A tough, adulterous traffic cop, after a night with his mistress, returns to his wife, the aforementioned painter's sister, and morosely gets into bed with her, only to be aroused by her foot massaging his genitals (all Altman).

Item: A young woman, a classical cellist, cannot get any affection from her mother, a nightclub crooner. The girl keeps inflicting real or imaginary injuries on herself, and will eventually gas herself in the garage. Earlier, she strips naked under the prying gaze of a pool repairman, and dives into the pool to float there like a corpse. (This entire inept tale was invented by Altman, so that the mother's nightclub songs can act as a musical bridge for the picture.)

Item: The pool repairman's unloving wife earns money at home by dispensing telephone sex, mostly sadistic, while changing a child's diapers or performing other household tasks, even as her shocked and neglected husband looks on with a hangdog air. Family quarrels and other loud noises do not seem to deter the clientele from fantasizing (all Altman).

Item: A couple spend agonizing hours by their eight-year-old son's bedside; he is comatose after having been hit by a car (Carver). The husband's father, living in another town and completely estranged from his son for thirty years upon being divorced by his wife, picks this moment to show up at the hospital, make a nuisance of himself, and keep his son from his comatose son with an endless self-exculpatory account of how he was seduced, once, by his wife's sister, which brought on the divorce (Altman).

The story "A Small, Good Thing" is the most moving of the lot. It tells how the dying boy's mother had ordered a fancy birthday cake and then, because the boy was injured on his very birthday, forgot the order. The hard-working, needy baker now keeps making phone calls to the family's home to demand pick-up and payment. The father doesn't even know about the cake, and the phone exchanges become ever nastier and, after the boy's death, downright spooky. Finally the parents angrily seek out the baker at work late at night; yelled at, he understands and becomes compassionate, making the hungry parents sit down, and comforting them with coffee and his fresh-baked rolls—"a small, good thing," as he calls it.

Thus in Carver; Altman, however, introduces on top of the baker's hate calls the nagging intrusion of the well-meaning but meddlesome and ludicrous father of the husband. This, of course, lessens the impact of the heckling and hectoring phone calls, and shifts the pathos away from the parents to the finally dejected old father.

But there is worse. Altman wants a unifying motif at the beginning and finish of the film. So he starts with an attack of medflies on Los Angeles, and sinister, spraying helicopters cruising the night sky, aerial shots interspersed with short takes of how the film's various characters react to this seeming menace from above. He ends with a menace from below, a 7.4 earthquake (accomplished by jiggling the camera), in which nobody dies. But it is enough to muck up the gentle, touching moment of the baker bearing the tray of rolls with the building shaking and the three characters hastily seeking shelter. Other stories, such as "Neighbors" and "Vitamins," completely lose their point in the movie.

Those supposedly unifying liminal and terminal disasters point to a major flaw in the film—that there is, in fact, nothing unifying here. Medflies, earthquakes, the jazz singer's dreary songs (which only some of the characters come to listen to) cannot really connect these disparate stories. Altman also makes the characters friends, neighbors, relatives, or has their paths cross fortuitously, but the basic arbitrariness is not overcome. Though he has changed the locale from the Northwest to L.A. (which he knows better, and is cheaper to film in), you do not get a sense of this being a true cross-section of a city. Why these characters and not others? Especially since Altman and Barhydt cannot successfully stretch out what works on the page in miniature: an incident, an epiphany.

So the vignette of an alcoholic chauffeur and his lunch-counter waitress wife has to be lengthened to make it conform to the others, but the new incidents and dialogue are mere corny fillers. And making the sympathetic waitress the little boy's accidental killer does not make her a more evolved or endearing character. A good short story functions because it has a structure, a shape, a style that, together, create a sense of character and atmosphere, a rising action, a climax, and a resolution. If the story is padded out or interspersed with other stories, its rhythm and internal logic suffer. The conflation of ten stories makes climaxes abut on other climaxes, moods clash with moods. How does a damaged marriage resonate if it is followed cheek by jowl with a dying boy and his parents' grief?

And all those hammy or sleazy effects! Why would a girl seeking out her mother at work for some sympathy lug a heavy cello with her for no reason? Why would a naked corpse be repeatedly dwelled on if not for prurient purposes? Why would each young actress have a, however brief or partial, nude scene? Why would a boy, after a weekend with one of his mother's lovers, call him by the name of another lover? In a star-studded cast, only Madeleine Stowe and Jennifer Jason Leigh manage to score, while some—Tom Waits, Robert Downey Jr., Matthew Modine—are nothing short of embarrassing. None of which prevents the critics from outsalivating Pavlov's dogs.

Farewell My Concubine

Farewell My Concubine, made in Hong Kong and China by Chen Kaige, a co-winner at the Cannes Festival, is a two-and-a-half-hour movie. The subject is Chinese opera, and, as seen through the eyes of two of its stars, the fortunes of China. The film takes us from the era of the warlords (the twenties) to that of the Cultural Revolution (the sixties); in between, there is the Japanese occupation, the Nationalist government, and, finally, Maoism. It is an outspoken picture, and has run into all sorts of trouble with the Chinese authorities. Alas, persecution does not, any more than the Cannes prize, confer automatic masterpiece status on its object.

Farewell My Concubine begins very strongly and ends equally powerfully, but has a long, sagging middle, where the opera turns pretty soapy. The story of two friends, Cheng Dieyi and Duan Xiaolou, apprenticed as boys to the Peking opera, it follows them through their arduous rise to stardom, through their troubled private lives and their downfall under Communist abuse. Kaige's film is not the easiest 154 minutes I ever spent. Still, the first 40 minutes or so are utterly absorbing in their tenaciously harrowing way. The tortures inflicted by their teachers on these young boys are related with a chilling objectivity that is not all that far from relish. The atmosphere is midway between that of *Oliver Twist* and that of Octave Mirbeau's protopornographic classic, *Torture Garden*.

These sequences explain a lot about why Chinese acrobats are unsurpassable, and why Far Eastern peoples can endure hardship better than most others can. The film, written by Lilian Lee and Lu Wei from the former's novel, is clearly in the popular, subartistic vein, but the impact of the subject matter and Kaige's forceful direction combine to rescue it from mediocrity.

Dieyi is delicate of build and a homosexual, and excels at women's roles. Xiaolou is burly, almost beefy, and specializes in warriors. We see them perform diverse roles, but especially the opera *Farewell My Concubine*, in which the mighty King of Chu (Xiaolou), finally defeated, wants his horse and his concubine Wu to escape to safety. Both noble creatures prefer to stay with their master, Wu (Dieyi) dancing for him one last time before slitting her throat with his sword. This opera becomes symbolic of the destinies of our principals. Dieyi is in love with the heterosexual Xiaolou, who, however, roisters in brothels, and ends up marrying the beautiful superwhore Juxian, who makes him a shrewd and loyal wife. The jealous Dieyi turns cold to Xiaolou and icy to Juxian, and gets involved in shady homosexual relationships with persons in power.

The ways in which politics and history impinge on these relationships is not without interest; neither is the connection between gender-bending in Chinese opera and Dieyi's sexuality. But the film opts for melodrama, starting with Dieyi's prostitute mother chopping off her boy's sixth finger to make him acceptable to the opera people. It treats us to frequent disciplinary beatings and other propaedeutic torments, goes on to a number of betrayals and sacrifices, introduces a couple of smooth villains right out of Josef von Sternberg, and becomes tiresome not through lack of incident, but through excess. It does, however, pick up tremendous power when the three principals fall victim to the Cultural Revolution. The manner in which the Red Guards, hardly more than children, manage to make three adults go morally to pieces is depicted with sickening authenticity. Psychological browbeating proves even worse than the physical tortures by the opera teachers, which, by the way, do not quite stop even after the boys become men.

The movie toys with all sorts of parallels: politics and private life, loving prostitutes (or concubines) of three separate but answering kinds, related instances of artists performing under enemy eyes, and echoes of life in art and vice versa. But it seems to score only through violence; nonviolent episodes never rise to comparable heights. And when Dieyi replicates the sacrifice of the concubine Wu in a way that makes art and life coincide a little too perfectly, the didacticism subverts the intended pathos.

How you will respond to *Farewell My Concubine* may also depend on your tolerance for Peking opera, of which there is quite a bit in the movie; it is, I'm sorry to have to confess, not music to my ears. But there are many rewards for the eyes, not least of them the portrayal of Juxian by the gorgeous and greatly gifted Gong Li, whom we have admired in the films of her husband, Zhang Yimou. She is just as good for Chen Kaige. All the acting is persuasive, as is the camera work of Gu Changwei. Yet there is one thing we never find out: What happened to the King of Chu's self-sacrificing steed? Perhaps because there is no ready parallel for it in the main story, the poor horse gets short shrift.

Fearless

Confronted with daily clinkers, a critic finds it hard to work up the passion to call a movie mendacious, detestable, and revolting, but *Fearless* provokes just such enthusiasm. One senses, of course, that its protagonist, meant to be both off-putting and sympathetic, must eventually die. But a two hours wait—not such a long time as movies go nowadays—seemed virtually interminable. And then to be cheated out of the well-earned death of the fatuous hero—horrible!

Fearless has a screenplay by Rafael Yglesias "based upon his novel." Whenever the dreaded *upon* appears instead of the unpretentious *on*, I know I am in for trouble; the only even surer sign is any sort of accolade at the Sundance Film Festival. Peter Weir, the Australian director, has already given us two of the world's most obnoxious films, *The Last Wave* and *Dead Poets Society*, and a couple of others not far behind. He is the sort of fellow for whom the German saying "*dem soll man das Handwerk legen*" was coined: this guy should be stripped of his trade. Moreover, the picture was produced by the husband-and-wife team Mark Rosenberg (deceased) and Paula Weinstein, about whom more below.

The architect Max Klein and his partner are flying on business from San Francisco to Houston, when the airliner develops serious hydraulic problems and catastrophe beckons. Max has been, as always, prey to fear of flying, but fear of dying somehow liberates him into an instant hero, the first of the whopping lies being peddled here. While the stewardesses try frantically and ineffectually to dispense help, Max rises from his partner's side and moves with a stately, almost floating walk toward an empty seat next to a scared little boy, some rows ahead of him, whom he spotted from way behind(!). Bestowing smiles on all and sundry, Max hunkers down next to the boy, Byron, goofily grins at him as they double up in crash position, and all is well. The movie actually begins right after the catastrophe, with Max carrying a baby and leading several kids through the tall corn back to the plane (how far were they ejected?) with poise the Pied Piper of Hamelin might envy.

The corn becomes ever taller. Max saw a blinding light, you see, that placed him beyond the concerns and worries of mere mortals. He takes his time to get back to his wife and children, who have been left in the dark about his fate, then proceeds to ignore them with sublime detachment. He treats both the airline's sympathetic psychiatrist and the eager-beaver lawyer of his wife and his partner's widow, trying to collect the utmost in damages, with amused contempt. He claims to be a ghost, and turns into a ruthless truthteller, which might be all right from a saint or sage, but, from this consistently disagreeable fellow, seems merely offensive.

The novel, I gather, views Max with a modicum of irony; the movie—thanks to Mr. Weir, I imagine—is wholly on his side. He walks through the onrushing cars on a freeway with unruffled nonchalance, balances on the narrow ledge of a high rooftop with ease and exhilaration, can even eat strawberries, to which he is mortally allergic; death has no dominion over him. The more smugly unreachable he gets, the more the movie gloatingly coasts along with him.

Out of desperation, Dr. Perlman, the psychiatrist, brings him together with Carla Rodrigo, the one other survivor beyond his ministrations. Carla was clutching her two-year-old son Bubble in her arms, but, from the impact of the crash, let go and lost him. She is now in a state of near-catatonia from guilt as well as grief, but Max, while alienating everyone else around him (he favors little Byron over his own son), proceeds to guide her out of it. Carla, neglecting husband and family, responds fully, and soon the unlikely pair live only for each other. On foot and in Max's Volvo, they rove through San Francisco, making idle talk.

The climax of their chaste *folie à deux* comes when they go on a Christmas-shopping spree for their dear departed: he for his long-dead father whom he was never close to, she for her adored Bubble. In this bubbleheaded orgy for socially and ethnically remote yet platonically loving partners, Mr. Weir surpasses himself—but there is worse to come. When he cannot quite exorcise Carla's guilt otherwise. Max straps her into the back of his car with a big box in her arms, and himself into the driver's seat, then crashes the Volvo full blast into a wall, just where a giant eye is painted on it—God's, no doubt. Both survive (Volvo must have made a handsome contribution to the production budget), but the box flies out of Carla's grasp, proving to her that she was innocent of Bubble's death, and to us that Max is a madman. (No, another Australian directed the Mad Max movies.)

In the end, redeemed, Carla resumes her humble Hispanic life, and bids Max a bittersweet farewell as she refuses to "disappear" with him. Rejecting his devoted, long-suffering Laura and their kids, Max once again bites the strawberry and, no longer sustained by his former sense of invulnerability, promptly falls down in lethal convulsions, as Laura fights desperately to keep him alive. The beyond, once again represented by blinding light, beckons to him at the end of the crashed plane's fuselage, which now turns into a blue-lit tunnel of supra-terrestrial love that draws him to his mystic destination. But, shucks, he coughs up the berry.

Throughout the film, the crash becomes, in Mr. Weir's hands, a supreme cheat. Although the initial failure of the hydraulic system is scary enough, other things are variously softened and muted. In the aftermath scene, we see dazed survivors, but no uncovered corpses. Whenever the story runs out of steam, we get further partial flashbacks on, as it were, the installment plan, teasing us along with promises (and dread) of the climactic crash. When this finally comes, the horror is toned down (or, for me, intensified) with the minimalist music of the abominable Henryk Gorecki's repellent Third Symphony, whose *lento sostenuto tranquillo ma cantabile* (get that?) movement descends on—upon!—the disaster like so much benignly all-enveloping soup.

But Weir will stop at nothing, and brings in another Pole, the maximalist no-talent Krzysztof Penderecki, and still other trendies to gussy up Maurice Jarre's already unsavory background score. A similar visual fakery has the gifted but often excessive cinematographer Allen Daviau bedizen the movie with every sort of unearned visual opulence as further aid in audience-besotting. Finally, there is the highly talented Jeff Bridges playing Max, though not even he can make the character sympathetic. Still, if you compare Mr. Bridges's work with that of Richard Gere, in a faintly similar yet even worse film, *Mr. Jones*, you can at least appreciate Mr. Bridges's honesty. In both films the hero stands or cavorts on a high ledge with magic impunity, but Mr. Bridges never stoops to Mr. Gere's intolerable cutesiness. On the other hand, by this very restraint, Mr. Bridges alienates anyone less weird than Mr. Weir.

Isabella Rossellini, an actress whose alleged charms were always lost on me, does some intense acting here as Laura, though her being Italian is never explained, any more than is anything else about anyone's past. Rosie Perez, albeit ethnically authentic, remains questionable otherwise. With her tiny stature and squeaky voice, she makes Carla cute rather than near-tragic, and when she shouts, as she is often called upon to do, her timbre and accent make her all but incomprehensible, which is annoying even when the lost dialogue is unlikely to contain many gems. Dubious, too, is the casting of John Turturro as Dr. Perlman. An excellent actor in rough-hewn proletarian or villainous roles, Turturro makes an unlikely psychiatrist. Others, however, notably Tom Hulce as the lawyer, hold their own staunchly. The film has received its share of raves, but what, these days, doesn't?

Praise Jack, Shoot *The Piano*

SHADOWLANDS; THE PIANO

Shadowlands, by William Nicholson, has already been a successful television movie and stage play, so that a theatrical film may have seemed redundant. Joss Ackland and Claire Bloom on TV, Nigel Hawthorne and Jane Alexander on stage, were everything one might ask for in this (broadly) true story of C. S. Lewis's belated marriage and all too early bereavement. The celebrated Oxford don, literary scholar, children's novelist, and Christian philosopher married, late in life, Joy Gresham, a minor American poet and ex-Communist, Jewish and the mother of one young boy (in real life, two). The movie makes their story as vivid and moving as if you had never seen it before.

C. S. Lewis (Jack to his friends) was an almost smugly devout Anglican; a confirmed, indeed ossified, bachelor, who shared his digs with his somewhat worldlier brother, Warnie, a retired army officer; and a person who probably never met a Jew or Communist in all his previous life. Joy Gresham, who had come to England to escape from her husband, a drunken and adulterous novelist, was, like her son, a great Lewis fan, so it was only natural for them to meet in London, and for the Greshams eventually to visit Lewis at Oxford. It was almost as natural for Lewis and Joy to become friends, even though her tartly outspoken ways raised many an Oxford eyebrow. What was less expectable was for Jack to marry Joy—to be sure, only in a marriage of convenience, to enable her to obtain British citizenship, but definitely not a place in his bed.

The Greshams remained in London until Joy was stricken with bone cancer too advanced for a cure. It was then that Lewis realized he truly loved this spirited, iconoclastic woman, and married her again—this time in a bedside Anglican ceremony, in the eyes of God, as he put it. Almost miraculously, Joy had a remission, and she and Jack enjoyed a real marriage for a brief while, though she warned him that, for this happiness, he would have to pay with a lifelong sorrow. After her death, Lewis sank into profound despair, mitigated only by his religion and having to look after Douglas, to whom shared grief brought him closer than before.

That is the story in essence, but Mr. Nicholson's sensitive and incisive reimagining of it makes it enormously rich in humor, drama, local color, and psychological detail. And surprisingly,

Richard Attenborough—who, for my money, never made a good movie (only overblown and naïve spectaculars or tiresome whimsies)—directed this with remarkable poise, empathy, and finesse. He captures the austere beauty of Oxford as tidily as its quaint rituals and academic bickering; also the slightly stiff yet companionable coexistence of the Lewis brothers. And he finds the right rhythms in which to tell the story of Jack and Joy—of how she thaws him out even as she wins over a harrumphing contingent of scholars and backbiters.

Less commanding than Joss Ackland's, less wry than Nigel Hawthorne's, Anthony Hopkins's Jack—more fumblingly introverted and emotionally corseted—is just as good, and possibly nearer the truth. Debra Winger has neither Claire Bloom's loveliness nor Jane Alexander's ironic hauteur, but she has a wonderfully idiosyncratic bounciness—almost a tomboyish *diablerie*—that befits this latter-day Madame Sans-Gêne to perfection. And when the going gets rough, she and Mr. Hopkins wring the heart with the best of them. When he, in the most unadorned language and with only slightly heightened inflection, tells her that he can't bear to lose her, the scene cuts quickly and unartily to the quick, to art.

Edward Hardwicke is a quietly winning Warnie; Joseph Mazzello a nicely unprecious, unprecocious Douglas; and John Wood, Maurice Denham, Peter Firth, along with many others, contribute handsomely. Roger Pratt's camera catches noble, history-laden stone exteriors as respectfully as warm, wooden interiors worn smooth with living. If George Fenton's music does not quite have the same tactful reticence, it is still tasteful enough. *Shadowlands* reports, but does not revel in, harsh realities, even as it unlipsmackingly savors happiness and humor. Every one of its tears, like every one of its laughs, is scrupulously earned, and understatement has never been deployed to better effect.

At a New York Film Festival press conference, Jane Campion said she had originally intended to have the Cannes grand-prize-winning *The Piano* end with the drowning of the heroine. Instead, she has her going off to live happily ever after with her lover. I wonder about a writer-director who ends up making the opposite of what she set out to do.

The film starts with Ada, a Scottish mail-order bride, arriving on a desolate New Zealand coast with her small daughter, Flora. It's sometime in the nineteenth century, and there is no dock: the sailors unceremoniously dump people and their belongings on a deserted beach. Next day, Stewart, the husband, arrives with some Maori carriers. As the return trek leads through muddy jungles, Stewart decrees that Ada's most precious possession, her piano, be temporarily left behind, exposed to the mercy of the waves and weather. Ada, by the way, is mute, and communicates with her daughter in a home-made sign language; with others, via a note-book she wears around her neck, on whose pages she furiously scribbles the notes she hands out. Early sequences of the film have voiceover narration in Ada's voice at age six, when she voluntarily stopped speaking. Don't inner voices mature?

We never find out anything about Ada's background, her first husband, and how Stewart acquired her in marriage. Or why she gave up speaking. Later, Flora will offer a wildly fanciful explana-tion that we, clearly, are not meant to believe. When mother and daughter spend that first cold night on the beach, they sleep under Ada's hoopskirt; who would have thought a crinoline could provide shelter for two?

Why would a welcoming husband abandon his bride's beloved piano, her chief mode of self-expression, when there are enough porters to carry it; and why not at least move it out of the reach of the waves? Later, it is Stewart's less affluent partner, Baines—an Englishman gone native, who sports Maori tattoos on his face—who buys the piano from Stewart, and seems to have no problem hauling it to his homestead. That the piano should play perfectly af-ter what it's been through is one of the film's most resounding lies.

Ada refuses to sleep with her husband, which he meekly ac-cepts: he'll wait. Baines tells Ada he'll let her have the piano back in exchange for lessons. She goes to his house to give them, each session earning her a black key or, if she is particularly complai-sant, more than one; the white keys, evidently, have no market value. Baines watches her from odd angles, including from below, often playing with her various extremities—with anything but the keyboard. Eventually, he presents himself to her naked and panting with desire; session by session, he has already removed quite a bit of her clothing. She succumbs, and they make wild, un-Victorian love. After that, things become rather more im-plausible.

Jane Campion prides herself on leaving much unexplained. She has every right to be proud: at leaving things unexplained, Miss Cam-pion is a champion. We do not even get a sense of topography of the distances between places, of what kind of settlement this is, of the reasons for the comings and goings of certain other white persons. As for the Maoris, they are lazy, giggling children, given to making rude jokes about the whites, which are sometimes, not always, translated by subtitles. Flora's actions consistently make no sense, but she at least has the excuse of being a child. What the adults do would make sense only as the wet dream of an inane woman, which *The Piano*, apparently, is not meant to be.

A final example. When Ada, who now plays teasing sexual games with her embarrassed husband (who had watched her through a window make love to Baines, and said nothing, only to keep her later under household arrest), decides to send a love message to Baines, she writes it on a key she rips from her piano— as if there were no paper, and as if Baines, who is illiterate, could read it. She entrusts the missive to Flora, who, perversely, walks miles to deliver it to Stewart instead, even though she bears him no particular allegiance. The consequences are dire, of course, but in an utterly loony way. Miss Campion claims kinship with Emily Brontë; but *Wuthering Heights*, another overheated spinsterish fantasy, makes a lot more sense, and has a little thing called genius going for it.

Even the music is absurd. Except for one piece of mauled Chopin, the score is by Michael Nyman, one of the most self-important, overrated, and, to my ears, worthless composers around; for this period piece, he has written his usual New Age claptrap. Yet, in other ways, Miss Campion is a stickler for accuracy, especially when such accuracy looks or sounds ridiculous to us, e.g., people wearing London street clothes and shoes to slosh through jungle mud.

Holly Hunter looks dismal and ghostly most of the time, her two white ears protruding through an oily, slicked-down carapace of black hair like a pair of stale shrimps. She plays piano and bizarre equally well. Harvey Keitel manages to act supremely randy in a childlike way, and wears his blue Morse-code-like tattoo with a straight face, which is an accomplishment. Sam Neill struggles with a role as unappetizing as it is thankless, and Anna Pacquin is an adorably precocious brat ripe for strangling. What possessed the Cannes judges to divide the Golden Palm between this and *Farewell My Concubine*, which is at least indisputably a film? The only similarity between the two lies in each having a main character one of whose fingers gets lustily chopped off.

From the Jaws of Death

SCHINDLER'S LIST

The old question of whether the Holocaust can be accosted head on in a work of art receives a resounding affirmative answer in Steven Spielberg's *Schindler's List*. The issue was raised most conspicuously apropos of Rolf Hochhuth's play *The Deputy*; the *New York Times Book Review* once concluded in an article that such monstrous horror could be tackled only by indirection, and held up Paul Celan's marvelous poem *"Todesfuge"* ("Death Fugue") as the proper solution. But it seems to me that Eastern European filmmakers had some noteworthy successes with frontal attacks, and now we have one too.

The film is based on a documentary novel by the Australian writer Thomas Keneally, whose work also underlies one of my all-time favorite movies, Fred Schepisi's *The Chant of Jimmie Blacksmith*. Keneally heard the true story of Oskar Schindler and the Schindler Jews from the owner of a Los Angeles leather goods store where the novelist had brought his briefcase for repair; the man was one of those Jews. Schindler was a minor Catholic Sudeten-German businessman who, when Hitler conquered Poland, moved to Krakow to strike it rich. Prospects for clever opportunists were good. Schindler joined the Nazi party, and acquired an enamelware factory confiscated from its Jewish owners, where he could manufacture kitchenware for the German troops.

A womanizer and a bon vivant, Schindler left his wife behind and soon became intimate with a number of young Polish women. He spent most of the money he had on treating German officers he befriended to food, drink, and women. By bribing young Polish black-marketeers, mostly Jews, he gained access to rare foods and luxury items with which he ingratiated himself to the conquerors. All this led to his factory's getting the precious army contracts, not to mention Jewish slave labor from the inmates of the nearby Plaszow concentration camp. Wanting, for purely materialistic reasons, workers in good shape, he built a special camp for them on factory grounds, where they got better food and were relatively protected from Nazi harassment. He also found a Jewish accountant, one Itzak Stern, a kind of genius, who helped him get Jewish financing for his enterprise, kept track of whose palm needed greasing in what way, and generally managed Schindler's affairs, Oskar himself being a terrific operator, but with a poor head for business.

Gradually, Schindler began to grasp the humanity of the Jews and the inhumanity of the Nazis. He managed to befriend Amon Goeth, the new and particularly bestial commandant of Plaszow, whose job it was to make the camp even deadlier than before. Schindler dealt deftly with Goeth, and was able, against ever-worsening odds, to save 1,100 Jews from certain death by placing them on his list of essential workers. This involved tricky and daring maneuvers and hair's breadth rescues, which you will have to experience for yourself.

What makes the film art? First, its ability to treat catastrophe with complete understatement and an objectivity that, though by no means feelingless, does not parade its feelings. In Steven Zaillian's screenplay, there is no speechifying, moralizing, or commentary of any sort. We are never buttonholed and instructed what to think about anyone or anything. Next, all about the film is unostentatiously but scrupulously authentic. The Polish is Polish, the German is German, the Hebrew, Hebrew. Having been made *in situ*, it used many locations preserved as they were fifty years ago, and rebuilt the rest with acute accuracy. Everything looks, sounds, even smells right. Though all that is of primary importance is spoken in English, a good deal is left in the actual languages, which enhances the atmosphere immeasurably. But then, the film lives especially in its images, which speak in one tongue for all.

Further, it is, except for the epilogue, shot in black-and-white. Mr. Spielberg has said that our knowledge of concentration camps comes from black-and-white photographs, and he wanted to hold fast to those associations. It works. Although absence of color might now seem as anachronistic as absence of sound, it gives the film a documentary look that it earns the hard way and puts to good use.

Again, Mr. Spielberg understands that with so many important minor characters, the film, to avoid confusing us, needs indelibly individualized faces. And most of them, memorably, are. In other words, the unfamiliar must be made familiar. But to work fully, the film must also make the familiar unfamiliar. We have all heard of individual Nazi soldiers taking instinctive interest in some little Jewish child they were about to consign to the ovens; of officers maintaining intimate contact with art and culture while engaged, willingly or not, in butchery. The way Mr. Spielberg introduces these details, they manage to ring new, true, and terrible. It has to do with underinsistence, the impersonal eye of history looking on unblinking and dispassionate.

And that is what gets you. People here die casually, like dogs, or worse. It is all shown with swift, stark impassivity, with total trust in the spare word and unsparing image. There is no editorializing, which is not even allowed to creep in by the back door, say, in Janusz Kaminski's cinematography or Michael Kahn's editing, and just barely in John Williams's score. (What an Arthur Honegger could have done here!) There is, for instance, a way of making black-and-white camera work take on a manichean perfection: angelic whites, diabolic blacks. Nothing like that here, thanks also to Allan Starski's production design and Anna Sheppard's costumes: each color was held accountable to the whole, and to the way it translated into the right shades of dismal grey.

Impressively, Spielberg's choices do not espouse artlessness in the interest of realism. Instead, there is fairly elaborate crosscutting, to contrast, as it were in parallel, the antithetical fates of the expropriators and the expropriated. There are matching shots that are distinctly artful, but do not feel arty, so compelling is their logic. There are camera angles and placements that are far from obvious, but do not feel *recherché*. They have an understated but discernible aesthetic value, as if to say that certain formal and pictorial niceties obtain even amid the ghastliest circumstances, which, far from lessening their ghastliness, heightens it.

It is also satisfying for the film to advert to color in the epilogue, which takes place in today's Israel, where Schindler, a thorough failure at everything after the war, was buried at his request in 1974, just short of his three-score and ten. The color is kept carefully restrained, almost home-movieish. Seeing the real Schindler Jews placing tokens on their savior's grave might have come out sentimental, but doesn't. The secret is matter-of-factness, and a certain tact. Take the way Schindler's marriage is handled. Both its strength and its weakness are in the film, conveyed with an economy as admirable as it is necessary. Any more about the Schindlers' marital problems, and you trivialize the main action. Any less, and you dehumanize a troubled but touching relationship.

In a film such as this, where certain novelistic elements must fill in the interstices between facts, false steps could be fatal. If the dialogue is too clever, it upstages the horror; if it is too pedestrian, it is unworthy of the surrounding truths. I don't know how much of the writing here is Mr. Keneally and how much Mr. Zaillian, but my, how it works! When a young German officer anguishedly plays the piano in a building where the others are savagely rounding up

the tenants, a soldier stops to wonder: "Bach?" Another replies condescendingly, "Nein. Mozart." To show that one man thinks he can
assuage his guilt with a piano, and that another can, amid a deadly
razzia, derive pride from irrelevant expertise—and to show this
with no more than four syllables of dialogue—*that* is superb.

For the record, I detect two false notes. Mr. Spielberg introduces
a couple of spots of color into his black-and-white. One is a candle
flame during a Jewish religious ritual, but this connects with the
epilogue and justifies the color. There is also, however, the red over-
coat of a tiny girl who seems to evade the Nazis in one scene, only to
turn up later on a cart as a diminutive corpse among so many others. The patch of color is meant to help us connect the two far-apart
images. Still, this strikes me as reaching, since the adorable face of
the child could have done the job by itself. The other misstep occurs when Schindler and one of his mistresses, out riding on a hill,
stop to stare at the savage roundup of Jews below; with the naked
eye they observe distant events in unlikely detail. But these are the
merest peccadilloes amid 185 minutes of sustained excellence.

The acting is impeccable. In the cast are mostly Polish, German,
Israeli, and other foreign actors, including many amateurs. No one
sticks out, which is the highest compliment I can pay. As Schindler,
Liam Neeson, an Irish giant of a man, is perfect. Looking like a large,
intelligent, sensual rat, he lets us see the stages of his awakening compassion as clearly as a glass does the rising level of the liquid poured
into it. Even more splendid, perhaps, is Ben Kingsley, the half-British,
half-Indian actor, who manages to look exactly as Stern, the Jewish accountant, should. His face hardly modulates its expression, his
voice barely changes volume or pitch, but his slightest emphasis tattoos itself on our minds even as his eyes burn holes into the screen.
As the horrific Goeth, the English actor Ralph Fiennes is a revelation. Like Neeson, he affects a slight accent, and, also like Neeson,
he makes it, atypically for Hollywood, perfect. I have never seen evil
given a more human—but not, therefore, humanizing—face.

The American Caroline Goodall is nicely contained as Mrs.
Schindler, and the Israeli Jonathan Sagalle as Poldek epitomizes
the petty knavery that, against a tragic background, becomes heroic
bravery. And as a Jewish beauty whom Goeth takes on as his maid,
lusts for, flirts with, and brutally takes out his rage on because, as
a good German officer, he dare not sexually molest her, Embeth
Davidtz is magnificent. She would quietly steal any other show but
this one, which cannot be stolen.

I don't know what it is that makes Steven Spielberg so hated in the worlds of Hollywood and film criticism, but hated he is. Already the Los Angeles and New York critics have voted his film best, while bypassing his direction. Ridiculous!

Romancing AIDS

PHILADELPHIA

AIDS has finally made it into mainline Hollywood cinema, and its first appearance has been hooplaed as if it were the Second Coming. *Philadelphia* was made by Jonathan Demme, whose *The Silence of the Lambs* was attacked in certain quarters because its murderer was a homosexual and transvestite, and the film was thus thought to be disrespectful to homosexuals, transvestites, and, for all I know, murderers. Unleashed, the minority mentality can sniff out disrespect in more places than a hyperactive dog can buried bones.

As an act of penance, Mr. Demme proceeded to make this *Philadelphia*, as it is called with heavy irony: the City of Brotherly Love exposed for its lack of fair play, decency, and brotherly love. But the trouble with genuflection is that, whatever its other uses, it is not the right posture for making movies. This one oozes reverence and self-righteousness in equal measure, and pins so many medals on its own chest that you can hardly see the movie beneath them.

It is the story—or such part of it as is deemed housebroken—of Andrew Beckett, a terrific young lawyer in a Philadelphia firm, who comes down with AIDS. He doesn't tell his employers, but when a lesion is spotted on his forehead, he is fired on grossly trumped-up charges of incompetence. He sues the firm, but the only lawyer he can get to represent him is Joe Miller, a black ambulance chaser who crassly promotes his services on TV. A macho man, Joe hates homosexuals; it is only when he happens to see how Andrew is discriminated against even in the reading room of the public library that the connection between discriminations dawns on him.

Already things are a bit too good to be true. What kind of name is Andrew Beckett? A prince or a Carnegie might be Andrew, and a saint or a Nobel laureate might be Beckett, but a lawyer who, on top of that, contracts AIDS? As for the rough-riding Joe Miller, he has a lovely and sagacious wife and a brand new girl baby, and is played by sexy Denzel Washington: clearly, a hustler with a heart of gold, not to mention a helluva head on his shoulders. And it is in a library, that temple of humanistic learning, that Joe sees the pitiful-looking Andrew boning up on the law—he'll have to represent himself—and notices how other readers recoil from him. So Saul becomes Paul.

The film avoids any closer examination of homosexuality, or even AIDS, and hurries to become a courtroom drama, which everyone can have good, wholesome fun with. To be sure, Andrew has a boyfriend, but that is as much as we learn about his lifestyle. Who is this companion, named Miguel Alvarez? He is sort of a painter, and is played by Antonio Banderas, perhaps the hottest of heterosexual Latin lovers on the current screen. It is not clear how he makes his living, where he comes from, or how he met Andrew—Heaven forfend that the movie should soil its hands with a scene in a gay bar. The relationship between Andrew and Miguel, as shown, could be that between two devoted brothers or, later, a sick man and his empathetic nurse.

Andrew's other relationships are equally sanitized. His loving mother knows all about his illness and is as understanding as his doctor—also a woman. When his father and his siblings and their spouses learn about his condition and lawsuit, they are all models of love, supportiveness, and pride, as if Andrew had received some great but controversial award. He is dandling a tiny niece on his knees as he and his extended family renew, as it were, their familial vows. It never crosses the mind of the dandled child's mother to worry, however supererogatorily, about possible infection, nor does Andrew's crude-looking father utter so much as one ambiguous word. This family reunion could have been painted by Norman Rockwell. Needless to say, they all love Miguel, too.

But what about Andrew's law firm? Well, its patriarch and linchpin, Charles Wheeler, is played by Jason Robards, who specializes in Crusty Old Men, Lovable, but here plays a Crusty Old Man, Hateful. This is good casting, for it proves how vicious even the best and most tailored among us can get when AIDS rears its head. The properly Philadelphian partners are solidly united against Andrew, except for one who wants to be decent, but fear silences his humanity. He is played by the well-known off-off Broadway actor Ron Vawter, who looks less clean-cut than the rest—midway between stuffy and scruffy, which is how, in the movies, one recognizes incipient humanity in a lawyer.

It is all slide-rule casting. The good mother is the lovable and oh, so liberal Joanne Woodward; the good doctoress is Karen Finley, the performance artist who smears her body with chocolate, and whose NEA grant was revoked and then reinstated. The low-echelon employee who speaks up for Andrew is played by the black performance artist Anna Deavere Smith. Too many noble women and blacks in the film? Mustn't let things look like PC, so the firm is represented by an unnerving woman lawyer (Mary Steenburgen) who, however, mutters at trial's end about how much she hated this case. And one of her legal adjuncts is a black man, but he never gets to say anything, lest he become too heinous.

But why pursue the mathematical ingenuity of the casting down to its least ramifications if the very lead is played by Tom Hanks, Hollywood's Mr. Lovable himself. The only actor who could have made Andrew even cuter is Robin Williams, but he would probably have done something wild along the line, whereas Hanks keeps him dignified all the way, except for a few slight ironic glints. He gives a very good performance, aided also by losing thirty pounds, and by the excellent makeup of Clark Fullerton, which may be the most honest and disturbing element in the entire movie.

I will mention only one more thing, the scene that even unenthusiastic critics have extolled. After Andrew has thrown a flamboyantly gay party (but gay in the manner of the New Orleans carnival), Joe stays on to discuss tomorrow's courtroom strategy with his host. Andrew, however, puts on one of his beloved operatic discs, something the like of which Joe has never heard: Maria Callas singing "La mamma morta" from Giordano's Andrea Chénier. And he proceeds to enlighten, civilize, and spiritually transform the culturally underprivileged Joe.

I find this scene tasteless, patronizing, and offensive. Mr. Demme and his scenarist, Ron Nyswaner, thought they could make Andrew lovable even to macho and black audiences as a fellow who, thanks to his homosexuality, has discovered the treasure trove of opera, and is now sharing his wealth with the less privileged. The scene is dawdled over, bedizened with fancy camera angles, and finally bathed in brazen scarlet light as Andrew dances around with his IV bottle for a partner. Homosexuals, it implies, have something wonderful to impart to the rest of us ignorant slobs. Yet Giordano's opera is one of the worst ever to make it into the standard repertoire, and Miss Callas's rendition is hammy. Andrew's glowingly passionate explication of "La mamma morta" is comparable to someone's spreading literary culture by lecturing on Danielle Steele.

According to Ron Nyswaner, Mr. Demme's motto is, "Let's entertain, and let's be truthful, and let's be bold." *Philadelphia* does poorly
by the first, worse by the second, and miserably by the third.

Like Father, Like Son

IN THE NAME OF THE FATHER

Jim Sheridan's *In the Name of the Father* is, not to mince words,
a great film, or, as the Irish would more appositely pronounce it,
fillum. It is something with which to bolster audiences: fill 'em up
with pity and terror, with laughter, sadness, and rage. And perhaps
even—the hardest reaction to elicit from moviegoers—thought.

It is based on the autobiography of Gerry Conlon, a young Belfast Catholic and ne'er-do-well, a fellow who dawdles, gambles, and
indulges in petty crime such as stealing the tin off a neighbor's
roof, much to the chagrin of his honest, hard-working father and
staunch, dedicated mother. Gerry's rooftop shenanigans (the British soldiery mistakes him for a sniper and a riot results) get him
into trouble with the IRA, some of whom might have been inadvertently compromised in that army crackdown. So, from the very
start, Gerry is at the center of a mistaken-identity ruckus.

Eventually he and his friend Paul Hill find themselves in London, drifting on a grander scale. They live in a curious free-love
commune when not sponging off Gerry's aunt, Annie Maguire. One
evening in 1974, as they sit talking to a bum on a park bench, an
explosion in a pub in Guildford kills five people. Similar IRA bombings have claimed further lives, and the newly devised Prevention of
Terrorism Act allows the police to hold suspects without a warrant
or formal charge for one week, grilling them in whatever brutal
fashion they please. On the flimsiest of quasi-evidence including
the jealous nattering of an English member of the commune—Gerry and Paul are arrested, along with another communard from Belfast, Paddy Armstrong, and his teenage English girlfriend, Carole
Richardson.

This quartet becomes known as the Guildford Four, and all the
understandable wrath of England descends on their heads after the
police, through various forms of physical and psychological torture, extract phony confessions from them. Inspector Dixon, who
heads the investigation, is a quiet, dapper, middle-aged man with

a sexy wife and neat kid; he seems to be thoughtful, gentlemanly, and controlled, but is, in fact, a wolf in police dog's clothing. Surrounding him is a crazy quilt of superiors and inferiors: isolated patches of decency encircled by ritualized sadism, as Kafkaesque innuendos, spoken or implied, crisscross the troubled air. Gerry's father, Giuseppe (the film misspells this as "Guiseppe"—or did he himself do so?), arrives at Aunt Annie's to lend support to his son. Promptly, he, Annie, and her family are also arrested, becoming the Maguire Seven.

Mr. Sheridan's screenplay, co-written with Terry George, takes some liberties with the facts, but, to my view, this dramatic tightening in no way tarnishes the basic truths. Outstanding here is the sense of detail, much of it evidenced in the quick cutting away to ancillary figures, who provide a kind of silent, choric comment on the main events. Thus we see a young policewoman carrying a candle-studded birthday cake along the corridor off which torture is in process. Later, we see her break down in tears.

But even the angle from which machine-gun-holding guards are shot—perched on high balconies or dominating the back of a courtroom—creates menace with quiet efficiency. Or take the nurse with the red-cross-marked first-aid coffer who trots after the accused or condemned in case they should be physically overcome. The very expression on her face—anxiety? disgust? weary solicitude?—as well as her funny canter in pursuit of hustled-off prisoners subtly conveys the complexities and contradictions of the law. A great deal is told in whispers, expressive looks, or blank silences throughout the film; also in such little touches as a bored Paul Hill, during the longueurs of the trial, braiding the wig of his attorney seated in front of him.

The casting of minor roles is masterly. Thus the prosecutor is played by Daniel Massey, who has specialized in gentle leading men, and who, his former good looks sabotaged by age, still exudes a sweet rationality belying wrongheadedness. Or take the defender, played by Bosco Hogan as a nerd, yet saying all the decent, sensible things. Or the judge, appearing to be the embodiment of impartiality, yet passing sentence with the unsolicited obiter dictum that he wished he could have made it hanging instead of thirty years' imprisonment, a hanging he would be happy to execute with his own hands. Aidan Grennell speaks these words in the butteriest of tones.

I don't know how much of this comes out of Mr. Conlon's memoir,

and how much of it is the script and the director, whom one benighted reviewer described as not having "a quarter of the cinematic
flair of Brian de Palma or Adrian Lyne"—the former an undisciplined
flounderer, the latter a slick hack. And once the film moves into the
prison, its mastery becomes unshowily overwhelming.

The irony of fate had Gerry and Giuseppe confined in the same
cell over the years: 15 for Gerry before his retrial and release; just a
little less for Giuseppe, carried off by illness before vindication. The
father-son relationship, poor during the years of freedom, slowly
evolves into love in this enforced closeness. A model prisoner, Giuseppe conducts an energetic campaign by mail for the Guildford
Four, for whom support was gradually building up all over Britain,
from high and low. But their most invaluable champion is Gareth
Peirce, activist woman lawyer, resented by Gerry both as a lawyer
and as a woman until her understated assiduity wins him over.

Earlier, Gerry, contemptuous of his father's methods, joined
cause with a very different prisoner, Joe McAndrew, a composite
character based on several IRA members, who proudly confessed
to being the real Guildford bomber a month after the Four were
tried. Furthermore, the police had located the bum, who confirmed
Gerry and Paul's alibi; but they swept this evidence under the carpet, not wishing to own up to a gross police and judicial error,
and perhaps considering all Irish Catholics ipso facto guilty. The
impressive thing about the film is that, though it obviously sides
with the victims, it does not idealize them, nor does it turn the
English authorities into stock heavies. A sense of general fallibility and insecurity prevails throughout, never more so than when
interrogators and suspects glower at one another in silence as the
malaise of history hangs over them like a malevolent smog.

Rather than tell you more of the story, let me enjoin you to watch
for the skill of the camera placements and movements within the
cramped prison quarters. Note especially two shots in which Giuseppe's head pops into the frame seemingly out of nowhere. This is
the essence of the man: an awkward but dutiful ubiquity, until the
respiratory illness keeps him in his cell. Observe how the film (fine
cinematography by Peter Biziou) conveys that particular seclusion
within a general sequestration. Milton may not have admired a
cloistered virtue, but this virtue, its cloisteredness imposed, shines
on and on, figuratively and even literally, as the dying man keeps
writing letters late into the night.

As Giuseppe, Pete Postlethwaite etches himself into the memory with a performance of such stripped-down integrity, such self-effacing determination that you believe the actor to be drawing on resources beyond the merely histrionic, great as those are. That blunt, blotchy pentagonal face, with its stubby nose and cluster of moles, radiates a sheer, patient, animal decency to knock your breath away. And, in smaller parts, what of the heart-wrenching bafflement of the innocently condemned, conveyed with aching simplicity by Britta Smith (Annie) and Beatie Edney (Carole)? Do not overlook either Gerald McSorley as a funny little balding detective from Belfast, or Don Baker as the bone-chilling McAndrew, whom Gerry finally turns away from in horror.

Corin Redgrave is a quietly scary Inspector Dixon, a soft-spoken tyrant who cannot comprehend that he could be wrong, and, in the end, can even cringe self-righteously. As the intrepid lawyer, there is the inevitable Emma Thompson. Her penchant for smugness is here either in abeyance or put to good use; even the upward-scooping tone of her voice objectifies the persistence with which the underdog digs his way into recognition. Miss Thompson is not mousy like the real-life Miss Peirce, but there is something very fetching about her sneer of triumph.

Finally, there is Daniel Day-Lewis. Superb as Liam Neeson, Anthony Hopkins, and Tom Hanks may be in their current stellar roles, and consistently splendid as Mr. Day-Lewis has been in wildly varied parts, the chameleon Gerry Conlon provides him with perhaps a finer opportunity to be charming, cynical, cocky, abject, childish, and finally profound. His way of aging 15 years, both outwardly and inwardly, into a wholly new person is nothing short of stunning. Mr. Day Lewis gets it all right—to say nothing of the accent—down to the dry crying, the incendiary laughter, the bumpkinish insouciance. Lovely as he was in Mr. Sheridan's *My Left Foot*, he has a wider range here to sweep across toward a deep concluding dignity. Perhaps in some dread way Gerry Conlon profited by his imprisonment; he certainly does from being portrayed by Daniel Day-Lewis.

Savage Nights

It isn't easy to make an honest film about homosexuality and AIDS, two topics that nowadays go almost as much hand in hand as love and marriage used to do. And just as a traditional love story tended to end with wedding bells, in today's homosexual story the knell of AIDS is, at least distantly, tolling. There are homosexual lifestyles that would not bring a blush to a dowager's cheek, or make a redneck see red. But once AIDS is addressed, so must be the indiscriminate sexuality that turned it into an epidemic, which, however, does not sit well with the grass-roots audiences on whose frayed greenbacks the movie industry depends. And so we get a bogus film such as *Philadelphia*, whose good box office smells of moral BO.

Now from France comes *Savage Nights*, which, without being a masterpiece, is honest, artistic, and disturbing: instead of providing glib answers, it asks difficult questions. It is written, directed, and starred in by Cyril Collard, a writer, musician, photographer, sailing instructor, and occasional actor, who adapted it from his second and last novel. One of the first French public figures to declare themselves HIV-positive at a time when this required real courage, Collard died of AIDS at 35, three days before his film won four Césars (French Oscars), including the one for best picture. The novel was statedly autobiographical; the, movie, on which Jacques Fieschi collaborated with Collard, departs from it in small but significant ways: it loses something in breadth, but gains in concentration.

Jean, the quasi-autobiographical hero, is first shown as a cameraman during the Algerian troubles, where he has some contact with a mysterious woman—the film is vague here—which may be the cause of his infection. Later, back in Paris, the bisexual Jean leads a life of, possibly infection-generated, excess. By day, he works as a cameraman; by night, he drives his red convertible at maniacal speeds, or has garish sex under bridges with strange men, often several at a time. He gets involved with two lovers: Laura, a 17-year-old would-be actress in commercials; and Samy, a young Spaniard, soccer player, and holder of odd jobs. Samy has a girlfriend whom he eventually leaves for Jean; Laura has a wise mother to whom she tearfully returns whenever Jean ditches her for Samy.

There are understatedly grim scenes with Jean at the hospital for tests, and lively ones showing him at work as a cameraman. A characteristic scene has, for instance, Jean and Samy picking up a prostitute (played by an improbably pretty young actress) who is an art student by day, and indulging in a threesome that ends poorly. Or Jean will be alone at night as Laura keeps phoning and leaving angry, weepy, pleading, or threatening messages on the answering machine, which Jean listens to as other people listen to records.

Samy is taken to M. André's, a house of heterosexual orgies and sadomasochistic male encounters, where he meets Pierre Ollivier, a man who organizes skinheads into vicious anti-Arab squads; Ollivier eventually recruits Samy as well. Alone, Jean and Laura enjoy passionate sex; with Samy around, the situation becomes more complicated and heterodox. When Jean first has intercourse with Laura, unable to accept his sickness, he does not tell her that he is HIV-positive. When, much later in the film, he tells her, she has an outburst of rage, but quickly forgives him. When they are about to have sex again, and he puts on a condom, the girl, tenderly and terrifyingly, removes it: she believes that her love alone can keep both of them from harm. In a still later scene, after one of Jean's periodic rejections, Laura shouts at him and the entire street from a balcony, accusing him of infecting and destroying her. We are never told whether she is telling the truth; the scene, regardless, is crushing.

However shattering, the scenes are artistically controlled in their violence: as when Laura discovers Samy, Jean, and an ex-girlfriend of his in a threesome; or when Samy (in an outburst of what?) repeatedly slashes his own chest with a razor; or when Laura, once again rejected, vandalizes her mother's apartment, which she shares; or when the mother, in an effort to negotiate peace, meets Laura and Jean at a fast-flood restaurant, and the meeting degenerates abominably. Yet the film is by no means unrelievedly gloomy; there are humorous, idyllic, intensely sensuous or sensual passages as well.

Laura finally finds someone else on the Riviera, whither Jean follows her, only to be ever so gently rejected in turn. But this is not the end, either. Rather, when Jean calls her from an assignment in Portugal, at the farthest tip of Europe, they have (less explicitly than in the book) telephonic sex, and Laura tells him that all he has to do is say he loves her and she'll come running. But he can't, and proceeds to immerse himself ever more desperately in nature.

This is a scary film, but only one scene rings untrue (it is not in the novel): to stop Ollivier, Samy, and the gang from mutilating an Arab, Jean cuts his finger and threatens to infect Ollivier with his tainted blood unless the thugs are called off. Otherwise, the movie feels ungainsayably factual. It certainly isn't pornographic: these are three-dimensional human beings experiencing genuine pain, not merely a simulacrum of suffering as an aphrodisiac for unwholesome audiences. It is a sadomasochism not of whips and chains, but of sexual rewards and withholdings, domination and submission, as everyone takes turns as tormentor and tormented.

You may find Laura's willingness, indeed eagerness, to risk infection incredible. (In the novel, that scene is played out between Samy and Jean.) But consider: Romane Bohringer, the young actress who plays Laura opposite Collard's Jean, knew that her leading man was HIV-positive, yet willingly acted these sex scenes with much open-mouthed kissing. Isn't this rather like the film's story: life imitating art, however improbable?

As a study of obsession, *Savage Nights* rises well above its sordid specifics. Jean and Samy's problem is that they desperately want love; Laura's is excess of love, utter and frenetic. The French title, *Les Nuits fauves*, is especially resonant. *Fauve* is not "savage," but "wild beast," the name adopted by a famous, coloristically ferocious school of painters. It also means "tawny," evoking nights of livid illumination, louche surroundings, and lurid passions. Further, it means a musky smell; here, the odor of sex. The film with its *fauve* nights, has something to say to people who are neither homosexual nor bisexual, neither unbridled sensualists nor slaves of passion.

Cyril Collard has acted and directed persuasively. All the actors are good, but the prize goes to Romane Bohringer as Laura: a young woman of unremarkable looks, her acting, like her face, is transfigured by the beauty of sheer truthfulness. The performance is not merely heart-rending; it is also a lesson in how inextricably beauty and abjectness can coexist in one face, one body, one soul. And Manuel Teran's frequently hand-held camera seems to burrow into Laura and the rest in its pursuit of unmediated, unmitigated reality.

What I found particularly moving is the film's clenched reluctance to let go. Toward the end, scene after scene looks to be the last, but isn't; always there is more. You can feel Collard hanging on, literally, for dear life: as if, as long as he was making his movie, he could not die.

Four Weddings and a Funeral

The good old Ealing comedies look better than ever in retrospect, as we search in vain for the likes of Alec Guinness, Dennis Price, Stanley Holloway, Joan Greenwood, Joyce Grenfell, Glynis Johns, and all the rest. Only Joan Plowright today captures that spirit, but, of course, those movies are no longer being made, which is why

British actors such as Gary Oldman and Tim Roth have to learn to make like Americans and appear in our unlikely clinkers in even unlikelier roles.

So I went with, so to speak, great expectations to *Four Weddings and a Funeral*, "filmed entirely on location in London and the home counties," with only one American in it, and playing, safely, an American. The mere word "wedding" in the title brought back memories of *A Quiet Wedding*, with the still undervalued Margaret Lockwood and a dream supporting cast. Let me tell you right off that *Four Weddings* is not in that league, and not even throwing in that one funeral by way of tragic relief adds much dimension to it.

This is the story of a group of friends seen from the perspective of four weddings and one funeral. The special focus allows the writer, Richard Curtis, to present the characters only as participants in weddings or mourners at a funeral. Such tunnel vision works well on stage in, say, a bedroom farce. On film, as time passes and the scene shifts, and people fall into bed or into their graves, confess secret loves they have been harboring for one another, despair over ever finding proper partners, a lot of emotional baggage accumulates, and the viewer cries out for more information: Who are these people really? What do they do for a living? Only one or two of them seem wealthy enough to do nothing whatsoever.

If the comedy were coruscating throughout, if the dialogue were consistently entrancing, these nagging questions might not obtrude. In the first episode, Charles, our hero, is the best man at a friend's wedding. He and his punker sister and roommate, Scarlett, barely get there on time (it's in one of those home counties), and then he finds he has forgotten the wedding rings. He spots among the wedding quests Carrie, a pretty American, and becomes besotted with her. Out of this, Curtis and his director, Mike Newell, manage to weave a reasonably tangled web, but the quick consummation of Charles and Carrie's infatuation, and her prompt departure for America, leave a peculiar taste in the mouth. The perfunctoriness with which the lovers are thrown together, the manipulativeness with which they are pulled apart, and so back and forth from wedding to funeral to wedding, shrieks contrivance at us a little too loudly.

Surrounding our storybook pair, there are benighted pairs, clumsy pairs, grotesque pairs. There is also a homosexual pair, and Charles has a deaf-mute brother with whom he communicates in sign language. Needless to say, the homosexual lovers display the most touching rapport, and the conversationally challenged brother proves to be the wisest member of the group. At one wedding, Charles is seated with a bunch of his catty former mistresses—could contrivance be more rampant? At another wedding, one member of the group, a newly minted clergyman, officiates, and commits verbal lapses on the order of "Holy Spigot" and "Holy Goat," etc. The comedian Rowan Atkinson does well by the part, but it is strictly a stand-up routine, not genuine comedy. And the film's tone calculatedly veers from the farcical to the poignant, the whole thing as formally straitjacketed as a fugue.

About one-fourth of the jokes—repartee and sight gags—come off. What is lacking is that seeming spontaneity of the best comedies: not being able to smell the scriptwriter behind the laughs. "There's nothing more off-putting at a wedding than a priest with an enormous erection" sounds somehow prefabricated to me, as does this piece of folk etymology for "honeymoon": "It's the first time a husband gets to see his wife's bottom." And I'm not sure everyone will relish the reminiscence of one male character about an old school friend: "Head of my house. Buggered me senseless. Still, taught me a lot of things."

The homosexual element is very strong here, and not only in the depiction of the homosexual couple: the flamboyant Gareth (Simon Callow, a bit over the top) and the devoted Matthew (John Hannah, subtle and effective). There is something, tendentious about allowing the bereaved Matthew, delivering Gareth's eulogy, the only truly literate dialogue—or monologue—in the film, complete with the reading of a poem by W. H. Auden; nowhere else is there even a passing reference to literature. Moreover, no woman in the film is as lovingly scrutinized as is Hugh Grant (Charles). From the very opening shots, as he wakes up in bed, the camera explores every part of him, leaving no nostril uninvaded. It is he who wears the lightest and most clinging garments, with ampler décolletage than any of the women; it is his former lovers who hover over him; it is he who is the film's chief love object.

It strikes me as a big—but under the circumstances perhaps unsurprising—mistake to have Carrie played by Andie MacDowell, whose feminine appeal is close to nil, and whose acting ability is rather less than that. She comes alive only in the scene where she tries on a number of wedding gowns; there her extensive modeling background briefly makes her look like a pro. The rest of the cast is accomplished, starting with Mr. Grant himself, who is not only a heartthrob (the Rupert Brooke look), but also an actor of intelligence and talent, whose only flaw is his very British, very helter-skelter teeth. Still, they are less troubling than Miss MacDowell's gums, with their equine way of gumming up her smile. There is especially strong support from Kristin Scott Thomas and James Fleet.

Mike Newell, an uneven director, has done rather well by this film, which also boasts sensitive camera work by Michael Coulter, and a fine score by Richard Rodney Bennett. And yes, there are funny lines, as when we hear at Gareth's funeral that "the recipe for duck à la banana fortunately goes to the grave with him." We read in the papers that Eeling Studios is about to be reactivated: perhaps the recipe for first-class comedy will come back from the grave.

The House of the Spirits

Having no stomach for magic realism—I tried twice to get through *A Hundred Years of Solitude*, but never made it past page 52—I certainly wasn't going to read Isabel Allende's *The House of the Spirits*, a sprawling family saga cum allegory of Chilean history by the niece of the assassinated Salvador Allende. But whatever that novel may be like, it's got to be better than the movie Bille August has made from it. Why? Because nothing could be worse than the movie, which is the very epitome of trash.

Sad, considering that the Danish filmmaker has previously given us the marvelous *Pelle the Conqueror* and the estimable *The Best Intentions*, from a script by Ingmar Bergman. I do not hold with those who glibly assert that a Dane has no business making a movie about South America, though here, for once, the smartasses may have a point. Much has been made by the scoffers of the motley cast. We have three Americans: Meryl Streep, Glenn Close, Winona Ryder; two Brits: Vanessa Redgrave, Jeremy Irons; one half-Brit, half-Indian: Sarita Choudury; one German: Armin Müller-Stahl; one (presumed) Austrian: Jan Niklas; one Spaniard (we are getting warmer): Antonio Banderas; one Venezuelan (hot, in both senses): Maria Conchita Alonso; and one Hispanic of uncertain nationality (probably American): Joaquin Martinez.

But this, too, is hogwash. A good actor can play any nationality if he can control his hair dye, makeup, and accent. As it happens, two Hispanics—Miss Alonso and Mr. Martinez—come off best here; but, in truth, they have rather undemanding roles. Conversely, Mr. Banderas as the *jeune premier* gives a routine, not to say boring, performance, doing nothing more than looking intense and Latino, as he also did, most recently, as Tom Hanks's lover in *Philadelphia*. There is no reason for the rest to be any worse, except that their parts are bigger and sillier, giving them more generous opportunities to hang themselves.

This is the story of a proper but poor young man, Esteban Trueba (Mr. Irons), who seeks to marry—way above his station—the beautiful young Rosa del Valle (Teri Polo, and really beautiful). Her rich bourgeois parents (Miss Redgrave and Mr. Müller-Stahl) advise him to get wealthy first, and married later. Meanwhile Rosa's little sister, Clara, already evinces a strong yearning for Esteban, but for now can only impress him with her occult talents, such as telekinesis, a small display of which she proffers. You'd think that such a handy (or handless) skill would be put to good use later on, but no: after moving a couple of objects about telekinetically, she seems never again to resort to it.

Esteban strikes lavish gold as a miner, but Rosa, as predicted by Clara (who may have practiced another useful gift, though the movie won't come out and say it), dies horribly, for no medically sound reason, but at least makes a very pretty cadaver until an explicit postmortem is performed on her, which may delight the more sadistic necrophiliacs in the audience. The hapless Esteban takes over an abandoned hacienda, Tres Marias, and converts it into a fabulous estate, and himself into a leading rightwing politician. Little Clara retreats into a mute, murky realm of visions, watched over by her mother, Nivea, a good name for a face cream, but no less so for a mother who'll protect her daughter's skin even after death. (Nivea is only one of several characters here who do not take death lying down.)

When Esteban comes back for Clara twenty years later, the girl has shed her fantasies and turned into Meryl Streep—well, win one, lose one. Her guessing why he has come amazes Esteban, who has obviously been too busy to see many movies. He takes his bride to Tres Marias, which is overseen by his spinster sister Ferula (Miss Close), who first had a sort of incestuous crush on her brother, and now develops a sort of lesbian one on his wife. But, mind you, all very properly, sort of.

There are two absolutely sure signs for spotting total trash. One is a whore with a heart of gold, the other is a one-shot tumble in the hay that results not only in a bastard, but also one (usually sinister) who'll play a major part in the plot. *The House of the Spirits* has both, which is like wearing belt and suspenders, only more indecent. I'll spare you the details, but must tell you (lest you get your hopes up) that the rape in question, like all the sex here, is rather tame, and that the bastard, though suitably evil, has some justification for his grudge, and turns in the end—if I understand the jerky story-telling and quirky editing correctly—into a bit of a softie. Well, since everyone else in the movie does, why not he? I realize that I haven't hit the really trashy parts yet, and haven't even brought in Winona Ryder, exquisitely mated with Mr. Banderas in their lack of talent. But space allows me at least coverage of my favorite bit.

Clara, you see, espoused mutism for twenty years. This may be because, unlike Esteban, she did find time for *The Piano*, or it may be because mute women are the coming thing in the cinema. Anyway, for years of her marriage she chattered away like a magpie, but when the boorish Esteban threatens to hit her, she warns him she will never speak to him again if he does. Well, he does, and she doesn't. She leaves him, but when, after another batch of years, they resume their marriage, everything is lovey-dovey save one thing; Clara, true to her vow, never speaks directly to her husband, only through third parties. Now that's what I call a stroke of narrative genius!

Jeremy Irons, who has been growing more and more unwholesomely overripe from film to film, surpasses himself: trying hard to look and sound Hispanic, mean as hell on the outside but vulnerable underneath, he is so overripe as to be rotten. Meryl Streep gives a quiet, restrained performance, but as I found her neither Latin nor appealing, my enthusiasm is similarly restrained. Glenn Close, on the other hand, has never looked, acted, or been costumed more like a wicked witch, and why it isn't she who has the telekinesis, I shall never know. The exteriors were shot in Portugal, which, whether or not it looks like Chile, is gorgeous, especially as photographed by the superb Swedish cinematographer Jörgen Persson, who, with the help of Anna Asp, Bergman's former production designer, has made the film look spectacular. If you can, by telekinesis or any other way, remove the plot, characters, and dialogue, you can have a perfectly grand time of it. Otherwise not.

A Dharma Bummer

LITTLE BUDDHA; BITTER MOON

Bernardo Bertolucci has always struck me as the perfect B-film-maker for middlebrow pseudo-intellectuals, but with *Little Buddha* he has finally made a pure abomination that is also something he hitherto managed to avoid: a crashing bore. This is the rare film that has almost nothing going for it: lousy story, dreadful dialogue, absolutely no suspense, pedestrian direction, and performances that are mostly bland or subliminal. It has a script by Rudy Wurlitzer, an American screenwriter and novelist of some repute, as rewritten by the Englishman Mark Peploe, who used to be one of Michelangelo Antonioni's scenarists while his sister was the director's girlfriend. (Now she is married to Mr. Bertolucci.) The cinematographer is Vittorio Storaro, one of the masters of the camera, and much of the film was made on location in Katmandu and Bhutan. All wasted; the sequences shot in Seattle actually look more exotic.

The film begins with the close-up of a miniature showing a Hindu priest about to sacrifice a goat, as the narrator tells how that goat—first by laughing, then by weeping, and finally by telling its own lives as a cautionary tale—converted the priest to never taking another creature's life. Clearly, that goat was as good a Buddhist as anyone, and indeed, the rest of the film is a two-hour anticlimax. Dorje, an important lama (of the two-footed kind) has died, and the members of his lamasery are desperately on the lookout for his reincarnation in a child born at the moment of his death. The chief contender seems to be Jesse Conrad, a blond, bright-eyed nine-year-old in Seattle, where his dad is an architect, his mom a schoolteacher. (Chris Isaak and Bridget Fonda play them as the most unlikely movie couple in recent memory.) Lama Norbu (played by the fine Chinese actor, politician, and speaker of English, Ying Ruocheng) sets out with a lesser but more garrulous lama for Seattle, where they are soon soliciting Dean and Lisa Conrad to lend them Jesse for a few weeks' sojourn at the lamasery. Incredibly, they agree; Dean, who has lately been sleepless in Seattle, will accompany his eager son.

It turns out that two other kids, the jolly urchin Raju of Katmandu, and the snooty little Gita of India, can also lay claim to Dorje's metempsychosis. As we travel to pick them up, the film manages to be as much about migration as about transmigration. All three end up duly at the lamasery, where Norbu and his fellow monks, in an act of unequaled egalitarianism, conclude that Dorje's soul is in all three children. Call it transmigration by triangulation.

As if this weren't enough, Norbu gives Jesse a book about the youth of Prince Siddhartha, who renounced all worldly power, sat under the bodhi tree, and meditated his way into becoming the Buddha. This story comes complete with ceremonial elephants through whose legs Mr. Bertolucci gets some of his artiest shots. Unless you prefer the ones of the three children and a bunch of monkeys gamboling around the bodhi tree as Buddha, played by Keanu Reeves, smiles mysteriously while five beautiful maidens tempt him, and an entire army shoots flaming arrows at him without affecting his meditation.

Keanu Reeves, or his hair, undergoes numerous avatars. It goes from a loose feather cut to total hirsuteness like a tree covered with kudzu, thence to a baroque court lady's coiffure as re-imagined by, say, Vidal Sassoon, without so much as once dislodging Mr. Reeves from his lotus position, or disrupting that beatific smile. I mean no disrespect to Buddhism, which has been with us for 25 centuries, only to Mr. Bertolucci's take on it, which ought to be forgotten in 25 days.

One might pass over *Bitter Moon* in silence, were it not made by the formerly brilliant Roman Polanski, and beginning to find an undeserved audience. Based on *Lunes de fiel*, by the French novelist Pascal Bruckner, it may have been of some interest before Polanski got through with it. It is now soft-core pornography devoid of genuine eroticism, affecting performances, or even incisive direction.

In the past, Mr. Polanski and his scenarist Gérard Brach (sometimes joined, as here, by John Brownjohn) have been able to whip up interest. Here they have contrived a confused and confusing story of sadomasochist sex, in which the novelist hero, Oscar, now wheelchair-bound, relates both a novel he has written and his stormy marriage to the much younger Mimi—two stories that manage only to detract from each other. The setting is an ocean crossing, where Oscar keeps luring Nigel, a young English fellow passenger, to come listen to him in his cabin, away from Fiona, Nigel's bride, who does not take kindly to hubby's absences, or his interest in Mimi, Oscar's sexy wife, around whom most of the action revolves.

Mimi is played by Emmanuelle Seigner, the granddaughter of the great Louis Seigner, but talent can skip two generations as easily as one. Her basically pretty face is made unappealing by what I can describe only as a look of stupidity. Intelligence, luckily, is not required in an actor, but Mlle Seigner, who may be bright as a button, has the misfortune of *looking* dumb, which acts as a powerful anaphrodisiac, and sabotages the film.

Peter Coyote, a San Francisco actor whom I've usually found wanting, and who now seems to be making a career of playing Americans in European movies (the last stop before the knacker's yard), portrays a successful novelist as a man who could at best write captions for horror comics. Far more interesting is the young British couple, effectively enacted by Hugh Grant and Kristin Scott-Thomas, but the film is only secondarily about them, which is a pity. Tonino delli Colli, the Italian cinematographer, works his usual wonders, but they are wasted on a mean-spirited little movie that comes across as a clean dirty joke, the worst kind of joke there is.

Polished Thriller, Polish Joke

SPEED; WHITE

At last an action picture out of Hollywood that satisfies—the first since *In the Line of Fire*. It is called *Speed*, which refers neither to amphetamines nor to any record-breaking velocity. The speed in question is 50 mph, which is not likely to provoke many arched eyebrows or batted eyelashes. But it is the speed below which a Los Angeles bus must not drop if it is not to be blown to smithereens by a device an ingenious and monstrous sociopath has attached to its underside.

The film, written by Graham Yost and directed by Jan De Bont, impresses first of all by its very structure. It has a sort of prologue, a main part, and a kind of epilogue. But unlike other prologues and epilogues, each of these has enough action, chills, and suspense to outfit an entire movie. There is even a kind of topographical symmetry involved. The prologue features a stalled elevator that may explode with its passengers above ground. The centerpiece, as mentioned, involves a hallucinatory ride on the ground, in which all riders plus an intrepid cop who jumps into the bus may find their destination, unscheduled by the L.A. Rapid Transit System, to be Kingdom Come. And the epilogue goes *under*ground, for a hellish subway ride, this time involving only the three principals, one handcuffed to a pole, the other two dueling to the death.

Good action movies are a reviewer's bane. How is one to fill out the allotted space without giving away too much plot? This is the sort of thing that stretches critical ingenuity to the breaking point, and sometimes beyond. The alternatives to telling too much of the story are to rehearse the director's and writer's previous credits, which can get pretty tiresome; or to rhapsodize about the actors, which is the stuff of fan magazines. So where does that leave us?

Film historians, perhaps, could make a go of it. They could tell you where *Speed* fits in the spectrum of cinematic thrillers between *The Cabinet of Dr. Caligari* and the many faces of James Bond. But that does not belong in this sort of publication.

Well, let me try to emulate the incomparable Pauline Kael, and see if I can analyze the personalities and audience appeal of the three main actors. First, the hero, Keanu Reeves. Last seen as the Buddha in *Little Buddha*—a catastrophe for all concerned—he has now happily transmigrated into Jack Traven, described as "an LAPD cop on SWAT detail." This is immediately engrossing: a hero with two acronyms (well, one bona fide, and one sort-of) pinned to him derives instant prestige, which Mr. Reeves makes the most of. A Canadian with a moniker that must be unique even in exotic Canada, Keanu (pronounced key-AH-noo) has an intense face with lean, limned features that would look great in intaglio or bas relief, but isn't half bad on the big screen either. For the longest time I used to get him mixed up with River Phoenix, not because they looked alike in the least, but because they were the two parallelly rising stars of their generation, and sported a vaguely similar aura. Now that poor Phoenix won't rise again, Reeves remains the undisputed champion.

Long locks, to be sure, do not suit him, which is partly why he was such a mess as Buddha. Here his close-cropped hair and sharply etched countenance, abetted by lithe, pantherish movements, stand him in good stead. Though a young man of action, he manages to look intermittently thoughtful: not slack-jawed and cow-eyed like Sly Stallone, or terminally obnoxious like Steven Seagal. Concerned but unsentimental, relentless in a good cause, and perfectly willing to shoot his partner in the leg if that will help apprehend the villain. As it happens, it doesn't.

As that villain, we have a past master, Dennis Hopper. When a part calls for wrongdoing, Mr. Hopper can do no wrong. Here he plays a fellow who wants $3.7 million to stop producing big bangs. Though foiled once, he may well succeed the next time: when it

comes to explosives, he can blow away the competition. He is casual, even ratty; but his way of taunting the LAPD is crisply, precisely exasperating. Hopper is less maniacal here than usual, and
the scarier for it.

As the obligatory young woman, there is Sandra Bullock, whom,
wearing my theater-critic hat, I had singled out in an off-Broadway
play, but whose first movie appearances were disappointing, until
she came into her own in *Wrestling Ernest Hemingway*, and now
this. As Annie, the free spirit who takes the wheel of the bus, she
manages to be plucky, witty, and enchanting, very much the girl
any man would want to sit next to on a bus. The writing for her
and Mr. Reeves, humorous as well as taut, and absolutely natural,
is in the best tradition of laconic lovers in action movies. It is one
of several things that make the Canadian performer-writer Graham
Yost, whose first screen feature this is, seem an enormously promising scenarist.

Of course, nothing about *Speed* can be taken seriously: it is lightweight stuff, and the multi-ethnic bus passengers are strictly a paper
rainbow. But nothing about the movie bores; sneeze at that who
dare! Jan De Bont, a fine Dutch cameraman who has been equally
impressive in Hollywood, is also making his debut here as director, and proves, to use an appositely automotive epithet, smashing.
With the help of the excellent Polish-American cinematographer
Andrzej Bartkowiak, Mr. De Bont nudges the camera effortlessly
into the trickiest spots (nooks, crannies, shafts, undersides—you
name it), where it ferrets out every conceivable bit of added excitement. He understands that, to keep dubiety at bay, he mustn't ever
slow down below 50 mph either. And he doesn't: this bus really
delivers. As do the elevator and the subway.

The Polish filmmaker Krzysztof Kieslowski's *White*, the second
part of his color trilogy, is every bit as irritating as was the first, *Blue*;
the third part, *Red*, has just been shown at Cannes, and augurs equally well. These are the three colors of the French flag, and the themes of
the three films allegedly derive from the French revolutionary slogan:
Liberty, Equality, Fraternity. Mr. Kieslowski likes these pseudo-pro-
found schemas: he has also made Decalogue, a sequence of ten films
about the Commandments, which I haven't seen, and the dreadful
Double Life of Véronique, in which a dead Polish girl and a living
French one are somehow corresponding alter egos. *Blue*, a maundering, meandering piece of complacent pretension about a woman

whose composer husband died in a car crash and who is lethargically picking up the pieces of her not particularly shattered life, has very little to tell us about Liberty, and *White* does equally poorly by Equality, besides being preposterous on any level.

Karol, a Polish hairdresser in Paris, has married a Frenchwoman; they don't speak each other's language, and now Karol cannot even make love to his beloved Dominique any more. Why? No explanation. There is a divorce hearing at which his lawyers have to translate every word for him into Polish, even *non*. Divorce granted, Dominique owns every *sou* Karol had, and he, apparently friendless, spends the night in what is now her hair salon, where Dominique discovers him. They try to make love, but he can't. Furious, she sets the curtains on fire, and sics the police on him as an arsonist. He ends up in the *métro*, playing a Polish song on his comb and begging.

A Polish passerby, Mikolaj, takes pity on Karol and smuggles him back into Poland by plane, hiding him in his trunk (a likely story!). Bandits steal the trunk, are disappointed by its contents, and brutally dump Karol—of all places—near his home, where his brother is running the old hair salon. By a far-fetched stratagem, Karol appropriates a corrupt land-grabbing scheme from a pair of crooks (who don't kill him for it), and gets filthy rich, and no longer inept in the least.

Karol pretends to die, leaves all his money to Dominique, and books a flight to Hong Kong, where Mikolaj has bought a house for him. Dominique comes to Warsaw for the funeral, becomes all teary, and is overjoyed when, at night in her hotel room, the putative ghost of Karol turns out to be the real thing, with whom she now makes mad, magnificent love. Even his French is vastly improved. Hong Kong is forgotten, but by some absurd plot twist (engineered by Karol?), the police arrest Dominique for her ex's murder. In the last scene, Karol is let into the prison courtyard by night, carrying a pie for his love. Although Dominique couldn't possibly see him from her cell window, she mimes her love for him, and Karol beams. I tell you this plot so you can see how stupid it is; the details I omit are stupider yet.

But this wretched Krzysztof Kieslowski is considered a major director. Julie Delpy (Dominique) is a charming actress, and deserves better. Zbigniew Zamachowski (Karol) is a pudgy, slimy nonentity—and one of the most popular actors in Poland today. The co-screenwriter with Mr. Kieslowski is his usual collaborator,

Krzysztof Piesiewicz, a lawyer, and thus presumably beyond feelings of shame. Mr. Kieslowski actually knows how to direct individual scenes, but I don't know why this should make people think he has anything to say.

Forrest Gump

Today's favorite movie heroes are the man who knows everything and the man who knows nothing. The one who knows everything is not threatening because he is so obviously a fabrication, a fiction on which our fond fantasies can hitch a ride. The one who knows nothing, the holy fool, is even better: we can all feel superior to him as he stumbles on to luck, love, and riches despite his mental deficiency, merely because he is sweet and good. Well, says the average moviegoer, I am not only as decent as this simpleton, but also a lot smarter. Good things must be just around the corner.

This week we have prime specimens of both these lies. The eponymous hero of *Forrest Gump* is a youngish Southerner sitting on a public bench in Savannah, telling a series of more or less interested benchmates his life story. He is the Little Man who was practically everywhere any kind of history was made—as an innocent bystander, unsuspecting initiator of great events, or heroic but unsung participant. I won't go into details, but Watergate, Elvis Presley, John Lennon, Sino-American relations, even a corner of the Vietnam War wouldn't have been the same but for Gump, the retardate as philosopher king. "Stupid is as stupid does," he retorts to those who would put him down, and because, however uncomprehendingly, he manages invariably to do the right thing, affliction emerges as an invaluable asset.

Robert Zemeckis's film, with a script by Eric Roth (who also wrote the maudlin *Mr. Jones*), is based on a novel by Winston Groom, which I take to be a belated offshoot of the Southern Gothic tradition as practiced by innumerable writers, high and low. It is a genre partaking of such antithetical ingredients as near-surreal absurdism and minutely scrutinized realism, and the movie serves up generous helpings of both. Running through it is a master image: running. It is by running away from unfairly superior persecutors or from undeserved predicaments that Forrest achieves his prodigious success—as college football player, war hero, Ping-Pong ace

(U.S.A. *v.* China), and finally sheer runner, racing for almost three years from one end of America to the other and back again.

Fleeing from life, he soon acquires followers: a large group of hangers-on who chase after him at a respectful distance, hoping for some sort of fulfillment. Along the way, persons with various projects that haven't quite jelled run alongside Forrest for a bit, and he helps them to the most successful slogans and thingamajigs of our era. His televised running further endears him to Jenny, the lovely girl who has been his lifelong girlfriend, as the poor sap imagines, even though, only platonically fond of him, she has ditched him in every conceivable way. Still, he was always there for her as she went from goodtime girl to stripper to folk singer to hippie activist, and finally to waitress.

Jenny started with all the advantages, being smart, pretty, and always on the go. But she had been an abused child, which may explain her seamier doings. Forrest, on the other hand, was the overprotected bastard of his loving, goofy, kookily wise mother, whose quirky precepts have guided him through life, along with Jenny's exhortation, "Run, Forrest, run!" Sure enough, Forrest ends up a millionaire businessman, and Jenny, who would come back to him periodically to be recharged, now comes to him for good. But the ending is not allowed to be happy, only bittersweet.

Mr. Zemeckis, who gave us *Roger Rabbit* and *Back to the Future*, among others, has always specialized in technical sleight-of-hand. *Forrest Gump* abounds in it: the hero is more or less seamlessly blended into scenes with Presidents Kennedy, Johnson, and Nixon, also with George Wallace and John Lennon, thanks to a technique pioneered by Woody Allen in *Zelig.* The confrontations, complete with dialogue, are visually and aurally convincing (except for the Lennon one, where John is rather too big for Gump), yet for all their crowd-pleasing aspect, they seem to me to undermine the story, at least in a visual medium.

Elvis, still young and unfamous, meets little Forrest in his mother's boarding house. Because both of them are actors, the scene works better than when Nixon is actually Nixon, or Lennon Lennon. We are not forced to admire the trickery, and can go with the amiably factitious flow. A novel, because we don't see what is described, can get away with much more. In the *New York Times,* Janet Maslin pointed out the script's pusillanimity: the novel's "Let me say this: being an idiot is no box of chocolates" is edulcorated into "My mother used to say life is like a box of chocolates: you never know what you're gonna get." That's a bonbon of a different flavor.

Gump wonders whether we are here for a purpose or whether everything is mere happenstance. He concludes that it is a blend of the two: we are purposeful drifters, savants and idiots; life, it would appear, is meaningfully meaningless. Such as this message is, the movie captures only the random side of it fully, and two and a quarter hours of randomness can wear pretty thin. If a millionaire decides to run around for a couple of years, wouldn't he at least have a backpack? I can respect an idiot savant, but not one who doesn't brush his teeth for three years. Even fantasy has to play by some sort of rules, however fanciful.

Tom Hanks does a neat balancing act of not letting either the idiot or the savant preponderate, and both his semivacuous gaze and his weird intonations (e.g., *buttocks* with the stress on *tocks*) come off with appositely fey pathos. Robin Wright is a properly flighty but also engaging Jenny, and the little girl who plays her as a child (Hanna Hall) is a stunner. Sally Field is inoffensive as Forrest's illegitimate mom, which, given the nature of the part, is no mean achievement. Gary Sinise and Mykelti Williamson do decently by supporting roles of limited interest. The winner, hands down, is technology (some very expensive stuff such as the choreographed flight of a feather) which can be a lot of things, but is rarely heart-warming. Yet that is what the movie strives to be. It emerges, rather like its hero, idiot-savantish.

Enduring the Indies

BARCELONA; SPANKING THE MONKEY

We tend to look to the independents for a relief from the majors, but, in film, the minor leaguers have their own ways of letting us down. Two of them are currently garnering good reviews even as they flounder with their admittedly off-beat material, which, to my view, sticks more in the craw than in the consciousness.

In 1990, Whit Stillman made a bit of a stir with *Metropolitan*, a comedy about the trivial traumas of debutantes and their escorts on the Park Avenue-Southampton axis. It seemed refreshing to have a young filmmaker who was unabashedly chronicling the tribulations of well-heeled WASPs rather than the aches and rages of various other minorities. Yet *Metropolitan* looked rather more impoverished than its subject matter warranted, and its invention was, at best, spotty. But Mr. Stillman was clearly his own man, possessed of a somewhat uneven but amiably idiosyncratic sense of humor.

He still is that with *Barcelona*, a comedy about two cousins who had a huge row at age ten, which pops up occasionally in flashback and adds little to the story. Now Ted is a sales rep for a Chicago company in Barcelona, where he is suddenly descended upon by cousin Fred, a junior naval officer here as an advance man for the Sixth Fleet. The time is the last decade of the Cold War, and NATO and Americans are powerfully unpopular in Spain, even though liberated young Spanish women put out for them rather liberally.

What Mr. Stillman has is a good situation, but no story. The movie is composed of slightly flaccid blackout skits, each of which could easily have been summed up by a *New Yorker* cartoon. The screenplay, if that is the word for it, tries to connect them, as if they were so many points in one of those by-the-numbers drawings to be joined by a counting pencil. But no picture emerges: the points could just as well have been random spots on a blank wall.

Ted tries to get rid of Fred, but Fred stays on and on. They bicker; they philosophize about feminine beauty, the tactics of salesmanship, and America's presence in Europe; and they do not really do much of anything. Ted works in a nice Art Nouveau office, but it is not clear at what; what Fred might possibly be accomplishing for the Navy as they amble around Barcelona a lot, which is a pretty sight but gets us nowhere is equally mysterious; at night, they go to jazz concerts, drink, dance, and debate with some fetching Spanish girls, and eventually go to bed with them, even though most of the girls have steady Spanish boyfriends. The chitchat between the cousins is sometimes amusing; the conversations and arguments between the Americans and Spaniards are less so, though they have a mild ironic edge. And every once in a while there is a spurt of political violence.

The few authentic Hispanics in the film speak an English that is barely comprehensible and grating; the girls, however, played by Americans with more or less convincing Spanish accents (mostly less), are easy on the eye, but no more believable than Ted and Fred. The views from a passing car of the Cathedral lit up at night are about as exciting as the movie gets. When someone hovers between life and death—or survival as a vegetable—we do not much care. Even at their best, these characters do little more than vegetate, though, unlike other household plants, you do not have to talk to them: *they* talk *your* head off.

To say that these superficial shadow-characters remain unexplored is a gross understatement. But nothing else is explored either: even a key theft is never satisfactorily cleared up. Money matters are treated in a particularly cavalier and vague manner, which may give the film a certain raffish insouciance. And there are some funny situations and intermittently funny lines. *Barcelona* also looks less home-movieish than *Metropolitan*. It is, however, even more disjointed.

The acting is not especially good or bad, but entirely apposite. Chris Eigeman, as Fred, may overdo the wide-eyed but unseeing stare in what would otherwise be an apt blend of self-righteousness and one-upmanship. He is droll the way the young Jack Nicholson used to be, but without his charm. Taylor Nichols is better as Ted, a sort of sophisticated nerd looking like a younger, gentrified Robert Duvall. The main girls, Tushka Bergen and Mira Sorvino, are attractive and likable, but have virtually nothing to do. *Barcelona* is the work of a clever, upbeat smartass, but hardly an artist. Though Mr. Stillman has spent some time in that city, and his American wife lived there even longer, the film could as readily have been made by a casual tourist; the great Catalan capital deserves better than that. But Mr. Stillman is consistent, flattening out his backgrounds as thoroughly as he does his characters.

Even so, *Barcelona* is a lot easier to take than the currently much-touted *Spanking the Monkey*, written and directed by the "young" David O. Russell, who, at 35, should know better. It is a film made on a financial as well as intellectual shoestring, and it shows it in every frame. If art lies in the concealing of art, as the Latin proverb has it, the art of shoestringery lies in hiding the shoestring. Here even the cinematography by Michael Mayers looks inept, possibly for reasons of financial limitations. But the cheapness in the writing, directing, and acting cannot be explained away in economic terms.

We have here the by now obligatory dysfunctional family, the Aibellis: father Tom is a traveling salesman for self-help video cassettes, always on the road, always in hotel rooms where a naked chippie seems to be part of the furniture. He is also a miser, tyrant, and fool, preventing his pre-med-student son, Raymond, from availing himself of a prestigious Washington summer scholarship, and forcing him instead to stay in their suburban Connecticut home taking care of his mother. Susan Aibelli has a broken leg in a cast, and a neglected wife's bruised ego casting about for compensation: Ray is to be her nurse, cook, sounding board, unpaid lady's companion, and, as it happens, bedmate. For, among other improbable things, *Spanking the Monkey* is about incest.

Incest is a difficult subject, to be accosted only by the greatest of artists. Even as good a filmmaker as Louis Malle treated it charmingly but unsatisfactorily in *Murmur of the Heart* (1970), turning incest into something as inconsequential as a mother and son drinking a cup of coffee from the same cup. *Monkey* strives to provide the equally briefly and irresponsibly treated incest with at least a more elaborate buildup, so we get endless massagings of the maternal leg and proppings up and pawings of the maternal body in the shower, along with appropriate oglings, wisecracks, and heavy breathing, but not a shred of genuine empathy or insight. These huffings and puffings are no more persuasive than the scenes of onanism that give the film its title, and are so poorly contrived and executed as to make it hard to tell whether the numerous tortuous and tasteless scenes on the toilet have to do with masturbation or with constipation.

Yet as whenever Ray retires to the bathroom for the eponymous pursuit, Frank, the family dog, whines and nuzzles away at the bathroom door until Ray admits him, the film lapses repeatedly into a tedious quasi-coitus interruptus—spoiling the mongrel rather than spanking the monkey. Alas, masturbation may be an even tougher cinematic topic than incest. Of course, there are other plot elements, too, such as two attempts by Ray to commit suicide—one comic, one dramatic—but both equally unsuccessful: Raymond is as much of a bust as a *felo-de-se* as Mr. Russell is as a filmmaker. There is also a youthful proto-romance with the neighboring psychiatrist's daughter (credibly played by Carla Gallo), but here, too, the authorial clumsiness precludes anything insightful, touching, or new.

Mr. Russell is, alas, less than lucky with his actors. Although Benjamin Hendrickson gets the father's loony self-contradictions across well enough, the other principals come up short. Alberta Watson, as the mother, wallows in a petulantly fixed stare for minutes on end, which becomes especially monotonous because it is shot mostly from the same angle (left semiprofile). But she fails to elicit sympathy for Susan, so that her solicitations of devotion from Ray are no more moving, and rather less funny, than Frank the dog's pesky tantrums at the bathroom door. As for Jeremy Davies, his Ray is nothing more than a nastier, less charming post-Tarkingtonian Penrod.

Natural Born Killers

How lamentable is Oliver Stone's latest and most horrible film, *Natural Born Killers*, from a story by another current hotshot, Quentin Tarantino. Mr. Stone's narcissism and megalomania, like badly driven horses, run away with this gross, pretentious, and ultimately senseless movie. Purporting to show how crime appeals to the American public, and how the media exploit it for their self-promotion and the public's cretinization, it is manifestly far too enamored of what it pretends to satirize, even if it knew how to do it.

Ostensibly, it is the story of Mickey and Mallory Knox, a parricidal and serial-killing young couple on an odyssey of manic self-indulgence and bloodshed. On that theme, Terrence Malick made the 1973 American classic, *Badlands*, from which *Killers* cribs a thing or two, but Mr. Stone and his hench-scribes, David Veloz and Richard Rutowski, turn the story into bestial excess, gimmicked up with every sort of irrelevant cinematic device: color and monochrome in meaningless alternation, sudden switches to videotape or drawn horror comix, handheld or tilted camera, constant cutaways to obtrusive irrelevancies—rattlesnakes particularly favored—and, in general, every known form of discrepancy and MTV-ish discontinuity, as if you were looking into a kaleidoscope manipulated by a whirling dervish.

Crassness is rampant, not least in the performances. Woody Harrelson's Mickey manages a certain idiosyncratically offhanded viciousness, but Juliette Lewis opts for all the tried and true hallmarks of cinematic psychopathy. Tom Sizemore contributes a manic cop, Tommy Lee Jones a maniacal prison warden, and Robert Downey Jr. a Geraldo-like voyeuristic and self-inflated TV talk-show host. None of these is a thought-through character, any more than the cheapest of all, Rodney Dangerfield's farcical-beastly father, and all of them swirl and caper about in a lunatic dance between hysteria and epilepsy.

Even the public's fascination with the lethal couple is only spottily conveyed, though Mr. Stone does occasionally stumble on striking images. But when the Knoxes end up as a happy family with two kiddies in a cozy van, what comes across is not *saeva indignatio* but hand-to-nose gloating. *Natural Born Killers* is neither wise nor witty enough for a satire, and displays only the depraved unhinged-ness of a hypertrophic ego.

Particularly offensive is the obtrusion of shots from the Menen-dez, Bobbitt, Tonya Harding, and O. J. Simpson telespectacles, lest a five-year-old should miss the movie's relevance; followed closely by cheap attempts at poetry, as when Mallory's bridal veil floats from a high bridge into a deep canyon, and stops midway in a freeze frame. Mr. Stone's real purpose must be to beat the public over the head with every blunt instrument he can muster: a subject on which the godfather of masochism, Count Leopold von Sacher Masoch, aptly pronounced, "Whoever allows himself to be whipped, deserves a whipping."

Questionable Questions

QUIZ SHOW; A GOOD MAN IN AFRICA

Among the great American ideals that do not often get mentioned aloud is getting rich quick. Though the hard-work ethic receives all the publicity, it is striking it rich that is considered the inalien-able right of the man in the street, always ready to trade in his two well-worn soles for four white-walled tires. But where is Lady Luck hiding?

Back in the late fifties—and still today—one of the answers would be the quiz shows. And here now is *Quiz Show*, a superproduction directed by Robert Redford, which deals with the famous scandal that surrounded and scuttled *Twenty-One* and *The $64,000 Question*, and the first thing that strikes me is, "Ah, the good old days, when $64,000 was still a lot of money." Nowadays it takes two-mil-lion-dollar tips to waitresses to make us sit up and take notice. The second thought that occurs is how able a filmmaker Robert Redford has become. With his screenwriter, Paul Attanasio—a Harvard man and former film critic for the *Washington Post*—Mr. Redford has put together a solid two-hour entertainment that also teaches us something about television, greed, and human nature, three phe-nomena that, it seems, will remain with us forever.

As some of you will recall, everybody watched *Twenty-One*, the jewel of the fabulous quiz shows, not only because it could make you wealthy, but also because it could make you wise. For those, as you may also recall, were the days when education still meant something beyond a foot in the door of opportunity, when, indeed, knowledge was still a good in itself, worth striving after for the sake of one's humanity and spiritual well-being. So even if the questions asked on the show were often (though not always) trivial, and if knowing the answers qualified one only as an idiot savant, it was splendid to see the contestants come up with those answers, and sometimes beat them to it oneself. One could learn things from the show, even hope to be on it someday, and what fun just to watch people enclosed in isolation booths in the act of sweating and thinking. Behind those glass partitions was thought made visible, and we could see as through a glass, brightly.

And then the revelation that it was all a put-up job, fakery, a con game! Contestants who seemed to have charisma, viewer appeal, were fed the answers beforehand. They often acted out a struggle for the answer—at other times not, with the golden facts simply leaping from their lips—and we thought it was a genuine fight, took sides, rooted for this or that valiant contestant, and we were royally had. Most painful was the downfall of Charles Van Doren, son of Mark, the Pulitzer Prize-winning poet and professor, and Dorothy, a novelist and editor, and the nephew of the famed Carl Van Doren. Charlie was, as the press kit rightly states, the intellectuals' answer to Elvis Presley. Until the Golden Boy came up with the wrong answer, and, worse yet, was proved a fraud. Many a person besides him lost his innocence with the fall of the scholar and gentleman Charles Van Doren.

The movie is based in part on the chapter on quiz shows in Richard Goodwin's *Remembering America*, and Goodwin himself was instrumental—but not crucial—in the unmasking. Unfortunately, the movie, for greater dramatic effect, vastly increases his importance in the investigation, and this strikes me as wrong. We are, to be sure, all used to historical fiction and film cheating a bit, but should a historical film about the evils of cheating also cheat? The story seems dramatic enough as it happened, and a strict documentary approach might have been no less rewarding. Certain confrontations that didn't occur, certain assumptions about what might have been said are helpful narrative devices, but I kept watching and wondering: Is this trick really necessary?

The movie honestly implicates both the sponsor, Geritol (the tonic that was to help you get rid of "tired blood"), and NBC and its chairman, and shows how and why those guilty parties got off scot free, with only the show's producers, Dan Enright and Al Freedman, taking the rap along with some of the contestants. Enright and Freedman argue that the whole thing was, after all, only show business. Just as sex and violence are faked for its sake, why shouldn't right answers be simulated for the sake of suspense and audience involvement?

Not an easy question to answer. Eventually, though, we must insist that the viewer knows that those movie stars aren't actually having intercourse or killing one another, whereas here the poor boobs glued to the tube were literally duped into perceiving charlatans as paragons. True, but what if those stars offscreen really indulged in those activities? And, more important, was Elvis really an artist or just a popular idol? Does it finally matter that much whether Charlie Van Doren was really omniscient or just a damn good impersonator of the perfect polymath?

We won't resolve these questions here. The movie, however, is hugely diverting and has quite often enough the ring of truth. The dialogue is deft and credible, the acting generally apt and persuasive, the pacing exemplary, the re-creation of times gone by accurate to seemingly the last detail (no cheating with production design—that *would* be a sin!), and there is consistently food for thought. Fast food, if you like, but not junk food.

That, granted, is a lot. The only performance I have trouble with is Rob Morrow's Dick Goodwin. Morrow is a personable actor, and has clearly studied the Boston accent assiduously, most likely from recordings of John F. and Robert Kennedy, both of whom were Goodwin's employers. But the accent comes out of Morrow too slickly; he is like one of those Katharine Hepburn impersonators who sound more Hepburn than Hepburn herself. There is also a certain oiliness at work: when this Dick Goodwin asserts that he would not have been on the take, I do not believe him. Or was that deliberate? I should hope not.

The others are superb. Take John Turturro, who plays Herbie Stempel, a nonentity from Queens, whom *Twenty-One* made into a folk hero and then, when his audience appeal seemed to wear thin, tried to drop like a hot potato. This Stempel, clearly a bright but unbalanced person, is incarnated with a dazzling incisiveness, a bountiful histrionic inventiveness that Mr. Turturro has always exhibited, but that here seems more riveting than ever. This is no longer mere naturalistic acting carried to its heights; it is subtly stylized, cutting

through to the essence, transcendent. You never know what to make
of this man, even when you think you know all about him.

Ralph Fiennes (the commandant in *Schindler's List*), playing
Charles Van Doren, is almost as good. The script provides him
with a fine, gradual, wholly believable progression from honesty
to collusion, and the actor traces every delicate scruple from its
inception to its demise with the most exquisite sense of gradation
and shading. Weakness has seldom been portrayed more charmingly and thus more pitiably. Apparently Eastern intellectuals in
the movies have to be portrayed by British actors, and so Mark Van
Doren, too, is played by a distinguished British actor, Paul Scofield,
who squeezes every drop of tragic dignity out of the part.

Particularly devastating, too, are David Paymer and Hank Azaria, as Dan and Al, the two friendly-fiendish producers of *Twenty-
One*. Enright's patronizingly Machiavellian evil contrasts beautifully
with Freedman's buffoonishly demotic one, and the two actors meld
perfectly into one of those con men's coins that is heads on both
sides. Altogether, the large cast, many of them stage actors, executes
the Redford bidding flawlessly, and Michael Ballhaus's fine, low-key
photography and Mark Isham's crisp score add polished finishing
touches to this sleek, adult entertainment.

Bruce Beresford, that good director, is being criticized as having
come a cropper with *A Good Man in Africa*. I haven't read William
Boyd's much-praised novel on which the screenplay, also by Mr.
Boyd, is based, and I can believe that the book is more complex,
subtle, and intellectually compelling. And I admit that the last reel
or two may have difficulties with tone, wobbling somewhat between trenchancy and absurdity, compassion and ridicule. Aside
from that, though, there is much to commend in this tale of Morgan
Leafy, a mid-level English diplomat in an emerging African country
where the British presence is still strongly felt.

Morgan Leafy (the very name is masterly) is a pure Evelyn Waugh
character, a slippery bachelor trying to juggle various women, black
and white, in his private life, while straining to pull off endless
sleights-of-hand to placate both his fatuous British superiors and
the African bosses and populace, mostly corrupt or superstitious.
Soon more than his livelihood—his life—is at stake, and we watch
his increasingly desperate, comic-horrible stratagems with unabat-
ing amusement. Everything intensifies further with the arrival of
a "Royal" in Kinjanja, and with Morgan's survival contingent on

subverting the one seemingly good white man in Africa.

Colin Friels, with perfect tact, makes Leafy neither too hateful nor too lovable. He is a fellow forever slipping on the banana peel of historic shifts, unconcerned with anything but cushioning his fall. Friels is surrounded by highly savvy comedians, white and black, some of whom may exaggerate a bit, but others, like Sean Connery and Louis Gossett Jr., get both the hilarity and the seriousness—or sinisterness—dead right. And Andrzej Bartkowiak's camera is no slouch, either. I suspect that much of the flak is due to political correctness. The Africans in the film are certainly not shown in a flattering light: but no more so are the whites. Rwanda is a tragedy: this not so mythical Kinjanja is a bloody comedy. Both are possible, historically and dramatically. *A Good Man in Africa* is a good film that goes slightly bad in the end. How much better than today's customary trajectory from bad to worse!

The Shawshank Redemption

As prison films go, *The Shawshank Redemption* is one of the more unredeemed ones; it is no *In the Name of the Father*, let alone *Un Condamné à mort s'est échappé*. The title of the Stephen King novella on which it is based is "Rita Hayworth and the Shawshank Redemption," which is longer but not better. It concerns a respectable young Maine banker, Andy Dufresne, sentenced to life without reprieve for the murder of his wife, which he did not commit. He is sent to Shawshank, a prison compared to which Devil's Island was a Palm Beach luxury hotel. Here he experiences the most satanic warden and guards, as well as fellow prisoners who, except for a few rotten apples, are a swell bunch, especially Red, the prison fixer and philosopher, who once in his youth rashly killed, but is now as good as gold. Yet the evil warden and stupid parole board see to it that he can't get out ever, which he takes with a stoicism worthy of Marcus Aurelius. Andy and Red become fast friends, each learning much from the other, until they end up living the life of Reilly in Mexico. I mention Reilly because when asked why they call him Red, he, a black man, replies. "I guess because I'm Irish." There you have the humor of it.

Before our guys hit Mexico, however, 19 years have to pass for them, and not much less for us. We are treated to 148 minutes of shock effects and didactics. Frank Darabont's screenplay and direction pile up the horrors rather too liberally (in both senses of the word), while not being particularly sparing with the homilies. Some horror is, of course, unavoidable (male rape, confinement in solitary, beatings), and a few platitudinous pieties may be inevitable, too. But you wonder when, on top of this, the warden is a Bible-thumping sadist and the head guard a beast out of hell, whether there isn't somewhere, buried in the profusion of credits, a billed dice-loader. Or perhaps the fact that Mr. Darabont, whose directorial debut this is, graduated from writing the likes of *A Nightmare on Elm Street 3* and *The Fly II* qualifies him as both Stygian helmsman and loader of cast-iron dice.

Great performances might help. Morgan Freeman, as Red, is fine as always, but hampered by the limitations of his role. Tim Robbins is a curious choice for a New England banker and Brahmin of imperturbable grit and wit, but he has his moments. As the warden, Bob Gunton belongs in the blackest of melodramas, and Clancy Brown, as the head guard, should head straight for Grand Guignol. James Whitmore is saddled with the unlikely role of a sweet old prison librarian who, when finally let out, finds freedom too hard to bear and hangs himself. There, again, you have the humor of it.

I don't know how much of this is Frank Darabont, how much Stephen King. But if I am to spend two-and-a-half hours with someone plumbing the depths of the human heart, I doubt that I would pick either of them. Best here is Roger Deakins's cinematography, which aptly lets the blue-grey of prison uniforms permeate the very air. Still, a heavy diet of slate blue can give anyone the blues.

From Pulp to Pap

PULP FICTION; VANYA ON 42ND STREET

No film arrives with more advance hype than *Pulp Fiction*. The winner at Cannes, it was the opener of the New York Film Festival, where its writer-director, Quentin Tarantino, began his presentation by thanking Janet Maslin for her dithyrambic review in the *New York Times*, now being reprinted as half of a two-page ad. Mr. Tarantino made his directorial debut with the mean and nasty *Reservoir Dogs*, and has provided similarly sniggering sadistic screenplays for other directors.

The *haute* audience at the Lincoln Center gala premiere laughed,

applauded, and cheered like a bunch of Saturday-night rowdies attending the latest horror film. During the most troubling scene,
when a woman who has OD'd has to be given a hypodermic straight
to the heart with a wallop sufficient to penetrate the chest cavity (is
this good medicine?), someone in the audience passed out, there
were calls for a doctor, and, in the near-panic, the film had to be
stopped, only to resume with an encore of the injection scene, making the premiere that much more prestigious and memorable.

Pulp Fiction consists of three interrelated stories and a framing
story. In the latter, two unlikely criminals (the grotesque Amanda
Plummer and the Mayfairish Tim Roth), who call each other Pumpkin and Honey Bunny, work up to the holdup of the coffee shop in
which they are breakfasting. They seem rank amateurs rather than
bona (or mala) fide crooks, but brandish compelling rods as they
leap up to proclaim the holdup. Freeze frame.

We move into the first tale, in which two hitmen—Jules, a philosophical black, and Vincent, a pragmatic Latino—liquidate some
delinquent associates of their boss, the awesome Marsellus Wallace,
a thuggish black married to a white sexpot, Mia. They are a bit early
for the job, so they keep up a dialectical inquiry begun in their
car about whether Marsellus was justified in having a henchman
thrown from a fourth-floor window for administering a foot massage to the seductive Mia. The innocence or indiscretion of such
a massage is argued in a quasi-Socratic dialogue until the chrono-
metrically correct moment to settle the hash of refractory business
partners who have absconded with a mysterious attaché case containing something priceless.

One of the prospective cadavers, all of whom are scared out
of their wits, was about to eat a burger, which Jules proceeds to
sample, gastronomically evaluate, and consume; he then launches
on Ezekiel's prophecy to the Philistines to terrorize the victims before he and the impassive Vincent blow them away. The guys look
like errant yuppies who, if involved in drugs, would never aspire
beyond contact with piddling street pushers, much less make off
with Marsellus's attaché case, containing—what? We are repeatedly
teased, but never find out.

You can see the whole game plan: accentuate the incongruous
and ludicrous, either by juxtaposing something elevated (quotations
from the Bible) with something low-down (gangland executions),
or by expatiating on the trivial (the ethics of foot massage) in tandem with the terrifying (casual defenestration). Endless smartass

chitchat is saturated with the detritus of seventies pop culture (the movie and TV references, the music on the soundtrack) that you'd expect from someone who, like Mr. Tarantino, got his education clerking in a video store and saw every movie in tarnation, which, please note, is an anagram for Tarantino.

The hitmen mixing comic palaver with lethal acts come out of Martin Scorsese's *GoodFellas* by way of David Mamet's cinematic oeuvre, and hark back all the way to Godard. The attaché case with the mighty but unshown contents derives from Buñuel's *Belle de jour*, where a Japanese client brings along a mysteriously charged but never explained box on his brothel visits. The Bible-spouting killer is cribbed from Charles Laughton's *Night of the Hunter*, and connoisseurs of seventies schlock, from QT's formative period, will surely spot many another *hommage* or plagiarism.

A fledgling filmmaker hatched in a video store presents another problem: old movies strike me as a poor substitute for life in the real world. If you catch Mr. Tarantino on the talk shows he is currently camping out on, you'll encounter a compulsive tongue-wagger who, like his characters, rattles on without substance or discernment, to say nothing of taste. *Pulp Fiction* is based on stories by Mr. Tarantino and Roger Avary, a Hollywood-besotted Frenchman whose own *film noir*, *Killing Chloe*, shows many traces of tarantinism (or is it tarantism, a mad urge to dance?). Much has been made of *Pulp Fiction*'s subdivision into three overlapping stories that lead into an epilogue dovetailing into the prologue, and that, moreover, play with chronological order. But titillation cures neither hollowness nor shallowness.

There are some amusing moments in the film, and some accomplished acting, notably from Samuel L. Jackson and John Travolta as the hitmen, and Bruce Willis as a boxer who refuses to throw a fight and must run from Marsellus's mob. But there is always something to undercut the pleasure, whether it is the rotten performance by the unappetizing Franco-Portuguese Maria de Medeiros, or some particularly blatant piece of copycattishness, as when Harvey Keitel is made to recycle the character he played in *Point of No Return*, itself a recycling of the French original, *La Femme Nikita*. Self-indulgence reaches its apogee when a character accuses another of being square and makes the appropriate gesture, whereupon a square in dotted outline appears on the screen. Truffaut did something similar but much better in *Shoot the Piano Player*. And the boxer story is so crammed with absurdities that just listing them would take up this entire column.

Still, the scene in which the not uninteresting Uma Thurman OD's and the hysterical John Travolta and drugged-out Eric Stoltz have to bring her back, literally, by the book (a long-moldering medical tome dug up from some forgotten cranny), which neither of them has ever read, is garish good fun. But from Mr. Tarantino's anything-goes filmmaking to true art is still quite a distance.

At the other end of the spectrum, there is *Vanya on 42nd Street*, which purports to be high, hieratic art and is really self-indulgent diddling. André Gregory, a second-rate avant-garde theater director (now practically inactive) and occasional actor, convened a number of performers, mostly old friends, and, to keep a hand in their craft, they started rehearsing Chekhov's *Uncle Vanya* in various locations, chiefly the Victory Theater, a decaying former movie house in New York's Tenderloin. They would knock off for a while as one or another of them got a job somewhere, then regather; so it continued for several years. There was no intention of ever opening the production to critics and audiences, but chosen friends and celebrities were allowed to attend occasionally in small groups of twelve to thirty.

Vanya was played by the actor-playwright Wallace Shawn, with whom Mr. Gregory had co-starred in Louis Malle's cult film *My Dinner with André*. Mr. Malle came to see this underground *Vanya*, and promptly proposed to film it. And filmed it was, in another derelict theater, the New Amsterdam, preserving bits of ruined gaudiness from its Ziegfeld Follies days. But there is a basic contradiction here: if Gregory & Co. wanted to keep the experience small and private, why throw it open to even bigger multitudes than random theatergoers—the film world's hoi polloi?

This aporia extends to the modern street clothes in which we see the cast arrive down 42nd Street and proceed to act, as well as to the scanty props, which go from the world of samovars to that of I LOVE NEW YORK paper cups. The older actors—George Gaynes as the Professor, Lynn Cohen as Maman, Phoebe Brand as Marina—look genuinely Chekhovian; the younger ones—notably Julianne Moore as Yelena, Larry Pine as Dr. Astrov—are strictly present-day. And why bring in the Indian actress Madhur Jaffrey impersonating a Mrs. Chao, who claims to be the granddaughter of Chekhov's Bengali translator?

David Mamet's so-called new translation sounds very much like whatever pre-existing British version Mr. Mamet fiddled with. We get, on the one hand, "Some people might appreciate this peevishness; I do not," "The weather, which looked so cloudy formerly," and "I entreat you, please, to exercise all your influence that my husband and myself quit this place"; and, on the other, "There's the deadbeat, the freeloader," "Where am I to go, and Sonya here, and my mother, if I may be so picayune?" and, best of all, "And you can go to hell."

Mr. Gregory has the cast do all kinds of out-of-period things— such as Vanya miming a hanged man with his tongue hanging out as he says "Excellent weather for suicide"—or lets Vanya pant and yap at Yelena like a comic dog, or has Vanya wave a trendy toodle-oo at the grimly departing doctor. These were probably the misguidedly indulged ideas of Wallace Shawn, a dwarfish and porcine creature who croaks, slobbers, and has hissy fits. Vanya is, of course, no such thing, and the main reason Mr. Shawn is an actor (besides being the son of the longtime editor of the *New Yorker*) is that Woody Allen, in casting *Manhattan*, needed, for a comic visual effect, a performer who would look appreciably homelier than Mr. Allen himself. To allow this Vanya to use words such as "swine" and "swinish" is, to say the least, unfortunate.

Louis Malle has simply turned a nonplay into a nonfilm, but one handsomely shot by Declan Quinn. The actors—especially Julianne Moore, Larry Pine, and Brooke Smith (Sonya)—have their affecting moments, but that is almost more of a tribute to Chekhov, whose ability to partly survive even such a treatment testifies yet again to his indestructible genius.

An Unforgettable Summer

Lucian Pintilie, who stunned us with *The Oak*, has done it again with *An Unforgettable Summer*. The title was imposed on him; he wanted *The Salad*, after the name of part one of the autobiography of a Romanian army captain, Petre Dumitriu, on which the film is based. This focuses on an incident in the officer's life in 1925, when he was transferred to a border outpost in the Dobruja by his superior, General (and Prince) Ipsilanti, who vainly lusted after Petre's beautiful wife, the half-Hungarian Marie-Thérèse. Nationalities and their languages are very important here: when the babble of tongues and dialects rises to Babelic heights, bloodshed ensues. Particularly in the Balkans.

The film quickly establishes the ethnic-linguistic cauldron threatening to boil over. Because a grand ball is about to take place nearby, a brothel must be temporarily closed and shuttered. The official bearing the edict is roundly abused with colorful (but anachronistic) Hungarian expletives by the liveliest of the whores, Erzsi, a Magyar. Later, from her window, the girl moons the army dignitaries arriving for the ball; they stare up in mixed horror and admiration at the familiar globe whose owner they promptly identify. When Ipsilanti sends a couple of junior officers to beat up the girl, she hurls at them the slogans of Béla Kún, the deposed Hungarian Communist leader.

At the ball, Ipsilanti dances with the longed-for Marie-Thérèse, while her jealous bantam-sized husband fumes, smokes, and wins at cards. Conversation is in mixed Romanian and French, as we learn that Marie-Thérèse is the daughter of a member of the aristocratic Lascari family who married a noble Hungarian, which the Romanians consider déclassé. Because the young woman is played by the spirited British actress Kristin Scott-Thomas, Mr. Pintilie, as his own screenwriter, invents a further background for her in England: "She speaks perfect Romanian with an Oxford accent." This may overcomplicate matters, but it fits in, as we hear her frequently speak English, in the aforementioned Babel.

Ipsilanti posts Dumitriu to the godforsaken Dobruja, a territory claimed by Bulgaria and infested with Comitaji, Macedonian rebels (or bandits, depending on your point of view) who keep raiding and killing whoever is in power, and slicing off the lips of the dead to feed them to their hogs. This is the fate that befell Captain Dumitriu's predecessor, and the general evidently hopes that it may befall the captain, so that Marie-Thérèse will fall to him. Or else that she will be so bored with their wretched surroundings as to become eager for some extramarital sport.

But Marie-Thérèse finds the primitive surroundings and pristine landscape, over which flocks of birds keep whirring and swooping, very much to her liking, and loves the stark mountain that dominates it. It looks, as she notes, like Fujiyama; only nicer than the prototype. And her three small children and the family setter have fun whipping around the camp and its sandy environs. The light on Fujiyama, as photographed by Calin Ghibu, is indeed of an almost unearthly beauty at sunset, and there are many shots of Petre's monocled, somewhat comic face and his wife's finely chiseled one laved by that otherworldly light as they take on the aspect of naive icons against the bare, white-gleaming walls of their abode.

The captain, trained in Germany, is a good fellow but a stickler for discipline. Marie-Thérèse is fun-loving, intelligent (she reads Proust in French—not bad for Dobruja in 1925), and sensitive. None of this is appreciated by the two boorish lieutenants under the captain (one of them the very fellow who roughed up Erzsi), or even by the common soldiers, to whom a seemingly flighty young beauty, gamboling children, and a befuddled nanny are an incomprehensible sight, and even the lady's intercession for them when maltreated by their lieutenants must seem somehow out of order.

There are disturbing omens. An elaborate Venetian pier glass on the wall is suddenly pierced by a projectile from without. A mischievous pebble, the Dumitrius assume; later, looking behind the mirror, they'll find a bullet in the wall. The tomatoes and lettuce for their salad, growing in sandy soil, prove unpalatable. Ten Bulgarian hostages become their slave gardeners, and the vegetables markedly improve. But the good gardeners are to be executed in retaliation for the latest Comitaji raid. This despite their innocence, and Marie-Thérèse's having befriended them to the point where she pays them out of her own pocket. When General Ipsilanti and his staff officers come to lunch, the salad is irresistible. Not so Marie-Thérèse's pro-Bulgarian remarks, which have the prince in a barely controlled rage.

But he did not come for the salad; rather, to reissue the oral orders Captain Dumitriu has thus far disregarded: that the Bulgarian hostages be shot. In various brilliant exchanges, the absurdity of Balkan politics becomes manifest. The Comitaji aren't even Bulgarian, and these Bulgarians, in any case, are harmless peasants, not even allowed to talk to their anxious wives who hover nearby. One of the hostages is, in fact, a Turk, who does not speak any Bulgarian. And there are no written orders for the execution, for obvious reasons; but Dumitriu, out of respect for military discipline (and perhaps love for his wife) insists on them, defying both his superiors' promises of preferment and their threats of nonpromotion.

The resultant imbroglio is capitally conveyed by Mr. Pintilie and his cast. The tiny outpost becomes a hotbed of tyranny and intrigue, with small individual decencies unable to stem the grinding wheels of satrapy. In the end, Marie-Thérèse and her husband are profoundly insulted by another, cruder general, who draws vile parallels between the captain's wife and Erzsi, the Hungarian Communist whore. Consider the fineness of the details. The insulted captain staggers to the stables to ride back from headquarters, then decides to shoot himself. First he sticks the pistol in his mouth, then decides (like Ibsen's Lövborg) that the temple is more fitting, but first dries the saliva on the pistol barrel carefully on his tunic. Then he notices that his hungry mount has been avidly chomping on the wooden rail of its stall. Petre falls weeping on his horse's flank, realizing (though the film does not spell this out) that, sometimes you have to eat wood, or dirt, or worse to survive.

This is a witty, harrowing, wonderful film; concidentally, it may even explain what is happening in Bosnia today. It understands full well how laughable absurdity can be without becoming any the less lacerating or lethal. There are ironies everywhere. What was the most horrible summer in the life of a young mother, driving her to drink and wasting away, was for her small son the most unforgettably lovely season of his life. The final tragic episode is not in Dumitriu's memoirs, and was invented by Pintilie. It is visually stunning and emotionally shattering, but it may be a bit too theatrical. Still, with such writing, directing, and acting—most prominently from Kristin Scott-Thomas and Claudiu Bleont as the Dumitriu, but also from the rest—what is a small faux pas? This film resonates in the memory, insistently and inspiredly.

Nobody's Fool

Let me tell you about *Nobody's Fool*, a modest movie that nevertheless gets to the root of truth about so-called ordinary people, showing them in their authentic complexity, their flavorous quirkiness.

As Robert Benton has directed his own adaptation of Richard Russo's novel, this is the story of Sully, an ornery but decent aging construction worker in an Upstate New York town, who long ago ran out on his family but, as he says, never got farther than five blocks away. He works mostly for Carl Roebuck, a rich young loafer, lecher, skinflint, who, however, is the only game in town for Sully, with whom he is locked in never-ending love-hate. Sully is the sole tenant and sort-of super in the house of Miss Beryl, the slightly eccentric but canny and kindly mother of a rapacious son, who manages to land the townsfolk in serious trouble with spurious land speculation. Sully's own son, Peter, is an English-lit professor unjustly let go by his college, and equally unjustly abandoned by his wife and one of their twins on Thanksgiving Day at his mother's house. But then, Sully's daughter-in-law can no more stand her

mother-in-law than Sully himself could when he was married to
her. Everyone, good or bad, has his reasons (as Jean Renoir discovered way back when), which is what makes life so bedeviling, and
movies that approach it honestly so interesting.

Sully is a flawed hero, not only because of a bad knee that makes
this handsome sexagenarian hobble awkwardly, but also because
his stubbornness about other people often makes him do senseless
things in preference to just as feasible smart ones. He is attracted
to the prettiest young woman in town, Toby, the wife Carl Roebuck
steadily and flagrantly cheats on. She, too, has a soft spot for him,
but can anything come of that? Still, life is strange. Why would
Peter, the abandoned son, happily consent to come and do manual
work for his scapegrace father? And why would Sully's only co-
worker and best friend, Rub, so bitterly resent the likable Peter's
coming to work with them? Many are the convolutions of the human mind, and near-infinite are the snakings of the human heart,
yet *Nobody's Fool* has a firm but unsuffocating grip on both.

There are many quiet pleasures here, first and foremost the late
Jessica Tandy in one of her last performances as Miss Beryl. The
temptation to overplay such an endearingly odd old lady must be
almost irresistible, but as the actress showed in *Driving Miss Daisy*
and several other films, she could get more out of dignified restraint
than others could out of the most dazzling pyrotechnics. Paul Newman, too, is a deftly judged Sully, skillfully juggling the oddball with
the universal in his nature, and making the most of every ironically
lowered eyelid and salty retort. As his one-legged, ineffectual but
scrappy lawyer, Gene Saks, better known as a director, gives a nice,
unsugary performance; as the forlorn and endearing Peter, Dylan
Walsh is superb. Alexander Goodwin is lovable as the nicer of two
grandsons, an unadulteratedly unadult kid; Bruce Willis and Melanie Griffith are tartly authentic as the warring Roebucks. In the tiny
parts of an aging barmaid and a pawky judge, Margo Martindale
and Philip Bosco contribute small but flawless gems.

The Madness of King George III

Alan Bennet's delightful play *The Madness of King George III* has
survived the transfer from stage to screen, and emerges equally
enjoyable on film. When you consider how very few stage works

make it in the movies, and how very few of those have any artistic merit, this is happy news indeed.

Something must, by definition, be lost in such a sea change. *The Madness of King George* (the film title jettisons the numeral) concerns the dementia that affected England's King George III, which is now believed to have been caused by porphyria, a metabolic imbalance that produces all the symptoms of mental illness. It was a curious business, what with the King reigning from 1760 to 1820, losing and regaining his senses until the final ten years of total obnubilation. It is helpful to read Alan Bennett's Introduction to the stage version, in which he discusses exactly what departures he made from historical fact, and gives his personal opinions on many of the personages involved. The play and the movie, though not strict history, then, remain for the most part faithful to the spirit of the story.

The play was more—how to put it?—theatrical. There was for instance prolepsis, wherein a doctor from the future was brought on to explain the King's illness. Furthermore, the ghastly tortures to which the King was subjected in the name of a medical science that, at the time, had not the vaguest notion of how to treat the illness in question, loomed much more terrifying on stage. Even confinement in a wooden chair by means of straps is scarier when performed by a live actor.

But there are other respects in which the film comes out ahead. Since the subject is, to a large extent, the discrepancy between the pomp and circumstance of rule and the sundry forms of pettiness in the monarch's private life, it helps if the splendors of royalty can be shown to the audience. Even if Arundel Castle (for the exteriors) and Wilmot House and Broughton Castle (for the interiors) aren't quite Windsor Castle, they seem to these uninitiated eyes close enough. And in the London scenes, which the film recreates *in situ*, there is all the panoply of uniforms, coaches, Parliament in session, and the rest.

Here, then, are Queen Charlotte, who has to fight and scheme to be admitted to the King's presence; Pitt, the prime minister, and his Whig sidekicks; Fox, leading the Tory opposition to ensconced Whiggery; the Prince of Wales and Duke of York acting sniffy or conniving; the menservants of the King fretting over his urine, which has turned blue; the King's physicians examining the royal stool and arguing with ludicrous ferocity about what's to be done. And here is "the Farmer King" himself, a basically decent albeit garrulous and dullish fellow, trying to fight off his illness and those who would turn it to their profit.

I am sorry that the film cut the clownish pair, Sir Boothby Skrymshir and his doltish nephew, but it compensates with an array of other minor characters who add denseness to the texture. What helps immeasurably is that Mr. Bennett wrote the screenplay, and that the gifted young stage director Nicholas Hytner also directed the movie. It is his first film, but it hardly looks like the work of a neophyte, though the expert production design by the marvelous Ken Adam and the full-blooded photography of Andrew Dunn lend considerable support.

Most important, Mr. Hytner was able to persuade the reluctant Nigel Hawthorne to re-create his George III on screen. This is one of those performances that engrave themselves on the memory: Mr. Hawthorne has a wonderfully warm, fleshy, pawky, rubicund face, with an unhandsome potato nose and small, restless eyes. But there is such canny vitality in his regard, such bantering bonhomie or indignant peckishness in his voice, such bouncy sprightliness in his movements, that you find yourself ducking without benefit of 3-D technology when he lunges at you, smiling conspiratorially at his little victories, amused by his absurd idiosyncrasies, and very nearly suffering his torments.

There are sterling performances from Helen Mirren as the frisky, German-accented Queen; Julian Wadham as a glacially ironic Pitt; Ian Holm as Dr. Willis, whose unorthodox early psychotherapeutic methods, though brutal, proved effective; Rupert Everett, whose Prince of Wales is so foppish he seems to exist in slow motion; Rupert Graves as Greville, a young equerry whose amiability bursts at the oddest moment; Amanda Donohoe as a Lady Pembroke as savvy as she is sexy; and not a few talented others. Only Jim Carter's Fox seems to me a little low on charisma. But this is as fun-filled a history (or near-history) lesson as anyone could wish for.

Ready to Wear

For a more than everyday fiasco, there is Robert Altman's, *Ready to Wear* (formerly *Prêt-à-porter*), a picture that only the director's mother could love. Correction: though almost all reviewers, even those who habitually slobber over Altman, considered it one of his rare failures ("rare"?—well, perhaps in the sense of "outstanding," as in "O rare Ben Jonson!"), a few diehards could be found who actually endorsed this ordure. It is the kind of movie made by a subliterate megalomaniac who has been sufficiently adulated by critics from Pauline Kael on down to believe that whatever he does is ipso facto magisterial. Failures could always be ascribed to his being ahead of his time.

In *Ready to Wear*, Mr. Altman and his co-scenarist, a certain Barbara Shulgasser—about whom the press kit keeps strangely mum—apparently intended a satirical exposé of the *couture* (sorry, we have to translate into English, so *fashion*) business, in much the same way as *The Player*, one of Altman's most undeserved hits, was supposedly lampooning Hollywood. But it should be clear to a ten-year-old that, if you are going to send up Hollywood, you do not enlist some of its biggest names to play bit parts in your movie, just as if you are going to mock the fashion industry, you do not litter the screen with some of the famous Paris and Milan designers, not to mention some of Tinseltown's best-dressed stars. The formula for such moviemaking is: Get yourself some thirty big names from film and fashion, include the latest designs from the willing fashion houses (the *really* big ones declined), and then pretend to laugh at them (Pretend-à-porter?) in such a way that it draws no blood. Blood stains would be hard to remove from all that costly high fashion.

For high fashion it is, despite the deceptive title, *Prêt-à-porter*, further diluted into *Ready to Wear*. People might be less eager to see Sophia Loren, Lauren Bacall, and Kim Basinger in mere ready-to-wear, but *Couture* doesn't have as good a ring to it as *Prêt-à-porter*, still less so if it had been translated into *Fashion*, a title that would suggest something you could pick up from the neighborhood tailor.

Ready to Wear lasts well over two hours, even though it wears out its welcome after ten minutes. In typically grandiose Altman fashion, it tries to tell half a dozen stories simultaneously, and does justice to none. As typically, it began as a much longer movie that was then frantically whittled down, leaving its truncated plot elements uneasily jostling, when not downright fighting, one another.

Even worse than the movie's disjointedness is its tastelessness. Thus several characters step into dog excrement (a gag to gag on); thus the aging stars, Marcello Mastroianni and Sophia Loren, are assigned a bedroom scene in which, after Mastroianni has let out several wolf howls at the partially disrobed Miss Loren, he falls asleep as she tries to crawl into bed with him—a scene that could give *coitus interruptus* a bad name; and thus, in the end, high-fashion models parade down the runway starkers, suggesting that *haute couture* is really the Emperor's New Clothes. To make the point still more obvious, Altman cuts to tiny tots gamboling sans clothes, a typical example of his muddleheadedness. For if high fashion is no different from female nudity, and that in turn no different from infant nakedness, the whole thing is really innocent, which is hardly what a satire should be telling us.

And the last straw is the pusillanimity with which the title was translated at the eleventh hour, because puzzled people were pronouncing *porter* as if it were a dark beer, so that it now appears both in English and in French, a two-headed monster like its producing company, Miramax, headed by Bob and Harvey Weinstein. To carry two-headedness even further, the cinematography is by two cut-rate cameramen, Pierre Mignot and Jean Lépine, who make shots that should be sharp and stylish look as fuzzy as the thinking behind this hapless venture.

Wrong-Note Waltz

BEFORE SUNRISE; COLONEL CHABERT

I missed Richard Linklater's previous and, I gather, very different films, but *Before Sunrise* does not instill in me an uncontrollable urge to ferret them out. Yes, *Before Sunrise* is atypical for our times, which lends it some interest. But from atypical to original and noteworthy can be quite a long way, which the movie lacks the stamina to traverse.

Céline, a graduate student, is returning from a visit to her grandmother in Budapest to her home in Paris; on the train, she meets Jesse, a young American who has just been ditched by his girlfriend in Madrid, but claims to have a cheaper flight home from Vienna. (It turns out he has a Eurail pass, and don't you rail at Eurail!) Céline, too, has had a recent romantic breakup. The stage is set when Jesse solicits Céline to interrupt her journey, so they can spend a platonic night roaming the streets and nightclubs of Vienna before they continue on their separate ways in the morning.

The girl has considered the youth cute ever since she moved into the seat next to him to avoid the proximity of an in-fighting Austrian couple; thus she does not require much prodding to jointly explore the "city of our dreams," to quote the song. The travelogue commences, subsidized in part by the Vienna Film Financing Fund. May the tribe of tourists in Vienna increase no less than Abou Ben Adhem's, but I would have preferred seeing the city in a less distorting mirror than this one.

The formula is as follows. Have these young people meet cute, continue cute, and part cute. Keep the audience guessing: will they or won't they, despite their ground rules, end up making love fetchingly among the Keep Off the Grass signs of one of Vienna's parks? Mr. Linklater leads up to what looks like an incipient sex scene, then cuts several hours ahead, leaving this particular answer to our imaginations, on the not unfounded assumption that they may be better than his. So, too, with the ambiguous ending: will the young persons keep their promise to meet again in the same place six months hence? (Where, by the way, have we heard that one before?) Frankly, Scarlett, I don't give a damn.

Still, as skeleton plots go, this one may not be worse than any another skeleton: the problem lies in the fleshing out. I find both Jesse and Céline crashing bores who never stop spouting thrice-told trivia: equally dull when they are being typical young people and when, in the filmmakers' opinions, they become clever or winsome or inventive, or whatever putative traits of theirs are supposed to beguile us. Clearly, such a story depends on so-called fragile charm, the very quality in shortest supply in these parts these days.

What moves the movie forward is twofold: the unfurling of the principals' past in their conversation, and the impact of encounters with the fabled city and its oddball denizens. And how delightful that, on top of Vienna, we get, in the score or the dialogue, such distinguished presences as Seurat, Auden, Purcell, Beethoven, Bach, Vivaldi, and numerous visual allusions to the movie *The Third Man*, not to mention the latest in Austrian and American pop music. One expects no less from co-authors such as Linklater, who studied literature and drama for two years at the University of Texas before dropping out to work on offshore oil rigs, and Kim Krizan, who is an actress and belly dancer, and earned her M.A. in literature with a thesis on "Anaïs Nin and the Psychology of Creativity," the one questionable item among otherwise impeccable credentials.

Representative of the movie is an interminable scene in the back of a Viennese trolley en route to the Prater amusement park and its giant ferris wheel, as Jesse and Céline rehearse their former love affairs. Perhaps to atone for the reputed fast cutting of his earlier films, Linklater (as also in other scenes) dawdles statically and relentlessly over an exchange of unenlightening confidences. How to approach this badinage? Are we to smile nostalgically as we re-encounter our former selves? Well now, if we ever were this banal and tiresome, the quicker we abjure and forget it, the better. And if we never were like this, why encumber us with alien regurgitations? One solution would be to satirize these pups, but nothing could be farther from the filmmakers' minds, especially since they encouraged their esteemed actors to draw on their own lives and vocabularies.

Alas, for us to share in this sentimental joyride, something would have to rise above the coy, the clichéd, and the cutesy. Take the dialogue. "Look, there's a rabbit!" "Hello, rabbit!" "He's cute." What was Céline like to Jesse? "She was literally like a Botticelli angel." Ah yes, literally. And what of "It kind of let me know how ambiguous everything was—even death"? I forgot to jot down the antecedent, but it's shuddery enough as is. And his parents, Jesse says, "stuck together for the well-being of my sister and I." "Well-being" may strike one as a bit fancy, but the ungrammatical nominative is only too believable, unironic as it is. People who write theses on Anaïs Nin can't be bothered with such trifles.

Or there could be great performances. Both Ethan Hawke and Julie Delpy are decent actors, but neither of them, as of now, is great. His main problem is something cultivatedly unwashed about his look and manner; hers, the Gallic (actually Swiss) charm she exudes a little too self-consciously. Moreover, Mr. Hawke tends toward smarminess; Miss Delpy, toward deliquescence. And forced to look at them this closely, this long, you get too much callowness from him, and a certain pasty-facedness from her. As for the minor Austrian characters who wander in and out, some of them are interesting, some of them merely irritating. When they speak German, there are no subtitles, which is too bad, because the German dialogue is marginally better than the English, the translators presumably improving on the screenwriters art. Or else, like the two avant-garde theater guys who appear briefly, they make up their own stuff better.

Watching the film invites free association. I was happy to see the little square outside the café that was the hangout of Peter Altenberg, the author of exquisitely humorous or lyrically poignant prose sketches; what a scenarist he might have made for this movie! The heroine's name, Céline, made me think of the homonymous French novelist, whose *Journey to the End of the Night*, though considerably longer than this one, is incomparably less exhausting.*

Apropos French novelists, *Colonel Chabert* has made it to the screen. As adapted by Jean Cosmos and Yves Angelo, and directed by the latter, this minor Balzac novel proves a major cinematic achievement. Angelo, a gifted cinematographer whose directorial debut this is, will be recalled for such gorgeously shot films as *Tous les matins du monde* and *Un Coeur en hiver*, and the undeservedly neglected *Germinal*, based on Zola. Angelo began as a first-prize winner in piano at the Paris Conservatory of Music, and so I expected this film to both look right and, musically, sound right.

The former expectation is neatly met by the camera of Bernard Lutic (a name new to me), but the music raises some problems. The composers here are Scarlatti, Mozart, Beethoven, Schubert, and Schumann, an even more impressive roster than Linklater's, but a bit topheavy: less of it—less of any soundtrack music—would go farther. Unfortunately, profitable sales of soundtrack albums have come to dictate film scoring to the point where silence seems more than golden—platinum.

The story is a splendid variation on the Martin Guerre theme. A rich widow who thinks she has lost her husband, an officer in the Napoleonic wars, has remarried into the aristocracy, given birth to charming offspring, and maneuvered her way to enormous wealth. The last thing she wants is for her ex-husband to show up and claim her. But such an alleged Colonel Chabert does show up, and may well be legitimate, even though the now Countess Ferraud will have nothing to do with him. Impostor or genuine article, Chabert cuts a seedy figure, yet manages, by sheer persistence, to gain access to the celebrated lawyer Derville, who is impressed enough to take on his case, even though he is also the Countess's lawyer. Never have the anfractuosities of the law been more Byzantine. To complicate matters further, Count Ferraud wants out of his marriage, as something better beckons.

With Balzac as co-screenwriter, you are in supremely good hands. And the riveting story and dialogue are matched here by superlative direction and acting. As Chabert, the ubiquitous Gérard Depardieu

---

* P.S. 2004. Linklater and his stars have produced a sequel, *Before Sunset*, in which Jesse and Céline, trysting again, finally consummate their affair after what may be the longest coitus interruptus in film history, and go off into the sunset together. If you have scant use for meeting, or re-meeting, cute, wait till you get mating cute.

proves yet again that his stardom is fully earned. His performance is both rock solid and subtly detailed; he inhabits the film like a giant meteorite crashed down here, and not to be easily removed or bypassed. Fanny Ardant makes a greedy, crafty, all too human Countess, and André Dussollier is superiorly swinish as the Count. But the film belongs to Fabrice Luchim, whose mercurial lawyer is a sublime bundle of contradictions, as complex a character as you've ever seen entrancingly enacted. And there is a fine supporting cast, from Claude Rich to Albert Delpy, easily as good as his famous daughter.

Boys on the Side

It is a rare and wonderful thing when an American movie comes along that is adult in every respect. Such a one is *Boys on the Side*, and I am quite prepared to be lenient about minor flaws in a work brimful of closely observed life, spontaneous feeling, pungent dialogue, and proper respect for the unpredictable. From the first moment to the last, the film exudes a sometimes quiet, sometimes rambunctious authenticity that does not grab you by the lapel, but slowly infiltrates the heart. You leave with the feeling of having acquired three new friends in the film's three heroines.

Jane (Whoopi Goldberg) is a second-rate barroom singer whose act in New York bombs, and who decides to try her luck in Los Angeles; she answers an ad for a co-driver to the Coast, placed by Robin (Mary-Louise Parker), her exact opposite. Jane is black, tough, and lesbian; Robin, white, proper, middle-class, a real-estate agent who thinks she can do better in San Diego. A relationship of Jane's has just broken up; Robin seems hardly to have had any kind of emotional experience. And so the cynical Jane and the finicky Robin set out in the latter's minivan. They amaze and amuse each other with their differences: Robin with her love for the songs of the Carpenters and her washing Jane's earphones with cologne before using them; Jane with her laughing indifference to a romantic movie on TV that makes Robin cry.

They head first for Pittsburgh, where Jane wants to look up Holly (Drew Barrymore), on whom she once had an unrequited crush. Holly lives in an indescribably messy apartment with Nick, a thug who pushes not only drugs but also her—against the wall, the better to pummel her. He roughs up Jane, too, when she comes to her friend's defense. To everyone's wonder, Robin stops the fighting with the force of reason, but when Nick becomes violent again, Holly clobbers him with a baseball bat, and the women tape him to a chair. At Robin's insistence, Holly takes only half of the drug money as the trio heads for St. Louis.

But Holly misses Nick, and catches a bus back to Pittsburgh. The other two catch a headline about a drug dealer found dead (the aftereffect of Holly's above-average batting), and they chase after her bus and comically get her off it. The camaraderie among them grows. They have droll little adventures and occasional surprises—as when Holly lets it slip out that Jane is a lesbian or when, in Tucson, Robin requires brief hospitalization: she is HIV-positive from her one fling with a New York bartender. So the girls decide to settle down in Tucson for a while; Holly falls for a cop, and Jane is in love with Robin.

I must not tell you more, though even what I have told you is not what really matters. What makes the movie so interesting is the small incidents, the exchanges of banter containing the odd occasional sting of lancinating truth, and the leisurely yet madcap way in which these three keep getting closer to one another—indeed, become family. Only Robin has a real mother, in San Diego, but one from whom she is totally estranged. Now each woman has two sisters as they start forging new lives for themselves. And everything could be lovely if Holly did not confess to her policeman lover, if Jane weren't so hopelessly in love with the straight Robin, and if AIDS did not act up in Robin just as she was coming fully alive.

The astounding thing is that this so correctly perceived story of feminine bonding, evoked in such telling and persuasive detail, was written by a man (Don Roos) and directed by a man (Herbert Ross). Throughout, Robin contributes an idealism that becomes more realistic, Jane a wisecracking skepticism that turns loving and protective of Robin, and Holly a savvy intuition underneath her oversexed ditsiness. But I must stress that nothing that is done or said here is conventional or predictable: the humor, the sadness, the everyday extraordinariness of it are always surprising.

It is, I repeat, all in the details. Details of travel on carefully caught highways, details of teasing or helping one another, details of contacts with passing or persisting strangers. Above all the pointed or poignant dialogue, often unforcedly witty, and sometimes quite plain, unadorned, and touching, Boys on the Side has a remarkable self-assurance about it, whether dealing in light-hearted badinage or encroaching devastation.

Part of that firmness comes from the solid performances. Whoopi Goldberg, whom I have always cordially disliked, displays here a gift for ironic understatement—a charged look, a corrosive inflection—that works with cool, suggestive incisiveness. Drew Barrymore creates a character out of more familiar material through an earnest naturalness with which she accosts other people's and her own absurdities. And Mary-Louise Parker reaffirms her status as one of our most fetching and affecting actresses: she acts with every part of her body, has oddly evocative resonances in her voice along with a delightful rubato in her delivery, and two huge eyes that seem to revolve worlds inside them.

Praise must also go to Donald E. Thorin for moody cinematography that puts both barroom darkness and outdoor brightness to striking uses, and features marvelous helicopter shots of the open road; to Ken Adam's customary skill in production design, deployed here in humbler locales, very different from the usual epic and exotic ones; and to David Newman's skillful blend of mostly found music. Even the supporting performances—Anita Gillette's doting mother, Dennis Boutsikaris's slimily slick DA, and Matthew McConaughey's sweetly obtuse Tucson cop—are outstanding.

Before the Rain

As I keep saying, any film that does well at the Sundance Festival is ipso facto a dud; *Before the Rain*, written and directed by the Macedonian Milcho Manchevski, is no exception. This is a pretentiously artsy concoction that plays tricks with chronology that do not fall into place, and that fails to create rounded, believable characters and situations. It profits from structural similarities to *Pulp Fiction*, a sorry thing to base one's success on.

In the first section, "Words," Kiril, a young monk in a Macedonian monastery who has taken a vow of silence, discovers Zamira, an Albanian Muslim girl in boy's clothing, hiding in his cell. She is running from a posse of Macedonian Christians from a neighboring village, one of whom she has, apparently, killed. (This is left cavalierly unclear.) The posse invades the monastery, wreaking havoc to the extent of machine-gunning the monastery cat for being a Muslim, though if ever there was a Greek Orthodox cat, this was it. Kiril immediately falls for Zamira; with the help of the monks, they escape together, but the girl is eventually shot by her own brother (heavy symbolism!).

In Section Two, "Faces," Anne, a London photograph agent, looks at pictures of the strife-torn Balkans taken by her lover, Aleksandar, a Macedonian photojournalist, among which are shots of Kiril and Zamira as we saw them in "Words." Aleksandar shows up, and he and Anne have sex in a moving taxi (the entire scene is shot as a reflection in the cab's window, superimposed on the passing London cityscape); but Anne finds it hard to commit herself to the fellow because she is also in love with her estranged husband, Nick. She and Nick discuss their problems in a restaurant where an ex-Yugoslav waiter somehow falls afoul of a patron who is his compatriot; the latter produces an Uzi and shoots the waiter and decimates the innocent clientele. Nick is among the dead. Aleksandar, incensed by Anne's hesitancy, returns to his Macedonian village, which he hasn't seen in 16 years.

Part Three, "Pictures," has Aleksandar involved with both his own Christian people and the neighboring Muslims, among them his ex-sweetheart, now widowed, with whom he hopes to reconnect. But the bloody religious divisions are such that he falls afoul of both factions, and, ends up getting shot by his own people—more weighty symbolism. This section, "Pictures," takes place just before "Words," so how could Aleksandar, dead, have taken the pictures Anne was looking at in "Faces"?

Such non-sequiturs do not bother the reviewers. As Janet Maslin writes: "Neither . . . such loose ends nor the film's slight [!] straining of its rain metaphor diminishes the final impact of an overwhelming vision." The quality of critical mercy is not strained; it droppeth like the Macedonian rain from Heaven. Yet there is no end to the movie's artsy-fartsiness. In the London sequence, there are endless panning shots of traffic, pedestrians, urban bustle; in Macedonia, there are endless panning shots of filter-enhanced mountains, sea, sunsets, clouds, rain. It is a veritable whoring after visual significance, while the words remain self-inflatedly sophomoric.

Because no Macedonian could be found to play the spiritual, delicate young monk, a French actor was recruited; so Kiril is saddled with a vow of silence unshared by any of the other monks. That saves money on dubbing, and when, at last, he does utter a few dubbed words, what poignancy, what art! There is no reason for starting the London section with Anne in the shower, but a discreet nude scene, what artistry! The restaurant massacre is gorily overdirected, but the more violence you spell out—with however faulty orthography—the more "overwhelming" your "vision."

Rade Šerbedžija, a leading ex-Yugoslav actor, is good, though a bit over the top, as Aleksandar; Katrin Cartlidge (last seen in Mike Leigh's dreadful *Naked*) is convincing as the vacillating Anne; the supporting cast of local characters exudes colorful authenticity. But *Before the Rain*, in its pretentiousness, is inauthentic. I find it fitting that Miss Maslin marvelingly compares Milcho Manchevski, with his "hauntingly oblique connections," to Krzysztof Kieslowski and Atom Egoyan, two of the smuggest phonies in today's barren cinema.

Subverted Summer

BURNT BY THE SUN
Nikita Mikhalkov has made some greatly admired movies that left me cold (though I missed his famed *Oblomov*), but with *Burnt by the Sun* he has completely won me over. It is a film in which we often don't know whether reality is surreal, or surreality real. And why, in Stalin's Russia of 1936, should we know? This was the moment when the Revolution lost all conceivable sense and began to devour its most faithful children to satisfy the insane lust for power of one of our century's two bloodiest dictators.

Colonel Sergei Kotov is a distinguished hero of Bolshevism, a friend of Stalin's, a leader in war, a popular favorite in peace. He now lives in a delectable dacha amid bounteous wheat-lands with his much younger, loving wife, Marusya, and their beguiling 6-year-old daughter, Nadya. They are surrounded by Marusya's extended family, which includes a great-grandmother and a devoted but benighted maid, made for teasing. It is a summer day of an intensity, preciousness, and lingering sweetness known only where winters are long and punishing, and where such a rare, irreplaceable day is felt as a matchless benison.

But there is trouble in paradise. Even as Sergei is enjoying an early-morning sauna with his wife and child, someone comes to fetch him because tanks on maneuver are about to overrun and destroy the farmers' wheat, and who but Colonel Kotov, the living legend whose uncannily Stalin-like face is a folk icon, could stop them? He does so, with a wonderful mixture of gruffness and charm, and the young lieutenant whom he jokily bullies into submission is so entranced that he momentarily forgets his own name.

It is a Chekhovian day; more precisely, a Chekhov-first-act day, before the clouds have gathered. But already we saw a prologue in which a young man, Mitya, returns to his well-appointed Moscow apartment at dawn, and contemplates shooting himself. A bit later in the film (but earlier in time), he shows up in comical disguise at the dacha. Absent for years, he is a family friend who, in extreme youth, had been Marusya's lover. His unexpected dropping in troubles Marusya and instills jealousy into Sergei.

Yet like a ubiquitous ray of sunshine (a good ray—there is also a destructive, fireball-like ray that burns a swath through the film), little Nadya spreads her now cajoling, now spunky warmth over all. Perkily precocious one minute, she is cozily cherubic the next and, in either mood, irresistible. But she is still a child, unable to comprehend, for example, that when Mitya left her mother to go abroad, Marusya tried to commit suicide, then waited over a year for him to return before yielding to Sergei's blandishments. What Marusya doesn't know is that Mitya, a former White, had to choose between jail or spying abroad for the Reds. All sorts of things emerge during this summer day on which various relatives, friends, and the maid indulge in their humdrum activities and ludicrous chatter, while something monstrous brews at the heart of farce.

Marusya behaves neurotically as Mitya twits and torments her, shuttling between buffoon and memory-wielding inquisitor. Some of this takes place on the lakeshore, where the uneasy Sergei takes Nadya boating so as to leave his wife and her ex-lover to their reminiscences. Meanwhile a nearby work crew is busy on what seems to be the launching pad for hot-air balloons; draped across it is a huge red banner proclaiming the glory of Stalin's balloon builders. A free concert of "music by a Soviet composer" is announced by loudspeakers to the holiday crowd, but what we hear mostly is swoony popular tango, first sung to small-band accompaniment, later played on a phonograph, and often tunelessly chirped by Nadya. Reminiscent of the andante of the Villa-Lobos String Quartet No. 7, and even more of Nino Rota's scores for Fellini, it has a lyric that begins with the eponymous words "Burnt by the sun." The soundtrack takes it up as a leitmotif, sometimes romantically appropriate, sometimes cruelly ironic; it should fill anyone who remembers the sentimental dance music of the European Thirties with a sympathetic tremor.

The movie achieves a unique aura of timelessness. You keenly feel a sense of transcendence, of the temporal falling away, of moments of joyously foolish activity spilling out of an inexhaustible cornucopia. Time appears as a fabulously wealthy benefactor who has invited these privileged guests to a never-ending house party to bestow upon them the gift of his standing still. And with that comes a sense of incomparable weightlessness.

That, however, is in the higher register, in the melody. Down in the bass, the accompaniment starts growling ominously. Mitya, who improvises a portentously doomy fairy-tale for Nadya—its threat not lost on the parents—is less of a prankster now and more of a veiled menace. And not unlike Eduard Artemiev's deceptively lulling music. Vilen Kaluta's cinematography is almost treacherously beautiful: the world takes on a lacquer that cannot but be brittle.

Let me mention one more marvel, a scene of conjugal lovemaking of discreet yet pervasive sensuality. Aroused again by Mitya, Marusya flees from Sergei, who chases her up into the attic, whence she threatens to jump if he comes any nearer. With infinite, fatherly tact, the husband woos his fragile wife back into his arms, and the ensuing coupling may just be the only one on film you experience not as a voyeur but as a participant. It is a hymn to married love, but also a trenchant image of the transience of bliss.

Nikita Mikhalkov co-wrote the screenplay, directed it, and plays Sergei, all three with equal finesse. As an actor, he can twirl his Stalin mustache with twinkling joviality, take command with more lightning than thunder, or suffer with wrenching bewilderment. I have problems with the Mitya of Oleg Menchikov: the comedian, the wastrel, the snake are all property in place, but I miss the charm, the seduction. As Marusya, Ingeborga Dapkunaite has all the feyness and volatility of this precariously balanced young woman, along with an otherworldliness that negates guilt. Nadya, played by Mikhalkov's daughter Nadya, is a child in a million, and an actor in rather more than that. Knowledge and innocence, coquetry and naïveté, bubbly brattiness and unself-conscious pathos exude from her as naturally as breath from the mouth. And she really was 6 at the time.

Some have found *Burnt by the Sun* slow-moving, yet this slowness is imbued with meaning, and a necessary foil for the dreadful accelerando of the last part, where surreal-seeming elements abound. We have heard much about the banality of evil; here we get its grotesquery. And its illogic. The questions that remain unreplied to are deeper than any answers.

Unusual Relationships

THE POSTMAN (IL POSTINO); SMOKE

I may have particular empathy for Mario Ruoppolo, the hero of Michael Radford's fetching and bittersweet *The Postman (Il Postino)*. Mario is a hapless fisherman's son on a small island off Naples, a fellow desperate for change. It comes when the celebrated Chilean poet Pablo Neruda, exiled for his leftist politics, settles on the island. So much mail arrives for Neruda from all over that an assistant mailman has to be hired to cycle with it up to the mountaintop villa the Nerudas are occupying. Mario, impressed by Neruda's reputation as a great lover first, and poet second, acquires a volume of his verse and requests a dedication. He gets an impersonal autograph, "Regards, Pablo Neruda"—which leaves him dissatisfied.

I did better upon encountering Neruda at a PEN congress. Knowing my man, I delegated my girlfriend to solicit an inscription in a Neruda tome. Told my given name, he wrote, "Para John, mi amigo, Pablo Neruda," plus the place and date. But unlike Mario, who uses Neruda to win the girl he longs for, I did my own wooing, and lost her. Life can also be less strange than fiction.

The Postman, however, is strangely rib-tickling and heart-melting, strange even in what went on behind the scenes, which, in this case, is not irrelevant, and further irradiates an already lucent movie. Antonio Skármeta's novella, *Burning Patience*, which underlies the film, is interesting in quite a different way. What the movie has made of it—as written by its Neapolitan star, British director, and three additional Italians—is a story in which friendship and romance interact fugally and then form a double canon with poetry and politics. For delicacy and intricacy of texture, *The Postman* is hard to match.

When Mario starts bicycling up the hill with Neruda's mail, he is at first almost resentful that most of the letters are from women. The postmaster, as good a Communist as Neruda, assures Mario that they are really, as befits a popular poet, from people; it's just that in Chile even the women are involved in politics. Still, if poetry can make you such a great ladies' man. Mario (one of the very few locals who can read and write, albeit "not very fast") starts poring over Neruda's verse. What adds to his fascination is that Neruda and his wife address each other as *amor*, which proves to Mario that the man is a poet.

A lonely dreamer in a community of illiterate fishermen, Mario feels like a fish out of water. His taciturn father substitutes loud soup-slurping for conversation, except when he reproves his son for having no job. So Mario eagerly takes on the barely remunerated task (no one else but Neruda gets letters around there), and starts fishing for tips about life along with monetary tips from the poet. He learns, amazedly, about something called metaphors, which Neruda explains to him, demonstrating that Mario, too, can do them.

They become particularly significant to Mario when he spots a new waitress at the village café, the boss lady's niece and a beauty, Beatrice Russo by name. Bedazzled by her looks, Mario sleepwalks into a game of pinball soccer with her, which he loses as resoundingly as his heart. When he tells his poet friend about his love, he confesses to having managed only a measly five words with her. Asked which ones, he proffers "What's your name?" When Neruda animadverts that this is only three, it emerges that the other two were a stunned repetition of "Beatrice Russo."

Mario implores the poet to write him a poem for Beatrice, which Neruda declines. But he comes with him to the café and makes clear to Beatrice that he is Mario's friend. Gradually, Mario learns a lot from Neruda: about history (a chap named Dante, who also had a Beatrice), poetry (there is no explanation for such a puzzling line as "the smell of barbershops makes me sob out loud" other than the poem itself), love (you have to find your own amorous metaphors), and life (the whole world may be a metaphor—which is something Mario points out to the astounded poet). And because Cala di Sotto is an island and Neruda is also a poet of the sea, and because the sea and love are shown as kindred phenomena, the film's picturesque vistas and intimate love story become tightly interwoven.

Politics enters in several ways. One involves the island's water supply, imported once a month by ship. When the waterless Neruda answers Mario's query by protesting that he uses only as much water as he needs, Mario explains, "That is too much." Here lies a political parable. But there is also the Christian Democrat who comes to the island soliciting votes with promises of providing an autonomous water supply—a promise forgotten as soon as his party is elected. Which only drives Mario more staunchly to Neruda's Communist politics, albeit with dire consequences.

Still, it is with Neruda's metaphors, clandestinely appropriated, that Mario makes romantic inroads. When the poet gently chides him for plagiarism, Mario rises to the occasion with, "Poetry doesn't belong to those who write it, but those who need it." Like the Ma-rio-Beatrice relationship, the Mario-Neruda one takes unexpected turns. So much depends on so little, such as the untutored Beatrice's responding to Mario's (borrowed) metaphors that shock her priest and scandalize her aunt. All this is told with a humor that, as special as the smell of barbershops, makes you cry out loud with joy.

Massimo Troisi, a beloved Neapolitan comedian, discovered Skármeta's novella and persuaded Michael Radford, who had ear-lier unsuccessfully solicited him for a British film, to come to Italy and direct this one. Making the venture even more ecumenical is the great French actor Philippe Noiret as Neruda. The voice that dubbed him into Italian is less interesting than his own, but the scenarists' invention of an Italo-Hispanic lingo for Neruda will be savored by linguists. Everyone, however, will savor the earthy, ir-resistible loveliness of Maria Grazia Cucinotta, who plays Beatrice with the kind of allure that waylays us only in Italy: a cross between ancient Mediterranean love-goddess-hood and unself-consciously sultry girlishness. It is enough to make you understand both Mario's passion and Neruda's poetry—even Dante's perhaps.

Noiret, who looks like Neruda, is perfect. He is not effusive, not the seigneurially patronizing, facilely benign poet. He is an inter-nalizing actor, and you must read his face, like a poetic text, by in-ference. His performance is all in the details: a bit of fraternal body language in the shoulders, an ache of compassion in the eyes.

Troisi needed a heart transplant but preferred to finish the movie first, though he could stand up for only a few minutes at a time and played much of it seated; Mario's touchingly befuddled expres-sions are suffused with Triosi's pectoral pain. But don't go dreading maudlin self-pity; what you get is the charming bewilderment of a man initiated simultaneously into passion, poetry, and political action. Also into the letdowns of friendships. That the actor, aged 41, died soon after principal photography ended is merely a fact of life, no more—and no less—mysterious than Beatrice's smile and bosom, Neruda's comradeship and forgetfulness, or the sob-elicit-ing odor of barbershops.

Let me also commend to you *Smoke*, one of the rare Ameri-can films that can hold their own against European artworks such as *The Postman* and *Burnt by the Sun*. Written by Paul Auster (a poet, novelist, and translator) and directed by Wayne Wang (in whose blood China and the United States commingle), this movie proceeds at a slower pace and along less traveled paths than the customary Hollywood product. It, too, is about an unusual relationship between a writer and an innocent, in this case a bright black adolescent escaping from school in search of a runaway father, and a white writer (an idealized Paul Auster) who becomes his father surrogate, there is also the story of the Brooklyn cigar-store owner in whose shop much of the action is laid, and his experiences with a suddenly reappearing ex-wife and an old black woman to whom he is led by a curious chain of circumstances.

Additionally, there are the tales of the boy's delinquent father, who owns an unprosperous gas station and a troubled conscience, and of the crack-addicted young woman who may be the cigarshop proprietor's daughter. This man, besides selling contraband Cuban cigars, has the strange habit of photographing the same intersection at the identical time day after day, and studying the infinitesimal differences. And there is also the tragically widowed white writer who comes to the smoke shop for cigarillos with which he tries to stimulate his blocked talent, and who may yet learn that, Kipling notwithstanding, a woman is more than a stogy.

These several stories jostle one another in *Smoke*, and although there are some loose ends, there is much racy dialogue, humane insight, and a sense of lived time, slowly but inexorably going up in smoke. There is also terrific performing, led by Harvey Keitel, who plays the tobacconist to the hilt—or, better yet, to the last drag of an aromatic cigar. This is a movie whose low-key veracity compels us by subtle infiltration—or perhaps inhalation, like nicotine.

From Waller to Wallace

THE BRIDGES OF MADISON COUNTY; BRAVEHEART

I have glanced at Robert James Waller's booklet *The Bridges of Madison County* just long enough to be able to put it down without bringing up my dinner. But I can see what, besides its sheer sticky sappiness, made it sell millions of copies. Herewith its messages. 1) Four rapturous days of love and sex are worth a lifetime: so, because everyone has had that much, no one has lived in vain. 2) Four days of adultery do not endanger a marriage; which justifies a lot of things. 3) Great parted lovers need not see each other again; their hearts will remain full of each other—consolation for all partings.

4) An Iowa farm can turn into Paradise; encouraging for all who live in stodgy surroundings. 5) Clichés and banalities are the true language of love; what greater comfort to illiterates?

Francesca Johnson is living in 1965 with Richard, her farmer husband, a son (17), and a daughter (16) on an Iowa farm, even though she was born in Bari, Italy, where she became a war bride. Richard and the kids have gone to a cattle show with their prize steer, and Francesca expects four days of uneventful relaxation from household chores. Instead, Robert Kincaid, a photographer on assignment from *National Geographic* to shoot the covered bridges of the county, having lost his way, drives onto the Johnson farm for directions. Francesca rides with him as guide, then invites him to dinner. Over the four days, the pair become lovers—that Robert spent some time in Bari helps, that both of them can quote Yeats clinches it—as each recognizes the perfect mate in the other.

Francesca yields to Robert's entreaty that she come away with him, but changes her mind at the last minute. She lives many more years as Mrs. Johnson, but when dull Richard finally dies, she cannot find Kincaid, who, in the meantime, has published a picture book about her. Then Robert, too, dies, leaving all sorts of memorabilia to her. Finally she dies, leaving a journal of her great love to her children. Her son is shocked and furious, but her daughter understands; eventually he too comes around. Their mother's story encourages both of them to put their own troubled marriages in some kind of order.

What I have just told you is not the story of the booklet, but a précis of the scenario, which is, astoundingly, less odious than was to be expected. Clint Eastwood has directed decently, and the screenplay by Richard LaGravenese manages to gloss over some of the sorest points. And Meryl Streep and Eastwood act the leads with sincere determination and genuine charm. The locations are authentic, and Jack N. Green's cinematography brings out the best in them. Only the last twenty or thirty minutes turn unendurably soggy, but because you care about the people thanks to the actors, you find it in your heart to be forgiving. More or less.

It is a simple story, verging on the simple-minded. Lines from Waller's booklet that survive include, "Francesca, do you think that what happened to us just happens to anyone?" Also the pivotal: "This kind of certainty comes but once, no matter how many lifetimes you live." (I love that *but*.) We also hear an encomium of the soil's "loamy" smell. But at least the movie doesn't have them go at it like bunny rabbits right off the bat, and makes the evolution of the relationship as gradual and believable as the four-day time span permits. Not especially believable, and distracting besides, is the periodic crosscutting to Francesca's grown children and their reactions, the son's especially broad as played by Victor Slezak.

What makes the tear- and cliché-drenched finale smell particularly loamy is that it really doesn't make sense. Since Richard is portrayed as a clod, and the children are old enough to cope, why wouldn't a woman like Francesca leave with her soulmate? Given, that is, how the situation is presented: she, with her tremulous, poetic, unfulfilled soul finally meeting a worldly man of equal sensitivity who picks flowers for her, modestly denies being an artist, and can talk about the restaurant across from the Bari train station. But no, they have to part, that being the rule of the genre.

A case, then, of having it both ways: your glorious fling, your subsequent lifelong fidelity; eating your cake, yet having its flavor forever in your memory. "We are the choices that we have made," the movie (and probably the booklet, too) observes; but we are also the choices that the author has carefully calculated. "I am no artist," says Kincaid, being "too well adjusted, too normal." On this evidence, Robert James Waller must be a paragon of mental health. I only wish that the score, by Lennie Niehaus, wouldn't repeatedly threaten to turn into the *Symphonie Pathétique*. But then, echoing one of the movie's finest lines "Good stuff. Yeats"), could one not say also, "Good stuff, Tchaikovsky"?

Braveheart is another film directed by its star, Mel Gibson. Close on the heels of *Rob Roy*, this is the second tribute to a legendary Scottish hero, this time round William Wallace, the great medieval warrior leader. Though less clever than its predecessor, it is much grander in its nearly three-hour epic sweep. The obvious comparison is with *Henry V* (the Olivier, not the Branagh), and even though Randall Wallace may not be quite so good a screenwriter as Shakespeare, the movie can hold its own.

Randall Wallace calls himself the spiritual descendant of William Wallace, and he has deftly incorporated the not many known facts about his namesake, and addressed the legend with gusto and eloquence. The result is an epic that, a few excessively romantic touches notwithstanding, is more realistic than most. These medieval Scots live in ferocious-looking hovels, seem (at least the men) heroically unwashed, and have coiffures in which a kestrel could nest. The friendly punches with which they communicate could easily kill a lesser fellow—an Englishman, say.

Braveheart aims to be a thinking man's epic. "It's our wits that make us men," young William's da tells him, and, after da and big brother are killed by the English, Uncle Argyll continues the boy's education along similar lines. Pretty soon William has turned into Mel Gibson, a young man who wants to settle down and live in peace. But the English are making things hard, what with such things as *ius primae noctis* (in the film, more tersely but less correctly, the *Prima nocte*) giving the English magistrate the right to deflower each lassie on her wedding night. Braveheartrending business, that.

Finally William secretly marries the bonniest of lasses, Murron—played by the breathtakingly beautiful and talented Catherine McCormack—but the English get wind of it, and when she won't put out for them, slit her throat in a shattering scene irradiated by Miss McCormack's performance. So William turns avenger and, by one small further step, leader of the Scottish populace (as opposed to the nobles, suborned by Edward Longshanks, the Machiavellian English king). There are plots and counterplots as the nobles sabotage William's efforts, and Robert the Bruce, who wants to help him, is prevented by his leprous father (well played by Ian Bannen), who expects the nobles to crown his son king. And much, much more.

The love-scenes are so-so, the political scenes ho-hum, but the fighting—both individual contests and mass battle scenes—is first-rate, barbaric, and sublime. You might think that so much battle stuff would pall after a while: how much slashing, chopping, stabbing, and skewering—not to mention mangling and incinerating—can there be without diminishing returns? Quite a bit; Gibson, to give him his due, comes up with new forms of warfare, better ways to turn charging men and horses into shishkebabs, new modes of battering down castle gates in a rain of boiling pitch from the battlements, fresh tricks to outsmart the enemy. And whereas this much violence with modern weapons would be unbearable, with medieval arms it becomes heroic and exhilarating.

There is something appealing about Mel Gibson—the ruggedly masculine countenance, the quick half-smile, the knack of conveying blue-eyed hurt (as when he discovers the Bruce under an enemy helmet), and a squarer-jawed determination than Dick Tracy's—that sustains *Braveheart* even through the unlikely scenes with Isabelle, the Princess of Wales (indifferently played by Sophie

Marceau), and through the Wallace's—or the Gibson's—unconvincing displays of polyglotism. Add to this the beauties of Scotland, searchingly chronicled by John Toll's inexhaustible camera, the solid supporting performances among which Patrick McGoohan's sardonic-sadistic Edward I is especially noteworthy (never before have terminal consonants been drawn out to such ironic length), and the intelligently deployed music by James Horner. A Scottish acquaintance, George Campbell, questions the use of the sweeter *uileann* (Irish) bagpipes rather than the fiercer Highland ones during the battle scenes, but these scenes are so exciting Horner could have used marimbas and I wouldn't have noticed.

The film put me in mind of a four-line poem by Scotland's greatest modern poet, Hugh MacDiarmid:

> The rose of all the world is not for me.
> I want for my part
> Only the little white rose of Scotland
> that smells sharp and sweet—
> And breaks the heart.

And that is high praise.

Spaced Out

KIDS; APOLLO 13

Kids was to be released by Miramax, which is part of Disney. But Disney boggled at the finished film, so Miramax created Excalibur, to release it, as it were, pseudomously on its own. It is the first film of the 52-year-old still photographer Larry Clark, author of three controversial picture books, the second of them *Teenage Lust* (1983), all unknown to me. It has been the longtime ambition of Larry Clark to make a film about how teenagers really are, which, according to him, has never been captured on screen.

Enthralled by the freedom and "culture" of skateboarders, Clark learned skateboarding along with his 9-year-old son; he also hung out in Washington Square Park photographing them, which attracted the attention of a 19-year-old high-school dropout, Harmony Korine, who claims to be the grandson of Huntz Hall of the Dead-End Kids and Bowery Boys. Asked by Clark to write him a screenplay, Korine delivered it in three weeks. The film was made with amateur actors, many of them skateboarders, though skateboarding is seen only fleetingly in the film. "I think all my work has been cinematic-like" says the Tulsa-born, subliterate-like Clark, "and my whole life was preparation for making this film."

The action takes place during the hottest day and night of summer in New York City. Supposedly every word was scripted, although the sudden disappearance of some major characters and emergence of others, and what feels like a certain haphazardness of plotting and some rambling dialogue, may suggest otherwise. We do not get to know the ages of any of the kids, though they seem to be mostly between 15 and 17, along with some very young ones and a couple of older ones. But only one parent is glimpsed briefly, the mother of the hero, Telly, nursing a baby as she smokes. She denies Telly the money he clamors for, which he promptly manages to swipe. Even during the film's final, all-night orgy, no parent is remotely in sight.

The movie begins with Telly's early morning seduction (how did he get there?) of a sweet, blonde virgin in her room. This winsome creature does not even rate a name; the press kit refers to her as Girl #1. Leaving, Telly joins his friend Casper waiting outside, and gives him a full account of the intimate details; it appears that Telly specializes in deflowering virgins and aspires to have two at a time. He is proud of not having meant a word of his declaration of love. The boys' language is utterly gutter, and doesn't change much when, later on, some girls join the gang.

This takes place on the Upper East Side, and everything suggests middle-class kids. Later, confusingly, other clues point toward a lower social milieu. The cinematography, by Eric Alan Edwards, is documentary-style: much handheld-camera work, randomly catching traffic and passers-by, the jetsam and flotsam of city life, with the sound recording often (deliberately?) muzzy. The boys steal a peach from a fruit stand; they blithely jump over subway turnstiles. They keep talking sex in ways that would do hardened cons proud, and head for the apartment of Paul, a young man of Levantine appearance, where, with a bunch of other boys, they do drugs and talk more sex.

Now the film's favorite technique takes over. Clark crosscuts between the boys and some girls in another apartment talking about *their* sexual experiences, extensive and varied and discussed in considerable detail. Jennie, a former girlfriend of Telly's, is surrounded by black and Hispanic friends, and oral intercourse is the chief topic. Back and forth we go between complementary exploits of the two groups. Then another element is introduced: a visit to the hospital by Jennie, who is Anglo, and Ruby (circa 15) who is a dark-skinned Hispanic. Ruby casually enumerates to the nurse the number of her lovers, her unprotected copulations and her indulgences in anal intercourse. Nevertheless she turns out to be clean; Jennie, whose only lover was Telly, is HIV positive. We never see Ruby and Girl #1, both charmers, again.

One of the main plot strands now is the tearful Jennie's search for Telly, whom she keeps missing. Another is the boys' hitting the park, buying and pinching some dope, skateboarding, fag-bashing, getting into a pointless fight with an older black youth whom they all stomp on, then leave lying there, possibly dead. Eventually, a bunch of boys and girls proceeds to collect Darcy, the virgin Telly intends to seduce next. Then they all sneak into a closed public swimming pool to disport themselves, including getting a couple of girls to kiss each other avidly although without feeling anything.

At night in a discotheque, Jennie is still vainly looking for Telly, but someone forces a pill down her throat. She takes taxis and more taxis (a rich kid, evidently), and ends up at that all-night orgy, witnessed by some very much younger kids turning on, talking dirty, and impatient to be old enough to participate. Telly has just given Darcy the same line he fed to Girl #1, and gets permission from the host, a buddy, to take her to the parents' bedroom. Overcoming Darcy's feeble defenses, he seduces her. Copulations in the film are long and fairly detailed, but shot cannily so as to reveal minimal flesh. It is during this seduction that Jennie bursts in on Darcy and Telly, who roughly orders her out. Disconsolate, she collapses among a bunch of inert bodies.

Casper is lying nearby, tries to talk to her, but finds that the pill has knocked her out completely. Promptly, he is having intercourse with Jennie, though the girl never fully awakens as the rape runs its course. On the morning after, in a quick final shot, Casper has just learned that he has possibly contracted the virus Jennie—and now perhaps Darcy—got from Telly, and is scared stiff.

I don't think I am doing a disservice to Clark and Korine by rapidly summarizing this plot that gestated 52 years and three weeks. Those who want to avoid such a movie will have heard enough about it from other sources; those who want to see *Kids* do not go for the surprise element. The interest here, in any case, is in the details, even in such seemingly irrelevant ones as the legless black beggar rolling through the subway cars on a sort of skateboard. Sporting a T-shirt reading, "Kiss me, I'm Polish," and chanting, "I have no legs"; he is ignored by all.

The question is, or course, is it really like that? The press kit cites authoritative-seeming figures that tend to corroborate these goings-on. Even so, certain particulars too clearly meant to shock (e.g., Telly brutally kicking his cat out of his way) make one wonder. Just what lurks under the quasi-documentary approach: a moralist's warning or a middle-aged man's envy? In neither case should one shoot the messenger: both good and harm can be done in spite of oneself. But the film is a bit too personal for a documentary, too impersonal for a work of fiction. A work of fixation, then, neither to be swallowed whole nor to be dismissed out of hand.

What to say about Ron Howard's *Apollo 13*? It is a technically accomplished piece about technology and true-life adventure. We know that the three astronauts headed for the moon and, although one oxygen tank blew up on them, came back alive; thus no real suspense. How the men at NASA headquarters toiled like Trojans to help bring them back is impressive to watch, but resembles too many fiction films we have seen. That the airborne trio had to make some risky, resolute moves, and that ingenuity and heroism, above and below, had to work wonders is, for me, undercut when all this centers on buttons, knobs, and switches, on a technology I find it hard to get with.

Yet the understated script, direction, and acting deserve praise. Tom Hanks, who has the aw-shucks, all-American charm with which to turn even a fictional half-wit into a hero, has no trouble making a real-life hero such as Jim Lovell enormously appealing. Kevin Bacon and Bill Paxton are similarly well cast as Swigert and Haise: the one first brash, then gingerly; the other bluffy jovial, then racked by fever in an icy, cramped capsule. In Houston, as the grounded astronaut Mattingly and flight commander Kranz, Gary Sinise and Ed Harris give engrossing performances. Kathleen Quinlan does her graceful best as the anxious wife in some cliché scenes of family ordeal, totally unsalvageable. And there is also the obnoxious score by James Horner, with yesteryear's celestial choirs dragged out of retirement, and cinematography by Dean Cundey that remains all too terrestrial. At least the pokes at commercial television are justified and apt. Patriotic viewers of this film, which opened on the Fourth of July, will get more uplift from it than from a thousand fireworks displays. Yet amid all the critical raves, I have seen no discussion of the cause of

the near-loss of three gallant lives: the malfunction of a superannuated coil that should have been replaced well before liftoff. Such a
miscue is conceivable "upon this sublunary stage," to quote William
Cowper; in lunar exploration, however, with so many NASA experts
at full throttle, it seems a trifle lax.

Novel Distractions

PERSUASION; HOW TO MAKE AN AMERICAN QUILT

Don't know what I would think today of the movie version of *Pride
and Prejudice*, which I loved back then; but with *that* cast, and Al-
dous Huxley for co-scenarist, it should please me still. I do, however, have trouble with the current adaptation of an even finer Austen
novel, *Persuasion*, for all the nice things it has to recommend it. Let
me state that, though I admire and enjoy Jane Austen, I am not a
Janeite, and would certainly not concur with Lord David Cecil's
declaration, "There are those who do not like her; as there are those
who do not like sunshine and unselfishness."

Miss Austen's dialogue is delightful, but her true forte is description, evocation, commentary; no voice in all her fiction is as sparkling as the authorial. And no character in the novels is quite as
worldly-wise as the omniscient narrator, who gives omniscience
a truly human tone. Yet there is something a bit constrained and
constraining about the fictional world in which everything revolves
around who will, or will not, marry whom. The traditional ending
of comedy may be a marriage, but here it is also the beginning and
the middle, with everything, like a stream or rivulet, panting for the
matrimonial river to debouch on.

From the standpoint of cinema, in any case, the authorial voice
is a major problem. A feature film can bear only so much voiceover,
and even the most scrupulously scrutinizing camera cannot catalogue as many details—or catalogue them as stylishly and wittily—
as Jane Austen's prose can. So a film adaptation of an Austen novel
must reconcile itself in advance to a substantial amount of loss,
even if it avoids some of the gratuitous errors here committed.

In the September *New Criterion*, that astute literary critic Brooke
Allen, in her essay "Jane Austen for the Nineties," touches briefly
on current film and TV versions. She refers to "an ungraceful adaptation of *Persuasion* (in their attempts to purify the movie of

Hollywood sheen and give it an air of naturalism, the producers…
have too zealously ripped away the romantic gauze: the distressing results are an unappealing Anne Elliot, a pockmarked Captain
Wentworth, a greasy-locked Benwick, and a slovenly-looking Lady
Russell)." I disagree only with those pockmarks: careful scanning of
every closeup of Ciaran Hinds's face failed to turn up a single one.

Amanda Root lets Anne Elliot and the movie down damnably.
"A few years before," we read in the novel, Anne "had been a very
pretty girl, but her bloom had vanished early." Miss Root, manifestly a different part of the plant, has no bloom whatsoever, and
seems never to have had. A competent actress, she lacks the charm
with which even much homelier performers have been known to
enchant an audience.

Even more disturbing, though less important, is the Lady Russell
of Susan Fleetwood, an actress I could never abide, and who, besides indeed looking slovenly here, towers physically over the tiny
Miss Root. You feel that to stop Anne from marrying Wentworth,
she might not so much have persuaded her as merely sat on her.
And yes, Benwick here is greasy not only of hair, but also of persona
and performance. Yet I find Ciaran Hinds a persuasive Wentworth,
and all other supporting roles well cast, with Corin Redgrave (Sir
Walter), Fiona Shaw (Mrs. Croft), and the wonderful John Wood-
vine (Admiral Croft) especially admirable.

The screenplay, by the gifted playwright Nick Dear, is adroit
enough, and John Daly's cinematography makes the most of what
appears to be period lighting (oh, such flickering candles!), while
Roger Michell's direction sedulously deconstructs what the young
South African calls "that particular glossy, classic look in period
drama". But then, the novel itself, written by Miss Austen not long
before she died, has about it a middle-aged matte finish, and Jeremy
Sams's music, for sober solo piano, spiritedly avoids excess. A few
anachronisms can be overlooked, but there is no getting around
that not-to-be-overlooked, or looked-at, heroine.

How wrong was I to believe I had plumbed the depths of terminal cuteness in a number of slobberingly sentimental films Hollywood has churned out lately along with its more violent fare.
What I mistook for the bottom proves merely the diving board
from which *How to Make an American Quilt* hurtles into yet more
deeply depraved emotional slatternliness that piles soggy platitude
on platitude for nearly two mind-dissolving hours.

The framework here is a quilting bee during which a handful of old and middle-aged quilters take turns spilling out to the young heroine (Winona Ryder, insufferable) their mostly miserable pasts and presents, ostensibly to help her choose wisely between a solid fiancé and a reckless lover. Stereotypical feuds, infidelities, self-sacrifices are banally heaped one upon another, often in duplicate as we hear the stories first from the now older women, then see them re-enacted by their younger selves. With ever-increasing histrionics, plot, character, and diction vie with one another in dimestore bathos. Jocelyn Moorhouse's disgusting direction wallows in this seemingly endless concatenation of attitudinizing clichés, dragging even the able cinematographer Janusz Kaminski (*Schindler's List*) down into flagrant picture-postcardiness, condignly matched by Thomas Newman's treacly score.

A huge cast, quite a few of them famous, make fools of themselves in actions and dialogue by Jane Anderson, one of America's worst playwrights, from a novel by Whitney Otto that makes Harlequin Romances look like Henry James. I allow for critical disagreement in most matters, but must declare anyone with the slightest use for this abomination beyond the pale of civilized discourse.

That Old S&V

SHOWGIRLS; ASSASSINS; STRANGE DAYS

Since everybody writing about film, and everybody not writing about film, has seen fit to carry on about sex and violence in the movies—as unsunderable, it appears, as a bicycle built for two, hence to be discussed only in tandem—I resolved to abstain. But a time comes for all good resolutions to be relinquished, when a bunch of pictures from *Seven* (which I have yet to see) to *Dead Presidents* (which I have yet to forget) is ravaging our screens, I must lock horns with the inevitable. Let me concentrate on *Strange Days*, which has garnered critical enthusiasm; *Assassins*, on which reviewers are divided; and *Showgirls*, which has aroused universal ridicule.

One problem with film criticism is that it is probably the most disregarded branch of reviewing. Books take time to read, serious music and fine arts require specialized knowledge, theater is expensive, and dance is bedevilingly ubiquitous. In all these, some guidance is welcome. But everyone knows everything there is to know about movies, right? So why bother with reviews? Considering who writes them these days, I must reluctantly agree.

A general consideration first. Sex and violence may or may not be damaging to young minds, but they are certainly stultifying to older ones. We must, of course, distinguish between films that *include* sex and/or violence, and films that *are* sex and/or violence from end to end. Abuses, possible among the former, are almost inevitable in the latter. Why? Because whereas other subjects—e.g., love, politics, war, human stupidity—are susceptible to endless permutations, sex and/or violence, stretched to fill an entire movie, can do only one thing: escalate. Sex must become bigger (in duration, number of participants, unsubtlety) or kinkier—usually both; violence has to become, simply or complicatedly, more violent. Those are the only possible progressions, and while intelligent people may disagree on the moral issues, anyone with an iota of aesthetic sensibility (a/k/a taste) ought to be able to spot surfeit, monotony, boredom.

Alas, it ain't so. To an entomologist, the dung beetle provides endless fascination; for the aficionados of sex or violence, the approach is similarly entomological. Many, probably most, people have some curiosity about sex and violence, and both can be decidedly photogenic. What I find hard to concede—or even to fathom—is the current insatiability: two to two and a half hours of S&V keeping viewers as contented as pigs in clover—the three-leafed variety at that, with no hope or desire for the four-leaf.

Showgirls, however, has managed to disappoint even the most assiduous seekers of sex in movies. Written by Joe Eszterhas, who gets millions for a screenplay, and directed by Paul Verhoeven, considered a specialist in sex, *Showgirls* (so much beneath this team's interesting *Basic Instinct*) merely shows that you cannot make hardcore pornography as a big-budget, major-studio release. Even though, as here, the NC-17 rating was happily accepted—indeed, sought—the kind of hardcore that thrives unrated in obscure fleabags was shied away from. Hence the movie was obliged to substitute for certain impermissibles a plot, a story—something, unconscionable in the realms of pristine pornography.

The idea was to explore what goes on in the hotels, dance halls, and strip joints of Las Vegas—to go behind the scenes and expose the private lives behind the publicly exposed bodies. I have no doubt that such backstage and bedroom goings-on are seamy, and that some of the language must be the kind used in this film. But to keep up my interest for 130 minutes would take more than generally splendid naked or near-naked bodies plastered all over, with generally trite and improbable dialogue and action filling the interstices.

The dialogue includes the possible, such as a showgirl saying "I want my nipples to press, but I don't want them to look like they're levitating." Also the impossible, such as the manager of the low-grade Cheetah coming to see his ex-star now featured at the hi-grade Stardust, and saying to her backstage, "Must be weird not to have anyone hitting on you." The latter also explains the raucous guffaws with which the audience generously salutes much here that is meant to be erotic or serious.

Assassins, directed by Richard Donner, is the kind of movie whose press kit lists seven producers, headed by the obnoxious Joel Silver, ahead of the three writers, who, however, prove to be equally obnoxious. And, further, the kind of movie whose plot you cannot really follow because it is a) convoluted beyond unscrambling by the ordinary brain, b) distasteful beyond endurance by a normal stomach, and c) stupid.

We are asked to concern ourselves with the rivalry between the world's No. 1 and No. 2 hitmen, sometimes almost friendly, but mostly lethal. There is Sylvester Stallone as the cool hitman, his features in a permanent mournful scowl, as if a hundred hangdog Hamlets were trying to squeeze through a hairnet. Challenging him is Antonio Banderas as the hot hitman, something like a trigger-happy laughing hyena, always over the top as well as over the sides and bottom. Both actors have a certain advantage vis-à-vis the screenplay "by Andy Wachowski & Larry Wachowski and Brian Helgeland" (where "&" in current credit parlance means collaboration, whereas "and" means earlier version or rewrite): Mr. Banderas because his thick Spanish accent makes him often unintelligible, Mr. Stallone because his lethargic delivery makes him frequently inaudible.

Julienne Moore—as the mark whom the one tries to kill and the other, despite his instructions, to protect—has no such advantage, and we get to hear her lines all too plainly. And apropos of plainly, this usually fetching actress is here shot by Vilmos Zsigmond and made up by whomever to look very nearly unsightly. She does, however, tote about a very sexy long-haired tabby that, coincidentally, gives the only attractive, unforced performance.

Assassins is a prime specimen of that odious genre in which a character, and especially the heavy, can take the most brutal beating, kicking, shooting, and other such inconveniences with only minimal damage—say, what you or I would incur while shaving or taking a mild stumble—to come back for more mischief, to the surprise and peril of those who think they have safely put him away. Call it the Rasputin motif, though, it makes the Russian monk a pushover by comparison. Here Mr. Banderas, having been shot several times and fallen through several floors of an admittedly crumbling building, rebounds to carry on just as murderously and unappetizingly as before.

Finally, *Strange Days*, directed by Kathryn Bigelow and co-written by her ex-husband, James Cameron, and the former *Time* critic Jay Cocks. This two-and-a-half-hour apocalypse is the story of the eve of the year 2000 and its millennial horrors in the streets of Los Angeles, now completely engulfed by mayhem. We begin with a tracking shot showing every imaginable and unimaginable crime in progress along the sidewalks, with cops and malefactors barely distinguishable. It is the kind of chaos that not even Los Angeles, the city prey to the most fateful visitations since Sodom and Gomorrah, could survive, although the movie wants us to believe it does, thanks largely to the efforts of its hero and heroine.

Having a much bigger budget than *Assassins*, *Strange Days* manages to be exponentially more loathsome. The plot concerns a gizmo called SQUID (Superconducting Quantum Interference Device), eminently portable and enabling a person to record not only the sights and sounds of an event, but also the thoughts and feelings of its participants, and later permitting anyone else to experience it all in cozily virtual reality. Thus we see the hero, Ralph Fiennes, savoring the virtual reality of a heist and shootout on what is presumably a nice SQUID. Subsequently, via the film's villain, he is treated to a not-so-nice SQUID that records the sender's perpetration of torture, rape, and murder on a young woman, the feelings and thoughts of both killer and victim all duly caught.

Mr. Fiennes is a fine actor, and he and the terrific Angela Bassett, as his sidekick, give remarkable performances under the circumstances. The villains—Tom Sizemore, Michael Wincott, and several more—are good and beastly; only Juliette Lewis is, as usual, unendurable. Incidentally, I remember when, many years ago, Jay Cocks spent most of our lunch together warning me against the cocaine addiction of a gorgeous young woman, my then girlfriend. His moral indignation knew no limit; as co-author of *Strange Days*, he has come a long way. And another thing. In the press kits of both *Assassins* and *Strange Days*, much is made of their makers' latest billion dollar efforts "outgrossing" their previous ones. From the mouths of babes and publicists . . .

Carrington; Seven

Scorned by most higher-brow reviewers, *Carrington* is a film I have a soft spot for. The playwright and scenarist Christopher Hampton has simplified and slightly sanitized the life of the painter Dora Carrington—her unrequited and unquenchable passion for the homosexual writer Lytton Strachey, and her other friendships, affairs, and marriage—but since even that brings in most of Bloomsbury, he could not delve deep below the surfaces. Yet, as his own director, he has striven for authenticity, using actual locations whenever possible, getting actors to look like the people they are portraying, and faithfully re-creating Carrington's and other Bloomsbury art work.

The film does have a somewhat unreal quality because it is told in brief, often disjointed scenes, and because it tends to dispense with extras: the characters who matter are largely left alone with their ideas, feelings, relationships, and talk, talk, talk. For me, this suffices, especially as subtly photographed by Denis Lenoir. As Strachey, Jonathan Pryce gives a performance that is idiomatic, zesty, finely textured, and, because wholly unsentimental, profoundly moving. Emma Thompson, though hardly the childlike and apple-cheeked creature Dora Carrington was, conveys those tomboyish qualities impressively in a performance scarcely behind Pryce's. The others are apt, too; only Rufus Sewell overacts the tempestuous painter and Dora-lover Mark Gertler.

The one serious drawback is the abominable score by the always atrocious Michael Nyman; when, late in the film, Schubert's C-major Quintet takes over, the relief is indescribable. *Carrington* is a somewhat sketchy but ultimately very affecting story; if it leads you eventually to Michael Holroyd's Strachey biography, so much the better.

Seven is one of the meanest, ugliest, most ferocious films ever made. It is also one of the most original, imaginative, and suspenseful of its kind. If you have nerves, if not of steel, at least of aluminum, you should find *Seven*, ingeniously directed by David Fincher and provocatively written by Andrew Kevin Walker, as absorbing as it is jolting, particularly given the moody cinematography of Darius Khondji. As two very different cops tracking a serial killer of demonic brilliance, Morgan Freeman and Brad Pitt give superb performances; in a supporting part that looms much larger than it is, Kevin Spacey shows yet again that he is the finest young character actor in Hollywood today. He performs a harrowing climactic scene with an understated intensity for the like of which we would have to reach back to Ralph Richardson. A must for those who can take it, the film is only slightly marred by the presence of the untalented and unprepossessive Gwyneth Paltrow.

Sense and Sensibility

Though *Sense and Sensibility* is not Jane Austen's best work, the screenplay that Emma Thompson drew from it, and the film that Ang Lee directed, capture the essence of the novel. There may be fewer earthy details here than in the recent *Persuasion* but neither are there any obvious anachronisms. The broadening of certain effects is, like the foreshortening necessitated by the film format, unavoidable. The film is one of the prettiest in a long time, thanks to the exquisite production design of Luciana Arrighi, nicely judged costuming of Jenny Beavan and John Bright, authentic period movement by Jane Gibson, and rapturous cinematography by Michael Coulter. The film truly looks right.

It also plays right. The Dashwood sisters may be more mature than stipulated, but "sense" is staunchly embodied by Miss Thompson's Elinor, and "sensibility" is impassionedly conveyed by Kate Winslet's Marianne. The very shapes of the actresses' faces and figures—Miss Thompson's ovals and elongations, Miss Winslet's fiercely compact rotundities—work as objective correlatives. Emilie François is enchantingly saucy as little Margaret, and Imogen Stubbs a wonderfully sanctimonious Lucy. Harriet Walter pulls out a few too many stops as the mean Fanny, but it pays off in her hilarious fight scene with Lucy.

The men are mostly fine, too. Alan Rickman, better suited to heavies, nevertheless awkwardly grows on you as a repressed Colonel Brandon. Greg Wise is all dashing recklessness as Willoughby, and Hugh Laurie a splendidly wry Mr. Palmer. Only Hugh Grant is much too adorably bumbling as Edward Ferrars; perhaps his off-screen misadventure may have added to his apologetic stance. He urgently needs to chasten his onscreen persona, and stop hunching his shoulders like a dromedary.

The riskiest move may have been picking Ang Lee, the young Taiwanese director of *The Wedding Banquet*, to shepherd so Occidental a venture, but East and West meet as never the twain have before. Add to this felicitous indoor and outdoor locations, and sparse but telling music by Patrick Doyle, and you have all the needed ingredients. Walter Allen has said of Jane Austen that "the main emphasis in her work is on manners, which she sees as morals in microcosm." This is an impeccably mannerly transposition to the cinematic medium.

And there is the amazing acting by our scenarist. Miss Thompson has been remarkable in most of her many films, but—improbably—she keeps getting better yet. Just when you think she has reached her acme, she goes ahead and tops herself. The scene at the end when Elinor, who believes she has lost Edward forever, finds him come back to woo her is simply unsurpassable. It requires the actress to sob and exult simultaneously—to release antithetical emotions in one long, liberating outburst, and what Miss Thompson does with it makes histrionic history. The distinguished scholar W. P. Ker once observed, "There is no name for the dominant quality in Miss Austen's work, except perhaps intelligence." This applies equally to Emma Thompson.

People, Politics, and Perversity

LAMERICA; NIXON

Before Bosnia, the most wretched Balkan country was Albania. For the Communist dictator Enver Hoxha, even Soviet Russia was too liberal; only Mao would do. But the miseries of this tiny, three-million-soul country go further back. In 1939, Mussolini's troops crossed the seventy miles of Adriatic Sea to rule Albania until 1943, when the Nazis took over. Under today's quasi-democracy, the country is still horribly poor. It reminded the filmmaker Gianni

Amelio (*Open Doors, Stolen Children*) of that immediately postwar
Italy that forced his grandfather to emigrate to *Lamerica*, as illiterate Italians refer to the United States, where he promptly failed.

Lamerica, Amelio's new film, is dedicated to all poor nations
whose paupers dream of distant salvation in a mythical America,
but either can't afford to leave or, like most Albanians who swarmed
to Italy after the dictator's fall, are sent back on the very ships they
came on. Equally tragic were the Italian soldiers who, upon the Duce's fall, changed their names, became Albanianized, and still ended
up in inhuman Albanian prisons, where many of them died.

The film takes place in 1991, when two Italian con men, Fiore and
young Gino, arrive in Albania to set up a bogus shoe factory, collect
subsidies from Italy, and then scamper off. They need an Albanian
figurehead to ostensibly run the company, and look for some abject
fellow they can boss around. They find Spiro, a poor wretch in his
seventies who languished in jail for decades and is too scared even
to speak, and make him president. They clean him up, provide him
with a decent suit that somehow refuses to hang right on him, and
temporarily park him in an orphanage run by nuns. But Spiro escapes, and Gino in his jeep sets out to retrieve him.

He finally catches him, and they head back for Tirana, the capital. Along the way, every removable part of the jeep is stolen. Next,
Gino's baggage and clothes; he even lands briefly in prison. Spiro,
however, refuses to talk, even though it emerges that he is, like
Gino, a Sicilian—Michele, a soldier who left a wife and child back
home. A half-century hiatus has befuddled his mind, just as greed
and impotent rage at Spiro and the depredations of the starving
Albanians have clouded Gino's. Meanwhile Fiore, unmasked by the
authorities, has fled back to Italy, and the scam is dead. Gino is left
hanging with a quirky and useless old man on his hands.

But Spiro-Michele now becomes friendly and communicative, and
harder for Gino to dump. He tries to do it kindly, but it's no go; the
two are stuck together until Spiro escapes again. Separately, though,
both he and Gino are headed for the coast and for Italy. En route, as
Gino becomes poorer and poorer, he mingles with fleeing Albanian
youths on an overcrowded truck, and his world view begins to change.
The very, landscape, stark and crisscrossed by escapees and police, is a
stern teacher. Yet the insipidities broadcast by Italian television seduce
the Albanians into believing paradise awaits them across the water.
Heartrendingly, Gino watches a little girl doing a frenzied dance she
copied from Italian TV as her mother approaches him with the chilling

suggestion that he take her child to Italy with him. Like so much in *Lamerica*, this actually happened; as it was being shot, the film kept incorporating real-life incidents into its screenplay.

Many things contribute to *Lamerica*'s potency. A terrible irony hovers over the goings-on. Frustration for every character—for the whole country—is everywhere, even hunger and death. Yet the horrors tend to wear a comic face. Whatever goes wrenchingly wrong is somehow also comic in its absurdity, its perverse contrariness, bureaucratic or existential. But misfortune's grinning mask is more appalling than outright horror; as a genuine skull would be, posturing as a Halloween pumpkin.

In its final sequences, *Lamerica* becomes incandescently moving. Even then this rigorously unsentimental film does not milk your tear ducts, however much it grips your heart and tightens your throat. From a screenplay partly by himself, Amelio has directed with his masterly trademark dryness. Yet it is not the soul that is dry, but the humor and the anger as suffering humanity is depicted in its shattered and audience-shattering essentials.

Michele Placido expertly balances the charm and menace of the charlatan Fiore; Enrico Lo Verso makes the transformation of the brash scoundrel Gino into a human being subtly gradual to the point of near-imperceptibility, Spiro-Michele is played by Carmelo di Mazzarelli, found by Amelio in the streets of a small Sicilian town where he had previously filmed. He lends the movie his bare-bones, no-frills presence, something few trained actors could have matched. Without imitating them, *Lamerica* transports us into the world of such masterworks as *Bicycle Thief* and *Umberto D*. It covers the enormous distance between despair and (probably unfounded) hope in less than two hours, but with enough insight to last you a lifetime.

Compared to this, a film such as Oliver Stone's *Nixon* is very small, and not especially new, potatoes. Stone and his sundry writers and consultants cannot make up their minds about what to think of Nixon: conspirator or political wizard, flawed superman or inflated opportunist marked by a hapless childhood, or unlucky loser in Washington's intrigue derby? Object for pity, terror, or grudging admiration? This is not the same thing as creative ambiguity, where the filmmaker sees all sides of a man and presents him in the paradoxical but total round. Rather, it is a matter of vacillation, inconsistency, trying to have it too many ways—not multivalent wisdom but shapelessly fuzzy thinking.

No one denies talent to Stone—individual scenes or, more often, parts of scenes in this three-hour-plus film play effectively—but you do not feel a ripe and judicious mind in control. Excess is like mother's milk to Stone. Better yet: like liquor to a drunkard; he could not lay off it even if he fully recognized its harmfulness, which is hardly the case.

There are further problems. A figure from the recent past like Nixon, whom we all remember all too clearly, should be played by an actor resembling him. Anthony Hopkins, gifted as he is, does not remotely look like Nixon and, as a Brit, has far too palpably tough a time trying to sound like him; I found his "yeah"s—or were they "ya"s?—especially hard to take. E. G. Marshall, unconvincing as Mitchell, would have made a far better Nixon, looking, more like him and able to suggest his particular brand of slippery unprepossessingness. Hopkins makes him beefy and bulldoggish, rather than oily and tricky—almost Kissingerish in fact. But Marshall may have been too old, and not (horrible concept!) a star.

James Woods, a fine actor, lacks Haldeman's deceptively handsome, solidly all-American façade, and J. T. Walsh manages no characterization as Ehrlichman. David Hyde Pierce is a touch too morose for John Dean; Brad Pitt would have had the right pretty-boy quality, but the part must have been too small for him. Thus the excellent Ed Harris is wasted on Gordon Liddy. And though Paul Sorvino is the correctly bloated size, his Kissinger, accentually as well as in general manner, is far less convincing than Ron Silver's was recently, on television. David Paymer is properly sweaty-under-the-collar as Ron Ziegler, but best of all is the Pat Nixon of Joan Allen, a fine and restrained actress who manages fully to look the part to boot.

As usual, Stone is obsessed with Kennedy, who figures too prominently; and with conspiracies, both of the millionaire-Texan anti-JFK and, more plausibly, U.S. anti-Castro varieties, in the latter of which Nixon is made out to be strongly but indistinctly implicated. Vagueness proliferates; even Watergate is handled anticlimatically. I suppose there are legal reasons for much of this, but unless you can say what you want, why bother? The idea seems to be to make Nixon into some sort of tragic hero, a man of strength, determination, and genuine achievements, but undercut by his strict puritanical upbringing, his lack of charm especially vis-à-vis Kennedy, and his not having the right school tie and social background.

These minuses are meant to add up to the *hamartia*, the tragic

flaw in Nixon's potentially heroic Stature. To me, despite his for-
eign-policy accomplishments, Nixon always seemed to be a non-
tragic nonentity, and Kissinger, though clever, something rather
worse. Maybe someday the full fishy story can be told, but even
then I doubt if Oliver Stone would be the man for the job.

Legal or Lethal?

DEAD MAN WALKING

The death penalty remains one of the trickier problems we find ourselves grappling with. Is taking a life for a life justice or barbarism?
Is the state entitled to turn killer under any circumstances? Is the
Old Testament "a tooth for a tooth" just? Or is some modified form
of the New Testament's not casting stones more appropriate? And
then the economics of it. What costs the taxpayer more: the death
penalty with all those appeals and stays of execution, or extensive
imprisonment and maintenance of the prisoners? And what about
the risk of recidivism—those news stories about parolees promptly
raping and murdering again?

I confess I don't know where I stand on all this. Which is partly why I am the proper audience for a movie such as *Dead Man
Walking*, and perhaps why I find it so absorbing. It is based on the
homonymous book by Sister Helen Prejean, a nun whose ministry
to the men on Death Row has turned her into a leading advocate
for the abolition of capital punishment. Her book is based principally, I gather, on two of the killers she dealt with: one repentant
and anxious, the other sullen and unfeeling. Tim Robbins, the actor
who adapted the book and directed the film, fused the two men into
one, Matthew Poncelet, creating a more interestingly complex character. It was certainly a clever move to have the guiltier of the two
accomplices—the one who remains unseen—get off with a lighter
sentence, whereas Poncelet, who merely came along for the ride
and was sucked into the rape of a young woman and the murder of
her and her fiancé, is condemned to death.

The movie's chief virtue is its genuine striving to be fair to all
concerned. This is particularly apparent in the treatment of the
crime. Verbal and pictorial references to it weave their way in increasing detail throughout the film. The rape has erotic aspects,
but is not wallowed in; its viciousness, and that of the killings, is

strongly but unexploitatively conveyed. The final punishment is crosscut with the crime, so that sympathy for the by now greatly humanized Poncelet is not allowed to outweigh our horror at what he did. The film is like one of those Platonic dialogues ending in the well-known Socratic aporia: nothing is spelled out, the viewer's mind must clear its own way through ironies and ambiguities.

Since Susan Sarandon, who plays Sister Helen, and Tim Robbins are life partners jointly active in liberal causes, we can extrapolate their stand against capital punishment. And careful scrutiny of the film suggests this position, albeit without shortchanging the contrary arguments. This balance is achieved largely through the attention paid to the parents of the victims (though the murderer's dysfunctional family is likewise cogently examined), and also through showing the contradictory goings-on both inside and outside Louisiana's Angola prison, and various other actual locations where much of the film was shot.

Helen Prejean also prayed and shared grief with the victims' families, even though it was hard to overcome their resistance to one whom they viewed as an ally of the guilty. The three parents in question neatly—but not too neatly—represent three points of view: realization that an execution might not be the best solution, insistence on a life for a life, and a transitional attitude in between. The three roles are superbly filled by Raymond J. Barry, Celia Weston and R. Lee Ermey. None of these actors is overfamiliar to moviegoers, which greatly heightens the quasi-documentary atmosphere. But even the stars in the two leads manage admirably to make you forget who they are.

Miss Sarandon has evolved over the years from sexy starlet, through seductive leading lady, to mature and magnificent actress for all occasions, emphasis having shifted from her commanding bosom to her enormous, eloquent eyes—two globes containing continents of compassion. She has that priceless reverse-baked-Alaska ability of being cool of face and voice while conveying fervor inside, yet staying scrupulously within the bounds of histrionic seemliness. There are things about nuns I have hitherto never fully understood; this actress, given this script, makes them lucently clear.

As Poncelet, Sean Penn is a revelation. Latterly a highly questionable writer-director, Penn has all along been a compelling actor. Here he is nothing short of stunning. Every physical detail of his characterization—looks, expressions, bearing, gestures, intonation, silences—is better than just correct: correct *and* unpredictable. There is also a nascent spiritual quality, growth of the soul, that the performance makes manifest. And there is no cheap plea for sympathy, only a certain flamboyance of the apposite kind; part Byronic, part defiantly aggressive, part pitiful. In short, a histrionic landmark.

Fascinating, too, are the performances by Roberta Maxwell as Poncelet's weirdly erratic yet not inhuman mother, and Lois Smith as an unidealized, idiomatic mother to Sister Helen—herself, needless to say, no unerring plaster saint. Even the smallest parts are accorded a flavorous authenticity, and Roger Deakins's camera is enlightenedly ironic as it traces inextricable moral entanglements with a worldly-wise, pictorially sensitive gaze. I am told on good authority that the film's initial three-hour version was by far the best; the reduction by half an hour, second-best; and the final cut demanded by the producers, two hours plus, only third-best. A sad comment on our times, when trash like *Heat* can go on for three hours, but *Dead Man Walking* must be severely curtailed.

Even so, plenty is left to be thankful for. Especially, the realization fostered here that questions exist to which there are no cut-and-dried answers, questions that must always be addressed afresh, and wrestled with for solutions that are, at best, provisional.

Dying Adults, Wounded Kids

VUKOVAR; THE WHITE BALLOON

A Yugoslav film that tries to come to grips with its country's tragedy is well worth attending to. *Vukovar* concerns life and death in a small Croatian town near the Serbian border, where, as the film begins, a young couple about to marry are painting the groom's family house. Ana, the Catholic Croat, and Toma, the Greek Orthodox Serb, are boundlessly in love. The TV announces the fall of the Berlin Wall along with that of Communism in Russia. All is well with the world, right? Wrong.

The two families get along nicely, though some neighbors frown at such a friendship. Suddenly, across the country just as in little Vukovar, small hostilities flare up, and Toma is drafted into the mostly Serbian Yugoslav army. Some members of the family emigrate to Sweden but both sets of parents elect to stand fast where they feel they belong. Eventually, almost all will wind up dead. "Look how smartly the Danube flows today," Toma had said to Ana as they walked entwined by their beloved river. Now dead bodies begin to float in it. "Fear not," someone remarks, "we're not in Beirut." But we are. "The world will prevent it," someone was saying. A wiser voice answered, "What are we to the world? A hunting ground."

Boro Drašković, who directed the movie, is a Serb of mixed Croat and Bosnian parentage, and he and his wife, the co-writer, have steered an almost mathematically evenhanded course, After a Croat outrage comes a Serbian one; after some worthy Serbs, we encounter some decent Croats. To my Yugoslav ears, there is true poignance in the variety of accents and dialects, especially in the army scenes, where the phenomenon no one there would have called multiculturalism surfaces most tellingly. One realizes both how easily these diverse people could get along, and how readily, goaded by circumstances, they could turn on one another.

The film is particularly apt in its portrayal of how small animosities escalate into big ones. When Ana, for her safety, returns to live with her Croat parents—she is expecting Toma's baby—two Croat militiamen come snooping. The younger's behavior is clearly, more menacing; he seems to eye Ana as a whore, and her folks as traitors. When the elder declines the offered glass of brandy, the younger, with ostentatious greed, drains both glasses. The scene, although restrained, throbs with threats for the future.

When full horror sets in, it is as powerful as anything seen on film. Ana's friend Ratka, who has lost her husband in the fighting, is with Ana when four Serbs, calling themselves "dogs of war," enter to pillage. As Ratka's little daughter watches, the men proceed to rape the women in the most bestial ways. The child looks on in blank bafflement, but when the women are left lying ravaged, an inscrutable half-smile suffuses her young face. It is almost more frightening than the rapes.

There is a heartbreaking meeting between the just-ravished Ana and Toma, who has fought his way back into the house. She tells him expressionlessly not to worry about her: "The important thing is that you are alive and well and on the right side."

"And which is the right side?" he asks dejectedly.

Vukovar is full of such incisive moments, though it sometimes overshoots the mark. Ana goes off to buy bread for her parents with the last gold trinket she has left. On the way home, a woman tries unsuccessfully to snatch the loaf; Ana runs after her and gives her half. Next, she arrives to see her shelled home go up in flames, with her parents inside. Haunted by the last look she caught on her mother's face, the dazed Ana wanders through the ruined nocturnal town to come upon some hideous *Macbeth*-ish hags stirring a foul-looking brew. Inviting her to partake, as they point out that the hogs they made it from fed on corpses, they ask, giggling, "Is this pork or human flesh?" Excessive, no doubt, but quite possibly true.

"Why this war in which everybody loses?" someone asks. The film hovers around this question, doggedly and helplessly. The final, wordless sequence is shot, like the rest, in Vukovar. From a plane and a car, the camera surveys mindless devastation. First ruined street upon street, beyond this, endless charred remnants of vegetation. The soundtrack plays the pop song Ana and Toma used to make love to, its lyrics now taking on a ghastly irony. Boris Isaković is very fine as Toma; Mirjana Joković sublime as Ana. Everything she does is nakedly real as, without one false move, she goes from the extremes of bliss to ultimate abjection. Perhaps more than anything else, her performance brings home truths that no amount of newspaper-reading or television-watching could. Want to understand the Yugoslav debacle in all its hopelessness? Here it is.

Few films are pure delight, but *The White Balloon* is one of these. An Iranian movie directed by Jafar Panahi and written by the distinguished director Abbas Kiarostami, it takes place in real time: the 85 minutes leading up to New Year's in Teheran. A seven-year-old girl, Razieh, wants a goldfish for the ceremonial occasion, but a fat and multi-finned one from the pet shop, not a skinny one from the pool outside the house, with which her mother would have her make do.

Eventually, helped by her adolescent brother, Ali, she wheedles the money out of Mom. On the way to the pet shop, she stops to observe some snake charmers who almost con the money from her, as an amused crowd looks on. But she does make it to the store, only to admit to the owner that she lost the money—a 500-toman bill, from which she is to return 400—but insists that he must not sell "her" fish. A kindly but absentminded old woman walks her back until they come upon the bill, just as it blows through a grate into an air vent below.

Razieh enlists Ali in rescuing the banknote. In the process, the kids get involved with assorted seniors: a tailor quarreling with a disgruntled customer over an allegedly ill-fitting shirt collar, a soldier on leave who tries to befriend Razieh (but there may be something suspect about his motive), a young Afghan balloon seller whose pole may help retrieve the banknote, the shopkeeper into whose cellar vent the money has fallen, and one or two others. The city throbs and pullulates around the children, who are constantly foiled by grown-up indifference to their momentous little problems.

Yet the kids are not sentimentalized. They can be dumb and ridiculous; a neighbor boy is even a bit of a crook. And they can be as callous as they perceive the adults to be. But they are charming. When Razieh forgets about the goldfish to gape at the snake-handling dervishes, it is because "I wanted to see what was not good for me to watch." Sweet. But when she and Ali no longer need the balloon-vending Afghan youth, they abandon him, alone on New Year's. Heartless.

The White Balloon far transcends its fragile plot. It fully conveys a society in which an argument over a shirt collar can become a neighborhood's spectator sport. Even the snake charmers with their conning spiel become fully felt presences. And what acting from these Iranian amateurs! Take Aïda Mohammadkhani as Razieh: the omnivorous eyes surrounded by tremulous baby fat can change from glow to gloom and back in a trice, adorably conveying the capricious climate of childhood. Just look at the way she removes a sweetmeat from inside her skirt, always turning modestly to face a wall. Or observe her and Ali (Mohsen Kalifi) sitting on either side of the money-devouring grate like two bundles of silent misery. Or watch hope and frustration turn those faces into battlegrounds.

Much of the picture was shot from Razieh's point of view in a world no more than waist-high. Yet how sympathetic is this mother (Fereshteh Sadr Orfani) as she struggles to ready the house for New Year's while contending with her children's demands and her husband's bellowed commands. In 85 minutes, *The White Balloon* conjures up lives antipodal to ours, but no farther removed from us than a child's smile from a child's tears.

Forgo *Fargo*

FARGO

The Coen brothers' *Fargo* is their best film so far, which isn't saying very much. Everything the brothers have sprung on us has been

far-out, arbitrary, and vastly overdone. Some of it was merely attitudinizing and bad; some of it, like *Barton Fink* and *The Hudsucker
Proxy*, asinine and insufferable.

Fargo could have been a nice little *film noir* if they hadn't compounded it with black comedy, absurdism, and folksy farce: Scan-
dinavian-American Midwesterners up, or down, to their hickish
shenanigans.

Some of this, surprisingly, works; some of it ranges from the
unpalatable to the indigestible. It may be that all these paltry
denizens of hyperborean Minnesota (and, in a few brief scenes,
North Dakota—or what passes for it) really exist like this: living
and talking in slow motion saying, "Let me fix you some eggs,"
five times over, and profusely punctuating their speech with *yah*
and *jeez*. Marge Gunderson, the pregnant small-town police chief
who is the film's hero as well as heroine, manages at one point
three *jeezes* in a row, which is cheesy enough to make you check
your cholesterol. Inasmuch as she is a smart one underneath, one
wonders where the line between homage and patronization may
lie, if indeed it exists.

The film begins with a title card informing us that *Fargo* is based
on a true story, with only the names changed "out of respect for the
dead." If this is indeed true—I don't mean the story, I mean the respect—it is the first time the brothers have exhibited this particular
trait: and, like all tyros, they are not very good at it. The film oozes
contempt, or at least condescension, for its characters, the brothers,
though originally Minnesotans, having made their triumphal getaway. The dramatis personae mostly bumble and bungle while still
alive, whatever respect they may achieve when dead. In the case of
one of them, death means being run through a wood chipper, with
one white-socked leg obstinately protruding.

I am, however, willing to grant the likelihood of this being based
on a true story: it is far too good for the brothers (Ethan writes,
Joel directs, both produce) to have invented it. What they have
done, though, is to encrust the story with their predilection for the
bizarre. Minor example: Marge, seven months pregnant, eats like
a horse. Her husband (expectably called Norm)—amateur painter,
fisherman and bumpkin—inspects a bagful of nightcrawlers right
at the table where Marge is eating, which nowise cuts her appetite.
Major example: Marge leaves her town of Brainerd for Minneapolis
on the criminals' trail. A high-school classmate, having caught her
being interviewed on television invites her to lunch at the Radis-

son. A Japanese-American, he talks about having been married to another classmate who just died. Playing on Marge's sympathy, he tries to make out. Later, Marge discovers that the man never married, and that his "wife" is alive.

This episode takes up considerable time, but to what purpose? It shows us the Radisson dining room, and allows a Japanese-American to contribute a few *yahs*, and Marge a passel of *jeezes*. (I feel like taking a hint from Lewis Carroll, and beating her when she jeezes.) The brothers do show guts in making a Japanese-American and, in another case, an Indian unsympathetic; but it would be even more daring for them to tell a story straightforwardly and economically, without their baroque curlicues.

What story? That of a milquetoasty Minneapolis car salesman, Jerry Lundegaard, who, having fallen into debt, gets the aforementioned Indian to put him in touch with two crooks: Showalter, a small, nervous, talkative weirdo (the ubiquitous Steve Buscemi), and the big, blond, menacingly taciturn Grimsrud (the unexpected Peter Stormare, ex-Bergman leading man). They agree to kidnap Jerry's wife for a sizable ransom, to be paid by her wealthy but stingy father, Wade Gustafson.

Things go wrong from the very start. The kidnapping, an effective mixture of the comic and the horrible, almost miscarries when, on the road back, the men are stopped by a state trooper whom they have to kill, ditto a couple of motorists who witness the crime. Holed up in their house in Fargo, missing the whores they like to shack up with, they quarrel with each other or with Jerry over the phone. Marge Gunderson enters the case amid some folksy banter with her husband (he hopes to get one of his duck paintings on a U.S. stamp), and further cozy badinage with her assisting subordinate.

In her slow way, Marge is shrewd on the job, even if her deductions are couched in verbiage such as "Oh, ya betcha, yah," and, ironically about her investigation "I'm doing really super here." And I'm not sure how many "Thanks a bunch"es I can take. But sometimes it all pays off, as when a prostitute who had sex with Showalter describes him only as small, funny-looking, and, in an afterthought, as uncircumcised. Marge asks demurely, "Was he funny-looking apart from that?"

The brothers have good taste in cinematographers, and have acquired one of the best in Roger Deakins. He shoots rural Minnesota as a huge blanket of snow, the image turning fuzzy at the edges to suggest recession into infinity, and even greater desolation. The violence, when it erupts, is sudden and grotesque, and all the more convincing. Marge and Norm's down-home lovey-doveyness seems a bit overdone, as is her byplay with her sidekicks. But her doggedly earnest interrogations have a slow, cumulative impact, and are shot in a way allowing the ambience to contribute richly to the aroma of a scene.

As Marge, Frances McDormand verges on the cutesy but manages in the nick of time to pull herself back from the verge. As Jerry, William H. Macy, his face as wrinkly as a Shar-Pei puppy's, makes masterly transitions from discomfiture to distress, his voice similarly progressing from an overeager quaver to a despairing whine. As his hapless spouse, Kristin Rudrüd etches a perfect cameo: simperingly unbearable in domesticity, she becomes heartbreakingly poignant in danger. As her blustering and conniving father, Harve Presnell is boomingly effective; as Norm, John Carroll Lynch is an inextricable weave of amiability and clunkiness.

As the kidnappers, Buscemi and Stormare are complementary creeps, but then Stormare, who otherwise utters only a few, short and basic words, will suddenly deliver himself of "unguent" in a characteristic Coen touch. And when Marge lectures the one surviving, handcuffed criminal with "There's more to life than a little money, you know," and adds, "Don't you *know* that?" folksiness and absurdity enjoy their preposterously entwined apogee.

For All Seasons

MA SAISON PRÉFÉRÉE

Andre Téchiné has always struck me as a profoundly spurious director, whose films were vapid and vague, pretentious and hollow, their texture threadbare, their craft rudimentary. Last year, his *Wild Reeds* won the Oscar for best foreign film, and though it was better than usual for him, it was still far from compelling. The year before (1993), he directed and co-wrote *Ma Saison Préférée*, and this strikes me as a major achievement. I do wish, however, that the French title had not been kept, giving the film a chichi, art-house aura. But someone must have been afraid (unfoundedly) of creating a confusion with *My Favorite Year*.

Anyway, *Saison* is an ambitious attempt to deal, with the interlocking problems of three generations within one family, and one outsider who impinges on them. Emilie (Catherine Deneuve) is in her mid-forties, a former great beauty still very handsome, and works, like her husband, Bruno (Jean-Pierre Bouvier), as a notary public in Toulouse. Her mother, Bertha (Martha Villalonga), is a zesty but stubborn widow of 76, living in a small country house but apparently no longer able to take care of herself. Emilie moves her in with Bruno and herself and their children. Anne (Chiara Mastroianni, and fine) is a first-year law student, who now has her own place. Lucien, an adopted son (Anthony Prada, and not very good), is raw-boned and surly, and has made it to nothing higher than bouncer in a Toulouse bar.

Emilie's somewhat younger brother, Antoine (Daniel Auteuil), a brain surgeon who often behaves erratically, has fallen out with Bruno, and so hasn't seen Emilie in years. A very neurotic neurologist, Antoine—it becomes progressively clearer—is unconsciously in love with his sister, who has strong, but not incestuous, feelings for him. No wonder Antoine and Bruno don't get along. But now that Bertha is living with them, Emilie needs help with this difficult mother who desperately misses her country house. So she secretly seeks out her brother at his hospital, and asks him to come visit. He does, and brings nothing but trouble.

The very first scenes of *Saison* attest to its mastery. Emilie is closing down Bertha's house, and systematically locks the shutters on window after window. Through these windows we got glimpses of an idyllic countryside; now, with each newly closed window, the house becomes ominously darker. It is as if Bertha's life were evaporating with the fading light inside, even as, outside, nature is at its most radiant. Mother will have to trade green spaciousness for a black oubliette.

Another early scene shows Bertha at dinner with Emilie and Bruno, and the table talk, sparse and forced, nicely conveys the unease of the spouses, which the old lady's presence exacerbates. Emilie and Bruno, whom we saw as highly efficient in their office, seem no longer quite at home in their home. Finally, Bertha escapes to sit alone outside by the nocturnal swimming pool. Emilie goes after her and watches in horror as her mother chats away with her dead husband and then calmly explains these visitations to her daughter. It is a scene as chilling as it is touching, and it prompts Emilie's surreptitious call on Antoine at the hospital. The serio-comic upheaval his coming to dinner causes leads to Emilie's leav-

ing her husband and setting up on her own. This, in turn induces
Antoine's feelings for her to come tumultuously to the fore, with
unsettling results for all.

Counterpointing the vicissitudes of the older generation are
those of the younger one. Khadija, nicknamed Radish (Carmen
Chaplin), is of North African parentage and works as a secretary to Bruno and Emilie. A slightly dusky stunner, she is a hard
worker, but also a sexually free spirit, currently the girlfriend of
Lucien with whom she enjoys terrific sex. But she also needs real
loving, which the youth finds hard to admit to. Even mousy Anne
has some proto-sexual feelings about Radish, as emerges from a
naïvely sensual striptease the girl performs for the siblings. The
theme here is how sexual attachment gradually leads to love, even
as the loss of it between Emilie and Bruno nibbles away at their
marriage. Unfortunately, Téchiné is not quite successful at inte-
grating these opposite movements into a convincing interplay;
indeed, we are never clear about why Lucien was adopted in the
first place, and why, given a solid middle-class upbringing, he
should still feel and behave like a lower-class interloper.

Anne's anxiety as a daughter torn between her father, with
whom she sides, and her mother, whom she misses, is presumably intensified by her lack of appeal to men; though this remains
a mere hint, it is nicely suggested. Lucien's emotional strangula-
tion is likewise effectively conveyed. And there are fascinating
sidelights on neurology, as exemplified by Antoine's intervention
in his mother's deteriorating mental processes. We experience the
striking contrast between his professional proficiency and private
awkwardness.

Even though the film works well enough as a whole, its chief
strength is in the individual scenes, some of them seemingly quite
ordinary. Thus a thoughtful talk between Antoine and Emilie about
their growing pains as children and escalating problems as adults
takes place at a roadside restaurant in what would be a charmingly rustic setting were it not for the cars whooshing by on the
highway just behind them. These cars function as a cacophonous
accompaniment to an apparently harmonious duet that, nevertheless, cannot end well.

Other scenes may border on the surreal. Take, for instance, Antoine's ludicrous attempt at suicide, brilliantly executed by actor
and director. More unsettling is the scene in a bar where a sixtyish
woman (Ingrid Caven) suddenly and loudly intones a song about

mortality and has to be escorted out. Most filmmakers would shy away form such weird, seemingly preposterous and certainly marginal, incidents; Téchiné risks them, and they pay off.

Most disturbing is this scene: Emilie has been living apart for some time now, is unnerved by the turn of events, and has not had any sex. Waiting for Antoine in the hospital cafeteria, she sits visibly dejected. A randy intern notices her—middle-aged but still beautiful, ostensibly an easy mark. He makes an obvious but wordless pass at her, which Emilie indignantly rejects. She hurries outside, sits down under a tree in the hospital garden and tries to regain her equilibrium. The intern follows her and starts groping her with bestial aggressiveness. We expect an even more summary rejection; instead, Emilie yields to a wild, wordless copulation on the lawn.

This may seem utterly improbable, but when you consider the unaccommodated female being's confusion and physical need, swift and anonymous relief may not be such a far-fetched solution. Either way, it is a brutal, grinding episode, but incisively acted as it is by Miss Deneuve, clearly exposing the contrary impulses in a tug-of-war underneath her crumbling composure, the scene is one to stay with you, like it or not.

Could it have happened this way, one wonders, when Chiara Mastroianni was conceived in the illegitimate union of two extraordinarily attractive actors, Marcello Mastroianni and Catherine Deneuve, whom their work had thrown together?

But, I repeat, the wistfully contemplative, indeed Chekhovian scenes are equally powerful. Thus, near the end, the principal characters are again sitting around a table, this time eating in the garden and speculating on what their favorite season might be. The personages in this al fresco meditation subtly affirm their allegiance to nature as her children, men and women rather than angels.

Catherine Deneuve is more deeply woman and human being in this movie than she has perhaps ever been; as her brother, the remarkable Daniel Auteuil manages to be both handsome and ugly (a *joli laid*), obliging and a pain, perceptive and obtuse. As he scrambles all this inside him and lets it dribble out gradually, his is a performance of shattering veracity. Carmen Chaplin (Radish) is an innocent enchantress with the most disarming appeal, and Marthe Villalonga's exasperating Bertha is all the more poignant for the utter refusal to play on our sentiments. *Ma Saison Préférée*, an uncommodious comedy, is a film for all seasons.

Someone Else's America

A modest but winning little movie is *Someone Else's America*, by the Yugoslav director Goran Paskaljevic, from a screenplay by Gordan Mihić. It concerns, mainly, the lives of two Brooklyn friends: Alonso, a timorous Spanish immigrant who owns a shabby bar, where he lets Bayo, a fierce illegal immigrant from Montenegro, live and clean up between a variety of other, underpaid and often dangerous, jobs. Alonso harbors a hopeless love for a Syrian girl in the melting-pot where they all live, and Bayo, for trying to help him, gets into all sorts of trouble.

Back in Montenegro, Anja, Bayo's mother, finds it impossible to survive with three grandchildren: Luka, a successful hustler who, nevertheless, is no match for a crooked postal clerk who steals Bayo's letters and the money they contain; Pepo, the sweet little accordion-playing younger brother; and Savka, the sister who, not hearing from her dad, will not eat or sleep. They manage to get themselves smuggled into the U.S.A., but, as they wade across the Rio Grande, Pepo's accordion is snatched away by the current; the boy swims after it and disappears.

The heartbroken others make it to Brooklyn, but Bayo, fanatically believing in the boy's survival, and helped in part by Alonso, conducts an obstinately self-deluding, endless search for Pepo. Back in Brooklyn, he irrationally blames Luka for everything. Meanwhile Anja can't get used to America, even as Alonso's blind, now deceased mother (played by the great Maria Casares, absent from the screen too long) couldn't until, with the help of a stone table, a fake well, and a genuine goat, Alonso and Bayo fooled her into believing herself back in Spain. Though sighted, Anja resigns herself through the same table, well, and goat into staying, and, with her cooking, turns Alonso's bar into a bustling eatery. Luka marries a Chinese-American girl from across the street, and is a better hustler than ever with his newly acquired green card, but finds it hard to cope with his father's wrath; Bayo even believes him to be another man's child.

For all these dramatic elements, the film is a racy, folksy comedy, handsomely shot in Greece, Mexico, and New York, especially a Brooklyn teeming with ethnic variety and zesty humor. Yorgos Arvanitis's camera helps create a place as exotic for the viewer as for its struggling inhabitants. Tom Conti plays Alonso with boundless gusto, investing even his crestfallen moments with comic verve; as Bayo the Yugoslav actor Miki Manojlović (a star also of the Cannes-prize-winning *Underground*, yet to be released here) gives a performance so explosive it practically leaps into your lap. No less fine is the Luka of Sergej Trifunović; in fact, only Manojlović's real-life mother is unimpressive as Anja.

Some of the dialogue is in Serbo-Croatian and somewhat skimpily subtitled, but Paskaljević's direction and Mihić's screenplay, though a bit repetitious at times, have a zesty feel for people of various backgrounds, and are good in both serious and comic moments, better yet when bittersweetly seriocomic. Only Andrew Dickson's self-consciously folk-tinted score is bothersome; the film itself is tangy and idiomatic. It is not unlike Bayo's beloved bantam rooster, small but plucky.

The Horseman on the Roof

What a relief to turn to *The Horseman on the Roof*, directed by Jean-Paul Rappeneau, who gave us *Cyrano*, and, sure enough, Gérard Depardieu pops up in a spirited cameo. The film is based on a 1951 novel by Jean Giono, a regional writer of ecumenical scope, and the author also of *The Baker's Wife*. His works are imbued with the love of his lovely native Provence. Here he tells of a young colonel in the Piedmontese cavalry, Angelo Pardi, who, like many other Carbonari (clandestine Republicans), fled to the south of France, pursued by the Austrian secret police. The time is the 1830s, cholera is sweeping through the land, and Angelo, entrusted with moneys collected to be taken back to Italy, must dodge not only the Austrians, but also French patrols quarantining all who try to leave Provence. And also the cholera itself, whose victims are dying in ghastly convulsions all around.

Fleeing from some villagers who foolishly perceive him as the poisoner of their wells with cholera, Angelo takes to the rooftops in the company of a spunky cat, until he drops through a skylight into the temporary home of Pauline, the young wife of the elderly Marquis de Théus, from whom she has become separated by the outbreak of the plague. Angelo gallantly postpones his return to Italy to act as Pauline's bodyguard as she searches for her husband through manifold perils. This has been aptly described as an equestrian road movie; it is also a magnificent swashbuckler, an ultraromantic but adult love story, and a brilliantly psychological, Stendhalian evocation of character in action.

There is Giono's love of the land captured with controlled lushness by the inspired camera of Thierry Arbogast (who also shot *Ma Saison Préférée*), and the growing love between the boyishly idealistic Angelo and the unhappily married but faithful Pauline. There are the depredations of the epidemic, and the meanness it brings out in some, nobility in others. There is intense passion without so much as one conventional kiss. There is the poetry of Giono's language, superbly translated to the screen by the gifted scenarists, who include the director himself. Quite a bit of it survives even in the subtitles.

For once, the well-publicized off-screen love affair of the principals, Juliette Binoche and Olivier Martinez, is critically relevant: their performances glow with the deepest and subtlest affection I may ever have encountered on screen. This is how strong-willed, tough-minded, idiosyncratic individuals undergo the purifying fire of love, to emerge fully human and ready for all the exigencies of life. Everyone, including the wonderful cat, acts to perfection; your role, dear reader, is to hasten to this unique adventure and have one of the sweetest times of your life.

Bernardo Bertolucci's Bottles

STEALING BEAUTY

In 1972, well before its commercial release, Pauline Kael pronounced Bernardo Bertolucci's *Last Tango in Paris* the film that made "the strongest impression on me in almost twenty years of reviewing. This must be the most powerfully erotic movie ever made, and it may turn out to be the most liberating," she wrote. "People will be arguing about it, I think, for as long as there are movies." When did you last hear people arguing about *Last Tango*? If it is remembered at all, it is for Marlon Brando's use of a stick of butter to bugger Maria Schneider with.

From his first feature, *The Grim Reaper*, and first *succès d'estime*, *Before the Revolution* Bertolucci looked to me like a three-lira bill. There was less to his films than met the eye, and much less than warranted the ooze of ohs and ahs. To be sure, he has carried pretentiousness to new heights, remotely basing his films on prestigious writers' fictions: *Before the Revolution* on Stendhal, the nonsensical *Partner* on Dostoyevsky, the equally impenetrable *The Spider's Stratagem* on Borges (who told me he had never heard of this movie that proudly displayed his name), *The Conformist* on Moravia, *The Sheltering Sky* on Paul Bowles (though, as David Thomson remarked, "he hardly seemed to notice the terrible darkness waiting beyond Paul Bowles's bright sky.").

Of all these, *The Conformist*, which bore some resemblance to its source, was the best. Other films that Bertolucci, sometimes with collaborators, wrote himself were worse; thus *Luna* and *Little Buddha*, two of the biggest crocks made by an allegedly major filmmaker. *The Last Emperor* did have some merit, partly because of the exotic and picturesque milieu, and partly because Bertolucci, like some other perennial amateurs, knows how to pick the right cameraman to do most of his work for him. For a long time, it was Vittorio Storaro; in the current film, it is Darius Khondji (*Before the Rain, Seven*).

What characterizes the work of this Marxist (or ex-Marxist) attitudinizer who has always been a solid bourgeois is a certain rivenness, an unsureness that often amounts to hysteria. As Robin Wood noted, "The split is not merely thematic (hence under the artist's control): it manifests itself at every level of his filmmaking," I am all for complexity and ambiguity, for raising difficult questions rather than disbursing easy answers, but I am not for nudging us toward sleazy revelations and then evading them. With hardly any exception, Bertolucci's films hint at, hover around, or briefly dip into homosexuality and lesbianism, but this ostensibly heterosexual filmmaker making purportedly heterosexual films has never faced the issue squarely.

Stealing Beauty, from a story by Bertolucci, was written by the American novelist Susan Minot, who spent 18 months on it in Italy with the director, though the sketchy, haphazard end result suggests something more like 18 days. It is one of those films called Chekhovian, a term that is sadly turning into a euphemism for boring. An English couple, Ian and Diana Grayson, inhabits a sprawling, romantic hilltop villa in the Chianti country between Florence and Siena. He is a sculptor; she is a homemaker, and in twenty years has turned their home into a museum. Not only are Ian's sculptures and drawings (the undistinguished work of Stephen Spender's son, Martin) all over the place, but also every conceivable artifact and object di virtù litters every nook and cranny, and most of the space in between.

Outside, there are painterly Tuscan landscapes for the camera to scan day and night. Inside, there are equally colorful house guests: Alex, a minor British playwright, is genteelly awaiting imminent death from cancer; Richard, a married American show-biz lawyer, is alternatingly copulating and quarreling with his likewise married girlfriend, Miranda, the Graysons' elder daughter, a jewelry designer. Christopher, her husband, is traveling about with his companion, Niccolò—midway into the film, they return.

"Those naughty boys," says Diana. "*I'm* sure they are being very naughty."

"I'm sure," retorts Miranda, "they've gone beyond naughty by now."

Noemi, an attractive middle-aged lonelyhearts columnist, is carrying on with a much younger fellow, and is furious when he makes her read Benjamin Constant's *Adolphe*, where such an affair ends badly. M. Guillaume appears to be Ian's powerful former art dealer; now old, he lounges about forlornly, uttering portentously vacuous aperçus in French, e.g., "There is no love—there are only proofs of love." Also around is a neighboring landowner and lecher, Carlo, whose son is Noemi's lover. Whether I have got all these relationships right is doubtful: of the three reviews of the film I have read, two got some of them wrong, the third confessed to total confusion. Blame Bertolucci's sloppiness.

Finally, though, it all centers on 19-year-old Lucy, a visitor from America. Still—and given her background, highly improbably—a virgin, she has come to the villa on a dual mission: to revisit the boy who gave her her first kiss five years ago, and to find out more about her dead mother, who spent much time here and may have conceived her by a man other than her husband. Mother, we are told wholly without irony by Alex, "was the best-dressed poet, writing transporting little verses between fashion shoots." In America, she married a poet five inches shorter than herself—the kind of meaningless detail Bertolucci likes to regale us with.

Lucy is very pretty and becomes the cynosure not only of the aforementioned characters, but also of several faceless and epicene young men who also loiter about. Wherever she looks, someone is poking someone of the opposite or same sex, and she is disturbed: "You're in need of a ravisher," Alex opines sagely. There is nude bathing and sunbathing at the pool, pseudosophisticated badinage everywhere ("We've become a nation of monologists," or "Let us bring up the rear, like Turgenev's poor Rakitin"), and one close call after another for Lucy's hymen. But the girl always bristles and runs. There is also one very shy, dark, and introverted youth who considers Lucy "plastic," but seems to have been the one who actually wrote her some lyrical letters. (Guess what his role will be.)

Perversion lurks around the corners. Richard and Miranda are glimpsed falling to sadomasochistic sex. At the annual summer ball at a nearby spectacular palazzo and grounds, orgiasts are everywhere. As Lucy is dancing with Carlo, a woman comes along, squats, and pees, asserting that this is what Carlo really likes. Lucy even takes a snaggle-toothed Young Brit home with her, but then insists on separate beds. Oddest, however, is a narcissistic episode before a mirror, triangular in cross-section, that runs along an entire wall in Lucy's room as a kind of dado. Richard gets down on all fours before it, has Lucy do so next to him; then he licks his image in the mirror and has the delighted Lucy follow suit. In between such incidents, she conducts coy colloquies, meant to be soul-searching, with her elders.

In due time, Lucy finds out what an olive grove looks like; what death means, as the aptly epigrammatizing Alex is carted off to the hospital; who her real father is; and how it feels to have sex. One is sorry for the decent actors—Donal McCann, Sinead Cusack, Carlo Cecchi, Stefania Sandrelli—mired in this smutty-adolescent stew. And even for the less decent ones, such as Jean Marais, whom one is glad to see still alive and handsome even if made to spout nonsense; and Jeremy Irons, insufferably mannered though he has become. D. W. Moffett (Richard) and Rachel Weisz (Miranda) pretty much deserve what they get, as do the shadowy young men flitting about.

As Lucy, there is Liv Tyler, who does have something, although it may not be acting talent. Tall, dark-haired, blue-eyed, heavy-lidded and sensually thick-lipped, this sexy 18-year-old daughter of a rock star and an ex-model is well on her way to stardom. But she has yet to be in a movie that offers her a chance to act, instead of merely surrounding her with unwholesome, aestheticizing innuendo, that strains to elevate indeterminacy into significance. Years ago, Bertolucci said in an interview with Joseph Gelmis, "Giorgio Morandi painted bottles all the time . . . And there are some directors who make always the same film. And poets who write always the same poem. This to me is very beautiful. Because the robins sing always the same song." Alas, obsessions are not all of the same value. The bullfrog may be just as obsessive in his song as the robin in his, but they are hardly equivalent. Morandi's bottles (and cups and salad bowls) came only after he had proved his mastery with superb landscapes. And still-lifes—think Chardin, think Cézanne—are something more forthright and ecumenical than smirking allusions to homosexuality and self-indulgent oglings of perversion as, for instance, in this scene from Bertolucci's *1900*, as described by David Shipman:

> There is a wedding ceremony during which the aristocratic Amelia (Laura Betti) shouts four-letter words before rushing off to the woodshed where she performs fellatio on the Fascist Attila (Donald Sutherland): discovered by a small boy, he and then she sodomize him before killing him by swinging him by his legs so that his head is crushed by the four walls—for which the rich young man allows his best friend to be blamed, despite his being miles away at the time.

The director pretends to be making a moral statement—this is how evil the Fascists were—but is really reveling in pathology. Bertolucci's Marxism was no more committed than his present dilettantism; politics was always merely an excuse for perverse suggestiveness.

Yet even this is never honest. Bertolucci keeps teasing you, in small matters as in large. Thus, in a bathtub scene in *Stealing Beauty*, he displays Liv Tyler's right breast: later, as she poses for Ian (whose final portrait of her is totally different), Bertolucci has her baring her left breast. In the film's penultimate scene of grunting sex, he carefully reveals nothing; it's all a nasty tease. Morandi's bottles are a wholly different matter as, with the passing years, the painter kept stripping them down more and more toward their essence. If Bertolucci is a master of anything, it is of the inessential.

Lone Star

John Sayles is one of our most interesting independent filmmakers, also one of the most productive and the most uneven. Ever since his debut with *The Return of the Secaucus Seven* (1980), he has made his own films, written screenplays for others, worked in television and music videos, and published novels and short stories. The two films he wrote, directed, and edited just before his current one are typical of his range both in theme and in quality: the very adult *Passion Fish* of 1992, and the very infantile *The Secret of Roan Inish* of 1994.

Now we get *Lone Star*, his most enterprising effort yet. Though only a partial success, it is a commendably ambitious—perhaps overambitious—undertaking that makes Texas emblematic of America's melting-pot essence, and examines the problems and possibilities of this multicultural identity. As a result, the 138-minute film takes on the characteristics of the epic: a rousing story with an overplot and related subplots that sweeps ahead carrying characters the way a flood carries debris, and is thus forced to give each shorter shrift than he deserves.

This problem is intensified by the action's taking place also in the past, indeed in the different pasts of several characters. One is torn between admiring Sayles's agility in juggling so many stories in two separate time frames, and frustration at not getting enough about any one individual, and too much about all of them cumulatively.

The small pseudonymous town of Frontera (note the symbolism!) on the Rio Grande is on the border between Texas and Mexico. Its current sheriff is Sam Deeds (remember Mr. Deeds?), the son of, as the synopsis puts it, "the late legendary lawman" Buddy Deeds, a good man but poor father, who drove Sam away from home. Next, we get the story of Pilar Cruz, a spunky young schoolteacher who was Sam's adolescent sweetheart until Buddy nipped the budding affair in the bud.

Pilar's widowed mother, Mercedes, is an affluent, assimilated restaurateur, embittered about a violent death in the family's past, uneasy about her roots and her daughter's stressing the role of Hispanic Americans in her history classes. Mercedes now vehemently opposes helping other Mexicans filter into Frontera. So: a motherdaughter conflict to match the father-son one.

Another notable Fronteran is Otis Payne, a black who runs the Big O Café, the only place in town where blacks can have a good old time. Known as the Mayor of Darktown, Otis was a bold maverick in his youth, sticking up perilously for his civic rights. But, like Buddy Deeds, he did less well by his son Delmore, whom he hasn't seen since Delmore was eight. Delmore joined the Army, became a superachieving colonel, and has just taken on the command of the soon-to-be-closed Army post at Frontera, largely, we suppose, to show his father. Ironically, he doesn't know how lovingly Otis has followed his career; even more ironically, he is repeating his father's mistakes with his own son, now a student in Pilar's high-school history class.

But Anglos, Hispanics, and blacks (whom, by the way, Sayles had to import into this Texas locale) do not yet a tapestry make. Accordingly, there is an episode involving a philosophical Indian road-side souvenir vendor, and a wrenching incident involving Mexican wetbacks. To show that Colonel Payne is a humane martinet, an episode has him temper severity with clemency in dealing with an errant woman soldier in his outfit. Still other episodes expose us to Sam's disturbed ex-wife (there must be marital trouble even in a good man's background), and to Otis's current, lovingly savvy woman (there must be redemption even for a formerly peccant father). This is fearful symmetry fearlessly accosted.

The main plot strand starts with the discovery of a skeleton wearing a rusty sheriff's badge in an abandoned rifle range. (You'd think the killer would have removed the badge, but then we'd have no movie.) It is the remains of Sheriff Charley Wade, a sadistic racist who killed or exploited members of minorities. Of his two deputies, Hollis Pogue feared and obeyed him; Buddy Deeds defied him, and probably shot him. As Sam begins to investigate the case, Hollis, now mayor of Frontera, is about to name the new courthouse after Buddy Deeds.

As this rather too neatly tangled web unravels, Sam and Pilar, hopeful symbols of intercultural understanding, fall in love all over again. But the big problems with *Lone Star* are that it bites off more than it can chew, and that its meliorist intentions seem a tad contrived, with too many schematic parallels proclaiming universal brotherhood for all but such varmints as Charley Wade. His all-black portrayal clashes excessively with the fastidiously meted out shades of grey for all others, except perhaps the hero and heroine, who may be a shade too white.

Tidily geometrical as the film is, it does not want for strong scenes, pungent dialogue, and the ability to sustain interest not only through well-managed suspense, but also through lively character sketches. But sketches, alas, is just what they are, material for a voluminous novel somewhat effortfully corralled into a mere movie, lengthy though it be. Moreover, Chris Cooper, who plays Sam, has a sagging hangdog look, as good as "Kick me!" writ large across the brow.

Yet he clearly appeals to Sayles, who has used him twice before. But Chris is a far cry from his homonym, Gary, who, besides his virile handsomeness, had that sincere, halting delivery that made visible the progression from thought to utterance, and who could convey nuances of feeling well beyond Chris's all-purpose earnestness.

The others are all good. As Pilar, Elizabeth Peña, without being pretty, offers a natural, animatedly attractive presence, and there are especially fine contributions from Clifton James (Hollis), Joe Morton (Delmore), Ron Canada (Otis), Miriam Colon (Mercedes), Frances McDormand (Sam's ex), and several others. In the thankless role of Wade, Kris Kristofferson aided by his beetling brow and recessed eyes, is most persuasive, and Stewart Dryburgh, cinematographer of *The Piano*, aptly catches the sun-burnt colors of Texas.

New Directors

THE SPITFIRE GRILL; TRAINSPOTTING

Sentimentality and melodrama are frequent partners in crime. The sentimental comedy or drama (depending on the ending) jerks tears; melodrama, always ending happily, thrives on chills and suspense. How does one marry the two? By taking, say, a poor but honest orphan girl, and exposing her to the machinations of a villain or villains: will she succumb or escape, yield or be rescued? This was the stuff of D. W. Griffith and his many legatees.

Nowadays, though melodrama continues to thrive, sentimentality is no longer a staple. Done in partly by greater sexual freedom, partly by pop psychology—the two combining to make virtue and vice less clear-cut matters—sentimentality has been replaced by spurious sophistication. What makes *The Spitfire Grill* noteworthy is its attempt to turn back the clock. It is surely no accident that its writer-director, Lee David Zlotoff, comes from television, that newish medium where ancient forms survive best. Nonstop mass entertainment postulates plunder of the past. In Zlotoff's feature-film debut, pretty Percy Talbot (or Talbott, depending on whether you go by the press kit or the screen credits), arrives in the small, soporific, and symbolically named Gilead, Maine, which this Ohioan has picked for her home after having completed a five-year prison term for manslaughter. She learned about the place while working as a telephonic tourist-bureau clerk in prison where this woodsy, hilly, and waterfally locale struck her as the perfect locus for regeneration. She becomes a waitress and cook at the Spitfire Grill, the town's only eatery, owned by the crusty, elderly Hannah Ferguson, who has been trying to sell it for years—ever since her son Eli, the town's spiritual sparkplug, failed to return from Vietnam.

Percy is viewed with suspicion by many, and outright hostility by two. One of these is the town's postmistress and chief busybody; the other is the realtor Nahum Goddard, Hannah's nephew, who always lived in Eli's shadow. He bullies his repressed wife, Shelby; tries unsuccessfully to dominate Hannah; and nurtures fantasies about the town's abandoned granite quarry, as well as other designs with which Percy could interfere. He becomes her relentless persecutor.

On plucky Percy's side, however, are Shelby, the bullied wife and mother, who eagerly helps the girl with her restaurant chores; Sheriff Walsh, impressed by all the Gilead lore Percy has acquired in jail; Joe Sperling, an inarticulate young mechanic who falls in love with her, and finally even Hannah, who, bedridden from a fall, finds Percy an able helper. What with the blossoming friendship between Percy and Shelby, and the town's gradual acceptance of the newcomer, things might have progressed serenely. But given a mysterious recluse in the nearby woods, an essay contest for ownership of the Spitfire that brings in a goodly sum for Hannah, and Nahum's underhanded maneuvering, the outcome is, at best, bittersweet.

Some things here are hard to believe. Why does that supposedly rich quarry remain unexploited, Why would the rest of the country know about the essay contest so much earlier than Gilead? How can a whole town participate in adjudicating it? Why would the hermit in the forest remain unknown to all but Hannah and Percy? But never mind: the movie is like a stray, eager-to-please puppy that has wandered into your yard—virtually impossible to kick out.

Much of this hinges on the likable performances, especially from what in rural Maine may still be called the distaff side. Alison Elliott as Percy, Ellen Burstyn as Hannah, and Marcia Gay Harden as Shelby are a good acting company, and good company for the audience. If you keep your expectations modest, you will find the fare at *The Spitfire Grill* to your liking. Especially as the Maine landscapes are elatingly evoked by Roger Draper's Wyethian camera.

It may be that if you speak Scots, do not care about narrative logic, relish scatology, and enjoy watching young heroin addicts go about their business (which includes crimes in obtaining the drugs), you will find *Trainspotting* a triumph. If not, you may wonder what's going on half the time, and why you should care the rest. The dialogue, which is occasionally quite funny, is only intermittently decipherable, although the soundtrack has been re-edited for ears not trained in spotting dialect-shrouded meanings.

The film sometimes turns surreal, as when a youth excretes his druggy suppositories into what styles itself "the worst toilet in Scotland," then crawls head-first into it and swims through, er, muddy waters to retrieve them. (You may be relieved to learn that in Irvine Wells's novel, this episode, like so much else, is even less savory.) At other times, the stuff, even without hitting the fan, flies through the air. Some of this is Rabelaisianly uproarious: most of it merely gross.

The film's continuity is deliberately discontinuous, but that is in keeping with nerves as raw as frayed jeans. Good acting all around, with the psychotic Begbie of Robert Carlyle most virtuosic, and Ewan McGregor's Renton, the protagonist, very nearly appealing. Danny Boyle has directed with condign jaggedness, and Brian Tufano's cinematography executes poster-art effects rivetingly. *Trainspotting* may well offer catchy fine points on second viewing, if only one could get over the first.

Emma Without Emma

EMMA

Of Jane Austen's *Emma*, Walter Allen writes in *The English Novel*, "It is the high point of Miss Austen's comedy"; Lord David Cecil accounts it "Austen's profoundest comedy"; Harold Bloom declares it "Austen's masterpiece." The Janeites, to be sure, are an excitable lot. So E.M. Forster begins a review, "I am a Jane Austenite, and therefore slightly imbecile about Jane Austen." "As a master of her craft," Cecil avers, "she outshines them all." Again: "So far from being a manufacturer of literary snuff-boxes, [she] is one of the few supreme novelists of the world." And, to top it all, "There are those who do not like her; as there are those who do not like sunshine or unselfishness. But the very nervous defiance with which they shout their dissatisfaction shows that they know they are a despised minority."

"There are in the world no compositions which approach nearer to perfection," Lord Macaulay raved. Hilaire Belloc awarded Austen an "alpha plus . . . because she has excelled in the quality of proportion—which is another way of saying in telling the truth." He compared her art to "an inlay of silver upon pale wood"—presumably not the wood of literary snuff-boxes. Others have been less enthusiastic. To Charlotte Brontë, Austen was "very incomplete and rather insensible"; to Emerson, "vulgar in tone, sterile in artistic invention." Mark Twain went further: "To me, Poe's prose is unreadable—like Jane Austen's. No, there is a difference. I could read his prose on a salary, but not Jane's."

Actually, if nervous defiance applies to anyone, it is rather to Austen's champions. So Dorothy Van Ghent has written, "It is wronging an Austen novel to expect of it what it makes no pretense to rival—the spiritual profundity of the very greatest novels. But if we expect artistic mastery of limited materials, we shall not be disappointed." That is relatively calm; Cecil is overwrought. While admitting that "Austen's imaginative range was, in some respects[!], a very limited one," he nonetheless makes a virtue of the author's "exclude[ing] from her books all aspects of life that cannot pass through the crucible of her imagination." True enough, but how much can one exclude and still be a major novelist?

The problem with *Emma*—both the novel and the movie written and directed by the American Douglas McGrath—is the smugness of the heroine. Or perhaps of the narrator. In *Critical Understanding*, Wayne C. Booth shrewdly observes, "Nobody was ever so marvelous as the implied author of *Emma*." Heroine or author-narrator, someone exudes a little too much priggishness and snobbery for me to swallow. Of course, we are to perceive these as defects, as Emma herself eventually realizes; but maybe meddlesome priggishness and snobbishness are harder to accept from a protagonist than murder and rapine.

The problem is compounded by the casting of the American Gwyneth Paltrow as Emma. An actress of charm, tact, and talent could reconcile us to Emma's (and Jane Austen's) smugness. The paltry Miss Paltrow has none of the above, and mostly mugs and postures. Instead of playing subtly against the grain, she minces and attitudinizes with it. Even so, thanks to viewers' and reviewers' benightedness and to media megahype, thin gruel is touted as milk and honey.

In what may be the best short discussion of Austen ("Regulated Hatred," in *Scrutiny*, March 1940), D. W. Harding argues persuasively: "In Jane Austen's treatment the natural order of things manages to reassert the heroine's proper pre-eminence without the intervention of any human or quasi-human helper. In this respect she allies the Cinderella theme to another fairy-tale theme which is often introduced—that of the princess brought up by unworthy parents but never losing the delicate sensibilities which are an inborn part of her."

Harding shows how with *Emma* Austen progresses beyond that stage: the heroine is less superior, and her parents are less inferior. For me, the problem remains; *Emma* is what Oscar Wilde lampooned about Victorian novels: "The good ended happily, and the bad unhappily. That is what fiction means." That is certainly what Austen's fiction means: a plain and obscure spinster's written revenge on an uncaring world. Austen punishes her enemies and rewards her friends. But the biggest plum always falls to her fictional alter ego: she marries the best man (here suggestively named Mr. Knightley) and lives happily ever after. Audiences lap it up; that rather than any literary merit explains Austen's success in the current cinema.

Yet this fearful symmetry leaves the works so predictable. McGrath's film version, like other such adaptations, can only make the predictability even greater: a film must cut to the chase faster than a leisurely paced novel, and cannot curtain the outcome behind so many descriptions, digressions, convolutions, and subplots. McGrath has adapted reasonably well, but he has directed with a number of contemporary cinematic tricks that feel anachronistic. Thus he will intercut an embellished account of a charitable expedition to the hovel of a starving family with quick—and embarrassingly funny—flashbacks to what actually happened. This is too jazzy—and too obvious—for Austen.

The British supporting cast does mainly well. Jeremy Northam offers a credibly dashing Knightley, as opposed to the incredibly dashing Darcy of Laurence Olivier in the Hollywood *Pride and Prejudice*. His transitions from irony to exasperation, from *hauteur* to involvement, are finely judged and smoothly executed. As Mr. Elton, the smarmy parson, Alan Cumming is exemplary. During the chaise ride in which he discovers that Emma's interest was solely in matching him up with the no-account Harriet Smith, and that his amorous advances to herself repelled her,

Cumming's eruption of thwarted passion and injured self-regard is a masterpiece of comic-pathetic bravura. The gorgeous Greta Scacchi, sadly showing her age, is winningly warm as Emma's beloved governess; Polly Walker, in the here shortchanged part of Jane Fairfax, makes up for truncation with great beauty and personal appeal. Edward Woodall does nicely by what is left of farmer Martin, Harriet's devoted suitor.

As the presumptuous chatterbox Mrs. Elton, Juliet Stevenson is comically bone-chilling; as the pitiful bore Miss Bates, Emma Thompson's sister, Sophie, overacts amusingly. Toni Collette's Harriet is properly befuddled and frustrated; only Ewan McGregor, good in a very different role in *Trainspotting*, is weak as the heart-throb Frank Churchill. Austen describes him as "very good-looking," and she specifies his "height"; neither applies to the callow and stubby actor. Ian Wilson's cinematography is uneven, but the score by Rachel Portman, incorporating period tunes, proves her yet again one of our finest soundtrack composers.

Witchery and Wonders

THE MIRROR HAS TWO FACES; BREAKING THE WAVES

I wish I could remember the André Cayette film on which *The Mirror Has Two Faces* is based. I recall only disliking it. The American version, which Barbra Streisand produced, directed, co-composed with Marvin Hamlisch, and, of course, stars in goes the French one better: it is loathsome. This should not prevent its being a hit: we live in a barbarous age.

At the time of her remake of *A Star Is Born*, Miss Streisand elicited from me: "O for the gift of Rostand's, Cyrano to invoke the vastness of that nose alone as it cleaves the giant screen from east to west, bisects it from north to south. It zigzags across our horizon like a bolt of fleshy lightning; it towers like a ziggurat made of meat." But the nose is only a symbol, or symptom, of what is wrong with Barbra Streisand.

She could easily have had it fixed; she had no problem, after all, shaving the middle "a" out of her given name. Her excuse was that it might have diminished her voice. But with electronics what they are, who would have known the difference? The nose, rather, is a monument to her ego: she'll force it down your craw whether you like it or not. It is like her unshed Brooklyn accent, as charming as bubble gum at a formal ball. She wants that face of hers to be in our face; that speech (like Rice Krispies if they could talk, I once called it) to ravish—i.e., violate—our ears.

In *The Mirror Has Two Faces*, Miss Streisand pretends to honesty by playing an alleged ugly duckling. But this duckling is a highly popular Columbia professor of literature (kind unspecified), radiating inner beauty and demotically passionate about baseball. On her blackboard are the names Roland Barthes and Michel Foucault, though her lecture seems to have nothing to do with them. The lecture room is the size of a minor railway station and is packed with students, auditing fellow teachers, and extras from central casting. She spouts platitudes and psychobabble punctuated with inane jokes that have the assembled multitude rocking with laughter, every laugh of the same volume and duration as the next. Even laugh tracks simulate a little variety.

The duckling sets her cap at a bumbling colleague, a mathematics professor played by Jeff Bridges, an actor who deserves better. He is a total nincompoop who needs Miss Streisand to coach him in how to keep his students awake. She instructs him not to face the blackboard while writing on it, and encourages him to turn mathematical demonstrations into stories with human interest. We don't see him doing it, but he is wildly grateful for alleged successes. So much so that, his marriage to a beauty having failed, he enters into a supposedly enlightened, entirely sexless marriage with Miss Streisand. Several attractive students are yearning for him, but he chooses her, for reasons that should be as plain as the nose on her face.

There are trials and tribulations. One morning Miss Streisand informs Mr. Bridges that she'd like some sex by nightfall, which has him choking on his breakfast coffee. He tries, but it doesn't work out, and she walks out on him. By the time he catches up with her, she has transformed herself into what is meant to be a gorgeous swan, yet looks to me merely different but equal. Mr. Bridges, clod that he is, is amazed, but not bowled over. Only when Miss Streisand removes herself from his grasp and is hotly panted after by her pretty sister's dreamboat husband does Jeff, now totally besotted, madly want her back. Miss Streisand's swanliness is complete. The ending, which could keep a coffee bar in artificial sweetener for a solid week, continues under the closing credits, which are endless.

What makes Barbra Streisand so successful? In the old Hollywood, there was no star of comparable sex repeal. Kay Francis, who came closest, was still ahead by a country mile. The mass attitude has changed in recent decades: the *profanum vulgus* has discovered the virtues of empowerment and entitlement, and the vices of elitism and lookism. In movie-star terms, this translates into: the plainer the better, because the more like us. If Miss Streisand can end up with the best of everything, so can we. As on the big screen, so in life, right?

Best about the movie is Lauren Bacall's performance as Miss Streisand's sardonic mom: boldest is Barbra's composing its "love theme." I can see it now: the director-star picks out a few sticky notes on the piano—unless she merely hums them—and Hamlisch orchestrates them into a big, shlurpy "love theme." Miss Streisand may have got the idea from Chaplin; but compare his catchy music for *Limelight* with the faceless one in *The Mirror Has Two Faces*, and there is, well, no comparison. For the record, the screenplay is by Richard LaGravenese, who also gave us *The Fisher King*, that landmark of bathos and bombast. How marvelously he and Miss Streisand must have hit it off.

Breaking the Waves, by the Dane Lars von Trier, won the Jury Prize at Cannes. If you believe in miracles—which might include von Trier making a sane movie—this could be the film for you. Bess, a sweet Scottish lass in a harbor town some twenty years ago, marries Jan, a macho Scandinavian oil-rig worker. They consummate their marriage in a lavatory, and all would be wonderful if Jan didn't have to be back on the job so soon. Bess has intimate conversations with God, requesting the prompt return of her husband. And back he comes, owing to a horrible accident that leaves him paralyzed, bed-ridden and at death's door.

Jan proceeds to persuade Bess that, for his sake, she must have sex with another: this, he tells her gallantly, will cure him if only she keeps recounting her sexual experiences to him. She resists at first, but love prevails. Bess becomes the strict Calvinist town's whore as she seeks out more and more brutal, indeed sadistic, affairs with men from the ships that put in at the harbor. When, as the press kit delicately puts it, she "plunges into the ultimate sacrifice," a whopping double miracle takes place.

Von Trier uses a handheld camera that must have become glued to its operator's hands. The most ordinary indoor scenes are shot so as to make you feel you're on a stormy ocean crossing and you've run out of Dramamine. Also, for no particular reason, the film is in chapters. Each chapter begins with a computer-generated quasi-landscape painting in which elaborate time and weather changes are compressed into one minute each. These artsy minutes seem almost longer than the hours of the rest of the film, in which the non-miraculous sequences are no more believable than the miracles.

Emily Watson is touching as Bess, and Katrin Cartlidge is equally fine as her devoted sister-in-law. Stellan Skarsgård, as Jan, is appropriately bearish, when vertical, and wheedling when horizontal. In the part of the chief pervert, pretty boy Udo Kier is, for once, properly cast. Robby Mueller is a master cinematographer, but visual bravura at the service of narrative and psychological absurdity becomes a case of packaging over substance. The film's score is an anthology of garish seventies pop, with a prestigious sprinkling of Bach. I am not quite sure what is meant by the title, *Breaking the Waves*, but after seeing the film, I can tell you all about stretching patience to the breaking point.

Play Rach 3 for Me

SHINE

The Australian *Shine* is yet another of those films surrounded by an aura of rapt veneration. It is the more or less true story of David Helfgott, the son of Peter, a Polish-Jewish refugee many of whose kin perished in the Holocaust. As a child, Peter scrimped for a violin, which his father prevented him from mastering. But Peter has taught his young son to play the piano. David proves a child prodigy, although Peter has great difficulty letting him go for lessons with a professional teacher nearby. When an offer comes for David to study in America, Peter puts his foot down: the family must not be broken up.

It is typical of this film written by Jan Sardi from a story by Scott Hicks, who also directed, that we find out next to nothing about Peter and his pathology—not even what he does for a living. David's talented siblings are dimly glimpsed in the background, his mother is a household drudge verging on a mute zombie. Yet we need to know more about this family Peter so desperately wants to hold together. Only his madly contradictory behavior toward David takes on a little life, largely because Armin Mueller-Stahl is an actor good at being quietly, ominously scary. But occasional telling details do

not connect into a story: the filmmaker's mistake being artily elliptical for art.

Again, the now somewhat older David's friendship with an elderly writer, Katharine, could be something touching and revelatory, especially as it is she who helps the youth defy his father and
go off to study at London's Royal College of Music. But this, too,
is sketched in with disjointed dabs, and nice as it is to see Goo-
gie Withers again, her Katharine is not allowed to register properly. In London, David studies with the splendidly eccentric Cecil
Parkes, and because the magnificent John Gielgud brings a jovially
demonic glow to a clichéd role, the teacher-student scenes have
some crackle to them.

Here it must be pointed out how musically unsophisticated the
film is. David's ambition all along, fanned by Peter, is to play the
Rachmaninov Third, or Rach 3, as they keep calling it. Rach 3 is
presented as the Everest of pianism, the summit of artistic greatness
and pianistic difficulty, which is hysterical hogwash. It is a complex
piece that professional players readily master. Yet one of the climactic scenes here is David's performing Rach 3 with the Royal College
student orchestra as Parkes gloats in the audience.

The scene pulls out enough stops to make a mere piano seem like
a giant organ. At times the music ceases and David is banging away
at dead keys; then again playing the piano becomes a cross between
a day in the salt mines of Siberia and soaring into the ether with
Mme. Blavatsky. That Noah Taylor, who plays the middle David, is
supremely unattractive—especially with long, flying tresses dripping pianistic sweat—doesn't help. At the end of the performance,
David passes out—the beginning of a breakdown that will keep
him, unable to play, in mental institutions for years.

It is typical of the filmmakers to linger over David's glasses with
their thick frames, and Peter's with their thin ones. In the last meeting between the father who has expelled and repudiated his son,
and the grown son who keeps slobbering about "Daddy," one of
Peter's lenses is even cracked: a reminder that David's fell off his face
as he conked out after Rach 3. This is banal and pretentious filmmaking whose empty glasses are supposed to fill up with profound
human and symbolic significance. Similarly, David's obsession with
water (unexplained) is supposed to be fraught with deeper implications, but remains a mere nuisance as David runs around bare-
assed, keeps taking baths, and creates floods in the bathroom. At
one point he even, touchingly, defecates into his bathwater.

So it is quite a mystery why the poised Gillian should fall in love with the gibbering David: since his breakdown, he has not stopped a rapid-fire, near-nonsensical chatter. Reader, she marries him. To be sure, she is an astrologer, and his chart, which she draws up on her computer, augurs favorably. Still, to those of us astrally challenged, this is the final insult. But everything ends well as David is concertizing again. Since Helfgott is no Pollini or Kissin, it would be even better if instead of starting to play he just stopped his prattle.

Geoffrey Rush, a noted Australian stage actor who can also play the piano a bit, is amazingly likable as the third and most garrulous David; his gibberish drops as cheerfully from his lips as his constant cigarette dangles from them. Lynn Redgrave is pleasant as Gillian, but the film is unable to convey why she would overflow with love for a bathroom-overflower. It ends with the couple's visit to Peter's grave in a pretty cemetery; this is meant to be an uplifting, conciliatory closure, but is merely a stereotype.

All the classical music heard in the movie has been arranged by David Hirschfelder and Ricky Edwards, whoever they are. It is all about bringing high culture to the masses, yet if the likes of Rachmaninov, Liszt, and Chopin must be adapted and diluted, instead of on Rach 3, the film should have concentrated on "Three Blind Mice."

Out-hamleting Hamlet

HAMLET

Kenneth Branagh suffers from the theatrical equivalent of a Napoleon complex: an Olivier complex. But where the old-time madmen were content to be Napoleon, Branagh must go one better: be a Roland for an Oliv(i)er. Now, though we know that the saying means tit for tat, we also know that Roland is really the bigger cheese. Of that most valiant of Charlemagne's paladins we know his famous sword Durandal, his famous horn Olivant, his heroic death at Roncesvalles. And Oliver (Olivier in French)? For all we know, he may have blown a pennywhistle and fought with a cudgel.

So Branagh made a *Henry V* meant to outdo Lord Olivier's—and in fighting in the mud it certainly did. And now he gives us a *Hamlet* to out-hamlet Olivier, or out-herod Herod (*Hamlet*, III, ii, 14). Whereas

Olivier cut his 1948 movie of *Hamlet* down to 144 minutes, Branagh in-
flates the customary First Folio text with enough of the Second Quarto
to boost the running time (with a brief intermission) to four hours and
two minutes. Like Olivier, he dyed his hair blond for the Prince, but
has added a mustache and goatee. And whereas Olivier chose a semi-
fluffy bob, Branagh opted for a more austere, military cut.

Either way, though, the blondining of Hamlet results in a kind
of Breck Shampoo ad, or, more succinctly, a sham. An anonymous
woman can go from brunette to blonde with impunity. But when
a male movie star pulls such a stunt, it stunts his performance by
focusing attention on his hair. (As if, incidentally, there were no
brown-haired Danes.) In Branagh's case, what emerges is a Teutonic
petty-functionary look: Hamlet as a prissy customs official or court
stenographer.

We know that Hamlets come in sundry guises. Mainly, though,
there have been mad Hamlets, poetic Hamlets, dreamy Hamlets,
and procrastinating Hamlets. Latterly, the inevitable backlash has
spawned vigorous, macho Hamlets—as it were, muscular-Chris-
tian Hamlets—whose dilatory tactics were just a strategic disguise.
These ultravirile Hamlets are often at odds with the text, but as we
know by now, texts are there only to be deconstructed.

So Branagh's Hamlet is an active, brawny one, but brawn with
guidance from the brain. When he soliloquizes, he shifts into a
somewhat countertenorish poetic gear; when he interacts with others, he is all businesslike efficiency, and none of that John-a-dreams
stuff. Such a split—not between action and dilatoriness, but between an affected recitalist and a barroom pianist—is possible to
condone, but not easy to like.

Even four hours won't do for novelty; the scenarist-director must
contribute flights of fancy of his own. One strategy is to supply explicitness where Shakespeare, in his woefully uncinematic way, set-
tled for subtlety or mere suggestion. Accordingly, we now see Hamlet and Ophelia carrying on in bed; Polonius, moralizing hypocrite
that he is, with a prostitute slinking out of his bedchamber; Ophelia,
this being a late-nineteenth-century *Hamlet*, in a padded cell and
straitjacket being hosed down; Fortinbras's army bursting through
the very walls of the throne room—an idea probably gleaned from
Ingmar Bergman's similarly questionable stage version.

Branagh the showman believes in gigantism: he may not be big
on thinking, but he does think big. Olivier was willing to settle
for a modestly historic Elsinore castle; Branagh needed Blenheim

Palace, Britain's biggest and grandest. The multi-mirrored throne-room, where much of the action takes place, is a kind of fun house out of Cecil B. De Mille, although C.B. would not have been ready to admit anachronistic two-way mirrors. Like De Mille, Branagh gives us a Norwegian army that looks to be easily Shakespeare's twenty thousand, and is particularly impressive when seen in the background marching over snow and ice while Branagh intones "How all occasions," etc. It is always nice to have such ample company for your soliloquies.

Another splendid innovation is the snow. Just as Scandinavians must be fair-haired, the ground under them must be snow-clad. Real snow is often not readily available, but that's where blon-dined—sorry, bleached—cornflakes come in. You've never seen such snow in non-polar-expedition movies, and I sincerely hope it can be recycled for a future remake of *Scott of the Antarctic*. Among minor wonders, let me cite the vast pool of blood around the slain Polonius (who would have thought the old man had so much blood in him?) and Claudius's demise via Hamlet's tossing a sword into his back from a considerable distance. Much as I have searched back issues of the Wittenberg University catalogue, I cannot find courses in circus skills such as knife-throwing.

Finally, with an unerring eye to the box office, Branagh has cast big-time international actors in bit parts. So we get Jack Lemmon, Charlton Heston, Rosemary Harris, Billy Crystal, Robin Williams, and the ubiquitous Gérard Depardieu as a cigar-chomping Rey-naldo. There are even fleeting, wordless glimpses of John Gielgud as Priam, Judi Dench as Hecuba, John Mills as Old Norway, person-ages merely alluded to in the text. But no Herod during the reference to him (see above). Of these, only Crystal's First Gravedigger manages to register positively.

Some of the casting works. Derek Jacobi is suitably slick and sleazy as Claudius (an actor-proof part if ever there was one), and, after a long absence and in an atypical role, Julie Christie is a love-ly and touching Gertrude. Richard Briers is a plausible Polonius. Brian Blessed does as well as can be by a horror-film Ghost, and Rufus Sewell contributes the fiercest Fortinbras ever. Particularly gratifying is the mute but splendid equestrian presence of the Duke of Marlborough as Fortinbras's general, in exchange, no doubt, for the loan of Blenheim Palace.

But Kate Winslet is a bovine milkmaid of an Ophelia, Nicholas Farrell a smarmy, vacant-faced Horatio, and Michael Maloney a pipsqueak of a Laertes—surely lest they compete in any way with Branagh. He himself asked from his cast "direct, accessible relation to modern life," and in the Hamlet-Ophelia copulation scene and Polonius's postcoital morning sequence, he certainly got it.

Citizen Ruth

True satire, it should be recalled, is equitable. It sees not black to the left and white to the right, but ridiculous and appalling mud-grey all over. That is how Swift, Voltaire, and Brecht did it, and that, in its sometimes a bit heavy-handed, not always quite funny enough way, is what *Citizen Ruth* does. It is quite simply the boldest satire out of Hollywood since, roughly, the year one.

Ruth (perfectly played by Laura Dern) is a complete tramp, whose chief joy is sniffing glue. Repeatedly in trouble with the law, she has already given up four illegitimate babies for adoption. The fifth time, to avoid imprisonment for endangering her fetus, she prepares to heed a judge's advice to have an abortion. Ruth now becomes the center of a wildly comic battle between a family of pro-lifers and a lesbian couple heading a pro-choice group. Both sides reduce Ruth to a pawn; Alexander Payne and Jim Taylor's screenplay, directed by the former, is impartially barbed in both directions.

Ruth turns into a national issue but maintains her selfish individuality as, at least, unhypocritical scum. And please don't tell me that abortion is too serious a subject for spoofing; a satire on an unserious subject is worthless.

Bal(lard)oney

CRASH

James Ballard and his wife, Catherine, are turned on by car crashes, and the wounds and deaths they lead to. If these do not by themselves induce orgasm, there is huggermugger sex in the front or back seat to get the job done. Alternatively, one can have intercourse anywhere, even in bed, so long as one fantasizes about automotive mayhem or its participants. This is the premise of David

Cronenberg's *Crash*, fairly but not altogether faithfully based on J. G. Ballard's novel, and a piece of failed pornography.

Pornography, in my view, is a work existing for the sole purpose of sexual arousal, without any regard for truth or existential relevance. I am not against it, so long as it is kept out of the hands of children. But of all pornography, *Crash* is least likely to be catching: few people would risk car crashes for sexual thrills; even fewer could afford it.

As the movie begins, Catherine enjoys sex with a stranger on top of an airplane engine, and James likes to snatch a quickie where the risk of discovery is greatest. (The even worse novel dispenses with such feeble attempts at etiology.) One day, James crashes into an oncoming car, whose driver is spectacularly killed; the victim's passenger and wife, Dr. Helen Remington, is so aroused that she instantly bares her breast to the wounded James. We cut to the hospital, where, by James's bedside, Catherine, too, is oddly affected, as is a stranger, Vaughan, who comes around to photograph Ballard's wounds. Thus is born a *folie à deux*, *trois*, or *quatre*, depending on your mode of counting.

Vaughan is the Canadian director's most egregious error. In the novel, he is a grubby, pockmarked weirdo who restages celebrity car crashes for audiences of like-mindless fanatics. In the film, he is played by Elias Koteas, an actor yet more repellent, so that no one—in his wrong mind even—would want to get involved with him, psychically or sexually, as James and Catherine do. Still, the only vaguely titillating scene has the couple in bed fantasizing intercourse with Vaughan-Koteas, which strikes me as sicker than humping a hood ornament. But Deborah Kara Unger, who plays Catherine, has a quality of ecstatic sensual absorption the other actresses cannot manage.

Holly Hunter wasn't Cronenberg's first choice for Helen, but shouldn't even have been his last. She earnestly says and does the perverse or merely sexual things demanded of her, as if reciting the Girl Scout manual or working out in an aerobics class. The equally unsexy Rosanna Arquette plays Gabrielle, a scarred waif who clanks about in a body suit and braces whose metallic content might be the envy of C3PO. Her copulations with James and, later, Helen in a car are even logistically preposterous: it's like trying to fit an ironing board into a microwave oven and then having sex with it. *Crash* is less lewd than ludicrous.

The film is most risible when Vaughan-Koteas goes metaphysical: "For the first time, the car crash is a fertilizing rather than a destructive event: a liberation of sexual energy that mediates the sexuality of those who died with an intensity impossible in any other form." Ballard wrote the novel in 1973, when Barthes and Foucault were still going strong, and such drivel was taken seriously; today, and on film, it is as if someone had crossbred the outtakes of Eric Rohmer and Peter Greenaway—in a car, of course. And when ever more fantastic games of murderous bumper cars are played with what seems to be the entire rush-hour traffic of Toronto, you lose all respect even for the Toronto highway police.

Peter Suschitzky shoots it all in gelid steel-blue and iron-grey tones, for clinical detachment as well as to highlight naked flesh and copious gore. Miss Unger is good only in the sexual scenes, but as James, James Spader is, I'm afraid, perfect for all of it. No other actor so oozes spineless, slack-jawed kinkiness even when it is not called for. Otherwise, the film is about as compelling as the endless interviews in which the director-scenarist has been explicating its profundities: a crashing bore.

Chasing Amy

Is there anything in the world more benighted than the typical movie reviewer who does not even rise to the grander incompetence of a Siskel or Ebert? The batrachian chorus is waxing rapturous over *Chasing Amy*, as it did, for instance, over *Flirting with Disaster*, a similar piece of attitudinizing persiflage. There is a kind of loose-limbed devil-may-care youth movie (*Fargo* is a slightly more proficient example) that tickles equally laid-back juveniles and trendy codgers, as if flashy anomie were an earnest of quality.

I missed Kevin Smith's acclaimed low-budget debut film *Clerks*, as well as its critically cold-shouldered sequel *Mallrats*, but segment three, *Chasing Amy*, despite a certain brio and some funny lines, is not calculated to make me feel deprived. The basic absurdity here is that when Holden, the hero, falls in love (for no compelling reason) with Alyssa, a confirmed lesbian, this converts the young woman (for no compelling reason) to passionate heterosexuality. There are, of course, also a number of ancillary inanities. I suspect that what Smith calls, rather grandly, his New Jersey Trilogy is a case of the whole nowhere near exceeding the sum of its parts. To be sure, I have no objection to the writer-director's casting his girlfriend in the lead, except when she is as untalented, unattractive, and mealy-mouthed as Joey Lauren Adams, about whom the ear and the eye will have to fight it out as to which is more victimized. Her leading man, Ben Affleck, is considerably better, except in the car scene in which he pours out his feelings in unison with the pouring rain outside, a bravura passage aimed at the heart, but hitting a somewhat lower organ.

There is good work from Jason Lee, as Holden's fellow cartoonist on Bluntman Comics and woman-hungry roommate (who may be unconsciously chasing Holden), and from Dwight Ewell, in the unsubtle but amusing role of a black homosexual. Kevin Smith repeats his running-gag cameo role as Silent Bob, who is not all that silent, alas, and gets to utter the key speech about everyone's having an Amy, a woman one carelessly lost and is doomed to chase forever. Yet even that is not the film's most bathetic scene, one that I'll let you discover for yourself, if you are desperado enough to seek it out. The ads for *Chasing Amy* show the heavily airbrushed face of Joey Lauren Adams with the caption, "It's not who you love. It's how." I would say, "It's not who you love, it's whom."

Prisoner of the Mountains

If the Academy Awards made any kind of sense—which, of course they don't—the foreign-language Oscar would have gone not to the insipid *Kolya*, but to Russia's powerful *Prisoner of the Mountains*. Based remotely on Tolstoy's *Prisoner of the Caucasus*, this is an updating to events in today's Chechnya. Many movies pretend to be pacifist in intent, but as long as they show wars with winners and losers, they are lying. In a true anti-war film such as this, even the winners are in some ways losers.

This is the story of two Russian soldiers captured by the Chechens and held for ransom by the town patriarch, Abdul-Murat, who would exchange them for his son, held by the Russians. The two are Sasha, a sergeant and cynical veteran, and Vanya, a recruit and naïve novice. Sasha begins with nothing but contempt for Vanya, refusing even to speak to him. But gradually the pair, often chained together, form human bonds as well. An exchange of prisoners fails,

and the Chechens exert pressure on Abdul-Murat to kill his cap-
tives. He refuses, and urges them to write to their mothers to in-
tercede. Meanwhile it is his 12-year-old but very mature daughter,
Dina, who looks after the men, and soon Vanya is in love with her,
even talking marriage. Up to a point, she reciprocates.

That much I can tell you. Let me add that hardly anything here
is conventional and predictable. There is unsentimental toughness
in story and dialogue, without a shadow of easy emotionalism. The
sweetest and roughest moments are done with lean truthfulness.
And always the action is surrounded by the cruelly beautiful Caucasus peaks, nature at its most austerely aloof, yet somehow epitomiz-
ing human courage and strength. Pavel Lebeshev's cinematography
catches both nature and human habitats in their uncompromising
starkness.

The director and co-scenarist, Sergei Bodrov, cast one of Russia's
most popular actors, Oleg Menshikov, as Sasha, and his own son,
Sergei Jr., as Vanya. Both are perfect: Menshikov with the easeful superiority of total self-confidence, Bodrov with youthful faith
in a caring universe. Their relationship and their interaction with
Dina evolve with matching insight and restraint. The Muslim girl
Susanna Mukhratyeva, discovered in a local school in Dagestan, is
immensely moving in her naturalness, simplicity, and understatement.

The script by Bodrov Sr., Boris Gilter, and Arif Aliev—with Aliev
contributing a discreet surreal element that works admirably—is
an exemplar of clean yet detailed storytelling. It sticks to essentials,
but without stinting on the pungently idiosyncratic. And nothing,
nothing is ever underlined.

Ponette

Ponette, by Jacques Doillon, is about a four-year-old who loses her
mother in a car crash, and whose father is often off on business.
Left with a nice aunt and cousins in another town, Ponette is inconsolable despite new school chums and a sympathetic teacher,
as well as a charming companion in her barely older boy cousin.
She searches for her mother everywhere, and is not helped by the
conflicting explanations of death all and sundry give her. At last, in
the cemetery, where Ponette tries to dig her up, *maman* appears in

something more than just a vision, and helps Ponette find peace.

Doillon, a paterfamilias of working-class origin, is smart and talented, and his method of finding the right children and working with them commends itself for originality and good sense. He established a splendid relationship with little Victoire Thivisol and the other kids, and made a film whose texture and dialogue are compelling, sometimes almost too good to be true. You question whether an adult, however sensitive and insightful, can lay claim to so much knowledge of how tots feel, think, and behave. Still, up to the supernatural ending, *Ponette* is absorbing: the adult actors lovely, the kids marvelous, and Victoire some kind of miracle.

She was voted best actress at the 1996 Venice Festival but, as Doillon told me, took the award coolly in her stride. To be sure, one wonders what "performance" means to a little girl, even if her achievement is the finest since Brigitte Fossey dazzled us in René Clément's *Forbidden Games* (1952), a masterpiece Doillon has some cavils with. In any case, Jacques Doillon and Victoire Thivisol make us look at their subject with fresh eyes, which is what all true art ultimately comes down to.

Brassed Off

Ewan McGregor appears in *Brassed Off*, an enormously likable film written and directed by Mark Herman. It is 1992 in northern England, and, all over, coal mines are closing—among other places, in the fictitious Yorkshire town of Grimley, populated by soon-to-be-unemployed colliers. Also endangered is the Grimley Colliery Band, the brass ensemble that is the precious baby of Danny Ormondroyd, its super-dedicated conductor, concerned only with making music. He even has his impoverished son, Phil, spend the money meant to stave off dispossession on a new trombone for the forthcoming semifinals of the national brass-band competition. Whereupon Phil's irate wife packs up the three kids and the furniture and clears out.

As the mine may close, the band may disband—until the sudden appearance of Gloria, granddaughter of a former band leader and the childhood sweetheart of Andy, a band member. She auditions for the band on the flugelhorn in the *Concierto de Aranjuez* of all things, and passes with flying colors, leaving all the musicians enchanted and rededicated. The band prospers in the semifinals, but the mine is closed. And Gloria, with whom Andy gets reinvolved, turns out to be a spy for the British Coal Board, making him into a shunned scab. But Gloria is soon on the band's and colliers' side, vainly fighting the management for them, when Danny collapses and is hospitalized just as the band faces the finals in Albert Hall.

The rest you must find out for yourselves. It is a delightful film, funny and serious by turns, perhaps a shade sentimental and manipulative. But whenever things threaten to get sticky comes some wry humor or just some sharply observed reality, aromatic, succulent, sassy. The Yorkshire locales and dialogue are pungently authentic, and the score by Trevor Jones, part original, part adapted, is beautifully played by the nonfictitious Grimethorpe Colliery Band. Never has brass music sounded more exhilarating.

As Danny, Pete Postlethwaite exudes his special brand of basic human dignity, usually goodhumoredly unflappable. But when emotion overcomes him, he becomes shattering as he confronts all the world's cruelty and injustice with a simple bone-deep decency, an utterly selfless pathos. His final tirade, which would sound unendurable from anyone else, issues from him rendingly right.

Scarcely less fine is Stephen Tompkinson as the large, lumbering, raw-boned Phil, who brings a sweetness and vulnerability wholly devoid of playing for sympathy. As the lovers, McGregor and the pertly toothsome Tara Fitzgerald have a wonderfully unactorish look and feel about them, and the entire supporting cast is so real you can (and this is high praise) smell them. These are some of the scruffiest actors and actresses you have recently seen, but their earthiness and doughtiness are as irresistible as that brass music. The punning title, *Brassed Off*, translates into American as "pissed off." The people and events need no translation: they are fully as universal as they are individual and idiosyncratic.

When the Cat's Away

By Cédric Klapisch, the gifted director of North African descent, *When the Cat's Away* has a mistranslated title. *Chacun cherche son Chat*—each of us seeks his cat—is not about unsurveyed mice making mischief, but about everyone's quest for what he is missing.

Chloé, a young Parisian makeup artist, is off on a vacation, and must find someone to take care of her cat, Gris-Gris, whom her roommate, the homosexual Michel, refuses to look after. He has just split up with his boyfriend and, embarking on a new affair, wants no distractions. After many frustrating inquiries, Chloé is directed to Madame Renée, a bustling old lady of the *quartier*, who owns a batch of cats and agrees to board Gris-Gris. Returning from her solitary vacation, cleverly summed up in cinematic shorthand, Chloé is told by the mortified Mme. Renée that Gris-Gris has vanished. The rest is mostly about the girl's desperate search for her pet.

Cat is a triumph of improvisation, authorial rather than thespian. It began as a short subject that blossomed midway into a feature. It was shot in the Bastille neighborhood, one of the most diversified, multicultural Paris milieus. Here the old and the new are jauntily jumbled, as in the two cafés where much of the action takes place: the time-worn, in-groupy Bar des Taillandiers and the modish, upscale Pause-Café. Half the cast are very young people, half old-timers; half professional actors, half amateurs. Half the film was written ahead of time, half each night before filming or even during next day's shooting. Characteristically, the trailer has almost nothing to do with the finished film.

What makes this heterodox stuff cohere? That it is really not about plot, but about a neighborhood and its denizens. An old church is being torn down, and we get troubling shots of that. Homeless men lolling about are coaxed into the proceedings; a couple dancing the salsa in the street was a plant, but a good one. Concierges, shopkeepers, a drummer whose banging keeps his neighbors from sleeping, a senile woman who repeatedly wanders off to be retrieved by the police, and sundry others figure amusingly. A slow-witted Arab, familiar with the territory, volunteers as co-searcher, and is more trouble than help as he falls in love with Chloé and wants to become her boyfriend.

We see Chloé at work at the ad-agency shoots, and the models, photographers, and supervisors who give her grief. We see her going out at night by herself. A painter who sings as he paints is nicknamed Bel Canto. He has painted Chloé through the window in postmodern distortion that flabbergasts her; still, he might become a boyfriend, but then he loses his lease and must move to the burbs. Guys at the bar horse around or try to make out. Cat-loving old ladies, friends of Mme Renée, keep watch for Gris-Gris from their windows or go out looking for him. There are a couple of seriocomic false alarms.

There is, further, Michel (Olivier Py, and funny) having his new lover move in with him. During the night, the lonely Chloé has to endure their loud sex across a translucent partition. In the morning, she has a curious encounter with the lover. There is more, much more: a wonder how a 95-minute film can contain such multitudes. Humor alternates with anxiety. And there are existential problems: why is Chloé's solid black cat named Gris-Gris, though it isn't always night, when all cats are *gris*? By the way, Garance Clavel, the charming actress who plays Chloé, supplied her own personal cat, Arapimou—that's the kind of film it is.

The ending is a bit far-fetched, but after such a frolic one feels forgiving. Why, one even got an insider's view of the genuine, non-touristy, everyday Paris: Laforgue's famous verse, *"Ah! que la vie est quotidienne . . ."* comes to mind. And, for once, one even felt at home among the xenophobic French.

A Beaut from LaBute

IN THE COMPANY OF MEN

No film within recent memory has aroused more public and private discussion than *In the Company of Men*, the 34-year-old Neil LaBute's first feature. Cheap at a quarter-million dollars, it was (though this doesn't get mentioned) clearly shot in 16 millimeters and imperfectly blown up: some sequences look rather muddy. Yet even that is turned into a virtue. In the *New York Times*, Janet Maslin writes, "In retrospect this colored film almost seems to have been in black and white. Its ideas are that stark." Or its cinematography that poor.

The movie's main problem is that it doesn't make sense. Two old school chums, Chad and Howard, work for the same company. Both have woman trouble: Chad's girlfriend apparently walked out; Howard's ex-girl importunes his mother on the phone. Chad, a handsome go-getter, proposes to the nerdy Howard joint vengeance on the female sex. They will find a specially vulnerable young woman, romance her for all they are worth, then leave her high and dry. Hesitant, Howard nevertheless agrees.

The company sends the pair out on a project to a branch office in another town for six weeks. Everything is left completely vague. We don't know what sort of company they work for, or what they are sent out to do. There is much talk about presentations, but we don't learn who is presenting what to whom. We don't even find out which two cities are involved.

At the new location, Chad discovers Christine, a sweet and pretty but deaf typist, her romantic life handicapped by her slurred speech—the ideal victim. Chad tells Howard, "Trust me, she'll be reaching for the sleeping pills in a week. And we'll be laughing about this till we are very old men." They start independently dating Christine, each not quite knowing what the other is up to. The guileless girl likes both, but prefers the handsome devil, goes to bed with him, and is utterly, blissfully in love. Yet she keeps platonically dating Howard.

The two men occasionally discuss their progress, though neither is fully open with the other. When Chad must return to the home office for a weekend, Howard, who has accidentally discovered that Chad has been seeing more of Christine, senses his chance. In a grim scene in his car, Christine confesses that she is in love with Chad, whereupon Howard, hurt and furious, spills the beans, lacerating the young woman. I wish I could tell you more, but maybe even this much is preposterous enough.

Why would the debonair and dashing Chad be that close to a nerd for so many years? Why would Howard, assuming that he would agree to such a dastardly plan, not keep closer tabs on Chad? Surely in such a joint scheme the plotters would compare notes more carefully. Can an executive be as nerdy as Howard? Can the sociopathic Chad get away with things undetected by all? As it turns out, Chad has it in for Howard as much as for Christine after so many years of friendship.

The basic idea is not all that new. It goes back to Choderlos de Laclos's *Les Liaisons dangereuses*, which has been variously dramatized and filmed. Recently the French film *La Discrète* by Christian Vincent had an even more similar story line. What distinguishes *In the Company of Men* is that it is set in America and has several twists near the end. Neither of the two main ones is plausible: the quasi-happy one contradicts the basic motivation for the plot; the drastic one turns Howard unwarrantedly into an idiot.

What LaBute wants to say, insofar as one can make it out, is that evil is mostly motiveless, and that (to quote the title of a Kurosawa film) the bad sleep well. Also that the corporate atmosphere somehow fosters individual nefariousness. Unfortunately, neither case is compellingly made. One also gets tired of some of LaBute's camera setups, notably his low-angle shots. I wasn't surprised to find the interview with LaBute in the press kit crawling with grammatical errors and stylistic lapses, despite his studies at three universities and literary fellowships at Sundance and at London's Royal Court Theatre. But Aaron Eckhart is a first-class Chad, and Stacy Edwards a magnificent Christine. Depending mostly on facial expressions and a few lines of clotted, guttural speech, she is quietly heartbreaking.

One scene has garnered special attention. In it, Chad brutalizes a young black employee, first with sarcasm ("Let me give you a professional tip: the word is *ask!*"), then by insisting that to qualify for advancement the youth must strip and show his balls. Since he reluctantly complies, it is in the brains department that he may be deficient.

Games People Play

THE FULL MONTY; MRS. BROWN

Even though it may be the worthiest new film around, I found *The Full Monty* offputting because I had serious trouble understanding it. There was a brief period when British films featuring Cockney or regional speech were subtitled, a practice I applauded. But the practice soon died out—whether for economic reasons or from shame at seeming condescension, I don't know. And here I was left struggling with the street talk of Sheffield.

It may have to do with my being foreign born, but the first twenty or thirty minutes proved well-nigh impenetrable, and even the remainder rather hit-or-miss. To be sure, I am not one of those who kid themselves into laughing along without full comprehension. In any case, though, *The Full Monty*, written by Simon Beaufoy and directed by Peter Cattaneo, is deft and interesting. Some unemployed steelworkers stumble onto a Chippendale club: male strippers performing for an all-female audience. Gaz, the protagonist, actually sneaks in with his young son, Nathan, and is astounded by the participatory zeal of four hundred women customers roaring their approval at handsome, muscular males who strip down to a g-string.

Meanwhile he and his mates, such as the overweight Dave and the perectly average Gerald, their office supervisor before he was let go, cannot find employment. Gerald has to lie to his wife and pretend he goes to work; Gaz cannot meet his child-support payments, and his remarried wife threatens him with a jail sentence. So the fellows conceive the desperate idea of becoming strippers even though they are scrawny or obese, over the hill or under a passel of inhibitions. But they propose to make up for such deficiencies by revealing the full monty—Australian slang for a horse that is a sure bet. In this case, total nudity.

The film contains riotous scenes, notably the audition for a few additional strippers with little Nathan handling the music from a ghetto-blaster. The men get into trouble with wives, mothers, and the law, and especially with one another, yet throughout their physical-fitness training and attempts to learn to dance their solidarity grows. One chap gets a job as a department-store floorwalker at the very place from which the others propose to steal clothes for the show, and more such shenanigans. It's funny, it's pathetic, and it's believable. Even so, I wish I had gotten more of it.

The cast is certainly a motley crew. Robert Carlyle (the sociopathic Begbie from *Trainspotters*) is a persuasive Gaz, but great Scot! (or great Yorkshireman!) is he hard on the eye. English teeth are notoriously bad, but Carlyle manages to look carious all over. Tom Wilkinson is solid as always as Gerald (he was, among other things, very fine as the clergyman living in concubinage in *Priest*); Mark Addy, as the adipose Dave, almost quitting from embarrassment at his fat, is fine; Emily Woof manages to register even in the tiny part of Gaz's ex-wife; and the nine-year-old neophyte William Snape is wonderfully unspoiled as Nathan. All the others are right too, scruffy and unstilted, and the locations positively ooze authenticity. The climactic scene—the big strip, and how the men and women take to it—couldn't be more awkwardly funny, eliciting both mischievous and compassionate merriment.

An additional bonus is the total absence of prurience. The dialogue, as far as I followed it, was amusing in a wholly natural way, and the production design and cinematography help make it, like Lear's hand, stink of humanity. Even if you get no more than half, you won't be half bored. Only a trifle frustrated.

For a truly great performance I recommend to you Judi Dench's Queen Victoria in *Mrs. Brown*. There are other good things about this respectable *Masterpiece Theater*-style picture—notably Anthony Sher's mischievous Disraeli and Geoffrey Palmer's grave Ponsonby—but the stunner is Miss Dench's Queen: a complex, ambivalent human being finely observed and embodied with almost unsettling realism.

L.A. *Confidential*

You must have noticed that in thrillers there is usually something that doesn't quite make sense. There was no reason for Amanda to wear a hat to the corner grocery, for the Brownstein twins to have missed school because of their mother's migraine, for there being an expert on Byzantine art on the bus that day. But that is how thrillers are—mostly.

I am happy to report that in *L.A. Confidential* there is nothing of the kind: everything is credible, fits in with all the rest, and goes from exciting to enthralling. The plot is absorbing, the characters are believable and even worth caring about, and the dialogue is tough and witty without ever sounding strained. This is as close to art as a *policier* can get, and that should be plenty for everyone. James Ellroy's underlying novel is, I gather, more complicated; all the more credit to the writers, Brian Helgeland (whose *Conspiracy Theory* failed to impress) and Curtis Hanson (who also directed), for getting at the essentials, and getting them right.

We are in the City of (Fallen) Angels in the fifties, the Eisenhower and Norman Rockwell decade. Here, at least in the movies, it is always midsummer arustle with palm fronds, although they are only a front behind which prostitution, pornography, drugs, and murder pullulate. Mickey Cohen, the crime czar, is safely behind bars, but the vacancy at the top merely invites rubouts as various contenders compete for the throne of crime. As the L.A. police employ ruthless tactics to rid the city of criminal elements, one wonders just how clean their own hands are.

Mainly, this is the story of three very different detectives. Bud White is thorough but unscrupulous in meting out punishment, even instant death, in what he perceives as the righting of wrong. He is particularly violent with abusers of women, harking back to his father's vile treatment of his mother. And an effective cop, though unwilling to testify against other cops, however culpable.

Bud's exact opposite is Ed Exley, a cerebral, bespectacled type ("You better lose those glasses," his superiors keep telling him, and sometimes he does), who, however, yearns for action. Above all, he hopes to match his late father's fine career in the Department, and perhaps even root out the old man's still unknown killer. Ed believes in ideal justice, which makes him and Bud natural enemies, especially after Ed testifies against some bad cops and ends up shunned by his colleagues.

The third, and most curious, principal is Jack Vincennes, a dapper, morally lax detective who not only acts as paid advisor on a dubious TV police show, but also teams up with Sid Hudgens, the sleazy editor of *Hush-Hush* magazine, which specializes in setting up movie celebrities in compromising situations. This involves much greasing of palms, fake publicity for Jack, who makes the well-photographed arrest, and good gossip for Sid. Jack, though, is very smart and, as it turns out, not such a bad guy.

Los Angeles needs all the police work it can get. Quickly, the movie establishes a sense of spreading evil, especially as we keep hearing about the Fleur de Lys, where all desires will be fulfilled. It turns out to be a place (which the film does not show in detail) where you can have sex with girls who have been made over into movie-star lookalikes; indeed, in a delightful throwaway scene, Ed mistakes—much to Jack's amusement—the real Lana Turner for such a knockoff. But isn't that the essence of Hollywood? Where even the real is make-believe, may not the make-believe be as good as real? Or as bad as real? It is Christmas Eve, yet a husband is beating the daylights out of his wife under the colored lights, and the cops at the station house are brutally working over some Mexicans who may not even be guilty. The former is punished by Bud; the latter, despite Ed's efforts, are not stopped.

It is to the movie's credit that it works mostly by suggestion. So Lynn Bracken, the blonde from Idaho who is the Veronica Lake of the Fleur de Lys, is amply characterized with utmost restraint. So, too, a corrupt D.A. and whoremongering politician are sketched in authoritatively with swift, subtle strokes. All locations are redolent of lived-in authenticity (and don't go telling me that Hollywood necessarily knows how to get L.A. down right). We believe a weatherbeaten type such as Police Captain Dudley Smith, more pragmatic than ethical, to be good at his job; or Pierce Patchett, the millionaire who makes as much from highway construction as from the byways of the Fleur de Lys, to be terrific at bending the law his way.

Everything has a fresh feel to it: Lynn's similar yet different effect on Bud and Ed; the uneasy alliances, first between Ed and

Jack, then between Ed and Bud; the seamy operations of the forces
of law in all their meanderings; the suddenness with which unconscionable violence strikes; the horrendous shootouts that register as more real than standard movie shootouts. The dead look
genuinely dead; more important the living are genuinely alive in
their imperfect, begrimed, vulnerable existences. And how cleverly the film is cast. Two of the leading roles have gone to an Australian and a New Zealander, sufficiently unfamiliar looking, yet
blending in seamlessly. Thus the babyfaced bully, Bud White, of
Russell Crowe and the slightly nerdy yet brilliant Ed Exley of Guy
Pearce. And how neat to cast James Cromwell, formerly Farmer
Hogett of *Babe* as the pawky Captain Smith. The recently too gorgeous Kim Basinger, now beginning to fade, is just right for the
disenchanted Lynn. Possibly the finest character actor in today's
Hollywood, Kevin Spacey gets across with wonderful irony both
the self-satisfaction and the self-loathing of Jack Vincennes. Perfect, too, are the slippery D.A. of Ron Rifkin and the exquisitely
unsavory nabob of David Strathairn. Also the cheerfully slimy
Hudgens of Danny DeVito, and the pathetic young actor for homosexual sale of Simon Baker Denny.

Dante Spinotti's cinematography, pretty but not too pretty, captures expertly this two-faced world, and Jerry Goldsmith, not always
my favorite composer, admirably blends lushness and menace in
his score. But top credit must go to Curtis Hanson for his astounding film-noir savoir faire: scene after tricky scene is directed with
quietly devastating command. *L.A. Confidential* conveys supremely
how brains and brawn must unite to achieve, however transiently
and with some compromise, the triumph of justice. It is sure to
become a classic of its genre.

Suburbia and Sub Rosa

THE ICE STORM; BOOGIE NIGHTS

Two of the most highly touted movies at the recent New York Film
Festival were *The Ice Storm* and *Boogie Nights*; I don't know which I
disliked more. Seeming opposites, the former is about upper-middle-class lives of quiet desperation in New Canaan, Connecticut;
the latter, about making pornographic movies in the San Fernando
Valley during the late seventies and early eighties. Yet they have

something in common: neither of them knows how to get inside its characters, however much it moans or moons about them.

The Ice Storm is based on a novel by Rick Moody that, on casual leafing through, seems more interesting than the film, but not much so. The screenplay is by James Schamus—a producer/ screenwriter/ film teacher at Columbia University—who has here dreamed up scenes that make no sense. Take the one wherein a girl apparently about to deliver oral sex to a youth passes out from a pill she took. He just sits and sits there for ages with her head between his knees. Then he finally gets up and goes home.

Even the eponymous ice storm is made to look preposterous, what with rime covering everything in bluish-silvery splendor, like a Disney wonderland. Or take a "key party," where jaded wives pick car keys from a bowl at evening's end and go off to bed down with whichever equally jaded husband the keys belong to. The movie doesn't know whether to play this for comedy, shock value, or pathos, and manages to flub them all.

Ang Lee, the Taiwan-born director, showed nice comic sense in his Taiwanese-American trilogy, and did remarkably well by the quite different *Sense and Sensibility*. But this story, these people, seem totally alien to him, and none of them comes to palpable life. Thus the superb Joan Allen, playing the hero's cheated-on wife, walks through the film like a zombie, giving her only poor performance in a career of nothing but winners, even in such inferior movies as *Nixon* and *The Crucible*. That, surely, is both the scenarist's and the director's fault. And the gifted Kevin Kline, as her gallivanting husband, makes an uncharacteristically flat showing, while as the object of his dalliance, his best friend's icy wife, the good Sigourney Weaver carries on like a silent-movie vamp.

Poorly cast, too, are the suffering children. As a charming but disturbed teenager, Christina Ricci, fine as a tiny tot in silly movies, has turned into a graceless young girl. As another confused youngster, Adam Hann-Byrd is so grotesque-looking as to elicit involuntary laughter. Add to this the garish cinematography of the hugely esteemed—and to my view coarse and inept—Frederick Elmes; also weirdly inapposite, gamelan-style music by the pretentious Mychael [*sic*] Danna; and, finally, insufferable, dragged-in sentimentality. Ugh!

Boogie Nights is a somewhat more complicated failure. To make a film about the porn-film industry requires tact and skill beyond

the reach of the young writer-director Paul Thomas Anderson, or
P.T., as he likes to call himself. He has to some extent managed to
avoid sensationalism, which is fine, but not enough. At the press
conference following the screening, his every sentence was liberally
sprinkled with "you know"s and "I don't know"s until he convinced
me that I know, and he hasn't a clue.

What, in any case, does a 26-year-old director know about conditions from 1977 to 1984, with which he purports to be familiar?
More important, what is his purpose in making such a film? If
purely to titillate, I could, without commending it, understand it.
However, he claims to have a higher goal: to show a moment in history when porn-movie makers thought they were on to an important new genre. Did they ever think that? Further, P.T. says: "These
characters are all searching for their dignity. They're just trying to
find themselves." If so, they are looking in mighty odd places, and
not very hard.

Eddie Adams, the juvenile lead, is a restless youth at odds with
his stridently carping mother; he is working as a busboy at a questionable Vegas joint where Jack Horner, the noted porn director,
likes to hang out. Horner spots Eddie as a likely Candide for the
sort of porn film in which a naïve young person is schooled in
all the ways and byways of sex. And when Eddie exhibits a penis
of epochal dimensions (not to us in the audience—*that* comes as
the film's climax after more than two and a half hours), his career
is clinched. He picks the *nom de—nom de* what, exactly?—Dirk
Diggler, and is promptly astounding all and sundry on the set with
his particular version of the one talent that, as he says, everyone
possesses.

He is, as it were, adopted by Jack Horner and the porn star Amber Waves, who lives with Jack. What is Jack and Amber's relationship? Unanswered. What is Jack's sexuality? Unanswered. There is
a suggestion that he may be asexual; but then why is he in this
profession? Unanswered. Why isn't more made of Amber's attempts
to regain her real son from her former husband? This subplot, like
so many others kicking around, pops up whenever it suits P.T., and
then not very persuasively. When Amber is up for a custody hearing, she, unlike her ex, does not bring a lawyer. Why? We see Eddie's
initiation into sex with the company ingenue, a high-school dropout who calls herself Rollergirl and never takes off her skates, not
even during intercourse. What is her story? The film is uninterested
in motivation.

On Horner's team, there are endless colorful characters. Thus Little Bill, an assistant director, whose wife (played by Nina Hartley, an actual porn star and technical advisor on the film) flagrantly cheats on him in ways such that Bill must always catch her in flagrante delicto. But if he is a perfect masochist, as he must be, how does he at long last summon strength for vengeance? There are several black performers in the Horner stable; why are they never shown in sexual action? A whole elaborate subplot which takes bizarre and irrelevant turns concerns one of them, Buck Swope, a fellow who keeps changing costumes, which also remains unexplored.

P.T. drags in whatever he can think of. Thus the fat, homely, male production assistant who develops an uncontrollable crush on Dirk. Thus an episode where Dirk, separated from his movie family, ends up as a male hustler beaten up by fag-bashers. Thus another episode where Dirk gets involved in the drug trade, with devastating results. Always there is a gaudy mixture of the smart-ass, the grotesque, and the bloodcurdling, as if P.T.'s chief aim were to outbid Quentin Tarantino—which, worse luck, may be the case. But when *Boogie Nights* is on to something truly interesting, such as the ambiguous relationship between Amber and Dirk—part mother and adopted son, part loving mistress and ardent young lover, part cynical fellow porn actors—the film fails to look any less superficially.

Instead, we are off on more subplots: the cornball action movies that Dirk and a sidekick, in rebellion from Horner, make unsuccessfully; the porn-movie producer who lands in jail for child molestation; another producer who vainly tries to make Horner & Co. switch from using film to using more cost-efficient video; the comical Hispanic who desperately wants to act in porn movies; and many more. What makes this overlong movie bearable is the fine performances.

Burt Reynolds, with probably a sense of his own manifold frustrations, infuses Jack with more than is in the screenplay. Julianne Moore, sweetly sexy, brings warmth and humanity to Amber. As Dirk, Mark Wahlberg (a/k/a Marky Mark, the former rapper and unwrapped Calvin Klein model) shuttles believably between befuddlement and cockiness. A large supporting cast contributes gamely. But nothing, not even careful period detail, can endow *Boogie Nights* with a sense of purpose—least of all the unearnedly cheerful final sequences.

The 14th-Worst Spot

WELCOME TO SARAJEVO

Michael Winterbottom's *Welcome to Sarajevo* is a scary and moving film that may also be great. It is loosely based on *Natasha's Story*, the account by the British journalist Michael Nicholson of his adoption of a nine-year-old Bosnian youngster. Winterbottom and his scenarist, Frank Cottrell Boyce, have considerably widened the focus—both factual and fictional—into a broad canvas of Sarajevo in 1992 and beyond, as the city gallantly clutches at normality under steady bombardment and sniper fire. It was filmed in Sarajevo right after the peace treaty of 1996, when the freshly contained rampage was still smoldering.

The film often switches to TV newsreels, and the wonder is that, despite obvious discrepancies between actual wide-screen and real or simulated television footage, a seamless blend emerges. Against a background of conflagration, individual figures—international correspondents and cameramen, TV producers, welfare workers, and all sorts of Sarajevans—coalesce into recognizable human beings. Specific stories, randomly or profoundly intertwined, thicken into involving identity. Yet the aura of confusion, rushing about, sudden death—an all but incomprehensible blur of fevered activity—never really lets up. All along, brave men and women journalists make zesty jokes or burst into apoplectic despair as they doggedly try to cover the unutterable.

And then the children. The inmates of a partly bombed-out orphanage that now mostly houses newly ravaged young lives, they are the ones for whom Henderson, the tough and wisecracking British TV correspondent, struggles to provide escape to the West. He gets particularly close to nine-year-old Emira, to whom he has casually promised safety in England, and whose quiet reproaches are shaming him into responsibility. Around them is a swirl of intrigue, profiteering, craven murder, hasty wartime sex, emotional and physical deprivation, but also genuine love and heroism, big or, no less touchingly, small.

It is, deliberately, hard to follow the details of what goes on. Some of the dialogue in the native tongue is translated, some of it isn't. (I speak the language, and found the untranslated stuff fascinating but nonessential.) This creates perplexity, as does the overlapping shouted, mumbled, or strangulated dialogue coming at you from all directions. Lights keep going off, gunfire punctuates everything, heavy weapons thunder from afar or alarmingly near. Horribly, as you watch, you get inured to the ubiquitous corpses as natural parts of the landscape, like pockmarked or crumbling buildings, torn-up and deserted streets, crippled and abandoned vehicles, and the occasional dead dog.

A woman killed by a sniper on camera promptly turns into a TV image as an offscreen voice informs us that no one dares remove the body. Journalists race after stories while others run for their lives. A mysterious choirboy hovers or gallops about muttering, popping up everywhere, silent or hurling imprecations. The name Živko turns up increasingly amid the omnipresent graffiti. And the visual refrain of the children, wide-eyed and absurdly brave. A group execution is carried out with chilling offhandedness; a father barely recognizes his emaciated son in a camp photograph. A decent young man is assassinated in his own apartment.

UN functionaries pronounce Sarajevo only the 14th-most dangerous spot in the world, which elicits all manner of sardonic merriment. A shattering story, considered routine in London, is bumped by the papers for marital troubles among the royals. Flynn, the hard-drinking, cynical American correspondent (Woody Harrelson), turns out to be human; Mrs. Savić, an empathetic caretaker, suddenly quits or disappears. The ingenuous young American welfare worker (Marisa Tomei) in charge of child evacuation is often cruelly foiled. There are also Jane (Kerry Fox), the British TV producer whose Bosnian lover gets killed, and Annie (Emily Lloyd), an inexperienced journalist who learns the hard way that news is only what an editor thinks it is.

Stephen Dillane is splendid as Henderson, danger-hardened yet unprofessionally drawn to Emira, played with affecting unsentimentality by ten-year-old Emira Nušević. Fine as well is Goran Višnjić as Risto, the Brits' chauffeur sucked into combat. Plenty of humor, too, at the Miss Besieged Sarajevo beauty contest, or in the constant repartee with which the journalists battle their fatigue. Winterbottom has a keen sense of how to use light. Many shots are in partial or near-total darkness suddenly irrupted into by blinding sunshine that however, brings anything but comfort. A good person says that killing his first enemy feels therapeutic; someone observes: "I used to think life and the siege were different things. Now I realize there is no life in Sarajevo apart from the siege." A cellist proposes a concert, but he'll wait until his city is declared the number-one trouble spot.

We see also historical figures making TV speeches: Bush, John Major, Karadžić, Boutros-Ghali. Some speak horrible lies; some, horrible truths. Often the camera (superbly handled by Daf Hobson) is in extreme closeup but, endangered, pans away at such speed that we don't know what we are seeing. The gift of three eggs to five hungry people turns an omelet into a solemn ritual. For it, a stove is lit with a page torn from a precious illustrated book. Explanation: "If you must burn books, you should at least enjoy it." The truest horror is in the understatement. Henderson tells Emira's delinquent but belatedly repentant mother he'll take the child to England. "Just for a short time," says the anxious woman. "Yes," he answers, "a short time. I hope so." Told over the phone that he is taking Emira to live with them, Mrs. Henderson, already toiling with her own children, says in hesitant voiceover, "It's good, I guess … it's good."

I could go on quoting and evoking, but you must really see for yourself. I urge, implore you to do so: as much as about them, this film is about you.

Souls at Sea

TITANIC; AMISTAD

Christmas is the time we film critics dread the most: more movies are showered on us than flesh can bear or mind absorb, and this year it has been even worse than usual. I have space for only three of them, dealt with rather laconically, but holiday guidance must supersede belletristics.

Titanic, made jointly by two major studios, is at two hundred million plus the costliest movie ever, but you can see where just about every dollar went. Here is a drama the world never tires of, but whose numerous ramifications even a 194-minute film can't quite cope with. This one, written and directed by James Cameron, is exciting in all but its central story, which, artistically, is the real disaster. It is the brief and tragic tale of Leonardo DiCaprio, a young American painter from steerage, and Kate Winslet, a not-so-affluent girl from first class, sailing with her mercenary mother, Frances Fisher, and her callous but wealthy fiancé, Billy Zane. (I am using the actors' real names to emphasize the story's hokiness.) Everything that happens to these people is utterly crass—including Leonardo's secretly drawing Kate in the nude and Billy's trying to shoot the love thief as the boat is already sinking—and not helped by Mr. Zane's and Miss Fisher's giving better perfomances than the leads.

Every cliché of young shipboard romance, visual and verbal, is proudly trotted out, along with a few far-fetched maneuvers. Thus Leonardo saves Kate from the unlikeliest of suicides, and deflowers her in a fancy motor car traveling across the ocean. Thus, too, Leonardo is unjustly accused of theft and handcuffed to a pole just as the catastrophe is about to occur; risking all, Kate saves him. And more such stuff. The crowning absurdity is the feel-good ending, with the entire cast lining the liner's grand staircase to cheer the young lovers as they embrace. Whether this is a statement about immortality or the wrap party being memorialized, it belongs in a long-overdue Museum of Cinematic Bathos.

There is a frame story involving the people trying to raise the *Titanic* (marvelous documentary footage) and a very old woman survivor of the disaster, who turns out to be—guess who. Throughout, whatever pertains to the historical aspects of the ship's life and death is absolutely splendid, and direction, production design, and cinematography (Russell Carpenter) deserve highest praise. *Titanic* is never boring, only often naggingly annoying, down to the preposterous way one of the principals survives and the other dies.

Amistad has been termed by its director, Steven Spielberg, "an extraordinarily important film," and who would know better? It shows that one can follow a factual outline reasonably closely and still come up with poster art for the delectation of knee-jerk liberals. I do not mind bringing together Cinque, the leader of the rebellion aboard the slaver *La Amistad* in 1839, with the man who defended the rebel slaves before the Supreme Court, John Quincy Adams, even though history records no such meeting. Nor do I mind other reasonable liberties of historical fiction.

I do, however, object to vulgarization. Take Anthony Hopkin's Adams, as bad a performance by a major actor as you'll ever see. Hopkins offers an anthology of mannerisms: fussy little gestures, quirky pauses, exaggerated absentmindedness, fingering of irrelevant objects (mostly plants—horticulture as monomania), aleatory vocal inflections, restless pacing about: a course in scene-stealing. And if what he produces is his idea of a Boston accent, Hopkins is full of beans.

Although the black performers were given careful instruction in Mende speech, what they say in authentic Mende is not translated for a very long time, and when it finally gets subtitled (screenplay by David Franzoni), you wonder whether you weren't better off before. My favorite bit is when Cinque gets a lesson in jail from one of his fellows, who learned English from reading the King James Bible in the standard monolingual edition—a minor miracle. Thus exposed to the New Testament, Cinque is understandably an instant convert.

As Roger Baldwin, the pawky lawyer hired by the abolitionists, and as Secretary of State Forsyth, Matthew McConaughey and David Paymer give performances devoid of a trace of period sense: remove their wigs and we are smack-dab in Grishamland. Even such incomparable character actors as Nigel Hawthorne and Pete Postlethwaite (Martin Van Buren and District Attorney Saunders) cannot turn bare bones into living flesh. With the exception of Morgan Freeman, as a composite of several black abolitionists, the major Americans are played by Brits and one Swede, Stellan Skarsgård, who comes closest to credible Yankeedom.

The absurdity is all-pervasive. Take a sequence in which a number of slaves are chained to a pile of rocks and thrown overboard to be dragged to their deaths. Spielberg positions the camera for a final shot deep underwater, so that the drowners emitting bubbles come at us like a lineup of holiday divers in for some aquatic fun. In an earlier sequence, Cinque and one of his henchmen, after killing most of the Spanish crew, contend for the captaincy of the ship. In extreme closeup, they howl at each other in an untranslated outburst, head to head. The effect is to make them as unsympathetic as possible: you expect that, at any moment, an ear will be bitten off. For background music, John Williams provides an almost ceaseless chorus of holier-than-thou pseudospirituals.

Some actors manage to register: Djimon Hounsou as Cinque, Arliss Howard as Calhoun, and Jeremy Northam as a young Catholic judge struggling with his conscience. Others, though, are painfully obvious, not least Anna Paquin as the adolescent Isabella II of Spain, jumping up and down on her royal bed in Spanish. I also relished the bit when the blacks objected to their lawyer's use of the word *should*, a word nonexistent in Mende, where things either are or aren't. The film presents this as clear proof of moral superiority. I feel great sympathy for all the actors who, having to wear irons on neck, wrists, and ankles, chafed those parts raw. But the filmmakers' awe-struck bended knees must have endured a no less liberal workout.

The Postman

Remember Kevin Costner's waterlogged *Waterworld*? In that apocalyptic stinker, post-Armageddon remnants of humanity jetsamed it up on the seven seas; in the current superturkey *The Postman*, we get a rerun on dry land. In the new dystopia, the United States is, by 2013, mostly unpeopled desolation, though an abandoned car, vacant house, or thriving township pops up whenever required to help Costner and the preposterous plot along. The actor-director seems determined to appear as the savior of the world, although the world has yet to figure out how to save itself from him.

As customary, an army of vicious marauders, here called Holnists and led by the beastly General Bethlehem, terrorizes the few remaining civilized communities. On horseback like the Huns, they exact inordinate tribute and abduct men for soldiering, women for lust. There is no one to oppose them, except, of course, Costner. A loner who was forcibly conscripted into the Holnists but managed to escape, he finds in an abandoned jeep a postman's uniform and a pouch full of old undelivered letters. To get food and shelter from the surviving towns, he assumes the role of the Postman, a representative of the supposedly restored United States Government.

Just how he manages to deliver the letters and even bring back replies is left vague, but mail delivery spells deliverance for him and all. Before long, other young men and women are having him anoint them as subsidiary postmen, only to have Bethlehem and the Holnists vow to destroy them and those who harbor them. I cannot begin to go into the details of this, after much last-minute cutting, three-and-a-quarter-hour movie, but I can assure you that, despite some unintended belly laughs, it provides little but self-indulgent flimflam.

Thus, in a sheltering town, Abby, a stunning young woman, accosts Postman Costner with the question, "So, as far as you know, you've got good semen?" It seems her beloved young husband has had "the bad mumps," which leaves you infertile. Postner, as for the sake of brevity I shall call him, hesitates, but when Abby disrobes and invades his bed, even he proves only flesh and blood. Conveniently, his good semen impregnates Abby on the first try; later, her husband is equally conveniently killed when he tries to stop Bethlehem from carrying her off. In this ravaged but ideal world, Bethlehem, much as he tries to possess her, remains impotent. Rescued later on, Abby, much as she tries to remain faithful to her husband's memory, cannot resist the Postner, just like those weak men who finance these dreadful Costner movies.

Mention must be made of the wit in this screenplay by Eric Roth and Brian Helgeland. When the Postner tries to persuade the people that order has been re-established, he lies to them about Broadway again mounting shows by Andrew Floyd [*sic*] Webber. Equally fetching is the allegory, as when Abby's child is presented as "My daughter: her name is Hope." (Costner, a good father, has cast his real-life children in the movie.)

Costner is heartwarming as the reluctant redeemer; as Bethlehem, the Dick Cavettish Will Patton knows Shakespeare and Latin tags, and smiles as he murders. As Abby, the young English actress Olivia Williams is much more than Costner deserves. Imagine a fellow not above calling his monster movie by the same title as that warmly remembered intimate charmer *Il Postino*. Couldn't he at least have had the decency to call his film *The Mailman*?

Minus Four

THE SWEET HEREAFTER; AFTERGLOW

Recent months produced a spat, of films even Argus couldn't have coped with. Let me dispatch a few with condign unceremoniousness. The Canadian Atom Egoyan's *The Sweet Hereafter*, from a seemingly better novel by Russell Banks—about a school bus that skids into icy waters drowning a number of children, and what that does to the morale of a small town—is marred by several things, chiefly Egoyan's screenplay. Ian Holm plays a well-meaning but officious lawyer who tries to make the grieving families sue for damages, but inhibiting skeletons come out of everyone's closet, including his own.

As usual, Egoyan cannot resist his terminal pretentiousness. He introduces visual/verbal quotations from the poem "The Pied Piper of Hamelin," as if Browning had bearing on Banks, which is manifest nonsense. He also invents an endless framing conversation on an airplane that detracts more than it adds. He allows the odiously attitudinizing Mychael [*sic*] Danna to compose a preposterous score, and casts a number of small-time actors in roles that make too large demands. Except for Holm's performance and the silverpoint-like wintry landscapes, everything about the film matches human disaster with artistic catastrophe.

Try as it might, this stinker cannot hold a candle to 1997's nadir, *Afterglow*, which, unsurprisingly, has garnered a number of (after)glowing reviews. The writer-director, Alan Rudolph, has learned only one thing in the 15 films he has churned out: how to make each worse than the one before. But even he will have serious difficulties trying to surpass the horror of his latest. Rudolph, a toady and protegé of Robert Altman, has all his master's defects, plus a few uniquely his own. *Afterglow* is an enchiridion of every known literary and cinematic cliché; racking my brains, I could come up with only one Rudolph overlooked. Even in that field, I guess, perfection eludes him.

How many times have we groaned at characters trying to remember the names of Disney's seven dwarfs? Or a woman pretending to talk about a friend when she means herself? Or leaning back, drained, against a door closing after a man in her life? Or a spouse tossing a snapshot of bygone connubial bliss into the fireplace? We get a man in a bar picking up the smoking woman next to him with "Smoke gets into your eyes," and promptly ordering "A bottle of Dom Pérignon and two glasses." (If at least it had been Cristalle!) "You're the most fascinating woman I met in my whole life," he adds.

Elsewhere we get, "Ever wonder about women being like fine wine?" Again, "The worst part is finding out late in life that nothing lasts," and "I like the way you smell—like a man." Also a more recent visual cliché (first seen in an Altman movie) of a woman (irrelevantly) using a toilet, and three separate gratuitous overhead shots with the camera rotating 360 degrees, not one of them—shot or degree—justified.

Rudolph excels at subtle sexual innuendo: e.g., "Turn me on; make it wet," from a young woman to her sexy plumber. Or explaining her skimpy dress to her sexually uncooperative husband, "I'm ovulating," a gentle hint to impregnate her. Or the middle-aged wife of the philandering plumber asking upon his return home, "How was work? Unplug a few tubes?" Or take this dazzling paradox: "I don't know what I like, but I know what art is." The story concerns two troubled couples, the middle-aged Lucky (!) and Phyllis, and the young Jeffrey and Marianne, in sexual interaction that results in nothing. The scene is Montreal, which seems to contain only one apartment building, the famous Habitat, with which Rudolph is obsessed.

Nick Nolte lets his Lion King mane do his acting, Jonny Lee Miller keeps squaring his already jutting jaw, and Lara Flynn Boyle carries on like a hard-porn actress compensating for being caught in soft-core. Julie Christie hams it up with silent-screen aplomb, and has already received several awards for her outrageous overacting.

As Good as It Gets

James L. Brooks is a producer/director/writer out of television who knows exactly how to make crowds laugh or cry or, better yet, do both at once. He has not always been successful, but with films such as *Terms of Endearment* and *Broadcast News* the great manipulator proved his mettle. He does it again with *As Good as It Gets*.

This is a comedy about Melvin Udall, a writer of popular romances, an obsessive-compulsive, and a total misanthrope. He cannot step on cracks between pavement squares; hates women, blacks, homosexuals, animals, and people in general with equal comic ferocity; and eats his regular artery-hardening breakfast at a coffee shop where Carol Connelly, alone among the waitresses, can endure his sarcastic tirades. She is the overprotective single mother of asthmatic young Spencer, of whom her easygoing mother, Beverly, takes care when Carol is at work.

Melvin's favorite butts are Simon Nye, the young homosexual painter who lives across the hall; Simon's black, homosexual art dealer, Frank Sachs, tough enough to crimp Melvin's style somewhat; and Verdell, Simon's pet Brussels griffon. At film's start, Melvin, annoyed by Verdell's yapping, throws the pooch down the garbage chute. But you cannot worry over the fate of a bowwow in American movies, where, unlike in Oliver Goldsmith's famous poem, dog is even more sacred than mom.

Can you, my friends, guess what happens next? You may not predict that Simon will be roughed up by rough trade (those nasty straight hustlers who sometimes beat up their gay clients), resulting in hospitalization and slow recovery. Or that Melvin will end up driving him down to Baltimore, where his conventional, estranged parents live, or that Carol will come along on the trip. But you will guess that Melvin and Carol will start falling in love until he dumbly spoils it all—and perhaps even that Simon's painter's block will vanish when Carol poses for him nude in the trio's hotel suite. What you will surely foretell is that, after all sorts of tribulations, all will turn out for the best for everyone.

How could it be otherwise when Melvin pays for a specialist's house call at Spencer's bedside, a privilege nowadays reserved for billionaires? You will, in any case, not worry for Spencer; kids, to be sure, have come to grief in Hollywood products, but not ones of this type, where the comedy is about as good as it gets. The dialogue is lively, often bitingly funny, in this screenplay by Mark Andrus and Brooks, whose direction jolts as well as it tickles. And obsessive-compulsive disorder lends itself to all kinds of sight gags—is, indeed, the most cinegenic of ailments.

As enacted by Jack Nicholson, Melvin is, you may be sure, as lovable as he is hateful. Oh, those squinty eyes aglitter with deviltry; that high-pitched, nerve-fraying drawl that not only inflicts wounds but also twists a smile inside them; those somewhat bestial good looks! Everything about Nicholson makes you love hating him, and not even begrudge him the girl.

And what a girl! Helen Hunt, inheriting the part relinquished by Holly Hunter (the hunt, I guess, is of the essence), gives a great comic performance in the Irene Dunne-Carole Lombard tradition. Her Carol, more sexy than pretty, is both nervy and nervous, fiercely female and meltingly feminine, gloriously fusing the natural with the histrionic.

Greg Kinnear (Simon), Cuba Gooding Jr. (Frank), and Shirley Knight (Beverly) lend impeccable support, and John Bailey's camera supplies oodles of colorfulness. Final praise must go to the six canines who played Verdell, with Timer doing most of the donkey work and Jill most of the star turns. The transition from Verdell's dreading Melvin to infuriatingly loving him more than his master is magisterially managed, whether by one dog or six. I wouldn't be surprised if Brussels became as famed for its griffons as for its sprouts.

The Boxer

You may think we need no more movies about the troubles in Northern Ireland. Or southern Ireland. And perhaps especially not from Jim Sheridan and Terry George, who have already given us the outstanding *In the Name of the Father* and the deserving

Some Mother's Son. Well, think again. *The Boxer* is a superb piece of work, of the sort Sean O'Casey would have appreciated, perhaps even written. It is a film replete with plot and multiform excitement, but at the center of it is a love story as moving as ever reached out from the screen, and one to which script, direction, acting, and cinematography contributed in equal measure.

Danny Flynn is a Belfast boxer finishing a 14-year jail term for IRA activities. He has not squealed on anyone, but neither has he fraternized with fellow political inmates. He has kept up his boxing exercises as much as possible, but has stopped writing to his girl, Maggie; he wanted to set her free, even though hoping she would nevertheless wait for him. Misunderstanding his silence, she lovelessly married his best friend, who fathered her child, Liam, but is now himself serving a long prison term. Danny now 32, gets out. But into what world, to what life?

As Terry George and Jim Sheridan wrote and the latter directed it, *The Boxer* does not tell all this right away. Instead, as a glum Danny is leaving, a prison wedding takes place, the bridegroom unhandcuffed just for the ceremony, whereupon the bride returns groomless to the wedding party. Boisterous as it is, a pair of young dancers are sternly separated: the girl is the wife of a prisoner and must abide by the exaggerated abstinence strictly enforced so as to maintain the morale of jailed husbands.

We also encounter Harry, the IRA district leader and chief firebrand, planning another bombing, then heading for a secret meeting with Joe Hamill, the IRA's top man. A tracking shot follows the entrants to the meeting past all sorts of guards to ever more interior rooms, until the final space is reached through a ragged man-sized hole in a wall, susceptible, no doubt, of instant cover-up. Above, throughout the film, the air teams with helicopters, ceaselessly surveying, but concerned only with interfaith clashes; to the Catholics in internecine slaughter, on whom the film focuses, these eyes of heaven are blind.

Danny's release goes unremarked. He checks into a flophouse where he is recognized by his former trainer, Ike Weir, now a drunken bum who proceeds to berate him boozily for having abandoned the ring for politics and jail. Yet the two end up breakfasting together just as one of Harry's bombs goes off in the distance. This despite Joe's order to abstain from violence as talks with the English are progressing hopefully. Danny and Ike resolve to resume their partnership.

But where? The gym of the Holy Family Boxing Club, their former purlieu, has been converted into a community center; group photos of young boxers, now scattered or killed, incongruously bedeck the walls. The place is dusty, ill lit, desolate, harboring ghostly, empty-eyed derelicts. The ring has been dismantled, its components locked away in a hiding place under the stairs. When Danny breaks into it, he finds there also packages of Harry's explosives, which he disgustedly dumps in the river.

Dinginess permeates the hall, somberly captured by the amazing camera of Chris Menges. A gifted film director in his own right, he has been the cameraman on such films as *The Killing Fields*, *Local Hero*, and *Michael Collins*; he has proved his ability with subjects requiring newsreel-like realism and has wrestled stark beauty from war, jungles, poverty, even grime. All picturesqueness, however, is strictly avoided.

The gym, which Danny and Ike resuscitate and make nonsectarian, open to Catholics, Protestants, and all needy children, takes on an extraordinary life thanks to Menges's lens. The prevailing color is an aqueous greenish blue, its quasi-aquatic denizens almost more piscine than human. In this glaucous and livid ambience, Danny trains frantically under Ike's supervision, but also under the hostile glances of Harry and others of his hotheaded persuasion.

The Boxer now artfully interweaves its threefold story line. There is Danny's budding boxing career, examined in naturalistic detail, but with a climax that, though stunning, is too noble for its own good. There are the political see-sawings, as Harry's warmongering clashes with Joe's maneuvering for a viable peace. Joe, the savvy, prison-tempered leader, is Maggie's widowed father. The young woman is now a schoolteacher, Liam's caring mom, and, yes, still in love with Danny, as he is with her. Slowly, with almost excruciating sobriety, these two restart their former romance against every handicap: the iron-clad rules for prisoners' wives, the censorious interference of menacing busybodies, the shocked and angry spying of young Liam, who suspects his mother of preparing to abandon him and run off to England with Danny.

Out of these elements, the film makes a complex yet cohesive tapestry. The progress of the love affair through infinitesimal increments—ambiguous glances, seemingly noncommittal salutations, furtive meetings that become gradually more defiant, dialogue that is impulsive, heartfelt, and pristinely free of cliché—is one of the rare triumphs of recent cinema. What makes this offhanded, awkward rapprochement so moving is, finally, the flawless acting of two magnificent performers.

Daniel Day-Lewis trained for nearly three years to make his boxing scenes absolutely professional, and they are equally impeccably directed and photographed. But it is in his shy, fumbling, circuitous approaches to a full-scale declaration of love that the actor scores with disciplined passion. His face and body become transparent as we watch ill-suppressed tremors eddy up into shamefaced half-smiles; hear his voice, with its accumulating retards, become more and more implication-laden, pleading for reciprocal corroboration. A man who, as he says, made a soothing compact with silence in his prison cell, is groping toward communication as his set features filter into tenderness.

No less amazing is the Maggie of Emily Watson. Her responses to Danny's return, public scrutiny, paternal warnings, and filial resentment are calibrated with a fineness of feeling whose evolution is scarcely more perceptible than the growth of a plant. Still, there it is, in expressions both inchoate and ambivalent, yet subtly evolving through stages of pretended indifference, guarded politesse, muted encouragement, and crumbling self-restraint. Through tiny bursts of complicity, a huge, dormant passion inches its way toward incandescence. You are sucked into the rapture these actors generate.

Here again Menges's camera rises to the occasion. Interiors have the burnished look of sparsely lighted rooms, but with faces radiating self-engendered wattage, becoming themselves ruddy and intense sources of illumination. Again, a walk on an empty beach, where the love relation reasserts itself, is aglimmer with grey-greens clamoring for the fuller palette of passion, soon to be released. Just so in the ring during a fight, the bleached-out glare bursts into crimson with the blood from Danny's battered face. And I haven't even mentioned the cunningly insinuating music of Gavin Friday and Maurice Seezer, or the great supporting performances of Ken Stott (Ike), Brian Cox (Joe), and several others. All good reasons not to miss *The Boxer*.

The Man in the Iron Mask

If inadvertent farce is your bag, *The Man in the Iron Mask* should provide you three bags full. It claims to be "based upon the novel by Alexandre Dumas," but never trust a "based upon"; the truth, when it exists in Hollywood, is always "based *on*." The movie was written and directed by Randall Wallace, who previously merely wrote *Braveheart*, but all this writing and directing and basing upon was too much for him. The resulting concoction has less to do with Dumas than with a shambles.

What to make of a movie in which "d'Artagnan" is pronounced four different ways? Correctly in the French manner, and also "dart onyon," "darTANNyan," and, as if it were Armenian, "dartainian"? Accents pullulate: Gérard Depardieu's Porthos sounds like Inspector Clouseau; Jeremy Irons's Aramis is pure British; John Malkovich's Athos (also variously pronounced), midwestern; Gabriel Byrne's d'Artagnan, Americanized Irish; Leonardo DiCaprio's man in the iron mask and Louis XIV are carefully learned stage-and-screen American.

If you feel that two Leonardo DiCaprios are too much for a single movie, I would add only that even one may be excessive. Yet weren't there always two of them? The one who, in some shots, is a very pretty young man, and the other who, in different shots, is a somewhat homely girl? I can't speak to his acting, so overwhelmed am I by his twinned unreality—as unreal as this supposed iron mask made out of, I think, hard rubber. The historical one was black velvet with iron hinges, but forget about history.

Wallace's writing falls somewhere between baroque and bizarre. The evil and lecherous young Louis causes the death of Athos's son in order to possess the boy's fiancée, Christine, and palavers as follows: "I know this day for you the world has spun round more than once and is still spinning; but let us sit down for dinner and perhaps you can bring it to a pause." Understandably, Christine puts up only the feeblest resistance, especially when also told, "Of all the wonders I have seen, I have never looked upon anything as wonderful," which, besides lame syntax, features that irresistible *upon*. The drunkard Porthos, about to fight against impossible odds, declares, "I would rather die like this than drown in my own piss," although his wit may escape an audience for which cracking a safe would be easier than penetrating Depardieu's English.

The plot hinges on the former musketeers' plan to replace the vicious young king with Philippe, his identical twin, a fine young man who, freed from his cumbersome mask, would make a model monarch. Their difficult scheme would prove easy were it not for d'Artagnan, who as captain of the royal guard (or something like that) is loyal to Louis, beastly though he be, and thus becomes the one of the famous foursome who is not for all. The poor sap is unaware that, as Queen Anne's lover, it is he who engendered the twins.

I confess that the script's finer points were wasted upon me, but I enjoyed the beauty of the French landscapes, châteaux, and actresses—Anne Parillaud (Anne) and Judith Godrèche (Christine). Peter Suschitzky's cinematography is accomplished, whereas Nick Glennie-Smith's score is merely perpetrated: a relentless criminal assault on the ear, of a piece with the dialogue. Should *The Man in the Iron Mask* dislodge *Titanic* from its No. 1 spot at the box office, I can envision a time when a film's success will depend on the number of DiCaprios it contains.

The Butcher Boy

Based on a novel by Patrick McCabe, Neil Jordan's *The Butcher Boy* is the story of how 12-year-old Francie Brady went to the dogs. His trumpet-player father, Benny, is an alcoholic; his mother, Annie, is mentally deranged. The time is that of the Cuban missile crisis: the good folk in Francie's small town in County Monaghan see communists in the bushes and atomic cataclysm round the corner. Francie and his best friend, Joe, play at Indians and Indians (no cowboys for them), watch monster movies on TV, play insidious pranks on their proper, bespectacled chum Philip and on his mother, Mrs. Nugent, a rather grand and officious neighbor, Francie's particular nemesis.

Strange things happen: madness, death of dear ones, escapes to Dublin, acts of accelerating violence against Mrs. Nugent, confinement in sundry institutions (medical, mental, educational, correctional). Escalating crimes lead to a huge one as Francie stands the town on its head. There are visions of the Virgin Mary dispensing motherly advice, and of Armageddon with a world of dead pigs ("pig" is what Mrs. Nugent called Francie, who adopts it as his *nom de guerre*), and all sorts of twists and shocks. We are exposed to a gallery of Irish types of every stripe, from priests to bums, sufficient to make O'Casey's and Synge's Hibernian green greener with envy. It is all funny, bizarre, horrific, and often incomprehensible.

That's because the characters speak the Monaghanian lingo,

which—when shouted, rattled off, or shrilled in childish treble—
turns impenetrable. (After two viewings, I have caught about 65
percent.) Admitting that he understood only half of what the protagonist said, David Denby concluded, "I find myself in an embarrassing position: I think this is a great movie, but I'm not sure." I
suspect that the film, written by McCabe and Jordan, is too slippery
for greatness: lightning shifts from farcical to sentimental, absurdist
to tragic, mundane to apocalyptic, cannot be absolved from hocus-
pocus.

But Jordan's direction is fluent, Elliot Goldenthal's score neatly
juggles pop and pseudo-classical, locations are authentic and cannily captured by Adrian Biddle's camera. The acting crackles. Well-
known actors such as Stephen Rea, Milo O'Shea, and Fiona Shaw
are evenly matched with less well-known but no less talented ones,
e.g., Sinead O'Connor, Rosaleen Linehan, Niall Buggy, Brendan
Gleeson (superb as Father Bubbles), and those two terrific boys,
classmates at a nearby school: Eamonn Owens (Francie) and Alan
Boyle (Joe). Even when you cannot quite follow the language, the
performances speak distinctly and attachingly. Still, what wouldn't
I have given for an occasional subtitle!

A Past Past Escaping

WILDE; THE TRUCE

There have been two previous films about Oscar Wilde. In the 1959
Oscar Wilde, Robert Morley re-created a stage performance, amusingly but without much charisma. In the 1960 *The Trials of Oscar
Wilde*, Peter Finch was a superb Wilde and John Frazer a very fine
Alfred Douglas. Neither film covered sufficient ground. *Wilde*,
written by the gifted Julian Mitchell and directed by Brian Gilbert,
whose *Tom and Viv* (about T.S. Eliot) was less than compelling, tries
to go farther and deeper, but doesn't quite come off either.

There is an unfortunate Masterpiece Theatre aura about *Wilde*,
which, it must be conceded, would have been hard to avoid. Put some
fine English actors into lavish costumes and opulent settings, photograph them resplendently, and what else will you get? Of course, this
story is more somber and seedy, but it is also illumined by Wilde's
charm and wit, and so that more or less balances out. The film shows
some of Wilde's sordid relations with servants and stable boys, and

does not shy away from all-male sex scenes. Yet it tends to senti-
mentalize, not least by Stephen Fry's rather too sweet and concerned
Oscar, and it does not go into those wretched post-prison years of
exile, poverty, drink, and degradation, leading to a pauper's death at
46. All that is laconically summed up in a title card.

Fry is an interesting actor (and a good writer as well), who does
manage to look rather like Wilde. But whereas Oscar was not exactly good-looking (Peter Finch, still my favorite Wilde, was perhaps too handsome), neither was he as funny-faced as Fry is. His
somewhat beady and close-set eyes, crooked nose going off to the
left, and mouth tending to curl to the right create a comic look
that works for some things but undercuts others. Still, he is of the
right large size, moves well, and delivers his lines stylishly. However,
helped by the script (based on Richard Ellmann's biography), he
does make Wilde into a rather more tender-hearted, even conscientious, figure than he must have been. Especially his relations with
Constance, the wife he mistreated, and the two sons he neglected
are artfully glossed over.

Mitchell's screenplay uses Wilde's story "The Selfish Giant" as
a sort of refrain or incremental repetition. We see Wilde reading
installments of the story (Constance, too, gets some) to the boys;
later, we hear him read passages in voiceover whenever the movie
returns to the kids. But as the story records the giant's coming to
love the children he at first hated, these prose-poetic passages put a
sentimental sheen on Wilde's treatment of Cyril and Vyvyan. Oscar,
other than superficially, remained a selfish giant.

Inexplicably, the film shortchanges the three trials that are at
the core of Wilde's downfall—tragic when you consider how many
other men, not a few of noble birth and high rank, indulged in
the same practices with impunity. We are not even given the key
moment in court when Edward Carson, cross-examining Wilde,
asked whether he had ever kissed the 16-year-old Walter Grainger.
"Oh, dear, no," was the reply. "He was, unfortunately, extremely
ugly." The jury was shocked, and this proved the turning point in
the case. But what also heavily contributed to Wilde's undoing was
the wit he exhibited on the witness stand. Though it elicited much
laughter, it also stirred up the resentment of the humorless; wit as
much as homosexuality condemned Oscar Wilde. But the movie
does not convey this.

The supporting roles are well taken. The handsome Jude Law is
a tempestuous, recklessly amoral, fickle yet demanding Lord Al-

fred; Jennifer Ehle is a touching yet unsappy Constance; Vanessa Redgrave does nicely by Oscar's mother (though the part, like some others, does not allow for detailed characterization); Tom Wilkinson manages to make the beastly Marquess of Queensberry just a bit ludicrously human as well; Zoe Wanamaker is a quietly sympathetic Ada Leverson. Although good otherwise, Michael Sheen is a somewhat batrachian Robert Ross, and one doubts whether Oscar would have wanted to kiss him.

The prison sequences, though brief, make their powerful point. I had no idea, for instance, that inmates exercising in the prison yard had to wear hideous masks, and the treadmill scenes are good and scary. Martin Fuhrer, new to me, delivers sensitive cinematography, and Debbie Wiseman's music makes its effects economically. The final title card quotes the famous epigram from Lady Windermere's Fan: "There are only two tragedies. One is not getting what one wants, and the other is getting it." Wilde, poor fellow, had his share of both. Even so, a film detailing his pathetic decline has yet to be made. Or would that be too shattering to bear?

That splendid Italian director Francesco Rosi has not had a film here for some time. Now we get his 1996 *The Truce*, based on Primo Levi's 1963 memoir, *The Reawakening*. It tells what happened to Levi between the Russians' liberation of the sick and crippled at Auschwitz (the healthy had been marched off to their deaths by the Nazis) in January 1945, and his arrival home in Turin nine months later. The young Jewish chemist and anti-Fascist activist had been captured by the Germans and sent to Auschwitz, which he had the luck to survive. There followed a tragicomic odyssey.

Levi's experiences have their share of horror, but are mostly grotesque. There are the three months in Katowice where Levi works for the Russians as a hospital orderly. Then it is staggering marches and crazy detours by whatever trains were available up and down Russia, Belarus, and Ukraine. Levi, who was to become a famous writer and successful businessman, never recovered from his past. In 1987, soon after hearing that *The Truce* was beginning to shoot, he committed suicide.

Perhaps the most colorful character Primo meets is a Greek, a cynical, sardonic opportunist who makes him carry his heavy bag, but also imparts lessons in survival. As they separate, the Greek gives Primo a pair of sturdy shoes, without which one cannot even forage for food. When they meet up again, the Greek is blithely running an itinerant brothel and offers Primo a girl at a much-reduced rate.

A Russian victory celebration is transformed by a recording of "Cheek to Cheek," to which a uniformed soldier does a clumsy Astaire imitation as a crowd of miserable deportees watches transfigured, their sexual longings reawakened. Another time, Primo and a starving band of his fellow Italians come across a farmer who is ready to shoot them. But when Primo does a comic impersonation of a chicken, he gets the amused farmer to give one to the gang. Still later, Primo comes across a young woman he saw the Nazis abuse at Auschwitz, and tentative, groping, bittersweet lovemaking ensues.

The film, written chiefly by Rosi and that old hand Tonino Guerra, is episodic and shapeless, but how else to convey desperate errings by foot and rail through a topsy-turvy Eastern Europe? John Turturro, who usually plays weirdos and maniacs, portrays Levi as introverted, bespectacled, soft-spoken, and shy. It is a good performance, though not quite a great one, somewhat overshadowed by that of the Serbian actor Rade Šerbedžia as the Greek.

The location photography, mostly in the Ukraine, and mostly by another fine old Italian hand, Pasqualino De Santis, is both vivid and stark: the present in color, the death-camp memories black-and-white. There are sentimental moments, but they are relatively few. And there are two tremendous lines. One is Primo's answer when told the war is over: "War is always." The other is Primo's observation, "God cannot exist if Auschwitz exists." Worth pondering, that.

Rappers and Whisperers

BULWORTH; THE HORSE WHISPERER

Two great stars, two heartthrobs, are coming out simultaneously with what may be their most ambitious projects: Warren Beatty with *Bulworth* and Robert Redford with *The Horse Whisperer*. Neither movie strikes me as very good, but the latter is at least inoffensive.

The parallels are noteworthy. At 61, both men are entering the last decade in which one can normally be a heartthrob. Both men are trying to convey ideas with their movies, to make more than entertainment—perhaps even art. And both have profiles running concurrently in important publications: Beatty in the *New York Times Magazine*, Redford in the *New Yorker*. One is dark and still boyish, the other blond and still boyish.

Bulworth is the story of a California senator seeking re-election. (Redford made such a movie years ago, *The Candidate*, and a good one it was.) Senator Jay Billington Bulworth starts out being a Clintonian middle-of-the-roader mouthing uplifting platitudes: we see him, alone, watching his campaign ad on the small screen, then burying his head in his hands. As well he might, hearing himself uttering over and over stuff like "We stand at the doorstep of a new millennium," as if that doorstep were covered with glue, and breaking loose a sticky business.

As the pictures on his wall indicate, Senator Bulworth was a liberal during the sixties, hanging out with the likes of Bobby Kennedy and Warren Beatty. Well he has now turned conservative, and has inveighed against welfare cheaters and such, but he is still not satisfied. He makes a deal with an insurance industry sleazeball: in exchange for foiling some anti-insurance-company legislation, he gets a juicy ten-mil life insurance policy payable to his daughter. Then, with a loathsome hit man, he takes out a contract on someone whose snapshots are in a manila envelope: himself. He is to be terminated when he gets back from Los Angeles (hit men seem to reside only in New York) for the final stage of his campaign.

Back in California, Bulworth buzzes around with his aides—one fat and slimy, one small and nerdy—and, figuring he has nothing more to lose, starts speaking out. In a black church, he makes caustic remarks about blacks. Before an audience of movie moguls, he makes fairly strong anti-capitalist and anti-Semitic remarks. And herewith the movie is in serious trouble: the big media can take only so much political incorrectness, and promptly Bulworth must backtrack. The Jewish capitalists are dropped as a theme, and we concentrate on the black question. "The real issue," Beatty is quoted as saying in the *Times Magazine* article, "is the disparity of wealth in this country. And that gets unattended and unacknowledged."

So how does he attend to and acknowledge it? By making Bulworth turn pro-black, mingling with, understanding, and espousing a supposedly prototypical black family: that of Nina, a beautiful young woman he has spotted in his audience, and whom he takes into his limousine along with two other young black women—rappers, whose routines he picks up.

But back to Nina. As played by Halle Berry, this black has gorgeous, perfectly Caucasian features and a barely milk-chocolate skin; she could be a Park Avenue debutante who just sunned herself a bit too intensely at Boca Raton. Even her speech is high-toned enough for a Smith College valedictorian, and when she is about to go into a clinch with Bulworth in the back seat of his limo, she launches instead on an oration—a lengthy, political one of the kind that even a Smith valedictorian couldn't deliver without a typescript or, better yet, a teleprompter. All the characters tend to speechify instead of speaking, but this is the most incredible example of it. Anyone in his right mind would shut her up with a kiss or throw her out of the car. Bulworth listens enraptured.

Of course, Nina turns out to be the lure who is supposed to coax Bulworth to the site of his doom, which someone else will execute. But the situation changes, and now Nina must be both seductress and executioner. She rebels, or does she? Then she falls for Bulworth, and then . . . suffice it to say that this is part screwball comedy, part Strangelovian absurdist satire, and part impassioned radical statement, a hard cocktail to mix or drink.

Despite the black family's being represented as both charming and sinister, the charming wins out. Before you know it, Bulworth, who has already been talking in jingles, starts dressing like the blackest of black rappers and so shows up in the TV studio to debate his political opponent, a WASP suit if ever there was one. To the interviewer's horror, Bulworth delivers his pro-poor-black and anti-fatcat-white message in perfect rap. 'Nuff said.

Like Beatty, Redford has also been directing, although, unlike him, not writing scripts. Whereas Beatty has played men of action on both sides of the law, he is thought of primarily as a lover boy; Redford, though he has always been a screen lover, is more often viewed as the man of action on either side of the law. For the novel *The Horse Whisperer*, Nicholas Evans, its British author, was paid hefty sums by both his publishers and Fox (for the movie rights) before the book was more than half written. And Redford just had to play Tom Booker, the Montana cattle rancher and famous horse doctor—or rather, horse psychotherapist—whom Annie MacLean, an Eastern magazine editor, seeks out after her 13-year-old daughter, Grace, in a freak riding accident, loses her best friend, her best friend's horse, her right leg, and, probably, her own horse, Pilgrim, badly scarred physically and mentally. Grace herself has turned morose, and thinks both she and her horse should have been put down.

Although Annie's brashness made Booker at first disinclined to take on Pilgrim, moved by mother and daughter's long trek to Montana with the horse (somewhat improbable, that journey), and the girl's artificial leg, he agrees. The treatment proves lengthy, and the MacLeans are invited to move into an unused cottage by the Bookers, who include Tom's brother, Frank, Frank's wife, Diane (Dianne Wiest, now of barrel size, and an unlikely Westerner), their children, the occasionally visiting mother of Tom and Frank, and an unexplained white-haired old man. The movie was at various times four and three hours long, and is now well over two and a half, with an often rocky continuity. Its first screenwriter was Eric Roth, of *Forrest Gump* fame, who put in a lot of time, only to be superseded by Richard LaGravenese, best known for the even worse *Fisher King*.

The movie is vague about time. Montana restores Grace's spiritual health, and Annie doesn't even mind too much being fired because of her long absence. Back East, Robert, Annie's lawyer husband (Sam Neill), waits patiently, even though an attraction between Annie and Tom is evolving. Tom, who has never loved since his cellist wife died, is so in love with Annie, he doesn't even want to listen to the Dvořák Cello Concerto any more. Perhaps Thomas Newton's lush score is enough for him.

The film is, first, about the Montana sky and landscape, which Robert Richardson shoots often and grandly enough for fifty Marlboro commercials. Next, about horses, especially Pilgrim, enacted by six horses good enough to start equine Equity. Lastly about people, who, unlike Beatty's, talk very little. Many a question elicits only a long silence, whether pregnant or not would require a rabbit test to determine.

Typically, the screenplay had for Tom and Annie a one-copulation, two-copulation, three-copulation and mountain-top copulation draft, but finally a no-copulation version was filmed. Robert comes to claim his wife and the by now cured Grace and Pilgrim. I won't tell you the outcome, and you will have to guess which man Annie (the excellent Kristin Scott Thomas) chooses. Hint: people refer to the movie as *The Horses of Madison County*.

Idle Idyll

THE TRUMAN SHOW; THE OPPOSITE OF SEX

The idea behind *The Truman Show* sounds ingenious. A baby, Truman Burbank, is born in a special enclave—a giant television studio somewhere in California—and grows up inside TV without realizing it. He thinks he is in the real world, but is actually surrounded by actors in the made-for-TV coastal town of Seahaven, which comes complete with pristinely Norman Rockwell houses, fake sun and moon, and a sizable bit of ocean. Everything in Truman's life is fictitious: his job as an insurance salesman, his cheery neighbors, his rough-hewn best friend, and his pretty wife, Meryl, a dedicated nurse.

The whole thing is the idea of a combination TV producer and mad scientist, Christof, who, from the control room, devises the day's events: when, for example, Truman is to be caught in the rain (a rain that, at first, maladroitly concentrates on him alone), or when his father is to drown in a sailing accident, though not when he is to fall in love with a young woman, Lauren, who wants to clue him in on the truth. Christof has her denounced as psychotic and whisked away; it is given out that she has moved to Fiji.

The idea is to supply American and world TV viewers with an ideal small town, an ideal bunch of down-home folks, an ideal marriage, and the perfect Everyman hero. As we are frequently shown, people the world over watch raptly this idyllic microcosm, this earthly (or unearthly) paradise, with Christof improvising peripeteias to make Truman's life more interesting, but never too disturbing. Right now Truman's chief hope is to get to Fiji, attempts to reach Lauren by phone having, of course, failed. At the travel agency, Truman is told he must book a month in advance, which seems to stump him. Also, pictures on the agency walls show aerial disasters to discourage Truman from flying; I wonder what they use to discourage him from thinking.

For it would take an idiot to be taken in by all this, and if Truman is an idiot, why should we care? But the actors involved in this hoax must be idiots too, to give up their real lives and participate full-time in this imposture. And how much money would it cost to stage such a gigantic charade? (To be sure, commercials are sneaked into the show.) And why would an attractive young actress become Meryl and be actually married to this dunce of a Truman?

The one believable thing about *The Truman Show* is Jim Carrey. If ever there was a Plasticman whose life could be pumped into him from the outside, he is it. In fact, he does not so much play Truman as be him, which in any other role might be an asset, but here comes across as stultifying.

Obviously, Andrew Niccol, who wrote the thing, and Peter Weir, who directed it, had something bigger in mind. Seahaven has to be at the very least America, with some kind of evil power pulling the strings—the media, big business, government, or even (gulp) God. As played by Ed Harris in a beret and rather monastic-looking suit, Christof is a quietly sinister despot with a pained expression of blue-eyed disbelief when things don't quite go his way, rare as that is. But what should please him particularly is that this harebrained movie he is in threatens to become a huge success.

Laura Linney is getting typecast as the smart, sleek blonde who is a real operator underneath, but would even such a one want to be bedmate to Jim Carrey? Natascha McElhone is appealing as Lauren, and Holland Taylor contributes her usual cool savvy to Truman's mother. Dennis Gassner's production design looks appropriately phony, and Peter Biziou's cinematography is suitably high-gloss, though why we need constant reminders from a kind of framing effect that we are looking at Truman through a hidden camera lens, or, as we learn, five thousand of them, I cannot say.

The score is fancy indeed: Mozart, Chopin, Brahms, Philip Glass, as well as some lesser lights (if anything can be lesser than Glass), plus some original music by Burkhard Dallwitz, who does rather better than some of the dull wits involved in the film. Is there anything more pitiful than a good idea fallen into the wrong hands?

A small film of considerable mischievous charm is *The Opposite of Sex*, written and directed by Don Roos. His screenplays, from *Love Field*, through *Single White Female*, to *Boys on the Side*, have been getting better all the time, and it's a sad comment on Hollywood that, in twenty years there, Roos has had only four of them produced.

This is the first time he has also directed, and the result augurs well. *The Opposite of Sex* concerns Dedee, a rebellious 16-year-old who runs away from a dismal life with mother and stepfather in a Louisiana backwater and seeks out, unannounced, her half-brother, Bill, a high-school English teacher in South Bend, Indiana. She doesn't know that Bill is homosexual, that he was deeply in love with Tom, who died of AIDS, but is now living with a new lover, Matt. Staying in their tastefully appointed house is Lucia, Tom's spinsterish sister, whose immediate dislike for Dedee is not hard to fathom.

Dedee has unusual taste in boyfriends. In Louisiana, Randy, who lived up to his name, had only one testicle. In South Bend she vamps Matt and, before long, is between the sheets with her gentle brother's lover. Bill is such a sweetheart that when he discovers a rude graffito about himself in the school lavatory, instead of administering correction to the scribe, he merely corrects the grammar on the wall. No wonder he also lovingly preserves Tom's ashes in an urn.

Matt, however, has impregnated Dedee and, relishing impending fatherhood, decides to elope with her. They steal Bill's savings and—to be used as a deterrent if necessary—Tom's ashes. Meanwhile Jason, an earlier lover of Bill's, unjustly accuses Bill of sexual harassment, causing trouble for him at his school. So Bill and Lucia set out in search of the runaways, who can disprove Jason's charges. Following them, in turn, is Carl Tippett, the local sheriff and a friend eager to help, who ends up falling for Lucia.

It gets even more complicated than that, but it works—partly because it is all narrated by Dedee with lusciously irreverent bitchiness; partly because the dialogue is, almost too relentlessly, witty; and partly because the young cast, under Roos's deft direction, perform like seasoned troupers. Moreover, the film's varied and far-flung locales were recreated in Southern California with stunning success.

What spices things up is political incorrectness. "He was one of those ACT UP people who think AIDS is a big conspiracy against homos. If it is, it isn't working. There are more of them than ever." Dedee, of course, is speaking. Again: "He made his bed, he can lie in it. If there's room." Or: "This is America, and we are Christians here. Except for a few Jewish people who were born that way." Why, there is even a joke that comes as close as legally possible to impugning Tom Cruise's heterosexuality.

The witticisms, though not all gems, come thick and fast enough to create a devil-may-care aura around the characters, and an atmosphere gayer (in the old sense) than the sum of its parts. Christina Ricci, much better here than in the atrocious *Fear and Loathing in Las Vegas*, makes Dedee's amorality into an inverted innocence, a precocious pseudosophistication that helped her through a rotten childhood and is ultimately rather touching. Martin Donovan is a nicely laid-back Bill, and Lisa Kudrow a surprisingly likable Lucia. Good work, too, from Johnny Galecki, Ivan Sergei, and William Scott Lee; only Lyle Lovett, as Carl, is hopeless. What makes a gifted movie director, or a lovely woman like Julia Roberts, fall for this homely and untalented man?

Un Air de famille (Family Resemblances)

Human beings take stage center in Cédric Klapisch's *Un Air de famille (Family Resemblances)*, a film based on a play by Agnès Jaoui and Jean-Pierre Bacri, who live together, write together, and often act together. They have written four highly successful films, and this is also Klapisch's fourth feature; I have reviewed his *When the Cat's Away* here. This one is even better, though it seemed more to my European taste than to my wife's American one.

Almost all of it takes place inside a café, Au Père Tranquille, which the subtitles render, perhaps too freely, as Sleepy Dad's. What goes on there this Friday evening is neither tranquil nor somnolent: a family reunion for a few drinks to be followed by dinner at a fancy restaurant. There is Henri, the café owner, unhappily married to Arlette, who phones to say she has moved in with a girlfriend, to meditate on whether or not to leave him. There is his sister, Betty, thirty and unmarried, an outspoken creature who has just given her boss what for and may lose her job. She enjoys drinking, and is sort of girlfriend to Denis, Henri's factotum, a bookish fellow much reproached for reading on the job.

The third sibling is Philippe, Maman's favorite and Number 4 at a big computer concern. He has just had his two minutes on a TV show and is preoccupied with how he performed, including whether he wore the wrong tie or smiled too much. He is polling everyone, either buttonholing or phoning them. Maman thinks he was sublime, as does, less convincingly, his mousy, dominated wife, Yoyo, whose birthday this is. She celebrates it with a couple of Suzes too many, eliciting more veritas than some family members can stand. Maman, by the way, left Papa long ago, which still occasions random sour remarks from her children.

These six manage to keep the joint jumping, mostly comically but with a persistent edge of misery. Even Caruso, Henri's dog, paralyzed with age and no longer singing (in his fashion), contributes his share, just lying there, "like a rug, only alive." Mother falls down the stairs to the bathroom; Henri steps outside to listen to the trains whooshing and whistling by; Philippe calls Number 5 at his firm and gets a devastating review. Denis becomes painfully jealous of Betty, who defiantly defends to Maman her single status. Henri drives off to retrieve Arlette, but is rebuffed. Yoyo mildly asserts herself. That is about it.

Yet almost every familial and extrafamilial relationship is put to the funny-sad test. Thus Yoyo gets wholly undesired birthday presents: a puppy that, she has good reason to believe, will end up like Caruso; a leash for this unwanted pup; a jewel-studded choker for herself, which she dejectedly mistakes for a dog collar. As shot in mostly subdued light by Bernard Delhomme, and racily directed by Klapisch, 107 minutes go by with a perfect blend of hilarity and agony. The co-writers play Betty and Henri, and are surrounded by no less apt others, including Claire Maurier, who, as Maman, brings back memories of herself as the young mother in *The 400 Blows*. Indeed, the spirit of Truffaut seems to watch over this movie infused with his antic sensibility.

Saving Private Ryan

Steven Spielberg is a director whose chief aim is to make movies to which terms such as most, biggest, or ultimate can be applied. He may labor under the delusion that they are synonyms for best. Having made, as he thinks, the ultimate extraterrestrial, dinosaur, Holocaust, and slavery movies, he has now applied himself to the ultimate World War II movie, *Saving Private Ryan*, for whose financing two film companies joined hands and pocketbooks. Such bedfellowship has precedent only in *Titanic*, with which *SPR* has more than one fateful aspect in common, starting with an overweening director.

SPR divides neatly into three acts. Act One: the allied invasion of Normandy, which Spielberg restages in full gory detail, with severed limbs flying, bloody bowels spilling, heads rolling in the mud, fright and heroism everywhere. The strategic planning, effort, and cost of this 26-minute re-enactment of D-Day seem not far behind those of the real thing. But we concentrate on Captain Miller and his squad ingeniously and intrepidly taking out a German pillbox from which machine-gun havoc was being wreaked on the landing forces.

Act Two: General George C. Marshall, informed that the Ryan farm family of Iowa has lost three sons, decrees that the last putatively surviving one, Private James Ryan, who parachuted somewhere behind enemy lines, be retrieved and sent home. The task of finding and bringing him back falls to Captain Miller and a few of his men. It may just be that, of all armies, the American would be sentimental enough for such a quixotic enterprise.

In this second act, the squad gets enmeshed in a sniper-terror-ized village with a French family whose small daughter one of the men tries preposterously to take along. They lose one man before a Bible-quoting Tennessee sharpshooter gets the sniper. There follow comic episodes in the search during which the men take bets on the captain's place of origin and civilian occupation. Miller playfully colludes with one of them as they wait for the jackpot to hit five hundred dollars. A skirmish with a German outpost has grotesque overtones; in a symphony, this would be the ominous scherzo.

Act Three: Ryan is discovered in a suitably offhanded way in a ruined village, and—surprise, surprise!—refuses to be rescued. The squad joins Ryan's platoon in defending a last remaining bridge against a German tank unit. Its sinister approaching rumble as the GIS hastily set up an ambush is the film's most powerful, because understated, sequence. The ensuing fight is even more elaborately staged than the Omaha Beach opening, as Spielberg not only plants his camera in the thick of things, but also races around with it to various margins for unusual views and angles. Technical mastery has a field day, but to what purpose? The tearful conclusion is not quite the end. An epilogue, connecting with the prologue, makes clear that what we saw was someone's memories—but a someone who wasn't there for most of it!

Authenticity, which Spielberg pursues relentlessly for 168 ex-hausting minutes, is a double-edged sword. It must not, except in a documentary, be an end in itself. It has to be transcended, in this case by making Miller and his men absorbing and memorable hu-man beings. Spielberg and his scenarist, Robert Rodat, pride them-selves on avoiding stereotypes; to the extent they do, it is only by providing ciphers. As you watch, they blur into one another; as you leave, you remember none of them—well, maybe the captain. As for the dialogue, the fraction that makes it through the shouting and the din does not prove particularly fresh or involving.

The actors were given ten days of rigorous boot camp under an ex-Marine captain. All uniforms, gear, and armament were re-created with scrupulous accuracy. Sea-incarnadining underwater deaths and brain-scattering ones on land are recorded in harrowing detail. An artificial river was dug. A village in ruins was built with painstaking realism. Dead fish and discarded Bibles were faithfully floated on Omaha Beach. The fine color cinematography of Janusz Kaminski was bleached out for documentary-style naturalism. But what does it get you, beyond cheap—or expensive—thrills? A history lesson?

Alas, those who know what war really is need no such reminders. And those who see it as a glorious macho adventure in which only others perish will merely be reinforced in their delusion. *Saving Private Ryan* isn't even that original: Bernhard Wicki's *The Last Bridge*, Kubrick's *Full Metal Jacket*, Oliver Stone's *Platoon*, among others, anticipated much of it, in some instances better. Only as a catalogue of horrors does *SPR* outdo the rest.

As Miller, Tom Hanks treats us to somewhat fewer of the habitual lovable Hanksisms; as a Brooklyn smartass and a couple of (in the current solecism) minorities, Edward Burns, Adam Goldberg, and Vin Diesel are—sob!—stereotypes. As an interpreter and obligatory ineffectual intellectual, Jeremy Davies enjoys many absurd escapes and a less absurd heroic redemption. Only Matt Damon, as Ryan, manages something a bit different. For the most part though, *Saving Private Ryan* is an exercise in gratuitousness.

Thieves of Hearts

THE THIEF; LOLITA

One of the better films out of the new Russia is Pavel Chukhraj's *The Thief*. It has a Chekhovian atmosphere verging on Gorkian as it unblinkingly surveys conditions at the close of the Stalin era. Katya, a young war widow, and her six-year-old son, Sanya, are aimlessly riding a train in search of security. A dashing young officer, Tolyan, enters their compartment and promptly takes control of their lives.

Sanya, who fantasizes about the father he never knew, resents this stranger who whisks his mother off to the dining car, but is thrilled to be left in charge of his handgun. Wasting no time, Tolyan has rough intercourse with Katya on the platform between cars. The smitten Katya, who sees in Tolyan her future husband, quickly overcomes her initial resistance. Sanya, looking for her, unsettlingly experiences the primal scene.

Tolyan is firmly in command. Getting off in a small town, the threesome passes for a fine young family hopefully headed for a better tomorrow. Katya is bursting with love, and even the ambivalent Sanya is impressed. In the communal flat where the "family" finds lodgings, Tolyan orders the boy to call him father. The kid refuses but otherwise acquiesces, save when again confronted with Tolyan and Katya's lovemaking. Put outside the door like a cat, he leaves the faucet on and starts a flood.

Tolyan, though, finds solutions for everything, as, for instance, teaching Sanya self-defense against a bunch of harassing boys, and personally wreaking exemplary vengeance on the chief tormentor. So Tolyan becomes a hard but efficacious paterfamilias, even if Sanya still has visions of his real father lovingly moving toward him.

Things progress nicely, and Tolyan, at a droll communal meal, invites the motley crew of oddball neighbors to be his guests at the circus. But Katya's rude awakening comes when Tolyan has the "family" leave the circus on a pretext, and wraps up all the apartment's silver and other valuables to make off with. Heartsick, Katya realizes that her handsome captain is a thief.

Her protests that she doesn't want her son to grow up a criminal are overridden as the "family" goes from domicile to domicile in different towns plying similar mischief. The unhappy but loving woman seeks comfort in the bottle and becomes addicted. Sanya, conversely, sees it all as a huge adventure, and warms to Tolyan as he learns how to steal. But this life can come to no good end; neither, as released, does the film.

When *The Thief* was submitted for last year's foreign Oscar, it was 10 or 15 minutes longer, which explains why, around the 75th minute, the continuity becomes jagged, with big jumps in time and place, and situations become puzzling if not inexplicable. There is a hugger-mugger to get to the conclusion, shaky though it be.

Originally, the movie took Sanya to his 48th year. But the writer-director himself, it seems, recut it to a mere 90 minutes for America, although the full version would still have been rather short by current standards. As summarized for me by those who saw it, the uncut version makes much better sense.

Still, Pavel Chukhraj, the son of the famous director Grigori Chukhraj (*Ballad of a Soldier*), has come up with an admirable movie most of the way. There is fine cinematography and background music, and a strong supporting cast. The portrayal is unsentimental, even when a crippled little girl falls in love with Sanya; there are arresting but unforced narrative and psychological twists, and an earthy sense of humor. Vladimir Mashkov is a compelling yet unglamorized Tolvan, and even the cuteness of the child actor Misha Filipchuk as Sanya is mitigated by wry realism. Nothing short of sensational, though, is the Katya of Ekaterina Rednikova, lovely in face, body, voice, and demeanor, and immensely moving in her performance. Best of all is that *The Thief* unemphatically glimpses the extraordinary in little things, and unattitudinizingly accepts the inevitability of the extraordinary. Despite alien circumstances, you get to see real people; you know them, and care about them.

The second movie version of *Lolita*, directed by Adrian Lyne, had the nowadays rare distinction of being rejected by every distributor. But only temporarily. There have been special screenings, a brief run in L.A., and airings on Showtime, which will release the film next month. The subject of Vladimir Nabokov's famous novel is pedophilia, of which our society is more frightened than of anything else. Even so, a serious film from a major work of fiction should not be banned.

Clearly the big problem here is how to deal with the sexual relations of the middle-aged professor Humbert Humbert and his 12-year-old beloved. In 1962, Stanley Kubrick cast a 15-year-old, and showed us no real sex. Lyne's Lolita was also 15, and there is one quick, fuzzy bedroom scene in which you can make out virtually nothing, and where a presumably older body double stands, or reclines, in for Dominique Swain, then a sophomore at Malibu High. Not much for the prurient here.

But, obviously, Lyne had to have sensuality. Since about the only flesh he could safely show was the girl's legs and feet, the almost always barefoot Lolita, using her feet as suggestively as possible, would be a foot fetishist's dream, except that her feet aren't particularly pretty. Otherwise, Miss Swain is fetching at moments, less so at others, and, except for somewhat overdone brattiness, handles herself well. However, she is not a true nymphet, Nabokov's famed term for a baby seductress. The ideal Lolita would have been poor little JonBenet Ramsey, had she been a bit older and not been killed.

As Lolita's mother, the man-and-culture-hungry Charlotte Haze, Melanie Griffith would be fine if she could erase Kubrick's Shelley Winters from memory. The deliberately scarcely seen (until the end) Clare Quilty, who steals Lolita from Humbert is well acted by Frank Langella, a specialist in cool loathsomeness.

The big mistake was casting Jeremy Irons as Humbert. Irons

has become progressively more decomposed with every appearance, and is now suited only for a literal-minded interpretation of Tolstoy's *The Living Corpse*. In films such as *Stealing Beauty* and *Chinese Box*, he refined cadaverousness into a high, or at least vertical, art, and by now his head looks like a moldy, greying aubergine, with plasticine features stuck on and a quavery British accent piped in. His every performance lays, if not an egg, an eggplant. Humbert is a tragicomic figure, with James Mason, for Kubrick, getting both the tragic and the comic dead right; Irons gets only the lugubrious and the ludicrous.

Stephen Schiff's screenplay is a decent simplification of Nabokov's baroque excesses, which barely stand up on the page and could not even be approximated on the screen. Lyne and Schiff had the sense to preserve much of the satire on America's road-and-motel culture which may be the novel's best part. The old master, Ennio Morricone, has composed some nice music, though less good than what he could muster as a young master. Howard Atherton's cinematography neatly captures both the strident and the soothing about the American landscape, and minor roles are effectively taken.

But Lyne's direction predictably fails in what could have been the subtler moments, and laughably overdoes the hospital scene in which Humbert discovers Lolita's abduction. Only the grotesque murder of Quilty entirely suits his souped-up style. Finally, though, the novel itself, its sensationalism faded, proves overwritten, pretentious, show-offy, and self-indulgent. For the problems of Nabokov the man, check out "Vlad the Impaler" in *New York* (August 3, 1998), where John Leonard raises all the right questions.

Your Friends & Neighbors

The writer-director Neil LaBute, whose *In the Company of Men* was admired by many and despised by me, has come up with his second effort, *Your Friends & Neighbors*. The former, which won awards at Sundance (always a bad sign) and from the New York Film Critics Circle, concerned a compact between two men to avenge themselves on women by seducing and destroying a sweet, blind office worker. It was the kind of movie only a fundamentally unpleasant person could have concocted; it shed no light and plumbed, except in quality, no depth.

Your Friends & Neighbors, which does not have the home-movie look of its predecessor, is otherwise an equally nasty piece of work, to whose cheapness even the characters rhyming names attest. Barry, Cary, and Jerry are best friends. Barry is married to Mary, Jerry is living with Terri; Cary screws, or tries to, everything in skirts. They live in an anonymous city, have (except for Jerry, a drama prof, and Cary, a gynecologist) unspecified jobs, and exist only as pawns for LaBute's mean-spirited games.

There is also a young woman, Cheri, some sort of art-gallery assistant. At one time or another, all the other characters come and stare at a photograph, not shown to us, in the gallery. Accosted by Cheri, they each conduct the identical dialogue with her, often pointing toward seduction. But an affair develops only with Terri. Why?

Because Jerry talks a lot during sex, which infuriates Terri. An excellent reason for her to turn lesbian, you'll agree. What further encourages her in that direction is the discovery that Jerry and Mary had a go at it—unsuccessfully, but she doesn't know that Barry is more or less impotent, and Jerry had scribbled a sexual overture to Mary in a lent volume of Camus, which Mary couldn't resist and Terri later stumbled onto. Mary breaks with both Jerry and Barry, and gets involved with Cary, a brute whose advances only Cheri, a lesbian, can withstand.

But Cheri is having problems with Terri because Cheri, also, talks too much, wanting to know which part of her lovemaking Terri enjoys most, something Terri doesn't wish to go into, especially not in the supermarket aisle where their heated altercation takes place. Other painful scenes erupt in a hotel room successively occupied by Jerry with Mary, and Mary with Barry—don't ask me to explain. Just about everyone beds everyone else, but always with dismal results, attesting to LaBute's high moral purpose.

As if this weren't enough, nearly everyone speaks in incomplete sentences, particularly Jerry, the professor, who is to blithering what Michael Jordan is to basketball. Terri is more coherent but almost always unpleasant, and Cary speaks only about sex, loathsomely. The sexual roundelay may derive—remotely—from Arthur Schnitzler's *Reigen*, but LaBute's drivel is light years away from Schnitzler's genius.

The one sympathetic character is Mary—not in the writing, but in the acting of the enormously charming, lovely, and gifted Amy Brenneman, whose infrequent casting can be chalked up to the indifference of the current cinema to so appealingly wholesome an actress. At the opposite extreme is the Terri of Catherine Keener: unprepossessing way beyond even the call of her role. Jason Patric, looking like a younger, macho Joel Grey, carries Cary to heights of obnoxiousness you wouldn't think scalable without crampons. Aaron Eckhart, the vile seducer of LaBute's previous film, is now the overweight and inept Barry, and at least proves he has some acting range. As Cheri, the formerly sexy Nastassja Kinski looks so unlike her old self that I did not even recognize her.

The nadir, however, is the Jerry of Ben Stiller. Stiller, whose physical repellence is matched only by his histrionic nullity, is in movies because he is the son of the well-known comedy couple Stiller and Meara. For all-around distastefulness he is equaled only by Nicolas Cage, in movies because he is the nephew of Francis Ford Coppola. (You can see Cage now in Brian De Palma's nonsensical and appalling *Snake Eyes*, with which I shall not detain you.)

Your Friends & Neighbors has vivid cinematography by Nancy Schreiber; it is not her fault that this always indoor film has a deliberately claustrophobic feel, and that sequences in an antiquarian bookshop are annoyingly souped up (Steadicam in excelsis), even as the ones in the art gallery are artily static. The score is mostly songs by Metallica, performed by Apocalyptica, and sounding like Emetica. For prestige, a bit of Schubert and Dvořák chamber music is thrown in, but in versions by Killer Tracks which their composers would be hard put to recognize.

Regeneration

Regeneration, which disappeared at record speed from our screens, is a beautiful and potent film you are, alas, unlikely to see. A Scottish-Canadian coproduction, it deals with the poet Siegfried Sassoon, who, after winning the Military Cross for bravery as a lieutenant in World War I, concluded in 1916 that this war was immoral, and bravely spoke out against it. He hoped to publicize his cause by a court martial, but his fellow poet and officer Robert Graves convinced him that would be counterproductive. So he let himself be declared mad and sent to Craiglockhart Castle in Scotland, a military hospital for the shell-shocked.

Here Sassoon comes under the care of Dr. William Rivers, one

of Britain's first Freudians, whose job it was to return his patients to
the war, an ambiguous cure that caused him considerable anxiety.
Now he was confronted with an even stranger situation: having to
treat someone entirely sane. What makes it all the more absorbing
is that Sassoon was neither a pacifist nor a coward, and that the film
is far from a simple antiwar screed. The therapy sessions become
a contest between two highly intelligent men in a paradox-laden
agony.

Rivers is also treating a young working-class officer, Bill Prior (a
fictional figure), whom shell shock has propelled into mutism. And
also the poet Wilfred Owen, whom Sassoon befriends at Craiglockhart and guides into writing his great poems about the war, which
Owen has previously avoided as a topic. The interplay of these three
men and Rivers is as intellectually stimulating as it is emotionally
involving.

There are further subplots. Rivers, on leave in London, studies
the methods of Dr. Yealland, who treats shell shock with electro-
shock, with much faster results but frightening means. And there
is a discreet but affecting love affair between Billy and a local girl
that elicits therapeutic benefits. And there are those scenes with the
medical boards where drama and irony wryly intertwine. The film
is based on a historical novel by Pat Barker, a woman who deals
with this seemingly masculine subject superlatively.

Gillies Mackinnon has directed with sensitivity and elegance,
mostly in stunning reconstruction of the thirteenth-century
Craiglockhart Castle. There are lovely scenes on its grounds em-
phasizing the patients' plight by contrast, and there are burnished-
looking indoor scenes moodily shot by Glen Macpherson. Allan
Scott's fine screenplay gives us terrific trench-warfare footage (not
in the novel) and scenes of as yet primitive shock therapy—with
John Neville a smilingly demonic Dr. Yealland—terrifying without
any exploitativeness. There is also a great deal of subtle wit, and only
a couple of sequences fail to ring true.

The acting is tremendous: understated, but without any of that
old-style-stiff-upper-lip hokum. As Rivers, Jonathan Pryce confirms his status as one Britain's supreme character actors, turning
in a performance of such complexity and penetrance as would require a separate column to assess. But the rest are not far behind:
James Wilby's quietly forceful Sassoon, Jonny Lee Miller's smoldering Billy, Stuart Bunce's touching Owen, along with John Neville,
David Hayman, and a host of others. That *Regeneration* is critically

slighted and publicly ignored, while *Saving Private Ryan* reaps journalistic hosannas and box-office bonanzas, is as good a comment on our times as I can think of.

The Eel

For those who miss the old Ealing comedies, there is *The Eel*, the latest from Japan's distinguished and venerable director Shohei Imamura—perhaps the finest now that Kurosawa is gone. Based on a novel by Akira Yoshimura, the film tells of Takuro Yamashita, a lowly white-collar worker who, goaded by an anonymous letter, catches his wife in flagrante delicto. He kills her, gives himself up, and spends eight years in jail, where he learns the barber's trade and acquires a pet eel to have soulful, albeit somewhat one-sided, conversations with. Paroled in the care of a kindly Buddhist priest and his motherly wife, Takuro restores a dilapidated barbershop in a small seaside town and starts a new life.

He has glimpsed a young woman who strongly resembles his dead wife, and one day he stumbles across her in the bushes, close to death from an overdose of pills. He rescues her and grudgingly accepts her as a shop assistant. This Keiko proves invaluable: not only does she turn the shop into a thriving concern, she is also deeply concerned for Takuro's creature comforts. She lodges with the priest and his wife rather than return to Tokyo, where a crazy mother and brutal ex-lover cause her miseries that, however, will not fail to catch up with her. Takuro, in turn, is harassed by a fellow ex-convict who is now a garbage man, a drunken bully and hypocrite, who insists that Takuro wallow in remorse. Since the dignified but withdrawn barber refuses, the lout reveals his past to Keiko. But she, by now, is in love with her boss, however much he may have abjured women.

Takuro's best friends are a man with whom he goes eel-fishing at night, and who instructs him in eel lore, and a young fellow who is tirelessly preparing an ideal site for a UFO to land on, and for this purpose keeps borrowing Takuro's barber pole. The film is full of such idiosyncratic characters, quaint not because they are Japanese but because they are human. Even the eel has its human characteristics, being, as in Eugenio Montale's famous poem, "the torch, whiplash, arrow of love on earth."

A bizarre, anguiliform film, *The Eel* displays the twists and turns of its titular character—and all the others, caught in the throes of love and hate, fear and frustration, as they wriggle their way through the currents of life. There are developments that are touching or burlesque, exquisite or ferocious, but all unpredictable, always. Keiko does not readily find the path to Takuro's frozen heart, and many ludicrous or harrowing mishaps block the man's passage from imprisoning reclusiveness to the light of recognition. Thus when Keiko prepares meals for him on his fishing expeditions, he callously rejects them: they remind him of the ones his wife packed for him on similar occasions while she, profiting from his angling absences, disported herself with her lover.

The stages by which Takuro realizes that he cannot run from his feelings and is drawn to Keiko, and the explosive events that crack his carapace, are evoked with a delicately quizzical charm or raucous hilarity edged with menace. It is an iridescent world of beauty turning to terror, of rage yielding to appeasement. Thus even the horror of watching one's beloved spouse making unleashed love to another is captured with the fascination of something beautiful, and the subsequent *crime passionnel* features a frenzy that partakes of the amorous.

The acting is flawless. Koji Yakusho, so splendid in the great *Shall We Dance?* is equally fine as Takuro. He is as moving in comic bewilderment as in arduous self-control, as touching when he opens up to his eel as when he shuts himself off from Keiko. His is as slow thawing into humanity from the robotic prison existence, and Yakusho endows every stage of the transition with exemplary restraint, yet also intimations of harbored warmth.

No less remarkable is the Keiko of Misa Shimizu, who, starting out from even greater negativity than Takuro's, learns faster the redemptive power of giving. Without a trace of sentimentality, the actress daintily conveys the arc from defensiveness to commitment, while resolutely contending with the demonism of her ex-lover and the dementia of her mom. It is, like Yakusho's, acting so self-effacing that it ceases to be anything but living. And the supporting roles are worthily taken under Imamura's direction, so finely balanced between comedy and drama that neither is ever wholly lost from sight. What we get is always a little more intense than mere naturalism (Imamura collaborated on the script), but when it deviates from the literal, it is only to espouse the poetic.

American History X

American History X has itself a strange history. Terry Kaye, a 46-year-old British MTV and commercial filmmaker, directed and shot this as a five-hour film. He was still fiddling with it after a year in post-production, costing another million and a half. Thereupon New Line Cinema snatched it away from him and let the star, Edward Norton, recut it, allegedly in the director's presence, to two hours. Kaye threatened to have his name removed and organize protests wherever the film was shown, but made good on neither threat. Self-admittedly, he suffers from a Kubrick complex, though (unadmittedly) lacking Kubrick's talent.

The film's cut version does manage to hustle along without too noticeable a limp. Inevitably, however, some scenes feel foreshortened, others merely indicated by an opening shot. The hero's change from rabid skinhead to solid citizen after his prison experience is made less persuasive by a certain jerky episodicity. Even so, the film is not without power in its crucial sequences, greatly helped by fine performances. Further, Kaye and his screenwriter, David McKenna, have a good eye or two for the telling detail.

Derek Vinyard and his adoring younger brother, Danny, become even closer after their fireman father is shot to death by a black man while putting out a blaze in a crack house. Even before that, their father was inculcating racism and xenophobia in them. Oddly—if not incredibly—both Doris, the mother, and Davina, the studious sister, remain staunch liberals throughout, although Doris is driven to heavy smoking and a racking cough.

One night while the now full-fledged skinhead Derek (shaved sconce, mustache curling into a goatee, large swastika tattooed on chest, further mean tattoos on back and arms, Nazi paraphernalia all over the bedroom) is having violent-sex with his neo-Nazi girlfriend (played by the obnoxious Fairuza Balk), three blacks are breaking into his car. Alerted by Danny, Derek charges out in his briefs and shoots two of the men as the third escapes. Of the others, one is merely wounded, and Derek kills him in the most horrifying way. Danny is awestruck.

Derek winds up in jail, where he first joins other skinheads, but is put off by their drug-trafficking with Mexicans. On laundry duty, he is befriended by Lamont, a young black who teaches him to relax and protects him from the ire of other black inmates. The skinheads, angered, gang rape Derek in the shower with the (un-explained) collusion of a white guard.

Out of prison, Derek is a changed man. He wants to break with the past and move away with his family. His good angel continues to be Sweeney, the black high-school history teacher who once taught him, and now teaches and tries to straighten out Danny. His evil angel is Cameron Alexander, the white supremacist ideologue, who has organized the West Coast's white gangs into one big neo-Nazi movement. Derek and his family, caught in the middle of a racial war, are headed for tragedy—and the film's melodramatic finish.

How to judge a movie cut down from five to two hours? And would the five-hour version—any five-hour version—be that much better? Tony Kaye's camera work is good, though verging on arty, and shooting the past in monochrome and the present in full color is effective. But Anne Dudley's score, which even resurrects the cliché disembodied choir, is annoying, as is the ponderous preachiness of Sweeney as played by Avery Brooks. Many others are fine, notably Beverly D'Angelo (Doris), Guy Torry (Lamont), and especially Edward Furlong (Danny). But the reason to see *American History X* is Edward Norton. His sensitive, various, nuanced, and powerful performance is a history-making achievement.

Of Blood and a Poet

THE THIN RED LINE; SHAKESPEARE IN LOVE

Modern war movies, like Tolstoy's happy families, are all alike. Old wars are another story: Salamis, Thermopylae, Cannae, Lepanto—those battles were different. But from World War I on, a certain sameness sets in. We are introduced all too briefly to far too many characters who remain interchangeable, especially so in helmets and battle gear. Shouted commands are often unintelligible, strategies and tactics hard to follow. Lately, men have begun dying more graphically, more gorily. And sometimes we see women at war. Still, though it was not coined for cinematic warfare, the old saw applies: *plus ça change . . .*

Nevertheless, some war films make it by concentrating on special aspects: ski troops, a submarine, a military hospital. Terrence Malick's *The Thin Red Line*, from James Jones's eyewitness novel about Guadalcanal, is largely straight fighting, yet it does achieve some genuine distinction. Thus there is a lot of Jonesian philoso-phizing in interior monologues of various characters, sometimes in rapid succession. Though frequently sophomoric, they come, after all, largely from very young and not especially educated persons, although one of them manages a Homeric tag in the original Greek. It would be nice, however, if the same character, Sgt. Welsh (well played by Sean Penn), did not almost simultaneously declare that "a man alone is nothing" and "you've got to shut your eyes and look out for yourself."

The film was shot partly on Guadalcanal, where some of the natives participate, and mostly in Australia. To my untutored eye, it all looks seamless and persuasive. Of course, it helps that this action takes place in exotic sea- and landscapes, that soldiers move through man-high grasses where the wind soughs, and bodies elicit a thwacking sound as they push through the often dry blades. Alter-natively, men move through towering forests, into which the light penetrates in seemingly separate rays, as if through tiny skylights or cathedral windows.

John Toll's cinematography works many wonders. His camera is often one of the soldiers, swaying a little side to side as it trudges on, or lurches, rushes, jumps about during battle. It captures fre-quent and sudden changes in weather: seas of grass undulate green and gold, water shimmers silvery-black. Periodically, the camera sidesteps into an idyllic glimpse of some bird or beast: a crocodile easing itself into a bath, an upside-down sloth, or pendent cluster of bats. At times we get blocks of color: everything blue-green or exploding orange and red. At night, a single match may illumine no more than one eye and a bit of nose. Everything seems to be—or really is—shot in natural light. The lens takes refuge, as the soldier's gaze might, in an expanse of unbesmirched sky or lushly gilded sunset cloud banks, or is jolted by a blood-spattered blade of grass. At times we are blinded by mist; at others, dazzled by eerie clarity.

Malick directs in psychological time. Some terrible moments stretch on and on, others race desperately by. Often more goes on in one shot than a single viewing can encompass. Pvt. Bell, de-moted from officer, is haunted by memories of his wife: of the two them in intimate situations, or her alone on a beach or a swing. Miranda Otto has that cozily homey look: pretty but not glamor-ous. When Bell (Ben Chaplin) gets a pitiful Dear John letter from her in voiceover, he wanders off forlornly with that scrap of white paper dangling like a slipped bandage from a limp arm. When men advance into danger, there is a special choreography as, capering to the right and left, they try to forestall an ambushing enemy.

The point of view changes restlessly. Now we look out of a Japanese hilltop bunker from which havoc is wreaked. Now we are privy to a walkie-talkie argument between the ambitious Colonel Tall (Nick Nolte), who orders a suicidal frontal attack, and Captain Staros (Elias Koteas, surprisingly good in an atypically sympathetic role), who refuses to sacrifice his men. Gunfire may natter sporadically or burst into sudden bombardment like an uncheckable firestorm. We may see a bullet go through someone, or we may come across a dead soldier with both legs torn off at the hip. Or, again, mere intense acting will convey that Sgt. Keck (Woody Harrelson) has blown off his own lower half.

But the emphasis is less on engulfing horror than on individual anxiety and resolve, frenzy or terror. Pvt. Witt from Kentucky, the nominal hero, often stares bemusedly as his mind monologizes; Jim Caviezel, a newish actor, has such a thoughtful, confidence-inspiring air that we easily immerse ourselves in his roving bewilderment. And so many poignant details! An old Melanesian walking unconcernedly past an army column marching in the opposite direction. Dogs (coming from where?) chomping on something (dead soldiers?) as no one heeds them. A native village that provides fleeting asylum—mothers with tots, children playing games, a singing procession—but also natives sharply bickering and an ossuary full of skulls to signal death in Arcadia.

Most of the acting is solid, nicely backed up by a score made out of Fauré's *Requiem*, Arvo Pärt, and original music by Hans Zimmer. This will surely be the year of heated debates between partisans of *Line* and of that other 160-or-so-minute epic, *Saving Private Ryan*. My vote goes to the more chaste and cohesive *Thin Red Line*.

The screenplay of *Shakespeare in Love* is credited to Marc Norman and Tom Stoppard, though the idea came from Norman's son, and the writing from Stoppard. This is a fantasy, which would be fine, save that it flagrantly defies known facts instead of working around and in between them. Still, fun is to be had with the concept of a Lady Viola de Lesseps, who, out of love of poetry and acting, gets the part of Romeo under the assumed identity of one Thomas Kent, women not being allowed on the stage. Unaware that she is right under his nose, Will falls in love with the distant Lady Viola and circuitously works his way into her bed.

For her family's social-climbing reasons, however, the young woman is promised to the nasty and impecunious Lord Wessex in a loveless marriage; he, in this year of 1593, would whisk her off to his estate in Virginia. (Anachronism runs rampant.) Many well-known figures appear: Marlowe (Rupert Everett), the manager Philip Henslowe (the excellent Geoffrey Rush), Richard Burbage, Ned Alleyn (Ben Affleck, strange among the sons of Albion), a bloody-minded young lout called John Webster, and Queen Elizabeth, sovereignly played by Judi Dench.

There are amusing inventions: the moneylender Fennyman (a supremely droll Tom Wilkinson), the ignoble nobleman Wessex (a funny Colin Firth), a stuttering tailor who becomes fluent onstage (Mark Williams), Anthony Sher as an astrologer who uncannily resembles a modern-day therapist, and Jim Carter, Imelda Staunton, and Simon Callow in other merry roles. Even Gwyneth Paltrow, whom I have never before liked, is a creditable Viola cum Thomas; only Joseph Fiennes, as Shakespeare, is a wimpy, calf-eyed nonentity. John Madden has directed with bounce and brio, and the picturesque, authentic-looking backgrounds are nicely rendered by Richard Greatrex, who, with a name like that, might as well have been in front of the camera as behind it.

The problem for me is the relentless crosscutting from bedroom to stage, with identical or similar dialogue surfacing both in Will and Viola's dalliance and in the rehearsals of a play—first called, *Romeo and Ethel, the Pirate's Daughter*, which gradually evolves into you-know-what. The conceit of life imitating art and vice versa becomes a bit too mechanical; certain other parallels, or bits of leering revisionism, are likewise labored. But when a gag works, it's a corker. So Viola remarks to Will, mourning Marlowe, that she never before heard him as admiring of his rival. Comes the reply, "He wasn't dead."

A Simple Plan

A Simple Plan begins in a small struggling midwestern town on the afternoon before New Year's Eve, which makes this snow-covered thriller as *blanc* as a film noir can get. Three men chasing a fox in nearby woods stumble on the snowed-over wreckage of a small plane, containing a duffel bag with $4 million in cash. Hank, the smartest, has a humble job in a feed store and a librarian wife, Sarah, who is expecting. Lou is a sort of good ole boy midwestern-style and unemployed, as is his friend Jacob, Hank's brother, not quite right in the head, but possessed of a certain moral sense.

After much debating, it is decided to let Hank hide the loot until such time he can decide whether it is safe to divvy it up or better to burn it. Predictably things go wrong in various ways; eventually, two of the three men, along with some others, will be dead, and no one will profit from the find. It is an old story—famed all the way from "The Pardoner's Tale" to *The Treasure of Sierra Madre*—but, as Heine said in a different context, it is ever new. Here it is decidedly full of the most bizarre twists and turns, as written by Scott B. Smith from his own novel, and directed by Sam Raimi, known hitherto only for horror films.

Horror-film elements duly pop up, notably in the form of threatening and aggressive crows in the trees around the wreck, one of which wounds Hank in the forehead—a kind of mark of Cain. In Alar Kivilo's apt cinematography, these birds of evil omen, so black against the surrounding whiteness, objectify the dark that lurks in human hearts. And though the snow is steadily falling, it can obliterate the tracks of the evildoers, but not cancel out their pangs of conscience.

From the initial shots of a fox raiding a chicken coop, an atmosphere of rapacity is established, to which even seemingly harmless slobs such as Jacob and Lou—the village idiot and the town drunk—readily fall prey. There is a good deal of gallows humor amid the cleverly managed violence, yet the laughter tends properly to stick in the craw. Danny Elfman's music, often mere electronic cacophony, is never overdone, and steadily suggestive. The dialogue and characterization are rich in detail, and the constant surprises do not, for the most part, strain credibility.

The ultimate strength is in the rendering of change. Thus the apparently sensible and somewhat mousy Sarah, admirably played by Bridget Fonda, first dispenses prudent advice, but turns into a master strategist of crime even while incongruously dandling, her baby in her arms. Both Hank, enacted with fine modulations by Bill Paxton, and Jacob, whose oafishness and decency are touchingly conveyed by Billy Bob Thornton, earn our sympathy despite their guilt, and the rest of the cast, notably Brent Briscoe as Lou, hardly lags behind. And, however it was achieved, the performance of the crows is something to crow about.

Lies Are Unbeautiful

LIFE IS BEAUTIFUL

Comic movies about the Nazis, whether by Lubitsch or Chaplin have always left me with a bad aftertaste. A comic movie about the Holocaust strikes me as unthinkable. Yet Roberto Benigni's *Life Is Beautiful,* hailed on all sides, awarded or nominated for numerous prizes, and a sure candidate for one or more Oscars, is just that, or almost. Two middle-aged women who recognized me and queried me about it on the bus simply could not get it through their heads that I was calling the film not excellent but execrable.

Benigni, a well-known comedian who co-wrote, directed, and stars in the film, stops just short of outright Holocaust comedy. The first, prewar part is a silly farce, not nearly so funny as forced. The second part, in a death camp, is sentimental comedy-drama, totally unbelievable and downright stupid. It intends to be sweet, wistful and touching, and to excuse itself with not wishing to be taken literally. I say it cannot be taken, period, unless you enjoy grossing out on imbecile lies.

Guido, the hero, is a waiter in Arezzo (the views of which, as shot by the veteran Tonino delli Colli, are the film's one asset), who comically meets the heroine, Dora, not once but some half-dozen times. He woos her with sundry pratfalls and by calling her Princess, and for the rest, chance takes over—and over and over.

For example, Guido notices that under a certain window when a man shouts "Maria!" a key is dropped for him, which, needless to say, beans Guido. On a rainy night, when he has snatched Dora away from her hated fiancé, who is also Guido's nemesis (Guido keeps snatching the fellow's expensive hats and substituting his own, for which the guy chases after him), they seek shelter under that window. Dora says she hasn't got her latchkey, whereupon Guido boasts that the Virgin Mary answers his prayers. "Maria!" he shouts, and, pronto, down flies the key. That it wouldn't fit Dora's lock isn't gone into.

When they get to Dora's gate, she remarks that Guido's hat has gotten all wet and she decides to address the Virgin herself. She asks for a dry hat, and who should pop up but her deserted fiancé and Guido's nemesis to angrily swap hats. Another miracle—no wonder Dora ends up marrying Guido.

We skip to the last year of World War II. The spouses Guido and Dora run a bookshop on which is painted in huge letters JEWISH

STORE. But otherwise they live in perfect bliss and a cozy house with their bright and adorable 6- or 7-year-old Giosuè. The Germans come and pick up Guido, his uncle, and Giosuè, and lead them onto a death-camp train. Dora, though unsummoned, insists on boarding another car full of women. Here sentimental comedy takes over. Guido tells Giosuè, who mourns a toy tank he left behind, that this is all a game, a giant contest with very rough play, but with a real giant tank for first prize. And he manages to persuade the boy that everything from being brutishly prodded into cattle cars to all the subsequent hardships and horrors of the camp is just a huge competition, to be won by whoever is first to amass 1,000 points for endurance. Hard to tell who is the bigger idiot: the smart, precocious kid who falls for this running lie, or the audience that falls for this movie.

Preposterousness piles up, even though the child is somehow spared the worst atrocities and never even wonders where his mother and great-uncle disappeared to. Instead, he lets his father's smokescreen screen the smoke from the crematoria, and everything turns to rough play with lots of jokiness. And again the most wonderful things keep happening by chance and more chance, or by the hand of the scriptwriters. In the end, the overjoyed kid faces a full-blown American tank as one of the G.I. liberators even hoists him up into it. Riding, he glimpses his mother, and jumps off the tank into her arms. True his father has been shot (discreetly off-camera) and he probably won't be allowed to keep that U.S. Army tank, but the film ends as mother and son laugh and embrace in a joyous freeze frame to chill any intelligent viewer's blood.

Comics do not have to be good-looking, but must they be as unappealing as the inverted-eggplant-headed, chinless wonder Benigni, with his passive-aggressive charmlessness and fish-eyed simpletonism? And then there is the angular ploddingness of his real-life spouse Nicoletta Braschi, and her by-the-numbers expressions. The little boy, appropriately not cherubically adorable is passable but nothing special. But the inane *Life Is Beautiful* thrives, while a fine Italian film such as Pupi Avati's *Best Man* vanishes.

My Name Is Joe

Ken Loach, born in 1936, has been called "Britain's last crusading leftist film director." "Leftist" the director of such movies as *Kes*,

Poor Cow, and *Raining Stones* certainly is; "crusading," though usually in a restrained way, as well. Not in any sense "last," though; rather, in some ways, first and foremost. Decidedly *My Name Is Joe*, though not flawless, proves him a major talent.

The title is unfortunate, doubly so because it invites being mistaken for *Meet Joe Black*, a recent elephantine flop. Like all of Loach's work, it is casually naturalistic on the surface, but with such sympathy for its characters, such insight into their small victories and not so small defeats, as to hold us spellbound from start to finish. A film able to imply so much more than it says, combining humor, heartache, mellowness, and drama (and only near the end some unfortunate melodrama), goes way beyond naturalism to the mysterious essence of our mundane yet extraordinary lives.

This is the story of Joe Kavanagh, an unemployed recovering alcoholic on the dole in Glasgow. The public-housing neighborhood he lives in (all cheerless cemer t), like his humble apartment, is more universal than Glaswegian—the realm of precarious survival. Joe has a friendly relationship with the parole officer in charge of him, who will even lend him some money. He has overcome ten years of booze with as many months of abstinence, and still counting. His one, alas unpaid, employment is coaching a hopeless neighborhood soccer team, sanguine in their bedraggled uniforms.

Joe is also responsible for chauffeuring his raggedy bunch to the playing field, though they are incapable even of giving him uncontradictory directions to their destination. And once the game starts, after considerable argument, some members of McGowan's drug-dealing gang show up and brutally work over one of the players. This is Joe's good friend Liam, who became addicted to the stuff he was peddling for them. Jailed, he incurred a further debt to the gang when Sabine, the mother of his child, took over for him, and appropriated the heroin she was hustling. Now the gang wants her to hustle her body for them, which Liam, out of jail, wishes to prevent.

Bleak, you say. Yes, but there is relief. Under amusing circumstances, Joe and his pals run into Sarah, a children's social worker whose apartment desperately needs wallpapering. Joe and a buddy hire out to do the job for her, even though the unemployed fellow is not allowed clandestine perquisites, and neither guy has ever put up so much as a poster. The scenes that follow are hilarious.

The job starts a friendship between Joe and Sarah that quickly develops into an affair. Since both he and she are insecure persons—he because of his alcoholic past when beating up his girl-friend queered him with the law, she because of her basic unsexi-ness—their movements toward each other are touchingly awkward, groping, overeager. They depend partly on chance, but more so on a basic decency that each discerns in the other. Another linking factor is that Sarah is the social worker assigned to Scott, the small child of Liam and Sabine, a family group for whom the kindly Joe involves himself in grave danger.

Where it all goes from there, I urge you to find out for yourself. But let me say that no one blends the harsh and the winsome better than Loach. Thus on a perilous drug-running mission that Joe undertakes for Liam in the Lake District, he waits for his contact while bemused-ly discussing a second-rate bagpipe player entertaining tourists with a measly repertory of three tunes. That little exchange, with a bored young female vendor in a nearby kiosk, perfectly encapsulates life's absurdities. Or take the moment when Joe and Sarah, to whom he has confessed his battering of that ex-girlfriend, have a quarrel in turn. In a scene almost unbearably sad and beautiful, Sarah asks qui-etly, "Are you going to hit me, too, Joe?"

Let's not forget the incisive scenario by Paul Laverty, the subdued but telling cinematography of Barry Ackroyd, and the flavorous music of George Fenton. Hail, above all, to the luminous acting of Peter Mullan, Louise Goodall, and their impeccable supporting cast. The climactic action scenes are not entirely convincing, but the minor-key ending is perfect for a film that captures with under-stated poignancy both the sublime and the all-too-human.

Of Gangs and Bands

ANALYZE THIS; THE HARMONISTS

What happens when two antithetical worlds collide? Different lan-guages, experiences, values, mentalities can spell disaster. Or, as in the case of *Analyze This*, crackling comedy. Of course, it helps if the Mafia don suddenly unable to whack an enemy is played by Robert De Niro, and if the extremely reluctant therapist whose services he enlists is Billy Crystal. Even the mere juxtaposition of Mafia lingo and Freudian jargon is good for tremors worthy of a minor earthquake.

Take this exchange. Mafia capo Vitti: "If you turn me into a fag, you die!" Therapist Ben Sobol: "Could we define fag?" Vitti (emphatically): "I go fag, you die." Or take the moment when the rival don, Primo Sindone (Chazz Palminteri), told that the situation needs closure, instructs a henchman: "You get a dictionary and find out what dis fucking closure is!" Or, when Vitti is told about his Oedipus complex, "Dis Freud was a sick fuck. I don't want to hear any more filth about my mother."

It all begins when Sobol accidentally rams a Mafia car, whose trunk springs open to reveal a bound and gagged, squirming victim. The trunk is instantly shut and taped down, but the stunned yet conscientious Sobol proffers his card, so as to be charged with the repair expenses. This card enables Paul's bodyguard, Jelly, to direct the panic-ridden boss to Sobol's office, where he immediately usurps the shrink's comfortable armchair. "When I got into family therapy," Ben bemoans, "this was not the family I had in mind."

Analyze This was written by Peter Tolan, who comes out of television; Kenneth Lonergan, the gifted playwright whose *This Is Our Youth* is a hit on the New York stage; and Harold Ramis, the film's director, best remembered for his droll *Groundhog Day*. Aside from a few slow patches, they have contrived a good many scenes and numerous one-liners funnier than any I have caught on film since… I can't remember, it's been so long.

De Niro, the beloved tough guy, started out comic in Brian De Palma's *Hi, Mom!*, and periodically proved himself adept at farce, from the underrated *King of Comedy* to the overrated *Wag the Dog*. But you have seldom seen him as rubber-faced as when Ben asks whether anyone has ever said no to him; only, he answers, in combination with such phrases as "Please don't kill me!" He illustrates this with facial accordion effects to do a Shar-Pei proud.

Crystal is just as amusing as the stuffy yet overeager (to get rid of Vitti) therapist, except in some scenes of the routine subplot about his engagement to a TV newscaster (Lisa Kudrow, in a part no one could wholly salvage). This engagement is an interruptus writ large as Ben is hauled off in the middle of the night or from his own wedding ceremony to provide instant therapy for Vitti. The internecine warfare between Paul's and Primo's Mafia factions is also, in both senses, hit-or-miss. But any scene with Ben, Paul, and Paul's sidekick Jelly (the terrific Joe Viterelli, fat and hang-dog-faced, but quick with a quip or a handgun) is undiluted fun. Much of it, to be sure, is in the delivery. I can't affirm that the answer to "What kind of sandwich isn't too fattening?"—"Half a sandwich"—would be as savory from a mouth other than Viterelli's.

I am told that *Analyze This* resembles TV's *The Sopranos*. I can't say just how they compare, but the film hits enough high notes to warrant a speedy revisit.

Joseph Vilsmaier's *The Harmonists*, from Germany, is the more or less true story of the Comedian Harmonists, six young Berliners who, in 1927, decide to start a close-harmony ensemble spiced with comedy. Harry Frommermann, an impecunious drama student reduced to filching peanuts from his pet parrot, advertises for young singers and, times being hard, an endless line promptly forms. How the five others were recruited, and their difficulties in finding the right syncopated style and a willing agent, is told with humor and even suspense by Vilsmaier, who both photographed and directed from a script by Klaus Richter.

There is genuine feeling for the fine, old-fashioned pop songs, and a skillfully applied shorthand for characterizing the Comedian Harmonists with terse pungency. There is Harry, the nice Jewish boy who faithfully visits his parents' grave to discuss his problems; Robert Biberti, the arrogant blond Aryan with a booming bass and shrewd business sense; Roman Cycowski, a displaced Polish opera singer and the group's conciliator; Erich Collin, a monocled baptized Jew with the bearing of a Prussian aristocrat; Ari Leschnikoff, a thickly accented Bulgarian-born waiter whose tenor voice women fall for; and the pianist Erwin Bootz, a sleepyhead who must be dragged from his lady's bed.

Already the opening sequence is splendidly managed—the last minutes before and first minutes after a Harmonists' concert. Both the frantic backstage bustle and the growing expectancy in the slowly filling hall are conveyed with a keen eye for detail, expert crosscutting, and a true sense of musical rhythm translated into the rhythm of cinema. When the group, immaculate in tails, takes the stage to sing the first of several charming numbers we get in the course of the movie, our fulfillment is overwhelming.

There are nice detours into the private lives of the group. Thus Cycowski literally bumps into a girl dancer, Mary, during an audition for the mighty impresario Erik Charell, as the boys are rushing onstage, and some girls off. Their love affair, his hard demand that she convert to Judaism, and their exuberant Jewish wedding are among the film's highlights. No less striking is Collin's finding a French bride among the whores of the bordello where the Harmonists seek shelter for their often stormy rehearsals. Or Bootz's cowardly dumping of his wife for being Jewish.

But the main love story is Frommermann and Biberti's competing for Ema Eggstein, an eternal history student doing her homework while employed in a Jewish music store, where the young men come calling on her. One of them, Hans, a fellow student and future Nazi will be the cause of considerable trouble.

The real drama is, of course, political, and involves the ever sterner pressure from Nazi authorities on the Harmonists to replace their Jewish members with Aryans. They ignore such demands, go on to ever greater international success, with Nazi bigwigs often applauding in the front rows and silencing lesser Nazis trying to disrupt the concert from the balcony. One of their biggest fans, the film claims, was the notorious Julius Streicher, later editor of the viciously anti-Semitic *Der Stürmer*, who invites the group to his house to sing German folk songs, a request that they daringly refuse to comply with. This and a few other incidents were questioned by the historian Peter Gay in a *New York Times* article.

Further high spots are the Harmonists' concert on a U.S. aircraft carrier in New York Harbor and the subsequent debate about whether to stay on in America, with Harry losing out to Robert, who argues the immunity of their group as an important propaganda weapon for German culture, and refuses to abandon his aged mother back home. I must also mention the group's farewell concert in Munich, fictionalized but very moving, as is also the closing scene at the Berlin train station, as the emigrating Jewish members bid goodbye to the Aryans staying on.

The performances are all exemplary, including those of some grand old German stars in supporting parts. The songs and production numbers are delightful, although the lyrics, like much of the dialogue, lose something in the translation. But what remains is more than enough. If you have access to Broadway, there is, currently and coincidentally, a show about the Comedian Harmonists, *Banned in Berlin*. It is not much of a play, but you can hear many more of the Harmonists' numbers nicely simulated by a group calling itself Hudson Shad.

New Angle on Angels

THE DREAMLIFE OF ANGELS

The surest way of testing a movie's greatness is seeing it a second time. If it is just as good, it is a good film. If it gets better in the

fineness and fullness of its detail, it is great. That is the case of Erick Zonca's *The Dreamlife of Angels*. Though riveting, it is no mere
entertainment, but a necessary work of art.

Two working-class French girls, Isa and Marie, meet in a sweat-
shop working sewing machines. They couldn't be more different. Isa
is an optimist, cheerful under the most trying circumstances. She
wanders from town to town with a backpack, only to discover in
bleak, chilly Lille that the fellow she hoped to crash with has moved
on without leaving a forwarding address. Undiscouraged, she raises
some money by cutting pictures out of magazines, mounting them
on colored cardboard, and selling them for a supposed charity on
the streets. And she takes odd jobs.

Marie is a sullen, unforthcoming creature who has left home
because she cannot stand her father. She does her work, but comes
alive only at night, though with little money to have much of a
nightlife. She is house-sitting a nice, big apartment for a mother
and daughter whom a car accident has left comatose in the hospital. She doesn't know much about them, and doesn't care to. But,
grudgingly, she lets Isa share the apartment.

At first, the girls hit it off: their very differences prove stimulating. They go pub-crawling and, penniless, decide to crash a disco.
But the two bouncers, Frédo, and Charly, won't let them in. A
jeering altercation arises. Later that night, at a café, the bouncers plant themselves in two empty chairs at the girls' table, and
a kind of friendship develops. Marie ends up lovelessly sleeping
with Frédo, Isa remains platonic with Charly; both accept money
from the boys. Isa finds a job as a sandwich-board-girl on roller-
skates, from which Marie abstains. She, however, tries to shoplift
an expensive leather jacket, and is caught. Chriss, a young man
the girls wished to pick up earlier, and whose headlight Marie
kicked in when he refused to give them a ride, happens to be
nearby; he pays for the jacket. But now Marie refuses to take it,
and won't even let him kiss her.

Spoiled rich kid that Chriss is—he owns both that disco and
the brasserie across the square—he is fascinated by a girl who resists him and determines to win her. He does so by treating her
like a whore, taking her to a hotel and making rough love to her.
Meanwhile Isa has discovered the diary of Sandrine, the comatose
girl whose room she inhabits, and starts reading it. Charmed by
its freshness, Isa seeks out Sandrine at the hospital. Although her
mother has died, the girl still has a slight chance of recovery. Isa is

drawn to her and is encouraged by the doctor and nurse to stay and talk to the unresponding patient.

That is only the beginning of the story, and, reduced to such an outline, it may not seem like much. But what the screenplay by Zonca and Roger Bohbot, and Zonca's direction, with the artistic collaboration of Virginie Wagon, do for it is irresistible. The language, in French (and even, largely, in the English subtitles), is a distillation of the zippy, slangy bravura of the urban young, yet at times obliquely affecting. Characters come alive with all their contradictions—surprises and predictabilities—and we become absorbed trying to read the thoughts off their manifestly toiling faces that nevertheless remain opaque. So much of this wonderful film is in suggestion, ambiguity, indirection: half-said or unsaid things—paradoxical behavior that yet makes a painful sort of sense.

Unlike in American films, where hack composers provide rampaging scores that tautologically hammer in obvious points—or, worse yet, blurt out that big moments are ahead—there is no score here—only music heard by the characters and one simple, effective song at the end. But we do get the most extraordinary—which is to say ordinary, but slightly amplified—everyday sounds: street noises, a train, birdsong, a dog barking, hammering, etc. At odd moments, bells are heard outside, or someone practicing scales next door. Objects—kitchen utensils, squeaky doors, hospital apparatus—join in the usually ignored symphony, the music of living.

And the director, combining with Agnès Godard's splendidly unobtrusive yet infinitely evocative cinematography, creates images that warm or chill, glow or threaten. Even the looks of various doorknobs tell part of the story. When Isa, at bedside, takes the comatose Sandrine's hand, the contrast between that pale, lifeless extremity and Isa's bitten nails with their sanguine but cracked polish speaks paragraphs. The closeups of Isa reading Sandrine's diary—its bouncy handwriting, the way the words race across the page, the suspense when a page must be turned in mid-sentence—are a dramatic event. Even more stunningly, we watch, again in extreme closeup, Isa making diary entries for Sandrine: the way she holds her pencil, how it moves sassily forward, the unexpected words coaxed into being, as well as the touching erasures. This is character in action, soul in self-revelation.

Every detail contributes, even the unruly shoulder straps of Isa's undershirt as they protrude from her boatnecked sweater. Or when Marie, smoking in bed, lets her cigarette briefly nudge the fringe of a curtain—playing with fire. Or the daring way Zonca holds the camera on a character for what seems an unconscionably long time, but that always pays off emotionally. And the final tracking shot should make history.

And the acting! Elodie Bouchez, as Isa, has a tomboyish haircut, ever-hopeful smile, sudden submersions in affliction. Her springy manner, disarming spontaneity, growing concern for and subsequent disconcertment with Marie, add up to a performance the like of which we haven't seen since the heyday of Giulietta Masina in Fellini's masterpieces.

Yet scarcely less astonishing is the Marie of Natacha Régnier, who infuses a basically unlikable person with pathos and despair, without, however, playing on our sympathy. Superficial and ungenerous as the character is, her tragic obsession is made to shine forth in terrible splendor. Both young actresses have unexceptional looks, yet transcend into searing beauty at crucial instants. Still, they remain natural, unaffected, real. As shattered as the dreamlife of these angels becomes, so shudderingly vivid is our participation in it. As the callow Chriss, Grégoire Colin is smoothly perfect; despite his abuse of her, you can see what rivets Marie to him. And the two bouncers, seemingly simple and alike, are yet discretely individuated by their telling portrayers.

Since writing these lines, I have seen *The Dreamlife of Angels* a third time, and, believe me, it is still growing. This is, after three short subjects, the first feature by Zonca, a man in his early 40s who discovered European films at the Bleecker Street Cinema while living in New York. I am told that his next film the made-for-TV *Un petit Garçon*, is even better. I can hardly wait.

A Walk on the Moon

It is rare for an American film about personal relations to be as sophisticated as *A Walk on the Moon*. Like *Cookie's Fortune*, it was written by a first-time woman scenarist, Pamela Gray, but there the similarity ends. The time is 1969, the revolutionary year, in one of those Catskill bungalow camps where lower-middle-class New York Jewish families summered. Husbands, however, worked in the city and drove up only for weekends. The Kantrowitzes are such a family, with Marty working in a TV-repair store, while his wife, Pearl, is left with their teenage daughter Alison, little and brattish son Daniel, and fussy mother-in-law Lilian (Bubbie) to get on her nerves.

The camp routine is punctuated by loudspeaker-heralded visits from the Ice Cream Man, the Knish Man, and the Blouse Man, the latter a handsome hippie, Walker Jerome. He sells women's clothing from a converted bus and manages to charm even the ungainliest customers. When the extremely pretty and frustrated Pearl drifts into his purview, he bestows a tie-dyed shirt on her without any obvious hidden agenda. Such beguiling unaggressiveness and liberated clothing set Pearl, step by innocent step, on a new sexual course.

That Alison is beginning to date and acts rebellious, that Marty despite his wife's encouragement cannot be more inventive sexually than to grab two toy guns and pretend he is John Wayne, that Walker is charming and not in the least importunate—all this and more contributes to Pearl's drifting into a heady affair. When the world watches the first moonwalk on TV, Marty does so alone in the city, while Pearl is blissfully in Walker's arms. But things come to a head when Alison, playing hooky at the Woodstock festival with her platonic boyfriend, espies her semi-nude and body-painted mother being lofted ecstatically by her lover. Adding to the ensuing crisis is Lilian's getting on Pearl's case and dragging in Marty for all hell to break loose.

The story is told with a fine sense of the little ironies and incongruities of life, as when Marty, amid his agony, remonstrates that Walker Jerome has a name that's the wrong way round; or when Walker, trying to persuade Pearl to run off with him, must instead attend to curing Daniel from a wasp sting and so earn Marty's gruff thanks. It's all terribly, funnily, infuriatingly real, down to every piece of music on the soundtrack and the outrage of the Jewish vacationers when some hippies come skinny-dipping in their lake.

It is a historical turning point as conventions begin to crumble, and also fresh departure for Tony Goldwyn, a so-so actor who does handsomely as a neophyte director. The British cinematographer Anthony Richmond has shot with a nice sense of atmosphere even though the Catskills are played by some Quebec mountains. Especially, heartbreakingly good as Pearl is Diane Lane, a former adorable child star who, as an adult, has hitherto received shabby treatment from Hollywood, which owes this refined, lovely, and talented actress considerable reparations.

But the others are no slouches either. Viggo Mortensen aptly bal-

ances Walker's genuine warmth and cool lifestyle; Leiv Schreiber's
Marty is deeply moving both in his clumsy loving and his helpless
rage; Anna Paquin is properly headstrong yet vulnerable as Alison,
and lesser roles are also well taken. Only Tovah Feldshuh as Lilian
gives her customary overripe performance. *A Walk on the Moon* is
as refreshing as a stroll in spring woods, and its love scenes—even
those for its teenagers—are the most convincing I have seen in
many a moon.

Treacle and Tea

NOTTING HILL; TEA WITH MUSSOLINI

Some cheeses are meant to be eaten rotten, others thrown away
when rot sets in. The cheesy Rotting—sorry—*Notting Hill* is of the
latter variety. A supposed romantic comedy, it is stale, soggy, and,
if it weren't so irritating, soporific. It concerns the glamorous Hollywood superstar Anna Scott, who wanders into William Thacker's
travel bookshop in London's multiculturally chic Notting Hill section. When the overeager William spills orange juice all over Anna's
blouse, she improbably agrees to come to his flat across the street
to repair the damage.

Forthwith, the rusty wheels of cutesy romance creak into motion,
and now it is only a matter of how long the screenwriter, Richard
Curtis, and the director, Roger Mitchell, can postpone the preposterous but predictable ending with every well-worn delaying tactic.

Absurdity would be forgivable if it were charming, witty, or sexy,
but all three qualities are in short supply here. The initially icy Anna
thaws out fairly quickly and becomes open to William's timid, gan-
gly courtship. You can tell that this is an English film by the way
the passive male dithers, blithers, and gets muddled, while the ag-
gressor female makes all the advances till the penultimate moment.
Unfortunately, reverse clichés are still clichés.

Hugh Grant's William, with the virginally blue eyes and carefully careless-seeming coiffure—two shocks of brown hair framing
his ingenuous countenance, the rest descending, neatly terraced,
onto his nape—is all adorable awkwardnesses, chief among them
a much-repeated long pause followed by a sheepish "Right!" Julia
Roberts's Anna, overcome by so much masculine sweetness, is first
to kiss, the first to make a date, the first to invite upstairs to her

suite at the Ritz—though not in years have we had a bedroom scene with so little eroticism, never mind bed, in it. Waking up together, the lovers discuss the uninterestingness of breasts, with William allowed one brief peek under Anna's decorously protective sheet, and the rest of us not even that.

There are more pauses in Nothing, sorry—*Notting Hill* than in a Pinter play, but only because the characters are bumblers, particularly William, whose tongue seems to be into advanced bondage, although he can deliver second-rate witticisms quite trippingly. He is saddled with a randy and foul-mouthed Welshman, Spike, for a flatmate, amusingly played by Rhys Ifans. Anna reminds us how hard her life as a star earning 15 million per picture is, which, of course, breaks the hearts of us making 14 or less. There are standard comic friends and relatives for William, including a punker sister and a happily married couple whose ardor isn't dampened by a fall that confines the wife to a wheelchair.

There are a few funny scenes, though, notably one in which William, to get to see Anna, must pretend to be an interviewing journalist from *Horse and Hound* and is forced into a bizarre line of questioning. The love story, however, which ends with William proposing to Anna during a huge press conference at the Savoy, is rather like a long bath in a tub of alternatingly hot and cold pineapple juice.

The mistimings and misconstruings and assorted contretemps that roughen the course of true love culminate in a scene where stellar Anna seeks out pining William in his shop and utters the soon-to-be-classic line, "I'm also just a girl standing in front of a boy asking him to love her." Not being able to stand yet another potential heartbreak, he sadly sends her away. That the still unwrapped present she brought him is the original of his favorite Chagall painting may contribute to his changing his mind.

At a movie whose every other moment makes you wince, and whose rock-music soundtrack makes you groan in between, you have to divert yourself in other ways. So you notice that Grant has tolerable upper teeth but, in best British dental tradition, disastrous lower ones, and start admiring his skill at smiling mostly with his upper lip. Or you marvel at how Miss Roberts's visage—despite excess nose, mouth, and ears—does not fail to captivate. But whenever you are diverted back to the film at hand, you merely feel like giving it the finger.

Tea with Mussolini is based on a couple of paragraphs of the Italian director Franco Zeffirelli's autobiography, in whose very foreword we read, "No one tells the full truth about themselves." The screenplay by Zeffirelli and John Mortimer is indeed highly fictionalized (mostly by Mortimer, I guess, as Mr. Z. says in the same foreword, "I am a raconteur rather than a writer"), and its content of truth seems about as full as a hunter's moon.

It concerns a gaggle of British ladies of a certain age leading a charmed life in Florence in the '30s, pursuing hobbies if affluent, and working at respectable jobs if not. They are known to the locals as the *scorpioni* for the sting of their meddling superiority. Their leader is Lady Hester (Maggie Smith), widow of a former British ambassador and great fan of Mussolini's because of a once-shared tea. Arabella (Judi Dench) officiously protects frescoes and fancies herself a singer. A butch American archeologist, Georgie (Lily Tomlin), is a showy lesbian. Most level-headed is Mary (Joan Plowright), a secretary and translator, who becomes de facto foster mother to little Luca, her boss's bastard and Zeffirelli's alter ego.

There are also other British ladies, but all are eclipsed by a flamboyant American, Elsa, a lucratively widowed ex-Ziegfeld girl (Cher), who generously and anonymously shares her wealth with the rest until, being Jewish, she lands in mortal danger. Though Mary does admirably by Luca, his proto-fascist father packs him off to Austria to learn German, as the Duce and the Führer form an axis, and war is about to break out. By the time Luca returns as a young man, the scorpions have been interned at picturesquely medieval San Gimignano, and it will be up to Luca and the partisans he valiantly joins to rescue them.

That is about as much as you need to know, though there are many incidents of mingled charm, sentimentality, and even suspense, laced with dollops of wit. Frankly, I didn't expect old Zeffirelli to show so much verve and viability at this late stage, yet he does better here than in his bejeweled prime. Credit also his shrewdly picked collaborators, notably the droll Mortimer and the great cinematographer David Watkin. Watkin keeps the exteriors fresco-like in tone (one sunset on the Arno is pure Giotto, had Giotto painted sunsets) and his interiors bursting with life. There is also intelligently spare background music, and Florence itself is enough to melt the eye.

All the smartly cast actresses perform yeoman's work, only Lily Tomlin may have been allowed a few balls too many. The two Lucas, child and youth, are equally adorable, Mr. Z. being especially fastidious about choosing his alter egos. But it is Joan Plowright who walks away with top honors in a performance that blends warmth and pawkiness, sparkle and gravitas, heart and backbone. So perfect a being could hardly exist, but the actress makes her grittily alive without allowing the occasionally circumambient sentimentality to creep into her work. Yet even the film's tear-jerking is executed with a certain restraint; there is not that much tea in *Tea with Mussolini*, but the sympathy is ubiquitous.

Boy Learns, Girl Runs

MY LIFE SO FAR; RUN LOLA RUN

More than ever, in movies, small is beautiful. As the blockbusters keep spewing out their predictable fare of frenzied action, unbounded violence, and heaving nudity, their success is not to their credit, merely to the debit of dumbed-down audiences. That is where charming small films come in as rescuers: *Enchanted April* or *Tea With Mussolini*, *A Walk on the Moon* or the much tougher *Dreamlife of Angels*. Now comes *My Life So Far*, a notch or two below, but still delightful and heartily recommendable.

The film is based on a section of *Son of Adam*, the childhood memoir of Sir Denis Forman, television executive and Royal Opera bigwig. The very setting is a winner: the home of the Pettigrews, Kiloran House, at Loch Fyne in the Scottish Highlands. The house is a cheeky blend of medieval castle and Edwardian mansion; its attics harbor legendary demons; in the woods bordering its lawns, the Hairy Man is roaming. Missing only is a monster in the loch.

The story is chiefly that of ten-year old Fraser and his eccentric inventor father, Edward, a veritable volcano of mostly useless inventions. But there are also Gamma (Granny) Macintosh, the matriarch and sometimes-benevolent tyrant; her ruthlessly acquisitive son, Uncle Morris to the six Pettigrew kids; and Moira, Edward's loving wife and a devoted mother.

My Life So Far begins further back, though—when Fraser, still a toddler, escapes to the roof, crawling about blithely in mortal danger as the family rushes around below trying frantically to retrieve him. The scene establishes the movie's ability to sound two notes simultaneously: comedy and suspense. When Edward climbs onto the roof, he communicates with the preverbal Fraser in their cherished dog language: a droll barking duet helps return the tot to the fold.

Edward revels in splendid contradictions. He is stern and teddy-bearish, puritanical and permissive, dedicated and outrageous by turns. He lives amid a congeries of abandoned inventions, some finished, some not—everything from a four-foot metal foghorn for communicating with the kitchen downstairs to a disastrous rubber wading outfit and a set of outlandish pyramidal speakers to enhance the gramophone. This last will be a battleground between him, a Beethoven fanatic, and Fraser, a zealous convert to jazz, which his father abominates.

Uncle Morris Macintosh can't wait to snatch Kiloran away from Edward Pettigrew, whose impracticality further emboldens his brother-in-law's greed. Besides, Morris has acquired a delicious French fiancée, Héloïse, for whom he considers the house just the right lagniappe. The young woman is a half-free spirit, flirting innocently with Edward and Fraser, both smitten, and Edward, at any rate, determines to do something about it. Occasionally dropping out of the sky is a happy-go-lucky French pilot, Gabriel Chenoux, who starts a dalliance with 16-year-old Elspeth, the eldest of the Pettigrew brood.

Two more remote presences also matter. Grandfather Macintosh, though dead, lives on in the illustrated sex books that, albeit hidden, fall into Fraser's hands; devoured but imperfectly digested, they will push the youngster into a number of resounding faux pas. And lurking in the not-too-distant future is World War II, in which Edward's most farfetched brainstorm, a sphagnum-moss factory, will prove highly useful for its product's antibacterial and absorbent properties.

Add to the comic potential of all this some more serious elements: Moira's discovery of her husband's infatuation with Héloïse, leading to an ill-considered bet during a picturesque curling tournament on the frozen loch, where Gamma also comes to grief.

Simon Donald's screenplay hurtles along merrily and sometimes poignantly, but not without some bumps. The Gabriel-Elspeth relationship is stinted on; we do not get a sense of what draws the lively Héloïse to the unpleasant Morris; a vast array of minor characters parades on and off before we can get a proper fix on any of them. And there is one major casting error: As Héloïse, the likable Irène Jacob is not, despite her talent, the head-turner and heart-scorcher she is meant to be.

Otherwise, Hugh Hudson, best remembered for *Chariots of Fire*, has directed with delicacy and sparkle. His imaginative French cinematographer, Bernard Lutic, has done wonders for the Scottish scenery, or is it vice versa? Lutic is no slouch indoors either, where he exploits the contrast between bright frilly gowns and brooding walls and furniture. The dialogue veering from madcap to grave contributes its own chiaroscuro, although I could have done with a little less Beethoven on the soundtrack and more of Howard Blake's original music, even if Blake is not one of the three B's.

Colin Firth is first-rate as the loopy Edward, dexterously juggling the character's contradictions; Rosemary Harris admirably blends steeliness and humanity as Gamma; Mary Elizabeth Mastrantonio, as Moira, may be imperfectly Scottish, but is perfectly lovable. Malcolm McDowell is a wryly amusing Morris, and child actors don't come more poised and affecting, without lapsing into cuteness, than the 11-year-old tyro Robbie Norman as Fraser.

It has been some time since a film from Germany has made waves among audiences and reviewers. Tom Tykwer's *Run Lola Run* has produced big billows. Yet, to my mind, the writer-director Tykwer suffers from an excess of originality and not much to vent it on.

Manni, a puny courier for a big gangster, loses a plastic bag with 100,000 marks in drug money on the Berlin subway, and a bum makes off with it. From a phone booth at the other end of town, he rings his girlfriend, Lola, in a panic: She must bring him a replacement sum to this out-of-the-way meeting place in 20 minutes, or else his life is forfeit.

From here on, everything and nothing happens. The same story is told several times, with some but not all particulars changed, and with a different ending. Lola keeps running most of the time, but the movie will turn her at times (literally) into a cartoon; at others, she bumps into or doesn't bump into certain passersby, is delayed buying cigarettes or not, has to dodge this or that bit of traffic—or not. The sequences involving Lola and Manni are shot on 35 mm, film; minor characters appear on synthetic-looking video. But when Lola runs through a video image, it too becomes film. Clocks observe the 20-minute time frame, but lengthy scenes, such as Lola trying to get money from her father's bank, clearly flout it. The father, by the way, is played by an actor scarcely older than Lola.

The music, by Tykwer and two others, is a crazy quilt, often defying the action. The camera can be as frisky as a puppy or as dogged as a Doberman unleashed. A typical statement from the director goes: "One really crazy aspect was all the clocks that keep coming into shots everywhere—we spent hours discussing whether it was seven minutes or six in some scenes." If you have difficulty following that statement, try following a film in which there is no boundary between fantasy and reality, most likely because the latter doesn't exist. Why, even the concluding crawl is contrary, with words scrolled in the opposite direction from the one we are used to.

There is not much room for acting amid all this trickery, and I wouldn't blame the actors for not creating characters. The worst thing about all this often ingenious technique is that it dies with this movie: It cannot be applied to another, better film than *Run Lola Run* and retain its freshness. And, by the way, how could a courier, however dumb, leave a bag of money on which his life depends in the subway?

Not with a Bang

EYES WIDE SHUT

If previous ages tended blindly to ignore their geniuses, ours is all to ready to crown as genius the nearest trendy hack. One of the very few masters not fully acknowledged even posthumously is the Viennese playwright-fiction writer Arthur Schnitzler (1862–1931), most of whose many works are poorly, if at all, translated into English.

Hence it may be unsurprising if, for his last movie, *Eyes Wide Shut*, Stanley Kubrick, along with his co-scenarist, Frederic Raphael, misread the work it was "inspired by," Schnitzler's *Traumnovelle* (Dream Story, 1926). That the director died four days after completing the film, and before putting in his usual last-minute finishing touches, makes the result even more damaging.

In the novella, Fridolin and Albertine are a young couple with a small daughter: he, a successful physician; she, a somewhat bored housewife; both basically happy. At a ball, he briefly flirts with a pair of masked girls; she dances with a stranger, charmed until a lewd remark shocks her. At home, the spouses are more amorous than ever, but then, out of a slight jealousy, confess that, on a long-ago shared holiday in Denmark she was attracted to a young officer at the next table, he to a glimpsed 15-year-old girl bathing naked on a deserted beach. Each of them felt briefly but intensely tempted.

A midnight call summons Fridolin to the bedside of a patient, who is dead by the time he gets there. The dead man's daughter, Marianne though engaged to another, suddenly confesses an overwhelming passion for Fridolin: Politely but hastily, he escapes. Not ready to go home, he follows a very young, rather touching prostitute to her digs, but the encounter ends platonically.

At a seedy café, he runs into Nachtigall, formerly a fellow medical student but now a somewhat shabby pianist. It emerges that tonight he will again play piano for a group of orgiasts who meet in different houses. Transported by a taciturn coachman, he will, as usual, play blindfolded, though he has noticed masked men dancing with comely nude women, then having sex with them. Fridolin extracts the password from his friend, then, under bizarre circumstances I can't go into here, acquires a monk's costume and follows Nachtigall to the orgy in an inconspicuous house on a small suburban street.

Strange things happen. He is recognized as an interloper, and would come to harm, were it not for a nude but masked girl who had previously urged him to bolt; she declares her readiness to take his unspecified punishment upon herself. He is packed off to near his home. The next morning, Albertine tells him her dream, wherein she made love to that young Danish officer while looking on unconcerned as strange men whipped and crucified Fridolin.

He, even more strongly piqued, seeks vengeance in the form of a real-life tryst of his own. But Marianne now proves both unattractive and unavailable; the young prostitute, for whom he brings a package of much-needed victuals, is off in the hospital, gravely ill, as her roommate, another prostitute, informs him. Searching for the stranger who sacrificed herself for him, he is told at Nachtigall's hotel that the pianist was hustled off at dawn by two men to an unknown destination. With some difficulty, he tracks down the orgy house, only to be handed by a servant at the gate a letter addressed to him by name. He is to stop making further useless inquiries or suffer the dire consequences.

In a newspaper, he reads about a beautiful young countess who took poison and was brought to a hospital by two gruff men. At the hospital, he learns of her death, but a doctor friend lets him look at her nude cadaver at the morgue. Never having seen her unmasked, he can't be sure whether she is his savior, but the body excites him uncommonly. Back home, he is horrified to find his wife asleep next to his last night's mask, which he had failed to return to the costumer.

He confesses his escapade. Forgiving, she tells him they ought to be thankful for emerging unscathed from their adventures, both real and dreamed. Here, when he asks, "Are you sure?" the film mistranslates her answer, "Just as sure as I am that the reality of one night, let alone that of a whole lifetime, is not the whole truth." Schnitzler ends the sentence: "and not even that of an entire human life represents its innermost truth." Then comes the movie's crowning vulgarity. Alice, as she is called in the film, tells her husband, Dr. Bill Harford, that there is one more thing they must promptly do. Asked what, she sassily declares, "Fuck." Blackout, end of film—and of any sympathy we could muster for Kubrick's swan song.

In the story, Schnitzler has the spouses, early on, talking gravely of "those hidden, barely sensed desires that can call forth dangerous eddies in the clearest and purest soul" and "the secret purlieus for which they had scant longing, but into which the winds of fate might yet, if only in a dream, someday sweep them." Schnitzler's tone is always subtle, poetic, and classically controlled. No explanation of the orgy and its consequences, who the dead woman was, and other, lesser mysteries. But both the real and dreamt adventures bespeak the dangers against which even a happy marriage must be on constant guard.

Kubrick, to do him justice, wanted to stick with the story, even though it was his disastrous idea to move the locale to present-day New York, which in mores and sensibility is not just a century but worlds removed from Schnitzler's Vienna. But, as we can gather from Raphael's book-length memoir of their collaboration, it was the screenwriter who insisted that moviegoers would not tolerate unresolved mystery and needed full explanations. So he invented an unlikely nabob, Victor Ziegler (played drably by Sydney Pollack), who gives the initial, huge Christmas party in his duplex at the Plaza. At that party, Victor, on the upper floor, was having sex with a call girl, Mandy, who overdosed; Bill, summoned upstairs, managed to resuscitate her. Near the film's end, Victor explains to Bill that he, too, was at that orgy where Bill was unmasked and recognized. Mandy was the young woman who "sacrificed" herself for him—a charade invented by Victor—and also the one who, having OD'd again, became the corpse at the morgue. Everything fits neatly and prosaically together—no profound unanswered questions here.

The screenplay's additions are crude and ugly. The pathetic young Vienna streetwalker becomes a ballsy Greenwich Village prostitute, and when Bill returns the next day with an unlikely box containing a cake, he lewdly sticks his hand into her roommate's cleavage, all but having sex with her. At Ziegler's party, Alice dances immodestly with a creepily suave Hungarian, who propositions her in a German accent. Nicole Kidman, a good actress, is made to play this and other scenes like a drunken nymphet. Tom Cruise, with many callow grins, is totally miscast as a doctor, whose midnight house call, by the way, is unimaginable in today's New York.

Kubrick, with characteristic grandiosity, turns the orgy into a Busby Berkeley extravaganza, with scores of participants in a spectacular Long Island mansion, the sort of thing that could not go undiscovered. But at least the film could have profited, had he been alive, from Warner Brothers' not bowdlerizing it clumsily: a girl fully naked in one shot wears a large, computer-generated G-string in the next.

Worse, though, Kubrick seems to have lost his sense of timing. Everything is slow-moving and protracted beyond endurance— much of it accompanied by three maddeningly repeated one-finger piano notes from the second movement of György Ligeti's *Musica Ricercata*—and there are enough deliberate gaps in the often stilted dialogue to supply a half-dozen Pinter and Mamet plays with pauses. Yet, clever showman that he was, Kubrick pulled off the ultimate trick: nothing succeeds like a director's prompt demise upon completing his film.

The Sixth Sense

I am by temper disinclined to sympathize with movies of a mystical bent, especially since movie mysticism is several notches below most other kinds. The *unio mystica* is imperfectly conveyed by a couple of hours of lurid plotting and sensationalistic images.

But there is that craving in people for more than pragmatic, palpable, everyday reality. Few are untempted by transcorporal, parapsychological, supranatural images that seem to slake the thirst for metaphysical transcendence. Though alternative worlds are currently favored, even primitive ghost stories often do the trick. *The Sixth Sense*, written and directed by the 28-year-old M. Night Shyamalan, is such a one.

Of Indian parentage but growing up in Philadelphia, Shyamalan seems to have received Catholic schooling. I have not seen either his *Wide Awake* or his debut feature, *Praying with Anger*, though that title tickles me. In *The Sixth Sense*, he tells of Dr. Malcolm Crowe, a happily married child psychologist. About to cozy up to his wife on the conjugal bed, he is suddenly confronted from the bathroom by Vincent Gray, a creepy-looking former patient whom he apparently badly failed professionally. In a long-delayed revenge, Gray shoots Crowe, then kills himself. But Crowe seemingly survives, and the film chronicles his attempt to make posthumous amends to Gray by helping Cole Sear, a deeply troubled eight-year-old.

Cole, it emerges, can see and hear the dead, who come to him for help or, sometimes, just to scare him, something he dares not confess to anyone. Some of these are newly dead, others are historic revenants, like the hanged family of three dangling in a doorway. Just why they single out Cole is left open, but this seems to be a quasi-autobiographical fantasy, and it figures that the dead would seek out a man who is Night to his friends. M. Night Shyamalan sheds darkness equitably all around; his child hero is Cole (as in coal), his principal adult is Crowe, and his shootist is (presumably Oxford) Gray.

I must not reveal to you why Crowe and the tormentedly un-communicative Cole hit it off so well so quickly, the boy previously not opening up even to his sympathetic, much put-upon mother, who misunderstands his oddness. But the air is rife with misunder-standings, not least those of the author. Night conceives an award-winning psychologist as someone who is thrown by an elementary Latin phrase (in a Catholic church, Cole exclaims, *De profundis clamo ad te*), and who must consult a rather simplistic textbook on child psychology. The idea for the film may have come to Night from Ambrose Bierce's famous short story "Incident at Owl Creek," or its superb movie version by Robert Enrico, a short film worth ten full-length efforts such as *The Sixth Sense*.

There are, however, some extenuating circumstances, chief among them the performance of eleven-year-old Haley Joel Os-ment as eight-year-old Cole. The young actor is spookily good, scarily adult for his age, with a face that can seamlessly go from being three years younger to being as old and tragic as time itself. In fact, Osment reminded me of Little Father Time in Hardy's *Jude the Obscure*, a child well beyond precocity delving into ancient doom. Osment's presence enriches every scene this fully mature actor is in, and doubtless helps elicit a respectable performance from Bruce Willis as Crowe.

We get high-level work also from Australian Toni Collette as

Cole's mother, and a couple of others. Tak Fujimoto's cinematography is splendid as always. Philadelphia provides some catchy exteriors, but Fujimoto knows also how to infuse an interior with an eerie glow or, alternatively, real enough to speak to your sense of touch.

And, for once, even the hokey score by James Newton Howard works, a phenomenon so rare from this routineer to seem almost supernatural.

Of Witches and Muses

THE BLAIR WITCH PROJECT; THE DINNER GAME

Why are people so benighted as to think *The Blair Witch Project* a terrific movie? Is it because it was made by five young kids? Because it cost only $35,000? Because it was a hit at the Sundance Festival (the worst possible reason)? Because they find it truly scary? For that, it would have to be, on some level, plausible; have characters that are, in some way, appealing. I find neither to be the case. Or because it is being sold with a monstrously effective hype? Now that is scary.

An opening title card announces that three young filmmakers vanished into a Maryland forest, where they had gone in search of a reputed witch. A year later, this film shot by them was found, and tells their story. The very first absurdity is that, as the two young men and one young woman each had a video camera, the film would really have to be three films. Edited into one, it predicates the work of editors, undercutting its documentary authenticity.

Next, these Maryland woods seem neither thick nor extensive enough to warrant such a disappearance. The young people, moreover, have only one map, which they read with difficulty, and which one of them, for no good reason, throws away. They also have only one compass, which they don't resort to till late in the game. When they come across a stream, they do not have brains enough to follow it; it would surely lead them to human habitations. Further, they keep fighting among themselves, which, under the circumstances, is imbecile. And finally, they keep shooting their film with their cumbersome equipment instead of jettisoning it and facilitating their escape.

The strength of the film supposedly resides in the invisibility of the enemy; the witch, or just some locals having fun with the trio. Only disturbing nocturnal sounds are heard, and disquieting manikins made of twigs hang in the trees near the campsites in the morning. That may, perhaps, be scarier than actual sightings, but when certain key things are shot so we can't quite make them out even up close, that is cheating.

What is imposing is the extensive and manifold hype the movie is getting. The press, TV, the Internet are full of it. I just read in the *New York Times* that "the voodoo doll-like stick figures… were based on an ancient runic figure called the Burning Man [plagiarized from a 1973 film, *The Wicker Man*]… [and] are drawing as much as $300 on the Internet." That is a bit steep; but if someone could inform me where I could get them for, say, $250, I would gladly order a dozen.

If you want to see how funny a movie can get, catch *The Dinner Game*, as *Le Dîner de cons* (*The Dinner of Jerks*) has been unsatisfactorily Englished. Written and directed by Francis Veber of *La Cage aux folles* fame, this concerns a weekly dinner given by pranksters, to which each guest must bring along a jerk dumb enough not even to know when he is mocked. At the bit of a dinner we see, an expert in boomerangs who gets himself knocked out by them has the others laughing inwardly as he delivers a paean to the boomerang.

The publisher Brochant intends to squire Pignon, a low-level clerk at the Ministry of Finance, who reproduces famous monuments with matchsticks and will regale you with the exact number of matches and tubes of glue it takes to build them. Brochant has invited Pignon to a pre-dinner drink at his apartment, but having just wrenched his back, can't go. Pignon stays on to be helpful, especially after a phone message from Christine Brochant announces that she is leaving her husband. Pignon's wife left with a friend of his two years ago, which makes Pignon especially sympathetic.

But beware of Pignon's helpfulness! Whatever he tries to do for Brochant lands the publisher in a worse mess, from little clumsinesses to catastrophic whoppers. When Brochant's mistress is to be gotten rid of, it is Pignon who opens the door. Not knowing that the woman he sees is not the mistress at all, but Christine, who has changed her mind, he tells her to be temporarily satisfied with the usual four to five visits a week. No wonder she departs with even firmer resolve this time.

It is hard to convey the humor of farce out of context and in cold print. What matters most is that Jacques Villeret, as Pignon, Thierry

Lhermitte as Brochant, and Francis Huster as a friend all have split-second timing and knockout facial expressions. Best of all may be Daniel Prévost, as a smug tax collector named Cheval, who horses around with exquisite dignity. See it!

Stardust Memories

MARCELLO MASTROIANNI: I REMEMBER

I don't usually write about documentaries, because most of them belong under the rubric of reportage rather than art. To be sure, most feature films, too, fall very far short of art, generally aspiring only to be popular entertainments, and failing even at that. Clearly outclassing the current copycat, featureless feature films, however, is the documentary *Marcello Mastroianni: I Remember*, by Anna Maria Tatò, whose name the press kit misspells Tató, which admittedly is nothing compared with the film's misnaming one of Mastroianni's favorite childhood movies as *Flaying Down to Rio*. Still, flaying alive might not qualify as excessive punishment for many in today's movie business.

Marcello Mastroianni (1923–1996) was a great film actor. It was not his fault he was dubbed "The Latin Lover," something he inveighs against in *I Remember*. Rightly so, for in several of his most important films he was not a lover at all: as the teacher-turned-labor-organizer in *The Organizer* (1963), a naïve youth shyly in love in *White Nights* (1957), a member of a gang of thieves in *Big Deal on Madonna Street* (1958), the caring older brother in *Family Diary* (1962), the impotent husband in *Il Bell' Antonio* (1960), the homosexual lusted after by Sophia Loren in *A Special Day* (1977), and several others. Even as the aging, lame Casanova of Ettore Scola's *That Night in Varennes* (1982), he is playing merely a human being, and no one in the movies has ever been more human than Mastroianni.

His was a startlingly handsome face that aged gracefully into a rueful palimpsest, where reading between the heavy lines of the present one could still discern the flawless alabaster past. When, as here, the posture has become slightly stooped, the walk somewhat hesitant, the viewer grows aware of his own aging. For we do not notice the tiny incremental stages of our own senescence, but in the sudden, shocking decrepitude of a movie idol we see our own mortality more truthfully than in any mirror. As *I Remember* moves freely forward, backward, and sideways, we get a fine perspective on Marcello's, our own, and everyone else's lives, and surely 200 minutes is not too long for a seminar on living.

Besides a ballooning wife (pasta, not helium) whom Marcello finally shed, there were well-publicized lovers such as his leading ladies Faye Dunaway and Catherine Deneuve, on whom he fathered the surprisingly unattractive and undependable actress-daughter Chiara. Could his then newly married co-star Brigitte Bardot also have been on the roster? In *I Remember*, he sings—or croaks—the famous Mozart aria about the number of Don Giovanni's conquests, and even his poor singing is not without charm. Conversely, his dancing, including the tap we see here, was good, except when, as in Fellini's *Ginger and Fred*, it was meant to be amateurish.

Anna Maria Tatò, a filmmaker and Mastroianni's companion for the last 22 years of his life, made this documentary in Portugal, where Marcello, then 73, was in his final movie, *Voyage to the Beginning of the World* (1996), directed by the 88-year-old Manoel de Oliveira. (Despite his age, Oliveira had "an irritating amount of energy," Mastroianni says, "I felt like his grandfather." It is a poor film (as I would have expected from that inept director), but Marcello brightens it considerably. Although the questions Tatò asked for *I Remember* were agreed upon beforehand, the answers were neither scripted nor rehearsed: only one camera, and always only one take. The result, with intercut sequences from Marcello's films (some of which were unseen in the U.S.) and a late stage appearance, is spontaneous and enchanting.

This was a man intelligent, witty, modest, honest, and charming to his fingertips—ah well, that was Marcello's only blemish: stubby, unaristocratic fingers. Fellini was well aware of them, as Marcello and he (Fellini makes several brief appearances) duly noted; the director even tried to lengthen them with plastic extensions. In the end, he took them as they were, as he also did what he jokingly called his star's "country-bumpkin face." He would tell his cherished cinematographer, Giuseppe Rotunno, who shot this film too, "Make him handsome! You must make him handsome!"

(Mastroianni took this sort of thing with a humility unknown in today's Hollywood. "He was right when he used to say, 'Make him handsome,' or 'make her beautiful,'" he said of Fellini, "because the actor is a hyphen between the filmmaker and the audience.")

I remember the dinner at Mastroianni's house on the fabled historic Appian Way to which the director Lina Wertmüller took me one evening. The food was delicious, our host delightful. I particularly recall his taking us around his art collection, including several discolored rectangles where paintings used to hang. "This was a Vespignani," Marcello would say with a shamefaced smile, "gone to pay the tax man."

In the movie, too, while musing about the absurdity of American actors turning their profession into something painful and tormented, he observes that this makes sense only if you are in arrears with tax payments or out of work. He compares acting to the cops-and-robbers games of his childhood: "This profession is marvelous. You are paid to play games, and everybody applauds. Of course, you need a little talent. But what more could anyone ask for?"

Against lively, shifting Portuguese backgrounds—mountains, rivers, the shady bench and table in front of a country Inn—the actor reminisces, reflects, makes graceful confessions, but without revealing any indiscreet details about himself or others. He is totally free of envy or malice, never mentioning the names of mediocrities he worked with on some of his 170 or so pictures, but always full of admiration for all sorts of people, including such rival leading men as Vittorio Gassman and Gian Maria Volontè. Gassman, in fact, secretly coached him out of his stage fright when both acted on the stage in Alfieri's *Oreste* for the sternly demanding Luchino Visconti. Gassman also had to drag the frightened novice out of the toilet, where nerves made him pee continually.

The actor claims to be not one for books, although quotations from Proust, Stendhal, Diderot, Kafka, and Chekhov come easefully to his lips. He hates TV ("Could it be old age, or is television really cretinous?"), except for old movies and documentaries about animals, but not fish or birds, which bore him. And there are sweet little anecdotes. Just once, Marcello's beloved younger brother Ruggero, a fine film editor, acted with his star sibling in a dismal historical movie about Scipio the African, a scene from which we see here. As always, Mamma Mastroianni caught the finished film, and commented, "Well Marcello, you were wonderful as usual, but the redhead [Ruggero] was better."

Or the time when the 19-year-old Marcello, on an absurd wartime journey with no lights allowed on a blacked-out hopelessly crowded train, was suddenly passionately kissed. "I never knew whom I kissed. But I am sure it was a woman—though I don't know if she was pretty or ugly. How many years have passed? And yet that moment is still present, truly, one of the intense memories of my life. Memory is bizarre, isn't it? Bizarre like love."

Thus speaks the self-disclaimed Latin lover but indisputable charmer. No wonder that, as we see in the film, busloads of tourists would briefly stop by that villa on the Via Appia. An offscreen voice says, "I know the Americans. First they go to the Coliseum, then to the catacombs, and then they come here to 'Mastroianni! Mastroianni!' And he's got to show his face." And speaking of shown faces—and bodies—another recurrent presence here is his frequent co-star, Sophia Loren, especially endearing in a striptease she performs for Marcello. To quote that happy man, "What more could anyone ask for?"

American Beauty

Six years ago, I reviewed a silly, frilly, very southern play, *Five Women Wearing the Same Dress*, by one Alan Ball, who subsequently became a producer of television's *Cybill*, among other unremarkable achievements. Now he has written a supposedly highly original screenplay, the cinematic debut of the noted British stage director Sam Mendes, entitled with portentous vagueness *American Beauty*. It has been hyped as well as reviewed ecstatically as the most important American film of the fall, the year, the ages.

It stars the gifted and currently most prestigious actor Kevin Spacey as Lester Burnham, a reporter who lives in a typical American suburb (aerial view, of course) and, as narrator, informs us that he is already dead (shades of *Sunset Boulevard*). But this was the year, he says, he started to live. His wife is Carolyn (Annette Bening), a hard-edged, somewhat fading fashion plate and not very successful realtor. They have a sullen teenage daughter, Jane, who, in a pre-title sequence, bemoans her "horny geek boy" dad, and seems to mean it when she asks her boyfriend to off him.

The film allegedly pushes the envelope. This consists of the following items: 1) Carolyn wakes up at night to find Lester masturbating next to her unrepentantly. 2) Lester falls madly in love with Angela, Jane's classmate and chum, a very blonde and extremely promiscuous brat ready to have an affair with him as soon as he builds up his physique. 3) Recording Lester's feverish workouts is Ricky, an 18-year-old neighboring voyeur with a video camera, surreptitiously shooting him, and more often Jane, through their windows. 4) Ricky's father, the despotic ex-Marine Colonel Fitts, with a pitifully repressed wife, spies on his son's every step and frequently mauls him. Even so, he is unaware that his son's affluence stems not from working for a caterer, but from pushing hard drugs, which the boy also consumes. 5) Frigid Carolyn, who won't have sex with Lester, has a liberating affair with her envied and admired "King of Realtors," pretty boy Buddy Kane (Peter Gallagher).

All right, I'll throw in 6) Colonel Fitts, who wrongly suspects Ricky's friendship with Lester to be sexual, reveals something previously hidden when he suddenly kisses Lester passionately on the mouth. Clearly the film should be called *Suburbia Confidential*, not *American Beauty*. Of course, the reference may be to the carpet of red rose petals amid which Lester keeps fantasizing the naked Angela. And now for my final plot revelation, 7) Lester, sick of his bourgeois existence, throws away his job to become a counterman at a hamburger joint. The only reason I withhold 8)—whether Lester actually beds Angela or not—is that the film turns opaque at this point. It happens (or doesn't) on what may or may not be the very couch where Carolyn refused herself to him, lest he spill his beer on the expensive fabric. Add to this the ever so groundbreaking feature of baring the breasts of both young actresses: Thora Birch (Jane) and Mena Suvari (Angela).

The dialogue has its moments, and Mendes has directed with a certain flair. The performances, except for Wes Bentley's wooden Ricky, are adequate, though with no great depths to plumb. The veteran cinematographer Conrad Hall gets nice effects, often in chiaroscuro, to prove that this is an art film. Thomas Newman's music tries to be arty, but is mostly irritating.

And now one more farewell gift to you, 9) The Burnhams' other neighbors are a homosexual pair, both cutely called Jim (Jim #1 and Jim #2). According to the film's press kit, the two are "probably the most normal people in the neighborhood." For the little we see of them, they may even be the most normal in the world. Or not.

Fight Club

Highly touted as the film of the season, *Fight Club* is actually a movie that could perhaps be used as an insect repellent if it did not also assault human sensibilities. The director, David Fincher, who scored with *Seven* and wobbled with *The Game*, now plummets to what, in better times, might have been deemed rock bottom. Fincher features weird gimmicks in his movies, gimmicks that have steadily gotten gimmickier. The one wagging *Fight Club* is so outlandish as to demonstrate how indistinguishable excessive cleverness can be from stupidity.

What regrettably shields Fincher, the screenwriter Jim Uhls, and Chuck Palahniuk, author of the underlying novel, is that no reviewer can, in good conscience, give away that preposterous gimmick. Too bad, too, that the film begins with a storyline that, though farfetched, is not without interest, but is soon dropped in favor of matchlessly sadomasochistic virulence combined with perfect incredibility.

We start with Narrator (no other name is given), a mid-level white-collar worker so bored with his job as to become addicted to amassing IKEA furniture he cannot use. To ease his malaise and insomnia, he seeks out all conceivable nocturnal support-group meetings, and, under an assumed name, pretends to be a fellow sufferer, just to feel something. His troubles begin when he meets Marla Singer, an attractive but hyperneurotic young woman who plays the same game, yet, at first, harshly snubs his attempts at co-conspiracy.

Soon, worse befalls both him and the movie. Tyler Durden, a young man who sat next to him on a plane, leads Narrator on night-prowling expeditions on which the two fight each other, or get a growing legion of fellow nightcrawlers to engage in bloody brawls. They form a fight club, heavily laden with overtly macho and covertly homoerotic symbolism, eventually leading to the unspeakable, or at least the not-to-be-divulged.

Do not, however, hold out the hope that if the whole is absurd, the parts, at any rate, might satisfy. How seriously can you take, for example, a reputable office-worker arriving on the job every day more bloodied, disfigured, and disreputable-looking without being fired by his prissy supervisor? If the more improbable stretches of *Fight Club* could be marketed, they might put rubber bands out of business. Also, bits of dialogue are so unintentionally laughable as to keep the wrong side of your mouth working overtime.

As Narrator, Edward Norton continues his recent predilection for unsavory roles well played. As the bisexually heartthrobby Tyler and the daintily dirty Marla, Brad Pitt and Helena Bonham

Carter also do their damnedest in a hopeless cause that, given current audience and critical tastes, may not be all that hopeless, alas. Conspicuous among a rogue's gallery of supporting players is the musician Meat Loaf, whom the *New York Times* once referred to as Mr. Loaf, and who here qualifies as Mr. Oaf. And let's not forget the Dust Brothers, whose music adds its not inconsiderable bit of wormwood to the rest.

Truth Up in Smoke

THE INSIDER; BOYS DON'T CRY

It is rare for a Hollywood movie to be both commercial and artistic, both a nail-biting exposé à la *All the President's Men* and a sociopolitical art film like those of Gillo Pontecorvo and Francesco Rosi. But *The Insider* is such a film: a superb quasi-documentary telling a real-life story (though not all of it, and with a few names changed), and a marvelous feature, 155 minutes of entertainment, exemplarily written, directed, and acted.

The film concerns Jeffrey Wigand, a scientist working for the third-largest tobacco company, Brown & Williamson, who, after much agonizing, blew the whistle on Big Tobacco's practices: he said that nicotine was addictive, with special additives making it even more insidious, and that the tobacco bigwigs lied to Congress and the nation, besides trying to silence him by fair means or foul. The man who aided and doggedly abetted him was Lowell Bergman, ex-radical firebrand and a news producer for *60 Minutes*, trying to bring about a segment of the show in which Wigand would spill the beans on camera to Mike Wallace.

This involved extraordinary amounts of planning and plotting, as B&W pulled all strings legal and illegal to block the enterprise, not least intimidation and a huge smear campaign, almost completely mendacious. But Bergman, Wigand, and *60 Minutes* were prevailing until the CBS board squelched the airing of that segment. There was a fear of a multi-million dollar lawsuit from B&W; Lawrence Tisch, the then-new CBS capo, was negotiating a merger with Westinghouse he did not want litigation to queer. Besides, Tisch owned Lorrillard, about to acquire some of B&W's discount brands, though the film is regrettably silent about this.

Wigand had signed a draconian confidentiality agreement with

B&W in exchange for considerable severance pay and health benefits especially needed by one of his daughters, chronically ill. This enabled B&W to hound him legally, and necessitated acrobatic maneuvers, such as his testifying in an anti-tobacco case in Mississippi, where B&W with its Kentucky law was hamstrung, and his getting certain things into the public record and thus usable on television. I cannot begin to go into the Byzantine ploys and counterploys chronicled by *The Insider*, making your heart race in time with the frames of the film, 24 beats a second.

There is, however, much more to the film than the suspenseful and literate screenplay by Eric Roth and the director, Michael Mann, based on expert reportage by Marie Brenner. Take, first, Wigand and Bergman as played by Russell Crowe and Al Pacino. Crowe magisterially conveys a character of intricate motivations: heroic largely out of compulsion; loving truth only a little more than economic and marital benefits (his wife, Liane, enjoys the amenities of corporate affluence). This is a fleshy man, an athlete on the verge of beefiness; but just what he does with his eyeglasses is artistry enough. The paranoia that creeps—not unjustifiably—into his life; the struggle to hang on to his wife and children, who nevertheless leave him, after repeated death threats; the endless all-hour phone calls, friendly or hostile, that buffet him as bells do experimental animals—Crowe suggests them with hard-won self-control: you can feel the sweat in this man's soul.

Pacino, who goes over the top as easily as one steps over a garden hose, stays within bounds as Bergman. He looks as emaciated and haunted as ever, his eyes barely contained in their sockets, his tousled hair propelled by a powerful additive; yet he suffers more than he rages, croons more than he croaks. His eruptions are the more powerful for coming from a nonsmoking volcano (as befits an anti-tobacco film). Best of all, the bleached-haired Crowe and the charcoal-tagliatelle-topped Pacino have a combustive chemistry unmatched since Clark Gable met Jean Harlow. Their combative love-hate percolates throughout, and has the movie crackling like Rice Krispies on Benzedrine.

I'd eulogize every player down to Wings Hauser, who, in one scene as a tobacco lawyer, is scarier than ten nights in a graveyard. There is Christopher Plummer's Mike Wallace, commandingly blending toughness and slipperiness, rectitude and opportunism. There is Diane Venora's memorable Mrs. Wigand, managing in a small part as layered a performance as Meryl Streep in her plummiest solo turn.

There is dear Lindsay Crouse, as Bergman's wife, radiating spousal supportiveness without an ounce of sugar. There is Michael Gambon's portrayal of a tobacco executive that, understated though it is, makes you wish for antifreeze for your bloodstream.

And what of Gina Gershon, as the CBS lawyer, who without one excessive move makes you hate lawyers and their employers with equal ardor? Why, even those very minor actors portraying hostile Arabs, in a prologue showing Bergman and Wallace tangling with some Middle Eastern terrorists, contribute to making that merely prefatory scene worth an Oscar or two.

Michael Mann, whose direction has at times been too mannered, puts his copious conceits to good use here. Extreme close-up, which can be distracting, here serves to rivet us to the gears of the plot. Telephones of every kind—sleekly cellular or clunkily coin-operated, on Lear jets or hectic street corners—crisscross the movie with talk oiled by cajoling suasion or driven by rocketing imprecations. They carry death threats or encouragements with equal urgency, and when their nocturnal rings remain unresponded to, your palms itch empathetically.

Seldom has film put backgrounds to better use. Whether they are exotic locations or merely murals, they heighten the tension by their insinuating irony, as Dante Spinotti's camera scoops drama out of every nook and cranny. There is even a scene with no partition for background, when Wigand, now deprived of his daughters' company, envisions their living presence as if right there. My only slight cavil is with the music by Lisa Gerrard and Pieter Bourke, which tries too hard to be different, but at least succeeds in being that. If *The Insider* does not strongly move you one way or the other—or both—you don't deserve movies; stay before the tube and let your tubers grow into the couch.

I missed the documentary on Brandon Teena, but here now is a first feature by Kimberly Peirce about him/her, *Boys Don't Cry*. It is the story of young Teena Brandon from Lincoln, Nebraska, who wanted to be a boy and changed herself into Brandon Teena in the dull neighboring burg of Falls City, where girls fell for this sensitive youth. One of them, Lana, though catching on, even consummated an affair with him. But when two ex-cons, one of them Lana's ex-boyfriend, found out, they first raped Brandon, then killed him.

The motif of the person who changes sex is well-known in life as in literature. The latter, at least, should provide some explanations, and a sense of how sexual partners could be so duped. The film, co-written by Peirce and Andy Bienen, has Teena declare that she is not a lesbian, but beyond that doesn't even try to enlighten us. But it does, as noted, explain the sex scenes.

Hilary Swank, an attractive and delicate actress, cuts an appealing ephebic figure in the lead that might have fooled the folks at Andover or Exeter, but among these beer-swilling, roughhousing hillbillies would hardly have passed. She strains to get her voice low and keeps flashing a toothily boyish smile, but earns our respect rather than belief. As Lana, Chloë Sevigny, a specialist in trashy roles, is more convincing. Other parts are underdeveloped, or stereotypical. The drab atmosphere of Falls City is well captured; the rest remains sketchy.

Holiday Hustle

THE HURRICANE; ANGELA'S ASHES; CIDER HOUSE RULES; CRADLE WILL ROCK; THE TALENTED MR. RIPLEY; SNOW FALLING ON CEDARS; TITUS; SLEEPY HOLLOW; MAGNOLIA

Given the preternatural plethora of holiday movies and their inordinate length, the best I can offer is a kind of checklist of those I've been able to see for your Yuletide guidance. To start with the cream: *The Hurricane* is the story of the black New Jersey boxing champion Rubin "Hurricane" Carter, who spent almost 20 years in jail for murders he did not commit. But for the self-sacrificing efforts of a black youth from Brooklyn and three white Canadians, he might have rotted there till his death. This true story is told with magnificent restraint in what may be Norman Jewison's finest directorial effort, with Denzel Washington superbly controlled in the lead and backed up by a fine supporting cast. The intelligent screenplay stays resolutely unhistrionic, and is all the more moving for it.

No less fine is *Angela's Ashes*, from Frank McCourt's bestselling memoir of his dreadfully deprived Irish childhood. The book profited from its lack of self-pity and strong sense of humor; much of this survives in the screenplay by Laura Jones and the director, Alan Parker. Parker's films have been wildly uneven, but here he maintains remarkable judiciousness throughout. Shooting on location in Dublin and Limerick, Michael Seresin captures the misery, grotesquery, and heroism of poverty with equal sharpness. The acting of both children and adults is nothing short of sublime, with Joe Breen particularly haunting as young Frank, and Robert Carlyle and Emily Watson shattering as his parents.

Readers of John Irving's *Cider House Rules* may find the author's screen adaptation procrustean and bowdlerizing. But taken just as a movie, it charms and entertains, and still has a little edge left. Lasse Hallström, the Swedish director of the delightful *My Life as a Dog*, has floundered in Hollywood, but here recovers his footing with his favorite subject, children, specifically orphans, perfectly cast and directed. Michael Caine is first-rate as the humane but fallible doctor running the orphanage, and Tobey Maguire is immensely winning as the brainy orphan who becomes his assistant. The marvelous supporting cast includes Kathy Baker, Jane Alexander, and Delroy Lindo; Oliver Stapleton's camera captures the colors of New England to burnished perfection.

In directing *Cradle Will Rock*, Tim Robbins deftly juggles the turmoil and fervor of the Depression-ravaged '30s in several public and private stories, historical and fictional. There are accounts of Marc Blitzstein's leftist opera, *The Cradle Will Rock*, which the authorities couldn't squelch, and of Diego Rivera's politicized Rockefeller Center murals, which were destroyed. Cherry Jones is wonderful as Hallie Flanagan, the embattled head of the Federal Theater, but Bill Murray, John Turturro, Ruben Blades, and Vanessa Redgrave are no slouches either in various historical or invented roles, and Emily Watson again breaks your heart. Only Joan Cusack and, as Orson Welles, Angus Macfadyen are disasters; otherwise, despite some oversimplifications, the film works.

The Talented Mr. Ripley, written and directed by Anthony Minghella, is a remake of René Clément's *Purple Noon*, based on Patricia Highsmith's admired mystery novel. In it, a nice but poor boy is sent to Italy by a millionaire father to retrieve his playboy son. But the virtuous youth, taken up by the jazz-loving and bisexually promiscuous ne'er-do-well and his would-be-writer girlfriend, develops a taste for the luxurious *dolce far niente* in a gorgeous seaside resort. Seduced by his newfound amenities, our hero cannot endure being just as suddenly dropped by the easily bored playboy, and, provoked by insults, kills him. He assumes his victim's identity and is gradually goaded into additional murders, and, though not without torment, gets away with them.

As in *The English Patient*, Minghella depends largely on lushly photographed picturesque surroundings. This time, however, he gets less good acting. Matt Damon works hard at conveying innocence dragged into viciousness, but does not quite convince at either extreme. As the main girlfriend, the hugely overrated Gwyneth Paltrow is abysmal. Still, Jude Law is excellent as the spoiled Lothario, and the travelogue through Italy's sea- and city-scapes is irresistible.

Lastly, the stinkers. Whatever the novel may be like, the movie *Snow Falling on Cedars* is a pretentious, artsy-fartsy catastrophe, with unconscionable visual and auditory distractions from the worthwhile story, for which the director Scott Hicks and his co-adapter Ron Bass should be hanged by their 20 thumbs. But the film also contains a performance by Max von Sydow that is as great as acting can get, well worth catching if you can keep from puking at the surrounding bilge.

Titus Andronicus is patently Shakespeare at love (a/k/a zero), though a clever stage production such as Peter Brook's (1955) can make theatrical history. Julie Taymor's film version, *Titus*, can only make cinematic calamity. An imaginative theater designer (as for *The Lion King*), Taymor is no film director, and has had the awful idea of combining ancient Rome with the present, presenting cheek-by-jowl quadrigas and Mercedes-Benzes, togas and tuxedos, and so on ad nauseam. As Titus, Anthony Hopkins again hams it up: the Roman matrons who scared their kids with "Hannibal is at the gates" probably switched to *Hannibal Lecter ante Portas*. Alan Cumming camps disgustingly as Saturninus, and Jessica Lange huffs and puffs as Tamora; the others do their bit, but are defeated by either the horror, or the boredom of it all.

Tim Burton's *Sleepy Hollow* is easily the silliest film of the season, and P.T. Anderson's *Magnolia* is the most certifiably insane, to be avoided like the plague of frogs it includes. Merry Christmas!

Criticism from

the 2000s

Comedies or Errors

TOPSY-TURVY; ALL ABOUT MY MOTHER

To continue with the survey of the slew of films that descended on us, like molten lava on Pompeii, at year's, or millennium's, end.

Topsy-Turvy is a departure for its director, Mike Leigh, who specializes in part-bleak, part-comic depictions of contemporary British lower-middle-class life, and improvises endlessly with his cast before beginning to shoot, which always struck me as rather masturbatory and yielded mostly drab films. A historical film about the lives of Gilbert and Sullivan, including many scenes of theatrical rehearsals and performances of their operettas, is the next-to-last thing you'd expect from Leigh, the last thing being that he would carry it off.

Well, he does, more or less, even if, at 160 minutes, at rather excessive length. Still, the down-to-earth Gilbert and the somewhat la-di-da Sullivan (who really wanted to compose serious operas and once, alas, did) make a fascinating team, the former with his wife, the latter with his mistress. Leigh, who is also a playwright, has a good grasp of theatrical life, and the onstage, backstage, and farther-behind-the-scenes sequences are tart and truthful. The financial aspect of production, the actors' demands for higher pay, the drink and the drugs, the dressing-room bickering are rendered with vivacity and humor.

Other scenes add very little, such as Sullivan's night in a Paris bordello or Gilbert's being accosted on a nocturnal ramble by a demented Irishwoman. But the feel of London life of the period is there, and the scenes from the Savoy operettas are reproduced with solicitous authenticity. Jim Broadbent (Gilbert) and Allan Corduner (Sullivan) are both fine, and so is the supporting cast in which Ron Cook, as the producer D'Oyly Carte, especially shines. Yet I couldn't help feeling nostalgic about a more modest 1953 film on this topic, wherein Maurice Evans, Peter Finch, and particularly Robert Morley as Gilbert enchanted me. To be sure, I was younger then.

The New York Film Critics Circle, with unsurprising obtuseness, ignored such masterpieces as *Dr. Akagi*, *The Dream Life of Angels*, and the modest but delightful *The Dinner Game*, to crown Pedro Almodóvar's *All About My Mother* as best foreign film. The film-maker is one of those homosexuals who adore imperious women and tormented young men, and he has turned his predilections to mildly amusing but greatly overrated movies, of which this may be the best, little as that is saying.

The problem is not that Almodóvar is homosexual, but that he is an inveterate fan. His film's title derives from *All About Eve*, which two of the principals watch on television. The film's two lesbian lovers are appearing as Blanche and Stella in *A Streetcar Named Desire*, which also figures importantly. Playacting is everywhere. The heroine, Manuela, is a nurse who plays a major role in a training film about organ donations. When her gifted 17-year-old son, a fan of Huma, the actress playing Blanche, is run over on a rainy night while chasing after Huma's cab for an autograph, Manuela sees fiction become reality as her son's heart is donated to a needy patient.

Grasping her dead son's diary-cum-autograph book, which ends protesting his mother's refusal to reveal anything about his father except that he died long ago, Manuela leaves Madrid for Barcelona. She is looking for that father, Esteban, to tell him about a son he doesn't know he had. She expects that Esteban, a male prostitute who had a sex-change operation and became Lola, will be found in an area known as the Field, where drugs and male prostitution thrive. Instead of Lola, she finds another transsexual, La Agrado, whom she saves from attack by an angry client. La Agrado lived with her and Esteban when they were married.

By a set of complicated circumstances, Manuela adopts Sister Rosa, a pregnant runaway nun who has fallen out with her family. Huma and her lover, Nina, now playing *Streetcar* in Barcelona, are fighting as usual over Nina's drug addiction. Everyone befriends everyone, and Manuela, who in her village once played Stella in *Streetcar*, even goes on for Nina, who has overdosed. What a memory that Manuela has!

This isn't the half of it, but it's enough for you to see how stage-, movie-, and star-struck Almodóvar is, with even the hospital becoming a place for cinema, which life promptly imitates. Life, for him, replicates stage and screen; everyone is actor or, preferably, an actress of the most outrageously showy sort. Granted, he knows the gay scene inside-out, and does have a certain campy sense of humor; but does that justify the awards he keeps winning from benighted reviewers?

Certainly the Argentine actress Cecilia Roth (Manuela) does a splendid job, but neither Marisa Paredes, as a repellent Huma-Blanche, nor Candela Peña, as a repugnant Nina-Stella, impresses. Even poorer is Toni Cantó, defeated by the tricky role of Esteban-Lola. But the film does have one bravura performance by Antonia San Juan as the transsexual prostitute La Agrado, which is not, however, enough to save a largely trashy film.

Life in the Slow Lane

THE STRAIGHT STORY; THE END OF THE AFFAIR

Alvin Straight is a nice old man living—we don't quite know off what—in Laurens, Iowa, with his daughter Rose, who talks haltingly and whose four children have been taken away from her because she is slightly retarded and because one of them was badly burned in a fire. Alvin says, "She is a little bit slow, but her mind is like a bear trap." Laurens is a small town, and on the sunny day when *The Straight Story* begins, Main Street is deserted but for four dogs (not together) who bound across it in canine bliss.

Alvin has to be helped up from the floor of his shack by Rose, who finally manages to drag him off to a doctor. He is henceforth to use a walker, eat more judiciously, and stop smoking cigars. For the walker, he substitutes two canes; the rest he ignores. As he and Rose are watching a lightning storm, a phone call from someone informs Rose that Alvin's brother, Lyle, has had a stroke. Although they haven't spoken in ten years, Alvin resolves to visit Lyle in Mt. Zion, Wisconsin, a goodly distance away. His eyes do not permit him to drive a car, so he decides to travel by his lawn mower, to which he attaches a flimsy trailer. The townsfolk think him crazy, his mission impossible. But this is a true story.

The lawn mower conks out fairly promptly, and he returns to buy another model, used but newer. Off he goes again, unperturbed by the fact that whatever moves on the road lets him eat its dust. He carries victuals with him, and doesn't even mind that he rides on a backless seat. Modest adventures befall him. Thus, a surly girl hitch-hiker, pregnant and running away from her family, comes upon his supper: toasting wieners on a campfire. He shares his meal and some good advice with her. Another time, he encounters a hysteri-cal woman who has just run over a deer. Its antlers end up on his trailer, its meat lands in his stomach.

When a group of young touring cyclists swarm around him and eventually share a bivouac with him, one of them asks what is worst about getting old. He tells them: remembering that one was once young. But he is content anyway, driving by day and sleeping by night, and dispensing bits of philosophy here and there, even if the wisdom is often derivative.

People, at least in the Midwest, are wonderfully kind. When his drive belt breaks on a steep incline, he nearly comes to grief. But some good folks from nearby come to his aid. One of them puts him up on his land, and summons a pair of comic repairmen to restore his vehicle. Alvin haggles with them pawkily. At times, the dialogue is very slow but it always hits home.

It is refreshing, for one thing, to see a film about an old person, many of whose encounters are with other old-timers. For another, the characters have a simple, earthy reality. Pathos is never milked, except perhaps in a barroom episode where Alvin and another geezer remi-nisce about terrible wartime memories, but even this scene does not go overboard. And the kindness of strangers never turns sappy. The rest is taken care of by the acting, directing, and cinematography.

David Lynch is known for having directed some of the meanest, ugliest films on record; here, suddenly, he goes antithetical, and gives us one of the gentlest movies of recent times. And it works. Even when the pacing dawdles, the camera will be on the face of Richard Farnsworth, that superb 79-year-old actor, equally fascinating in quirkiness and in quietude. And the scenes on the road, amid typical uneventfully flat landscapes, are shot with unfailing eloquence by Freddie Francis, the marvelous 82-year-old British cinematographer (and sometimes di-rector), who manages to wrest a rich palette from wheat, asphalt, and some greenery. Also, the night sky with stars, a poetic leitmotif.

The screenplay by John Roach and the film's editor, Mary Sweeney, is humane and only occasionally a bit weirdly Lynchian, and the usually overwrought composer Angelo Badalamenti remains decently restrained. With Sissy Spacek (Rose) and Harry Dean Stanton (Lyle) leading an utterly believable supporting cast, *The Straight Story* gets it pretty much right.

Neil Jordan gives us a remake Graham Greene's semiautobiographical novel *The End of the Affair*, with Stephen Rea, Julianne Moore, and Ralph Fiennes playing, respectively the husband, the wife, and the friend/lover. This triangle, set against the London Blitz and including even a direct hit on the house where adultery is in progress, makes for the melodrama of tortured conscience and Catholic guilt that was Greene's forte, and Jordan brings it vividly to the screen.

But Jordan must be more Catholic than—not quite the Pope—but Graham Greene, and has more nocturnal rain in his film than even London can usually produce. This, then, is a movie top-heavy with atmosphere, especially since Stephen Rea is always caught without an umbrella—most unlikely for a British civil servant, proverbially well-brollied. There are some fine moments, a plethora of sex, moody cinematography by Roger Pratt; but something is lacking, or too much for the lay viewer. Moore, an American, impresses with her accent as much as with her acting, and Stephen Rea, in an atypical part, is even better. But Fiennes is becoming a bit of a cliché: the genteel, delicate British romantic lover, capable of outbursts of ever-so-sensitive passion before relapsing into his standard sensitive British dorkiness.

Not One Less

The leading Chinese filmmaker Zhag Yimou brings us *Not One Less*. Though he has lost his gorgeous companion and star, Gong Li, his art is undiminished, as this film, despite its ungrammatical English title, proves.

It is the story of Wei Minzhi, a 13-year-old girl recruited as a substitute for a backwoods primary-school teacher given a month-long emergency leave to tend to his gravely ill mother. No one else would undertake this thankless job, and Wei is at first intimidated by her 28 prospective wards and her own youthful inexperience. But she desperately needs the fee: 50 yuan, plus, if none of the kids defects as some already have, ten yuan more. Hence the title, which ought to be "Not One Fewer," although *Not One Less* has a better ring.

How this simple village girl, scarcely older than her pupils and under dire circumstances—the school is so poor that even chalk is stringently rationed—makes a go of it is both absorbing and profoundly moving. Peasant stubborness translates itself into pedagogic ingenuity, and the great need for those 60 yuan spurs Wei to almost superhuman feats of endurance and canniness. Everyone in the cast is an amateur and, in Zhang's masterstroke, plays a role identical with or close to his real-life status. Everybody also retains his real-life name, and a good deal of the film was improvised.

Just when things begin to go smoothly for Wei, the little student troublemaker, whom she managed to tame, is sent off to the big city by his sick, widowed and destitute mother to earn money toward paying off her creditors. Wei resolves to retrieve the boy for that extra ten yuan, though she doesn't even have the money for the fare to the distant and scary city that she has never seen.

What happens from then on is almost indescribably touching, but also, like the rest of the film, not devoid of humor, and crowned by an irresistible performance from the slightly stolid, but all the more gripping, Wei Minzhi. If you miss this marvelously written, directed, acted and shot film, you will cheat yourself out of a good deal more than 60 yuan.

Mifune

A group of Danish filmmakers signed a vow of chastity, called "Dogma 95." All shooting is to be done on location, with no smuggled-in props. The sound must always be simultaneous with the images, not added later. The light must be natural, the camera handheld. The unsensational action must take place here and now, and the director must not be credited. This may seem excessive, but some of it is strangely fruitful. Certainly, Søren Kragh-Jacobsen's *Mifune* is a heartening success.

Kresten, a young arriviste, marries the rich Claire without revealing anything about his family and penurious childhood on a dilapidated and distant island farm. The day after the wedding, he is summoned to the home he left years ago, to help bury his father and take care of his semicretinous older brother Rud. When the upper-crust Claire finds out the truth, she promptly divorces him. To help care for the helpless Rud, and run the run-down farm, he advertises for a housekeeper.

Liva, a Copenhagen call girl (to put her rebellious younger brother, Bjarke, through private school), is fed up with her creepy clients, brutal pimp, and obscene phone calls. She takes on the farm job, as she thinks temporarily. Gradually, farm life begins to appeal to her, as does Kresten, and even poor, retarded Rud, who warmly responds to her. There is trouble with a lecherously envious and violent neighbor, and even Liva's fellow call girls, thinking her in grave danger, come comically and mistakenly to her rescue. Kresten, turned into an all too casual lover, nevertheless allows Liva to bring Bjarke to the farm; recalcitrant at first, the boy adapts. In the end, Kresten and Liva, on their now revivified farm, dance amorously in the soft lamplight allowed by the tenets of Dogma 95.

Mifune, whose title derives from a charming episode alluding to *The Seven Samurai*, reeks of true, basic humanity, virtually unknown in American movies. Country life is captured with stunning veracity and no less impressive Dogma 95 cinematography. Mostly sunless skies supply a silverpoint background against which the colors of nature and humanity come to pungently idiosyncratic life. The sparse indoor lighting makes for exquisite chiaroscuro by night, and avoids a blanketing sheen by day. But the finest light is shed on the human soul. The writer-director Kragh-Jacobsen is keenly and compassionately cognizant of the inconsistent murk in the human heart, yielding both petty nastiness and amazing generosity. Rather than flaunt skin-deep Hollywood profundities, the film humanely probes our paradoxical essence.

As Liva, Iben Hjejle has the moody vivacity of changeable weather, one moment radiantly lovely, another sullenly overcast. Her face and bearing are an Aeolian harp played on by inner winds, but her spirit's faithful compass always points to the truth. Anders W. Berthelsen's Kresten is likewise unvarnishedly natural, and Jesper Asholt's Rud is, admirably, neither patronized nor sentimentalized.

Beautiful People

Jasmin Dizdar, a Bosnian filmmaker living in London, has come up with *Beautiful People*, a film so dazzling and dizzying that I feel

JOHN SIMON ON FILM

rash to review it after just one seeing. It concerns four families, British and Bosnian, whose intersecting lives make for farce and satire, sadness and anguish, a carousel of carefreeness, carelessness, and caring. The characters are so numerous, the crosscutting so rapid, the situations so bizarre, the editing so elliptical as to require utmost, but never unrewarded, concentration.

Connections can be made only gradually, but the very confusion makes dramatic and philosophical contributions. The survey here is from upper-crust to lower-class, from the benighted to the sentient, from Croat to Serb. Only briefly does the action move to war-torn Bosnia, but the offhanded horror—comic if it were not so dreadful—makes a huge impact. Throughout, suffering verges on grotesquery, madness, and absurdity, as when two ethnic adversaries, wounded and hospitalized, still keep fighting, and the British nurse admonishes, "You're here to heal, not to fight. So start healing." There is a strange, detached sympathy, or sympathetic detachment, and Dizdar's language is as penetrating as his direction.

Shot with astringence by Barry Ackroyd, this film boasts a large, multinational cast, which forms an ensemble as seamless as it is internecine. Some here may be amateurs, but as good as professionals, even as the professionals cannily pass for just plain people, sometimes even beautiful. Watching *Beautiful People* is to descend into a maelstrom of the sublime and the ridiculous and emerge, if such a thing can be, richer and wiser.

Miniskirted Crusader

ERIN BROCKOVICH

Many who concede that Julia Roberts is beautiful doubt whether she can act. Yet though probably not destined for Shakespeare and Sophocles, she has been dependable on screen. With *Erin Brockovich*, she should persuade even doubting Thomases that she is both a movie star (lovely, sexy, adored by the camera) and an actress (damn talented).

This is the true story of an ex–Miss Wichita, twice divorced and the mother of three, who, guiltless in a nasty traffic accident, is nevertheless awarded no compensation for her injuries. With not even enough money for baby-sitters, she browbeats the middle-aged ambulance chaser Ed Masry, who lost the court case, into at least giving her a job. Erin Brockovich is tall and toothsome, dresses in the miniest of skirts, and lets part of her bra, much of her bosom, and all of her feelings hang out. Under stress she becomes foulmouthed, which may have helped lose her case for her and adds to her unpopularity with her officemates.

Though hired at a low salary with no benefits, she goes at her file clerk's job with a determination lacking in many with a better education and legal training. She is puzzled by the inclusion of medical records in some dossiers and on impulse, visits some claimants in the little town of Hinkley. Its adults and children suffer from a cornucopia of ghastly maladies, caused, as she slowly figures out, by Chromium 6, a toxic substance Pacific Gas & Electric is dumping there. The sick are uneager to talk to lawyers, but Erin's earthiness and compassion wins them over, and she compiles a list of grievances that convinces even the hard-boiled Ed Masry. The zeal to do right by others—with profit also to himself—captures him, and he and Erin become a droll detective team.

Looking for someone to watch her kids while she is away, Erin hooks up with George, a biker neighbor, who genuinely likes children, and also enjoys an affair with her. Yet as her pursuit of evidence against PG&E becomes all-consuming, she loses the finally restive George, for whom she has come to care. Meanwhile, as the damage claims become bigger, Ed joins up with a major specialist law firm, but most of the grunt work still devolves on Erin.

This is where the scenarist Susannah Grant and the director Steven Soderburgh could fall into the trap of the stereotypical David *vs.* Goliath story—but it is impressive how many clichés they largely manage to avoid. The byplay between Erin and Ed, pawkily played by the wily veteran Albert Finney, always sparkles; Erin's investigations in Hinkley and elsewhere are honestly suspenseful; the reactions of the locals, whose ailments are graphically but unexploitatively portrayed, ring true; minor characters have lives of their own, notably a suspicious and uncooperative woman splendidly played by Cherry Jones. The subsidiary lawyers on both sides of what becomes a $333 million case are vividly characterized, and you feel for the put-upon George (nicely played by Aaron Eckhart) and the loved but neglected Brockovich children.

Soderbergh has always been an annoyingly gimmicky director, sometimes almost unbearable. Here, however, he restrains himself, and though he is still keen on tricky cuts and dissolves and the odd *recherché* camera angle, these manage to entice rather than interfere. He has rounded up fine supporting players, notably Marg Helgenberger as a woman afflicted with cancer, Veanne Cox as a frostily buttoned-up lawyer, and Tracey Walter as Erin's seeming stalker. And the joy at the victims' hard-won victory that the movie communicates is as infectious as Chromium 6, and much more salubrious.

East-West

In Régis Wargnier's *East-West*, based on a true story, East and West meet over the very screenplay, which is by Rustam Ibragimbekov, Sergei Bodrov, Louis Garde, and Wargnier. Though the film is mostly in French, quite a bit of it is in Russian, and the cast is both Russian and French. The story concerns a number of Russian émigrés who, after World War II, were coaxed by the Soviets into returning to live in their homeland. Instead of the promised warm reception, they are sent to labor camps or executed. Our hero, Aleksei Golovin, a much-needed doctor, is spared. He and his French wife, Marie, and young son, Seryozha, are assigned to a single room in a communal apartment in Kiev, where Aleksei is posted to the infirmary of a textile factory.

The crampedness, lack of privacy, petty wrangling among the tenants, snooping informers within the *komunalka*, make the Golovins' life appalling. When Marie tries to get a visa to go back to France, the vicious (and often murderous) commissar Pirogov merely tears up her passport. Aleksei, partly out of love for the motherland, partly out of necessity, pursues a cunctatory course, playing along with the authorities while hoping for some future amelioration. Over this, the marriage deteriorates. The head of the *komunalka*, a nice old lady who commiserated with Marie (in French!) is denounced and executed, her 17-year-old grandson, Sasha becomes Marie's only confidant.

She helps Sasha develop into an Olympic swimmer, which should lead to competing abroad and defection. She also befriends Gabrielle, a famous French actress on tour in Kiev, who promises to help her get out. By this time, Aleksei has become a seemingly perfect government toady, and even intercepts Gabrielle's letters to Marie. Marital relations between them cease, and Aleksei becomes involved with his factory's female director.

Years pass, but Marie and Sasha are repeatedly foiled in their escape plans, even as their relationship becomes closer. There are scary, depressing, and sometimes even exhilarating adventures as Aleksei becomes the bedmate of a vulgar neighbor woman, and Seryozha is buffeted between his parents. That is enough plot summary, though there is plenty more.

East-West is a mixture of sharply observed political and psychological detail with melodramatic events that, however true, preclude much deepening beyond the thriller level. Yet the mixture is artfully handled, and, except for Pirogov, the characters tend not to be all black or white. Marie herself becomes hard, but in the end manages some conjugal feelings for Aleksei, who proves to have genuinely redeeming features.

The dialogue is intelligent throughout, the suspense always riveting. Amazingly, two of the principals—Oleg Menchikov as Aleksei, and Sergei Bodrov Jr. as Sasha—being monolingual, had to learn their French lines by rote. They came through remarkably, although Sandrine Bonnaire (Marie) later observed how weird it was when Menchikov, with whom she hardly communicated offscreen, suddenly spoke his part in near-perfect French. Under such difficult circumstances, the smoothness achieved is impressive; as Gabrielle, Catherine Deneuve provides condignly staunch support.

Backed up by an efficient score from Patrick Doyle and atmospheric cinematography from Laurent Dailland, Wargnier has directed with a fine sense for minute particulars and powerful use of crosscutting. Mlle Bonnaire, always a trenchant actress, has grown with age into a softer, maturer, more womanly presence. *East-West* is not a great film, but, until such a one comes along, will do very nicely.

What, No Orgy?

GLADIATOR

By one of fate's sardonic ironies, the very week that brought the demise of Steve Reeves, the body builder actor whose Hercules initiated the popularity of sword-and-sandal (or blood-and-sand) epics, also produced the opening of Ridley Scott's *Gladiator*, the first such film in many a lustrum, the public's blood lust having switched to more up-to-date genres. Although Anthony Mann's *Fall of the Ro-*

man Empire (1964) covered some of the same ground—so much so that it has, unfairly, been removed from video stores—*Gladiator* is bigger, costlier, and beastlier.

It begins in A.D. 180, at the end of Marcus Aurelius's rule, with the emperor fighting the barbarians in what, with touching classicism, is referred to as Germania. Commanding the SPQR forces is a fictitious general, Maximus, whose name the screenwriters—David Franzoni, John Logan, and William Nicholson—most likely plucked out of Marcus Aurelius's famous *Meditations*, where the itinerant lecturer Maximus is mentioned as a mentor. A Maximus, to be sure, very different from the grim and growling warrior whom Russell Crowe portrays with unyielding prowess and unsmiling probity, but who, we read, likewise "thought as he spoke," though perhaps not with an Australian accent.

Aided by only minor anachronisms, Maximus defeats the antique Krauts, hairier than the worst hippies, in grandiose nocturnal battle sequences, the forest battleground crisscrossed by somewhat unlikely but wildly photogenic flaming arrows. As a reward, Marcus—played by Richard Harris as only a hair or two less hirsute than the furibund Teutons and about as Roman as Monty Python—picks him as his heir. This naturally angers the heir apparent, Commodus, who, with his sister, Lucilla, has kept well to the rear of the fighting. He promptly throttles his father and dispatches a few trusties to decapitate Maximus, who, however, proves too agile for them and instead cooks their goose, or geese.

Just how he does this is hard to tell, because Scott's chief technique through much of the film is lightning-fast cutting, so that chopped-off limbs, severed heads, gushing blood, etc., fly by so quickly that you can't be sure of what you saw, or whether indeed you saw it—a reasonably good tactic for assuaging the censor while titillating the audience. After a while I found this irritating, because pruned or manicured bestiality has a way of looking more insinuatingly nasty than outright brutishness.

While Commodus enters Rome in ill-gained triumph, Maximus rides himself to a frazzle back to his farm in Spain, but finds that Commodus's men have already done in his wife and little boy by a mélange of rape, burning, and crucifixion. During his swoon of grief, he is apprehended by some slave traders, who trundle him off to an exotic North African location and school for gladiators. It is owned by Proximo, a freed ex-gladiator—juicily played by the grizzled veteran Oliver Reed—who now trades in such *morituri*.

Reed died during the filming, thus depriving us of a few more much-needed comic moments. Maximus's favorite fellow student at gladiatorial school is a black giant, Juba (Djimon Hounsou), with whom the equally but differently pious ex-general exchanges views of the afterlife and hopes of a reunion with his slain family that should be of interest to all comparative religionists.

Before long, Maximus, Juba, and their colorful colleagues are in the Colosseum, which computer imaging has turned into the awesome eighth wonder of the world. Computer graphics, moreover, have restored the glory that was Rome into a triumph of virtuality, which, as we know, is its own reward. For the plot makes scant sense, least of all a previous love affair between Maximus and Lucilla, who now tries to help him organize a gladiator rebellion (shades of *Spartacus*). We see one chaste kiss between Lucilla (the charming Danish actress Connie Nielsen) and our hero, who remains faithful to his dead wife. But there a e plentiful histrionics from Joaquin Phoenix as a Commodus, part effete homosexual, part incestuous lecher, planning to marry his sister.

Historical truth is once lightly brushed against, in that Commodus did actually fight gladiators, though these knew better than to win against him. Here everything culminates in a circus duel to the death between him and Maximus, as tricky surprises pile up toward the film's end. But Ridley Scott (of *Alien* and *Blade Runner* fame) is too much in love with effects to be an effective director. We do get, however, two-and-a-half laughable hours of lavish hokum, a word of obscure origin, perhaps derived from a late Latin term signifying "hundred-million-dollar Hollywood rubbish."

More Clouds than Sun

SUNSHINE

Considerable as is the artistic achievement of *Sunshine*, its historical, social, and philosophical importance is greater yet. Compressed into three hours is a family chronicle that could be fully encompassed only by a long novel or TV series. It is the story of the Jewish Sonnenschein family in Hungary, from the late 19th to the late 20th century.

Aaron Sonnenschein invented a highly profitable herbal elixir named Sunshine, which is what the family name means in German.

Aaron's inventiveness also caused his death in an explosion at his Eastern European distillery. His son Emmanuel escapes to Budapest with the formula, where thriving, large-scale business with the elixir makes the family wealthy. As the new century arrives, they naively toast it as an age of peace and prosperity.

The renowned Hungarian director István Szabó made the movie from a script written by himself and the American playwright-scenarist Israel Horovitz. The main thread is the relationship between Jews and Gentiles under various forms of government, and how tolerance and persecution alternated or even coexisted, sometimes ludicrously, at other times tragically.

Another theme is adherence to or rebellion against ancient Judaic laws. Thus when Emmanuel's son Ignatz falls in love with his orphaned cousin and adoptive sister Valerie, they marry despite intense parental opposition on religious grounds. Then there is the political thread: Ignatz, a liberal imperialist, worships Emperor Franz Joseph; his younger brother, Gustave, outraged by social injustice, turns radical socialist. Valerie, whom both love, stays in the middle as an enlightened Hungarian nationalist.

The question of assimilation is a further thread as the Sonnenscheins, under pressure, change their name to Sors—the Hungarian, as well as the Latin, for fate—with symbolic and also socioeconomic implications. The liberal lawyer Ignatz can thus become a judge, whose politics so alienate Valerie that she leaves him for Gustave, to return only when her husband becomes mortally ill.

Hungary, under its fascist dictator Horthy, drifts ever closer to Nazism. Ignatz and Valerie's older son, Istvan, is a doctor married to the fierce Greta; Adam, the younger, becomes a champion fencer, who, for admission to the elite military fencing club, must convert to Catholicism. Receiving religious instruction with the Sorses is the beautiful Hanna; though already affianced, she falls for Adam's impassioned wooing and superb fencing, and marries him. Adam leads the Hungarian fencing team to a gold medal at the 1936 Berlin Olympics, even as Greta, ferociously in love with him, overcomes his staunch sexual resistance.

Despite warnings and job offers from America, Adam, a loyal Hungarian, rejects emigration. A national sports hero, he foresees no danger to Jews until, at the advent of World War II, he and his son, Ivan, end up in the same forced-labor battalion. When Adam refuses to play the groveling Jew to a military bully, he is put to a particularly hideous death while his son, like the others, impotently looks on. Later, Hanna, Istvan, and Greta also perish, but Valerie, as wise as she is good, is hidden by friends and survives.

Ivan witnesses his father's posthumous vindication and, to help ferret out former Nazis, joins the secret police. There follow pell-mell betrayals and remorse, prison and liberation, expropriation and partial reinstatement. Throughout, Valerie remains the unwobbling pivot, lending moral support to all, especially to Ivan, and is joined by her son Gustave, back from political exile in France and still a dedicated radical. When she dies serenely in a crowded hospital ward, her silvertipped cane is left to Ivan. Like the golden pocket watch, passed in *Sunshine* from fathers to sons, this, too, becomes a symbol: paternal gold and maternal silver.

The film may be a bit fraught with symbols, like those two Meissen cups broken in different times and circumstances, their shards gathered each time with loving care. Valerie takes up photography, often making group portraits of her evolving family. The camera is the eye of history, and justifies inclusion in the film also of technically dissimilar newsreel sequences of momentous occasions.

Some details defy categorization. Early on, Valerie accidentally takes a snapshot of herself removing something (a pebble?) from her bare toes; much later, on a museum visit abroad, the spellbound Adam views the antique statue of the Boy Removing a Thorn, in the same pose as Valerie's in the photograph. For me, this speaks of a confluence of life and art, of eternal recurrence, and of beauty even in painful situations. You must similarly derive your own interpretations of the fate of the black booklet containing the formula of the elixir, and of another significant name change at film's end.

Certain objections to the movie raised elsewhere seem to me unfounded. The brutality of Adam's death shows both the moral victory to be snatched from horrible, humiliating defeat and the permanence of anti-Semitism that, often dormant, never dies. The frequent sex scenes are not gratuitous; the sex, wholesome or not, is life-sustaining. As the great Hungarian poet Miklós Radnóti, himself a victim of fascism, wrote in a poem, "the taste of kisses in my mouth is now honey, now cranberry": lovemaking varies pointedly. Ignatz and Valerie's premarital sex is rapturous; Adam's adulterous sex with his sister-in-law, Greta, is the meeting of two diverse furies; Ivan's sex with Major Carola Kovacs, the opportunistic wife of a high-ranking Communist, is, during the time of purges, anguished, frenetic, desperate. Significantly, we never see the lovemaking of Adam and his gentle wife, Hanna.

The *New York Times* reviewer questioned the film's language, e.g., Ignatz's grantedly clichéd postcoital comment to Valerie, "When I'm lying in your arms, I feel I've come home." But consider: The scene is Vienna, where Ignatz is studying and homesick for Budapest; bear in mind, too, the not fully assimilated Jew's hunger for a true home. Besides, this is immediately followed by Ignatz's deflationary "I have to pee," and Valerie's giggly "So do I."

Sunshine enjoys the consistently expert direction of Szabó and the masterly cinematography of Lajos Koltai, a force both in Europe and in Hollywood. The grandmaster of movie music, Maurice Jarre, has composed a score based on Schubert's two-piano Fantasy in F Minor, which we also hear in an orchestral, a one-piano, and, poignantly, one-finger version from a child.

The ultimate triumph is the acting. Ralph Fiennes changes just enough to be equally right, both similar and dissimilar, as Ignatz, Adam, and Ivan; Jennifer Ehle is adorable as the young Valerie; so, too is her real-life mother, Rosemary Harris, as the older one. Noteworthy too are James Frain and John Neville as the youthful and the elderly Gustave, respectively; Molly Parker (Hanna); Rachel Weisz (Greta); William Hurt as a decent commissar; and the great Hungarian actress Mari Töröcsik as an elderly servant. (Töröcsik's is a nonspeaking part, for the simple reason that the actress doesn't speak English.) I always have problems with Deborah Kara Unger, but her grasping, fickle Carola is properly predatory.

Sunshine is the cinematic equivalent of what the French call *roman fleuve*, the novel as a sweeping river. In the present case, the mighty flow more than excuses the footling flaws.

It All Starts Today

Bertrand Tavernier is the most enterprising, various, humane, and sensitive filmmaker in France today—or, more simply put, the finest. Starting with *The Clockmaker*, the now-59-year-old director has turned out every kind of film. Some may remember him best for the thriller *The Judge and the Assassin*, others for the historical *Let the Feast Begin*, many for the family saga *A Sunday in the Country* or the antiwar *Life and Nothing But*. Still others for the jazz film *Round Midnight*, shot partly in New York. There are several other films just as good, and now comes his 19th feature, the masterly *It All Starts Today.*

This is a film about a kindergarten somewhere in the north of France. The actual one used is in Anzin, a suburb of Valenciennes. It is in the heart of what was once coal-mining country; Zola's *Germinal* takes place nearby. Always poor, these folk—with the closing of the mines and widespread unemployment—are now at rock bottom. The kindergarten teachers try to keep the minds and spirits of the tots going, despite a lack of money, hygiene, and even food in most of the homes they come from.

Tavernier's daughter, Tiffany, and her husband, Dominique Sampiero, collaborated on the script with the director. Sampiero has taught in just such schools for years, even though he is a novelist with twelve books to his credit. The film's protagonist, Daniel Lefebvre, is freely modeled on him, and incorporates numerous characters and incidents from his teaching career. What inspired the film was a particular recollection of a young single mother he reprimanded for falling behind on the 30-francs' ($4.50) monthly payment for tiny treats for the children. Thirty francs, she replied, was what she kept herself and her children alive with each month on stale crackers dipped in milk.

Such stories accumulated from Sampiero's memories. There was the kid who would not rat on the "uncle" (really his mother's lover) who beat him savagely; the student whose loving mother collapsed drunk in the schoolyard; another mother, unable to pay the electric bill, whose family was living in darkness for months; the parents who could not face getting out of bed and shepherding their boy to and from school; the kids who did not know what a trade is; and so on and on.

Daniel, head of the school, copes prodigiously. But he has other problems as well. Valeria, with whom he lives, is a sculptress cum waitress, with a child of her own. The boy resents not being told who his (worthless) father is, and takes it out on Daniel. Valeria would like to be married, but Daniel is reluctant. Their story alone could make up a whole movie.

Then there is Daniel's aged father, unwilling to move from the house in which he lived as a miner, and a problem for his wife. That Daniel unrenumeratively teaches tots, instead of going into business like his brother, torments the old man. And then he has a stroke. In all this there is a movie, too.

And then the stories of all those unemployed fathers, desperate mothers and deprived kids. Yet this film is far from being solidly gloomy; it is also full of smiles—in the interaction among teachers and pupils, teachers and teachers, diverse social workers, a mayor, school inspector, a policeman, and others. Daniel's skirmishes with the child-support agency, the mayor, the whole bureaucracy, are often horribly ludicrous, and the way lack of money can stimulate ingenuity is frequently charming.

There are other threads. Daniel's (really Dominique's) prose poems weave their way through the film, beautifully cosmic yet also specific. Tavernier and his gifted cinematographer, Alain Choquart, work in stark cityscapes as well as severely comely landscapes. And always the faces of the children, mostly the 33 pupils in a class of the Anzin kindergarten, whose parents, reduced to watching American television, have absurdly named them William or Kevin or Kelly, or even, in the case of a pair of twins, Starsky and Hutch. Yet when Daniel and the kids sing French nursery songs together, God is in his heaven.

There are other memorable characters: Sarnia, a novice social worker, who becomes Daniel's staunchest ally, notably in getting the children medical treatment. Or Mme Delacourt, the most senior teacher, who exudes a wonderfully melancholy tenacity. Or the overextended Communist mayor, or the maid who becomes a surrogate mother to young and old.

Daniel, with tough love, unsentimental empathy, and heroic indignation, is at the center of unremitting onslaughts, drama lurking everywhere. But there are also moments of relaxation, lovemaking, shared meals, dancing, and sometimes humorous quarrels. Quite a bit is improvised, but so skillfully that it never becomes, as so often in movies, embarrassingly obvious. And almost no one, not even the child-support bureaucrats who hang up on Daniel, is treated as a villain.

The wonder is how Tavernier keeps more stories going in under two hours than a tabloid has articles, how he manages to connect them smoothly without losing the narrative thread or the audience's involvement. The camera rushes around quite a lot, yet does not induce dizziness; chaos is kept in a firm directorial hand.

Philippe Torreton of the Comédie Française, these days Tavernier's favorite leading man, has a face and body language that convey Daniel's fundamental innocence and experience-hardened practicality to lovably pigheaded perfection. He is splendidly supported by Maria Pitaresi as Valeria, and everybody else, including local amateurs pungent in their bit parts. But this is a film that does not conform to American expectations, and may be short-lived on our screens. If you can possibly catch *It All Starts Today*, do so today. Tomorrow may be too late.

You Can Count on Me

The one thing American movies don't know how to do is grow up. Whatever money and technology can achieve, Hollywood does in spades; but produce mature movies? Fuggeddaboutit. Partly this has to do with primitive, uneducated consumers; partly with greedy and not much less primitive purveyors. Things are black and white: In the end, the good guys blow the bad guys to smithereens, the triumphant hero gets the alluring heroine and we all go home happy.

Even the rare mature film, such as *The Insider*, must have at least an ambiguous enough ending not to depress anyone too much; regardless, it fails at the box office and the Oscars. Small independent films are better: They show the steamy side of life only to exalt it or to wallow in self-pity and we all go home not exactly happy but with the gratifying sensation of having seen something really grown-up, perhaps indeed art.

Lacking are the films that face reality foursquare and, delving below the surface, attain insights, perspective, perhaps indeed art. So hail to a fine new, fully mature American movie that meets all my standards for intelligence, originality, subtlety, wit, and artistry: Kenneth Lonergan's *You Can Count on Me*, which I hope breaks the barriers of obtuseness and succeeds despite its virtues. But don't count on it.

Kenneth Lonergan is a profusely gifted young playwright whose *This Is Our Youth* was one of the finest seriocomic plays of recent years. He also co-wrote the screenplay for one of 1999's funniest movies, *Analyze This*, unjustly overshadowed by a somewhat similar TV favorite, *The Sopranos*. For *You Can Count on Me*, he is writer, director, and supporting actor, and shines at all three.

Samantha "Sammy" Prescott and her younger brother, Terry, were orphaned early when their parents perished in a car crash. Sammy stayed in their small Catskills town of Scottsville (actually Phoenicia, N.Y.), married a brute, and divorced him two years later.

She now has an eight-year-old son, Rudy, a decent but unexciting lover, Bob, and a responsible position at the town bank. Terry left town, wandered all over doing odd jobs and getting into barroom brawls, once even, unbeknown to his loving and beloved sister, landing in jail.

Right now, Terry and his current pregnant squeeze are broke in Massachusetts, and he heads for Scottsville to borrow money from Sammy, who hasn't heard from him in a long while and is overjoyed at his coming. Meanwhile her bank has acquired a new manager, Brian, a soft-spoken stickler for discipline who resents Sammy's somewhat early departures to fetch Rudy from school. Her brother's arrival is a godsend: Rudy and Terry bond together, and Terry resolves to stay on and look after Rudy's automotive and other needs.

But Terry, whose very speech is that of an unreconstructed hippie, is soon bored by Scottsville. Meanwhile Sammy gets a surprise marriage proposal from Bob, just after she starts a torrid affair with her boss, who is married to a pregnant but cold wife. Terry does pick up Rudy at school when he remembers, and takes him fishing, which is good, but also for a nocturnal visit to a pool hall (while Sammy is in a motel with Brian), which isn't. The differences between the devoted siblings come to a boil.

Terry is an atheist, Sammy (despite her affairs) a steady church-goer. She recommends to her restless brother that he seek counseling from her priest, Ron, a bumbler sweetly played by Lonergan. Nothing much comes of it, but when Terry yields to Rudy's curiosity about his father and drives him to a shack in a neighboring town shared by Rudy Sr. and his girlfriend, real trouble erupts.

Scottsville and its beautiful hilly environs come to idiosyncratic life. The paternal sheriff, the befuddled priest, a bank employee who likes her computer screen in brash colors (played by Lonergan's real-life mate J. Smith Cameron) contribute sharply etched cameos. The dialogue is pungent, the scenes are terse; Stephen Kazmierski's cinematography is pretty without being postcardish; the country music on the soundtrack is more ironic than obtrusive. And the acting is radiant.

Laura Linney is a superb Sammy: decent, understanding, but also impulsive and sharp-tongued, slightly harried, and enormously likable. As Terry, Mark Ruffalo, is the quintessential charming ne'er-do-well, his soul a perpetually unmade bed. Their interaction is conceived and executed to hilarious and heartbreaking perfection. Brian is impeccably played by Matthew Broderick, with that eternally juvenile quality that makes his pedantry seem all the more comical. Rory Culkin, Macaulay's younger brother, brings a touching gravity to the role of the fatherless boy.

The film's honesty is in the absence of resolution. Nothing terrible happens, but a sense of the insoluble casts its bittersweet shadow. The sweetness is in the gallant optimism about Terry's future in which neither sibling believes but to which both valiantly adhere. It makes the film's closing scene irresistibly poignant.

Traffic

Steven Soderbergh, the not untalented but show-offy writer-director, has come up with *Traffic*, a film based on a BBC TV serial, transposed by him to Mexico, San Diego, Cincinnati, and points beyond. It concerns rival Mexican drug cartels battling each other for supremacy in exporting their unholy wares to our pristine shores. Robert Wakefield, a worthy Ohio judge newly appointed U.S. drug czar, has a bit of a handicap in his 16-year-old daughter Caroline, a druggie and mild orgiast, but really a good girl merely overreacting to paternal neglect in however noble a cause.

The movie careers frantically among four or more stories. There is Robert, the worried father (Michael Douglas, who knows how to worry in a resolute, manly way), his wife, Barbara (Amy Irving, looking drawn but still lovely), and the addicted Caroline (remarkably played by Erika Christensen). Then there are the two Mexican policemen, Javier and Manolo (the hip Benicio Del Toro and vulnerable Jacob Vargas), good actors playing would-be good guys hopelessly buffeted between drug lords—one of them a police chief—more powerful than the police.

Next, there are the two American DEA agents, the Hispanic Ray Castro (Luis Guzman) and the black Montel Gordon (Don Cheadle), guarding a key witness in the trial of Carlos Ayala, an Americanized Mexican drug king in San Diego. The witness is recalcitrant and assassins are after both him and his guards. And there are Carlos himself and his wife Helena (Catherine Zeta-Jones), who either doesn't know his racket or pretends not to. He being jailed, she takes over his shady business with near-superhuman acumen, while also trying to get him out of jail and fending off the amorous advances of his sleazy lawyer (Dennis Quaid).

There is, furthermore, the rise and fall of the chief Mexican drug fighter, General Salazar, not to mention the tragedy of Ana, Manolo's anxious wife. And also the anguish of a youth from a good American family, Caroline's seducer and fellow junkie, whom Robert roughs up in a concerned fatherly way. And a Mexican killer who gets very thoroughly tortured by the police, but misbehaves again the moment he is free. All in all, two-and-a-half hours of nonstop action, made harder to follow by Soderbergh's fancy film-making. But what fun you can have afterward, trying to unravel what you saw.

The film is also a little longer than it needs to be, but it must be granted that it is more adult than most American movies. Best about it is that it perceives drug addiction and the crimes surrounding it as a problem of human nature, not confined to this or that underprivileged group, and that it sees no easy, or even arduous, solution. Although it concludes on a guardedly upbeat note, it offers no panacea, no feel-good ending. *Traffic* promises to be the most award-winning movie of the year, what with raves from most of my colleagues.

Cast Away

Tom Hanks is the kind of beloved actor who can make a retardate look like a prince, and a smartass seem lovable. In *Cast Away* (why two words instead of one?), he is Chuck Noland, a fervent FedEx engineer whom we watch plying his efficiency-fanaticism in Moscow and the American heartland, and who, when a FedEx plane crashes—rather more spectacularly than any previous movie plane crash—ends up as a castaway on an uninhabited South Pacific island.

Chuck's beloved speed no longer exists, and time stands nighmarishly still. Dedicated actor that he is, Hanks dieted away a good chunk of his avoirdupois during a year-long break in the filming while the director, Robert Zemeckis, went off to make another movie. The struggles of a ship-wrecked (well, plane-wrecked) man are scrupulously conveyed in the main part of the film, including the relentless, monotonous sound of wind and waves, which the soundtrack lets us endure with minimal edulcoration by music.

The English classics of shipwreck are, of course, Defoe's *Rob-

inson Crusoe and, for the dramatic return of the stranded sailor, Tennyson's *Enoch Arden*. The movie harks back to both. It is, as it were, in three acts: before, during, and after the island. Though by far the best, even the long middle part has its problems. Film needs dialogue (at least since the invention of sound) and can sustain silence and interior monologue only so long.

True, Chuck has the picture of his girlfriend, Kelly, whom he foolishly just missed getting engaged to, inside the cover of the family-heirloom pocket watch she gave him, to emote to. Depending largely on whatever FedEx packages the surf washes ashore, he also has a pair of girls' ice skates (with which he extracts a tormenting tooth in one of the film's most harrowing scenes), some video tape (with whose help he'll build a raft), and a white volleyball (on which he paints a face with his blood). He dubs it Wilson, after the manufacturer's name, and converses with it, but volleyballs don't have much conversation.

Cast Away is good about the slow and painful discovery of edibles, tools, fire, etc., as well as about the frustrated escape attempts and other setbacks. There is, however, a certain cuteness about William Broyles Jr.'s script, Zemeckis's direction, and Hanks's acting. The "Four Years Later" title, which allows the film to jump from Chuck's first weeks on the island to his last, is also a bit of an evasion, and Chuck's escape on that homemade raft is a trifle too good to be true.

The real trouble, though, is the last part. Both what happens with Kelly (although the ubiquitous Helen Hunt gives yet another of her fine performances) and what happens without her are sweaty efforts for a not-too-sweet and not-too-bitter ending, and make strained-for veracity feel factitious. And how can we possibly worry about such a darling of the gods and the public as Tom Hanks?

The Pledge

When, in 1957, the Swiss playwright and novelist Friedrich Dürrenmatt wrote his novella *Das Versprechen* (*The Pledge*), he subtitled it *Requiem for the Crime Novel*. It has a framing story: a retired Zurich police chief reminisces to Dürrenmatt, author of thrillers, about a poor, semi-demented gas-station operator, waiting for someone the fellow keeps insisting will come. This wreck of a man is the former inspector Matthäi, once the chief's most gifted sleuth.

Years ago, when he was about to retire, Matthäi was nevertheless drawn into the case of a murdered 14-year-old girl found in the bushes. In the movie version of *The Pledge*, directed by Sean Penn, the girl becomes an eight-year-old who was also raped, which, presumably, makes things more interesting for American moviegoers. The screenwriters, the Pole Jerzy Kromolowski and his American wife, Mary Olson-Kromolowski, met as students at the University of Copenhagen, and have had fetchingly motley careers.

These are no garden-variety scenarists. Their script, transposing the action to the vicinity of Reno, and greatly expanding the novella while remaining faithful to its essence, is far superior to Penn's two previous directorial ventures, *Indian Runner* and *The Crossing Guard*. Matthäi has become detective Jerry Black (Jack Nicholson), who likewise promises the victim's distraught mother that he'll find the killer, and goes to almost insane lengths to do it.

The process whereby a fellow cop (the good Aaron Eckhart) extracts a confession from a retarded Indian (the always fascinating Benicio Del Toro) is as subduedly harrowing as a scene can get, and the fanatical way Jerry, disbelieving the confession, goes on his epic wild-goose chase is riveting. This may indeed be Jack Nicholson's crowning performance. The actor's naturally ogival eyebrows, looking like naves of mini-cathedrals, his forehead crisscrossed by lines as if for a game of tic-tac-toe, the gaze alternately cozy and perforating, the mustache rugged, the receding hair hedgehoggishly erect—all this cuts deep. And then there is his mercurial, moving performance.

Penn has directed artfully, but, this time, not artily, and in Chris Menges he has a cinematographer who can make nature as poetic as Dürrenmatt described it. Everyone acts compellingly, not least Sam Shepard as Jerry's boss, and Lois Smith in an all-too-tiny role. That said, I can't help wondering what those Brits are doing in Nevada: Vanessa Redgrave, as the victim's grandmother who spouts an accent no one ever heard before; Helen Mirren as the psychiatrist who remains unabashedly British. As the prostitute in the novel—upgraded in the movie to a husband-battered waitress—Robin Wright Penn (Mrs. Sean Penn in real life) does nicely, as does also little Pauline Roberts as her daughter and Jerry's lure for the killer.

The worthwhile point is that no matter how astute and thorough the detective, chance can trip him up (yet why this should be a requiem for the crime novel, I don't know). It makes a haunting movie, though, even if the ending is deliberately fudged.

Faithless

Even though he only wrote it, and didn't direct it, *Faithless* may be Ingmar Bergman's most personal film. But then, it was directed by Liv Ullmann, who has known him as intimately and as long as anyone. The film deals with a painful story from Bergman's past that seems to have been a thorn in his side. In many of his films, Bergman has allowed bits of it to dribble out, but here he confronts it head-on with an expiating heart. He concentrates on the woman he wronged, a long-ago mistress now dead. Miss Ullmann, herself a longtime former mistress, who contributes much more than routine direction, was the right person to add the woman's-eye view.

Faithless is the tale of the happily married Marianne, an actress (Lena Endre); her husband, Markus, a world-famous conductor (Thomas Hanzon); and David, a stage and screen director and their closest friend (Krister Henriksson). Out of this true friendship, there evolves a treacherous triangle with tragic consequences. When Marianne gets a scholarship to study theater in Paris, the divorced and womanizing David, on a pretext, joins her there for three weeks of overflowing passion in a small hotel. But the affair continues back in Stockholm, where it wreaks havoc on all involved, not least on Marianne's nine-year-old daughter Isabelle (touchingly played by Michelle Gylemo).

I do not wish to give away a plot full of ominous, even lethal, surprises. But I must state that nobody is entirely innocent here; before two and one-half hours elapse, everyone will have betrayed everyone else with disastrous results, in a story that, like a trick box, has many false bottoms. Still, it is the woman who comes off best: the only one who acts from genuine passion, whose instincts are mostly good, who seems capable of sustaining a relationship, and whose love for her daughter never wavers.

Bergman's strategy is fascinating. The story is told, basically, from the point of view of the lonely old writer, called Bergman, who lives (like Ingmar) on the isolated island of Fårö. This writer is going over his diaries, perhaps to write a book; to help him do so, he conjures up the image of the dead woman he calls Marianne

Vogler (a name recurrent in Bergman's oeuvre), and lets her take over the storytelling. This memory-Marianne that comes to partly independent life for him, says, near the end, "I do not much like your Marianne," adding yet another dimension to the story, another bottom to the box. Indeed, that there are trendily ambiguous counterindications that this may be a real woman impersonating Marianne for Bergman is the only thing I don't like about the film.

Old Bergman is played—largely in grieving, open-mouthed silence—by the admirable Erland Josephson, as the film shuttles between Bergman and Marianne in the present, and Marianne, Markus, and David (Bergman as a youngish man) in the past. Intercut, too, are moments from the Fårö seashore, shots of exquisite beauty from the camera of the splendid Jörgen Persson, best remembered hereabouts for his work on *Elvira Madigan*. One of the film's remarkable features is the preponderance of scenes tightly confined within four walls, yet such is Persson's artistry with light and shadow and shades of color that his cinematography contributes as much emotion as some filmmakers' entire movies.

All the actors excel, but the triumph is that of Lena Endre, whose Marianne transcends even what Bergman profoundly wrote and Ullmann magisterially directed. Endre's performance may well be the greatest by an actress on film known to me, and beggars attempts to translate it into words.

Miss Endre is, offscreen, a warm, charming, intelligent, and understatedly lovely fortyish woman. Onscreen, she becomes all women of all ages, and in all modes that ever were: from surpassing beauty, through heartbreaking common humanity, all the way to the distorted, frightening visages of extreme rage and crushing agony. Of course, she acts with every part of her lissome body, and her low, slightly husky, hypnotic voice—both in dialogue and in extensive narration—is irresistible.

But the great, unforgettable thing about Miss Endre is her face. Throughout the film she wears several different hairdos, some of which—pushed forward loosely, pulled back, or spread across a pillow—multiply her looks further. She becomes—though not only through them—many different women, from the trusting schoolgirl to the unleashed bacchante, from the voluptuously womanly to the savagely martyred, from blissfully transfigured to distorted with ineffable pain. Everything about this face is miraculous: the perfect oval, the noble brow, the eloquent eyebrows, the aristocratic nose, the full mouth that speaks no less in silence or in little inchoate sounds of dolor or delight.

Supreme, however, are the eyes—those enormous-seeming, bottomless eyes. Their gaze comes from unsoundable depths and sees far beyond its immediate object. There is, even in happiness, a soupçon of sadness in it, as if aware of the fragility of joy, of the danger, deceptions, and death lying in wait. These eyes alone, at the thin frontier between bright wonder and the tragic sense of life, warrant seeing the film a second time. Lena Endre will make all women viewers proud of their womanhood, and all men a little more loving toward their women for being her sisters.

Dangerous Game

ENEMY AT THE GATES; MEMENTO

The French filmmaker Jean-Jacques Annaud has had a checkered career. His first film, *Black and White in Color* (1976), about inept colonial warfare between the French and Germans in 1915 West Africa, was an absolute gem. Ranging from drolly farcical to sharply satirical, it was comedy at its brainiest and most biting. His next, *Hothead*, a comedy about two competing factory soccer teams (and much else), was intelligent, but slightly offside.

After that, Annaud went commercial. *Quest for Fire*, based on one of J. H. Rosny's once-popular novels about prehistoric tribal wars and caveman romance, benefited from the linguistic contribution of Anthony Burgess, movement-consulting by Desmond Morris, and some nice woolly mammoths. But the film's authenticity was marred by the filmmaker's anachronistic sentimentality. Later, Annaud's version of *The Name of the Rose*, softened by a preposterous happy ending, misfired.

The Bear, about an orphaned bear cub's coming of age, told from the bear's point of view, had a lot of charm, not least in the sounds of nature substituting for dialogue, but could not escape a soupçon of Disneyism.

The Lover, based on Marguerite Duras's self-serving novel about coming of sexual age in prewar Vietnam, had some wonderfully authentic touches, but the central love story failed to ignite. *Seven Years in Tibet* was a glossy picture postcard about strange doings in a forbidden city, but emerged as a bit of a Lhasa apso. It also glossed over some queasy political questions.

Now comes *Enemy at the Gates*, centering on the duel to the death of two master snipers, young Vasily Zaitsev, a historical figure, and the German Major König, who may or may not have been. Vasily was a shepherd boy from the Urals, whose grandfather trained him to shoot by hunting wolves; König, if he existed, ran a prestigious school for Nazi sharpshooters. In the middle of one of World War II's most crucial battles, the six-month siege of Stalingrad with perhaps as many as 2 million dead, these men are locked in mortal combat, seeing each other only, if at all, through their telescopic rifle sights.

It is a curious love-hate story between Vasily and König, simple, barely literate shepherd and gold-tipped-cigarette-smoking aristocrat. Each is admiringly fascinated by the other, studying his minutest quirks, and trying to shoot him dead. Each man does mighty devastation in the enemy lines, and tracks the other through spectacular stratagems across eccentric battlegrounds and from bizarre hiding places. But, until the very end, neither can nail the other.

The inferno of war—burning and smoking Stalingrad in jagged ruins, a German air attack on Russian reinforcements crossing the Volga in boats, and assorted other horrors—is depicted spectacularly in the best Spielbergian fashion. Annaud, however, not content with this epic canvas, insists on adding a gratuitous love triangle involving the relationship between the ingenuous Vasily and Danilov, a brilliant but neurotic officer and propagandist, who turns Vasily into a morale-boosting national hero. Both fall in love with Tanya, a university-educated young Jewish girl who, thanks to her knowledge of German, has a cushy office job, but yearns to go out to fight and avenge her slaughtered Jewish parents. Because Danilov, too, is Jewish, he hopes to win Tanya; she, however, prefers Vasily, with melodramatic consequences.

There are some fairly stereotypical figures: the brave Russian mother, the grizzled soldier who has seen it all, the valiant young Russian boy who shines König's boots and pretends to be a German sympathizer, but spies for his beloved Vasily. And there are some worse yet, including Bob Hoskins as a menacing but comic Khrushchev, made more comic by (inadvertently) mispronouncing his own name. More subtly, the unembellished shadow of Stalin hovers over all.

The acting is consistently good, with Joseph Fiennes a nicely unpredictable but ultimately noble Danilov, Rachel Weisz a spunky but tenderhearted Tanya, and Jude Law as a star-quality-notwith-standing believable Vasily. Best of all is Ed Harris's König, able to make the film's most complex character entirely believable. Only Gabriel Marshall-Thomson, as the shoeshine boy, is too adorable and, even for the most naïve moviegoers, presages a sticky end. Also distracting is the unrelentingly god-awful score (by James Horner, who should be made to stand in a corner for at least a month), plus a lot of rather questionable dialogue by Annaud and Alain Godard. Robert Fraisse's cinematography contributes powerfully to a flawed but by no means unimpressive movie.

If anyone tells you he could follow *Memento*, be assured he is a liar. Or worse yet, a *Memento* cultist, trying to turn a clinker into a classic. The writer-director Christopher Nolan has taken what seems to be a fairly unremarkable film noir, sliced it to ribbons, and more or less arbitrarily scrambled the pieces.

The insurance investigator Leonard Shelby, after seeing his wife raped and murdered, gets a knock on the head and loses his short-term memory. Everything before the blow he remembers clearly, but now he forgets everything that happens to him after 15 minutes or so. I doubt if such a condition actually exists, but that is the least problem here.

The film moves both forward and (mainly) backward in time, ostensibly to simulate how Leonard discovers things. To compen-sate for his sieve-like memory, he depends on annotated Polaroids, scraps of paper handed him, information (possibly false and cer-tainly conflicting) tendered by strangers, and most of all, tattoos on his torso and limbs. Particularly irritating is that neither the back-ward nor the forward movement of the story is clearly indicated (in *Betrayal*, with a similar two-way movement, Harold Pinter gives you dates). And several scenes recur as bothersomely as a party bore whom you cannot shake.

Nolan does everything he can to confound you. There are black-and-white scenes telling the barely related story of another man with like memory loss. But some, though not all, of Leonard's past is also in monochrome. There are subliminal flashes of who-knows-what. I never figured out whether the barmaid Natalie (with whom the grieving husband shacks up) and the mysterious Teddy (who may be cop or killer) are friends or foes. The short-term memory lasts 15 minutes, yet when Natalie and a barfly spit, in full view, into his beer, Leonard drinks it without demur.

When chased by a murderous character, Leonard forgets whether he is the chased or the chaser—funny, but phony as a three-dol-
lar bill. Under the circumstances, it is hard to care about our hero,
however ably the gifted Guy Pearce portrays him. As Natalie, Car-
rie-Anne Moss is good if she is meant to be antipathetic; less so if
not. As Teddy, Joe Pantoliano scores either way.

If ever a movie was smartass, *Memento* is it. Christopher Nolan
made it from a story by his brother, Jonathan. Brotherly love, like
all good things, can be carried too far.

Amores Perros

The best Mexican films hitherto were the works of the Spaniard
Luis Buñuel. Now comes a Mexican movie just as powerful made
by Mexicans: *Amores Perros*, directed by Alejandro González Iñár-
ritu, and written by the novelist Guillermo Arriaga. It comprises
three very tough interrelated Mexico City stories, seamlessly connected even though the principals in one have only brief contact
with those in another. What does connect the tales more tellingly
is the presence of dogs.

Here the untranslatable title comes in. The official "Love's a
Bitch," provided in the credits, won't quite do. *Amores perros* means
rotten or lousy loves, with the adjectival *perro* a common pejora-
tive. But the noun *perro*, dog, also matters. Each story contains
both love of dogs and love affairs that go to the dogs. Ultimately,
comparisons of canines and humans impose themselves, with the
dogs coming out ahead.

In the first story, "Octavio and Susana," feckless Octavio is in love
with Susana, the wife of his criminal older brother, Ramiro. Susana
and Ramiro have a baby, with another on its way, but Ramiro is brutal
to everyone and a robber to boot. Their drunken mother is barely
capable of baby-sitting, and the shabby family house is overcrowded.
There is also Cofi, the brothers' Rottweiler, which Octavio, eager to
make easy money and escape with Susana, forces into the brutish dog
fights that are rather graphically shown. (We are assured no dog was
hurt; the same may not hold for all viewers.) Cofi does so well that the
vicious owner of a defeated dog shoots him almost dead. Whereupon
Octavio stabs the shooter and drives off with Cofi to a vet, with the
shooter's accomplices pursuing and shooting.

The first story blends into the second when Octavio's car crashes into another, driven by Valeria, a sexy supermodel for whom the besotted middle-aged businessman Daniel has left his wife and child. Daniel, Valeria, and her insanely adored lapdog, Richie, have set up housekeeping in an unfinished house, whose floor has a big hole in it. Valeria, her leg in a cast after the crash, throws a ball for Richie to fetch, but the dog, alas, ends up down in a rat-infested sub-basement. Trying to extricate him, Valeria further damages, and eventually loses, her leg. She can't go back to her career on the runway, Daniel can't go back to his wife. Daniel and Valeria stay together in hate.

The third story is the most ingenious. It is about heartbreakingly frustrated paternal love, about a lost soul's partial redemption, and about a grotesquely fratricidal Cain and Abel—or Cain and Cain. In it, the dog Cofi, nursed back to life by a reformed hired killer, also gets redeemed. Almost, but not quite, everyone in all three stories comes to terrible grief, but there is also a subtle undertone of Christian symbolism and, at least for some, salvation. The acting is inspired throughout, the direction incisive and inventive, and the often deliberately grainy but always apt cinematography by Rodrigo Prieto a further triumph. *Amores Perros* is the kind of film you want to see twice to absorb the fullness of its intricate details. But even one viewing will stay with you for a long time.

Moulin Rouge

The Australian director Baz Luhrmann's *William Shakespeare's Romeo and Juliet* was clearly a misnomer. The work's reduction to the taste of the MTV generation was plainly *Baz Luhrmann's Romeo and Juliet*. About his *Moulin Rouge*, the buzz from Cannes was pretty bad; as it turns out, its Baz is worse than its buzz.

Luhrmann's forte—if it can be called that—is splash, swirl, and frenetic cutting, to leave the viewers breathless and unthinking. Since his audience tends to come equipped with the latter attribute, he can concentrate on gaudiness and breakneck speed. In this *Moulin Rouge* there is far more décor and frippery than plot and character, and the dialogue is a blend of the cribbed and the clichéd. But the tempo is such that hardly a shot exceeds six or seven seconds—many shots, in fact, are virtually subliminal—and the crass display of opulence is a veritable nouveau-riche banquet. Whatever else it lacks, the film suffocates in sheer razzmatazz, or, more exactly, Bazmatazz.

You had best come to it supplied with Dramamine or some other anti-seasickness drug; it is easily the equivalent of a stormy Atlantic crossing, though the shipboard orchestras are far more chaste and melodious than a Luhrmann soundtrack. The only times this one's fury abates is when Nicole Kidman—as Satine, the "Sparkling Diamond" of the Moulin floor show—chirps in her own fragile voice, so dainty that even electronic enhancement sits on it like falsies on a flat chest. When the men vocalize—Ewan McGregor in more than *mezza voce*, and Jim Broadbent in spunky *sprechstimme*—I suspect that the two masculine names billed in the credits as "vocal doubles" deserve the applause.

The story is a brazen concoction from *La Traviata* (lovely courtesan dying of consumption sacrifices herself for her beloved's good by pretending to prefer a rich nobleman), *La Bohème* (hero surrounded by merry bohemian friends, heroine succumbing to obligatory consumption after loving reconciliation with him), the musical *On Your Toes* (while hero is on stage, killer stalks him with gun but must find proper moment to shoot him), and heaven knows where else.

Our hero, a young Englishman named Christian (McGregor), is trying to make it as a writer in turn-of-the-century Paree (a setup borrowed from George du Maurier's *Trilby*, and countless others). Never before in love, he falls fatally for Satine, the courtesan-dancer who herself has never before loved, but reciprocates, harboring as she does under her lust for gold a repressed heart of same. But roughening the course of true love are Harold Zidler (Jim Broadbent), the near bankrupt owner of the Moulin, and the wealthy Duke of Worcester (Richard Roxburgh), who will finance the "spectacular spectacular" Christian is writing for Zidler and Satine in exchange for the lady's utter and undivided favors.

The banalities of the meager plot will not be rehearsed here; suffice it to say that Christian's pal Toulouse-Lautrec (whom his intimates here call Toulouse; Henri might confuse a Luhrmannite audience) is played wretchedly by John Leguizamo, who doesn't even manage to look as convincing as José Ferrer in John Huston's 1952 version. As Satine expires in the arms of the sobbing Christian, she exhorts him that he must go on, having so much to give to the world. Earlier, in her Camille mode, she said, "The difference between you and I [*sic*] is that you can leave anytime, but this is my home, the Moulin Rouge." By a cruel irony of the Grim Reaper, it is she who is leaving, but she assures Christian, "I'll always be with you." We see him throughout typing his musical, entitled *Moulin Rouge*, on his trusty vintage '99 Underwood. If Satine is truly watching from above, she may not, alas, see his work crowned at the box office.

John Huston's *Moulin Rouge* at least had a fine score by Georges Auric, and did not depend on musical scavenging. Here we have recycled old songs along with new ones by Lil' Kim, Mya & Pink, Fatboy Slim, and David Bowie and Massive Attack. The film's attack on the eyeballs is massive indeed; mine started throbbing at midpoint.

Sexy Beast

All of the characters in the British film noir *Sexy Beast* have extensive past or present criminal records, and in the course of the story a major heist and two murders are committed; yet nowhere is there the slightest evidence of a past or present brush with the law. Whatever troubles they have are with one another, and information about their past is sketchy. So the plot unfolds in a field almost hermetically sealed off from any sort of real-world context.

This could have been a major flaw if it weren't for other very considerable compensations. The superior screenplay is by Louis Mellis and David Scinto, who, apparently, are playwrights and have come up with literate, but nowise literary, dialogue, unusual in your typical gangster films. For example, they are not afraid of having the fiendish sociopath Don Logan (Ben Kingsley) do such things as sarcastically repeat what is said to him verbatim, but with a sinisterly sardonic spin. Or express his fierce disapproval by uttering the one word "no" more times than the dying Lear exclaims "Never." Or conduct a brutish conversation with his own mirror image while shaving.

Sexy Beast begins by introducing us to Gary "Gal" Dove (Ray Winstone), a retired safecracker taking it easy in his modern hillside villa on Spain's Costa del Sol, which he shares with his beloved wife DeeDee (Amanda Redman), a former porn actress. Nearby are his former fellow in crime, Aitch (Cavan Kendall), and Aitch's

consort, Jackie (Julianne White), with whom Gal and DeeDee share
eating, drinking, and perhaps other pleasures.

The opening sequence has Gal sunning himself by his pool, trying to give his by now somewhat flabby, pinky-white British body
some Mediterranean tan, even as a Murilloesque houseboy is languidly sweeping up around the pool. The lazily sultry atmosphere
is suddenly ripped apart by a boulder that comes thundering down
the hillside and, narrowly missing Gal, crashes into the pool, coming to rest atop the colored tiles arranged in the shape of a pair of
entwined hearts.

This is canny foreshadowing: out of left field comes danger, possibly deadly, and certainly threatening Gal and DeeDee's middle-
aged bliss. That danger is Don Logan, who has been sent by Gal's
former boss, Teddy Bass (Ian McShane), to corral him out of retirement and into one more heist: cracking the supposedly impreg-
nable underwater vault operated by the aristocratic and decadent
Harry (James Fox). The long middle part of the film concerns Don's
scare tactics, designed to bully Gal back into crime and terrorize
Jackie and Aitch. He humiliates DeeDee (who doesn't scare easily)
with ugly references to her unchaste past, and Jackie with gloating
mentions of when he used to have his way with her.

Don's dominance is much less physical than verbal and psychological—or symbolic. Thus he deliberately finishes urinating outside his host's toilet bowl, or uses his ramrod-stiff body to lunge
diagonally, like a falling plank, at Gal, several times in rapid succession, stopping just short of actual contact. And the clever director,
Jonathan Glazer, shoots this from a certain distance and from such
an angle that Don, at first outside the frame and invisible, keeps
hurtling into it, not unlike that initial boulder.

Glazer, whose background is in commercials and music videos,
directs with great skill and originality. He has learned how to convey
a strong message with utmost concision (commercials), and how
to get elaborately choreographed movement into a spontaneous-
seeming shot (music videos). Here he works wonders. He shoots
from odd, disorienting, emotionally loaded angles; he places four
or five persons within a shot in quaint, stylized, but highly expressive positions; he keeps the nearest head in blurry close-up, with
others at lesser or greater distance, so as to convey depth of field; he
cuts profusely and adroitly, often leaving us deprived of establishing
shots and thus anxious, uncertain; he varies his tempos cunningly;
and he uses light or its lack to disturbingly vivid effect, as when

Teddy's carnivorous teeth shine out of the surrounding shadows, or the mere white of an ominous eye glistens in the dark.

One huge miscalculation is showing us Gal's nightmares, which involve some grotesque, hairy, and horned monster making mischief, right out of a second-rate horror movie. It may also be that crosscutting the heist in London with a previous murder in Spain, merely hinted at before, creates needless confusion rather than doubled suspense. Yet you must admire a director who stages Don's arrival at a Spanish airport by introducing the bald, skinny little fellow in a rear tracking shot, which the able Ben Kingsley, acting with his swinging shoulders and arrogantly jaunty walk, manages to imbue with consummate menace.

Kingsley gives us the ultimate psychopath in look, speech, and demeanor, the like of which we haven't seen since Robert Mitchum's performance in *The Night of the Hunter*. By injecting a sneering humor into his beastliness, he makes it, perhaps not sexier, but surely more frightening. Opposite him, Ray Winstone's Gal is his very antithesis: a big, quasi-somnolent hippo, slowly reacting to the tauntings of an unpredictable wolverine, but suggesting that it, too, can throw its weight around when aroused.

Excellent performances, as well, by Ian McShane, whose dapper Teddy, with his slicked-down hair, sharklike smile, and inscrutably intense gaze, is no less chilling than Don; by Amanda Redman, as a comfortably seedy DeeDee capable of mustering unsuspected pluck; by Julianne White as a lively but deflatable Jackie; by Cavan Kendall, as the sweaty-under-the-collar Aitch; and by James Fox as Harry, the perfect upperclass twit. Add versatile cinematography by Ivan Bird and twitchy music by Roque Baños, and you've got a complexly unsettling, dazzlingly colorful film noir.

Pinocchio Was Here

A.I.: ARTIFICIAL INTELLIGENCE

Asked whom he considered the most important French poet, André Gide famously replied, "Victor Hugo, alas." Asked who the most important American film director is today, I answer, "Steven Spielberg, alas." He is a great technician, has a terrific eye, and knows how to reach a large audience.

But Spielberg's shortcomings are also considerable. The reason so many of his films deal with children or extraterrestrials—or with sensational topics such as killer sharks, dinosaurs, and the Holocaust—is that these are ways of avoiding adults with their everyday existential problems, at which Spielberg is no good. And then there is his sentimentality, about which more anon.

Spielberg's latest, *A.I.* (for Artificial Intelligence), is by any standards a lesser, by mine a much lesser, performance. It is a project Stanley Kubrick had been piddling with and talking to Spielberg about, based on a 1969 short story by Brian Aldiss. In Kubrick's hands, it was to have been a black dystopia; bequeathed to Spielberg, who wrote his own screenplay, it becomes an uneasy mix of trauma and treacle.

In a future where global warming has caused coastal cities (including New York) to be flooded, humanity has been decimated, and highly evolved humanoid robots serve numerous functions, from gardening to sexual pleasuring: everything except love, of which they are incapable. Now Prof. Hobby, the head of the Cybertronics lab, has come up with a robot boy, David, programmed to give undying love to his "parents." A Cybertronic employee, Henry Swinton, and his wife, Monica, whose mortally ill child has been cryogenically frozen and awaits a cure, are given David on a trial basis. After a number of contretemps, the wary Monica is won over and decides to make the adoption permanent. For some reason, David's love does not extend to Henry.

Everything is fine until the Swintons' natural son, Martin, is cured and returns home. Intense sibling rivalry ensues—Martin is odious, David angelic—and the Swintons, misled about some incidents, decide to jettison David. His grim "mother" drives him out into the woods and abandons the devastated kid in a scene guaranteed to melt the most robotic human heart. Here ends what is in essence the first movie. The second concerns David's wanderings with Teddy, his speaking and thinking supertoy teddy bear. They encounter a robot junkpile where less-damaged robots scavenge for replacement body parts, and where human robot hunters (threatened by robot proliferation) hunt down with robot dogs any stray mecha. (The robots are mechas, i.e., mechanicals; the humans, orgas, i.e., organics.) David meets up with Gigolo Joe, a cavorting, merry, adult mecha who services orga women better than an orga can. They strike up a friendship as David, yearning to become fully human and loved by Mommy, seeks the miracle granting Blue Fairy he heard about in the fairy tales Monica read to him.

By now you must realize that this is a retelling of Pinocchio, with the trusty Teddy as Jiminy Cricket, and so on. Joe and David wander into a Flesh Fair, a hideous circus where doomed robots go heroically to their grisly deaths, as ferocious orga crowds watch and even brutally participate: the Roman arena and Nazi death camps are evoked. I spare you sundry adventures—including an encounter with Dr. Know, a hologram that answers questions in Robin Williams's voice—and skip to where we arrive in a semi-submerged New York City. Gigolo Joe has been dragged off to annihilation, and the despairing David dives off Radio City Music Hall into freezing waters and a 2,000-year sleep.

By now, in film No. 3, humans are extinct and the world is inhabited by elongated, benevolent, large but wispy creatures that help David and Teddy find the Blue Fairy, who looks like a primitive Madonna in an Italian village church and speaks with the voice of Meryl Streep. David's wish is sort of granted: by means of a lock of Monica's hair that Teddy has secreted, she is brought back alive for one day on David's birthday. He is a real boy now with a birthday cake and an adoring Mommy for a day. He even gets to sleep in her bed. We are not shown the aftermath, but surely, the second and final loss of Mommy must be even more—and eternally—wrenching.

Among all the echoes and overtones, the Pinocchio parallel is particularly damaging: The rapscallion puppet had more unruly, idiosyncratic vitality than soppy David ever will. The talking Teddy (voiced by Jack Angel) is very cute, and rather steals the show from David. Henry, played by the dull Sam Robards, might as well be a second-rate robot; Frances O'Connor, as the neurotic Monica, looks polished and manicured enough for a first-class robot, but is a very poor mother. As Joe, Jude Law, with a now blond, now black crest of a hairdo and what looks like polyurethane cheeks, has some amusing lines, but does not really fit into the story.

Perhaps the best scene comes early. It has Prof. Hobby (William Hurt) demonstrating to a group of scientific onlookers how a robot works (but don't they know that already?). He pushes the upper half of an attractive woman's face up like the visor on a helmet, revealing the inner mechanism, then pushes it down again, whereupon she calmly refreshes her makeup. But she, like Joe, seems metallic and hard—scarcely the kind of bed partner one would wish for.

Haley Joel Osment (David) is an accomplished actor, and with a little help from his excellent makeup, conveys the convergence of creature and machine with moving conviction. But he must stop playing weird, preternatural beings, lest he become typecast, if not indeed deprived of his boyhood.

The various designers, and the fine cinematographer Janusz Kaminski, conjure up hauntingly beautiful or houndingly scary images, but the clash of the Kubrick imp and the Spielberg sentimentalist undermines whatever cohesion the movie might have. Artificial intelligence veers into genuine silliness.

INDEX OF FILMS REVIEWED